D0203726

ESSAYS IN MEDICAL SOCIOLOGY

ESSAYS IN MEDICAL SOCIOLOGY

Journeys into the Field

Renée C. Fox

Transaction Books
New Brunswick (USA) and Oxford (UK)

Library of Congress Catalog Number: 87-5092
ISBN 0-88738-148-0 (cloth); 0-88738-682-2 (paper)
Printed in the United States of America

Library of Congress Cataloging in Publication Data

Fox, Renée C. (Renée Claire), 1928-
Essays in medical sociology.

Includes bibliographies and index.
1. Social medicine. 2. Medicine—Research—Social aspects. I. Title. [DNLM: 1. Social Medicine—essays. 2. Sociology, Medical—essays. WA 31 F793e]
RA418.F66 1987 306 87-5092
ISBN 0-88738-148-0

In memory of
my Teacher

TALCOTT PARSONS
(1902–1979)

Contents

Introduction to the Transaction Edition: Endings, Beginnings, and Continuities

The work goes on. As the new section of this second edition of *Essays in Medical Sociology* indicates, my "journeys into the field" continue. Most of the physical and social landscapes are the same ones that I have traversed for years, in the United States, and beyond it: medical schools, hospitals and laboratories; "experiment perilous" enclaves of clinical research, grave illness, and proximity to death; daunting and dauntless universes, dominated by the whirring of artificial, mechanical organs, and the transplantation of natural, human ones; and the microcosmic, European world of Belgium, with its ironic ("small country, no problems") sense of itself.

Human comedy and human tragedy pervade my inner and outer travels, to places that have both empirical and metaphoric significance. Lying deeply below the "hard surfaces"[1] of the reality that I continuously explore are the symbolic spheres of social life, its moral and existential dimensions, and its endless mysteries. These summon me, as they always have.

The women and men who people the terrain that I cover are still primarily doctors and nurses, patients and families, medical students and scientists. Singly and collectively (along with the participant-observer sociologist), they belong to a larger human condition:

1. This is a phrase used by Clifford Geertz in his essay, "Thick Description: Toward an Interpretive Theory of Culture," in Clifford Geertz, *The Interpretation of Cultures: Selected Essays* (New York: Basic Books, 1973), p. 30.

> I can . . . see the white, Grecian-temple style building of the medical school gleaming outside the windows of Ward F-Second, with its Hippocratic aphorism, "Life is short, the art long, moment difficult, experiment perilous"—as though it had been placed there like some cosmic signboard. I see myself going down that long, enclosed corridor that led to the far end of the hospital where Ward F-Second and the laboratories and conference room of the Metabolic Group were located . . . . Down the long corridor, far away from the street and the front door of the hospital, deep inside it, toward a sequestered and, in some ways, secret world . . . .
>
> In this romantic, tragic, comic, courageous, heroic, and mock-heroic world, we were young together—the doctors, the nurses, the patients, and the sociologist. We suffered together. We laughed together . . . . F-Second is burned into my soul. I have seen it again and again in other hospital settings. For me, it is the iconic expression of a "hospital society."
>
> The ward and laboratory and conference room are no longer there, physically. And the old hospital building that housed them has been replaced by a new one. But all that I studied and experienced there still exists in medicine and science and the human condition. And Hippocrates' aphorism, chiseled in white marble on a medical temple, still looms over it, silently.[2]

The themes that I pursue are remarkably constant: uncertainty; detached concern; the gift of life; the never-perfect nature of medical science, research, and practice, and the ceaseless cycle of problem-solving and problem-creating that they generate;[3] and the courage to try, to cease and desist, to succeed, and to fail. "The Human Condition of Health Professionals," "The Evolution of Medical Uncertainty," and "'It's the Same, but Different'"—three essays that I have added to this new edition—attest to my thematic steadfastness.

"'It's the Same, but Different'" tells the story of the implantation of an artificial heart in Dr. Barney Clark, in the Mormon setting of the University of Utah Medical Center, analyzing how this bold, experimental-therapeutic act was like and unlike other trail-blazing clinical research ventures. The phrase "it's the same, but different" also aphoristically expresses some of the ways that my work and my relationship to it have changed, despite all that has

2. Renée C. Fox, "Ethics in the Hospital Society," unpublished talk delivered at the Henry Knox Sherrill Symposium on Ethics, Massachusetts General Hospital, Boston, April 8, 1983.

3. Using the Daedalus myth as a metaphor, physician-biologist Baruch Blumberg and I have coined the term "Daedalus effect" to identify and describe these properties of medical research and practice. See Baruch S. Blumberg and Renée C. Fox, "The Daedalus Effect: Changes in Ethical Questions Relating to the Hepatitis B Virus," *Annals of Internal Medicine,* Vol. 102, No. 3 (March 1985), 390-394.

not changed, since 1978 when I wrote the introduction to the first edition of this book.

There are a number of geographic differences that are more than geographic. I have not gone back to the dialysis center on Majuro in the Marshall Islands that I visited in 1977, and I probably never will. That miniscule atoll, a coral dot in the Pacific Ocean, so far in space and time from any mainland, and forever in danger of being engulfed by a huge tidal wave, seems an almost mythic embodiment of the brave and pathetic efforts being made in the world to provide kidney machines for all persons in renal failure, no matter what the surrounding circumstances may be.

Nor have I physically returned to Congo-Zaire. I maintain as much contact as I can with this "heart of darkness" Central African society, once a Belgian frontier and "dreaming space," through newspaper accounts, the journal *Zaire-Afrique,*[4] occasional correspondence, my visits to Belgium, and rereading portions of my own fieldnotes, in anticipation of writing I am planning to do. But the contact is vicarious, sporadic, and distant. There are political reasons for which it seems neither practical nor prudent to make another field trip to Zaire. It might endanger African colleagues and friends to be involved as sociological respondents and informants. I do hope to see Zaire again some day, although I am wistfully reconciled to the fact that I am no longer as youthfully venturesome as I was in 1964-65 when, in collaboration with Willy De Craemer, I made a first-hand study of the Congo Rebellion, physically following the rebels into the various regions of the country that they invaded.[5]

More hauntingly than ever, Belgium remains at the center of my sociological life. Over the course of the twenty-five consecutive years of fieldwork that I have conducted in this country, what began as a social and cultural exploration of its medical research was progressively transformed into a study of "Belgium through the windows of its medical laboratories." It has become a chronicle of the lived-in, post-World War II history of a small, emblematically West European land. It is also a record of a personal odyssey.

My sustained research in Belgium has ended. I have painfully broken the

4. *Zaire-Afrique* is a monthly review, published in Kinshasa, by the Centre d'Etudes pour l'Action Sociale (CEPAS).

5. See, Renée C. Fox, Willy De Craemer and Jean-Marie Ribeaucourt, "'The Second Independence': A Case Study of the Kwilu Rebellion in the Congo," *Comparative Studies in Society and History,* Vol. VIII, No. 1 (October 1965), 78-109.

pattern of annual commuting to Belgium that I established in 1959, as I prepare to write what I simply call "the Belgian book." But "it is around me and inside me";[6] the overt and the subterranean culture of Belgium—the symbols and images, the atmosphere and the angle of vision that permeate the Belgian essay ("Is Religion Important in Belgium?"), added to this volume. Belgium grips and pursues me wherever I am—all the more so now that I have arrived at this ultimate, book-writing relationship to it.

In 1983 Judith Swazey and I coauthored an essay called "Leaving the Field." Its subtitle was "Personal Reflections on the Human Condition of Two Participant Observers and Their Relationship to Transplantation and Dialysis."[7] In this essay, we summarized and examined the course and content of our studies of dialysis and transplantation. What the Chinese dubbed our "team of two" work began in 1968 and continues to this day. It has been strengthened and enriched over the years, and as the mention of the Chinese indicates, in 1981 it carried us as far as the People's Republic of China.[8]

"Leaving the Field" was not only an analytic summing-up of our research experiences, but also a celebration of our colleagueship. It was a kind of testimony that described the cumulative sadness, anxiety, and problems of meaning that we were experiencing as participant observers of transplantation and dialysis. We concluded that we were suffering from the fieldworker's equivalent of "burnout," and that the time had come to depart from this area of research. We recognized that our decision resembled the clinical moratoriums called by pioneering cardiac and transplant surgeons that we had repeat-

6. Michel de Ghelderode, "The Ostend Interviews (*Entretiens d'Ostende*)," in Michel de Ghelderode, *Seven Plays,* Volume I. Translated from French, and with an introduction by George Hauger (New York: Hill and Wang, 1960), p. 6. (Cited in my article, "Is Religion Important in Belgium?", included in this second edition of *Essays in Medical Sociology*).

7. This essay was written under the auspices and with the support of the James Picker Foundation Program on the Human Qualities in Medicine.

8. There was a *double entendre* to the collective name we acquired. In the summer of 1981, in China, there was much talk and writing about the evil-doing and destructiveness of the so-called Gang of Four during the Cultural Revolution, and about the need to repair the damage they had done, and move rapidly forward and upward in the present period of the "Four Modernizations." With ironically flattering wit, Chinese colleagues referred to us invidiously, as the "Team of Two" rather than the "Gang of Four."

edly observed and studied.[9] Toward the end of the essay, we admitted that "our declared disengagement from the field . . . made us feel at times as though we are going through a divorce, leaving a religious order, or deserting comrades in crisis." We also noted "with some amusement, the rapidity and zest with which we [were] making plans for a field trip to Utah in the spring to gather material for an article on the case of the Jarvik VII artificial heart."

That article became "'It's the Same, but Different': A Sociological Perspective on the Case of the Utah Artificial Heart." "Leaving the Field" is still unpublished, for an obvious reason. The trip to Utah marked the beginning of our *in situ* research on the development of the artificial heart, a therapeutic innovation that has grown directly out of the history of organ transplantation and the artificial kidney machine. During the past year, Judith Swazey, the principal investigator, has spent a great deal of time in the field at the Humana Heart Institute in Louisville, Kentucky, the site to which the organized attempt to permanently implant an artificial heart in desperately ill patients has moved, along with its determined, paramount surgeon, Dr. William De Vries. This summer (1986) we will make two brief, focused field trips together, to Louisville and Salt Lake City. Another book is aborning.

Of all the journeys into the field that have transpired since 1979 when *Essays in Medical Sociology* was first published, the most unexpected have been my three trips to China. They have also been the most renewing.

The first trip took place in November 1978, when the Board of Directors of the American Association for the Advancement of Science (AAAS), of which I was then a member, spent three weeks in China (in Beijing, Shanghai, Canton, and Kweilin), as the guests of the China Association for Science and Technology (CAST). Those weeks were historic. They occurred at the end of the Cultural Revolution, just two months before the normalization of relations between China and the United States. Our "unofficially official" visit, smiled upon by the American and Chinese governments, expedited the opening up of scientific exchanges between the two countries. My second trip was the one I made with Judith Swazey in the summer of 1981, at the height of the

9. See Judith P. Swazey and Renée C. Fox, "The Clinical Moratorium," in Paul A. Freund, ed., *Experimentation with Human Subjects* (New York: George Braziller, 1970), pp. 315-357. (Reprinted in *Essays in Medical Sociology,* pp. 325-363.) See also Renée C. Fox and Judith P. Swazey, "The Heart Transplant Moratorium," chapter 6 of our coauthored book, *The Courage to Fail: A Social View of Organ Transplants and Dialysis* (Chicago: University of Chicago Press, 1974), pp. 122-148. Another recent paper extends the concept of the clinical moratorium to the case of the artificial heart: Judith P. Swazey, Judith C. Watkins, and Renée C. Fox, "Assessing the Artificial Heart: The Clinical Moratorium Revisited," *International Journal of Technology Assessment in Health Care*, Vol. 2, No. 3 (1986), 387–410.

"Four Modernizations" era, under the joint auspices of AAAS and CAST. As a team of two, we did six weeks of medical sociological fieldwork and teaching, principally in Tianjin First Central Hospital, an important locus of medical modernization, of what the Chinese call "medical morality," and of the post-Gang of Four rehabilitation and development of the Chinese nursing profession. "Medical Morality is Not Bioethics—Medical Ethics in China and the United States," reprinted in this volume, is one of three articles that were published as a consequence of this visit.[10] My third experience in China was a solo one, this time in a period when a national "open door," "market socialism" policy was being emphasized. During the summer of 1985, I spent two months in the field, supported by CAST, and the United States National Academy of Sciences' Distinguished Scholar Exchange Program of the Committee on Scholarly Communication with the People's Republic of China. I requested and was granted the opportunity to do research in the setting of an urban cancer hospital, where I could observe how medical scientists, clinically-involved doctors and nurses, and patients and patients' families deal with the illness that (along with cardiovascular disease and stroke) has become one of the country's major health problems and causes of death. Most of my time was spent at the Beijing Cancer Hospital and Institute of the Chinese Academy of Medical Sciences, and the Yang-Pu District Tumor Hospital of Shanghai. (I also made a sentimental revisit to Tianjin First Central Hospital.)

I never dreamt that I would see China, much less do field research and teaching there. As a consequence, I have come to this China phase of my career in a state of cultural, social, historical, and linguistic unpreparedness that violates the intellectual and moral tenets of my own training, and runs counter to what I teach students about the training they should have to do competent work in societies and cultures other then their own. I feel too strongly about these principles to minimize the inadequacy of my Chinese qualifications. It would be absurdly arrogant to suppose that three short field trips to China—an enormous, teeming, complex, traditional and revolutionary Asian society, with a civilization and written history thousands of years old—make me any kind of Sinological expert. However, there is one unanticipated, quite interesting way in which my long experience as a fieldworking

10. The other two are: Renée C. Fox and Judith P. Swazey, "Critical Care at Tianjin's First Central Hospital and the Fourth Modernization," *Science,* Vol. 217, No. 4561 (August 20, 1982), 700-705; and Bonnie Bilyeu Gordon, "Making Rounds in the People's Republic of China: Four Vignettes of Urban Chinese Medicine," *Science 83,* Vol. 4, No. 3 (April 1983), 56-63 (photographs by Margot Crabtree). The "vignettes" in the Gordon article were drawn from our field notes and her interviews with us about them.

sociologist in Europe, Africa, and the United States has helped me in China. It seems to have given me transferable skill in recognizing and recording cultural patterns. My field notes, I have been told by able China scholars with whom I have shared them, are surprisingly rich in patterns that are integrally, and often anciently, Chinese.

China has catapulted me beyond what I had known or ever expected to know. As the essay ''Medical Morality is Not Bioethics'' indicates, it has also provided me with a societal telescope through which, from a great historical, cultural, and physical distance, I can more clearly see the contours of American society, its distinctive cultural tradition, and the current state of ideas, values, and beliefs that are basic to its collective conscience. Comparing our own, very American bioethics with the very Chinese medical morality has been especially illuminating to me in this regard (although an American philosopher, prominent in the field, views my analysis as ''bioethics baiting'').[11]

''Seeing things through a societal telescope'' describes more than the power of a Chinese perspective, or the general value of a cross-cultural outlook. It refers as well to the relationship between the minutely detailed, close-to-the-ground fieldwork that I do in a specialized medical sphere of sociology, and the panoramic societal and cultural inferences that I incrementally make from this first-hand observation. The progression from micro- to macro-levels of analysis and interpretation is particularly apparent in the essays on ''The Evolution of Medical Uncertainty,'' and on ''Medicine, Science, and Technology'' that are included in this second edition. Searching for the large in the small, and whatever ability I have to find it, were fostered in me by my master-teacher, Talcott Parsons, the ''incurable theorist,'' for whom the human condition was an endlessly intriguing, everyday reality, and also the broadest ''action system'' of all.

So, there have been endings and new beginnings since the first edition of this book was published. And through it all, continuity, fidelity, and commitment give unbroken meaning to my journeys into and out of the field.

RENÉE C. FOX
Philadelphia,
June 1986

11. Samuel Gorovitz, ''Baiting Bioethics'' (survey article), *Ethics,* Vol. 96 (January 1986), 356-374.

Introduction

Assembling a collection of one's own essays obliges one to look back, in a sustained and systematic way, on many years of research and writing, thinking and feeling, and of professional and personal experience. Planning this particular collection involved reviewing almost thirty years of first-hand fieldwork in the area of the sociology of medicine (1950–1979). It entailed rereading a good deal of what I have written and published in the past, and doing so not only from the inside, but also from the outside, as if those writings had been authored by somebody other than myself. In addition, it meant trying to "re-see" the situations that I studied, and the ways that I analyzed and interpreted them. And it invited me to look for deep structure, as well as surface patterns, in the things that I "happened" to study, and in the ways in which I wrote about them. Preparing this volume recast me in a role that I have played throughout most of my professional life, that of participant observer—although in this context, that role became even more reflexive and self-reflexive than usual.

Reviewing my work for this purpose, in these ways, revealed that I have been consistently concerned with chronic and terminal illness, medical research, therapeutic innovation, and medical education and socialization, and with what has come to be known (since the mid-1960s) as "bioethics." The continuous exploration of certain empirical phenomena has been central to my pursuit of these concerns. Three "cases" in particular have been paradigmatic in this regard: the process of becoming a physician; the development of hemodialysis (the use of the artificial kidney machine) and organ transplantation; and the evolution of medical research in Belgium. Not only have a considerable number of my published articles grown out of these cases, but so too have the major books that I have written (*Experiment Perilous* and *The Courage to Fail*), and the one on which I am currently working—what I have long referred to as my "Belgian book," or "Belgium Through the Windows of its Medical Laboratories."[1]

Over the years, I have also worked on what might be called "occasional cases": that is, relatively short-term, one-time, and often more circumscribed phenomena that are related to the principal foci of my socio-medical interests. These have included the cases of the "floppy-eared rabbits" and "serendipity gained and lost" in laboratory experiments with papain, and of "physicians on the drug-industry side of the prescription blank" (both with Bernard Barber); of the "clinical moratorium" and the history of mitral valve surgery (with Judith P. Swazey); and of the Medical Assistants and first African physicians in Congo/Zaïre (with Willy De Craemer).[2] One of the intriguing patterns

1. *Experiment Perilous.* (Glencoe, Illinois: The Free Press, 1959.) Reprinted in a paperback edition with a new introduction, Philadelphia: The University of Pennsylvania Press, 1974. *The Courage to Fail: A Social View of Organ Transplants and Dialysis* (with Judith P. Swazey). (Chicago: The University of Chicago Press, 1974.) Revised, paperback edition, Chicago: University of Chicago Press, 1978.

I am also finishing a monograph on the sociology of medicine for the Prentice-Hall Foundations of Modern Sociology series, under the editorship of Alex Inkeles.

It is notable that these published books do not include one that tells the "story" of the socialization of medical students from the day that they enter the anatomy laboratory at the inception of their training, until the day that they take the Hippocratic or Maimonidean Oath and officially graduate into physicianhood. In fact, during my years as a member of the so-called "Medical School Project" of the Columbia University Department of Sociology and Bureau of Applied Social Research, I worked on such a book. It was based on my four years of participant observation at Cornell University Medical College, one of the primary sites of the project's research, and in the in-group code of the research team, it was referred to as the "sociological calendar" of the medical school. As can happen in group research, where the data are collectively managed as well as gathered and all manuscripts must be approved and released by the project director, the sociological calendar—along with numerous manuscripts written by other members of the project—was never defined as sufficiently complete or satisfactory to be published.

2. "The Case of the Floppy-Eared Rabbits: An Instance of Serendipity Gained and Serendipity Lost" (with Bernard Barber), *American Journal of Sociology*, Vol. 64, No. 2 (September 1958), 128–136; "Physicians on the Drug Industry Side of the Prescription Blank: Their Dual Commitment to Medical Science and Business," *Journal of Health and Human Behavior,* Vol. 2 (Spring 1961), 3–16; "The Clinical Moratorium: A Case Study of Mitral Valve Surgery" (with Judith P. Swazey), in Paul A. Freund, ed., *Experimentation with Human Subjects,* New York: George Braziller, Inc., 1970, 315–357; *The Emerging Physician: A Sociological Approach to the Development of a Congolese Medical Profession* (with Willy De Craemer), Stanford: Hoover Institution Press, Stanford University, 1968.

that I discovered through the retrospective overview of my work is that all these special case studies have been done collaboratively, with colleagues whose competence and experience have complemented and enlarged my own.

From the foregoing, it can be seen that what I have considered to be cases have ranged in size and scope from a particular set of laboratory experiments, therapeutic innovations, or medical roles and training sequences, to the development of a national medical profession, and, beyond that, to those characteristics of a whole society that can be gleaned through a social, cultural, and historical perspective on medicine. In most instances, the initial choice of the micro- and the macro-cases I studied was partly adventitious—for example, the Columbia University Medical School Project was organized toward the end of my graduate work in the Department of Social Relations at Harvard University, and I was hired by that project to be its chief fieldworker at Cornell University Medical College. Still, this did not happen by "chance" alone, for, by 1953, I had already done several years' worth of relevant fieldwork in another medical school setting, principally in connection with my Ph.D. dissertation study of the metabolic research ward (F-Second), at Harvard's Peter Bent Brigham Hospital (later published as *Experiment Perilous*). Furthermore, 1953 was not a year in which jobs for new Ph.D.'s were scarce, as they are at the present time, and so I was not pressured by employment anxieties to accept the Columbia offer. I did so out of inherent intellectual interest in studying the socialization of medical students, and also because the opportunity touched some deeper wellsprings in me that had already been tapped by my previous research.

In this latter regard, it is significant that one of the first attitude-learning sequences that attracted my attention was the "training for uncertainty" that medical students undergo[3] and that the same "theme" of uncertainty had figured so prominently in my previous study of the social world created by patients and physicians on Ward F-Second. (I will return to the uncertainty theme later in this introductory essay.) In any case, it seems altogether appropriate that a sociologist like myself who has been continually interested in the serendipitous and nonserendipitous elements in scientific research should recognize, in an *ex post facto* way, that chance and nonchance factors have entered into her own research undertakings as well. (In my essay "Why Belgium?",[4] included

3. "Training for Uncertainty," in Robert K. Merton, George C. Reader, and Patricia L. Kendall, eds., *The Student-Physician* (Cambridge, Mass.: Harvard University Press, 1957), 207–241.

4. "Why Belgium?", *Archives Européennes de Sociologie*, Vol. 19 (1978), 2–25.

in this collection, I have tried to spell out in some detail how the intermingling of these factors led to my studying and restudying Belgian medical research over the years.)

In the course of these initial remarks, I have referred several times to my research in Continental Europe and Central Africa, as well as in Boston and New York City, U.S.A. The cross-cultural nature of my work has been deliberate. As I have explained in the early pages of "Why Belgium?", my sociological training occurred during a post-World War II period that could aptly be described as a "cross-cultural time" in the orientation of American social science. I was educated and socialized in a comparative institutional framework, through which I came to believe that all sociological analysis is at least implicitly, if not always explicitly, comparative; that "one could not identify distinctively American structural and cultural traits without systematic, knowledgeable reference to other societies"; and that, ideally, each sociologist should progressively and painstakingly develop knowledge of at least several societies other than her (his) own. Furthermore, in the climate of the late 1940s and early 1950s, this kind of cross-cultural competence and range was viewed as a moral as well as an intellectual stance, in support of a one-world spirit of internationalism, and as a safeguard against isolationism, provincialism, and chauvinism. The convictions that I formed in that era have not been shaken over the years. To this day, they are fundamental to the cognitive and ethical premises in which my work as a general sociologist and as a sociologist of medicine is rooted.

Thus, I intentionally undertook research outside the United States. What was not planned or predictable was exactly where that work would be situated. It would be unduly theatrical and essentially false to say that I was "destined" to study Belgian society. However, my returning to Belgium again and again may have some unconscious as well as some self-consciously intellectual significance. In an interview that filmmaker Ingmar Bergman once granted to a *New York Times* reporter, he referred to the island off the coast of Sweden to which he periodically retreats as a place where he "recognized the contours of [him]self." Belgium may have that kind of meaning for me. It may also be more generally true that any place, at home or abroad, that becomes an important research site for a fieldworking social scientist involves some degree of self-recognition in this Bergmanian sense.

Belgium subsequently led me to Congo/Zaïre. When I first arrived in Belgium in 1959, the Congo was still a Belgian colony, scheduled to receive its independence on June 30, 1960. It was not inevitable that my work should transport me to the Congo, but it was both logical and sociological. It was also very Belgian in certain ways because, as I have written elsewhere, in addition to the great economic and geopolitical value that the Congo had for Belgians, it was also a vast open frontier and a "dreaming space" for them. Psychically and physically, they traveled in great numbers toward Belgian, and later ex-Belgian, Africa—from their highly particularistic and conformity-exacting lives in their own small and constricting land. In and through my research, I joined this Belgian exodus. Seeing the mighty Congo River for the first time at dawn, as I looked out of the windows of my descending jet airliner; then, driving past a procession of "African women draped in *pagnes,* carrying bundles on their heads" and babies on their backs, and "moving with silent grace down an early-morning road"[5] to Léopoldville; and, at the end of that first day, experiencing a "heart of darkness" sunset that with terrifying swiftness removed all sound as well as light from the universe—these catapulted me into a personal and professional encounter with Congo/Zaïre that culminated in five intensive years of sociological research on many aspects and in most regions of the country.[6] My exposure to anthropology in graduate school, the romantic images that reading monographs by Radcliffe-Brown, Evans-Pritchard, and Bronislaw Malinowski evoked in me, and a literary conception of Central Africa conveyed by the works of Aimé Césaire, Joseph Conrad, André Gide, and Graham Greene may also have quickened my response to the Congo.

The cross-section of sociology of medicine-related research in the American, Belgian, and Zaïrean societies that this volume of essays represents was conducted largely through the medium of fieldwork, *sur le terrain:* participant observation, face-to-face interviewing, the taking of oral histories, the collection and analysis of primary and secondary documentary materials, and, occasionally, the examination of artifacts. My initial field experience occurred in 1950, at the end of my first year in graduate school. At the Massachusetts General Hospital, under the supervision of Professor of Psychiatry Eric Lindemann, and in collaboration with another graduate student in the Harvard Department of Social Relations, Doris Gilbert, who was working toward her Ph.D. in Clinical Psychology, I observed group therapy sessions with in-patients on the hospital's psychiatric service. These sessions, conceived by Dr. Lindemann and run by Mrs. Gilbert, were designed to strengthen the

5. Acceptance Speech, Radcliffe Graduate Society Medal, Cambridge, Mass., June 14, 1977.

6. From 1963 through 1967, I was a member of and scientific advisor for the Centre de Recherches Sociologiques, located in Kinshasa, Zaïre, and directed by Willy De Craemer. I have made a number of revisits to Zaïre since 1967 (the last one in 1977), but only for relatively short periods of time.

patients' "healthiest," most "mature defenses," enhance their sense of self-worth, reinforce their capacity accurately and insightfully to observe their "reality situation," and involve them in a then-pioneering "patient government." From the discussions that took place in that group, and also from the teaching sessions based on recordings and verbatim transcripts of those meetings that Dr. Lindemann conducted with the young psychiatrist-residents who were the patients' primary therapists,[7] I learned a great deal about the social system of the psychiatric unit. In the end, in order to clarify my thoughts about what I had observed and further my understanding of it, I wrote a paper that I never sought to publish.[8] It analyzed the structural strains that existed between the ward maids and the patients on the unit; identified the unanticipated degree to which the resident psychiatrists were threatened by the fact that their patients sounded much less "sick" in group therapy than in their individual psychotherapy sessions with their physicians; and showed the partly conscious and partly unconscious ways in which the residents succeeded in ending the group-therapy experiment.

Outside of my continuing cycle of American, Belgian, and Zaïrean fieldwork, one of my more recent field trips (in April 1977) was made to the atoll of Majuro in the Marshall Islands. With Linda Alexander, a medical anthropologist, I conducted an exploratory study of the history and operation of a dialysis center on that tiny Pacific atoll (3.5 square miles in land mass), surrounded by sea and sky. In this Oceanic setting, for the first time, I had the experience of working with audio-visual means of recording observations, as well as my usual paper-and-pen ways of proceeding.[9]

The question of "Why fieldwork?"—as well as, "Why Majuro, Zaïre, and Belgium?"—might be raised about my research. Too often in the discipline of sociology (and also in other social sciences), it is assumed that a researcher has chosen a particular set of methods out of the partisan conviction that they are inherently superior to other modes of inquiry. Although my primary research instruments have been partici-

7. The recordings were made with the informed, voluntary consent of the patients, who also gave their permission for the psychiatric residents to hear them.

8. "My Experience as a Sociological Observer on the Psychiatric Service of Massachusetts General Hospital: Some Reflections on Patterned Biases of Psychiatric Practitioners and on Ward B-7 as a Social System," March 1951 (40 pp.).

9. Ms. Cinda Weber accompanied Linda Alexander and me on this field trip to Majuro and did all the filming and the sound recording in close collaboration with us. The three of us are currently editing some of these materials with the goal of making a teaching film about "dialysis on a coral island" that we hope might be useful for technicians, nurses, physicians, nursing and medical students, and social scientists interested in medicine.

pant observation and focused, "on-the-hoof" interviewing, I am as aware of their limitations as of their assets. My teaching of fieldwork to students and others has always been embedded in a larger methodological framework: one in which I have systematically identified the special properties of each of the gamut of social research methods available to investigators, including their particular advantages and disadvantages.

It is probably true that field methods fit my temperament, some of my basic personality traits, and certain of my talents in ways not easy to analyze. Developing my ability to use this repertoire of methods also has some relationship to the yearning writer in me. But what is most important about my recurrent use of field methods is that my decisions to do so have been consistently based on my professional judgment that they were culturally suited to the social milieux in which my research has taken place, and scientifically appropriate for the kinds of data that I wished to gather in those settings. For example, during my 1962–1967 period in Zaïre, the administration of a survey research questionnaire presented great physical as well as cultural difficulties, including problems of paper, pen, and pencil supplies; printing facilities; reliable postal services; translations into the many different languages of the country; and eliciting responses with an impersonal, long-distance instrument. On the other hand, participant observation, face-to-face interviewing, oral history taking, and the study of local documents enabled my colleagues at the Centre de Recherches Sociologiques and me to deal with some of these obstacles by traveling personally to our research sites, where we enlisted the collaborative aid of informants and respondents native to those regions, and carried out our inquiries on the terrain in an observable, *in vivo* way. To take another example, although Belgium is justifiably proud of its postal system, its printing tradition, and its paper industry, the extreme particularism of that society and the high levels of institutionalized shyness, reserve, and distrust that characterize it—along with widespread, negatively inclined unfamiliarity with how sociologists work—combined to create certain disadvantages for a survey researcher that a fieldworker might hope to overcome. In the sorts of clinical medical research and medical educational contexts that I have investigated in American society (despite some of the scientistic tendencies that physicians, nurses, medical students, and patients often exhibited), a fieldworking sociologist has been more likely to be accepted and approved than one engaged in survey research. In my own case, my research behavior has been regarded by most medical professionals and patients (and also by their families) as compatible with some of the paramount norms and values of their own social systems and subcultures. By and large, I have been viewed as clinically oriented and trained;

demonstrably interested in medicine; humanistic as well as scientific in outlook; sufficiently motivated and caring to share the frequently stressful and tragic predicaments of the persons in the situations I was studying; and able to cope with its elements of ordeal.

By this time, it has become abundantly clear that, without ignoring social structural and social organizational factors, I have been more concerned with cultural, psychological, historical, biological, and phenomenological aspects of health, illness, and medicine than many other sociologists of medicine. Field methods have provided me with apt and penetrating means for probing and presenting these facets of social reality. My choice of methods, then, has been associated with still another characteristic of my work: its interdisciplinary perspective. For that perspective, as for my cross-cultural orientation, I am not only indebted to the general ethos and ambience of American social science in the era in which I did graduate work, but to the education that I received in the Harvard Department of Social Relations in particular and, above all, to the example of my major teacher, Talcott Parsons and the opportunities for anthropological, psychological, psychiatric, and biomedical training that he made available to me.

The impact of clinical psychology and psychoanalytic psychiatry on my thinking is especially visible in those aspects of my writings about medical students, research physicians, and dialysis and transplant patients that deal with the stresses they experienced and the ways they developed for coming to terms with those stresses. Certain Freudian conceptions about defense mechanisms that I have reformulated in order to make them applicable to a social-system level of analysis underlie these accounts. In addition, biomedical notions about the dynamics of stress, principally those associated with research on the adrenal cortex (to which I was intensively exposed on Ward F-Second), have influenced me.

The sociology of medical science and medical research dimensions of my work have obliged me to acquire sufficient biomedical knowledge and understanding to deal competently with the cases through which I have pursued these interests. In addition, I have always proceeded on the assumption that exempting oneself from exploring biological aspects of medicine on the grounds that they fall outside the orbit of sociologically relevant considerations is to overlook some of the important ways in which attitudes, values, beliefs, symbols, and myths are coded into the language, concepts, facts, and modes of reasoning of the various fields that make up medicine. This assumption, for example, was basic to my demonstration of the relationship between anatomy, pharmacology, and pathology, and medical students' training for uncertainty and detached concern; to my deciphering of the electrolyte balance language of the research physicians of Ward F-Second in *Experiment Perilous* and my discovery of their several forms of "scientific magic"; and, more recently, in the revised edition of *The Courage to Fail,* to the analysis that Judith Swazey and I made of changing medical attitudes toward kidney, heart, liver, and bone marrow transplantation, and toward the probability of an imminent "breakthrough" in understanding and controlling the rejection reaction.

My collaboration with Judith Swazey, a trained historian of medicine and science, has professionalized and greatly enriched the historical perspective that I have tried to incorporate into my work. I have done so out of a vivid interest in the relationship between the present, the past, and the future, and in the structure and dynamics of social and cultural change and nonchange. Furthermore, I have always believed that viewing contemporaneous events within an historical framework can help a sociologist to avoid the kinds of interpretive distortions that often result from dealing with social and cultural phenomena in a strictly here-and-now, static, and *sui generis* way. The primary respect in which my research has been historical lies in my study and re-study of the case of dialysis and transplantation since 1951; of the socialization of American medical students since 1953; and of Belgian medical research since 1959. Occasionally, as in the study of the clinical moratorium and mitral valve surgery, I have focused on historical aspects of a contemporaneous case that antedate the 1950s and that I did not personally observe.

But if I were asked to identify the primary way in which the work represented in this volume is interdisciplinary in scope and outlook, I would cite its preoccupation with cultural phenomena and questions. Not only is the work cross-cultural in orientation, and concerned with values, beliefs, symbols, rites, and the nuances of language, but, in a more comprehensive way, it deals continually with interrelationships between medicine, science, religion, and magic. This overarching characteristic of the work owes much to the writings of cultural anthropologists Malinowski, Mauss, Evans-Pritchard, and Geertz, as well as to sociologists Durkheim, Weber, Parsons, and Bellah. My interest in these relationships is emblematically expressed in the titles of some of my books and articles: *Experiment Perilous, The Courage to Fail,* "Training for Uncertainty," "The 'Gift of Life' and Its Reciprocation," and "Medical Scientists in a Château," among others. It is most clearly and explicitly apparent in what I have written about death, suffering, chance, "gallows humor," "scientific magic," gift exchange, the "tyranny of the gift," and the allocation of scarce nonmaterial resources like caring, compassion, and commitment. It is manifest in my collaborative publications about Congo/Zaïre (especially in " 'The Second Independence': A Case Study of the Kwilu Rebellion in the Congo," and "Religious Movements in Central Africa").[10] It will have an important place in the book that I am writing about medical research in predominantly (and in many ways subtly) Catholic Belgium. And it has converged with the recent development of bioethics in the United States (about which I have written several essays),[11] and with the society-wide moral and existential concerns that this new field represents.

The book and article titles that I have cited are cultural in still another sense. They are connected with what (at the risk of sounding grandiose) might be termed my underlying world view. In a speech to the Radcliffe College Graduate Society, I tried to describe that view and how it has affected my work:[12]

> . . . Wonder over the vastness and complexity of the human condition, and over the similarities as well as the differences in what people experience, how they think and feel, imagine and act has impelled me to search beyond the boundaries of my own society. . . . A lived-out rather than a verbalized conviction that I ought to be sufficiently open and unafraid, questing yet committed to go where my work carries me, and the need to do so underlie its voyaging contemplativeness. A romantic kind of mysticism, too: the sort of recognition and ultimacy that I felt looking down on Majuro; or seeing the Congo River for the first time. . . . The feeling of ultimacy is associated with a tragic sense that underlies and animates my work. By tragic, I do not mean melancholy or pessimistic. Quite to the contrary, the continual awareness that life is finite, and death is a part of it makes me marvel all the more over how much there is to learn, and understand, and try to communicate while we are here, and has given me enough joyous conviction to undertake the study, the research, the writing, the traveling, and the teaching despite the "natural" shyness from which we all suffer and, in my own case, in spite of a great deal of existential anxiety as well. . . .

From wherever it comes, this kind of relationship to life and death is not only inherent to the fact that a great deal of my work has centered on the

10. " 'The Second Independence': A Case Study of the Kwilu Rebellion in the Congo" (with Willy De Craemer and Jean-Marie Ribeaucourt), *Comparative Studies in Society and History,* Vol. VIII, No. 1 (October 1965), 78–109; "Religious Movements in Central Africa" (with Willy De Craemer and Jan Vansina), *Comparative Studies in Society and History,* Vol. 18, No. 4 (October 1978), 458–475.

11. "Ethical and Existential Developments in Contemporaneous American Medicine: Their Implications for Culture and Society," The Milbank Memorial Fund Quarterly, *Health and Society,* Vol. II (1976), 231–268; "Ethical Aspects of Biomedical Advance," *Acta Hospitalia,* Vol. XVI, No. 4 (Winter 1976), 280–293; "*L'éthique dans les sciences médicales: Les cas de la dialyse et de la transplantation des organes,*" unpublished talk to the Groupe de Synthèse, Maison Saint Jean, Heverlee, Belgium, May 21, 1977.

12. Acceptance Speech, Radcliffe Graduate Society Medal, Cambridge, Mass., June 14, 1977.

> sociology of health, illness, and medicine, but in a deep-structure way, it has influenced the phenomena I have studied, the questions I have asked, and the themes with which I have been preoccupied. . . . From a certain point of view I could, and perhaps should, be faulted for having written too little about "ordinary" medical concerns and acute health policy issues in our society, and too much about "extraordinary" [ones]. . . . But these foci of interest and concern have both allowed and obliged me to deal continually with some of the most basic and transcendent questions of the human condition and of its meaning. . . .
>
> As a participant observer, and an observing participant, I have shared the predicament of physicians, nurses, patients, and their families, working and living and dying on the edge of what is known, scrutable, and remediable, and the predicament of medical students confronted with the . . . existential as well as cognitive reality of all that doctorhood ideally asks of one. . . . I have watched how . . . patients and their kin, medical professionals and students have tried to cope with these situations and issues. Without unduly glorifying them (for though patienthood or doctorhood may transform persons in certain ways, it does not necessarily sanctify them), I have learned priceless things from these men and women. Cosmic laughter, for one: appreciation of the unexpected whimsy of seeing rabbits' ears droop and progressively collapse around their heads as a consequence of an injection of papain that they received in the course of a laboratory experiment; the poignancy and bravado of the black humor of besieged patients and physicians, especially when, either directly or vicariously, they find themselves face to face with death; the Kafkaesque absurdity of holding a medical scientific colloquium in a still functioning royal palace; and what often seems to be the "game of chance"-like capriciousness of how the experiments we conduct or the therapies we administer turn out. I have learned, too, that in the face of such ultimate experiences, Job-like questions are wrenched out of most people, and that it is the quality of their *Angst,* rather than of their education, that determines how lucidly and lyrically these questions are answered. Finally, I have learned, as did Job, that God does not lean down out of heaven like a benevolent, didactically spoon-feeding professor and give us clear, certain answers that we can neatly copy into our human-condition notebooks.

One of the analytic exercises in which I engaged as I reread my writings and planned this book was to list some of the broad themes that repeatedly appear in those pages:

- Life/Death (including Birth and Survival)
- Suffering/Healing
- Uncertainty/Certainty
- Chance/Necessity
- Freedom/Responsibility

- Risk/Benefit
- Detachment/Concern
- Participation/Observation
- Protest/Acceptance
- Intervention/Restraint
- Persistence/Desistence
- Courage/Hubris
- Success/Failure
- Abundance/Scarcity
- Justice/Equity
- Individuality/Solidarity
- Particularism/Universalism (my brother's [sister's] keeper / my stranger's keeper)

These pairs constitute some of the principal cultural, social, and psychological ambiguities, dilemmas, ambivalences, countertendencies, tensions, conflicts, and choices with which the actors have frequently been faced, and that they have been called upon to resolve in individual and collective ways. The themes and the human predicaments they represent are integrally related to some of the moral questions and problems of meaning that are central to the Jewish-Christian religious tradition of Western society.

In reflecting on these thematic pairs, it occurred to me that a tendency to see dualities of various kinds in social and cultural life, and to grapple with their interrelationships and significance, is one of the most general conceptual characteristics of my work. Is it "accidental" that I studied physicians who are researchers and clinicians; members of a hospital ward community who are patients and human subjects; organ transplantation that juxtaposes the acts of giving and receiving; Congolese medical assistants who are "neither nurses nor doctors, but fall somewhere in between"; drug industry physicians who have professional and business role attributes; training for detachment/concern; Belgians who are Flemish and Walloon, Catholic and Free Mason, in a country that is highly centralized in some ways, and decentralized in others—and that I have used the method of participation-cum-observation to inquire into all these things? What accounts for the dualities with which my work is laced? My own medical and life-history experiences? Basic personality tendencies? My metaphysical sense? The enduring impact of Talcott Parsons's pattern variable pairs and paradigm on my thinking? Or perhaps there are properties inherent to the health/illness/medicine sector of a society, and to the situations and roles of patients, their families, medical professionals, and the sociologists studying them that engender such dualities, bring them to the surface, and infuse them with more than everyday significance.[13]

I leave these questions to readers to pursue if it interests them to do so, for I find that raising them has brought me to the end of my capacity to go any further with this insider/outsider analysis of the patterns in my own work. In the closing paragraphs of this introductory essay, I want briefly to explain how the essays in this book were chosen and ordered, and to acknowledge at least a few of the many persons who have accompanied me on my journeys in the United States, Belgium, and Congo/Zaïre, into the tragicomic worlds of Ward F-Second, the medical laboratory, the medical school, the medical assistants, live and cadaveric organ transplantations, artificial kidneys and artificial hearts, out of which most of these essays have grown.

Both chronological and conceptual factors have determined how the essays that I have selected are arranged. In principle, the volume should have begun with one of my best-known publications, "Illness, Therapy, and the Modern Urban American Family," *The Journal of Social Issues*, Vol. 8, No. 4 (1952), 31–44, written with Talcott Parsons.[14] Not only was this the first article that I published, but it documents the fact that it was Parsons's teaching, personal influence, and writings that launched me on my work in the sociology of medicine. During my second year in graduate school, Parsons was in the midst of writing *The Social System*,[15] and I was a member of a small seminar of students who worked with him on the parts of the book that dealt with the pattern variables, socialization, social control, and his famous Chapter X on "Social Structure and Dynamic Process: The Case of Modern Medical Practice," in which his concept of the "sick role" and of the uncertainty dimension in the physician's role were set forth in early form.[16] "Illness, Therapy, and the Modern Urban American Family" was written in that context and pe-

13. In his introductory essay to *The Student-Physician* (Cambridge, Mass.: Harvard University Press, 1957), Robert K. Merton suggests that one of the major socialization tasks with which medical students are faced is learning to reconcile and blend a series of dualistic expectations and obligations that are part of the physician's role: "Medical education can be conceived as facing the task of enabling students to learn *how to blend* incompatible or potentially incompatible norms into a functional consistent whole. Indeed, the process of learning to be a physician can be conceived as largely the learning of blending seeming or actual incompatibles into consistent and stable patterns of professional behavior" (p. 72).

14. "Illness, Therapy, and the Modern Urban American Family," *The Journal of Social Issues*, Vol. 8, No. 4 (1952), 31–44.

15. Talcott Parsons, *The Social System* (Glencoe, Ill.: The Free Press, 1951).

16. *Ibid.*, 428–479. The other students in this seminar were François Bourricaud, Miriam Massey, the Rev. John V. Martin, Robert N. Wilson, and Dr. Lyman Wynne.

riod, after I had begun my own research on Ward F-Second, which also contributed to the content and the conceptualization of the Parsons-Fox article. I have not included it in this volume because it has been reprinted many times and is still widely available. However, the essence of that article has been summarized in my essay "Medical Evolution," written for the *Festschrift* volume in honor of Talcott Parsons (edited by Jan J. Loubser, Rainer C. Baum, Andrew Effrat, and Victor M. Lidz), which I have included in Part VI of this book.[17]

Parts I through IV are devoted to the major cases that I have studied over the years: medical education and socialization, organ transplantation and hemodialysis, and American and Belgian medical research. If I had been strictly chronological in deciding on the sequence of essays, I would have put the section on transplantation and dialysis first, because my original encounter with these therapeutic innovations occurred on Ward F-Second, the site of my doctoral dissertation research, which antedates all the other work encompassed by this book. But it seemed more sociological to begin with several essays on the education and socialization of medical students—physicians-in-becoming. In this first section of the book, I have chosen to present the "training for detached concern" aspect of medical socialization through an unpublished essay on "The Autopsy," rather than through the article on "Training for 'Detached Concern' in Medical Students" that I published with Harold I. Lief.[18] I have done so because the papers overlap considerably, and although the autopsy piece was written in 1958 (before the Lief-Fox article), I continue to receive many requests for this paper, which has never been available in print.

In Part III, the focus shifts from the medical student and physician side of the "experiment perilous" aspects of medical practice and research to those experienced by patients and human subjects, individually and communally, and by persons cast in the at once transcendent and binding roles of donors and recipients.

Part IV moves from the land of American medical research to the land of Belgian medical research.

Part V consists of an assortment of special, "occasional" case studies that I have undertaken.

Part VI is composed of two essays on bioethics: one in which I not only described the concrete phenomena associated with the emergence of this new field, but also tried to analyze and interpret its larger social and

17. "Medical Evolution," in Jan J. Loubser, Rainer C. Baum, Andrew Effrat, and Victor M. Lidz, eds. (New York: The Free Press, 1976), 773–787.

18. "Training for 'Detached Concern' in Medical Students," in Harold I. Lief et al., eds., *The Psychological Basis of Medical Practice* (New York: Harper and Row, 1963), 12–35.

cultural meaning and impact; and the other, in which I reviewed the relatively sparse work of sociologists in this area, inquired into their seeming reluctance to enter the field, and identified some of the social and intellectual characteristics of the philosophers, theologians, lawyers, and physicians who are the chief contributors to the bioethics literature.

The final section of the book (VII) brings together three macroanalytic essays that synthesize various of the insights and findings of my medical sociological research by placing them in a broad societal and cultural framework. In fact, the whole book moves progressively from micro- to macro-levels of analysis, both with respect to the way that the individual essays are grouped within each of the seven sections and the way that the sections have been ordered.

One additional and timely note: I have left the pronomial usage—currently outmoded though it might be—as it was in the original forms of these essays. Thus, the reader will note "his" rather than "his or hers." When these essays were written, of course, the former was the more accurate.

Over the course of the years that this collection of essays spans, I have received a special "gift of life" from the following special people:

My mother and father, who brought me into the world, and gave me my upbringing, my education, the example of their own lives, and their love.

Talcott Parsons, my great teacher, to whom I not only owe whatever sociological competence I have, but who, along with his wife, Helen, and his daughter, Anne, has graced my life with an extraordinary friendship.

Willy De Craemer, who gave me the *courage/moed* to continue my work in Belgium (and elsewhere), who taught me all that I know about Zaïre and Central Africa, and who understands better than anyone else the existential wellsprings of my work.

Judith P. Swazey and her family, with whom I have shared "the courage to fail" and not to fail, and the deep personal as well as professional things that this has implied.

Paul O'Brian—a pseudonym—of Ward F-Second and *Experiment Perilous,* who has continued to personify for me the hope and the despair of all the patients, families, physicians, and nurses I have known.

In gratitude, reciprocity, and unity, I offer this book to them.

Paris, France
August 1978

PART ONE

MEDICAL EDUCATION AND SOCIALIZATION

Training for Uncertainty

There are areas of experience where we know that uncertainty is the certainty.
—James B. Conant

Voluminous texts, crammed notebooks, and tightly packed memories of students at Cornell University Medical College attest to the "enormous amount"[1] of established medical knowledge they are expected to learn. It is less commonly recognized that they also learn much about the uncertainties of medicine and how to cope with them. Because training for uncertainty in the preparation of a doctor has been largely overlooked, the following discussion will be focused exclusively on this aspect of medical education, but with full realization that it is counterbalanced by "all the material [students] learn that is as solid and real as a hospital building."

There is of course marked variation among students in the degree to which uncertainty is recognized or acknowledged. Some students, more

1. Unless otherwise indicated, all the quoted phrases and passages in this paper are drawn from the diaries that eleven Cornell students at various points along the medical school continuum have kept for us over the course of the past three years; from interviews with these student diarists and some of their classmates; and from close-to-verbatim student dialogue recorded by the sociologist who carried out day-by-day observations in some of the medical school situations cited in this paper.

Robert K. Merton et al., eds., from *The Student-Physician* (Cambridge, Mass.: Harvard University Press, 1957), 207–241.

inclined than others to equate knowing with pages covered and facts memorized, may think they have "really accomplished a lot . . . gained valuable knowledge," and that what they have learned is "firmly embedded and clear in their minds." Other students are more sensitive to the "vastness of medicine," and more conscious of ignorance and superficiality in the face of all they "should know," and of all the "puzzling questions" they glimpse but cannot answer. Many students fall somewhere between these two extremes, half-aware in the course of diligent learning that there is much they do not understand, yet not disposed "at this point to stop and lament." Discussion will be limited to the training for uncertainty that seems to apply to the largest number of students, admitting at the outset that inferences from the data must be provisional.

THE KINDS OF UNCERTAINTY THAT THE DOCTOR FACES

In Western society, where disease is presumed to yield to application of scientific method, the doctor is regarded as an expert, a man professionally trained in matters pertaining to sickness and health and able by his medical competence to cure our ills and keep us well. It would be good to think that he has only to make a diagnosis and to apply appropriate treatment for alleviation of ills to follow. But such a utopian view of the physician is at variance with facts. His knowledge and skill are not always adequate, and there are many times when his most vigorous efforts to understand illness and to rectify its consequences may be of no avail. Despite unprecedented scientific advances, the life of the modern physician is still full of uncertainty.[2]

Two basic types of uncertainty may be recognized. The first results from incomplete or imperfect mastery of available knowledge. No one can have at his command all skills and all knowledge of the lore of medicine. The second depends upon limitations in current medical knowledge. There are innumerable questions to which no physician, however well trained, can as yet provide answers. A third source of uncertainty derives from the first two. This consists of difficulty in distinguishing between personal ignorance or ineptitude and the limitations of present medical knowledge. It is inevitable that every doctor

2. It is not only the doctor, of course, who must deal with the problem of uncertainty. To some extent this problem presents itself in all forms of responsible human action. The business executive or the parent, for example, has no assurance that his decisions will have the desired results. But the doctor is particularly subject to this problem, for his decisions are likely to have profound and directly observable consequences for his patients.

must constantly cope with these forms of uncertainty and that grave consequences may result if he is not able to do so. It is for this reason that training for uncertainty in a medical curriculum and in early professional experiences is an important part of becoming a physician.

An effort will be made to identify some experiences as well as some agencies and mechanisms in medical school that prepare students for uncertainty and to designate patterns by which students may gradually come to terms with uncertainty. In the initial inquiry we shall content ourselves with a general view of the sequence through which most students pass, but in a concluding section we shall suggest some variations that might be considered in further investigation of training for uncertainty.

THE PRECLINICAL YEARS

Learning to Acknowledge Uncertainty

The first kind of uncertainty that the student encounters has its source in his role as a student. It derives from the avoidance of "spoon-feeding," a philosophy of the preclinical years at Cornell Medical College (as at many other medical schools).

> You will from the start be given the major responsibility for learning [students are told on the first day that they enter medical school]. Most of your undergraduate courses to date have had fixed and circumscribed limits; your textbooks have been of ponderable dimensions. . . . Not so with your medical college courses. . . . We do not use the comfortable method of spoon-feeding. . . .[3] Limits are not fixed. Each field will be opened up somewhat sketchily. . . . You will begin to paint a picture on a vast canvas but only the center of the picture will be worked in any detail. The periphery will gradually blur into the hazy background. And the more you work out the peripheral pattern, the more you will realize the vastness of that which stretches an unknown distance beyond. . . . Another common collegiate goal is to excel in competition with others. . . . [But] because an overly competitive environment can hinder learning, student ratings are never divulged [in this medical school], except to the extent that once a

3. This particular sentence was taken from the "Address of Welcome to the Class of 1957" delivered by Dr. Lawrence W. Hanlon. Everything else in the paragraph quoted above is extracted from "Some Steps in the Maturation of the Medical Student," a speech delivered by Dr. Robert F. Pitts at Opening Day Exercises, September 1952.

> year each student is privately informed as to which quarter of the class he is in.

From the first, the medical school rookie is thus confronted with the challenge of a situation only hazily defined for him. Information is not presented "in neat packets"[4]; precise boundaries are not set on the amount of work expected. Under these conditions the uncertainty that the beginning student faces lies in determining how much he ought to know, exactly what he should learn, and how he ought to go about his studies.

This uncertainty, great as it is, is further accentuated for the beginner by the fact that he does not receive grades, and therefore does not have the usual concrete evidence by which to discover whether he is in fact doing well:

> In college, if you decide to work very hard in a course, the usual result is that you do very well in it, and you have the feeling that studying hard leads to good grades. You may tell yourself that you don't give a damn about grades, but nevertheless, they do give you some reassurance when you ask yourself if the work was worth it. . . . In medical school, there is no such relationship. Studying does not always lead to doing well—it is quite easy to study hard, but to study the wrong things and do poorly. And if you should do well, you never know it. . . . In my own case, I honestly think the thing that bothers me most is not the lack of grades, but rather the feeling that even after studying some in a given course, I always end up knowing so little of what I should know about it. . . . Medicine is such an enormous proposition that one cannot help but fall short of what he feels he should get done. . . .

Thus, it would seem that avoidance of spoon-feeding by the preclinical faculty encourages the student to take responsibility in a relatively unstructured situation, perhaps providing him with a foretaste of the ambiguities he may encounter when he assumes responsibility for a patient.

From the latter parts of the comment under review it would appear that the same teaching philosophy also leads to the beginning awareness of a second type of uncertainty: by making the student conscious of how vast medicine is, the absence of spoon-feeding readies him for the fact that even as a mature physician he will not always experience the certainty that comes with knowing "all there is to know" about the medical problems with which he is faced. He begins to realize that, no matter how

4. Pitts, *ibid.*

skilled and well informed he may gradually become, his mastery of all that is known in medicine will never be complete.

It is perhaps during the course of studying gross anatomy that the student experiences this type of uncertainty most intensely. Over the centuries this science has gradually traced out what one medical student describes as the "blueprint of the body." As a result of his struggle to master a "huge body of facts," he comes to see more clearly that medicine is such an "enormous proposition" he can never hope to command it in a way both encompassing and sure:

> . . . Men have been able to study the body for thousands of years . . . to dissect the cadaver . . . and to work on it with the naked eye. They may not know everything about the biochemistry of the body, or understand it all microscopically . . . but when it comes to the gross anatomy, they know just about all there is to know. . . . This vast sea of information that we have to keep from going out the other ear is overwhelming. . . . There's a sense in which even before I came to medical school I knew that I didn't know anything. But I never *realized* it before, if you know what I mean—not to the extent that it was actually a gripping part of me. Basically, I guess what I thought before was, sure, I was ignorant *now*—but I'd be pretty smart after a while. Well, at this point it's evident to me that even after four years, I'll still be ignorant. . . . I'm now in the process of learning how much there is to learn. . . .[5]

As in this case, the student's own sense of personal inadequacy may be further reinforced by the contrast he draws between his knowledge and that which he attributes to his instructors. Believing as he does that "when it comes to the gross anatomy, they know just about all there is to know," he is made increasingly aware of how imperfect his own mastery really is.

There are other courses and situations in preclinical years that acquaint the Cornell student with uncertainties that result, not from his own inadequacies, but from the limitations in the current state of medical knowledge. For example, standing in distinction to the amassed knowledge of a discipline such as gross anatomy is a science like phar-

5. Such a felt sense that there will always be more to learn in medicine than he can possibly make his own is the beginning of the medical student's acceptance of limitation. It might also be said that this same realization is often one of the attitudinal first signs of a later decision on the part of a student to enter a specialized medical field. This is of some relevance to the discussion of specialization by Patricia L. Kendall and Hanan C. Selvin, "Tendencies toward Specialization in Medical Training," also printed in *The Student-Physician.*

macology, which only in recent years has begun to emerge from a trial-and-error state of experimentation:

> Throughout the history of pharmacology, it would appear that the ultimate goal was to expedite the search for agents with actions on living systems and to provide explanations for these actions, to the practical end of providing drugs which might be used in the treatment of the disease of man. As a result of many searches there now exist such great numbers of drugs that the task of organizing them is a formidable one. The need for the development of generalizations and simplifying assumptions is great. It is to be hoped that laws and theories of drug action will be forthcoming, but the student should at this point appreciate that few of them, as yet, exist.[6]

The tentativeness of pharmacology as a science, then, advances the student's recognition that not all the gaps in his knowledge indicate deficiencies on his part. In effect, pharmacology helps teach medical students that, because "there are so many voids" in medical knowledge, the practice of medicine is sometimes largely "a matter of conjuring . . . possibilities and probabilities."

> When Charles was over for dinner last week, I remarked at the time that I was coming to the conclusion that medicine was certainly no precise science, but rather, it is simply a matter of probabilities. Even these drugs today, for example, were noted as to their wide range of action. One dose will be too small to elicit a response in one individual; the same dose will be sufficient to get just the right response in another; and in yet another individual, the same dose will produce hypersensitive toxic results. So, there is nothing exact in this, I guess. It's a matter of conjuring the possibilities and probabilities and then drawing conclusions as to the most likely response and the proper thing to do. And Charles last week agreed that a doctor is just an artist who has learned to derive these probabilities and then prescribe a treatment.

In pharmacology (and in the other basic medical sciences as well) it is assumed that "laws and theories will be forthcoming" so that the uncertainties resulting from limited knowledge in the field will gradually yield to greater certainty. However, the "experimental point of view" pervading much of early teaching at the Cornell Medical College promotes the idea that an irreducible minimum of uncertainty is inherent in medicine, in spite of the promise of further scientific advance. The

6. Joseph A. Wells, "Historical Background and General Principles of Drug Action," in Victor A. Drill, ed., *Pharmacology in Medicine* (New York: McGraw-Hill Book Company, 1945), p. 6.

preclinical instructors presenting this point of view have as a basic premise the idea that medical knowledge thus far attained must be regarded as no more than tentative, and must be constantly subjected to further inquiry. It is their assumption that few absolutes exist:

> If you were having a great deal of trouble finding some simple sort of cell in histology and you asked him about it, Dr. A. always made a point to give you information from the experimental point of view. He would (a) point out that this cell has five different names; (b) point out that this cell might actually be a ——— cell or a ——— cell that has undergone a transformation and that indeed this cell might be able to change into almost anything; (c) also mention that even though the cell has five names, it may not, in fact, exist in the first place—perhaps it's just an artifact.
>
> Or, take the way the Bacteriology Department pushes the theme of "individual differences"—how one person will contract a disease he's been exposed to, while another one won't. The person may have a chill, or not; the agent may be virulent or not; and that determines whether pneumonia will occur or not. . . . "The occurrence, progression and outcome of a disease is a function of the offense of the microorganism and the defense of the host." That's the formula they keep pounding home. . . .
>
> . . . In the course of the demonstration of drugs affecting respiration, Dr. S. quoted Goodman and Gilman [a pharmacology textbook universally recommended and respected] as to the dramatic effect of one certain drug in respiratory failure. And then they proceeded to show the falsity of that statement. So pharmacologists are now debunking pharmacologists! Heretofore they simply showed the drugs commonly used by many physicians had no effect. If this keeps up, we will all be first-class skeptics!

This is not to say, a student cautions, that we don't learn "a lot of established facts . . . tried and true things about which there is little or no argument." But in course after course during the preclinical years at Cornell, emphasis is also placed on the provisional nature of much that is assumed to be medically known. The experimental point of view set forth by his teachers makes it more apparent than it might otherwise be that medicine is something less than a powerful, exact science, based on nicely invariant principles. In this way, the student is encouraged to acknowledge uncertainty and, more than this, to tolerate it. He is made aware, not only that it is possible to act in spite of uncertainties, but that some of his teachers make such uncertainties the basis of their own experimental work.

Up to this point we have reviewed some of the courses and situations in the preclinical years at Cornell that make the beginning student aware of his own inadequacies and others that lead him to recognize limitations in current medical knowledge. The student has other experiences during the early years of medical school that present him with the problem of distinguishing between these two types of uncertainty—that is, there are times when he is unsure where his limitations leave off and the limitations of medical science begin. The difficulty is particularly evident in situations where he is called upon to make observations.

Whether he is trying to visualize an anatomical entity, studying gross or microscopic specimens in pathology, utilizing the method of percussion in physical diagnosis, or taking a personal history in psychiatry, the preclinical student is being asked to glean whatever information he can from the processes of looking, feeling, and listening.[7] In all these situations, students are often expected to see before they know how to look or what to look for. For the ability to "see what you ought to see," "feel what you ought to feel," and "hear what you ought to hear," students assure us, is premised upon "a knowledge of what you're supposed to observe," an ordered method for making these observations, and a great deal of practice in medical ways of perceiving. ("We see only what we look for. We look for only what we know," the famous Goethe axiom goes.)

Nowhere does this kind of uncertainty become more salient for medical students during their preclinical years than in physical diagnosis:

> Physical diagnosis is the one course I don't feel quite right about. I still have a great deal of difficulty making observations, and I usually don't feel certain about them. . . . Dick and I had a forty-year-old woman as our patient this morning. Though I thought we were doing better than usual at the time, we nevertheless missed several important things—a murmur and an enlarged spleen. . . .

"This sort of thing happens often in a course like physical diagnosis," the same student continues, and "it raises a question that gives me quite a bit of concern—*why* do I have . . . difficulty making observations?"

There are at least two reasons why a student may "miss" an important clinical sign, or feel uncertain about its presence or absence. On the one hand, his oversight or doubt may be largely attributable to lack of knowledge or skill on his part:

> One of the problems now is that we don't know the primary clinical signs of various disease processes. . . . For example, today we suspected subacute bacterial endocarditis, but we didn't know that the spleen is usually enlarged, and as a result, we didn't feel as hard as we should have. . . .

7. The physician is called upon to use his sense of smell and of taste on occasion, too, but not as frequently as those of sight, touch, and hearing.

On the other hand, missing a spleen, for example, or "not being sure you hear a murmur" is sometimes more the "fault of the field" (as one student puts it) than "your own fault." That is, given the limitations in current medical knowledge and technique, the enlargement of a spleen may be too slight, the sound of a murmur too subtle, for "even the experts to agree upon it."

The uncertainty for a student, then, lies in trying to determine how much of his own "trouble . . . hearing, feeling or seeing is personal," and how much of it "has to do with factors outside of himself." (Or, as another student phrases the problem: "How do you make the distinction between yourself and objectivity?")

Generically, the student's uncertainty in this respect is no different from that to which every responsible, self-critical doctor is often subject. But because he has not yet developed the discrimination and judgment of a skilled diagnostician, a student is usually less sure than a mature physician about where to draw the line between his own limitations and those of medical science. When in doubt, a student seems more likely than an experienced practitioner to question and "blame" himself.

His course in gross anatomy, it has been suggested, gives a Cornell student some awareness of his own inadequacies; pharmacology emphasizes the limitations of current medical knowledge; and his training in observation, particularly in physical diagnosis, confronts him with the problem of distinguishing between his own limitations and those in the field of medicine. But in his second year his participation in autopsies simultaneously exposes the student to all these uncertainties. The autopsy both epitomizes and summarizes various other experiences that together make up the preclinical student's training for uncertainty.

Before witnessing their first autopsy, second-year students may, on occasion, sound rather complacent about the questions death poses. For example, speculating on the causes of death, one group of sophomores decided to their satisfaction that the cessation of life could be explained in simple physiological terms and that, armed with this knowledge, the doctor stands a good chance of "winning the fight" against death:

> We found that one very important matter could be traced back to one of two basic actions. The important matter—death. The two basic actions—the heart and respiration. For death is caused, finally, by the stopping of one of these two actions. As long as they both continue, there is life. . . . It's all a fight to keep the heart beating, the lungs breathing, and, in man, a third factor—the brain unharmed. . . . With all the multitude of actions and reactions which are found in this medical business, it seems strange and satisfying to find something that can really be narrowed down. . . .

But the conviction that death "can really be narrowed down" is not long-lasting. Only a short time later, commenting on an autopsy he had just witnessed, one of these same students referred to death with "disquietude" as something you "can't pinpoint" or easily prevent.

One of the chief consequences of the student's participation in an autopsy is that it heightens his awareness of the uncertainties that result from limited medical knowledge and of the implications these uncertainties have for the practicing doctor. This is effected in a number of ways. To begin with, the experience of being "on call" for an autopsy ("waiting around for someone to die") makes a student more conscious of the fact that, even when death is expected, it is seldom wholly predictable:

> In groups of threes, we all watch at least one autopsy—and my group is the third one in line. The first group went in for theirs this morning; this means that ours may come any time now. You can't be sure when, though, so you have to stay pretty close to home where you can be reached. . . .

In other words, although ultimate death is certain, medical science is still not far enough advanced so that the physicians can state with assurance exactly when an individual will die.

Of even greater importance, perhaps, in impressing the student with the limitations of current medical knowledge is the fact that, although the pathologist may be able to provide a satisfactory explanation of the patient's death, the student usually finds these "causes of death" less "dramatic" and specific than he expected them to be:

> While our case was unusual, it was a bit of a letdown to me, for there was nothing dramatic to be pointed to as the cause of death. The clinician reported that the patient had lost 1,000 cc. of blood from internal bleeding from the G.I. tract. . . . Well, we saw no gaping hole there. There was no place you could pinpoint and say: "This is where the hemorrhage took place." . . . Rather, it was a culmination of a condition relating to various factors. I suppose most causes of death are this way. But still . . . (though I'm not really sure why it should be) . . . it was somewhat disquieting to me.

A third limitation of the field is implied in lack of control over death. For example, the student observes that "the various doctors connected with the case being autopsied . . . wander in while the procedure is going on." This serves to remind him that the "body on the autopsy table" belongs to a patient whose death no physician was able to prevent.

It is not only the limits of the field that are impressed upon the student during his participation in an autopsy. This experience also serves to make him aware of the personal limitations of even the most skilled practitioners. For instance, an autopsy gives a student an opportunity to observe that "the doctors aren't always sure what caused the patient's death"; rather, as one student puts it, "they come . . . to find out what was really wrong." Furthermore, the student may be present at an autopsy in which the pathologist's findings make it apparent that the physician was mistaken in his diagnosis (when, for example, the pathologist "doesn't find any of the things in the doctors' diagnoses"). From experiences such as these the student learns that, not only he, but also his instructors have only an imperfect mastery of all there is to know in medicine.

These varied aspects of the autopsy, in other words, give it central significance in the student's training for uncertainty.

Learning to Cope with Uncertainty

In describing the various kinds of uncertainty to which a student is exposed during his preclinical years at Cornell, we do not mean to portray him as groping helplessly around in the midst of them. On the contrary, as time goes on, a student begins to develop effective ways of dealing with these forms of uncertainty, so that, gradually, he becomes more capable of meeting them with the competence and equipoise of a mature physician.

To begin with, as a student acquires medical knowledge and skill, some of his uncertainty gives way. "A more complete and satisfying picture of the organism takes shape" in his mind. Gradually, "the missing jig-saw puzzle pieces seem to fall into place, and [he] sees interconnections and interrelationships between all subjects." The student also feels more at home looking in a microscope; he finds it easier to draw slides; he begins to have more confidence in what he sees and hears in physical diagnosis; and he becomes more adept at talking to patients. In all these respects, cognitive learning and a greater sense of certainty go hand in hand.

Growing competence and more experience decrease the student's uncertainty about his personal knowledge and skills; this, in turn, modifies his attitude toward the uncertainties which arise from limitations in the current state of medical knowledge. It will be remembered that, at first, the preclinical student goes through a period in which he is inclined to regard his uncertainty as reflecting his personal inadequacy. During his early days in physical diagnosis, for example, a student is likely to dismiss the uncertainty he may feel about "how much percussion tells [him]" in a particular instance by saying that he thinks he is "probably wrong" to have doubts in the first place and that giving vent to these doubts might make him "look like a fool":

> For example, I can see that percussion *does* tell you a lot, and that in most cases, the borders of the heart *can* be percussed. What it amounts to really is not that I doubt it, but that I can't do it. . . . It's all very well and good [to express your doubt], but if it turns out that you're the only one who seems to be having so much trouble, you begin to look like a fool after a while if you do. . . . We don't really know enough yet so that we can afford not to take a positive stand. . . .

With the growth of his knowledge and skill, however, and the widening and deepening of his experience, a student's perspective on his own uncertainty changes. Now that he "knows a little more" and is a "little more sure of himself," a student says, he realizes that although some of his uncertainty is attributable to his "ignorance," some of it is "really well-justified." By this he means that he is better able to distinguish between those aspects of his uncertainty that derive from his own lack of knowledge and those that are inherent in medicine. He is therefore less apt to think of his uncertainty as largely personal and now considers it more appropriate to give voice to the doubts he feels.

This more "affirmative attitude" toward doubting (as one student calls it) is not only a product of book knowledge and skill in the techniques of physical diagnosis. It also results from what a student learns about the uncertainties of medicine through his daily contact with members of the faculty. From time to time in the classroom, for example, a student will ask what he considers a "well-chosen question" only to discover that his teacher "does not have immediate command of the known medical facts on that point" or to be told that the problem into which he is inquiring "represents one of the big gaps in medical knowledge at present." In the autopsy room, as we have seen, a student is struck by the fact that the pathologist cannot always explain the causes of death and that, although the "doctors' diagnoses are often right, they can also be wrong." Examining patients under the supervision of clinical faculty, a student discovers that when "different instructors listen to (or feel or see) the exact same thing, they frequently come up with different impressions . . . and have to consult one another before they reach a final conclusion."

In short, observing his teachers in various classroom and clinical situations makes a student more aware of the fact that they are subject to the same kinds of uncertainty that he himself is experiencing. Furthermore, the student notes that, when his instructors experience these uncertainties, they usually deal with them in a forthright manner, acknowledging them with the consistency of what one student has termed a "philosophy of doubting." Thus, a student's relationship to the faculty, like his advances in knowledge and skill, encourages him to accept some of his uncertainty as "inevitable" and thoroughly "legitimate" and to handle that uncertainty by openly conceding that he is unsure.

Another process by which the student learns to face up to uncertainty in an unequivocal manner is connected with his membership in the "little society" of medical students, for a medical school class is a closely knit, self-regulating community, with its own method of "tackling a big problem" like that of uncertainty.

Through a process of "feeling each other out," the group first establishes that uncertainty is experienced by "everyone," thereby reassuring a student that his own difficulties in this regard are not unique:

> As always, the biggest lift comes from talking to other students and finding that they have felt the same way. You may do this by a few casual jokes, but you know there is more to it than that. . . .

Second, out of the more than "casual joking, asking around and talking to others" that constantly go on among students, a set of standards for dealing with uncertainty gradually emerges—standards that tend to coincide with those of the faculty:

> Suppose I should talk real enthusiastically about the job of dissection I did [a freshman explains]. Well, Earl will say, "Gee, I'm a great guy, too, you know," or something to that effect. From that remark, I can tell I'm bragging too much. That cues me in, so I make a mental note not to brag so much the next time. . . . Because you don't talk about your successes to the group as a whole. It's sort of understood that you don't try to impress each other. . . . A lot of the fellows belittle themselves. . . . I mean, a fellow will say, for example, that he thought a certain structure was a lymph node and that it turned out to be something entirely different. Then he and everyone else will laugh a lot over that. . . .

If he acts presumptuous about his knowledge, a student will be reproached by his classmates, whereas an admission of ignorance on his part may evoke their approval. From their positive and negative reactions, a student learns that his classmates, like his teachers, expect him to be uncertain about what he knows and candid about his uncertainty. (As one student puts it, "It really isn't fashionable to believe much or to be overly sure.")

"Summing up is pretty tough," a sophomore writes, taking stock as his second year draws to a close:

> The uncertainty of first year is missing. You feel now as though you have a very shaky hold on a great deal of knowledge. You rather expect that the next two years will be spent getting a better hold on the things you are already familiar with. . . . We are halfway through. To some people this is quite a milestone. . . . The realization that one day we will be doctors—finished with medical school—is now in the back of our minds. But few people have a definite idea of what they want to do. . . . For the most part, I think our class is looking forward to the third year, although there is a certain uneasiness about the idea of presenting yourself to the patient as a doctor. . . .

In some respects confident and knowing, in others uneasy and not sure, a student feels variously certain and uncertain as he makes the transition from the preclinical to the clinical years of medical school.

THE CLINICAL YEARS

The Kinds of Uncertainty Facing the Third-Year Student

The kinds of uncertainty experienced by a third-year student are qualitatively the same as those he encountered in his preclinical years. First, there is the uncertainty that comes with realizing that, despite all the medicine a student has mastered and all he will learn, he can never hope to "shovel out more than a corner of what there is to know":

> Studying medicine is a lot like digging a hole in the sand. You get down there and start digging, but it seems as though for every shovelful you toss out, some more slides in. And of course, when you dig *any* hole, you never get to the bottom. . . . If you were to ask me how I felt about medicine now, and you happened to catch me in a moment of honesty, I'd tell you that I'm completely overwhelmed by a feeling of lack of knowledge. . . .

Second, when he meets clinical problems that "even stump the experts," a third-year student is confronted with uncertainty that derives from the limitations of medical science:

> Ted and I got to talking about some of the revelations of third year, and one of the things that has struck him is that there isn't a diagnosis for everything. He has more or less assumed that there was always a diagnosis that could be made, and especially that a resident or attending should have no trouble making one. But this year, he has discovered that even a sharp attending like Dr. ——— can be stumped. . . .

Uncertainty over how to distinguish his own inadequacies from those general to the field continues to pose a problem for the student. If he has trouble with a venipuncture, for example, or does what he considers a "hack job" in "working up" a patient, a student wonders if "it's mostly due to the fact that [his] talents just don't run toward being a doctor" or if his difficulty is largely attributable to the poor condition of the patient's veins and to the objective intricacy of her case.

But if the uncertainties of third year are like those with which a student is already acquainted and to which he has become partly inured, there is a sense in which the third year at Cornell seems to intensify the *degree* of uncertainty. As one student puts it:

> Starting third year is a little like starting medical school all over. Everything is new, and you don't know what to expect or to plan for. . . .[8]

Because the third year represents a major transition point in a student's training—it is the beginning of his total immersion in clinical medicine—the uncertainties he encounters at first seem greater to him than those he encountered as a sophomore.

In spite of his enthusiasm over working on the wards and in the clinics of the hospital, a third-year student looks back somewhat wistfully on what he regards as the relative "organization and continuity of the

8. Within the limited confines of this paper, we have chosen to treat the third year as a unit—for the most part ignoring the fact that it is actually made up of a series of microcosms. The third year at Cornell is divided into three terms: (1) medicine; (2) surgery; (3) obstetrics-gynecology; pediatrics; public health; psychiatry. And the class itself is divided into three groups that rotate through these various terms—some taking medicine first, some surgery, some obstetrics-gynecology, etc. Further, these three groups are, in turn, subdivided—half taking their medical clerkships at New York Hospital first, half at Bellevue first (and then interchanging); half taking pediatrics first, half obstetrics-gynecology first (and interchanging, too). Again, within each of these terms, even more subdivisions take place. For example, the students go two by two to the palpation clinic while on obstetrics-gynecology; on medicine, they are broken up into tutorial groups containing five students apiece; and so on. In the section that follows, we will only allude to the differences between the trimesters of the year and the wide dispersion of the student group. Though our discussion of it here is cursory, the effect that the "geometry" of third year has on students merits future study.

academic classroom." How do you "approach learning," he wonders, "now that things are no longer grouped by courses—and the choice of what to study is so completely your own?"

> For example, suppose you want to read up on headache. . . . You can read a two-page section in the Merck Manual, a five-page section in Cecil,[9] a thirty-page section in a book called *Signs and Symptoms*, or recent articles in the journals. . . .

"Which is best is very hard to decide." Part of the student's difficulty in evolving a plan of study lies in the fact that what he is really seeking is nothing less than an organized way of learning to think like a doctor. During the third year at Cornell the student reaches out to make the process of differential diagnosis and the logic of rational treatment more conclusively his own.

As a student quickly discovers, however, the way of thought of the doctor is something other than a sum total of the ideas he has already mastered. Neither the principles he has learned in the basic medical sciences nor his book knowledge of disease processes automatically equip him to think like a doctor:

> The basic principles of medicine are very difficult things to catch hold of [a third-year student writes]. In engineering, once you really understand a principle, it stays with you, and you feel confident you will be able to use it in attacking a wide range of new problems. If you really understand mechanics, you can do anything with it, and you don't have to worry so much about whether certain things are true in one case and not in another. . . . The problems may be new tomorrow, but the basic principles don't change (much). . . . With medicine, it's different. . . . There are as many exceptions as there are rules . . . and the important things in one case don't count in another. . . . You can't read the chapter and "figure out the problem" in medicine. And it is the greatest folly to argue with an instructor (a good one) with only the chapter behind you. You can say, "Cecil says . . ." but if he's seen patients with such-and-such for twenty years, then he probably has you. In other words, years of experience don't modify the principles of the engineering book, but in medicine they do. . . .

Along with the change in organization and the different way of thought, the divided nature of the third year augments the uncertainty to which a student is subject:

9. Russell L. Cecil, Robert F. Loeb, and associates, *Textbook of Medicine* (Philadelphia: W. B. Saunders Company, 1955).

> The class is pretty split up these days. . . . Lunch is the only time you see friends you are otherwise completely out of contact with. You are all doing different things, and it is really very nice to get a chance to eat together and talk about them. . . .

Separated from some of the people on whom he depended for confirmation and support and now asked to see patients alone, a third-year student is called upon to meet uncertainty in a more solitary fashion:

> Last year, if you thought you felt a liver, for instance, but you weren't quite sure, there were always two or three other fellows there, and you could ask them if they felt it too. But this year we see patients alone. So we're more on our own now. . . .

Perhaps most important of all in quickening a student's sense of uncertainty is his conviction that "third year is the year when the whole jump is made, and you learn to be a doctor." What is called for now, he says, is "knowing enough to do justice to your patients."

> . . . You get to the point where you say I should know these things. . . . Otherwise I'll be cheating my patients. . . . In that respect, I feel like a doctor already. . . .

In general, then, the uncertainty of third year is compounded for a student by his "developing sense of responsibility." As he becomes aware of the imminence of his doctorhood, "gaps in [his] knowledge" or unsureness on his part seem more serious to a beginning third-year student than they formerly did.

The Certitude of the Third-Year Student

Although a student may tell you at the outset of the third year that he feels "a little bit like a pea on a griddle" (dwarfed by medicine and alone in some ways), he does not continue to sound so unsure of himself. As the year unfolds, a student's initial uncertainty gradually gives way to a manner of certitude. One gains the impression that students are more uncertain during the first part of the third year than they were before, but that they become less uncertain than before during the later part of the third year. There seem to be several reasons for this.

In the atmosphere of the "clinical situation," a student can feel his medical knowledge take root. The "chance to see many of the things [he] has read about" reinforces what he has previously learned; and the fact that "there is a patient lying there in bed proves" to him that what he is currently learning is "really important."

However, the growing assurance of a third-year student does not result only from his greater knowledge and his conviction that what he is doing is important. It results also from the fact that in the third year he is relatively insulated from some of the diagnostic and therapeutic uncertainties he will encounter later. For one thing, the acute illnesses he sees on the wards and the explicit problems he handles in the clinics are often "classic" or so manifest that he says they seem almost "obvious" to him. For another, the responsibilities a third-year student is asked to assume are carefully circumscribed. Although he now has more responsibility than he did when he was a preclinical student, he has considerably less than he will have later, as a fourth-year student or practicing physician. His duties on the wards do not go beyond taking a history, doing a physical examination, and carrying out indicated laboratory tests. When it comes to the problems of treating a patient, the student is largely an onlooker. He does not have to decide upon medicaments and other therapeutic procedures—weighing the potential risks involved against the possible benefits that may accrue to his patients. A student's responsibilities in the clinic are equally limited and specific. In the surgery specialty clinics, for example, his diagnoses are restricted to those facets of a patient's problems that are encompassed by the particular specialty he is representing at the time. The only therapy for which he is responsible is "fairly simple and concrete": treating infections, removing sutures, and dressing wounds, for example, such as he does on minor surgery.

In effect, the delimited nature of his responsibilities frees a student from the necessity of coping with diagnostic and therapeutic uncertainties that fall outside a narrow orbit.[10] Even in the general surgery clinic where he deals with a wider range of medical problems in a more comprehensive way, the student is protected from many clinical uncertainties. In general surgery (and in his other clinics as well) a student rarely sees a patient more than once. It is usually only in retrospect that he catches a glimpse of the uncertainties he might have encountered had his relationship with patients been continuous. For example, reviewing the charts of patients he examined in general surgery as a junior, a

10. One of the factors that may persuade a student to enter a specialized field within medicine is that narrowing the scope of practice also narrows the range of potential uncertainty with which he will have to deal as a doctor. For further discussion of this point, see Patricia L. Kendall and Hanan C. Selvin, "Tendencies toward Specialization in Medical Training," also in *The Student-Physician*.

fourth-year student was "amazed to discover" that some of the cases he saw were never resolved:

> . . . One poor woman had a negative GB series (I thought she had gall bladder disease); was seen by someone else and had a negative GI series (he thought she had an ulcer); was seen by someone else and had a negative proctoscopy and Ba. enema (he thought she had Ca. of the colon). She then went to another clinic and had two more negative GI series because someone there thought she had a Meckel's diverticulum. On her last visit, someone wrote down "irritable colon" and treated her with "reassurance." . . .

His close relationship to the clinical faculty is another source of a third-year student's increasing assurance:

> During the first two years it was possible to remain completely removed from the faculty and yet still do O.K. by reading and going to lectures. While some departments made an effort to develop a close student-faculty relationship, you never had to depend on this to get the things you were supposed to. But now only 50% of what we need can come from books. The other 50% has to come from the teachers we work with. And so, there is a 180-degree shift in the class' relation to the faculty. . . .

Because he finds that listening to experienced doctors reason out loud is the only way he can get "a sense of how to approach clinical problems," the third-year student welcomes the opportunity to learn through direct contact with his instructors. Meeting with members of the faculty or house staff in small intimate groups and discussing patients with them is "the heart of clinical medical education," so far as a student is concerned. Sessions like these, he says, "give [him] insight into how a doctor organizes and uses his information," and a "real sense of colleagueship." ("You catch the feeling you must have in a craft: the father passing the secrets of the craft on to the son.") The closeness of his relationship to the faculty in the third year helps a student to think and feel more like a doctor, and consequently fosters his sense of certainty.

In these respects, the student acquires greater assurance during the course of his third year at Cornell. He also adopts a *manner* of certitude, for he has come to realize that it may be important for him to "act like a savant" even when he does not actually feel sure. From his instructors and patients alike a student learns this lesson: that if he is to meet his clinical responsibilities, he cannot allow himself to doubt as openly or to the same extent that he did during his preclinical years. Instead, he must commit himself to some of the tentative judgments he makes and move decisively on behalf of his patients:

> Dr. T.'s philosophy goes something like this. . . . "You boys are to handle the case as you see best. I put no restrictions on you from this point of view. You do the work-up, decide what's to be done, and whatever you decide is all right. But I insist on this much—you must stand up for your decisions, never apologize for what you are doing, and never start getting humble and say you don't know. . . ."

The third-year student learns from his instructors that too great a display of unsureness on his part may elicit criticism; from his patients he learns that it may evoke alarm:

> To say that the patient "searches your face" for clues is no overstatement. An example—while on OB, when trying to palpate a baby once, I got a little confused and frowned in puzzlement. Sensed at once that the mother saw the frown and was alarmed. So I reassured her that everything was all right. I have always tried to remember not to do it again. . . .

Yielding to the point of view of his instructors, who enjoin him to be "firm and take a position," to the desire of his patients to be assured, and to his own "need for definiteness" as well, a third-year student generally makes it his policy to "believe."

> I'm sure that on the higher levels of medicine you *do* admit your ignorance and avoid stereotyped thinking. But we are at the point now where you have to believe in the rule rather than the exception. . . . Perhaps this is a phase you must pass through on the way up, just as you must learn that the heart *does* have a pacemaker before you learn that it *doesn't*. . . .

In sum, the assurance of a third-year student results from his progress in learning and his unawareness of many clinical uncertainties. He assumes a sure manner also because of his belief that "it is a mistake for a medical student at [his] stage of the game to doubt too much."

Training for Uncertainty in the Comprehensive Care and Teaching Program

The sense of sureness expressed by students about to complete their third year at Cornell is, in some respects, premature. At any rate, the fourth-year student's perspective on the uncertainties of medicine is usually different from that of a junior:

> Experience makes you less sure of yourself, [a senior explains]. What you realize is that, even when you've been out of medical school twenty years, there'll be many times when you won't be able to make a diagnosis or cure a patient. . . . Instead of looking for the day, then, when all the knowledge you need will be in your possession, you learn that such a day will never come. . . .

A fourth-year student who faces up to uncertainty in this way has departed considerably from his third-year self. Part of this change seems attributable to experiences in the comprehensive care and teaching program.[11] A central feature of the program is the extensive responsibility for patients it allows students. Each student is assigned a number of patients who are defined as *his* patients, and he is expected to deal with all the problems that each case presents.[12] Stemming from this degree of responsibility are varied situations and experiences that make the fourth-year student more aware of the uncertainties of medicine.[13]

One important way in which students exercise the broad responsibility offered them is by following their patients over a period of months. This gives them more insight into the prevalence of uncertainties in the practice of medicine. What began as the "classical case" of Mrs. B., for example, illustrates this fact:

> My new patient arrived first . . . Mrs. B., a thirty-two year old housewife and mother of two children, who had a sudden onset of typical thyroid symptoms complete with the physical findings to go with them. . . . I ordered several diagnostic tests for her and advised her to return in a week. . . .

11. Though the fourth year at Cornell is made up of three terms, we will discuss only the medicine semester (comprehensive care) in this paper. The qualitative data (diaries, interviews, and observations) are not sufficient to do justice to the surgery and obstetrics-gynecology terms that also form part of the fourth year.

12. For a more detailed description of the comprehensive care and teaching program and the kinds of experiences which students have in it, see George G. Reader, "The Cornell Comprehensive Care and Teaching Program," and Margaret Olencki, "Range of Patient Contacts in the Comprehensive Care and Teaching Program," both in *The Student-Physician* volume.

13. The types of uncertainties a student encounters in the comprehensive care and teaching program seem to be like those he has dealt with recurrently since his days as a freshman. However, it is no longer so easily possible to distinguish which fourth-year experiences are salient for which types of uncertainty. Rather, in the situations in which the fourth-year student finds himself all types of uncertainty seem to converge and to be intertwined. For this reason we have found it necessary here to modify the pattern set in earlier sections of this paper, and we talk now largely in terms of undifferentiated uncertainties.

In this initial contact, the student-physician considered Mrs. B.'s case "typical," and the tests which he ordered were presumably intended merely to confirm his diagnosis. There is no indication that he anticipated special difficulty in handling Mrs. B.'s problems.

On the second visit the student and the attending physician who was supervising him agreed that Mrs. B.'s case was clear-cut, and that surgery would be appropriate. But they did not reckon with the response of the patient to that proposal:

> By the time I got to my second re-visit, Mrs. B., my toxic thyroid case, she had been waiting some time. . . . She gave me the story of continuation of her previous symptoms with shaking even more apparent at present. Of the tests ordered, only the BMR came back, but this was conclusive, being 59% above normal. I informed her that all her problems were related to these findings, and after discussing her with Dr. D. told her that hospitalization and surgery were her best chance for a permanent cure. At this she broke down in tears, and after composing herself, made many arguments against surgery. . . . Dr. D. and I quickly agreed that I should treat her with propylthiouracil on an ambulatory basis until she has quieted down. This is an unnatural response to hospitalization and surgery, and I'll be interested in seeing if she becomes more logical with the quiescence of her toxic symptoms. . . .

The patient's fear of an operation forced the student and the attending physician to adopt a plan of therapy they believed was less effective than the one they originally set forth.

On a later visit the full complexity of Mrs. B.'s case became more apparent:

> I went in to see Mrs. B. and found that the threat of her husband's quitting his job was related to hysterical crying most of the day. She admitted that her reaction wasn't wholly because of her disease state, but that she had been easily unnerved prior to this. I assured her that, although this might be so, her thyroid was making it much worse, and that we would shortly be rid of part of it. . . . She mentioned that a lump on her daughter's wrist was bothering her, and I suggested that she bring her in on the next visit. . . . We discussed surgery at her initiation, and arrived at the same conclusion as before: my insisting that surgery was the best solution to her problem, and her insisting that she, her husband, and friends all agreed that if a cure is possible without surgery, that it is to be embarked on. . . .

Mrs. B.'s emotional response to the diagnosis and recommendations made by the student-physician, her eagerness to accept the antisurgical opinions of her family and friends, and her anxiety over her husband's job and her daughter's health all proved relevant to the appraisal and management of her case. With each visit it became more apparent to the student-physician that Mrs. B.'s problems were psychological as well as physical, and this realization evoked new questions. Was Mrs. B.'s long-standing nervousness wholly attributable to her disease state? Would it be possible to "ever get this woman over some of her anxious moments" and thus ready her for a needed operation? "I'm not too certain about any of these things," Mrs. B.'s student-physician reported at the end of his third visit with her. But, had he seen her only once, this student would not have had any reason to alter his original impression that the case of Mrs. B. was diagnostically and therapeutically "clear cut."

The continuous nature of his contact with patients in the program, then, alerts a student to some of the clinical uncertainties that lie beyond first medical judgments and the appearance of things. Furthermore, it confronts him with the problem of managing a long-term doctor-patient relationship in the face of these uncertainties. For example:

> I saw Mr. T. again and gave him the sad news—no ulcer demonstrated. What could this be if it wasn't an ulcer? I tried my best to put him off so that I wouldn't be obligated to further diagnostic procedures that would be useless and expensive. I did my best to convince him that it sounded like nothing but ulcer, and that we planned to treat it as such because not all ulcers are demonstrated by X ray. This wasn't good enough. . . .

> Mrs. J. puts up a pretty good front, but I think she worries a good deal about her problem. And today she asked me what she had. I was kind of up a tree. . . . I told her that what she had was somewhat different in that it didn't respond to the usual therapy—but that we had many other weapons and she shouldn't be concerned. . . .

With every revisit, the need for a solution may grow more intense in both the patient and the student-physician. Mr. T., for example, becomes harder to convince or reassure. Mrs. J. shows evidence of worrying a great deal and begins to press her doctor for an explanation of her problem. And the student, feeling responsible for the welfare of this man and woman (defined by the program as *his* patients), is likely to feel frustrated and disappointed by his inability to resolve their cases.

These frustrations may be all the more provoking because the student has not been completely prepared for them by his earlier experiences. His relatively brief and circumscribed contact with patients in the third year had led him to assume that a good doctor ought to be able to arrive at a "definitive diagnosis" and to evolve a successful plan of treatment for most of the cases with which he deals. But the broad and continuous experience provided by the program teaches a student that cases like those of Mr. T. and Mrs. J. are more widespread than he had supposed them to be.

Not only do his continuing relationships with patients and the growing magnitude of his responsibility for them increase a student's awareness of the uncertain aspects of the cases with which he deals; they often lead to his being deeply affected by these uncertainties. Because he is working with patients in a sustained way, a student is more susceptible to positive and negative countertransference than he was before entering the program. As time goes on, he may become attached to some patients and alienated from others. Furthermore, the relatively large degree of responsibility assigned to him by the program makes a student feel more accountable for what happens to patients than he formerly did. As a result, the uncertainties that a student experiences in the program "make an emotional impact on [him]," so that he is sometimes inclined to react subjectively to the uncertain features of cases he cannot bring to a satisfactory conclusion. Usually these reactions involve the placing of "blame," either on himself or on his patient:

> I blame myself, not Mrs. H. [her student-physician declares]. I can't get her to reduce, and I don't know what I'm doing wrong. I have remained pleasant and sympathetic, but have applied strong urging and have registered disappointment (not wrath) at her failure to cooperate. . . . The reason I find her so difficult is that I feel, if someone else were handling her, he could get the pounds off her. . . .

> Mrs. C. has caused me quite a bit of consternation [another student asserts]. Though we have taken adequate physical measures to ascertain that her difficulty is on an emotional basis, she's still showing bodily overconcern. . . . She complains of pains in her legs; that her arms are too weak; that she's tired; that she feels pressure in her abdomen. . . . And then, these gripes about her husband. I can understand them in a way—because he's the type of man who comes home from work, picks up his paper, looks at TV for a while, and then goes to bed without saying a word. . . . But she makes no effort to do anything about the situation. . . . She just sits there and tells me, "That's the way he is. . . ." Another thing about this woman is, in all instances she will discontinue whatever treatment you prescribe and proceed on her own conception. . . .

The "failure" is his, the first student claims; it's the "fault" of the patient and her environment, says the second.

As the cases of Mrs. H. and Mrs. C. suggest, a student is particularly apt to respond in one or the other of these affectual ways when the uncertainty he faces concerns either the social and psychological aspects of a patient's illness or his own management of the doctor-patient relationship. Partly because psychiatry and the social sciences are in a more embryonic stage of development than the disciplines from which medicine derives its understanding of the human body, the student encounters uncertainty more frequently in trying to handle the emotional and environmental components of his patient's disorder than in trying to cope with problems that are largely physical in nature. The classification of psychological disturbances thus far evolved, for example, is not precise enough to permit a high degree of diagnostic exactitude. The relationship between social factors and illness is only beginning to be systematically explored. And most of the available methods for treating sociopsychological difficulties are still grossly empirical, their relative merits and demerits a focus of present day medical controversy, interest, and concern.

Intellectually, a student is aware of these things before he enters the comprehensive care program; but he has not yet fully learned to acknowledge the uncertainties and limitations in this realm, or to proceed comfortably within the framework of such a realization. This is partly because, prior to his semester in the program, a student has had little opportunity to take active responsibility for the "personal problems" of his patients. In the third year, for example, as we have seen, a student's work centers primarily on physical diagnosis. The only personal therapy he has occasion to administer to his patients is a simple and limited form of reassurance, which, on the whole, he judges to be effective. His success in this respect he deems "understandable," for he is inclined to feel that the so-called art-of-medicine skills are based not so much on trained experience as they are on personal qualities. Such an attitude is reflected, for example, in the way that a number of third-year students look upon their psychiatry instructors:

> There is a general feeling of great respect for most of the psychiatry people we have come in contact with [one student tells us]. We are impressed to note that the psychiatrist almost always suggests the honest, straightforward, direct approach to things . . . and most of us feel these people make sense. . . .

Yet "the regard we have for psychiatrists is not the same as the respect we have for surgeons," this student goes on to say. In the case of surgery, "it's a matter of respecting skill," in the case of psychiatry, "respecting common sense."

This distinction is one that students carry with them into the program. It helps explain the observed tendency of many students in comprehensive care to reproach themselves when they are unable to formulate the "human aspects of a patient's case" or to decide upon an effective way of dealing with those aspects. ("I can't get Mrs. H. to reduce . . . and I don't know what I'm doing wrong.") For a student who tends to regard problems like "getting the patient to lose weight" as more contingent on personal attributes than on learned skill, the case of Mrs. H. may seem to represent a personal failure on his part.

The more common tendency of a student to blame the patient under such circumstances is a different manifestation of the same emotional involvement. In the face of medical uncertainties that may impede his attempts to be decisive about the sociopsychological dimensions of the cases he handles, a student often projects his own sense of inadequacy upon the patient. In comprehensive care, for example, students frequently apply the epithet "crock" to "patients who do not have an organic lesion" or whose behavior appears to be "psychoneurotic." "The central feature in all these patients we call 'crocks' is that they threaten our ability as doctors," one student points out. This is both because such patients do not respond to the diagnostic and therapeutic efforts of the student-physician in the way he would like ("You don't get a foothold anywhere and do something to give them a better adjustment. . . ."), and because the student is emotionally "more vulnerable when thinking about the human aspects of a case, rather than just the strict medical problems involved."

> Whether you're conscious of it or not, a lot of the things disturbed patients talk to you about are the kinds of things you're likely to react to very strongly in a positive or negative way. . . . I mean, it's all very well to say you're not judging these people, for instance. But you can get annoyed as heck with some of them, or lose your sympathy though you know they're psychoneurotic. . . .

To sum up: the fourth-year student is repeatedly impressed by the diagnostic and therapeutic uncertainties he encounters in dealing with patients during his semester in comprehensive care. Some of these uncertainties, he realizes, result from his own lack of medical knowledge and some from the limitations of medicine itself. In this respect, they are no different from those he has met at earlier points in his training. However, the physician-like responsibilities ascribed to him by the program, along with the continuing and holistic nature of his relationship to patients, magnify the problem of uncertainty for the student and make it harder for him to deal with it in a dispassionate way. In turn, the student's emotional involvement increases the difficulty he has in distinguishing between those uncertainties that grow out of his personal ignorance and those that stem from the current limitations of medical science. It is particularly when he feels unsure about how to classify the ulcer-like symptoms of a Mr. T., or what to do about the obesity of a Mrs. H., that a student "doesn't know whether [his] uncertainty is a reflection of his lack of knowledge and technique or whether such cases would be perplexing" even to more experienced physicians. As we have seen, a student is at first more apt to blame himself or, by projection, the patient, than he is to attribute his uncertainty to gaps in medical science.

Coming to Terms with Uncertainty in Comprehensive Care

The student's increased awareness of uncertainties in medicine is of course not the chief by-product of his term in comprehensive care. The same experiences that lead to such awareness also enlarge his skills in the realms of diagnosis and patient management. From the absence of expected findings in a case like that presented by Mr. T., for example, he learns how to appraise conflicting evidence in arriving at a diagnosis. From the complex problems of Mrs. B. he learns something of the connection between emotional stress and physical illness and gains some experience in dealing with patients who are under such stress. When he leaves the program the student, therefore, has considerably more confidence about his ability to cope with these problems than he did six months before.

Moreover, the fourth-year student finds ways of adjusting to his remaining uncertainties. The organization of the comprehensive care program and some of its precepts help the student to recognize that he shares part of his uncertainty with fellow classmates and instructors. This enables him to meet his uncertainty with greater confidence and equipoise.[14]

In contrast to the many small groups into which the class is divided during the third year, half of the senior class is enrolled in comprehen-

14. An indication of the marked increase in confidence is contained in a simple statistical result. In May 1955, all four classes at Cornell were asked how capable they felt about dealing with a number of problems encountered by practicing physicians. One of these problems concerned "the uncertainties of diagnosis and therapy that one meets in practice." The class-by-class distribution of replies on this item was as follows:

	Percentage of each class			
Problem of "uncertainties"	First year	Second year	Third year	Fourth year
Quite sure I can deal with this	10	11	21	25
Fairly sure I can deal with this	52	61	60	72
Not sure I can deal with this	38	28	19	3
No. of students	(82)	(82)	(85)	(85)

sive care at one time, spending a continuous six months together in the program. This arrangement facilitates that kind of interchange between students that from the earliest days of medical school provided them with mutual aid and the supportive knowledge that "others feel the way [they] do."

> In the process of a routine physical, I performed a pelvic and rectal, and the glove specimen of the stool was strongly guaiac positive! And I didn't quite know what to do. The patient lives in upstate New York and can come to the city only when her husband drives in once a month. A decent GI workup would require her spending four full days at the hospital. To further complicate matters, I wasn't sure of the significance of the positive test. I had rinsed my glove between pelvic and rectal, but the possibility of a positive test from blood in the vagina remains. . . . In the course of describing this experience at lunch . . . one of my classmates suggested that it was a crime to let her out of the building without a GI series, Ba. enema, and proctoscopy. He felt that even if subsequent stool examinations are negative, such a workup is obligatory. . . . This is the sort of decision I would prefer to force on someone else. I would feel foolish if such a workup showed nothing and subsequent stools were negative, but I'd feel worse if she showed up with an inoperable cancer a few months hence. . . . The lunch table of four was evenly divided on the question of what one should do if such a circumstance arose in general practice. . . . This problem is a real threat to the young physician. . . .

Although uncertainties such as these are "threatening," the student can perhaps find some reassurance in the fact that his classmates experience the same difficulties in deciding on appropriate action.

The opportunity to work as coequal with the attending physicians of comprehensive care also gives the student a chance to see that, at times, expert doctors are no more facile than he in making a diagnosis or deciding upon a course of treatment:

> My second case was a three-year old girl with a swollen, red, warm left hand, which seemed to itch more than it hurt. No signs of infected wound—only a history of a possible insect bite. I felt this was a contact dermatitis. The pediatrician felt it was obvious cellulitis, but insisted we call in a surgeon to confirm him. The surgeon leaned toward my diagnosis—and we called in a dermatologist who felt this was definitely infection—which was very amusing. . . .

Finally, the experimental milieu of the program also furthers the student's realization that neither his classmates nor his instructors have sure and easy answers to some of the questions he finds puzzling. Because one of the primary aims of the program is self-critically to develop a more comprehensive type of medical care, students and staff are continuously engaged in a process of inquiry. Conjoined by a living experiment, they openly express their feelings of doubt and uncertainty and systematically try to resolve them. In one of the weekly comprehensive care conferences, for example, we can see this process taking place. A fourth-year student is presenting the history of the Gonzales family, whom he serves as general physician:

> The Gonzales family is a Puerto Rican family that has been in this country for sixteen months. It consists of eight members: Mr. Gonzales, a thirty-eight-year old unskilled laborer; Mrs. Gonzales, his twenty-five-year old uneducated wife; and their six children. . . . They live in a three-room, unheated apartment on 60th Street. From the outset of our contact with this family, it was obvious that there were a number of interrelated sociological, economic, and medical problems, all of which could not be treated at the same time. We have tried to proceed in the most logical manner, but often our efforts have had to be side-tracked by the appearance of new problems. First, there was the real possibility of the family breaking up under the existing stresses. This immediate crisis passed. Then, there was the problem of tuberculosis with the diagnosis of Anna's active case, the question of Mrs. Gonzales' status, and the necessity of evaluating other members of the family. Coincidental with this investigation was the series of upper respiratory infections, otitis medias, episodes of gastro-enteritis and pyelitis, Carlo's seizure disorder, and, finally, Mr. Gonzales' admission to the Hospital. Many of the family are known to be anemic, so following our satisfaction that none of the other children had tuberculosis, it was agreed that the known parasitic infections should be next attacked. . . . It seems certain that poor nutrition is another contributing factor to the anemias, and we have taken steps along this line as well. . . . One of the family's food difficulties has been the inability to shop properly. Previous to our contact with them, they purchased all of their groceries from a store uptown where Spanish was spoken, and high prices asked. On our advice, Mr. Gonzales now does most of his shopping at the A & P. . . . The situation has been in a constant state of flux since we first came in contact with the family, and shows every evidence of continuing in the same state. . . . All our efforts still leave many of the major problems of the family unsolved. . . . We will welcome any suggestions and opinions you may have. . . .

A series of student comments followed upon this presentation, gradually crystallizing around one of the major ideas of the program. "There is consensus that adequate care must include preventive, emotional, environmental, and familial aspects if it is to offer the most that modern knowledge can supply in the management of those who are ill."[15] But it

15. From a report of the comprehensive care and teaching program to the Commonwealth Fund, March 30, 1954.

has not yet been determined how inclusive "adequate care" can and should be:

> I was thinking as I sat there listening to the Gonzales case . . . is it or isn't it part of the doctor's job to be concerned with such things as where his patients buy their food?
>
> Theoretically, I guess it's part of the doctor's job. . . . But from my own point of view, I'm afraid that if I had a family like this, all I'd want to do is throw up my hands completely. . . .
>
> As far as the question of whether or not the doctor is obligated to look into such matters as the food people buy is concerned, I'd say yes . . . so long as those things pertain to medical illness. And in this particular family, it's especially important because they're all anemic. . . . But as for the social problems of this Puerto Rican family, they're beyond the scope of an everyday doctor to crack, in my opinion. . . .
>
> What we have here is a group of Americans coming from highly sordid conditions to live in highly sordid conditions. . . . Well, I think it's part of our responsibility to do something about this problem. . . .
>
> We had another case in a session on Thursday that bears on this. This is an Irish woman who's tied down with arthritis and who has a number of problems in addition. Among them is the fact that she lives in a one-room flat—dirty and with no heat. Well, the question arose as to whether it's the doctor's responsibility to get her another apartment and encourage her to move . . . or whether it's beyond the scope of the physician's work. . . .

The variety of opinion voiced in the course of such a conference provides a student with intimations that not only his classmates, but his instructors and physicians in general, are as perplexed as he is by questions about such matters as the boundaries of the doctor's professional task and the unsolved problems of patients like the Gonzales family. In the words of a faculty member who spoke up at the end of this conference:

> These questions don't only concern students. . . . They concern doctors as well. . . . There just aren't many "ground rules" in this area. . . .

CONCLUSION

This paper reviews some experiences that acquaint the medical student with the different types of uncertainty he will encounter later as a practicing physician and some of the ways in which he learns to deal with these uncertainties.

Because this is a preliminary description of what, it turns out, are rather complex processes, we have not organized the analysis around several basic distinctions that could be made. But it seems appropriate to introduce these now so that lines of a more systematic analysis can begin to emerge.

One basic type of uncertainty distinguished at the onset is that deriving from limitations in the current state of medical knowledge. Clearly, the different medical sciences vary in this respect. It has been indicated, for example, that limitations in a field like pharmacology are now considerably greater than they are in, say, anatomy. There are comparable differences among the clinical sciences. There would probably be general agreement that gaps in psychiatric knowledge are considerably greater than those in the field of obstetrics and gynecology. Such distinctions would provide a focus for further and more rigorous study of training for uncertainty. The different fields would be arranged according to the degree of uncertainty that characterizes them in order to see whether this ranking is paralleled by what the student learns from his different courses about the uncertainties of medicine. Are students made most aware of uncertainties when they are exposed to fields in which these uncertainties are greatest? More important, perhaps, is the question whether those fields in which limitations of knowledge are particularly prominent offer more or fewer means of coming to terms with uncertainty.

The second type of uncertainty, resulting from imperfect mastery of what is currently known in the various fields of medicine, was not analyzed in terms of its variability. We chose rather to concentrate on the "typical" or "modal" student at different phases of his medical school career. But, obviously, there are significant individual differences, and these could provide a second focus in a more systematic study of training for uncertainty. Students vary in the level of skill they achieve at any particular stage of their training. For example, those who find it easy to memorize details may have an advantage over their classmates in the study of anatomy; those whose manual dexterity is highly developed may not experience the same degree of personal inadequacy as the less adroit students when they begin to carry out surgical procedures; extroverted students may find it easier to get along with patients than introverted classmates. These variations in aptitudes, skill, and knowledge may lead to individual differences in the extent to which students experience the uncertainties derived from limitations of skill and knowledge. Students probably differ also in awareness of their own limitations and in response to these limitations. Some may be more sensitive than others to their real or imagined lack of skill. Some may be more able than others to tolerate the uncertainties of which they are aware. As we have seen, distinctions such as these would have to be considered in a more precise investigation of training for uncertainty. Are relatively skilled students less likely than relatively unskilled students to become aware of those uncertainties that derive from limits of medical knowledge? Are students especially sensitive to the uncertainties that confront them better able than less sensitive classmates to cope with such uncertainties? Or, to raise a somewhat different sort of problem, do students with a low level of tolerance for such uncertainty perform less effectively in their medical studies than students who are able to accommodate themselves to uncertainty? The level of tolerance might also affect the choice of a career: for example, do students who find it difficult to accept the uncertainties they encounter elect to go into fields of medicine in which there is less likelihood of meeting these uncertainties?

A third distinction involves the experiences through which the student becomes acquainted with the uncertainties of medicine. Some of them are directly comparable with those a mature physician would encounter. For example, when he meets the tentative and experimental point of view of pharmacologists or when inconsistent findings make a definitive diagnosis problematic, the student is faced with exactly the same sort of unsurenesses met by a practicing physician. But other experiences seem to derive their elements of uncertainty from the teaching philosophies or curricular organization of the medical school. For instance, the uncertainties a student experiences as a result of the avoidance of spoon-feeding by the basic science faculty at Cornell or the atomistic division of his class in the third year are by-products of particular conditions in the medical school, although they may have their analogues in actual practice. This distinction would consequently have to be incorporated into a more detailed analysis of training for uncertainty. Which type of experience is more conducive to recognition of the uncertainties in medicine? Which is more easily handled by students? In view of the wide range of experiences in medical school that have a bearing on training for uncertainty, what is the relative balance between those experiences that are inherent in the role of physician and those that inhere in the role of student?

This concluding section is clearly not a summary of what has gone before. Instead, we have chosen this opportunity to make explicit some of the variables and distinctions that were only implicit in earlier pages in order to indicate further problems for the more systematic qualitative analysis of a process like training for uncertainty.

The Autopsy: Its Place in the Attitude-Learning of Second-Year Medical Students

This essay examines an event experienced by all second-year students at a medical college: the first autopsy they attend as part of their course in general pathology. It begins with the premise, shared by many medical educators, that the autopsy room is one of the important "halls of learning"[1] in which medical students are trained to be physicians, and it goes on to suggest that the experience of the autopsy serves to transmit to students, in ways planned and unplanned, some of the attitudes and

1. See Averill A. Liebow, M.D., "The Autopsy Room as a Hall of Learning," *The American Journal of Medicine*, Vol. 21 (Oct. 1956), 485–486.

In 1952 the Bureau of Applied Social Research of Columbia University began long-term studies in the sociology of medical education, with support by the Commonwealth Fund. The central objective of these studies was to characterize the social and psychological environment of the medical school and to determine the bearing of that environment upon the student's acquisition of knowledge and skills and the development of his attitudes and values: his professional socialization. This unpublished essay was written in the mid-1950s while I was associated with the Columbia "medical school project." The data on which it was based were collected over the course of my four years of participant-observation-based field research at Cornell University Medical College, one of the four medical schools in which the Columbia team carried out its study of the professional socialization of medical students.

values, as well as knowledge and skills, required for the effective performance of the role of physician.

STUDENT PARTICIPATION IN AN AUTOPSY: A "LANDMARK" EXPERIENCE

As part of the course in general pathology, all second-year second-trimester students are required to take part in at least one autopsy. This is an event students regard as especially important, one of the "landmark" or "milestone" experiences of their training in medical school. Students recognize the special role of the autopsy in launching them on the study of disease; it is partly for this reason that they regard the autopsy as a "big experience" in a "big course." However, they do not consider it important only because it advances their intellectual development as student-physicians. They also describe participation in an autopsy as "an emotionally important experience . . . one of the hurdles you have to get over along the way to becoming a doctor." By this students apparently mean both that the autopsy significantly challenges their ability to act and feel like doctors, and that it plays an especially important role in teaching them some of the attitudes and values that will enable them to regard themselves as physicians and to conduct themselves in a suitably professional manner.

From this point of view the autopsy advances not just one, but several aspects of attitudinal learning of students. Taking part in an autopsy seems to have relevance for their training in detached concern, uncertainty, the management of time, and medical morality, and, partly as a consequence, for their development of a professional self-image. Because the autopsy advances their attitude-learning in these several ways, it is experienced by almost every student as an event of special import.

DESCRIPTION OF THE AUTOPSY SITUATION

Before we examine the kinds of attitude-learning that seem to take place in the autopsy and consider some of the processes by which this learning is effected, some description of the autopsy as experienced by second-year students is in order.

The sophomore class is divided into alphabetically determined groups of threes and assigned autopsies in rotation, according to a schedule posted in the microscopic laboratory. Each group is put "on call" when the preceding one has participated in an autopsy. Students are told that they are "next up" for an autopsy, and from then on they are expected to be available by telephone so that they can report to the hospital quickly, on short notice.

When a group of three students is called for an autopsy, they immediately go to a dressing room where they change from street clothes into white scrub suits similar to those worn in an operating room. (For many students this is the first time in medical school that they wear "all whites.") They cover their white uniforms with long plastic aprons and are given rubber gloves, which they are required to wear when they handle unfixed tissues. As part of the precautions that are taken to avoid the dissemination of infected materials in the autopsy room, students wash their hands carefully before they put gloves on.

The room in which autopsies are conducted is as immaculate, well-organized and brightly lit as a modern laboratory or surgical amphitheater. The walls and floor are constructed of well-scrubbed gray tile. The room is illuminated by overhead fluorescent lighting. Most of the equipment is made of stainless steel or white enamel. There are two stainless steel autopsy tables and a high, narrow stainless steel table on which a Bunsen burner, a rack of test tubes, and several small jars filled with solution are set. (The burner and test tubes are used to take various cultures, the jars to preserve some of the specimens of tissue that the prosector takes as the dissection proceeds.) The instruments the prosector uses are carefully arranged on a cork board. Some of these are surgical instruments—for example, steel scissors and retractors. In addition, there are larger, heavier pieces of equipment with unpainted wooden handles that look more like tools than the finer, stainless steel instruments of the operating room usually do. Affixed to the far wall are a special camera and timer for taking photographic slides of pathological specimens. The metallic properties of this equipment along with the white enamel of the scales in which vital organs are weighed, of the pans in which they are placed, and of the sinks along the walls contribute to the aseptic, efficient atmosphere of the autopsy room.

A wall telephone, a desk, and a blackboard on wheels complete the major fixtures in the room. Among the papers on the top of the desk are the hospital chart of the patient on whom the autopsy will be conducted, a "Permission for the Performance of an Autopsy" slip signed by the patient's nearest of kin, and a death certificate that has not yet been filled out. A list of the major organs and cavities of the body has been painted in white on the surface of the blackboard. As the autopsy proceeds, vital data about these organs and cavities are recorded on the blackboard in the places designated for them.

When students enter the autopsy room, the body on which they will help to conduct a post-mortem examination is usually already there. Generally, when students first see it, it is still on the stretcher and wrapped from head to toe in a white sheet. There is, however, some variation from autopsy to autopsy in all these respects. For example, sometimes students report to the autopsy room before the body is wheeled in; on other occasions, by the time students arrive the body has been moved from the stretcher to the autopsy table, where it lies with only the face and genitalia covered by small white cloths.

The first thing that students do is read as much as they can of the patient's medical history in his hospital chart. They then discuss some of its highlights with the pathologist who will be conducting the autopsy to which they have been assigned. Next, the prosector starts the examination by carrying out a quick, rough inspection of the body, beginning with the head and proceeding downward toward the feet. Generally, he invites two students to assist him; the third student acts as recorder for the group.

When this superficial examination is completed, the prosector walks back to the desk and checks the "Permission for Autopsy" form to make sure that it has been signed by a relative of the patient. (One pathologist tells us that he not only does this as a legal precaution, but also to "impress students with the solemnity" of the procedure.) At this point, the prosector is likely to remind students that the right to perform autopsies is a privilege exclusively granted to members of the medical profession; and that it is their responsibility to handle the parts of the body they are about to dissect with respect for their being human tissues.

The prosector returns to the autopsy table, mounts a stainless steel stool, and, taking one of the larger instruments in hand, makes the first incision. With this, the actual dissection begins.

On the whole, students are observers rather than active participants in this technically intricate and physically strenuous phase of the dissection. Working rapidly and deftly, the prosector frees the vital organs from the body cavity. To the extent that students assist the prosector at all during this part of the autopsy, it is mainly in carrying out routine minor tasks, such as holding back various structures and tissues with retractors. Their verbal interchange with him, however, is vigorous. Throughout the entire autopsy there is a continuous flow of conversation between the prosector and students: questions and answers, explanations and opinions, all centering primarily about the case being examined. In fact, even though the atmosphere of the room in which the autopsy takes place is serious, dignified and intensely work-oriented, it is by no means hushed. On the contrary, the room hums with the constant arrival and departure of members of the pathology department, members of the house staff, attending physicians, and second-, third-, and fourth-year students who in some way were connected with the case or who are specially interested in it either from a research or clinical point of view. They come and go and add their voices to the stream of talk about the case. In the background the phone rings intermittently, bringing calls both for persons already in the autopsy room, and from persons in other parts of the hospital who want to know how far the dissection has proceeded and how much longer it will probably be before the most crucial findings begin to emerge.

The next phase of the autopsy entails working on the patient's head: removing the calvarium and the brain. In this part of the autopsy, the prosector receives assistance from an orderly rather than from students.

Once the evisceration of the body is completed, the orderly sponges off the body, and he and the prosector close various skin flaps over the open cavities. The body is moved from the table to a stretcher, and, after the prosector signs the death certificate, the body is wheeled from the room toward a special elevator that opens directly into the morgue, where it is turned over to the undertaker. Typically, all that has ensued in the autopsy room until now has taken place in approximately one hour.

The vital organs and tissue that have been removed from the body are placed in enamel pans. Further dissection and examination of them now begins. Though not invariably the case, many prosectors permit students to play a more active role in this phase of the autopsy than they did earlier. It is not unusual for the prosector to ask students to weigh the organs, trace out their blood supplies, and even do a considerable part of the subsequent dissection.

Dissection and examination of these organs continue until the pathologist decides that he has reached a definitive enough understanding of the case to terminate the autopsy. He then arranges some of the organs on photographic plates and takes pictures of the most significant and interesting findings. He also sets aside fresh specimens for the second-year class in pathology to study. Three or four hours have probably elapsed, and the autopsy may then be said to be over.

Students return to the dressing room, where they remove their white scrub outfits and put their street clothes back on. There is some talk among them about medical scientific aspects of the autopsy in which they have just assisted.

The foregoing is a description of some of the situational features of the autopsy relevant to the contribution this experience makes in the attitude-learning of second-year students. These descriptive details provide a conception of what the autopsy is like from which analysis of the socio-psychological import of this significant medical school event can now proceed.

TRAINING IN DETACHED CONCERN

Perhaps the most potent impact of the autopsy is in the realm of what we have termed students' training in "detached concern." This is the process by which students gradually learn to combine the counterattitudes of detachment and concern to attain the balance between objectivity and empathy expected of mature physicians in the various kinds of professional situations they encounter.[2]

In the context of the autopsy, students are called upon to meet death and to carry out the dissection of a human body with the relatively "impersonal attitude of scientists." At the same time, they are also expected to maintain some degree of sensitivity to the "human implications" of what they are doing—in the words of a sophomore, to "preserve a certain amount of feeling" about "working on the body of a person who was once alive and now is dead."

Second-year students generally experience their first autopsy as a challenge to their objectivity. One student, for example, refers to the autopsy as a "test of [your] constitution and reactions . . . a real workout in objectivity." This is primarily because "an autopsy is the first place where you get the feeling of death as recent life," another student explains. It "gives you the feeling that what [they are] doing is working on the body of a real person who not very long ago was very much alive."

Aspects of the Autopsy Conducive to Emotional Response

Various features of the autopsy situation challenge the ability of students to manage their feelings. One of these is the experience of being put "on call" for an autopsy. Because no one knows just when the next patient in the hospital will die, or whether the physician will be able to obtain permission for an autopsy from the patient's next of kin, students who

2. Because the autopsy makes such an important contribution to students' development of detached concern, the largest section of this article will be devoted to a discussion of this aspect of their training.

are "up for the next autopsy" often have to "stand by" for quite a while before they are finally summoned.

For some students, this "waiting around for someone to die is really quite disturbing." Being on call gives such students time to contemplate the fact that somewhere in the hospital the person they will see in the autopsy room is in the process of dying, and that they are waiting for this to occur so they can dissect the body. They find themselves thinking of death "in terms of an individual" and of the organs they will dissect as "once a vital, functioning part" of that individual. As a consequence, even before the autopsy begins such students are reacting to it in what one described as a somewhat "personal, subjective way."

Later, various other aspects of the situation and procedure in the autopsy room tend to remind students that they are dissecting the body of someone who has just died. These are the parts of the autopsy to which they are most likely to respond with emotion.

For example, some students are "bothered" by the extent to which the body on the autopsy table is exposed. They contrast it with the relatively well-swathed cadaver in the anatomy laboratory. Since the body in the autopsy is less covered than the cadaver, its connection with human life and personality is more apparent to students. In turn, this makes it hard for them to think of the autopsy as impersonally as they did the dissection in anatomy.

> [In anatomy] the cadaver is pretty well mummified. . . . As a result, you don't consider the cadaver as a former human being—but as a species of anatomy. Its personality is wrapped up, so to speak. . . . But in the autopsy . . . you can see the whole body. . . . You . . . have the feeling that here is a person who was alive a few minutes before. . . .

Some of the specific attributes of the body on the autopsy table, as well as its general appearance, convey a "sense of the human and the living" to students. For example, students contrast the life-like color and "feel" of the body dissected in the autopsy with the cadaver in anatomy:

> In anatomy, everything was in tones of gray—literally. . . . But the recently living tissue you see in the autopsy is much brighter in color. . . . Red, yellow and brown are the outstanding hues. . . . Also, the organs seem soft and floppy compared to the hard entrails of the cadaver. . . . The cadaver has been dead and gone for a long time. You might say the spirit has gone out of it, so it's like cutting into a wooden box or something. The body doesn't feel like a body. It's hard: a good deal like rawhide . . . and it's cold. . . . The body in the autopsy is still warm. . . .

Practically all students are forcibly struck by the characteristic odor of the body at autopsy.[3] They find it hard to describe this "autopsy smell." ("It is organic." . . . "It is subtle, but all-pervasive." . . . "It has no circumference." . . . "You only become fully aware of it after you have left the autopsy room.") Students agree that this diffuse, fleshly, evasive, but lingering odor makes them think of death and dissection in the context of human life. As a consequence, they often feel uncomfortable about these aspects of the autopsy. For example, one student says that "watching the prosector cut away with that big knife" at the soft, vividly colored tissues and seeing them "jiggle like jelly" made him "feel funny." Another student "admits" that the smell of the first autopsy he attended "would have made [him] sick sooner or later if [he] had not breathed through [his] mouth."

At two stages of the autopsy in particular the physical concomitants of the dissection tend to increase students' awareness of "the body as a person."

> When you see the initial incision and the first bleeding, [a sophomore says], that's a point at which you're very aware of the whole person. . . . You realize this is someone who has died, and that what you're going to do is look inside that person. . . .

Students also report that the dissection of the head makes them more conscious of the body as a person than in other phases of the autopsy. This is apparently because they regard the face and brain as representing the thinking and feeling life of a person. When the prosector "uncovers the face, saws into the skull, and peels the scalp down," they are "reminded of the personality" of the individual on the table, as one student puts it. During these phases of the dissection students are especially susceptible to "feeling poorly" or "somewhat queasy."

Just as certain physical characteristics of the body tend to activate students' awareness of its connection with human life, so other characteristics of the autopsy remind them that they are examining the body of "someone who was a patient in the hospital." As we have seen, the patient's hospital chart is in the autopsy room, and before the examination begins, students are expected to read portions of it. Frequently the

3. For the many years that this paper has circulated as an underground document among medical students and doctors, they have responded to this section by saying what a vivid impression of the autopsy my "description" has produced. In fact, the following three sentences have been added for this version—earlier medical readers' strong (and inaccurate) reaction to my "description" testifies to the intensity of their own sense-memory of the autopsy. The error forms an interesting datum in itself.

prosector supplements the student's cursory review of the chart with an oral summary of the patient's clinical history. Furthermore, the attending physician and members of the house staff who were connected with the case usually make an appearance during the autopsy and enter into a certain amount of discussion with the prosector about the patient's hospital course, as well as about the post-mortem findings that seem to be emerging. In these several ways, students learn something about the patient when he was alive. One consequence of this is that some students find themselves "looking at a group of vital organs . . . and thinking, [for example, that] 'This woman was sixty-seven years old.'" By tending to make students conscious of the personal attributes of the body they are dissecting, knowledge of the clinical history tends to increase the emotionality of their response to the autopsy.

Along with what students experience as the "hospital-like atmosphere" of the autopsy room, their information about the patient's clinical course makes them feel "closer to the actual practice of medicine":

> First we look at the medical history for a few minutes and browse over it; and then we discuss it. The prosector goes over significant parts of it with us . . . what we will be particularly interested in looking for. . . . I don't know how to put it exactly . . . but the autopsy seems to be more concerned with the hospital [than the anatomy laboratory was] . . . concerned with a disease process and the death of a patient that just happened a few hours ago. . . . The anatomy room is a drab, laboratory-looking place. But the autopsy room has bright, shiny chrome. . . . There are only two tables . . . instruments on the shelf. . . . It's more like what you would expect in a hospital. It's kind of like an operating room . . . like a minor operation. . . . You seem to be dealing with something closer to medicine. It's nearer to you. It's more like doctoring. . . .

Finding some comparability between the autopsy and a doctor's work with live patients can be a source of disturbance to students. It reminds them, as one student puts it, that

> Many of our patients in the wards of learning will die. This, of course, is something we must get used to, [he continued], but this still makes me stop momentarily and get my breath. . . .

Those aspects of the situation that make them conscious of the patient's family also make it difficult for students to react to the autopsy impersonally. This, more than their work in the anatomy laboratory, leads the autopsy to be a challenge to objectivity.

> The reason you have the cadaver in anatomy, [a student points out], is because the body is unclaimed. Since there's no family in the picture, it's more impersonal. In the autopsy, you're more aware of the patient's family. You know that someone's broken up about her death. . . .

The patient's family can enter into students' consciousness in a number of ways. First, as we have noted, an autopsy is performed only if the written consent of the patient's next of kin is obtained. A "permission for autopsy" form, signed by this close relative, is affixed to the patient's chart, where it is seen by students when they look through the medical history. Second, the conduct of students in the autopsy is partly conditioned by having to take into account the way a patient's family is likely to feel about his death and about granting permission for a post-mortem examination. In the words of the students' pathology syllabus:

> . . . For physicians to be in a position to request a post-mortem examination, they must be assured that the Department of Pathology will treat the body with due respect and consideration. Discussion at the autopsy table should be limited to relevant scientific considerations. Students seeing autopsy materials are bound by rules of professional secrecy not to relate any facts about a given case outside of professional circles. In general, autopsy materials should be described as #11,456, not Mr. Brown, Mrs. Smith or Miss Jones. . . .

Third, the pace at which the autopsy proceeds and the technique of dissection are somewhat affected by the wishes and sentiments of the patient's family regarding his funeral and burial. In the guide drawn up by hospital administrators and funeral directors, for example, pathologists are enjoined to carry out the autopsy "promptly so as not to inconvenience the family of the deceased," to avoid destroying the vessels of the body that are needed for embalming, and to desist from excising those parts of the body that will be exposed when the patient is laid out for the funeral. From this guide, from their own observation, and from some of the remarks and behavior of the prosector, students become aware of the influence exerted by the patient's family over the autopsy. Because all this reminds students that the body on the table is a person mourned by relatives, it is apt to contribute to whatever difficulty students experience in approaching their first autopsy with the "scientific objectivity" of mature physicians.

Yet, in spite of these tendencies for reacting in a disturbed, emotional way, most students seem able to maintain relative equanimity in the autopsy situation. In the face of these inclinations to feel strongly and "personally" about the autopsy, what accounts for the fact that students generally meet it with equipoise?

Experiences That Prepare Students for the Autopsy

To a certain extent, students are prepared for the autopsy by earlier experiences in medical school. As the tendency to compare it with the anatomy laboratory implies, one of these important experiences is their work on a cadaver in first-year anatomy. Students have already told us that from their point of view the autopsy and the anatomy laboratory differ in at least one crucial respect: "There is more of an indication of the living" at an autopsy. But students also indicate that they regard the autopsy as "an extension" of their introduction to death and dissection in first-year anatomy.

As one sophomore puts it, students generally "do not have a real acquaintance with death" when they first enter medical school. For many, the anatomy laboratory represents the first sustained contact with the death of a human being (although they have all dissected animals in the course of their pre-medical studies). Anatomy is also the place where students first have the experience of dissecting a human body. As a result, they are inclined to react with some emotion to their first sight of the cadaver, to the first incisions they make on the cadaver, and to dissecting those parts of the cadaver, such as the face and the hands, that tend to convey a sense of its "humanness." Nevertheless, most students soon develop a comparatively "objective . . . loose . . . workaday" attitude toward these things. In short, their work on a cadaver in first-year anatomy helps students to cope with death and the dissection of a body in a detached way.

Experiments on laboratory animals in other pre-clinical courses (especially physiology and pharmacology) also help to ready students emotionally for the autopsy. They imply that there is something like a progression in this aspect of their training in detachment. The nature of this sequence is made explicit by a first-year student. Referring to a pharmacology experiment that "involved a little surgery on cats," he writes:

> . . . It seems to me that these experiences are some of the most important along the way. You start out by cutting up a dead frog or pig or cat in college, and advance by stages. Each new thing bothers you a little at first, and then it's O.K. . . .

From their pre-medical experience in dissecting nonliving animals, students move to their freshman year in medical school where, after working on a "very dead" human cadaver, they operate on live animals—first on cats, and then on dogs. Students regard each of these experiences as one step closer to working on the bodies of alive and recently alive patients—and each one as more difficult to manage with equanimity than the related experiences that preceded it. Thus, students consider it emotionally harder to work on the human cadaver than on dead laboratory animals; harder still to carry out procedures on live animals; and, within this general category, more difficult to work with live dogs than with live cats.[4] At first, each situation "bothers [students] a little"; but gradually, as one sophomore puts it, they learn to be "more objectively cool about it." This helps to prepare them to meet the next, more advanced stage in the sequence with relative detachment. By the time they assist in their first autopsy, then, students have achieved some objectivity about "cutting up" a body, and, in the words of a student, they have "gotten more used to death and things dying."

Other medical school experiences contribute directly to the degree of detachment about the autopsy that students generally attain before they are called upon to take active part in one. In conjunction with first-year anatomy, many students have occasion to be spectators at an autopsy. "Watching an autopsy from the sidelines" seems to develop students' capacity for detachment in this situation in two ways. First, it provides them with a "first-hand view of what an autopsy is like" and in doing so "eases the shock" of the autopsy in which students assist when they are sophomores. Simply because they know more about what to expect, the second autopsy is likely to have less of an emotional impact on them.

Students' attendance at an autopsy as freshmen usually advances their objectivity in another way. It helps allay some of their anxiety about how they will react later: "Most of the fellows are very eager to be good doctors," a first-year student explains, and so they would like to be able to meet the autopsy in the "objective, scientific spirit" that they regard as characteristic of good doctors. Until they attend an autopsy, however, most students are uncertain about their ability to summon up this spirit. In the course of observing an autopsy when they are freshmen, students learn something about the extent of their emotional response to it. They generally find themselves able to manage their feelings relatively well. They take this to mean that they have successfully passed a crucial "test"

4. Some students suggest that one reason they find it more difficult to conduct experiments on dogs than on cats is that they were "brought up with a dog," which "gives them the feeling that a dog is more like a person . . . closer to a human being."

of their objectivity—or, as one student phrases it, that they have "gotten over an important emotional hurdle in [their] medical development." As a result, they seem less apprehensive about their reactions to an autopsy when they participate in one as second-year students.

The early phases of their second-year work in gross pathology, students say, also help to "break them in emotionally" for the autopsy. The gross specimens examined in these laboratory sessions are the vital organs of deceased hospital patients and they are usually presented to students "in individual case terms." At first, some students are inclined to react emotionally to the fact that "these are the organs of a human being." But before long they begin to think more "impersonally" about the organs they are examining:

> Now when I see a lung, for example, I concentrate on its structure. . . . I don't picture its being in someone who was once living, breathing, and talking. . . .

Some students report that the objectivity they achieve in the gross pathology laboratory carries over to some extent into the autopsy, making it easier for them to approach it with the same kind of scientific detachment.

Certain features of the autopsy situation itself also facilitate students' detachment.

Features of the Autopsy Promoting Detachment

First, the appearance of the autopsy room helps students to cope with some of their emotional reactions. Its "extreme cleanliness," bright lights, "shiny stainless steel," and gleaming white enamel partly offset the tendency of some students to "feel revulsion" over such physical concomitants of the dissection as bleeding and the characteristic "autopsy smell." (As one sophomore puts it, the appearance of the autopsy room makes it seem "less like a butcher shop" and "more like an operating room.")

This immaculate surgical milieu partly results from the necessity for the prosector and his student assistants to observe aseptic techniques. Adherence to this strict ritual of procedure seems to aid students' detachment. It focuses their attention on such matters as wearing gloves, rolling up the sleeves of their laboratory gowns, washing their hands, using a pan to carry tissues from one table to another, etc., and it may distract students from what they regard as the "butchery" aspects of the autopsy.

Other procedures and precautions in the autopsy room also seem to promote student detachment. For example, as we noted earlier, students are advised by their pathology syllabus that "in general, autopsy material should be described as #11,456, not Mr. Brown, Mrs. Smith or Miss Jones." The ostensible reason given for the importance of conforming to this rule of medical etiquette is "in order for physicians to be in a position to request a post-mortem examination from relatives." It is assumed that to confine comments around the autopsy table strictly to the scientific task, and to maintain the anonymity of deceased patients by referring to them by number rather than by name, will insure the decorum that will encourage a patient's family to consent to an autopsy. Along with this manifest purpose, we suggest, this rule of behavior serves the latent function of fostering detachment in the autopsy situation. It facilitates and justifies an impersonal attitude toward the patient being autopsied and toward the phenomenon of death.

Some procedures followed in the process of dissection also help to "depersonalize" the autopsy for students. For example, during the early part of the dissection the face and the genitalia of the body are kept covered. As we noted before, these parts of the body are perceived by students as especially connected with "human, personal" qualities.

Students also "associate hands with people more than [they] do some other parts of the body." ("There's something about the hand that's . . . intimate and personal.") Because they feel this way, many freshmen experience working on the hands of the cadaver in anatomy as one of the more emotion-provoking points in the dissection. This lends significance to the fact that the hands are not excised in the autopsy, because they are exposed to view at a funeral. Any cuts on them would disturb the family and friends of the deceased, physicians and pathologists assume. If such episodes were frequent, they suppose, physicians might find it difficult to obtain permission from relatives for autopsies. Thus, in their view, not dissecting the hands takes the feelings of the mourners into consideration and so reinforces the effectiveness of the system for getting permission to carry out autopsies. The policy of not dissecting the hands also seems to have the latent function of making it easier for students to maintain equanimity during the autopsy, for, as we have seen, it exempts them from having to witness or to carry out a phase of the dissection that disturbed them in the past.

Another aspect of the autopsy that contributes to student detachment is the procedure of having the body taken out of the room (to be prepared for the undertaker) as soon as the vital organs are removed:

> Before the organs are taken out and the body is taken away, you're more aware of the person, [a student explains], but once the body goes, you're down to tissues and it's very depersonalized after that. . . .

Finally, the skill of the prosector in doing the dissection is another technical feature of the autopsy conducive to a "depersonalized" objective attitude among students. Both because it makes the autopsy a "neater, more bloodless" procedure than it would otherwise be, and, because it engages their intellectual interest, the prosector's "deft" technique helps students to think of the autopsy "scientifically" rather than "emotionally."

Scientific Orientation as an Aid to Detachment

As we have seen, students do more than observe the "technical know-how aspects" of the autopsy. They are instructed in the pathology and medicine of the autopsy by the prosector who keeps up a running stream of commentary and questioning as the dissection progresses. They assist the prosector in certain tasks: in the inspection of the body with which the autopsy begins, the recording of findings, and some of the less intricate and delicate parts of the dissection itself. To some extent students become involved in the exchange of remarks and opinions between the prosector, and the pathologists, clinicians, and students interested in the case who file continuously in and out of the autopsy room. Through their observation of the technical work of the autopsy, their participation in it, and in the discussions that take place as the work proceeds, students often become so "engrossed in the scientific angles" of the autopsy that (in the words of a sophomore) "its emotional aspects are obscured" for them. Intellectual absorption in the autopsy is thus another source of student detachment in the situation.

Most students are interested in the medical science of the autopsy in its own right. Some also make a self-conscious effort to enhance their objectivity by deliberately focusing on its scientific aspects. As one student observes,

> Most of the fellows are so eager to be good doctors that they force themselves to look at things in a scientific way. I was noticing that at the autopsy. Nobody was hanging back away from the table. Everyone was leaning forward and trying to see everything they could. Every guy was interested in the facts . . . asking questions and wanting to learn what had happened. . . .

What students perceive as the pathologist's attitude toward the autopsy also seems to facilitate their detachment in the situation. From such things as the care with which he handles the organs and his serious demeanor in the autopsy room, the prosector generally conveys to student assistants his respectful awareness that he is dissecting the body of a dead human being. Students note that the pathologist nevertheless approaches the autopsy in a relatively impersonal, matter-of-course way. By helping to create what students experience as the "scientific atmosphere" of the autopsy room, the composed attitude of the pathologist that "it's part of a day's work" reinforces students' capacity for detachment in the autopsy. It provides them with a standard to follow. For the prosector's conduct shows students that he himself is not "bothered" by the autopsy and that he "doesn't expect that students will be either." The pathologist's expectation that students should and can maintain their equanimity in the autopsy, and the example of objectivity that he sets, make it easier for students to conduct themselves in the autopsy with relative detachment.

Limiting Discussion and Maintaining Detachment

Finally, students seem to limit the extent to which they discuss the autopsy. They evidently believe this will help them avert an excessively emotional response to it. In keeping with their practice regarding important events in medical school that they share, students talk with one another about their autopsy experience. But their comments seem impersonal and stylized:

> We pretty much talk about the autopsy the way you would if you were presenting a case, [a student explains]. "This was a sixty-some-odd-year-old man who had such-and-such a set of signs and symptoms. This is what it was thought he had. This is what we found. . . ."
>
> You may talk about what you did in the autopsy . . . about the medicine and pathology, [another student agrees], but you don't talk about the autopsy from an emotional point of view. . . .

The closest that students usually come to discussing their "personal reactions" to the autopsy is that they sometimes allude to its smell.

Students' preoccupation with the pathology and medicine of the autopsy and their unwillingness to discuss their feelings about it suggest that they are predominantly interested in the contribution the autopsy makes to their scientific knowledge. But it may also result from the students' difficulty in describing their emotional reactions to the autopsy. Student feelings about death and the dissection of the human body seem to run deep. But they are attenuated and made more subtle by the medical school experiences that prepare students for the autopsy, and by the features of the autopsy that tend to offset an emotional response. Both factors seem to lie behind the difficulty that students experience when they "try to put their feelings about the autopsy into words."

The usual absence of talk among students about their reactions to the autopsy is not simply a product of their intellectual involvement in the medical science of the autopsy or their relative inarticulateness about how they feel. Students seem to have a tacit agreement to curtail such discussions:

> We don't talk very much about such things, [a student explains]. Each person more or less handles [his] feelings individually. . . . Everyone has the idea you should be objective in situations like the autopsy. . . . There's almost something like an unwritten law about not discussing such things. . . .

Students share the unspoken conviction that "admitting you had qualms about the autopsy" or that "it made you feel queasy" is not in keeping with standards of professional objectivity. Some students are guided by the belief that restricting discussion about their reactions to the autopsy will make it easier for them to manage their feelings. As one puts it,

> You don't bare your heart about the autopsy. . . . You sort of sit on the lid of your feelings. . . .

For both reasons, a norm restraining talk about other than scientific aspects of the autopsy develops in the student group. Since most students assent to this "unwritten law," comments made by a student who transgresses it by telling how he felt in the autopsy are likely to be "passed over" or "cut short."

Although their participation in an autopsy makes some students "think a little, and see if the pieces of [their] philosophy still fit," there is less speculation of this sort among them than might be expected. Students tend not to reflect on what one sophomore terms such "enigmatic questions" as "What is life? What is death? What exactly is the difference between them?" Such reflections, apparently, are felt not to be in accord with the kind of objectivity they regard as befitting a doctor. Students seem to agree that—because "trying to determine the whys and wherefores of things" leads away from the "objective, factual approach" of medical science into the realm of personal feelings and beliefs—"speculation" of this sort should be kept at a minimum.

Students themselves take note of their "more detached" outlook:

> We find ourselves not taking as personal an attitude, [a student explains]. For example, not thinking and feeling, "Here is a person who was living and is now dead" to the extent that we once would have. . . . It's something that seems to have happened to us in medical school. . . .

These students claim that their reaction to the autopsy was not as intense as it probably would have been a year earlier, that their medical school experiences have curbed their "tendency to react emotionally."

Students have mixed feelings about the perceived changes in their perceptions and attitudes. They welcome their greater composure as a "sign of [their] progression" in achieving the "professional detachment [they] need to develop." But they also express some uneasiness over the possibility that perhaps they are becoming "insensitive," "callous," or "blasé":

> . . . You have to overcome some of your emotion . . . and learn to look at things objectively and scientifically. . . . But you also have to preserve a certain amount of feeling. . . . Because if you're a cold fish, you won't be good with patients. . . . So you worry about becoming over-callous to things you were once sensitive to. . . .

In his own words, a second-year student is still striving to attain his balance between "feeling things" and "looking at things objectively" that he considers essential for a "good practicing physician."

We turn from this discussion of detached concern to consider how the autopsy contributes to the development of other student attitudes. The first of these is the attitude of students toward uncertainty.

TRAINING FOR UNCERTAINTY

The autopsy plays a major role in training students for uncertainty, the process by which students learn about some of the uncertainties of medicine and develop ways of coping with them.[5]

5. Some of what follows is a restatement or elaboration of ideas and material that formed part of my paper on "Training for Uncertainty" in Merton's *The Student-Physician* (and in this volume).

Kinds of Uncertainty in the Autopsy

Every doctor encounters three basic types of uncertainty: uncertainty that derives from limits on the state of medical knowledge; uncertainty that grows out of his imperfect mastery of all that is known; and uncertainty over how to distinguish between his own ignorance or ineptitude and the restricted powers of medicine itself. Second-year students are exposed simultaneously to all three kinds of uncertainty when they take part in autopsies. Since an autopsy is an organized attempt of pathologists and clinicians to resolve some of the uncertainties of a case by conducting a post-mortem examination, students are also being introduced to one of the institutionalized ways in which physicians in a teaching and research center deal with uncertainty. Finally, the autopsy tests and advances the ability of students to come to terms with uncertainty.

Participation in an autopsy makes students more aware in various ways of the uncertainties that result from limited medical knowledge. To begin with, being put on call for an autopsy reminds them that even when death is expected, the exact time of death is seldom predictable.

Students become impressed by the limitations of current medical knowledge when they see that the autopsy—the final and presumably exhaustive examination of the patient—often fails to tell what was the cause of the patient's death. Even when the autopsy provides an answer, it is often less "dramatic" and "specific" than students expected it to be:

> While our case was unusual, it was a bit of a letdown to me, for there was nothing dramatic to be pointed to as the cause of death. The clinician reported that the patient had lost 1000 cc. of blood from internal bleeding in the G.I. tract. . . . Well, we saw no gaping hole there. There was no one place you could pinpoint and say: "This is where the hemorrhage took place." . . . Rather, it was a culmination of a condition relating to various factors. I suppose most causes of death are this way. But still . . . it was somewhat disquieting to me. . . .

The extent of uncertainty at the end of an autopsy is often greater than students had anticipated. As a result, students sometimes have difficulty in determining when the autopsy is over:

> I didn't know the autopsy was over until I was told that it was. . . . After going over each of the organs, Dr. L. continued to cut and to take pictures. Finally, at a certain point he had to tell us, "I guess that just about does it. You can go now." . . . But there's really no finite point. You can't say it ends here. . . .

No matter how definitive an understanding of the "causes of the patient's death" that emerges from the autopsy, it remains obvious that physicians did not know how to prevent his death. This is conveyed to students primarily through the presence of "various doctors connected with the case" in the autopsy room and by the doctors' discussions with the pathologist. In this way, students become increasingly aware of another limitation in the field of medicine: its lack of control over death and the uncertainty with which physicians are confronted as a result of this limitation.

Not only the limits of the field, but the relationship between the personal limitations of physicians and the uncertainties they face become impressed upon students during their participation in an autopsy. For example, the autopsy gives students an opportunity to observe that "the doctors aren't always sure what caused the patient's death" or whether they could have done something to forestall it. As one student puts it, "they come to the autopsy . . . to find [these things] out."

Students may be present at an autopsy in which it becomes apparent that the physician was mistaken in his medical judgments:

> . . . My roommate had his autopsy last week. . . . And there were lots of things supposed to be wrong with this case. . . . Well, as you know, the various doctors who were involved in the case wander down while the autopsy is going on, and come in to see what was wrong with the patient. . . . In my roommate's case, they just weren't finding anything in the doctor's diagnoses. . . .

From experiences such as these, students may learn that because "medical knowledge is so vast" and "there's always so much to be taken into account, even the finest physicians" do not command all the available information relevant to each case they handle. Their medical knowledge, of course, is greater and more seasoned than that of medical students. But students have an opportunity to see in the autopsy that, nevertheless, mature physicians—like the students themselves—are confronted with uncertainties of diagnosis, therapy, and prognosis that grow out of their imperfect mastery of all there is to know in medicine. What is more, students can observe that lack of knowledge and its attendant uncertainty may have led "the best of doctors" to misjudge a case, or to have "made mistakes" that sometimes affected the welfare of the patient.

The third type of uncertainty the autopsy presents students derives from the first two: uncertainty over how to tell where the personal limitations of physicians leave off and the limitations of medical science begin. This is the kind of uncertainty that an autopsy ought ideally to resolve. If the clinicians could not make a diagnosis in a specific case, or failed to make a correct one, should they have been able to? Did they make the right therapeutic decisions? In short, given the current state of medical knowledge, could the death of the patient have been prevented? Unless unusual circumstances surround a case, such as the possibility that the patient's death was due to "unnatural" causes, or that some form of malpractice was involved, the pathologist who conducts the autopsy does not explicitly address himself to these questions. Nevertheless, they are always implicit in his post-mortem examination.

The pathologist is often unable to answer some of the questions that were left unsolved by clinicians. When this is the case, it is generally because of the limitations of current medical knowledge rather than the ignorance or ineptitude of the clinicians responsible for the case. But, as we have seen, at some autopsies that students attend the pathologist is able to clear up some of the diagnostic and therapeutic uncertainties that clinicians left unsettled; in others, the findings of the pathologist contradict those previously arrived at by clinicians. When the latter happens, students may at first regard it as proof of the clinicians' inadequacy in handling the case. But in many instances, the pathologist helps them see that "it is not as cut and dried as all that":

> In the first autopsy I did with students this year, [a pathologist told us], the man was diagnosed as having a carcinoma of the stomach. During the course of the work-up on the patient, he suddenly died. It turned out that the pain in the patient's stomach was not in the stomach, but in the liver. And what the patient died of was a tumor of the lung that was completely unsuspected. The students' first reaction to this was, "What a 'boo-boo' on the part of the clinician!" What I did was say, "Here's the chest X-ray done on the patient. Now *you* show me the cancer." . . . Which they couldn't. It wasn't that visible. . . . [I also tell students that] we try to write the autopsy up in such a way that doesn't say, "Nyah, nyah, it was your fault." Because it's usually not as cut and dried as all that. . . .

Students who assist a prosector with this point of view learn directly from him that it is often hard to distinguish between the "fault" of the doctor and the "fault" of the field of medicine.

In sum, students learn from their first autopsies that, although death is inevitable, it presents physicians with several kinds of uncertainty that even a post-mortem examination cannot always dispel. As we have seen, students react to these uncertainties with surprise, discomfort, and chagrin. The realization that death is something the doctor can neither "pinpoint" nor easily prevent becomes especially "disquieting" and "disappointing" to them. On the whole, however, students seem able to cope successfully with the uncertainties presented by the autopsy.

Basis of Coping with Uncertainty

By the time they are put on call for their first autopsy, second-year students have already had much training for uncertainty.[6] For one thing, even when they were freshmen students were "given the major responsibility for learning." In the non-spoon-feeding milieu of the first year at some medical schools, including the one under review, information is not presented to them "in neat packets"; precise boundaries are not set on the amount of work expected of them; and they do not receive grades. Students have to find out for themselves how much they are expected to know, what they should learn, how they should go about it, and how well they are doing. Insofar as it teaches students to take responsibility in a relatively undefined situation, the non-spoon-feeding approach of their first year can be thought of as providing them with a foretaste of the ambiguities a physician encounters when he assumes responsibility for a patient.

First-year anatomy gave students their beginning awareness of the specific kind of uncertainty that results from personal limitation. The venerable science of anatomy represents such a "huge body of facts" that, no matter how much time and energy they devoted to it, students found that they were unable to master all this knowledge. This experience helped students to see more clearly that they would always be faced with uncertainties derived from their inability to "know all there is to know."

Their course in pharmacology confronted students with the kind of uncertainty that stemmed from limitations of current medical knowledge. Pharmacology is a relatively tentative science, one that is only beginning to emerge from a trial-and-error state of experimentation. The study of pharmacology helped students to realize that not all the gaps in their knowledge indicated personal deficiencies.

Chiefly through their training in observation, students were also introduced to another kind of uncertainty before they assisted in their first autopsy. On the many occasions when they had trouble making some of the observations that their courses required of them (for example, visualizing anatomical entities or seeing what they were "supposed" to on an histological slide), they did not find it easy to decide how much

6. See "Training for Uncertainty."

of their difficulty was "personal" and how much of it "had to do with factors outside [themselves]." Their uncertainty was that of how to distinguish between their own limitations and those of medical knowledge itself.

Although the autopsy may be unique in exposing them simultaneously to all these types of uncertainty, students have had some prior experience with each type.

The "spirit" in which they see pathologists and clinicians approach the autopsy also helps students to cope with these uncertainties. Students note that, in general, pathologists and clinicians at an autopsy freely acknowledge their uncertainties about the diagnosis and treatment of the case they are considering. (In fact, the autopsy is premised on their mutual willingness to do so, in order to learn from those uncertainties and thereby possibly to resolve some of them.) Because it gives students a chance to see mature scientists and physicians handle uncertainty in an open, affirmative way, the autopsy helps students to come to terms with their own uncertainties. It encourages them to accept their own uncertainty—to define some of it as "inevitable" and "thoroughly legitimate"—and to begin to cope with it by freely expressing that they are unsure.

Finally, the strains to which the uncertainties of the autopsy subject students are offset to some extent by these uncertainties deepening their scientific interest in the case being examined:

> . . . Before the autopsy even began, you could tell from the clinical record that they hadn't been too sure of what was wrong with the patient. In a way, I was hoping it wouldn't be a clear-cut case. . . . Because it wasn't clear-cut, it gave me a real desire to see the autopsy and try to find out what had really been the matter. . . . I guess that's one of the reasons why the emotional aspects of it were obscured. . . . There was the excitement of expecting one thing and finding another, and also many small things that hadn't been anticipated. . . .

In sum, the autopsy presents students with various kinds of uncertainty and helps them to cope with each kind. It makes students more nearly aware that some of their uncertainty does not differ from that facing doctors and that candor about such uncertainties is expected and approved. This realization, along with their previous experiences with uncertainty and their intellectual attraction to cases that have some elements of unexpectedness, seem to enable students to come to terms with the uncertainties of the autopsy.

Apart from advancing students' training for uncertainty and training in detached concern, the autopsy also contributes to their training in the management of time.

TRAINING IN THE MANAGEMENT OF TIME

Illness, birth, and death, the major events for which a doctor is summoned, involve actual or potential exigencies, and they are typically accompanied by anxiety on the part of the patient and the patient's family. For this reason physicians are generally subject to the special demands of being on call. They are expected to be accessible (if only by telephone) whenever their patients need them.

Being on call for autopsies gives students their first direct experience with this characteristic demand made on the time of physicians in practice. Many students react unfavorably to the restrictions it imposes on their personal plans and sense of "freedom." ("There's the feeling of something pending, hanging over you. . . .") A few students carry this further. For them the experience of being on call is a preview of the heavy inroads professional responsibilities will make on their time when they are doctors:

> . . . [Being on call] meant to me that my life was not my own any more. We got called on Saturday afternoon, which meant I had to stick around school after classes were over. . . . My fiancée came, but because I was on call I couldn't leave. . . . I thought "Shades of things to come!" and "What have I gotten myself into?" . . .

Generally students do not experience being on call solely as a responsibility that interferes with their nonmedical activities, or as a disturbing preview of the kinds of demands that will be made on them as doctors. Because they associate being on call with "what it's really like to be a doctor," many students take pride in having this obligation:

> We felt great excitement about waiting around for our autopsy to come up. . . . It was one of the first times we were really doctors. . . . You know, "I can't come home this week, Ma—I'm on call," kind of thing. . . .

> Our autopsy came on a Saturday afternoon. I had tickets for the theater that afternoon. I got a real kick out of telling the people there that I was Dr. Scott and was on call at the hospital, if a phone call should come in for me. . . .

In other words, although students respond somewhat negatively to the restraints of being on call, they also tend to see it as an opportunity both to act like doctors and to be perceived as such by lay people.

Participating in an autopsy has consequences for students' training in medical morality, and this, too, is part of its significance as a landmark experience.

TRAINING IN MEDICAL MORALITY

By training in medical morality, we mean the process by which students learn the special rights and obligations of their chosen profession and come to grips with some of the moral problems of these rights and obligations. Through the autopsy, this part of student training is advanced in several ways.

First, from the pathology syllabus, the "Guide for Pathologists, Hospital Administrators and Funeral Directors," and from the prosector, students learn about the legal and ethical prescriptions that apply to an autopsy and about how to meet these requirements. Taking part in an autopsy is "one of the many rights and privileges of doctors" extended to students in the course of their medical school training. On the whole, students accept such rights as a matter of course; they are regarded as a necessary and justifiable part of becoming a physician. But the autopsy represents an extraordinary privilege: the right to dissect the body of someone who has just died. This is a prerogative granted only to people associated with the medical profession, and one that runs counter to deep-rooted beliefs in society regarding the sacredness of the human body and of the dead. Because it involves a unique and serious privilege, the autopsy helps make students aware that they are entering a profession with a code of morality that is "very different" from that of lay people in certain important respects.

One aspect of the autopsy in particular contributes to this awareness: the rules of professional secrecy that govern it. (In the words of the pathology syllabus, medical personnel attending an autopsy are "bound not to relate any facts about the case outside of professional circles.") In protecting the dignity and privacy of the deceased and their families, this rule is in keeping with the cultural belief in the sacrosanct nature of death. It accords special respect and consideration to patients and their families when they are confronted with death. But the instructions given to students imply that it is not always easy for doctors to obtain permission for a post-mortem examination from a patient's family, and that maintaining secrecy about the details of an autopsy will make it more likely that families will give their consent. Being pledged to secrecy tends to deepen the awareness among students of the discrepancy between the conviction of most physicians that the performance of autopsies is intellectually and morally necessary to advance medical knowledge, and the feeling of many lay people that it is morally dubious or unacceptable because it "imposes upon" those who have died or desecrates them.

The rule of professional secrecy also brings students face to face with a kind of conflict between professional and personal loyalties that is inherent in the role of doctor. There is a "problem cropping up now," one student explains, regarding "what you can and cannot talk about with the [nonmedical] members of your own family" and with nonmedical friends. This problem extends beyond medical school years, he goes on to say, "because one of the things a doctor has to learn is to keep his patients' confidence."

DEVELOPMENT OF A PROFESSIONAL SELF-IMAGE[7]

Finally, as the foregoing suggests, the autopsy has major significance for students' development of a professional self-image. By this we mean that their participation in an autopsy makes most students feel considerably more like doctors and less like lay people than they did before. Because the right to observe and assist in an autopsy is usually granted only to people affiliated with the medical profession, the simple experience of participation in an autopsy gives some students the sense that they are entering a new phase of their professional development (". . . when you enter the autopsy room, you pass through an important door . . .").

The autopsy makes students feel in other ways that they are graduating into doctorhood. As we have already noted, for example, students experience being put on call for an autopsy as one of the first times in medical school that they have a chance to act as "real doctors" do. The requirement that they wear white uniforms for the autopsy and practice aseptic techniques often gives them the feeling that, in appearance and behavior, they are acquiring some important characteristics of physicians.

Second, we have seen that the autopsy is conducted in a setting that appears "hospital-like" to students, that it centers on the examination of a recently deceased patient whose hospital chart students read, and that it is attended by clinicians as well as pathologists. All this converges to make students feel that they are "dealing with something close to the actual practice of medicine . . . more like doctoring" than was true of earlier stages in their training.

7. The process by which medical students develop a professional self-image has been investigated by Mary Jean Huntington as part of the studies in the sociology of medical education of the Bureau. See her first published paper on this process, "The Development of a Professional Self-Image," also in *The Student-Physician.*

Finally, the contribution of the autopsy to the professional self-image of students encompasses all the attitude-learning they undergo in this situation. By advancing their training in detached concern, training for uncertainty, training in the management of time, and training in medical morality, the autopsy variously modifies the attitudes and values of students. These changes in their attitudes and values in turn make students feel that their outlook is becoming quite different from that of persons outside the medical profession.

The autopsy also deepens the students' feeling of identification with one another. Through the shared experience of the autopsy, students develop a greater similarity of attitudes and values. As a consequence, their sense of "really becoming a unit with . . . [a] common background to hold [them] together" is enhanced. Thus, by making them feel distinct from nonphysicians and more united with one another, the autopsy plays a role in developing students' conception of themselves as doctors and professional colleagues.

Because participation in autopsies (1) is an experience common to all persons who have undergone medical school training; (2) differs sharply from the experiences of most nonphysicians; (3) contributes importantly to the attitude-learning of doctors; and (4) to some extent is recognized as doing so by medical students and graduate physicians, the first autopsy has a symbolic significance for the profession that reaches beyond the years of medical school. "What binds our profession together," Dr. Alan Gregg wrote, "is not so much the facts we agree upon or the knowledge we share, as the experiences we have all gone through, and the way we understand them and fit them to the pattern of our values."[8] The participation in autopsies, with all its implications for the learning of similar attitudes and values, seems to be one such cardinal experience.[9]

In these respects, the first autopsy is a "*rite de passage,*" a "landmark" or "milestone" event along the road to becoming a doctor that attitudinally and symbolically incorporates students more fully into the medical profession.

8. Alan Gregg, M.D., "Our Anabasis," *The Pharos of Alpha Omega Alpha,* Vol. 18, No. 2 (February 1955), p. 24.

9. *Ibid.*

Is There a "New" Medical Student?: A Comparative View of Medical Socialization in the 1950s and the 1970s

Writing about the socialization of physicians in the 1970s is a paradoxical intellectual experience. Due notice is being taken of the dramatic increase in the number of persons applying for admission to medical school. Discussion regarding not only the intellectual and scientific qualifications of the men and women deciding on medical careers, but also their social backgrounds, life experiences, attitudes, and convictions is rampant. The advantages and drawbacks of actual and potential curriculum changes are being debated throughout the country by medical educators, who are attempting to evaluate the impact of these changes on the competence and outlook of physicians now in training. In many educational and professional circles, and in the public arena, there is great preoccupation with the quality as well as the distribution and cost of health care in the society. To what is perhaps an unprece-

---

Prepared for presentation at the Conference on Health Care and Changing Values, sponsored by the Institute of Medicine, Committee on Human Value Issues in Health Care, National Academy of Sciences, Washington, D.C., November 27–29, 1973. Published in Laurence R. Tancredi, ed., *Ethics of Health Care* (Washington, D.C.: National Academy of Sciences, 1974), 197–227.

dented degree, this concerned interest has come to include questions about the ethical and existential dimensions of modern medicine, along with its scientific and technical aspects. These various developments are accompanied by general recognition that there is a significant relationship between the perceived strengths and weaknesses of the American medical system and the process of socialization for physicianhood that is an integral part of medical training. It could even be said that another characteristic of the present medical historical juncture is heightened awareness of the professional socialization process. Today's medical students, house officers, and their teachers seem to be impressed with the fact that the educational sequences in which they are participating not only convey knowledge and skills, but also professionally relevant values, attitudes and behavior patterns.

One would expect these characteristics of present-day medical educational milieux to generate significant, clinically perceptive, and socially sensitive research on the process of becoming a physician. But, to our knowledge, no such major study is being conducted. This stands in sharp contrast to the late 1950s, when a number of important social scientific inquiries into the process of becoming a physician were undertaken.[1] Why there is currently a paucity of work on medical socialization is a subject for study in and of itself. Its explanation is intricately associated with the stage of development and the collective mood both of social science and medicine and with more general cultural, economic, and political trends in the society that affect these disciplines. But, whatever its origins, the lack of research on this subject means that any discussion of medical socialization in the 1970s is necessarily speculative. This is as regrettable as it is curious. For it occurs at a time when both for social scientific and medical educational reasons it would be valuable to

1. Major publications based on these studies include: Howard S. Becker, Blanche Geer, Everett C. Hughes and Anselm L. Strauss, *Boys in White: Student Culture in Medical School* (Chicago: University of Chicago Press, 1961); Kenneth R. Hammond and Fred Kern, Jr., *Teaching Comprehensive Medical Care* (Cambridge, Mass.: Harvard University Press, 1959); Milton J. Horowitz, *Educating Tomorrow's Doctors* (New York: Appleton-Century-Crofts, 1964); Robert K. Merton, George Reader, and Patricia L. Kendall, eds., *The Student-Physician: Introductory Studies in the Sociology of Medical Education* (Cambridge, Mass.: Harvard University Press, 1957); George E. Miller, *Teaching and Learning in Medical School* (Cambridge, Mass.: Harvard University Press, 1961). In addition, at least two major books on the house officership phase of medical training came out of that period: Stephen J. Miller, *Prescription for Leadership: Training for the Medical Elite* (Chicago: Aldine Publishing Co., 1970) and Emily Mumford, *Interns: From Students to Physicians* (Cambridge, Mass.: Harvard University Press, 1970). For a state of the field review of these and other sociology of medical education studies, see Samuel W. Bloom, "The Sociology of Medical Education: Some Comments on the State of the Field," *Milbank Memorial Fund Quarterly,* Vol. 43, No. 2 (April 1965), 143–184.

study the social and cultural changes that seem to be taking place in the attitudes and values of medical students, the education they are undergoing, and the profession into which they are graduating. Instead, what is happening is that the many strongly felt but undocumented opinions that are being expressed on these matters are being presented and accepted as fact and are beginning to influence policy decisions about present and future medical training.

This paper is based on social scientific observations made in various medical school settings, principally in the 1950s and in the 1970s. One set of materials on which I draw are my own first-hand research experiences as a member of the Bureau of Applied Social Research-Columbia University team that undertook studies in the sociology of medical education in the mid-1950s at Cornell University, the University of Pennsylvania, Western Reserve University, and the University of Colorado. I was the chief fieldworker for the project, and in this capacity spent four years as a participant observer at Cornell University Medical College, watching and taking part in the academic, clinical, and interpersonal events that contributed to the processes of medical education and socialization through which students passed. I also had access to the data that my colleagues obtained from students in the four medical schools under study, through the periodic administration of a panel-type survey questionnaire.[2] As already implied, this was a golden era of research on professional socialization. Not only were several studies of psychosocial aspects of becoming a physician in progress, but a continual exchange of insights and information characterized them. Thus, my data from the 1950s include unpublished as well as published observations made available to me by social scientists and physicians associated with the University of Chicago, the University of Kansas, Tulane University, and Harvard University, among others.

As already implied, my data from the late 1960s and early 1970s are more impressionistic: they have not been gathered within the framework of a large, systematic study. Rather, they are the product of my own, more sporadically collected observations and documentation, which several of the roles that I now occupy have made possible. Since 1969, in my capacity as professor of sociology in the departments of psychiatry and of medicine at the University of Pennsylvania, I have been engaged in teaching medical students and also in observing and interviewing them

2. For a sample of the questionnaire and a discussion of how it was developed and administered, see Robert K. Merton, et al., eds., *The Student-Physician,* Appendix D, 307–351.

in order to help appraise the consequences of certain curriculum reforms. In addition, I have served both on the admissions and the curriculum committees of the medical school. Beyond those functions—because I have now done research, writing, and teaching in the field of the sociology of medicine for more than twenty years—I am often invited to visit and lecture at other medical schools. These activities have enabled me to have various kinds of contact with medical students and faculty in different medical schools. I have kept a fieldworker's record of these experiences, and these notes are the primary source for the account of medical socialization in the 1970s that I shall present.

Medical education in the 1950s was more tightly and uniformly organized than it is now. Looking at it from the perspective of the 1970s, the medical school curriculum was arranged in a "lockstep" way, with little room for individual variation or choice. The first two years of training were devoted *en bloc* to lecture hall presentations and laboratory work in the so-called "pre-clinical" or "basic" sciences. Patient contact was minimal, largely confined to the cadaver in the anatomy laboratory, the newly deceased patient in the autopsy room, and the live patients who were briefly presented to the class by an instructor, generally to demonstrate some biological principle or phenomenon. Only toward the end of the second year, in the context of their physical diagnosis course, where students learned to take medical histories and conduct physical examinations, did they have more sustained and clinically oriented exposure to patients. Although students were divided into smaller working groups for some of their laboratory and clinical tasks, assignment to these groups was determined by alphabetical order. The third year of medical school represented the great crossing over to the clinical phase of training. The third and fourth years were largely made up of a series of clinical clerkships in the various branches of medicine and surgery. The same alphabetical criterion that applied to the first two years ordered the sequence in which students rotated through their clerkships.

The highly patterned, collective, and relatively unvarying nature of each stage of medical school training was reflected in the students' characteristic dress and equipage. For, although they were not expressly required to wear uniforms and were not aware that they did so, the self-presentation of each cohort of students was so similar that one could identify the phase of their training by their costume. First-year students in the fifties tended to dress in long white laboratory coats, worn over khaki pants and sports shirts. They moved through the corridors of the medical school, arms laden with clipboards, notebooks and large, atlas-like texts. Toward the end of second year, when they were beginning to see patients in physical diagnosis, students looked more freshly barbered, donned neckties and more formal woolen trousers, and self-consciously carried unmistakably new little black bags wherever they went. During the clinical clerkships of third and fourth years, the long white coats gave way to short, jacket-length ones. Students pinned identifying name tags on their lapels and allowed their stethoscopes to hang conspicuously out of their hospital coat pockets. Some fourth-year students, emulating the interns they would soon become, knotted a rubber tourniquet around one of their belt loops, as if they were perpetually ready to draw bloods or start an intravenous infusion.

In certain medical schools (among them, the four that were studied by the Columbia team of sociologists), the 1950s were also a time when various educational innovations were being tried. The most extensive changes were those initiated by the school of medicine at Western Reserve University, where the traditional curriculum was razed and another put in its place. By and large, the experiments in medical education that were launched during this decade were oriented around a number of common themes.[3] Organized attempts were made to design opportunities for students to have earlier patient contact. Ways were also devised to introduce students to patients with "normal" health problems, such as those of uncomplicated pregnancy or everyday pediatrics, at the same time that they were being introduced to the more tragic and extraordinary dimensions of medicine through the anatomy laboratory, the autopsy, and their first encounters with chronically ill and dying patients. Various modes of more broadly defining the physician's role were tried, and of effectively emphasizing the role of social and psychological factors in the genesis and treatment of illness. These included developing and conveying the concept of "comprehensive care" and teaching, as well as efforts to incorporate more behavioral science into the medical curriculum. They also entailed trying to upgrade the importance of experience in outpatient clinics, based on the conviction that providing students with continuing responsibility for ambulatory patient care would train them in a more inclusive approach to medicine. Finally, there were some endeavors to increase the amount of free or elective time in medical students' programs. As the foregoing suggests, although these modifications in the curriculum were oriented to greater "liberalization" of medical training in several senses, they were as structured as the aspects of the traditional curriculum that they sought to modify.

3. As the citations listed under Footnote 1 suggest, numerous of these experiments in medical education, and the studies that described, analyzed and attempted to evaluate them were sponsored by the Commonwealth Fund.

The medical curriculum of the 1950s was not only highly organized: it was also characterized by a remarkable degree of internal logic. The learning sequences that it embodied unfolded in a systematic way, with each new step building on the ones that preceded it. This kind of order was a distinguishing feature of the attitude-learning, as well as the cognitive learning, that took place in medical school. Students were as progressively trained in certain values, attitudes, and norms as they were in biomedical knowledge and skills. This is all the more impressive because, by and large, these psychosocial aspects of learning built into the curriculum were not planned as such by medical educators. To a significant degree, they were unanticipated and unrecognized consequences of the more deliberately arranged scientific and clinical training that students received and of the kinds of relationships with faculty, patients, and each other that students typically developed in medical school. In fact, one of the primary tasks that the social scientists involved in the socialization studies of the 1950s performed for medical educators was to identify the formal and informal medical school contexts in which professionally relevant attitude-learning inadvertently occurred.

The nonrandom nature and the psychosocial logic of attitude-learning in medical schools of the 1950s can be illustrated by several examples drawn from my own observations. Two such learning sequences in which I became particularly interested were what I came to call training for uncertainty and training for detached concern.[4]

Training for uncertainty consisted of the flow of medical school experiences that taught students progressively to perceive the uncertainties of medicine, to acknowledge some of their implications for the role of physician and the welfare of patients, and to cope with them. Students were confronted with three basic types of uncertainty as they advanced from one phase of the curriculum to another. These were: (1) the uncertainties that stem from the incomplete mastery of the vast and growing body of medical concepts, information, and skills; (2) the uncertainties that come from limitations in current medical knowledge and techniques; and (3) the uncertainties that grow out of difficulties in distinguishing between personal ignorance or ineptitude and the open-ended, imperfect state of medical science, technology, and art.

In the preclinical years, gross anatomy—the first and most massive course that students experienced—played an important role in confronting them with the realization that, no matter how well informed or

4. See Renée C. Fox, "Training for Uncertainty," in Robert K. Merton et al., eds., *The Student-Physician,* 207–241, and Harold I. Lief and Renée C. Fox, "The Medical Student's Training for 'Detached Concern,'" in Harold I. Lief, Victor F. Lief and Nina R. Lief, eds., *The Psychological Basis of Medical Practice* (New York: Harper and Row, 1963), 12–35.

skilled they might become, their mastery of all that is known in medicine would never be complete. For, over the centuries, this field has gradually traced out what students described as nothing less than the "blueprint of the body." The "huge body of [anatomical] facts" symbolized for students the "enormity" of medicine and the impossibility of commanding it all. Pharmacology, which came later in the pre-clinical curriculum, significantly contributed to acquainting students with uncertainties that result from limitations in the current state of medical knowledge, rather than from their own inadequacies. The lack of a general theory of drug action that characterizes this science, along with the associated difficulties of predicting how individuals will respond to any given drug, dramatized for students the fact that "there are so many voids" in medical knowledge that the practice of medicine sometimes seems largely "a matter of conjuring . . . possibilities and probabilities." The third kind of uncertainty—that of determining where personal limitations leave off and those of medical science and technique begin—became more salient for medical students at the end of their pre-clinical years in physical diagnosis. Here, as they learned examination, observational, and history-taking methods relevant to defining the nature of the patient's problem, students were acutely faced with difficulties in ascertaining how much of their "trouble . . . hearing, feeling or seeing [was] personal" and how much of it had to do with "factors outside of themselves," with "the fault of the field, so to speak."

The range of course-related experiences bearing upon students' training for uncertainty was as broad as it was systematic. Throughout the curriculum, students were recurrently exposed to experiences that contributed to this aspect of the attitude-learning they underwent. In the clinical years, for example, the several forms of medical uncertainty to which they were subject were compounded for them by their contact with patients and their developing sense of professional responsibility. As students' awareness of the imminence of their doctorhood grew, their obligation to "know enough to do justice to [their] patients" also increased. And they came to regard "gaps in their knowledge" or "unsureness" on their part as more serious than in earlier stages of their training.

One of the cardinal experiences that linked students' training for uncertainty in the pre-clinical and clinical years were the various contexts and guises in which they faced death. These included dissecting a human cadaver in anatomy, witnessing and contributing to the death of some of the laboratory animals on which students worked in their basic science courses, observing the conduct of autopsies, and meeting terminally ill and dying patients. Students were astonished and disquieted to learn that, although death is an ultimate and finite certainty for human beings as for all living creatures, it is also more ambiguous and even more mysterious than they had supposed. Whether death will occur in a given case, when it will come to pass, and what causes it, students discovered, are all questions that in many instances cannot be easily or categorically answered. Furthermore, they began to see that the relationship between the physician's knowledgeable and skillful intervention in a patient's condition and his ability to forestall or prevent that patient's death is more tenuous than they had assumed.

There was a structured discontinuity in students' experiences during the pre-clinical and clinical years that also significantly contributed to their training for uncertainty. The ethos created by their instructors in the first two years of medical school were what students described as an "experimental" and "philosophy of doubting" point of view. Pervading the basic science teaching that they received was the "message" that an irreducible minimum of uncertainty is inherent in medicine, that uncertainty is "legitimate" as well as "inevitable," that it can be conducive to medical scientific creativity and progress, and that, in any case, it is best handled by openly facing up to it. In the clinical years, this systematic doubting continued. But from their clinical instructors and from their patients, students now began to learn about some of the undesirable consequences of "doubting too much." However exquisitely aware the physician may be of the ambiguous and indeterminate aspects of a case, students were made to realize, he nonetheless must sufficiently commit himself to some tentative diagnostic and therapeutic judgments so that he can act on behalf of his patient. And although patients may welcome the physician's willingness to admit his uncertainty and that of the field, too great a display of unsureness may alarm them or undermine their confidence and trust. These insights were gradually assimilated and applied by students in their third and fourth years of medical school, so that by the time they reached graduation, most had achieved some balance between Hamlet-like doubting and its opposite extreme, super-certitude.

The training for detached concern dimension of students' attitude-learning unfolded with an equally impressive orderliness. What it entailed was progressively acquiring the ability to bring the objectivity and empathy, the equanimity and compassion expected of physicians into a supple balance with one another so that the care they rendered was at once competent, clear-sighted, and humane. Over the course of the four medical school years, students were recurrently involved in experiences that had powerful implications for their training in detachment and concern and the dynamic equilibrium between them. As with all medical school sequences, it began in the anatomy laboratory, where students were introduced simultaneously to the cadaver, death, nudity, and anonymity and to both the obligation and prerogative to cut and explore the human body. However potentially stressful these encounters were, as students put it, the "very dead" appearance and texture of the cadaver helped to shield them against the full emotional realization that the body on which they were working was a once-human being. Only when they dissected the hands, face, and genitalia did the "humanness" of the cadaver become acutely problematic for them. Students' scientific involvement in learning anatomy and in performing well in the laboratory, their teamwork, and the gallows humor in which they mutually engaged were their chief ways of coping with the evocative aspects of dissecting a cadaver.

From anatomy, students moved on to work with live laboratory animals in various of their pre-clinical courses. Both because students were no longer working on the human form and because the anatomy laboratory had given them some emotional as well as technical preparation for manipulating and cutting into a body, this set of experiences was not as disturbing in certain regards as contact with the cadaver. At the same time, students testified, the new experience that challenged their equanimity somewhat was the fact that unlike the cadaver, these animals were alive, moved, bled and, in courses like pharmacology, as the expression went, were "sacrificed" as part of the process of training doctors. It is interesting that in this sequence of laboratory exercises students worked on cats before they carried out procedures on dogs. By and large, they found it emotionally more difficult to practice on dogs, attributing their sentiments to the fact that more of them had had dogs as pets to whom they had been attached than cats. Although this arrangement made a great deal of socialization sense, its latent consequences were neither anticipated nor recognized by medical educators.

In their second year of medical school, students underwent a major *rite de passage* experience that had great import for their training in detached concern. This was their first autopsy in their pathology course.[5] In many ways, students reported, the autopsy reminded them of the anatomy laboratory. Now, however, they found themselves simultaneously confronted with death as "recent life," as an ultimate certainty and an irreducible mystery, and with the chastening realization, as one of them put it, that "on the wards of learning" and throughout our professional careers "some of our patients will die." Despite the anticipatory socialization that they received through their prior work on the human cadaver and on live laboratory animals, students were profoundly af-

5. See Renée C. Fox, "The Autopsy: Its Place in the Attitude-Learning of Second-Year Medical Students," in this volume.

fected by the autopsy. Once again, engrossment in the scientific, technical, and learning tasks at hand helped them to handle their feelings, along with their strong motivation to "do well" and "act professional." But in this setting, by tacit agreement ("unwritten law") they dealt with their deepest emotions in mutual silence. ("You don't bare your heart about the autopsy. . . . You sort of sit on the lid of your feelings. . ."). This stood in sharp contrast to the easy verbalizing and vigorous discussing that generally characterized the student group and particularly to the counterphobic black humor that they used to cope with death in the anatomy laboratory.

Still later in the second year, in anticipation of the approaching clinical phase of their training, students began to try certain procedures on themselves and on their classmates. In some of their basic science courses and in physical diagnosis, for example, they became the subjects of urinalyses, glucose tolerance tests, capillary punctures, venipunctures, auscultation, percussion, blood pressure determinations, nose and throat swabs, fluoroscopy of the gastrointestinal tract, typhoid vaccinations, and personal and psychiatric case histories. This phase of their experience and development was notable for the collective state of hypochondriasis that it elicited. The sociodynamics of this reaction were incisively analyzed by one student, who explained: "We are now in the process of contracting the diseases we are studying, in order to develop emotional immunity to them."

The ultimate focus and raison d'être of the training in detached concern that students received was their relationship with patients. In a sense, the cadaver, the laboratory animals, the deceased person on the autopsy table, and the classmates on whom students worked were all "pre-patients." It was not until the end of the second year, chiefly in physical diagnosis, that students began to have face-to-face contact with "real patients." The process was very gradual, beginning with short, task-delimited, group visits to hospitalized patients, chaperoned by instructors. Gradually, these patient contacts were lengthened, came to include more interaction and responsibility, and were no longer flanked by supporting clusters of classmates and faculty supervisors. Finally, the day arrived when the medical student "soloed," taking a patient's entire medical history and carrying out a complete physical examination without the presence or aid of anyone else.

Certain aspects of the history and physical were particularly embarrassing and emotion-laden experiences for students: taking a sexual history, for example, examining a woman's breasts, doing a vaginal or pelvic examination, palpating a man's testicles or a person's abdomen, carrying out a rectal examination. These intimate and potentially erotic aspects of the clinical tasks they were learning to perform, along with "any very emotional reaction" by a patient were likely to be disturbing to students. For, at this point in their training, most students were struggling to manage their own overabundance of concerned feelings and to achieve greater detachment, as they undertook their still very new physician-like role.

The third and fourth years of medical school—the clinical phase—were organized around interviewing and examining patients. Although, with experience, students gained more skill and poise in these functions, particular kinds of patients were likely to make them feel anxious, frustrated, or sad. Sick children, psychiatric patients, alcoholics, hostile, "uncooperative" patients, the elderly, and dying patients confronted students with problems of suffering, vulnerability, competence, adequacy, mortality, and meaning that challenged their equilibrium and control.

Somewhere in the course of the third year, students' difficulties in relating to patients shifted from what they had previously experienced as too much concern to that of too much detachment. They were no longer so preoccupied with how to manage superfluous emotion as they were troubled about what had happened to their former capacity to respond feelingly to patients and their predicaments. This was a period that students apprehensively described as a time of "emotional numbness." In part, they were taking note of a degree of overdeterminism in the greater capacity for detachment that their medical training seemed to have instilled in them. But this was a temporary socialization phase. By the time students reached their senior year, they had progressed beyond this hyperdetachment to a new level of integration, which enabled them more effectively to blend objectivity and equipoise with compassionate concern.

There were at least three fundamental differences in the studies of medical socialization conducted in the 1950s. Some of the inquiries were more psychodynamically than sociologically oriented, emphasizing the personal development of medical students, the impact of their medical school experiences on them as individuals, and the inner or unconscious meaning of those experiences.[6]

6. Notable among these are the studies carried out by Daniel H. Funkenstein and Harold I. Lief, as well as Milton J. Horowitz's *Educating Tomorrow's Doctors* already mentioned. See, for example, Daniel H. Funkenstein, "Medical Students, Medical Schools, and Society During Three Eras," paper presented at the Conference on Medical Students at the Bowman Gray School of Medicine, Winston-Salem, North Carolina, June 25, 1969 (unpublished); Daniel H. Funkenstein, "The Learning and Personal Development of Medical Students: Reconsidered," *The New Physician,* Vol. 19 (September 1970), 740–755; and Harold I. Lief, et al., "A Psychodynamic Study of Medical Students and Their Adaptational Problems: Preliminary Report," *Journal of Medical Education,* Vol. 35 (July 1960), 696–704.

A second major difference in the studies of the 1950s has been the subject of commentary and debate in the social science literature. Whereas Columbia University sociologists viewed the medical school as training "student-physicians," University of Chicago sociologists saw it as training "boys in white." The Columbia group was impressed with the extent to which the medical school curriculum provided both latent and manifest forms of "anticipatory socialization" for values, attitudes and behavior patterns relevant to the role of physician. In their view, medical school courses and experiences made up an ordered continuum that progressively moved students toward physicianhood attitudinally, as well as intellectually and technically. In contrast, the Chicago group saw whatever socialization medical school effected as much more dissociated from becoming a physician and assuming the physicianly role. Rather, it seemed to them that the greater part of the training that students underwent in this respect entailed learning to adroitly play the *student* ("boy") role, so as to excel academically in ways that would enable them to master the vast amount of knowledge and technique they had to assimilate, earn them high grades, curry favor with their teachers, and make them eligible for the professionally critical reward of a "good internship." According to this perspective, becoming a physician in deeper, less expedient senses was almost a luxury that had to be postponed until the hurdle of medical school was successfully passed—and students were neither granted nor did they take the kind of responsibility that made them feel successively more like physicians. As the foregoing implies, unlike their Columbia colleagues, the Chicago group was disinclined to argue that, below the surface of the manifest learning experiences, students were undergoing more latent learning, which was shaping their future attitudes and behavior as physicians. The utilitarian, achievement-oriented, competitive outlook and actions of the medical students reported by the Chicago sociologists would have been interpreted by the Columbia group as socialization for physicianhood and not just for "studentry."

Whether the disparities in the Chicago and Columbia studies were more a reflection of the divergent assumptions that the two groups brought to their research or of the differences in the milieux of the medical schools where they did their respective field work has never been resolved. Probably both sets of factors contributed to the "student-physician" versus "boys in white" pictures of socialization that emerged from their inquiries. The University of Kansas School of Medicine studied by Chicago is a state-supported, Midwestern institution that in the 1950s had a curriculum and an educational philosophy that were relatively traditional. Cornell University Medical College, where the major part of the fieldwork for the Columbia study was conducted, is a private Ivy League school; it had a greater commitment than Kansas to educational experimentation and innovation. In addition, however, it could be said that the implicit world views of the Chicago and Columbia schools of sociology varied sufficiently to account for some of the differences in the ways they perceived and reported the medical socialization process. This is made apparent by a third basic distinction between the 1950s studies. The Chicago group—renowned for its first-hand work on the sociology of deviance and for its insights into "cooling the mark" attitudes and behaviors—found evidence of these phenomena in the subculture of the medical students that they observed, while the Columbia group did not. Furthermore, the Columbia study described the self-regulating "little society" of medical students as a straightforward, informal organization of peers that openly supported and reinforced values and norms espoused by faculty as well as themselves. According to the Columbia observations, they had no "undercover" aspect to their group, such as that portrayed by the Chicago sociologists, who reported that the medical student world that they came to know was one that presented a conformist public face to the faculty, while, in private, students collectively believed in deviating from some of the rigorous standards of excellence and etiquette that the faculty expected them to meet.

These differences notwithstanding, the medical socialization studies of the 1950s were significantly alike in ways that reflected the perspective on becoming and being a doctor that medical educators, social scientists, and medical students shared in that decade. Attention was focused on students' interaction with their teachers, with patients, and with each other. Although their relationships with nonphysician members of the medical team were not ignored, they were subordinated to other aspects of students' role set. There was consensus that medical students formed a subculture that importantly influenced the direction and content of socialization. Peer relations were thus acknowledged as critical to nascent physicianhood and, by implication, to the practice of medicine by mature physicians. Teachers were viewed more as positive than as negative role models. But the sacred center and ultimate goal of medical education and socialization was taken to be the relationship that medical students learned to develop with patients. Ideally, it was supposed to combine high competence in the most advanced, specialized, and vigorous medical scientific treatment of the patient's problems with a comprehensive, humanistic approach to what was sloganistically called "the patient as a whole person." Medical practice was implicitly depicted as a chain of dyadic relationships between individual physicians and their individual patients. Teamwork with fellow physicians, nurses, social workers, and other medical and paramedical professionals was invoked, but there was virtually no reference to the medical care system qua system or as more than the sum of its interpersonal parts. The medical school was studied as a microcosm. Outside its doors lay the larger medical profession that it was training students to enter. Yet physicians, patients, and medical professionals whose trajectories extended beyond the medical school and university medical center were rarely seen or merely glimpsed in passing. The organization of the medical profession was only occasionally mentioned. And even the social system of the medical school was examined in a selective way. Its academic structure was thoroughly explored, but its economic and political dimensions and their potential impact on the educational and socialization process were hardly considered.

The 1950s studies concentrated on certain attitude-learning sequences to which the medical school seemed to contribute. Training for uncertainty and limitation, training in detached concern, and training in teamwork have already been mentioned. In addition, training in the allocation and management of scarce time was studied, not only for its own sake, but also as indicative of both the values and skills that students were acquiring. The so-called "fate of idealism"[7] was followed through medical school: that is, the process by which students came to temper their olympian medical standards, their sense of calling, and their high commitment to the profession with the "reality-situation" factors of which they progressively became aware. There was considerable interest in how students learned to deal with the competitive, achievement-and-success-oriented aspects of their medical school experiences, and with how they reconciled these self-interested aspects of their role with the disinterested professional obligation to be primarily concerned with the welfare of patients. Students' training for responsibility and their training in medical morality—rather specifically conceived—were other foci of attention.

An interesting common pattern that emerged from the 1950s studies was that a good deal of the socialization that took place in medical school seemed to entail the blending of counterattitudes: uncertainty with certainty, detachment with concern, idealism with realism, self- with other-orientation, and active responsibility and meliorism with humility and the ability to desist. Furthermore, each of the attitude-learning sequences traced out was characterized by a phase that generally occurred

7. Howard S. Becker, "The Fate of Idealism in Medical School," *American Sociological Review,* Vol. 23 (February 1958), 50–56.

midway in the curriculum, when students seemed to have temporarily *over*-learned one of a set of counterattitudes. Thus, at a certain point in their third year of medical school, for example, students were inclined to behave with exaggerated "certitude," often complained of feeling "emotionally numb," and they appeared to be more "cynical" than "idealistic." Yet by the end of their fourth year these attitudes seemed to be more equitably balanced in what we earlier described as a dynamic equilibrium. It has not been determined whether this attitude-learning pattern is distinctive to medical education or whether it is applicable to professional and adult socialization in other contexts as well. This is a question of potential basic and applied significance that merits further attention.

Medical education and socialization in the 1970s are proceeding under circumstances markedly different from those of the 1950s. To begin with, as already stated, an unprecedented number of young men and women are now aspiring to the career of physician. Although the 1950s were marked by a post-World War II increase in applicants to medical school, what was then considered a "boom" period in this regard did not approach the ratio of at least three applicants for every one medical school place that characterizes the 1970s. At the present, this tendency continues unabated, even appears to be gaining momentum. The attraction of so many young people to medicine is occurring at the same time that law schools are experiencing a comparable increase in applicants. This suggests that a more generalized movement toward the liberal professions may be taking place. Why this is happening, what attributes of medicine and law are motivating college students to try to gain entrance to a professional school, and from what social backgrounds these students are being drawn are all questions that have not yet been systematically investigated.

There is a great deal of speculation among medical educators about whether the men and women now enrolled in a medical school or hoping to be accepted by one constitute a "new" type of medical student with different conceptions of the profession and their future roles in it than their predecessors. Those who contend that there is, indeed, a new medical student say that he (or now she) is socially concerned, critical of the way that health care is organized and delivered in American society (particularly to the disadvantaged), determined to practice a more equitable, feeling, and less driven medicine than his elders, and committed to actively reforming medicine in ways that he hopes will also ramify into nonmedical sectors of the society. Those who argue that the present generation of medical students is not really "new" in these or other respects tend to regard the social criticism and social commitment statements made by students as "rhetoric"—ideology that, however sincere, is ephemerally idealistic. What is more, these skeptical observers maintain, the students who articulate these new values are not representative of the present generation of medical students. They come from privileged backgrounds and attend certain elite Eastern medical schools, where they constitute a vociferous minority of the student body. Once again, the data needed to resolve the question, "is there a 'new' medical student?" are lacking.[8] But those who believe and those who disbelieve in the existence and importance of the new medical student are reacting to the same phenomena of which they have mutually taken note. And it seems to us that medical students of the 1970s must be sufficiently different from those to whom medical educators were previously accustomed to have elicited all this discussion and controversy about them.

In addition to the fact that many more students are now applying to medical school than in the past, and that numbers of those who are admitted begin their study of medicine with a "new" socially conscious and critical ideology, medical curricula have changed in ways that distinguish them from the programs of the 1950s.[9] Organized attempts have been taken to loosen and diversify the "lockstep" curriculum. Both elective and free time have been expanded. Multiple tracks have been created so that there now exist a number of patterns in which students can proceed through medical school, in accordance with their present interests and future career plans. Combined M.D.-Ph.D. programs have been created that allow students to broaden, intensify, and accelerate their competence in a variety of medically relevant fields. The course of studies is no longer sharply dichotomized into pre-clinical and clinical years; rather, a required "core curriculum" has been instituted, which from the first medical school year on tries to integrate the various basic sciences with each other and with clinical training. Numerous medical schools have been experimenting with ways of shortening the duration of professional training. Chiefly, these take the form of selectively granting students early admission or advanced placement, making it

8. Daniel H. Funkenstein is virtually singular in providing data supporting the contention that a "new breed" of what he calls "community era" medical students has emerged, and "first became the majority of an entering class in the Harvard Medical School in 1968." See his unpublished paper, "Medical Students, Medical Schools, and Society During Three Eras."

9. For a useful summary of the major characteristics of these curriculum changes, and also some speculative comments on the new medical student, see Barrie Thorne, "Professional Education in Medicine" in Everett C. Hughes, Barrie Thorne, Agostino M. DeBaggis, Arnold Gurin and David Williams, *Education for the Professions of Medicine, Law, Theology, and Social Welfare,* a report prepared for The Carnegie Commission on Higher Education (New York: McGraw-Hill Book Company, 1973), 17–99.

possible for them to complete the medical curriculum in three years and eliminating required internships in some fields. Medical school departments and programs of community medicine, social medicine, preventive medicine, and family medicine have been created. Students have been given opportunities for fieldwork and practicum experiences outside the walls of academic medical centers. The aim here has been to acquaint them with more than "ivory tower" medicine, to familiarize them with the health and medical care delivery problems of disadvantaged groups in the society, and to develop their general ability to think of health, illness, and care in a social system framework. (It is interesting to note that some of these extramural experiences were originally sought out or created by students and subsequently accepted for credit by faculty.) Greater emphasis has been placed on the hypothesized relevance of behavioral science training to physicians' collective ability to improve the health care system, as well as to their development as humanely competent individual practitioners. Courses—and even programs—in medical ethics have been launched by medical schools throughout the country. These courses go beyond the "do's and dont's of doctorhood" to consider the ethical component in medical decision making, and to ponder such issues as death and dying and the moral and metaphysical implications of particular biomedical advances. Along with all these other changes, many medical schools have replaced their traditional "A through F" grading systems with a "pass-fail" type of evaluation. And an increasing number of medical schools have been making concerted efforts both to recruit and admit more minority-group students (especially nonwhite, nonaffluent, and women students) to training for physicianhood.

These sorts of modifications of the curriculum and ethos of medical schools have all come about in the past decade. They constitute a set of educational arrangements and perspectives that grow largely out of the criticism and self-criticism to which the American medical profession and health care system have been subject in recent years. In turn, these alterations and the inner and outer pressures that have helped to produce them are part of a much broader process of social and cultural change that surfaced in the 1960s and continues into the seventies. During this period, medical schools, like many other institutions, have been questioned, challenged, and reproached. Various medical professional, student, government, patient, and community groups have held them responsible for often practicing medicine in ways that have contributed to the keenly felt problems with which the American medical system is currently faced. The innovations in medical school curricula already described represent ad hoc, organized attempts to meet this criticism. Medical educators have introduced these changes on the assumption that they may influence physicians-in-becoming actively to participate in the development of a high-quality, reasonably priced national system of health care, which is also more equitably distributed, accessible, universalistic, socially aware, and humane.

More explicitly than in the 1950s, then, the new curriculum is premised on the notion that medical education not only affects the outlook and comportment of individual physicians, but also the attributes of the profession and the contours of the larger medical system of which doctors are part. In this respect, the present generation of medical educators has high "socialization consciousness." Yet there are several anomalous features that characterize their view of professional socialization that would seem to belie such an attribution. As mentioned earlier, by and large the evaluations of what impact curriculum changes have had on students that medical schools are now conducting do not include attempts systematically to appraise attitude-learning. Rather, the tendency is to measure the amount and quality of cognitive learning that is taking place, chiefly in the form of National Board Examination scores, and to ascertain what aspects of particular courses students and faculty like and dislike. The following sorts of questions are not explored: Does the supposedly less invidious pass-fail grading system actually quell acquisitively competitive tendencies in students? What effect does it have on students to be alternately dissecting a cadaver in the anatomy laboratory and seeing gravely ill patients in the hospital during their first medical school year, instead of having these two sets of experiences separated in time from one another as they were in the traditional curriculum? Does the increased contact with poor and deprived patients now provided strengthen students' belief that, as physicians, they should and can do something to improve the health of such people and the medical care they receive, or does it discourage and dissuade them from this conviction? Do the core curriculum and multiple track educational sequences result in as coherent and cumulative a socialization process as the one that existed in the 1950s? Are there any discernable subpatterns in the more diversified effects that the curriculum can be expected to have on students now that it is not as monolithic as it formerly was? Does the increased individuation of course work and medical school experiences that is permitted and fostered by the curriculum reduce the socialization role played by the corporate student peer group? If so, what are the intellectual and psychosocial consequences of such a change in students' role set?

Along with their failure to inquire into such matters, medical educators seem more reluctant than they were in the past to admit verbally that what they teach significantly shapes attitudes as well as conveying knowledge, and that these attitudes may have long-range implications for how students will enact the role of physician. Medical educators proceed on this supposition in their daily round and in their curriculum planning, as we have seen. However, they are inclined to disavow that they really believe this when they are called upon to discuss their sentiments and convictions about professional education.[10] The source of such faculty ambivalence about the socialization dimension of the medical educational process is not easy to identify. It is almost as if medical faculty members were protecting themselves against being held too accountable for whatever the beliefs, attitudes, and conduct of the new generation of physicians may turn out to be. This stance may be a defense mechanism to which medical (and other) educators have resorted in an era when they have been continuously subject to criticism concerning the social attitudes that they do and do not successfully convey. It may also be a way of implicitly acknowledging that a perplexing "generation gap" exists between them and their students for which they cannot thoroughly account and do not wish to be held largely responsible.

Medical students' attitudes toward their own professional socialization seems more ambivalent than those of their instructors. Many students begin their medical school training with the determined hope that it will not transform them into the kinds of persons and physicians that they are trying not to become. As compared with their counterparts in the fifties, students now tend to view their teachers as negative role models, not necessarily with rancor or loss of esteem, but more as a symbolic expression of their resolve to be "different," "better," and more socially responsible physicians than the medical "establishment" with which they identify their instructors. From the outset, however, students are convinced that "the System" the medical school both represents and comprises is seductive and powerful. In their eyes, it has the insidious capacity to change them into what they are resolved not to be. When asked to predict what effect they think their medical education will ultimately have upon them, they are inclined to the opinion that, both because of the forcefulness of the system and their own potential pliancy in the face of it, they are likely to end up replicating the past generation's professional attitudes, behavior, and even their personal style of life.[11]

10. In the way of an illustrative anecdote, at a recent dinner discussion meeting about premedical and medical education at the University of Pennsylvania, all the medical faculty members present heartily agreed with a professor of religion who affirmed that it was "too messianic to believe that education forms moral character."

11. It would be interesting to explore the psychodynamic as well as social reasons for which this generation of medical students feels so malleable in the face of what they conceive to be "the System." This is the kind of question that lends itself to an Erik Erikson type of analysis.

Thus, in the medical school climate of the 1970s, change-oriented students who are persuaded that the latent socializing impact of their professional education is subtly but irresistibly converting them to the status quo meet faculty members who deny that medical education per se has potent socializing effects—but who have nonetheless altered the traditional curriculum in order better to train young physicians, attitudinally as well as intellectually, to tackle the health care and medical services delivery problems now facing the profession and the society. Complicating the socialization picture further are the attitudes expressed by some of the social scientists with whom medical faculty and students have conferred about the present and future education of physicians. As already noted, no studies of medical socialization of the magnitude of *Boys in White* and *The Student-Physician* are currently in progress. In our opinion, this is as much a consequence of social scientists' brand of ambivalence toward the socialization process as it is a question of medical schools' receptivity to such undertakings or the availability of funds to carry them out. In recent years, for example, several prominent sociologists of medicine have become critical of the importance that they and their colleagues formerly attached to medical education and socialization. They now contend that the physician's "immediate work environment,"[12] the "exigencies . . . and realities of practice"[13] are more significant determinants of the way a man or woman performs in the physician's role than the anticipatory socialization that medical schools supposedly provide. Partly for this reason, they are not enthusiastic about launching studies of becoming a physician in the 1970s, and even less disposed to cast them in the conceptual framework of the 1950s. Insofar as they would be at all willing to conduct research in medical school rather than in medical practice settings, these sociologists would lay greater stress on studying the faculty, the social organization of the medical school, and especially its organization of power, than on inquiring into student attitudes, experiences, and culture.[14] They seem to be more interested in political and economic facets of the medical school than sociologists were in the fifties, and more intent on doing research that will have policy implications. One detects in their orienta-

12. See, for example, Eliot Freidson, *The Profession of Medicine* (New York: Dodd, Mead & Company, Inc., 1970), p. 89.

13. Eliot Freidson, *Professional Dominance: The Social Structure of Medical Care* (New York: Aldine-Atherton Press, 1970), 17–18.

14. These sentiments were forcefully and recurrently expressed by the social scientists who participated in a two day meeting on medical education research convened by the National Center for Health Services Research and Development, of the Department of Health, Education and Welfare, and held on November 22 and 23, 1971, in Rockville, Maryland. In the verbatim transcript that was made of these sessions, see, for example, the comments of sociologist, Samuel W. Bloom.

tion a certain undercurrent of disappointment that the sociology of medical school inquiries carried out 20 years ago did not lead to reforms in the educational process that significantly improved the way that medicine is organized and practiced in our society. These activist yearnings and regrets on the part of sociologists, along with their increased social structural determinism, are not conducive to their undertaking studies of medical socialization in the seventies.

Meanwhile, a new generation of students is passing through a greatly changed medical school en route to becoming physicians. We know remarkably little about these students or about the impress that their medical education is making on them. Yet, at the present time, a number of medical schools are considering "rolling back" certain of the curriculum reforms of the 1960s, on the grounds that they have already had some undesirable consequences for the intellectual and attitude-learning of medical students.[15] Is this an accurate diagnosis and an appropriate set of responses to it? Will such revisions become widespread and, if so, will they usher in a state of retrenchment in the medical profession and the process of being educated and socialized for it? There is little data on such matters, either available or being collected.

In the way of a conclusion, I would like to essay a portrait of the "new" medical student, based on my observations and constructed out of my field notes.[16] Whether such students exist in significant numbers, what role the medical school, relative to other institutions, is playing in their development, and what effect their graduation into physicianhood will have on the medical profession are questions to which there are as yet no valid or reliable answers.

Despite the efforts being made to recruit young persons into medical school from minority groups and nonprivileged social class backgrounds, the new medical student is still likely to be a white middle-class man. He arrives in medical school garbed as he was in college—in blue jeans or modishly colored sports slacks and tieless shirt. His hair is long, though usually not unkempt, and he may have grown a moderate beard. When he begins to see patients, he often starts wearing a tie and sometimes a jacket. He may also cut his hair on the short side of long and shave more closely.

15. See Samuel Z. Goldhaber, "Medical Education: Harvard Reverts to Tradition," *Science*, Vol. 181 (September 14, 1973), 1027–1032. Although this article somewhat simplifies and exaggerates the "strong trend toward retrenchment and reinstating the traditional educational system" at Yale as well as Harvard, it is nevertheless a significant and perhaps even a premonitory piece.

16. All the quotations in the "portrait" that follows are taken from verbatim spoken or written comments made by medical students.

Although he is fiercely intent on being accepted by a medical school, unlike his counterparts in the 1950s the new medical student is generally a "late decider." It is not uncommon for him to have committed himself to becoming a doctor in the second half of his college career. Because of his "delayed" decision, he may have had to take his pre-medical courses in summer school or in a concentrated post-undergraduate year. In any case, he worked hard and competitively as a college student in order to earn the very high grade-point average that made him eligible for admission to medical school. He is aggressively achievement-oriented, but deplores it in himself, his classmates, his teachers, the medical profession, his parents, and American society generally. As engaged as he is by medicine, he wonders continually whether it is really his "vocation." The "on call twenty-four hours a day" demands associated with the traditions and responsibilities of many branches of medicine contribute to these doubts. For, he is concerned about what this kind of relentlessness may do to his person, his relationships to patients and colleagues, his family life, and his capacity to participate in the cultural, civic, and recreational activities that he considers healthy and humanizing, as well as pleasurable.

Such a student is likely to have come to medical school with declared interests in fields like community medicine, public health, family medicine, psychiatry, and pediatrics (the latter, he feels obliged to explain, because it is "holistic" medicine and entails caring for "new and future generations"). In the end, these may not be the fields that he will actually enter. But they express the interpersonal, moral, and societal perspective on physicianhood that he brings with him from college. He is actively committed to such humane and social goals as peace, the furtherance of civil rights, the reduction of poverty, the protection of the environment, population control, and improvement in the "quality of life" for all. He extends the principles that underlie these commitments to medicine and the role of doctor. In his view, health and health care are fundamental rights that ought to be as equitably distributed as possible. For this reason, as he sees it, the physician should not only care for the psychological, social, and physical aspects of his own patients' illness; he should have a "genuine concern for the total health of mankind." He should take initiative in dealing with some of the factors at work in the society that adversely affect health and keep the medical care system from functioning optimally to maintain and restore it. Although the doctor's social dedication should be universalistic, the new student believes, he has special obligations to those who are disadvantaged or deprived.

The new medical student is also staunchly egalitarian in his conception of the doctor and of the doctor's relationship to patients and to nonphysician members of the medical team. The student disapproves of "all-knowing" or "omnipotent" attitudes and behavior on the part of physicians. ("The doctor is not a king . . . a high priest . . . or a technological master who can control or dominate all.") He maintains that physicians should approach patients "as human beings" with "respect for their feelings and opinions," rather than as "diseased specimens" or persons incapable of understanding their own medical condition and the treatment prescribed for it. Ideally, a collegial and "nonauthoritarian" relationship with patients ought to be developed, one that is "honest," "open," and nonmanipulative. ("The physician should reach people through conversation that is not like that of a salesman. . . . He should have open communication with patients . . . and hide as little as possible from them.") "Integrity" that is emotional and moral, as well as intellectual, is basic to this relationship, too. It entails more than being honest and consistent in what one says and does: it is actively critical and self-critical, involving the "questioning of self, colleagues, teachers, physicians and the intentions of the institution."

A "detached concern" model of relating to patients is not one that the new medical student admires or would like to exemplify. Rather, he places the highest value on feeling with the patient. Although he recognizes the need for maintaining some objectivity in this relationship, he does so with regret. For him, he says, to feel is to be human and compassionate; it dignifies and heals; and the more one feels, the better. However scientifically and intellectually inclined he may be, the student believes that it is all too easy to distance oneself from patients (and from one's own humanity) by approaching the problems for which they seek the doctor's aid in an overly conceptual and technical way. He considers "direct experience"—or what one student calls, "phenomenological contact"—to be the method *par excellence* by which the physician should learn and come to understand. It allows him to maintain close contact with patients and "reality" and also to seek knowledge and truth that go beyond the passive acceptance and mastery of what is handed down to him by past generations. ("We are experiencing physical diagnosis in relative virginity. . . . We still don't know the 'rules of the game' and are therefore likely to violate them in worthwhile ways.")

Finally, although the new medical student would not downgrade the importance of training, knowledge, skill, and experience for competent physicianhood, he also insists that the doctor's values, beliefs, and commitments are a critical part of his ability to help patients, reform the health care system, and "improve society." ("Ethical, moral, and social issues are a base on which a superstructure of scientific knowledge should be built, rather than the over-Flexnerian tradition in which scientific schema formed the base. . . .") And so the physician must be more than just a "good human being." He must also concern himself with the "philosophical" problems of life and death, suffering and evil, justice and equity, human solidarity, and ultimate meaning in which his chosen profession and the human condition are grounded.[17]

This is the at once critical, activist, and meditative ideology or world view that the new student brings to medical school. How predominant it is, whether it will prevail, whether in interaction with the medical school environment and the social climate of the seventies it will produce a new type of physician, time, the professional socialization process, and, one hopes, studies of it will eventually tell.

17. Talcott Parsons, Renée C. Fox and Victor M. Lidz, "The 'Gift of Life' and Its Reciprocation," *Social Research,* Vol. 39, No. 3 (Autumn 1972), especially 405–410.

PART TWO

ORGAN TRANSPLANTATION AND HEMODIALYSIS

Kidney Dialysis and Transplantation

RENÉE C. FOX AND JUDITH P. SWAZEY

When all other therapies have failed to control the course of their disease, patients in the end-stage of chronic renal failure have two modes of treatment available to them that may prolong their lives: hemodialysis (the use of the artificial kidney), and a kidney transplant. The clinical use of renal dialysis began in the early 1940s when a pioneering version of this machine was first tried on a few patients who were in acute kidney failure. In 1951, the first human kidney transplantations (which were also the world's first human organ transplantations) were carried out on patients whose conditions were considered to be medically beyond the help that dialysis could offer. In 1960, the invention of a cannula-shunt apparatus made possible long-term or chronic dialysis for patients with end-stage kidney disease. And in the early 1960s the development of immunosuppressive chemotherapy began enabling physicians to forestall the body's rejection of "foreign" transplanted tissue.

According to the latest available data, in the United States alone, close to 7500 kidney transplants had been performed by the end of 1972, and by July 1974 nearly 12,000 patients were being maintained on chronic dialysis. Thus, over the course of the past thirty years, dialysis and

---

From *Encyclopedia of Bioethics* (New York: The Free Press, 1978, 811–816).

transplantation have developed in therapeutic efficacy, and they have been used to sustain the lives of thousands of people. Nevertheless, these entwined forms of treatment are still fraught with medical ambiguities and ethical dilemmas for medical scientists, health professionals, renal patients and their families, the lay public, and the body politic alike.

Many of the medical and ethical issues associated with renal transplantation and dialysis are common to most areas of therapeutic innovation, particularly those which involve critically or terminally ill patients. Among these issues are: the often stressful and conflicting double roles played both by the physician who is also a clinical investigator, and the patient who is also a research subject; problems of uncertainty that arise from current limitations in medical knowledge and technique; ambiguities about the stage of development of a relatively new treatment—that is, how "experimental" or "therapeutic" it is; concerns about the ethical and legal requirements of human experimentation, notably, the difficulties of obtaining truly informed, voluntary consent from a patient-subject, or striking a proper balance between the potential benefits and risks to such a subject, and of protecting his (her) integrity and privacy; decisions about the allocation of scarce material and nonmaterial resources (including human organs) that must be made at individual, institutional, and larger societal levels; and finally, the personal and social implications of the medical commitment to use extraordinary means to prolong the lives of terminally ill patients.

In addition to the problems shared with other forms of therapeutic innovation, dialysis and renal transplantation have contributed to the development of certain more distinctive issues. These include questions about: the relative "quality of life" that dialysis (in a hospital, at a proprietary center, or at home) and transplantation (of a live or a cadaveric kidney) have to offer; the "gift of life" significance of these modes of treatment—the transcendent meaning that givers and receivers can experience both in the dialysis and transplant situations, and the mutual tyranny that these ways of exchanging life for death can also impose on those who participate in them; the justification for inflicting a major surgical injury on a live donor in order to help a dying recipient; and the operational definition of death that is proper as well as necessary to use when the transplantation of cadaveric organs is involved. Paradoxically, now that full financial coverage for dialysis and renal transplantation has been insured through public law, these treatments also present equality and equity problems that are forerunners of difficulties that will probably become more salient and widespread in the American health care system of the future.

This article will focus on some of the socioethical phenomena that accompany dialysis and renal transplantation: particularly the experiment-therapy dilemmas they entail, their gift-exchange aspects, and both the quality of life and allocation of scarce resources questions that they pose.

Despite the thousands of patients who have undergone dialysis and/or transplantation since these procedures were introduced, the question of where they fall on the experiment-therapy spectrum remains a core ambiguity, of import both to physicians and patients. For the question of how experimental or how routinely therapeutic a given procedure is judged to be has far more than semantic meaning. The definition of a treatment's status plays a major role in physicians' decisions about the circumstances under which that treatment may justifiably be used, and about the types of patients on whom it may properly be tried. Physicians find it difficult to define the overall experimental-therapeutic status of procedures like dialysis and renal transplantation. The types of criteria that are employed, sometimes implicitly, include quantitatively expressed probability estimates of the patient's medical prognosis with a transplant or dialysis compared to other possible treatments, as well as his prognosis with a transplant compared with dialysis, and qualitative judgments about the type of life that one or the other treatment may offer the patient, however long or short his period of survival.

A host of uncertainties about how well or poorly a given patient may do with a transplant or with dialysis, medically and sociopsychologically, contribute to the difficulty of establishing quantitative and qualitative criteria by which to locate these treatments on the experiment-therapy continuum. A cardinal example of the uncertainties that confront transplant physicians and their patients is whether the kidney recipient will be able to "walk the therapeutic tightrope": to prevent his body's rejection of the transplanted kidney, the recipient must continuously take doses of immunosuppressive drugs that vastly increase his susceptibility to severe, massive, and often lethal kinds of infection. The course of the chronic dialysis patient also is difficult to predict with accuracy. For example, there are few explicit medical criteria for predicting how a patient will respond to dialysis, physiologically and chemically, or how he will cope with the psychological and social stresses that accompany life-dependency on an artificial kidney machine.

Because of such uncertainties, dialysis and transplantation continue to be utilized only for patients in the terminal stages of chronic renal failure, when all other treatments have been exhausted. Thus, although numerous physicians contend that transplantation and dialysis have become "accepted" clinical procedures, they remain less than "routine" treatments in the "ordinary practice of medicine." As the Advisory Committee to the Renal Transplantation Registry acknowledged in its 11th Registry Report (1972), for example, "the exact place of transplantation in the care of end-stage renal failure has yet to be defined."

A particularly complex and pivotal set of issues inherent to transplantation are those associated with the fact that it constitutes a gift of such magnitude and moment. A vital organ is donated by one individual in order to "give life" to another person who is terminally ill. Like other forms of gift exchange, organ donation is implicitly structured and regulated by a set of norms. These are the same "symmetrical" and "reciprocal" norms that Marcel Mauss identified in his classical monograph on *The Gift*: the obligations to give, to receive, and to repay. Failure to live up to any of these expectations produces social strains that affect the giver, the receiver, and those associated with them.

The dynamics of organ gift exchange can be especially intricate in the case of renal transplantation. The kidneys are paired vital organs, with the consequence that the loss of one kidney is not immediately life threatening. Because one kidney can safely do the work of two, the medical profession, and the larger society of which it is part, permit live as well as cadaveric renal transplants to take place. The live transplantation of any other vital organ is forbidden, since its removal would cause the death of the donor.

In situations where a live renal transplant is contemplated, the members of the prospective recipient's family face strong normative pressure to offer a gift of a kidney. This is partly because a live transplant from a donor who is genetically related to the recipient (his parents, siblings, or children), and who is a "good tissue match," has a better medical prognosis than a cadaveric transplant. The rejection reaction engendered by all transplants except those between identical twins is less likely to occur rapidly, and with a severity that jeopardizes the functioning of the implanted organ. Furthermore, the honor, intimacy and generosity of the family and of each of its members are symbolically involved in the individual and collective willingness of these close kin to give of themselves to their dying relative in this supreme, life-sustaining way. Because the biomedical and psychosocial pressures on prospective live family donors are so compelling, medical teams involved in the renal transplantation situation have felt obliged to devise "gatekeeping" mechanisms that protect relatives against an excessively coerced or self-coerced gift of a kidney.

The terminally ill patient who is offered such a gift is subject to complementary normative pressures to accept the live kidney from the candidate-donor. To refuse the organ transplant implies a rejection of a gift of life, of the person who proffered it, and of the family unit to which the donor and recipient jointly belong.

If the live transplant does take place, then, in keeping with the Maussian paradigm, there is a sense in which the donor-recipient relationship takes on a debtor-creditor dimension. The donor has made the utmost gift; the recipient has received something that is inherently unrepayable. Under some circumstances, the extraordinary meaning of what has been interchanged may reinforce the solidarity of the donor and recipient so that their mutual self-esteem is enhanced without jeopardizing their autonomy. But it is also possible that the essentially unreciprocal gift that links them may bind them one to the other in a mutually tyrannical way. The donor may hover over the person and life of the individual who has received his kidney, and the recipient may feel that because he can never hope to repay the gift of life that he has received, he must allow, even encourage this.

As the foregoing implies, the complex impact of the triple norms of gift exchange makes it difficult for transplant teams, patients, and their families to predict and evaluate the psychological, social, and moral consequences that a live kidney transplant will have for the donor, the recipient, and their kin.

Although dialysis does not involve offering and accepting a vital bodily part in the same literal sense that a kidney transplant does, its life-giving implications are as momentous. Whether dialysis is conducted in a medical center or at home, it entails the continuous exchange of life for death through the donation of time, energy, skill, and concern by the persons who help run the kidney machine and attend the dialysis patient. In the case of home dialysis, this exchange is all the more remarkable, because it requires and permits a lay person (usually the patient's spouse) to assume an unprecedented amount of medical responsibility for operating a complex life-support system. As a consequence, home dialysis especially confronts patients with the problem of receiving and reciprocating a recurrent gift of life.

As already suggested, the quality of life that dialysis and transplantation offer to persons with end-stage kidney disease is a matter of deep and constant concern to the medical professionals, patients, and families involved. As with many other medical interventions, there are few reliable predictive measures that accurately forecast how well a patient will respond to these modes of treatment. Moreover, there is no ready set of criteria to define and measure a "good" or "bad" quality of life: different individuals and social groups have their own indices by which they judge how "successfully" a person's life is being extended by a procedure like transplantation or dialysis.

Numerous transplant and dialysis patients "do well," leading what they and others consider to be active, rewarding lives, particularly when contrasted with their pre-treatment existence. Other patients fare less well. But irrespective of the ostensible differences in adjustment that may characterize them, all transplant and dialysis patients face certain stresses that may significantly undermine the quality of their prolonged lives.

The potential "gift of life" burdens that a kidney transplant can impose are preeminent among these stresses. In addition, the renal transplant recipient may find it difficult to tolerate (1) the medical uncertainties surrounding the constant threat that his body will reject the transplanted kidney and (2) his increased vulnerability to grave infections as a consequence of the immunosuppressive drugs that he is taking to forestall such a rejection reaction. The unpredictable inevitability of an eventual rejection, and the ever-present possibility that, for unknown reasons, his original renal disease may redevelop in his transplanted kidney confront the recipient with the stress of knowing that someday he probably will have to return to life on the dialysis machine, and to the prospect of being a candidate for another transplantation. He must also deal with the psychosocial as well as the biomedical side-effects of the immunosuppressive drugs he is receiving: for example, with cosmetic changes in his appearance due to high doses of steroids, which may alter his self-image and his presentation of self.

Many patients undergoing long-term dialysis seem to experience even greater strain than the recipients of transplants. Among the difficulties they report are the severe dietary restrictions that they are required to observe, the general state of enervation to which they are prone, the sexual impotency that some patients develop, and, above all, the degree to which they feel that they are "unnaturally tied to a machine." For some patients and their families, the kidney machine becomes a major anthropomorphic presence in their existence, a presence that they characteristically feel is as "monstrous" as it is "miraculous." Perhaps the best indicator of how oppressed by their life with the machine many dialysands and their families feel is the almost millennarian expectation with which they look forward to their "deliverance" through the medium of a kidney transplant, though they have enough expert knowledge to recognize that even the best-matched live kidney transplant will not provide "salvation."

The quality of life questions that chronic hemodialysis raises are further complicated by the unresolved debate about the advantages and disadvantages of in-center versus at-home dialysis that is still occurring among different groups of physicians, nurses, and technicians administering the procedure. All agree that home dialysis is far less costly, in the strictly financial sense of the term. The most unqualified proponents of home dialysis contend that, in addition to its economic assets, it frees patients and their families from the vise of triweekly, six-to-eight-hour visits to a hospital or center for treatment. And they insist that virtually all patients can be taught to manage dialysis successfully at home. Other medical professionals are more skeptical about the general applicability of home dialysis. Particularly medical teams conducting dialysis in large cities, with populations who are ethnically and socioeconomically heterogeneous, claim that home dialysis is too risky or unviable for many patients whom they treat, because of their family situations, cultural traditions, personal life styles, and/or the physical layout and facilities of their residences. Some of the same physicians, nurses, and technicians are also impressed by the degree of stress that the responsibility for conducting dialysis at home creates for the patients, their spouses, and other close kin, even when they are comparatively well suited and equipped to attempt it. What makes it all the more difficult to appraise the assets and liabilities of different types of dialysis is the element of self-fulfilling prophecy that seems to influence the outcome of this procedure. Evidence suggests that those medical teams that are the most convinced that home dialysis is an efficacious and desirable mode of treatment are also the ones that obtain the best results with it.

From a certain point of view, no matter how well a patient seems to be adjusting to life with dialysis or a transplant, the fact remains that he is chronically dying. For the extraordinary treatment that he is receiving is superimposed on the end-stage kidney disease with which he is afflicted, and that cannot be cured or even ameliorated at the present stage in the development of medicine. Because this is so, when a transplant patient who has lost one or more donor kidneys through rejection, or a dialysis patient who is struggling with his machine-dependent life, decides that dying is a lesser evil than the treatments available to him, the medical team is faced with a peculiar set of moral and metaphysical questions. The most common ways that patients on dialysis signal their desire to die are by requesting their physicians to stop treatment or by engaging in overtly or covertly suicidal behavior, such as pulling out their cannula shunt or going on dietary binges. In this situation, if the medical team decides to acccede to the patient's wish to discontinue his life by tapering off or not initiating further treatment, are they legitimizing and facilitating suicide? Are they performing euthanasia? Or are they merely allowing a terminally ill patient to die a "natural" death?

The experiment-therapy dilemmas, gift exchange phenomena and the quality of life issues related to dialysis and renal transplantation all bear upon the allocation of scarce resources problems that these treatments also present. The most fundamental resource allocation questions concerning these procedures are: in the light of their present phase of development, the prevalence of end-stage kidney disease that they are designed to treat, and the net balance of suffering, reprieve and fulfillment with which they imbue the lives of dialysis and transplant patients and their families, to what extent ought monies, equipment, technical competence, personnel, time, hospital space, vital organs, concern, anguish and hope be invested in these particular ways of keeping terminally ill persons alive? And what proportion of such inherently scarce, precious resources should be allotted to dialysis and transplantation as compared to: life-prolonging therapies for *other* catastrophic diseases; the treatment of less grave, more "ordinary" medical conditions; the implementation of preventive medicine procedures of various sorts; the furtherance of medical knowledge through medical research; the education of new generations of health professionals? On the macroscopic level, the issue becomes: how much should our society invest in the health-illness-medicine sector taken as a whole, as compared with other needed and valued activities?

The case of hemodialysis and renal transplantation is a particularly illuminating one in these regards. For, with the passage of Public Law 92-603 in 1972, financial coverage under Medicare has been extended to the treatment costs both of dialysis and kidney transplants. Ostensibly, this constitutes a felicitous solution to the overwhelming financial problems with which end-stage renal patients and their families were formerly confronted. But, in fact, the law has not resolved many of the scarce resources questions associated with these procedures, and has helped to create some new ones. For example, passage of the law has intensified uncertainty and debate over the projected long-range costs of treating large numbers of patients with terminal kidney disease, and whether our society can afford to defray them. It has created a problem of equity by singling out persons suffering from renal disease for special financial coverage while many other equally expensive catastrophic illnesses have been ignored. Furthermore, the act of making financial help equally available to persons with end-stage kidney disease has increased the pressure on physicians not to deny any such patients access to dialysis and transplantation, no matter what the medical, psychic, or social contraindications may be. Is the most just and proper system of allocating scarce medical resources, then, one that entails no patient selection or triage whatsoever? This is an issue which has become more acute and unsettling for medical teams caring for renal patients since

Public Law 92-603 was passed. It converges with the problems of quality of life and of intervention in the human condition already confronting medical professionals involved in the dialysis-transplantation enterprise. Finally, although the law provides economic resources for patients with terminal kidney disease, it does not eliminate other types of scarcity. The sheer availability of monies does not command the services of the many highly trained persons, the specialized facilities and equipment, particularly dialysis machines and beds, and the abundant supply of donor kidneys that are requisite for hemodialysis and renal transplantation.

In our opinion, dialysis and kidney transplantation have received so much public and professional attention not only because they represent dramatic medical advances, but also because of the crucial ethical and existential issues that they have evoked. Together, they constitute a paradigm of some of the basic questions of value and belief with which modern Western society is currently wrestling.

BIBLIOGRAPHY

Abram, H. S. "The Psychiatrist, The Treatment of Chronic Renal Failure, and the Prolongation of Life." *American Journal of Psychiatry* 124, 1968, pp. 1351–1358.

Abram, H. S., Moore, G. L., and Westervelt, F. B. "Suicidal Behavior in Chronic Dialysis Patients." *American Journal of Psychiatry* 127, 1971, pp. 1119–1204.

Advisory Committee to the Renal Transplant Registry. "The 11th Report of the Human Renal Transplant Registry." *Journal of the American Medical Association* 226, 3 Dec. 1973, pp. 1197–1204. (Reports by the Human Renal Transplant Registry and the American College of Surgeons/National Institutes of Health Organ Transplant Registry are published yearly in the Journal.)

Blagg, C. R., Hickman, R. O., Eschback, J. W., and Scribner, B. H. "Home Dialysis: Six Years' Experience." *New England Journal of Medicine* 283, 19 Nov. 1970, pp. 1126–1131.

Crammond, W. A. "Renal Transplantation: Experiences with Recipients and Donors." *Seminars in Psychiatry* 3, Feb. 1971, pp. 116–132.

Dukeminier, J., Jr., "Supplying Organs for Transplantation." *Michigan Law Review* 68, Apr. 1970, pp. 811–866.

Fellner, C. H. "Selection of Living Kidney Donors and the Problem of Informed Consent." *Seminars in Psychiatry* 3, Feb. 1971, pp. 79–85.

Fellner, C. H., and Schwartz, S. H. "Altruism in Disrepute: Medical vs. Public Attitudes Towards the Living Organ Donor." *New England Journal of Medicine* 284, March 1971, pp. 582–612.

Fox, R. C., and Swazey, J. P. *The Courage to Fail: A Social View of Organ Transplants and Dialysis*. Chicago: University of Chicago Press, 1974.

Friedman, E. A., and Kountz, S. L. "Impact of HR-1 on the Therapy of End-stage Uremia." *New England Journal of Medicine* 288, 14 June 1973, p. 1287.

Kaplan de Nour, A., and Czackes, J. "Emotional Problems and Reactions of the Medical Team in a Chronic Hemodialysis Unit." *Lancet*, 9 Nov. 1968, pp. 986–991.

Kemph, J. P. "Psychotherapy with Donors and Recipients of Kidney Transplants." *Seminars in Psychiatry* 3, Feb. 1971, pp. 145–158.

Mauss, M. *The Gift.* Translated by I. Cunnison, Glencoe, Illinois: The Free Press, 1954.

McKengeny, F. P., and Lange, P. "The Decision to No Longer Live on Hemodialysis." *American Journal of Psychiatry* 128, 1971, pp. 264–274.

Moore, F. D. *Transplant: The Give and Take of Tissue Transplantation*. New York: Simon and Schuster, 1972.

Simmons, R. G., Hickey, K., Kjellstrand, C. M., and Simmons, R. L. "Donors and Non-donors: The Role of the Family and the Physician in Kidney Transplantation." *Seminars in Psychiatry* 3, Feb. 1971, pp. 102–115.

Starzl, T. E. *Experience in Renal Transplantation.* Philadelphia: W. B. Saunders, 1964.

Swazey, J. P. "The Scribner Dialysis Shunt." *The Management of Health Care*. Edited by W. J. Abernathy, A. Sheldon, C. K. Prahalad. Cambridge, Mass.: Ballinger, 1975, pp. 229–252.

Thorwald, J. *The Patients*. New York: Harcourt Brace Jovanovich, 1971.

Wolstenholme, G. E. W., and O'Connor, M., eds. *Ethics in Medical Progress*. Boston: Little, Brown, 1966.

Organ Transplantation: Sociocultural Aspects

. . . I know only a little about the donor [of the kidney I received]. They [the medical team] told me a little: much too much, and yet not enough . . . and I still suffer from it. . . . She was a little girl, nine-years old, who was killed in an automobile accident. . . . Ever since the transplant, I have a recurrent dream. It's not about the little girl, but about her mother, or at least I assume that it's her mother. For all I know she, too, may have died in the same accident as her daughter. But in my dream, I see this woman, all dressed in black, with a black veil over her face. She is crying, and she has a reproach in her eyes. I try to communicate with her, to console her, but I can't. Because there is a pane of glass between her and me: a pane just like the one that was in the isolation room where I was hospitalized during the first days after the transplant. . . . When certain of my friends learned that I had received a kidney from a little girl, they made jokes about it, saying that maybe I'd get back the youth and virility that I hadn't had for a long time. This so upset and disgusted me that I broke off all relations with those people, and I haven't seen or spoken with them since. . . . But there was another patient, a woman, who received a kidney at the same time that I did from the same little girl. We have become brother and sister. This is because our kidneys come from the same donor. We don't talk about it, but the feeling is there. We see each other often, and telephone each other regularly, even if there is no news to report. . . . The transplants have created something between us: brotherly love, or what have you. . . .

From *Encyclopedia of Bioethics* (New York: The Free Press, 1978, 1166–1169).

This recipient's eloquent account of how the implantation of a kidney from someone else's body into his own has affected his sleeping and waking life focuses on the most distinctive aspects of the transplant experience. The phenomena he describes were not anticipated by the medical profession, partly because they run counter to the rational-empirical ethos of modern medical science. But they are integral to the deepest philosophical questions that are evoked by the donation and receipt of human organs.

Organ donation entails a very special kind of gift. A vital organ is surgically removed from a live or a recently dead person, and is offered to a dying individual, whose survival and quality of life depend on his (her) physical and psychic capacity to accept and retain it. This "gift of life" is what the philosopher Hans Jonas terms a "supererogatory gift . . . beyond duty and claim." Paradoxically, it so perfectly expresses the ultimate Judeo-Christian injunction to give of one's self to others that it transcends what is ordinarily asked even of persons who are members of societies that belong to this religious tradition. In principle, then, one would expect an organ transplant to be experienced as a sublime gift, one whose symbolic meaning would enrich and unite all who participated in it: the live donor, the family of the cadaver donor, the recipient, his or her kin, and the medical professionals involved.

But, as the quoted comments of the transplant recipient vividly suggest, the significance of receiving an organ is more complex and potentially more problematic. To begin with, however animistic it may appear to be, the transplantation of a vital organ from one person to another is often accompanied by the at once apprehensive and hopeful belief that some of the physical, social, and psychic qualities of the donor are transferred along with it. Thus, as in the case cited, receiving a kidney from a very young, healthy individual, who was a girl rather than a person of his own sex, conveyed both a promise and a threat to a man whose fatal renal disease had also rendered him impotent. And other persons in his entourage expressed comparable sentiments about their friend's transplant through their counterphobically humorous remarks.

"My blood has adopted a child who shuffles through my chest carrying a doll," wrote J. D. Reed in a poem about the "girl's heart" he "wears" as a consequence of a cardiac transplant. The sense that part of the donor's self or personhood has been transmitted along with his organ is likely to be most pronounced with cardiac transplants. If interviewed about their conception of the human heart, the majority of persons in a modern, secularized society would probably attest to the fact that it is a muscle, a pump, an organ that is no more exalted than the kidney, for example. But the way that recipients have reacted to cardiac implants suggests that on deeper, less conscious levels it is widely viewed as the seat of the soul or spirit, the source and repository of love, courage, and the highest, most human emotions.

Even when the transplanted organ is not associated with a silhouette of the donor's traits, it is often perceived as having a life of its own. One recipient verbalized these feelings in the following way: "No matter what you say, it's a foreign body, and there are moments when it's painful to keep it. . . . I have a theory that if you don't like the organ, it contributes to a rejection reaction. . . . But as for us [pointing to his transplanted kidney], we don't have that problem. We have understood each other very well for four years already."

In the case of cadaveric organ transplants, it may not be the donor himself or herself with whom the recipient feels so hauntingly unified. The close relatives of the donor may preoccupy him even more: "the woman all dressed in black with the black veil over her face," who at the time of her deepest loss and grief made a sacrificial gift of a part of the person she loved. The inestimable debt that the recipient may feel he owes to the donor's family, his unrequited desire to thank them for a "gift of life," and to assure them that there is a sense in which the donor "lives on" in and through him may enhance his guilty concern about the relatives. And just as a kind of "brotherly love" may be forged between two individuals who have received organs from the same person, so the identification that a recipient may feel with the donor's kin may be analogous to that of a family member who has become "flesh of their flesh."

A live organ transplantation potentially confronts the recipient with the same phenomena as those associated with a cadaver implant. But these experiences are often heightened by the fact that, with a live transplant, the donor and recipient are not only known to one another; they are also intimately related.

The only type of live transplant that is currently permitted by the medical profession, and the larger society from which it receives its mandate, is that of a kidney. This is allowed because the kidneys are paired organs, with the consequence that the loss of one of them is not synonymous with death, or necessarily life-threatening, as would be the case with the live transplantation of other vital organs like the heart or the liver. Furthermore, a live kidney that is a "good match" with the recipient's tissue type has a better chance of functioning well in his body, and of being retained for a long period of time before it is finally rejected, than a cadaveric transplant. For genetic reasons, the parents, siblings, or children of a person terminally ill with renal disease who is a candidate for a live kidney transplant are the only ones eligible to make such a well-matched donation. (Even a spouse is not biologically qualified to contribute a live kidney for, in modern Western societies, at any rate, husband and wife are related by marriage but not genetically, or "by blood," as the expression goes.) This means that the donor from whom a person receives a live organ is not only someone who was willing and able to give a living part of himself to prevent the recipient's death, but (with the exception of the spouse) is also one of his closest relatives. The "face" of the donor is not "veiled," then, as it is in a cadaveric transplant; it is very familiar indeed. Furthermore, in comparison with a cadaveric transplant, it is the live donor himself who offers the "gift of life" to the recipient, personally and directly, rather than through the intermediary of a donor card or of surviving relatives. And the making of this gift subjects the donor to a major surgical procedure with its attendant discomforts and risks. Under these circumstances, the recipient's identification with the live donor is likely to be greater than with an unknown, deceased donor or his kin. His sense that a part of the donor lives inside of him is likely to be more powerful. And his feelings of gratitude and indebtedness are likely to be stronger. Furthermore, these sentiments may be increased by the intensification of contact between the donor and recipient that often ensues from the transplantation experience.

As might be expected, the reactions of the recipient have their counterparts in the ways that the live donor or the relatives of a cadaver donor respond to the transplant situation. The live donor often feels closer to the relative who has received his kidney and more unified with him. In addition, it is not uncommon for the donor to exhibit a great degree of "proprietary interest" in the state of health and activities of the recipient than he did before the transplant occurred. As W. A. Crammond has reported, there are donors who insinuate themselves into the life of the recipient, with the stated or unstated conviction that, "After all, it's my kidney. . . . That's me in there." It has also been noted that when the recipient's body rejects a transplanted kidney, the donor may experience chagrin, anger, or loss, as if a part of himself had proven inadequate, or been repudiated, wasted, or destroyed. (The technical medical term, "rejection reaction," has an unfortunate connotation that may reinforce these sentiments.)

The family of a cadaver donor, on the other hand, usually exhibits a great deal of interest in knowing who has received their relative's donated organ(s), what kind of a person he is, what sort of life he has led, and, above all, how well he is doing with the implant. In many instances, when the relatives of a cadaver donor have been given such information, they have made contact with the recipient and his kin. Particularly in the case of heart transplants, a close and continuing relationship has sometimes been established and has even developed to the point where the donor's bereaved kin have emotionally "adopted" the recipient as a substitute family member.

However surreal these concomitants of organ donation and receipt may seem from one point of view, from another they are sociologically and psychologically related to the dynamics of gift exchange. Like other forms of gift-giving and -receiving, organ transplantation is structured by a set of norms that shape the feelings and behavior of both donors and recipients. These are the norms that Marcel Mauss analyzed in his anthropological essay *The Gift*: the obligations to give, to receive, and to repay. This trinity of giving, receiving, and reciprocating constitutes an exchange cycle that draws participants into an intimate, involved relationship with one another. In organ transplantation what is interchanged is so extraordinary—a literal as well as symbolic gift of life—that donor, recipient, and kin can become linked in ways that are at once mutually enhancing and self-transcending. But the exceptional nature of what they have come to share through their entwined acts of giving and receiving may also create a symbiotic relationship between them that fetters rather than frees them. The fact that the recipient has received and accepted an inherently unreciprocal gift from the donor makes this more probable. The recipient can never totally repay the donor for his priceless gift. As a consequence, the giver, the receiver and their families may find themselves perpetually locked in a creditor-debtor vise that constricts their autonomy and their ability to reach out to others.

It is these dimensions of organ donation that raise the most important philosophical questions about this medical option: questions that concern what Mauss called "the theme of the gift," above all, "freedom and obligation in the gift." One of the ultimate values in the Judeo-Christian tradition of Western societies is the conviction that to give to others, especially to give of one's self, is a supreme good. A widely accepted corollary to this principle is the belief that the more generously and disinterestedly this gift of self is made, the more virtuous it is. The consequences of such gift-giving are assumed to be beneficial and uplifting to donor and recipient alike, and to the broader society. For, in this view, the more widespread the personal and collective commitment to a concept of the gift that (to use Richard Titmuss's phrase) makes us our "strangers' keepers" as well as our "brothers' keepers," the more ideal the society is supposed to be. (It is of fundamental significance that in the Judeo-Christian tradition out of which these notions come, "charity" not only means giving help or relief to those in need, but also God's love for human beings and the love of human beings for each other.)

The case of organ donation dramatically suggests that this perspective on the gift is both too simple and sentimental. To be sure, a transplantation can be a transfiguring experience for those directly implicated. It may epitomize for them, and even for onlookers, the highest capacity of human beings to make a sacrificial gift of life in the face of death. But it is also true that organ transplantation has caused new forms of suffering, through the "tyranny of the gift." The degree of responsibility and indebtedness that giving and receiving an organ entails, the kind of mutually indentured relationships into which it can bind the donor, the recipient, and their kin, and the degree of anthropomorphic influence that the transplanted organ can exert over all their lives are the sources of this "tyranny."

The action implications of these insights are not self-obvious. To repudiate organ transplantation because the gift of sustained life that it involves is not anguish-free seems excessive. To ignore the pain and burden of the gift does not seem justifiable. To try to reduce this suffering, although the most reasoned and humane alternative, is not easy to effect. For example, out of their gradual recognition of the problems of the gift, the medical profession in North America and Europe has instituted the custom of keeping the identity of the cadaver donor and the live recipient unknown to each other and to their kin. But this does not protect the recipient and the donor family from the painfully ambivalent feeling that, as a consequence of the enforced anonymity, they now know both "too much and too little."

In the final analysis, as Parsons, Fox and Lidz have written, perhaps the only satisfactory conclusion is a religious rather than a philosophical one:

> Organ transplantation suggests that the only perfect, truly redemptive gifts are divine ones. These are the gifts of life and death from God, which constitute the at once sacred and flawed materials on which medicine acts: our essential humanity.

BIBLIOGRAPHY

Crammond, W. A. "Renal Homotransplantation: Some Observations on Recipients and Donors." *British Journal of Psychiatry* 113, 1967, pp. 1223–1230.

Christopherson, L. K., and Lunde, D. T. "Heart Transplant Donors and Their Families." *Seminars in Psychiatry* 3, February 1971, pp. 26–35.

Fox, R. C. and Swazey, J. P. *The Courage to Fail: A Social View of Organ Transplants and Dialysis*. Chicago: The University of Chicago Press, 1974.

Jonas, H. "Philosophical Reflections on Experimenting with Human Subjects." *Experimentation with Human Subjects.* Edited by P. A. Freund. New York: George Braziller, 1970, pp. 1–31.

Kemph, J. P. "Psychotherapy with Donors and Recipients of Kidney Transplants." *Seminars in Psychiatry* 3, February 1971, pp. 145–158.

Mauss, M. *The Gift*. Translated by I. Cunnison. Glencoe: The Free Press, 1954.

Parsons, T., Fox, R. C., and Lidz, V. M. "The 'Gift of Life' and Its Reciprocation." *Social Research* 39, Autumn 1972, pp. 367–415.

Reed, J. D. "Organ Transplant." *The New Yorker*, September 26, 1970, p. 126.

Titmuss, R. M. *The Gift Relationship: From Human Blood to Social Policy*. New York: Pantheon Books, 1971.

The Medical Profession's Changing Outlook on Hemodialysis (1950–1976)

INTRODUCTION

The systematic observations and reflections on hemodialysis that I will present in this paper cover an historical period of almost forty years. I intend to describe and chronicle the changing preoccupation of the medical profession with hemodialysis from the end of the 1930s (when Dr. Willem J. Kolff developed the first model of the artificial kidney machine) to the present, focusing the more analytic aspects of my history on the factors that have contributed to the changing configuration of the medical profession's perception of hemodialysis throughout the last quarter of a century, 1950 through 1976. My perspective on the development and evolution of hemodialysis highlights the complex interplay between biological, medical, technological, social, cultural, and psychological factors that have contributed to the medical profession's changing view of hemodialysis over this time span.

Hemodialysis has reached a rather curious historical juncture, one that is as instructive and prognostic in certain respects as it is ironic in others. Over the course of the years, since Kolff invented and built the

---

Paper presented at a conference on "Emerging Medical, Moral, and Legal Concerns: Extraordinary Therapeutic Procedures," organized by the Institute of Renal Diseases, St. Francis Hospital, Honolulu, Hawaii, August 9–13, 1976.

first model of the rotating-drum artificial kidney machine and began to dialyze patients experimentally, this procedure has undergone impressive technical improvements. It has become a life-sustaining and life-prolonging mechanism for tens of thousands of patients in the United States and in other countries of the world. It has been related to still another extraordinary therapeutic procedure, renal transplantation; with renal transplantation, it has become the only expensive, sustained treatment for a catastrophic, end-stage disease to enjoy national health insurance-like financial coverage in this country.

In principle, the evolution of hemodialysis in these respects should have progressively dispelled the problems faced by physicians, nurses, technicians, patients, and patients' families who were pioneers and earlier participants in the development of dialysis. But, in fact, those involved in the dialysis enterprise today are confronted with many of the same problems as their predecessors, albeit in more refined and subtle forms. To these have been added new questions and difficulties that have resulted from the advance of dialysis and transplantation, and from the larger medical and social context within which this advance has occurred. To put it another way, one of my basic assumptions is that, if hemodialysis had developed over the years 1900–1930 instead of during the period that spans the 1940s into the 1970s, or if we were considering its evolution in a society other than the United States, the medical profession's perspective on it would be significantly different in specifiable ways—even if the essential technical features of the machine had been conceivable earlier.

The case of hemodialysis can be used to exemplify some of the problems and concerns that characteristically accompany an extraordinary therapeutic procedure at successive stages in its development (at least in a modern Western society with the structural and cultural features of our own). Furthermore, I regard this conference as a manifestation of how salient such issues have become in American society in recent years (and increasingly in Japan and various Western and Eastern European societies, it now seems), and of one of the ways that the medical profession is trying both comtemplatively and actively to deal with what our conference organizers have called these "emerging medical, moral and legal concerns."

MY PROFESSIONAL RELATIONSHIP TO HEMODIALYSIS (AND TRANSPLANTATION)

From 1951 through 1954, in the role of participant observer, I made a sociological study of the clinical research unit of the Peter Bent Brigham

Hospital in Boston ("Ward F-Second"). During this period, the Renal-Metabolic Division, under the supervision of Dr. John P. Merrill, was involved in its early experimental work with a modified model of the Kolff artificial kidney, and subsequently developed new experimental types of artificial kidney. Furthermore, in collaboration with Dr. J. Hartwell Harrison, Dr. Joseph E. Murray, and Dr. David Hume, this group went on to perform the world's first human kidney transplants. During this same period on Ward F-Second, ACTH, cortisone, Compound F, and *Rauwolfia serpentina* were being assayed on the unit's very sick patients; early mitral valve and aortic valve surgery was being performed; and total bilateral adrenalectomy was being carried out on patients with terminal, malignant hypertension and carcinoma of the prostate, as well as on those with Cushing's disease. My first-hand ethnographic study of the research physicians and patients of Ward F-Second initiated me into the sociology of medicine and formed the basis of my Ph.D. dissertation, which in 1959 was published as a book entitled *Experiment Perilous.*[1]

My second intensive immersion in the "world" of hemodialysis and renal transplantation occurred in the years 1968 through 1972 when—in collaboration with Dr. Judith P. Swazey, a biologist and historian of science—I undertook the research that in 1974 resulted in our coauthored book *The Courage To Fail: A Social View of Organ Transplants and Dialysis.*[2] Our research for this book was more geographically encompassing than my earlier inquiry which concentrated on the small universe of F-Second. Dr. Swazey and I traveled throughout the United States (and also into Canada), spending several days to a week at most of the country's major dialysis and transplant centers. There were three renal units in particular that we studied more continuously and intensively: those at the Massachusetts General Hospital in Boston, the Hospital of the University of Pennsylvania in Philadelphia, and the Northwest Kidney Center in Seattle. In addition, during the period from 1959 to the present, through my continuing study of social and cultural factors that affect clinical medical research and research careers in Continental Europe, I have had the chance recurrently to observe the evolution of hemodialysis and transplantation in various European milieux: in France, Switzerland, England, and especially in Belgium, where my overseas work has been concentrated. Thus I have directly observed and, in the role of sociologist, participated in the unfolding of dialysis and transplantation in the United States and abroad, at various

1. R. C. Fox, *Experiment Perilous* (The Free Press, 1959), hardback. (University of Pennsylvania Press, 1974), paperback.

2. R. C. Fox and J. P. Swazey, *The Courage to Fail: A Social View of Organ Transplants and Dialysis* (University of Chicago Press, 1974).

time intervals during the fifties, sixties, and seventies. I have also tried to keep abreast of the relevant medical literature. It is not an exaggeration to say that I have been centrally involved throughout my entire sociological career in the unfolding of the renal dialysis/transplantation "story."

THE MEDICAL PROFESSION'S PERSPECTIVE ON DIALYSIS IN THE 1950s

Briefly, before moving into an historical perspective that begins with 1950, it will be useful to consider the earliest stages of the development of the artificial kidney machine by Dr. Kolff.[3] The kind of problems Dr. Kolff faced in the initial phase of the artificial kidney's development are all too familiar to medical professionals who have conducted early clinical trials with a new therapy: problems relating to desperately ill, dying patients, unresponsive to established medical therapies, and to the scientific, clinical, and technical risks and uncertainties that trying new procedures on such patients entails. For example, because knowledge of anticoagulation therapy was then in its infancy, Dr. Kolff used ten times as much heparin as would be prescribed today; furthermore, there was no drug available as yet to counteract the effect of heparin. Protamine sulfate was developed much later. Out of the first fifteen patients whom Dr. Kolff put on the artificial kidney machine, only one person did well enough to encourage him to go on with his trials or to dare to believe that they were morally justifiable. This kind of outcome is characteristic of pioneering clinical trials for which the research physician is ethically obliged to use terminally ill patients.

The years that Dr. Kolff experienced in developing the hemodialysis machine are prototypical of what Francis D. Moore has termed the "black years" phase of clinical investigation.[4] It is at this juncture in therapeutic innovation involving the use of human subjects that "clinical moratoria" are most likely to occur. Faced with the overwhelming mortality rate of their patient-subjects, despite the extraordinary therapeutic measures they have launched, physician-investigators may find it emotionally and morally impossible to continue their trials.[5]

3. J. Thorwald, *The Patients* (Harcourt Brace Jovanovich, 1971).

4. F. D. Moore, *Give and Take: the Biology of Tissue Transplantation* (Doubleday Anchor Books, 1965).

5. Fox, *The Courage to Fail,* Ch. 6, pp. 122–148. See also J. P. Swazey and R. C. Fox, "The Clinical Moratorium: A Case Study of Mitral Valve Surgery," in *Experimentation with Human Subjects.* Edited by P. A. Freund. (George Braziller, 1970), pp. 315–357.

In order to detail the prevailing attitudes, expectations, and perspectives characterizing the domain of hemodialysis in the 1950s, a few hallmarks of that decade should be noted:

- Artificial kidney machines, based on Kolff's rotating-drum model and his pioneering clinical trials in Holland, were built and used in a limited number of medical centers (in England, Canada, and the United States), experimentally tried on patients, modified, and improved. (In 1950, Kolff came to the United States permanently.)
- The twin-coil artificial kidney was developed.[6]
- Gradually a larger, but still highly restricted population of patients was dialyzed. Only short-term treatment was possible, primarily because each time a patient was dialyzed, he/she had to undergo surgery for the insertion of cannulas into an artery and vein to connect his/her circulation to the machine. Since each artery and vein could only be used once, the number of possible treatments was limited (10–12).
- Kolff gave the rights to manufacture the artificial kidney machine to Travenol. This marked the beginning of its nationwide and worldwide use.
- Human renal transplantation, both cadaveric and live related homografts, was initiated. The problem of the rejection reaction was discovered to be applicable to human recipients as well as to laboratory animals. Massive doses of whole body irradiation were used to suppress the immune reaction.

In 1951, there were no more than twelve artificial kidney machines in the entire world. One of the models of that machine being experimentally used was in the Peter Bent Brigham Hospital—a modified version of Kolff's original machine. It was about 4 feet long, with 125 feet of cellophane tubing, and resembled, it was said, a miniature tank car, an iron lung, or a giant washing machine. During the 1950s, the medical profession continued developing the artificial kidney and the process of hemodialysis in a relatively few university centers, in a limited number of countries, among which the United States figured prominently. These medical centers were heavily involved during this decade in teaching other medical professionals to use the machine: physicians, nurses, and technicians, from the United States and abroad, working in military as well as civilian settings.

6. W. J. Kolff and B. Watschinger, "Further Development of a Coil Kidney: Disposable Artificial Kidney," *J. Lab. & Clin. Med.*, Vol. 47 (1956), pp. 969–977.

This phase of the medical profession's relationship to dialysis took place in a post-World War II "golden days" atmosphere of enthusiastic commitment to medical research. This was particularly characteristic of the United States at that time. Belief in the unequivocal "goodness" and promise of medical research was at its height, as was federal support for biomedical research. For example, at the Brigham, research on the artificial kidney in this era was supported by the National Institutes of Health, Public Health Service, American Heart Association, Department of the Army, Sharp & Dohme, and Renal and Vascular Disease Research Fund of the Hospital.

Professional teams like the Brigham group were confronted with a "research versus therapy" conflict that bothered them a great deal. They felt fiscally and ethically as well as scientifically and technically obliged to spend a great deal of their time and energy developing and improving the dialysis machine and doing basic, renal physiological research. Yet they were confronted with an ever-swelling stream of patients—terminally ill patients with chronic, irreversible kidney failure, who were sent by their own physicians or who came on their own volition, urgently hoping to be treated and "saved" by this "wonder machine," which had received a considerable amount of mass media as well as medical journal attention. These research physicians found it hard and even questionable not to respond to the immediate life-and-death clinical needs of the patients who appeared on the hospital's doorstep. Yet, if they invested too much of their activity in nonselectively treating such patients with the machine, they sacrificed a certain amount of the basic and applied research they might otherwise have done—research that might contribute to new "breakthroughs" in knowledge and in therapeutic effectiveness. The dilemma that these teams faced was heightened by the fact that a considerable proportion of the patients seeking treatment were in chronic renal failure, in an era of the development of hemodialysis when it could only definitively reverse certain forms of acute renal failure. "The kidney machine is turning into a Frankenstein monster, which is very much in danger of destroying itself and all of us in the process!" exclaimed one anguished Ward F-Second research physician of this era.

As the foregoing implies, the major clinical trials with hemodialysis being conducted at that time were with patients in acute renal failure, due to intoxication with drugs (carbon tetrachloride poisoning, bromide poisoning, barbiturate intoxication), third-degree burns, "crush syndrome,"* mismatched transfusions, or eclampsia in pregnancy. These

*"Crush syndrome" denotes those symptoms of renal failure following crushing of a part.

were the conditions in which patients' kidneys were assumed to be temporarily shut down. If given a short period of "rest" by virtue of dialysis, such patients' kidneys could be expected to "take over again" and resume normal functioning. The repertoire of such acute conditions to which dialysis proved applicable was gradually expanded and confirmed during this decade.

The attitude of the medical profession toward the use of dialysis for chronic renal failure was more complex and ambivalent. Patients were continuously referred (self- and family-referred, as well as physician-referred) and sent to centers like the Brigham in the uremic stage of chronic kidney disease. On the one hand, renal groups like the one at the Brigham aspired to the clinico-philosophical wisdom in treating renal disease that a physician such as Dr. Thomas Addis personified for them. (Dr. Addis was a Scotch physician who worked many years in the Nephritis Clinic of the Out-Patient Department of Stanford University Medical School in San Francisco, and who was the author of a famous monograph on the diagnosis and treatment of glomerular nephritis.[7]) This perspective can be glimpsed in the following excerpt, from the introduction and conclusion of his book:

> This book is written because we have come to the conclusion that the present-day treatment of patients with renal disease is inadequate and sometimes dangerous. There is no universally accepted plan of treatment, but none of the current proposals takes cognizance of the therapeutic efficacy of rest. In the past the giving of rest to the diseased kidney was explicitly recognized as the theoretical justification for various dietary prohibitions and as the reason for the administration of drugs that induced sweating and purging. . . . Today, though we know something about the work of the kidney, we find the principle of rest implicitly, if not explicitly denied . . . the leaders of investigation in the field treat patients with renal disease, particularly those with edema, in such a way as to impose an unnecessary amount of work on the kidneys. On theoretical, experimental, and clinical grounds we have slowly reached the conclusion that this is a dangerous error. This whole book may be taken as a reasoned exposition of that view. . . .
>
> As our patient passes from the degenerative into the terminal stage, it does not seem to him that anything noteworthy is happening. . . . This is what we spoke of as the wisdom of the patient that grows slowly in the dark. It is an instinctive adaptation. We cannot do anything to forward its development and we ought not to try, for if we did we should almost surely blunder. . . . In this particular instance . . . the social importance of our patient's life is

7. T. Addis, *Glomerular Nephritis: Diagnosis and Treatment* (Macmillan, 1948).

> very obvious, but in a measure that we often cannot evaluate, it is true of the lives of all our patients. It is our job to do our best to keep them on the firing line to the very last gasp. Since our best endeavor amounts to almost nothing, we need not take ourselves too seriously. The situation is now more clearly than ever not in our hands and can no longer be influenced appreciably by us. More and more we cease to play even a minor role in the drama. We retreat to the wings to watch the last act of the tragedy. . . . Finally, the day comes when he vomits so frequently that he loses considerably more fluid than he is able to keep down. He is moved to the hospital. Sugar and salt solution are given by vein. The vomiting continues. His face is slightly swollen, almost as it was on the day we first saw him. The urine volume is now less than 1,000 cc, and the sediment shows hundreds and thousands of broad casts. . . . The blood urea concentration has risen to over 300 mgm per 100 cc. Petechiae appear on his skin. His breathing is at times Cheyne-Stokes. He is utterly exhausted. Yet on occasion his mind is still alert. . . . In the art of anesthesia, as practiced by the obstetrician, there are techniques that can be of value when we are trying to help deeply uremic patients out of this life as smoothly and gently as possible.
>
> We want a twilight sleep. . . . Our experience is that paraldehyde given by rectum is the most useful drug. . . . It is the quiet drowsiness we want. The disease itself will soon bring the deep sleep. . . .

Though they admired the Addis perspective, groups like the Brigham did try to treat such patients more vigorously with the still experimental artificial kidney machine, did "take [them]selves . . . seriously" and did not "retreat to the wings." They dialyzed such patients numerous times, making a new "cut-down" for each run—in some cases until there was no usable vein left. In so doing, they raised their own hopes, as well as those of the patients and their families, especially when there was a short-lived improvement before uremic failure took over again. Often they experienced a highly emotional reaction to such a patient's death when it inevitably and rapidly occurred—but not as swiftly, "smoothly and gently" as it might have without the calling into play of the artificial kidney.

In this era of a limited number of kidney machines and persons trained to use them, when the therapeutic capacity of the machine was more restricted than now, dialysis received more and more publicity. Along with other factors this raised hopes and expectations, and brought additional patients to dialysis centers for treatment:

> . . . The cardiorenal group . . . notes that the number of patient dialyses on the artificial kidney has now reached the tremendous total of 526 [since 1948]. Many of these procedures have been critical in restoring health to

patients with acute forms of kidney disease and intoxications from drugs and other substances.[8]

In summary, medical professionals working with hemodialysis in the 1950s were caught in the intense throes of role conflicts between research and therapy obligations, and between more basic and more applied research, as well as between treating patients with acute and chronic renal failure. In looking over my fieldnotes and the Brigham annual reports from those years, I note that in 1951–1952 Merrill's team arrived at a structural or organizational way of dealing with this conflict, through an expansion of staff and a clear-cut division of labor between those responsible for therapy and those for research. In 1951, a "new system" was established whereby one full-time fellow and a number of junior resident assistants rotated for a three-month period and were responsible for "routine therapeutic procedure with the kidney," which, according to the report, "free[d] the research group from the daily routine of the use of the artificial kidney."

By the end of the 1950s, the artificial kidney and hemodialysis had come sufficiently into use, especially during the oliguric phase of reversible renal failure, for the *Journal of the American Medical Association* to publish a lengthy "official" editorial codifying its technical and therapeutic properties, in which it was stated that "dialysis should no longer be considered a final desperate measure because if it is to be effective it should be applied long before the patient is moribund or even comatose."[9] What were considered to be the first successful human renal transplants (between twins) had also been carried out before the fifties were over.

THE MEDICAL PROFESSION'S PERSPECTIVE ON DIALYSIS IN THE 1960s

The following are the major axes around which dialysis and transplantation developed in the decade of the 1960s:

- In 1960, the era of long-term dialysis began. With the invention, trial, and adoption of Dr. Belding Scribner's cannula shunt, chronic intermittent hemodialysis became extensively possible. Standardized dialy-

8. From "Forty-third Annual Report of the Peter Bent Brigham Hospital," for the fiscal year ending September 30, 1956, p. 22.

9. See *Journal of American Medical Association,* Vol. 166, No. 6 (February 8, 1958), pp. 642ff.

sis regimens and programs for patients were established (number of dialyses per week, number of hours on dialysis, diet, etc.).

- Home dialysis was launched (1963).
- Long-term peritoneal dialysis was improved, and limited home treatment with this method was introduced.
- Profit-making, proprietary dialysis centers were developed in the mid-1960s.
- Human liver transplantation was begun, suspended, and relaunched. Human heart transplants were inaugurated, skyrocketed, and tapered down.
- Chemical (drug) immunosuppressive agents were developed to deal with the rejection reaction (antimetabolites, steroids, ALS/ALG). Total body irradiation for other than bone marrow transplants was suspended (1961–1964).
- A Special Committee on Chronic Kidney Disease was appointed by the federal government.
- New criteria were set forth by the Ad Hoc Committee of Harvard Medical School for ascertaining whether or not death has occurred and for "pronouncing" it: "a definition of irreversible coma" and of "brain death" (1968).
- In 1968, the Uniform Anatomical Gift Act was drafted and promulgated, and it began its passage through all the jurisdictions of the United States.
- A series of organ "banks" were created.
- The Human Kidney Transplant Registry was established (around 1963).
- Significant progress in organ preservation and transportation occurred.

The most important medical-technical event that made 1960 a watershed year for the history of hemodialysis was the design, development, and clinical application by Dr. Belding Scribner of the cannula-shunt apparatus, which made possible long-term treatment on an artificial kidney machine. The immediate precipitating event for this invention was the death of Mr. Joe Saunders, an exceptionally sick patient who, at first, did well on the artificial kidney machine. His death was particularly traumatic for Scribner and his colleagues because initially Saunders had had such an "amazing result" from dialysis; he was subsequently discovered to have irreversible kidney disease, rather than acute renal failure, as had been originally supposed. The frustrating helplessness that Scribner and other team members felt in the face of this death was analogous to the sentiments that Willem Kolff experienced in connection with the death of a patient whom he treated as a young physician, and which he considered to be one of the cardinal events that precipitated his development of the artificial kidney. The patient was twenty-seven-year-old Jan Bruning, Kolff's first patient to die of uremia (in 1938).[10]

The other major dialysis development that took place in the 1960s was also made possible by the cannula shunt and by the long-term treatment option that it brought into being: home dialysis. (As will be seen, in addition to this technical factor, certain economic and quality of life considerations contributed to the adoption of home dialysis as a treatment modality.) Once again, in the early 1960s, as in the early 1950s, a good deal of medical thought and energy went into the resolution of technical and clinical problems associated with dialysis. In the 1960s, these were focused on the shunt and long-term dialysis regimens, in medical centers and at home. Many of the problems were gradually worked out by trial and error in collaboration with patients and their families.

Running parallel to this in time was the medical profession's scientific, technical, and clinical involvement in organ transplantation. Cadaveric as well as live-related kidney transplant, the development of chemotherapy for immunosuppression, studies to understand and control rejection reaction better, and the transplantation of other organs, notably the heart and liver, were intense concerns of the medical profession in this decade. Related problems of organ supply, banking, and distribution also occupied medical professional attention.

Partly as a result of advances in hemodialysis and organ transplantation, and partly as a consequence of broader societal developments, the medical profession now found itself confronted with a series of issues that no longer were as confined to biotechnical matters, as was characteristic of the 1950s. Fundamental to these issues was the fact that, although both dialysis and renal transplantation had become applicable, more long-term and effective, and somewhat less experimental, extraordinary forms of therapy for end-stage chronic kidney disease, there were not enough monies, machines, trained personnel, medical centers, live and cadaveric organs to treat all, or even most of the patients in this condition.[11] This state of affairs was fundamental to the problems of

10. Thorwald, *The Patients*.

11. A. H. Katz and D. M. Proctor, "Social-Psychological Characteristics of Patients Receiving Hemodialysis in Treatment for Chronic Renal Failure." Public Health Service, Kidney Disease Control Program, July 1969.

allocation of scarce material and nonmaterial resources and the selection, nonselection, and de-selection of patients in which the medical profession found itself increasingly involved. These scarcity/selection/allocation problems, along with the choices that could now be made between in-center and home dialysis, live-related and cadaveric renal transplants, and various combinations of them, also contributed to the quality of life and quality of death questions with which the medical profession, patients with kidney disease, their families, the public, and the polity became progressively concerned.

A general attempt was made to select patients for dialysis with the best prognosis for doing well on the artificial kidney. Biomedical criteria were used, but given the "state of the art" and medical "problems of uncertainty," only the roughest kind of consensus existed about indications and contraindications in this regard. In their 1967 survey, Katz and Proctor reported that only half of the dialysis centers in the United States had explicit medical criteria for selecting or rejecting a patient. Recurrently used contraindications were: age (patients considered too young because dialysis would severely retard their growth and development, or too old to benefit) and the existence of other major disease states, such as severe diabetes, severe cardiovascular disease, and carcinoma. Accumulating evidence indicated that patients with glomerulonephritis did better than those with pyelonephritis or polycystic kidney disease.[12]

So-called "psychological and social suitability" criteria were also used. These tended to blur over into social background, social status, and "social worth" considerations. In addition to these supposedly prognosis-relevant criteria, first come, first served, random lottery, and ability to pay bases of selection were tried. Selection committees made up of teams of medical professionals (physicians, nurses, social workers, psychologists, psychiatrists, and, in certain centers, clergymen, lawyers, and laypeople) were organized. The Katz and Proctor study shows, however, that the predominant role in voting on patient selection was played by physicians, who were the primary gatekeepers.[13]

By and large, the medical profession was not happy with the overall problem of having to select, nonselect, and de-select dialysis patients in the face of scarce resources problems, nor did they find any of the criteria used entirely satisfactory. Even the biomedical criteria seemed too scientifically and clinically uncertain; the "first come" and the "random lottery" criteria were too capricious, arbitrary, and extramedical;

12. *Ibid.*
13. *Ibid.*

and the economic, psychological, and social criteria were too "unmedical," incompatible with principles of justice and equity, and too likely to discriminate in favor of those already socially and economically privileged.

The problem of deciding which treatment a kidney patient should receive preoccupied the medical profession as much as the questions of who should be treated, who not, and who should make that decision. Biomedical and psychological suitability and prognostic criteria were used here, too. But the particular medical team's or medical center's outlook on each of these therapies influenced not just the attitudes of patients and their families toward each of the treatment options: it also latently affected how well the patients responded to these various therapies. Different medical groups committed themselves philosophically and programatically to different treatment options; and, to an indeterminate but seemingly significant degree, their results were influenced by a "self-fulfilling prophecy" factor. The more a team "believed in" and practiced one or another of these alternative therapies, the more patients were likely to elect it if given the choice, and the better they were likely to do with that treatment.

Thus, for example, under the aegis of Belding Scribner, the Northwest Kidney Center in Seattle committed itself primarily to home dialysis and has had especially positive results with it from a mortality, morbidity, and quality of life point of view. In Boston, on the other hand, at the Brigham, under the influence of John P. Merrill emphasis was placed on providing renal transplants for end-stage kidney patients, using dialysis principally as a "holding procedure" until a donor organ became available or as a "back-up therapy" should a recipient reject his transplant. Home dialysis was no more favored here than in-hospital and in-center dialysis; all these forms of dialysis were used as adjuncts to transplantation. The Brigham has had notably good results with kidney transplants.

Attempts on the part of the medical profession to objectively evaluate the comparative merits and results of each of these therapies went on throughout the 1960s and continues in the 1970s. They have not been totally dissociated from advocacy for one or another approach. Too, they have been accompanied by a limited amount of self-awareness of the self-confirming, observer, and placebo-like effect phenomena.

The 1960s also confronted the medical profession for the first time with the question of whether in some instances the medical profession should enable, or at least allow, certain patients on long-term dialysis to terminate treatment (and not undergo transplantation). If so, which patients by virtue of what kind of decision-making process and by what means? These questions were evoked by three recurrent kinds of patient happenings: outright requests by patients that treatment be discontinued; flagrantly self-destructive, suicidal acts by patients, particularly ripping out the cannula shunt; more unconscious, symbolic acts, which could be covertly suicidal, such as drinking and dietary binges and failure to take proper care of the shunt.[14] Do patients have the right to stop as well as start life-sustaining treatment for a terminal disease? Do they have a "right to die" and to "death with dignity," as well as a "right to live"? Is the termination of an extraordinary treatment like dialysis an act of suicide or of euthanasia, or should it be more appropriately thought of as allowing a patient to die a "natural" death? What is the proper role for the medical profession in this connection? Does medicine have the unequivocal responsibility to maintain life at all costs and under all circumstances? Or are there any conditions under which medical professionals may qualify this commandment? How actively or passively, using what means?

Different medical groups took different positions on these questions, which over the course of the 1960s were debated more openly and widely, in many nonmedical as well as medical milieux, in connection with dialysis, transplantation, and other extraordinary therapeutic procedures and life-support systems as well. In fact, as part of a larger and deeper set of social and cultural developments that surfaced in this decade, terms like "the quality of life," "the right to die," and "death with dignity" were coined in the 1960s and entered into common parlance. By the end of the 1960s, new criteria for the pronouncement of death—on the basis of irreversible brain coma rather than cessation of respiration and heart beat—had been medically proposed and were also being discussed on a society-wide basis.

During the 1960s, hemodialysis and transplantation and the various scarcity, allocation, and selection and the life-and-death issues associated with it became important symbolic foci of fundamental questions of values, beliefs, and meaning (what Durkheim called "collective conscience" issues) with which American society was strenuously grappling. Dialysis and transplantation, for example, were invoked in connection with our national debate about the justifiability of our involvement in the war in Southeast Asia. If we really believe in health and life rather than death and destruction, it was argued, then why have we been willing to invest seemingly limitless funds in a war in Vietnam, and unwilling to

14. Dr. Harry Abram has substantially reviewed these problems—e.g., with G. Moore and F. Westervelt, Jr., "Suicidal Behavior in Chronic Dialysis Patients." *American Journal of Psychiatry,* Vol. 127, No. 9 (1971), pp. 1199–1203.

designate comparable funds for treating catastrophic kidney disease—providing kidney machines and dialysis treatment for all who need them? Dialysis and transplantation also received a great deal of attention from the new area of concern, inquiry, and action that emerged in the mid-1960s and has come to be known as bioethics. Bioethicists have figured prominently in the progressive outpouring of publications and the convoking of conferences, workshops, and the like on the social, ethical, theological, and legal implications of developments in biomedical research and technology. In this context, dialysis has been repeatedly cited in connection with discussions about scarcity, equity, and distributive justice; the right to health and health care; the proper definition of death, and the human treatment of the dying; what it means to be a truly alive, fulfilled, autonomous, purposive human being; whether, and to what extent we are morally obliged to be our "stranger's keeper"[15] as well as our "brother's keeper"; and about how vigorously we ought or ought not intervene in the human condition. It is interesting that such themes have also been central to a variety of nonmedical issues that surfaced in American society during the same decade: for example, in the civil rights, peace, antipoverty, ecology, and women's movements.

These themes and issues continue to be of concern in the 1970s both in medical and nonmedical contexts. To a sociologist, this suggests that the dialysis/transplantation/bioethics preoccupations of the sixties are part of a more extensive, long-term process of cultural reflection and change.

THE MEDICAL PROFESSION'S PERSPECTIVE ON DIALYSIS IN THE 1970s

In the present decade, much less of the medical profession's energies are focused on bioengineering aspects of the kidney machine, on the technical improvement of the dialysis process, and on renal research than in the 1950s and 1960s. To be sure, progress has been made in developing a so-called "suitcase kidney," which is lighter, more compact, and portable and may help to make it possible for patients on dialysis to travel. Kolff and others believe that a wearable artificial kidney (WAK) is in sight and are working hard on this project. The A-V fistula (which was developed in the late 1960s by Brescia and colleagues)[16] is an improve-

15. R. Titmuss, *The Gift Relationship: From Human Blood to Social Policy* (Pantheon Books, 1971).

16. M. J. Brescia, J. E. Cimino, K. Appel, et al., "Chronic Hemodialysis Using Venipuncture and a Surgically Created Arteriovenous Fistula," *New England Journal of Medicine,* Vol. 275 (November 17, 1966), pp. 1089–1092.

ment over the Scribner cannula shunt in a number of ways. In contrast to a shunt, the morbidity associated with making a fistula is nearly zero. It can be put in and allowed to "mature" three to six months before the patient goes into uremic failure and dialysis must begin. (On the other hand, if precipitously, without forewarning and time to prepare, a patient must be put on dialysis immediately, a shunt is still indicated, because a fistula cannot be used right away.) Since it is "internal" rather than "external," a shunt does not have to be so carefully protected by the patient and, by and large, it lasts longer without having to be replaced, in comparison with the shunt, whose characteristic life span was six to nine months to a year before a different one had to be established at another site. Even more recently developed bovine and dacron heterografts (initiated in the 1970s by Swartz and associates) make effective dialysis possible for those whose arteries and veins are not in good enough condition either for a shunt or a fistula. Somewhat more experimental but promising are the trials with the direct puncture of the femoral vein in which certain renal groups are involved, which would eliminate the need for a fistula or a shunt.

In addition, during the late sixties and early seventies, significant advances were made in the medical management of problems of anemia, nutrition, and bone disease and with peripheral nerve disorders that affect patients on the artificial kidney machine, both as concomitants of their chronic renal disease, and as consequences of the dialysis process itself. The medical profession has improved in its capacity to dialyze patients with complicated multiple-disease states. Basic and clinical medical research relevant to kidney disease continues as well.

But the magnitude and importance of these activities is not as great as in the 1950s and 1960s. The artificial kidney is outwardly modified (miniaturized, for example, so that it looks more like a Xerox machine than a respirator), but inwardly it is not very different than it was in the 1950s. Although some progress has been made in understanding the mechanisms involved in kidney disease, little has been learned about its etiology, prevention, or therapy. There have been no real breakthroughs in renal research, nor does there seem to be an imminent promise of one. Furthermore, on a broader medical profession and societal basis, the same kind of enthusiasm about medical research, belief in it, and moral and fiscal support for it that characterized the fifties and early sixties does not exist in the seventies. Not only has much of the pioneering exuberance and expectancy of the 1950s and early 1960s been lost, but the medical staffs of numerous renal units I have visited during the last few years are experiencing problems of morale. Some are passing through crises of confidence in dialysis and of commitment to it. At the present time, the medical profession is fraught with questions about what it ought and ought not to be doing with and through dialysis. And one has the impression that it is difficult for the profession to reach consensus on the questions, old and new, with which it is acutely faced.

One important factor that has contributed to the notable loss of zeal and expectancy about hemodialysis in certain units is the plateau that renal research has reached in the 1970s. The sense of an imminent "breakthrough" in a basic understanding of normal and abnormal kidney functioning has greatly diminished, and many of the once challenging technical problems of dialysis have been "routinized."

In another context, I have made the point that involvement in research can have the "scientifically magical" function of "ritualizing the optimism" of medical professionals and patients alike. It can provide them with a vista: a sense of hope that new knowledge and greater therapeutic efficacy will soon be forthcoming. Partly because of the present stage of development of basic and applied renal research, there is now less of a "vista" in this respect than in the 1950s. This has had a demoralizing effect on some dialysis teams and patients.[17]

An incipient succession of generations phenomenon is also contributing to the "atmosphere" and "consensus" problems of the 1970s. For the first time, a "second generation of physician-dialyzers" is on board, trained by the original physicians involved in the earlier development of the artificial kidney machine and the dialysis process, but different from them in significant ways that we need better to understand. For example, in a group interview that Judith Swazey and I conducted recently with senior and junior members of an important university hospital renal group, one of the younger physicians was amazed and intrigued to learn from an older physician who was involved in the earlier phases of the development of dialysis that physicians, in general, and that the older man, in particular, had run the kidney machine.

Among dialysis nurses, I have noticed some tendency for those who are relatively new to the field to be somewhat less vulnerable to the strains associated with carrying out dialysis in the mid-1970s, and less prone to engage in doubting questions about the enterprise and their relationship to it, than nurses who have been involved in dialysis for many years. The "older" group of nurses are prone to make invidious comparisons between the present situation, and what they regard as the "good old (pioneering) days" of dialysis, which they feel to have been a time of greater hope, belief, and unity than presently exists.

In addition to the state of knowledge and art, and succession of

17. Clinicosociologic Conference on "Long-Term Dialysis," *American Journal of Medicine*, Vol. 59 (1975), pp. 702–712.

generations phenomena, the passage of Public Law 92-603 is a major precipitant of the shift in emphasis and atmosphere in the dialysis field. One of the most significant consequences of Public Law 92-603, which funds hemodialysis and renal transplantation, is the way that it has affected the medical profession's attitudes and actions concerning selection of patients for hemodialysis. In principle, physicians and centers caring for patients with end-stage chronic renal disease still employ certain medical criteria to determine whether or not it is appropriate to put a terminally ill patient in uremic failure on dialysis. But, by and large, the kinds of "social worth" criteria of selection used in the 1960s and a number of the "psychological suitability" criteria formerly employed have been abandoned, now that the shortage of dialysis machines, centers, personnel, and monies is no longer so acute. Dialysis became increasingly available to a larger number of people even before the passage of the Public Law, but the extensive financial coverage that the legislation made possible is the major factor that accounts for the dramatic change in accessibility of dialysis. There seems to be general agreement among medical professionals that evolution toward the minimization of psychosocial criteria of selection is desirable.

Many physicians still claim, however, that certain more biologically based criteria not only *are* but ideally *should* be used to discourage dialysis treatment for various categories of patients who it is medically assumed would not benefit from this therapy, and might even be harmed by it. *Grosso modo,* these presumed contraindications are: overage or underage (the most suitable patients are considered those over fifteen and under fifty years of age), and the coexistence of chronic renal disease with other severe or life-threatening conditions (most particularly, advanced diabetes, cardiovascular disease, liver disease, and organic brain syndrome). But in fact, partly as a consequence of the degree of financial coverage that now exists, what is happening progressively is that virtually *all* criteria of negative selection are being abandoned and the medical profession appears to be rapidly moving toward the point where almost every patient with end-stage kidney disease will receive dialysis and/or transplantation. In fact, the General Accounting Office of the federal government favors this goal and has brought pressure on the medical profession to achieve it.

As compared with the 1960s, the problem has become what Belding Scribner has termed one of "negative selection" rather than positive selection. The medical triage system has not only been altered under the impact of greater financial coverage for kidney disease and less scarcity in this sense; to a considerable degree, it has been suspended. What seems notable to the sociological observer is that government-supported funding of dialysis has contributed to the slackening, if not elimination of *biomedical* criteria of judgment and selection, as well as social and psychological ones. It highlights the degree to which this kind of medical decison-making can be and, in this case, has been influenced by economic and political factors. Whether these aspects of medical decision-making ideally ought to be so affected by such nonmedical factors is a complex question.

Different physicians and medical groups have different opinions about whether they consider it desirable or undesirable to "liberalize" selection to this degree.[18] But they are all aware that as a consequence of this reorientation in patient selection, they are now caring for a much larger number of patients on dialysis who are sicker in more complex ways than was true of dialysands in the 1960s. Many of these patients do not do well on dialysis, which, in turn, intensifies the doubt-filled questioning in which the medical personnel of numerous renal centers are currently engaged, concerning the medical wisdom, the humanity, and the ethical and economic justifiability of having put such patients on dialysis to begin with.

The passage of Public Law 92-603 has also made dialysis financially accessible to patients who are less socioeconomically privileged and who come from working-class and indigent populations as well as middle- and upper-class strata.[19] The greater democratization and inclusiveness of dialysis in this regard has presented the medical profession with still another painful dilemma. In this case, there is general value consensus that income, social class, and racial, ethnic, and religious factors associated with them ideally should not exclude patients from dialysis, or act as deterring factors. But the more universalistic bases of selection that the Public Law has made possible have also created a medical situation in which it is becoming apparent to numerous dialysis groups that many of their patients from less fortunate socioeconomic backgrounds are not as likely to do well on dialysis as their more privileged patients. This is especially true of patients on home dialysis.

In a recent article,[20] Dr. James Roberts reports on an "Analysis and Outcome of 1063 Patients Trained for Home Dialysis." From the point of

18. On this point, see U.S. General Accounting Office Report to Congress on "Treatment of Chronic Kidney Failure," June 24, 1975; and HEW response to it, particularly pp. 16 and 66.

19. Note, however, that because this legislation is part of the Social Security Amendments of 1972, patients who are not themselves covered by Social Security, or are not dependents of family members who are, are not eligible for funding of their renal dialysis and/or transplantation.

20. Published in *Kidney International*, Vol. 9 (1976), pp. 363–374.

view of mortality statistics, the "best" dialysis center in his sample was one with a predominantly suburban population of elderly patients whose general health status was poor. Eighty-five percent of the patients in this center survived at least two years, as compared with the "worst" dialysis center in the sample, which had a preponderantly indigent inner-city population of relatively young patients with better health status, where only 30 percent of the patients survived two years.[21]

According to American values of equality, universalism, and social justice, this is not the way that it "ought" to come out. I have visited a number of dialysis groups in these last few, post-Public Law 92-603 years that are as troubled as they are astounded by this pattern. In some instances, the staff feels guiltily responsible for the fact that these patients are not doing well. At one university hospital, for example, the dialysis nurses have gone through a rocky time of blaming themselves for harboring unconscious prejudice against poor black patients from the inner city, and for their inability to communicate effectively with such patients. They attribute the relatively poor response of patients from this background to dialysis to their (the nurses') personal limitations and failings rather than to more "objective" medical, psychological, and social factors.

One of the largest issues with which the medical profession and the society more generally are faced as a result of this legislation is a new variant of the macro-allocation of resources problems that surrounded dialysis in the 1960s. Whereas 10 years ago the question centered around why we were spending so many valuable and scarce resources on life-taking wars rather than on life-saving medical therapies like dialysis and transplantation, the question, as it is now posed asks, "Why are we spending all these resources on such extraordinary forms of treatment for a relatively small number of persons, rather than investing more in the delivery of basic medical care for the entire population, and in preventive medicine and health care?" The irony of the Vietnam-like status that dialysis has acquired in this connection does not escape those physicians, nurses, and technicians who were also dialyzers in the sixties.

This problem has become acute for a number of reasons. Thus far, this is the only catastrophic disease for which the federal government pays treatment costs. Why this is so, and whether or not it should be so, are strongly felt issues for many. In a national and international period of economic troubles, financial coverage for dialysis and renal transplantation is costing more than was originally estimated by the promot-

21. This article was brought to my attention by Dr. Robert Goldstein, a member of the Renal Unit of the Massachusetts General Hospital.

ers, planners, and drafters of the Law ($240 million for the first year post-Public Law 92-603). At the present time, $8 million per week nationwide is allocated to dialyze approximately 18,000 patients. It is now predicted that, within the next few years, it will begin to cost no less than $1 billion a year to cover all dialysis and renal transplantation. Aside from the complex question of whether this is too much to be spending on kidney disease at a time when the prospect of national health insurance is being seriously contemplated, even for those who favor it, the case of dialysis and transplantation has raised disturbing questions about how much of the GNP such insurance is likely to cost.

As it is presently set up, federal funding for treatment of chronic kidney disease does not provide encouragement, incentives, or rewards for home dialysis, the least expensive form of dialysis treatment. (In fact, in its original form, now rectified, the law discriminated against those on home rather than center dialysis. It still does not require centers to provide training programs for home dialysis.) Whereas for a single patient, after the first year of treatment, home dialysis costs somewhere between $6000 and $8000 per year (depending on whether or not one includes extra medical costs), center dialysis costs $23,000 to $25,000 annually.

Different groups of physicians have different opinions and, beyond that, different philosophies about the degree to which home dialysis can and ought to be emphasized, and about what categories of patients are appropriate for it. Those who argue vigorously for it do so on psychological and social as well as financial grounds, contending that it offers patients a greater degree of self-determination, flexibility, and freedom from excessive dependence on the medical profession. This fits the "take care of yourself" exhortations which have been made on a broader medical and societal scale in recent years. As discussed earlier, there is a self-fulfilling prophecy dimension to this question, with those groups most enthusiastic about home dialysis tending to use this modality more extensively than those who are not, and to obtain better results with it. Thus, for example, at the Northwest Kidney Center in Seattle, Washington, under the influence of Belding Scribner—the inventor-godfather of long-term hemodialysis who is also a "believer" in home dialysis—all patients dialyze at home with results that, by and large, are impressive. Eli Friedman and Samuel Kountz at Downstate Medical Center, on the other hand, are more skeptical about the advisability of such an omni-home dialysis program, and about its feasibility. They have argued that not only the medical condition of patients, and the attitudes of the medical team treating them, but also the social composition of the particular patient population affect how many persons can be put on home dialysis. They contend that in the Brooklyn/New York City area in which they practice, with many very sick, indigent patients who live alone, or in broken homes, in a tenement flat, without the necessary plumbing and other physical facilities, the more than 90 percent of patients on home dialysis ratio that cities such as Seattle and Spokane have attained is not possible.* Physicians like Scribner have come to recognize the role that such social factors play in the home dialysis situation. There is now rough general agreement that nationwide, perhaps no more than about half of all treatable patients may be suitable for home dialysis. Yet, to the distress of many physicians, the percentage of home dialysis patients in the United States has dropped from 47.4 percent in 1972–1973 to 24.0 percent in 1976, and still seems to be on the decline.[22]

The fact that the proportion of patients on home dialysis is so low and that the most recent trend is downward rather than upward has not only raised acute questions about the influence and wisdom of our national policy in this respect.[23] It has also intensified discussion within the medical profession as well as outside of it about the ethicality of physicians establishing and running proprietary centers for dialysis. The number of such centers has increased in the last few years. They are profit-making establishments, although what margin of profit they make and whether that margin is or is not justifiable is a matter of some dispute. It is argued by some that medical professionals who are involved in such centers, directly or as stockholders, have a vested interest in their continuing existence and in siphoning off patients from other modes of treatment, most particularly home dialysis. There are those who believe that various physicians among them have acted as a political pressure group against home dialysis.

Finally, the process by which Public Law 92-603 was enacted has raised new, medical-political questions. It was partly because the National Kidney Foundation and the National Association of Patients on Hemodialysis and Transplantation (NAPHT) lobbied strenuously that this particular disease group received financial coverage under law. (One particularly dramatic and effective tactic used was the appearance of the Vice-President of NAPHT before the Ways and Means Committee of the

*Since the writing of this essay, Eli Friedman has modified this stance and is now more optimistic about the possibility and desirability of offering home dialysis to the patients he treats in Brooklyn. For further discussion of this issue, see the revised edition of *The Courage to Fail,* 1978.

22. Personal communication from Belding Scribner.

23. See, in comparison, for example, the United Kingdom statistics of 65.8 percent on home dialysis.

House of Representatives, where he was publicly dialyzed by his wife to demonstrate to the congressmen and women what this treatment was like.) Certain medical and nonmedical persons alike have expressed concern over the political pressures and public relations techniques that contributed to the law's passage. They hope that the history of this law will not invite representatives of other groups to lobby for their particular set of medical problems, rather than collaborating on the larger societal problem of allocating resources for a whole range of catastrophic, and noncatastrophic medical conditions and problems.

It would be both foolhardy and irresponsible to attempt to write a definitive analytic summary of the evolution of hemodialysis and of the American medical profession's relationship to it over the past 40 years. But, in the way of a conclusion, several major patterns have emerged in the course of this at once historical and sociological account that merit re-emphasis.

First, it would seem that the development of hemodialysis and of the medical profession's perspective on it exemplifies some of the promises and achievements, and the problems and dilemmas associated with therapeutic innovation and human experimentation in a modern Western society. But the "story" of dialysis in the United States has certain distinctively American structural and cultural traits: notably, a nonnationalized health system, on the one hand, and an especially optimistic and energetic kind of melioristic attitude towards health and illness, on the other.

What is particularly striking is that the problems with which dialysis has confronted the medical profession have progressively shifted ground, becoming less focused on biomedical, bioengineering and psychological questions, and more oriented toward social, economic, political, moral and existential concerns.

In fact, hemodialysis and the medical profession's involvement in it have become empirically and symbolically associated with the broadest kinds of social and cultural issues—nonmedical as well as medical—that have surfaced in American, European (and Japanese) societies in the past ten to fifteen years. In this sense, it has served as a paradigmatic and pioneering center of what has come to be called "bioethical" questions. The term bioethics is misleading in at least one respect. It implies that the social concerns and cultural themes that developments like dialysis have helped to evoke have been directly and unilaterally *caused* by such biomedical advances. But there is persuasive evidence to suggest that the questions of value, belief, and meaning to which this paper and this conference are addressed are part of a process of social and cultural review and reformulation that go beyond the scope of hemodialysis, therapeutic innovation, and even medicine.[24] What role hemodialysis and the medical profession will play with respect to these issues in the 1980s remains to be seen.

24. I have presented this analysis more fully and some of the supporting evidence for it in the following papers: "Ethical and Existential Developments in Contemporaneous American Medicine: Their Implications for Culture and Society," *Health and Society,* Fall 1974, pp. 445–483; "Advanced Medical Technology—Social and Ethical Implications," *Annual Review of Sociology,* Vol. 2 (1976), pp. 231–268; "The Medicalization and Demedicalization of American Society," *Daedalus,* Vol. 106, No. 1 (Winter 1977), pp. 9–22; "Ethical Aspects of Biomedical Advance," *Acta Hospitalia,* Vol. 16, No. 4 (1976), pp. 280–293.

PART THREE

PATIENTS AND HUMAN SUBJECTS, DONORS AND RECIPIENTS

The patients on whom these essays focus—Paul O'Brian, Leo Angelico, Jackie Foote, Mark J., and Ernie Crowfeather—represent more than themselves. Their case histories are an integral part of the social worlds of chronic and terminal illness, clinical medical research, and organ transplantation and dialysis portrayed and analyzed in *Experiment Perilous* and *The Courage to Fail.* In an ideal-typical way, they personify the most significant experiences and predicaments, satisfactions and solutions that are shared and structured by patients and research subjects, donors and recipients, medical professionals and family members who are participants in these settings.

Three Patients: Paul O'Brian, Leo Angelico and Jackie Foote

. . . [T]he patients of Ward F-Second did not all come to terms with their problems in exactly the same manner. The ward community provided patients with certain patterned ways of thinking about their situation and dealing with it: preferred attitudes, values, and behaviors which were taught to new members and were to some extent enforced. However, this still left room for variation between patients, both with respect to how they felt about these recommended ways of coming to terms, and precisely how they made use of them. Such factors as the personality characteristics of each patient, the type of disease he had, his prognosis, age, marital status, occupation, religion, and ethnic background undoubtedly made for differences in the nature and intensity of the patients' commitment to the ward's designated solutions and the ways they combined them.

The differences in outlook and behavior of individual patients we have encountered suggest something of the variation that existed; and several times we have noted that differences in the ethnic origins of patients seemed to affect the ways in which they experienced and managed their problems. A detailed, systematic treatment of the bearing that

---

From *Experiment Perilous* (Glencoe, Ill.: The Free Press, 1959, and Philadelphia: University of Pennsylvania Press, 1974), pp. 186–188 and 191–207.

such factors had on the ways in which patients responded to their situation falls outside the scope of this study, as does a consideration of patients in terms of their individuating life histories and special personality traits.

However, there are three patients among those we have met to whom we wish to devote this chapter. These are patients who seem to have had symbolic importance for the ward community as a whole, primarily because each personified an archetypical mode of coming to terms with the problems and stresses which F-Seconders shared. Learning more about these patients, letting them speak for themselves, and hearing what other F-Seconders said about them will accomplish a number of things. It will quicken our appreciation of the fact that Ward F-Second was comprised of real persons, each of whom was an important and unique human being in his own right. It will deepen our felt understanding of at least three patients as individuals. At the same time, it will provide concrete, case-history examples of different ways in which patients evaluated, combined, and utilized the ward's patterned solutions, and of some of their functional and dysfunctional consequences. Finally, it will enable us to listen in as the basic question around which Ward F-Second was built is openly debated. What is a good adjustment to the situation we share? F-Seconders asked themselves—the "best way" of coming to terms? Two diametrically opposed answers came back: the reply of a Paul O'Brian and the response of a Leo Angelico.

Face up to the fact that you will probably never get well, and that death is imminent, Paul O'Brian advocated. Have faith; but protest against illness and death. Live as long and fully and deeply as you can in terms of the world outside and wellness. Stay out of bed as much as possible. Make jokes and laugh with the fellows on the ward. But don't become too attached to them, or to the doctors. And don't succumb to the allure of medical stardom by committing yourself to the laboratory or to the notion of furthering medical science.

Accept the fact that you are paralyzed and probably always will be, Leo Angelico maintained. "Try to take what the Lord has decided [and] make the best of it." Put out of your mind things like "walking on the street," going to work, being at home with your family. Don't think too much about leaving the hospital. Find solace, pleasure, inspiration, and important work to do for the patients and doctors, right here and now on Ward F-Second. Get up in a wheelchair as much as possible and try to help patients who are "having a hard time" by visiting them and talking to them. Beyond that, assist the doctors, achieve "fame," and accomplish the "mission" of bringing health and happiness to "thousands," by acting as a volunteer for the Metabolic Group's experiments.

Finally, standing midway between the rebellious acquiescence of a Paul O'Brian and the active resignation of a Leo Angelico—symbolizing the way in which they could be reconciled—was a patient we never came to know but "always heard about." This was Jackie Foote, the seventeen-year-old boy who represented Ward F-Second's image of the "ideal" adjustment.

PAUL O'BRIAN

> *Hodgkin's Disease:* a painless, progressive and fatal enlargement of the lymph nodes, spleen, and general lymphoid tissues, which often begins in the neck, and spreads over the body. . . .
>
> —*The American Illustrated Medical Dictionary*

> I only know that one must do what one can to cease being plague-stricken, and that's the only way we can hope for some peace or, failing that, a decent death. . . .
>
> —Albert Camus, *The Plague*

> Disease so adjusts its man that it and he can come to terms: there are sensory appeasements, short circuits, a merciful narcosis. . . . But one must fight against them, after all, for they are two-faced. If you are not meant to get home, they are a benefaction, they are merciful; but if you mean to get home, they become sinister.
>
> —Thomas Mann, *The Magic Mountain*

> Our family doctor's a good doctor, but he's not very good at handling patients in a social way, if you know what I mean. When I got sick, he told my father that I had only five years to live. If he had told *me,* I wouldn't have cared at all. But Dopey there had to go and tell my father and worry him half to death! That's why he won't believe my sister when she tells him how well I'm getting along in the hospital this time. . . . Because this is the fifth year, you see . . . .

With full knowledge of the nature of his disease, and the imminence of his death, Paul O'Brian, twenty-seven, lived out his days. From his doctors, he had demanded and received this merciless knowledge. ("I asked him whether he could tell me anything about the progress of Hodgkin's disease; how far it had gone. . . . I asked him how long he thought I had to live. . . .") His ferocious drive to "find out" had made it imperative for him to ask these questions; and with a kind of savageness, he had come to terms with the unequivocal answers.

The coming-to-terms struggle had been a desperate one: a literal life-and-death battle. At first, a terrible void seemed to stretch before him:

> I wasn't working. And I was looking for a job, but not really very hard. I slept late every morning; went to bed late every night. And I had nothing to do . . . absolutely nothing to do. Nothing to look forward to . . . no one to see. I even went out one day and got drunk, thinking maybe that would help. But it didn't. . . . You see, before I was sick, I was so active. I went to school, and to work. I had dates, and went dancing and to parties. I just never had a moment to spare, my life was so full. . . . So to have my life so empty and so unbusy was a hard thing to get used to. . . .

Paul's days were taken up by strenuous treatments, but they still seemed "empty" to him—without meaning, beginning or end:

> I don't know which of the two treatments they're going to give me this time: mustard or X ray. I'd rather have X ray, I think. No, I'd rather have mustard. I don't know. . . . [pointing to his upper chest] I guess I'd rather have X ray if it's going to be from here up, and mustard if it's going to be from here down. Because X ray goes on forever. Day after day they drag you down for your treatment, and you're as limp as a rag. Nitrogen mustard gas only lasts two days, and most of the time you don't know what's going on. . . .

All of this involved "coming to the hospital, and going out—coming in and going out": a senseless repetition of arrivals and departures. There were days when Paul O'Brian longed for the ultimate certainty of his death:

> Listen, Dr. W., this is all stupid. What's the use of going on with these treatments? Just let me go home and forget about it. It's going to get me sometime or other, anyway.
>
> You know, if I thought I was going to have to go on like this for years—for more than five years, even . . . coming in and going out, coming in and going out—with only short intervals in between—I'd rather not live. Really, I'd rather die and get it over with.

And yet, Paul O'Brian refused to surrender himself. Move in the pattern of wellness, he affirmed. And "keep endless watch . . . lest you join forces with pestilence."[1]

1. Albert Camus, *The Plague* (New York: Alfred A. Knopf, 1950), p. 229.

> This time when I go home, I'm not going to wear a suit like I did last time. Last time, I sent for my favorite blue suit, and a special tie and shirt. And then, when I put them on, I discovered I'd lost so much weight that nothing fit and I looked just terrible. Like death warmed over. . . . This time, I'm going to wear slacks, and a sport shirt, and a sweater. . . . What I'd really like to do is drive my car home from the hospital. And when I finally do get to my house, I'd like to open the front door, run upstairs carrying my suitcase, and then rush downstairs again to the kitchen, and take a nice, cold beer out of the refrigerator. . . . If I did all those things, then my family would really believe that I was well . . . and home to stay. . . .
>
> I hope I get out of this hospital mood before I get out of here, though. Like I'm sitting here now and saying to myself as I watch the people in the corridor and on the ward, "That's a nurse; and that's a dietician; and that's a famous doctor." I wish I didn't know anything about anything here—about who people are, and what's going on. I'd like it if I could feel and act as if I'd never been here. . . . When I get out of here, I'll probably have to come back for a check-up once a week, for about a month or so. But do you know something? No matter how many times I have to come in for a check-up, I'll never come up to this ward. Never! Once I get out, I want to leave it all behind me. . . .

Even when the ward claimed him, Paul O'Brian kept faith with nonappeasement. Every drop swallowed, every pound gained, he regarded as a triumph. For with each progression, no matter how small, he advanced his return to the outside world:

> I remember when I was so sick for a while when I first came in . . . I'd lie there in bed and say to myself, "All I want for tomorrow is to be able to swallow a little tea." And when I finally succeeded in keeping that down, I'd say, "All I want now is to be able to drink a little tea, and eat a piece of toast, too." . . .

Paul had no tolerance for the supine. There was "something *wrong*" with a patient who "rested all day long," he declared. And when the whole of F-Second turned into a "stay-abed ward . . . with everyone in his cubicle by 9:30 at night"—that was the time Paul "*really* wished [he] could get out of the dump!" For him, a "quiet" ward was a "half-dead" place. And Paul O'Brian craved the "bustle," the clamor of life. As he envisioned it, the "perfect ward" would be a living defiance. "Graveyard roses" and "sickroom bonbons" would be outlawed. Beds and wheelchairs would stand empty. And "from every cubicle . . . you would hear all this laughter."

Death and disease would have no sovereignty in a world of Paul's making. They were his mortal enemies. Against all the ways in which they could seduce or overtake a man, Paul fought his never-ending battle:

> So far as I'm concerned, Mac is a bore and a regular hypochondriac. Do you know, he keeps a record of everything that has happened to him since his operation? He writes it all down in that big fat notebook of his. His temperature, his weight, his headaches—even a pain in his toe. That annoys me to death!
>
> When I look at Sam, I do more than wonder about that adrenalectomy operation. It certainly doesn't seem to have done him much good! All that trouble with his eyes. There's something terribly wrong with them. This morning he could hardly find his orange juice or his toast on his tray. His hands kept reaching in the wrong direction. His eyes must be all out of focus. . . . So far as I'm concerned, it's just not worth having that operation. One thing for sure—they're not going to get *my* adrenals! . . . I don't see why anyone would want to be experimented on, anyhow!
>
> This place keeps drawing you in toward itself, and the world outside starts to get smaller and smaller—farther and farther away. . . . I wouldn't want to adjust perfectly to any place. And particularly not to *this* place.

> 10/22/51: *Discharge Note*
> 27-year-old white male with Hodgkin's disease known for four years. Entered hospital 21 days ago for sixth admission. Ran a progressive downhill course with increasing pulmonary difficulty and pain. For the past four days patient has been in severe respiratory distress, and during past 36 hours has required constant oxygen and large amounts of sedation. For the past 10 hours has been cyanotic, chest filled with large rhonci, gurgles, etc. Conscious until last hour when respirations became irregular, gasping and quite noisy. Patient finally stopped breathing, and some 30–50 seconds later heart sounds ceased. He was discharged to Ward X at 9:55 P.M.

Paul O'Brian's last days were a testament to his credo. He cried bitterly because he was "coming back to the hospital." ("The tears kept rolling down my face.") In spite of "a temperature of about a hundred-and-three," the morning of the day (October 1) he left home, he shaved himself. And he arrived on the ward resolutely determined to "do nothing but get well and go home again." ("This is the Jewish New Year, isn't it? Well, maybe things will start afresh for me.") Feverishly, he battled narcosis. ("I don't even know if I slept last night. That's how befuddled I am. It's all that dope I'm getting. It's changing my personality so that I hardly know myself. And I don't like it one bit. I'm just not going to take any more medication.") With unblurred contempt, he looked out on the ward. ("This place is dead! No one on the ward is funny anymore. And everyone's in bed all the time. It's awful! A bunch of mourners, that's what they are. Take Mr. Kaye, for instance. He looks as if you could hire him to cry.") Shattering the funereal silence, Paul's voice rang out: "Come on, somebody! Make a little noise, won't you? Talk! Laugh! Do anything! But don't just lie there like a bunch of mummies!"

On October 13 Paul was still not "bedridden." On October 15, he launched himself on a "rehabilitation program":

> They're going to try to rehabilitate me—Miss P., and the others. She's going to get someone up here to show me how to make a wallet. And she's going to bring me a book of funny stories. And I've asked her to get Father Mac to come up and see me. . . . All that's to get me out of the apathy I'm in. . . . Because it's not natural to feel as hopeless as I do now. . . .

On October 19, Paul was put on the Danger List. ("My sister told me that I was on it, and I couldn't take it. I shouldn't care about dying. But I do. . . .") On October 22, Paul O'Brian was "discharged to Ward X."

The day he died, Paul held fast to consciousness. (Dr. L.: "I've never seen anything like it! Most people aren't aware of everything happening to them like Paul is.") Through his oxygen mask, in a loud unmodulated voice, he talked on and on. ("How's everyone on the ward? Go see if my bed in the cubicle is made up, will you? Because I intend to get back there.") His family arrived. ("Hi. I had a pretty good night, last night. . . . Why did you all come? It wasn't necessary. That means you had to leave work and everything. How did you get here? Did you take the car? . . .") Paul lapsed into unconsciousness, and then aroused himself with a bitter reproach. ("You can go on talking to me, you know, even when I can't talk to you! I can hear every word you say! What's new in the outside world?") The O'Brian family departed. ("They're too sentimental. I don't want consolation.")

Paul had a choking spell. ("Open the windows! All the way from the top!") He said he felt "very hungry" and wanted "something to eat." ("Chow! I want some chow!") In spite of his difficulty in breathing and swallowing, Paul downed a glass of orange juice, a poached egg, and a cup of coffee, in huge, frenetic gulps. ("Hurry, hurry! The next bite!") The nurse arrived with the medicine tray, and Paul swallowed three pills at once.

Before he became unconscious for the last time, he asked for his "square crucifix with the special blessing"; and he made a deadly joke with the newspaper boy who appeared in the doorway. ("No, I don't want a paper! I'm dying!") Reverence-and-blasphemy.

At 9:45 and-a-half, Paul "finally stopped breathing." At 9:55 P.M. when his "heart sounds ceased" and he was "discharged to Ward X,"* the battle Paul O'Brian had waged ended.

LEO ANGELICO

> This 40-year-old male developd progressive muscular weakness of both lower extremities and left upper extremity leading to evaluation and operation in 1943. Exploration of the cord revealed a reddish-grey mass which was thought to be an intramedullary spinal cord tumor at the level of C-4 to C-6. Resection could not be carried out. There has been no progression since that time; both lower extremities and the left upper extremity are paralyzed. The right upper extremity is functionally intact. Since 1950, this patient has been admitted every year to the Metabolic Ward as a volunteer for metabolic studies. As a rule, he has been discharged for two to three months every summer, and has usually spent this time with his family.
>
> A well-developed, well-nourished, healthy-appearing, young-looking, middle-aged male who shows no abnormalities other than paraplegia of the lower extremities and flaccid paralysis of the left arm. On the ward, he stays in a wheelchair during the day, and requires the help of an orderly to be put to bed at night and in his wheelchair in the morning. He is pleasant and seems to be well-adjusted. . . .
>
> Although he has found a fairly satisfactory solution to his problem by serving as a permanent volunteer for metabolic studies, this is a solution which is only secure on a year-to-year basis. It depends entirely on the availability of funds for his support and the support of a research ward. This has been pointed out to him every year, and he and his family have been encouraged to use at least the summer months for an attempt at vocational rehabilitation, taking advantage of his general good health, his adequate mental faculties, and his intact right arm. This has never been carried out to any satisfactory degree. . . . As a result of this, he has spent his summers going from relative to relative for one to two weeks at a time. This is an unsatisfactory solution. . . . It should be kept in mind that this man is now 40 years old, that his condition has been essentially stationary for ten years, that his general health is excellent, and that he will have to try to find a solution for twenty years or so. . . .
>
> —From the medical chart of Leo Angelico

*A euphemism for "died."

> Disease so adjusts its man that it and he can come to terms; there are sensory appeasements, short circuits, a merciful narcosis. . . .
>
> The day routine . . . so piously observed, had taken on in his eyes . . . a character of sanctity. When . . . he considered life as lived down in the flat-land, it seemed somehow queer and unnatural.
>
> —Thomas Mann, *The Magic Mountain*

> I'm a realist . . . not an idle dreamer [Leo Angelico claimed]. And I don't kid myself into thinking that I'm going to get out of this chair and walk out of here. Because that's a lot of baloney, and I know it.
>
> Of course, I've gotten worse as time has gone on. I can remember when it was only my foot that wouldn't work right. When I first went to the General Hospital, I was getting along very well with a cane. Over there, they put me through all sorts of tests, and gave me all sorts of pills, and put me in casts, and recommended that I use crutches—and God only knows what else. And they didn't find nothing.
>
> But no matter what I did, I kept getting worse. Finally, I went to ——— Clinic. And there, Dr. P. wanted to operate on me. He thought that maybe as a kid I had a fall or something, that had injured my spine and made my brain slip down too far over my spinal cord. He thought if by operating he could put the brain back where it belonged and removed the pressure, why, it might be all right.
>
> So, I went home and thought about it for a while. And I decided to go through with it—by this time, I was desperate, because there didn't seem to be anything else I could do. So he operated, and in a couple of days I come out all right. But he didn't find what he thought he would. All he found was a greyish-red mass on the spinal cord. At first he thought it was a tumor. But the biopsy said it wasn't.
>
> So there I was . . . up against a stone wall. They couldn't do anything about removing that mass, because they figured if they started fooling around, they might paralyze me completely. . . .

This, in Leo's own words, was the story of his disease—a mysterious illness that had run its course. Like the swellings in Paul O'Brian's neck, Leo's paralysis could not be reversed. Although he had been spared the ultimacy of death, Leo Angelico faced another finality—the walls and the bars of an inexorable, imprisoning condition:

> Just suppose there were a brick wall over there, and you made up your mind you were going to walk right through it. Do you think it would make much difference to put mind over matter? That's how the idea of making

> up my mind to walk is. You know how my legs feel? As though there were twenty-five-pound cement blocks on the end of each of them!
>
> No matter who you are, you never really get adjusted to being in the hospital all the time. . . . A man wasn't made to stay inside in one place all his life. Does a canary ever feel completely happy in his cage? Does a lion enjoy being in his cage?

It was in rare instances, however, that Leo Angelico decried his fate. The days of bewilderment were over for him; the angry protest had been put aside:

> I'm forty. So, obviously things happened to me before I came in here. . . . I was married—I had a wife, and I had a son. But my wife divorced me. I was served with the papers the day I went to the hospital for the operation. My son will be twelve this October, I guess. I've never seen him since.
>
> In the beginning, I was bewildered-like. I didn't know what the hell was happening to me. I didn't know what was wrong. And I kept going from doctor to doctor—and getting worse all the time. Slipping and slipping. I was like up in a cloud—and I was cross then. And bitter. I couldn't see why God had made such a big decision on me. I saw my brothers and sisters walking around so healthy-like—and I couldn't understand why it had happened to me and not to them. Things like that . . . But, after a while, I decided you've got to take what the Lord decides, and make the best of it. . . .

Give up the fight, Leo advocated. Smilingly, acceptingly, "take things as they are," and live in terms of the present:

> I made up my mind long ago that I wasn't going to be grumpy or cranky if I could help it. Because if you have a long face all the time, people get pretty tired of you. . . . I made up my mind that I was going to take things as they are, and get as much good and benefit from them as I can. There's no point in being any other way. You're only hurting yourself. . . . I just don't think very much about what could have been or what might have been if this hadn't happened. Like one fellow I know. He's always talking about what he was cheated of—what he would have been able to do that he can't now. I told him . . . he should try to make the best out of this. . . .

For if you win out over rage and self-pity, the world of F-Second becomes a "wonderful" place:

> You know, in all the time I've been here I've only seen maybe one or two men who I thought were disagreeable. All the rest were pretty wonderful. . . . I've met some remarkable people on this ward. Like Mr. Willis. He went

> blind suddenly. He was a swell old gent—so cheerful and brave. Or Jackie Foote. He's a wonderful kid. Seventeen years old and sick all his life with a kidney disease. The things he does for people on this ward! I've seen him get up four times in a night to answer a patient's bell. . . . Then there are Pat and Louis. What characters they are! Pat can make a joke out of anything—and Louis's even better at it. . . . Or Paul O'Brian—so young! He was planning on so many things when he left last time. Like driving his car, and going to dances . . . .

The "Pauls" of the ward—Leo maintained—they're part of the reason "you can't spend time feeling sorry for yourself":

> When you see people suffering like that, you feel you're lucky. There are so many worse things than what I have, for instance. Being born blind, or an idiot. Or man-made things—like being shot up in the war. Compared to that . . . compared to a lot of guys here on the ward, I'm really well off. . . . The boy down the ward is having a rough time. He had an I.V. running all night. And the one across the way's been suffering something terrible. He threw up all night. Billy's a little better, but he's far from his old self. And they say that J.W.'s a pretty sick boy. . . . But as for me, I don't have any pain. My physical condition's good, and I feel well most of the time. Except for a little aching in damp weather . . . In a place like this, you always see somebody worse off than you are. So, how long can you go on thinking about your own troubles?

Wheeling himself from bed to bed, Leo made physicianly calls upon suffering and dying patients:

> SAM: Oy, oy. Leo, Leo.
> LEO: Hello, Sam. How are you?
> SAM: I feel lousy. How are you?
> LEO: I'm pretty good, Sam. I wish you felt as well as I do.
> SAM: I feel lousy. Oh, God, oh, God. Oh, dear, oh, dear.
> LEO: I would have been down to see you before this, Sam. But I've been busy up there with the I.V.'s, you know.
> SAM: Oh, well, oh, well. Poor Sam, poor Sam.
> LEO: I'm sorry you're feeling so lousy, Sam.
> SAM: How is your friend, Leo?
> LEO: Who do you mean, Sam? Do you mean Will? He's fine. He comes in a couple of times a week to the clinic and to see Dr. J.
> SAM: How's Mr. Flanders?
> LEO: You know what happened to him? He's fine. Was out of the Hospital for a while and then went home to California.
> SAM: That's good.
> LEO: Have you been eating, Sam?

SAM: Not yet.
LEO: Are you trying?
SAM: Yes.
LEO: That's good. Because it's very important—look, Sam, you get some rest, and I'll be back to see you later.
SAM: Okay, Leo. Thanks.

Like Hans Castorp in Thomas Mann's *The Magic Mountain*, Leo Angelico concerned himself with "the severe cases and the moribund" because he did not wish to take flight from the world of disease. This is a community of sickness and death, he asserted, and we ought not to "act as though we had nothing to do with it."[2] Rather, it is our moral responsibility to draw close to our fellow patients in their time of greatest need. Nor is this the only humanitarian service we can perform as F-Seconders. There is also the "job" of experimental subject, through which we can aid our "fellow-men in need."

In the realm of the laboratory, Leo Angelico had achieved ward supremacy. Three years as "standard human assay subject"; a record of hundreds of I.V.'s; a personal I.V. pole (adapted for wheelchair use); a stopwatch for timing and regulating ACTH infusions; a stack of reprints from the *New England Journal of Medicine* ("We are much indebted to Mr. Leo Angelico, whose unfailing cooperation enabled us to work out the fundamentals of intravenous administration of ACTH . . .")—all these attested to Leo's stardom. Like the "young man" in the projective story he related to a psychologist, Leo was one of Ward F-Second's "main attractions":[3]

> This is a young man . . . who has dreams of attaining great fame. As he ascends the swings above . . . he is thinking about how some day he will get the center ring. . . . Finally, after working very hard, he does get to the main attraction and great fame in which we find him . . . which makes him very happy because he brings great joy to thousands. . . .

Though he was doomed to a wheelchair existence, Leo's participation in "research" gave him the sense that he had "ascend[ed] . . . above" his paralyzed state, was a "main attraction," and was bringing "great joy to thousands."

> Having received IV ACTH on several hundred occasions, he shows no evidence of resistance to the material when administered by this route.

2. Thomas Mann, *The Magic Mountain.* Translated by H. T. Lowe-Pozter (New York: Alfred A. Knopf, 1948), p. 295.

3. Card Number Seven in the Thematic Apperception Test: administered to Leo Angelico by the clinical psychologist affiliated with the Psychiatric group of the Hospital.

> Although there has been some variation in his control 17-ketosteroids, this response is still essentially predictable.

Hours of submission to his task had made Leo a "perfect research patient." "No evidence of resistance . . . response . . . essentially predictable"—Leo had become as synchronized as his stopwatch:

> Where are those damn doctors? I was supposed to give them a urine specimen and they were supposed to start at 10:30 on the button. Here it is a quarter to eleven now. Well, if they want to spoil the experiment, that's their business.

When the doctors were "off schedule" and the I.V.'s did not "run on time," Leo was very disturbed, for his certitude depended on the "daily round." There was always the possibility that at the completion of each series of assays he might be permanently discharged because his services as a research subject were no longer needed or wanted. Thus, a deferred I.V. could mean the beginning of no I.V.'s at all. And Leo Angelico wanted to "make sure" that such a day was not close at hand:

> I want to keep these veins as good as I can for as long as I can. Otherwise, I'll be out of a job!
>
> I just asked Dr. D. how long I could go on taking ACTH without overloading my adrenal glands. He said the way they did it, spacing the I.V.'s and all, it wasn't too likely to happen. . . . Dr. D. said so far as they're concerned I'm still having a normal response to it. So he says maybe I could go on five years or more taking ACTH like this. . . .

Unlike Paul O'Brian, who dreamed of "leaving the ward behind" and "going home for good," Leo Angelico looked with fear upon the prospect of such a journey:

> Poor Paul. He was planning on so many things. . . . Like he was going to a dance when he got out, he said. I don't plan like that anymore. I'll tell you the truth, I get a nervous stomach every time I have to make a change. Even a little one . . . For me, this hospital and this ward are like no other hospital and no other ward I've ever been in. . . . I get cold chills when I think of leaving it. . . .

For Leo was a stranger in the world outside F-Second:

> When I'm home and all the people in the room start talking at once—even if they're my own family—I get nervous and tired. Like one night there last summer, my brothers got into this political discussion, and it wore me out

just listening. That's why I feel I'm not made to be with strong, healthy people anymore.

"Seeing my brothers come in full of vim and vigor," Leo said, "listening to them going real hard at discussions—I can't really believe I ever did all the things I see them doing." The Leo Angelico who "used to go deer hunting," play an instrument, and parade in a marching band, and romp with his baby son existed only in the faded snapshots he kept in a night-table drawer. "All I know now is what goes on in here."

PAUL: If Leo were suddenly to get well . . . if he were to discover that he could walk and get out of that chair . . . they'd have to do a terrific job of rehabilitation on him. . . .

LEO: If it should happen in the middle of the night that suddenly I was well, I'd get up in my pajamas and bare feet, and no matter how crazy it looked, I'd walk home just that way. . . . But after that—well, I haven't really gotten much farther in my own mind. . . .

PAUL VERSUS LEO

Around the smiling immobility of Leo Angelico, a controversy raged.

For Paul O'Brian, so fiercely enamored of wellness, Leo symbolized all the "adjustments" to disease that he so bitterly opposed. "Worse than anything, I'd hate to be like he is," Paul avowed. "Not physically. I wouldn't mind that so much. But mentally, I mean . . . Such a goody-goody. So nice and sweet about everything . . ." A man ought to "get mad," Paul felt. Years of paralysis should not deaden his anger, or silence his protest against the sick-day:

> Emptiness. Nothing but emptiness. You would think that with all the years that he's been sick, and the fact that he's still a pretty young man, and that he's never been in pain . . . You would think that he would have studied something, learned something during that time. But he's never tried to. As it is, day after day passes for him in exactly the same way. . . .

Life in the outside world, Paul declared, is not attuned to such a "fixed pattern." What is more, it is a ceaseless round of activities:

> At home, we just don't live in that set, routine kind of way. Like on Sundays . . . we just get dinner whenever one of us feels like starting in. And sometimes, after dinner is over, we'll sit around the table talking and smoking and drinking coffee 'til maybe 9 o'clock, or something like that.

. . . We don't have a fixed pattern about anything. Why, do you know, when I drive to work every morning, I try to take a slightly different route so I can see something different. . . .

Before I was sick, I went to school, and to work. I had dates, went dancing, and to parties. I just never had a minute to spare, my life was so full. . . .

Illness excluded you from activities such as these. But the alternative, Paul maintained, did not lie in bondage to the sick world. Rather than offering his arm to the laboratory, Leo Angelico ought to use it for *healthy* pursuits:

You know, I know a girl as bad—worse off than Leo is. Because she can't even sit in a wheelchair. She had only the use of one hand, too. But she taught herself to paint. And she paints these wonderful flower pictures and trays. My sister used to go to classes she taught in that sort of thing.

Taking a paintbrush in his hand, turning his head to face the window, a man should keep the well world alive within him. "But Leo doesn't really know what the outside world is like anymore," Paul claimed.

He's forgotten. . . . I know a fellow at home who's completely paralyzed. Even more so than Leo. He's been in bed for years with just one tiny window to look out of. But he's not like Leo. . . . He's interested in lots of things outside that one little sickroom. . . .

Not Leo—he admitted that all he "knows now is what goes on in here," and that for him, "this ward and this hospital [were] like no other ward and no other hospital" on the face of the earth. "But I know for a fact," Paul argued, "that everyone on this ward isn't as nice as you think they are."

Take Mac, for instance. I don't see what's so swell about him like you were just saying. So far as I'm concerned, he's a bore and a regular hypochondriac. . . . And what about that guy from Dorchester who has the cubicle across the way from mine? He used to send his wife running to the kitchen all the time. "My Henry would like another piece of toast," she'd say. . . . Me, I think there's a lot of bad things in the people here, as well as the good ones. You make it sound too rosy. . . .

PAUL: Did you hear what Leo just said to me? He said, "You ought to be here at Christmas time; it's really nice then." Be here at Christmas time! That's all I need! I'm sure sorry I'm not going to be here to enjoy it!

LEO: I didn't mean it that way, Paul. I just meant it's really pretty here. Last year they had a silver tree in the middle of the ward—and they decorated every other cubicle—and all the nurses sang carols. . . .

Silver trees and singing nurses—these, Paul contended, were some of the real "dangers" of F-Second. For, in the "rosy" aspects of ward life, seduction lay. Unless a man took active precautions, the hospital would "pull you in toward itself":

> LEO: Why didn't Jackie come up to visit if he was in the hospital, I wonder?
>
> PAUL: Why should he have?
>
> LEO: I don't see why he wouldn't. He liked it here in the hospital.
>
> PAUL: Well, there are ways in which I've liked it, too. But I can tell you right now, that even though I'll have to come back every week for a check-up, I'll hardly ever come up here. . . . I just don't believe in it.

Paul did not "believe in" visiting the ward often or in maintaining a great deal of interest in how patients still on the ward were "coming along." These were Leo-like ways—ways of surrendering to the sick world. "I wouldn't call that the perfect adjustment by any means!"[4]

HOW OTHER PATIENTS REGARDED LEO ANGELICO

Many F-Seconders reacted more favorably to Leo Angelico than Paul O'Brian did. Particularly for the new patients on the ward, Leo was a "guiding light"—a tragic and radiant figure. Paralyzed, confined to a wheelchair, he seemed to them the very incarnation of the suffering world they had just entered. Twelve years of illness, and "no hope of recovery!" The new F-Seconder had "never dreamed of a sickness so terrible":

> You take Leo. He's been sick for twelve years, he tells me. You don't realize how lucky you are until you encounter something like that.
>
> That sickness of Leo's is a terrible thing. There's not much hope for him getting better, is there?
>
> Believe me, he's got it rough! His back's up against the wall.

4. The "tropistic" nature of the relationship between Paul O'Brian and Leo Angelico suggests that, psychologically speaking, they may have represented two sides of the same ambivalent motivation: the one rebellious, the other acquiescent. It may have been partly because Paul was involuntarily drawn toward Leo's solution that he felt compelled to attack him, and thus to strike out against all those things in Leo that he battled within himself (compliance, passivity, dependence, fixity). Analogously, Leo may have drawn close to Paul, out of his own inner needs for rebellion. ("I wanted to have as much to do with Paul as I possibly could," Leo once said.)

And yet, over his bleak and paralyzed fight, Leo's cheerfulness shone forth:

> He's such a sweet boy, with such a good disposition. He smiles all the time.
>
> He certainly deserves a lot of credit for the way he looks at his illness. He's very good about it. . . .

The neophyte was awed by such serenity. To a man who had "never been in a hospital before . . . never been sick," an attitude of smiling acceptance seemed a "real accomplishment."

Leo Angelico was also "admired" by many F-Seconders because "he had a sense of vocation about being sick." He was not simply reconciled to his illness. He was "doing important work" by acting as one of the "top subjects" for the Metabolic Group's experiments, and he was "very dedicated to his job."

Because he seemed to be at peace with illness, "at home" in the hospital, and to have found meaning in his predicament, Leo was "a great help in helping others adjust themselves to strange hospital life."

Although most patients "liked Leo very much," some were less enthusiastic about the kind of adjustment he had made. A number of veteran F-Seconders who had graduated beyond the turbulent first stages of illness and who, like Paul, had come to terms with their situation in a more active, unresigned, well-world-oriented way than Leo felt that his "outlook" was too docile. "Out of the mouth of babes," the old saying goes. It was a boy patient who put this feeling into words when he was "kidding around with Leo one day":

> LEO: Ray has another bright idea. This is *really* a good one!
> RAY: I think if we took Leo's legs off, and got him two artificial limbs like the veterans have—well, then, maybe he could walk.
> LEO: It wouldn't work.
> RAY: You know, Leo, I don't think you really want to leave here. I guess you never had it so good! But to give up, and to stop trying—that's the easy and scared way out. . . .

JACKIE FOOTE: THE "PERFECT" ADJUSTMENT

("Angel with a Baseball Bat")

> . . . Patient is at home now. . . . He goes to baseball games for recreation, but exercise has been limited by doctors' orders. He seems very well

adjusted to his illness, cooperative, cheerful, and from the stories of his previous admissions, a great favorite around the ward. . . .

—From the hospital chart of Jackie Foote

Ward F-Second's most uncontroversial, luminous figure was an "angel with a baseball bat." "Sick all his life with kidney disease . . . practically raised in the hospital," Jackie Foote, a seventeen-year-old towhead, symbolized the "perfect adjustment." "*Everyone* loved Jackie. No one," it was asserted, "could be more wonderful, more perfect than he."[5]

He usually arrived at the hospital "all swollen up something terrible—his whole face, his arms, his legs." And yet, "no matter how sick he was, he was always doing something to help other patients or cheer them up." Many times, he had been known to "get up at night and help a patient, when he felt worse himself than the patient who was calling for help." Not only that, but "he was very precocious. He could reel off the names of those drugs, one after another, without any effort at all." In short, Jackie could cope so well with the challenges of illness and the hospital, that he was always ready and equipped to reach out a helping hand to others less well-adjusted than he.

"But Jackie was not an angel, by any means. He was all boy. . . . He had a swell sense of humor. . . . He was a happy-go-lucky kid, always joking. . . ." Most characteristic of all, "he just loved baseball." He "went around all day long swinging an imaginary baseball bat." He was "natura ," had "lots of interests," was "vigorous," and "thoroughly alive."

Thus, in the eyes of Ward F-Second, Jackie was more than a "hospital angel." He was a "normal," mischievous, baseball-enamored adolescent, as well. Ward F-Second's all-perfect boy stood poised between the sick world and the well world—exquisitely adjusted to the demands of both.

At the time this study was made, "for the first time in many years Jackie [had] managed to stay out of the hospital for months." "He still comes in to the O.P.D. from time to time, but the doctors now have the feeling that maybe he'll get well," patients said. They were not in favor of "having him come up and visit the ward." ("It's not a good idea. . . . It just might jinx him. . . .")

"Jackie ought to get well," patients felt. "He deserves to." If, in fact, he had, it would have been a triumph for "everyone" on Ward F-Second.

5. I only caught a glimpse of Jackie Foote once, during a visit he made to the ward one morning. Therefore, I have no way of distinguishing reality elements from projective elements in the ward's image of Jackie. Though some of the attributes ascribed to him may have been mythological in nature, it does not seem as important to try to establish this fact as to understand the symbolic meaning which they had for the patient community.

"FOLLOW-UP"

The last entries in Jackie Foote's chart and a letter from Leo Angelico tell us what subsequently happened to these patients:

> This was the sixteenth admission of this 18-year-old boy who has been suffering from terminal glomerular nephritis for the past 9 months. Under medical management, the prognosis was hopeless. The homologous kidney transplant was offered as a possible therapeutic measure after the risk of the operation and the limitations of the procedure were explained to his parents. . . . Before the operation . . . Jackie became quite an analgesic problem. . . . Following a visit by his brother who was full of summer plans of all his friends, Jackie became very despondent, and then agitated. He slept not at all one Saturday night, and got out of bed many times, requiring someone at the bedside. . . . He was unsedated, and allowed to get up in a chair. . . . On July 20th, a homologous kidney transplant was performed. . . . On the 27th post-operative day, after 6 days of steady downhill course despite hemodialysis, the patient became increasingly lethargic, and finally unresponsive. . . . Discharged to Ward X, 10:45 A.M.

> November 22, 1957.
>
> Hi, Renée,
>
> At last here it is. I do write once in a while. Well, how are you? I do hope everything is just fine with you. I have been thinking about you and the book you are going to write, or are writing. And how is it progressing? This year I did not go back to the Hospital, as I usually do in September. I feel a need for a change from research for a while anyway. But I do miss the Hospital very much—so much that I am forever thinking about it and the wonderful people I knew.
>
> Four weeks ago I left my brother and family and am now in a nursing home for a while. You see, this month and next the hunting season is on for deer. And the men in our family, well, they just have to get out and into the woods and look for game.
>
> Where are you on these lovely fall days? . . . When your story on F-Second is finished and in book form, please let me know about it. I'd love to have and read what you thought about that grand gang we knew. If I can be of help in finding addresses of people, I'd be happy to. When you have the time, please write. I'd love to hear.
>
> My best wishes to you and yours, and happy Thanksgiving.
>
> Your F-Second friend,
>
> Leo [Angelico][6]

6. Since Leo Angelico and I have had no more than a Christmas card correspondence since 1952, this letter I received from him in the Fall of 1957 came as a surprise. Perhaps one of the most interesting things about its contents is that it suggests that Leo regarded helping me with this book as a substitute for contributing to the research of the Metabolic Group.

Some of the patients on Ward F-Second got well and went home to stay. But for patients like Leo Angelico, Jackie Foote, and Paul O'Brian, what *would* have been the "perfect adjustment"? There was a time when this sociologist would have been more inclined to offer a simple and somewhat partisan answer. However, partly as a consequence of the kinds of experience and learning that participant observation on Ward F-Second and in the laboratory and conference room of the Metabolic Group entailed, such pat answers and personal judgments now come harder and seem less satisfactory.

Chronicle of a Cadaver Transplant

RENÉE C. FOX AND JUDITH P. SWAZEY

The impersonal professional vocabulary that members of a transplant team generally employ in their formal accounts of the donation-recipient process mutes the inherent emotionality of what actually takes place.

> Cardiac donors used at Stanford have most often been emergency cases receiving their initial medical care at another hospital. . . . The patient (possible donor) is brought to the emergency room of that hospital critically ill. The family is informed within a limited amount of time that there is no hope for the patient's survival—or family members may take this presumption independently. . . . Serious thought about donorship usually begins slightly following the impact of pending death. Although family members still must struggle with their decision about donating, little question typically exists for them that the potential donor is dying or dead. . . .

From Renée C. Fox and Judith P. Swazey, *The Courage to Fail: A Social View of Organ Transplant and Dialysis* (Chicago: University of Chicago Press, 1974), pp. 94–99. Reprinted in *The Hastings Center Report* Vol. 3, No. 6 (December 1973).

> Stanford transplant team members seek to develop or reinforce this feeling by trying to separate the pronouncement of death from the decision for donorship (the determination and pronouncement of brain death is made by three physicians who have no connection with the transplant team); by offering help to the donor family in dealing with the death and grief process; and by immediate exploration of signs that the family might be thinking of the recipient as a substitute family member (the latter is always discouraged).
>
> If the family decides that the patient is to be used as a donor, good-byes are essentially said at that time. If the donor is at another hospital, the body is then brought to Stanford, but the family rarely accompanies it. If the donor is at Stanford, the family typically leaves some time prior to transplantation. Although the family has contact with the transplant surgeon and social worker, the family's energy is directed primarily toward coping with the death and funeral arrangements. Transplantation occurs within hours after the decision is made.[1]

The use of such uncharged vocabulary meets the norms of objective, dignified medical reporting. It also serves the more latent function of encouraging transplanters to conceptualize what they are doing, to themselves as well as to others, in terms that enhance their equanimity in the at once life-saving and death-ridden situation in which they function. Hidden behind the carefully controlled presentation is the highly stressful affective reality of what the members of a medical team (nurses and social workers as well as physicians) actually experience when they undertake responsibility for a transplant.

The protective screen of professionalism lifted for us one weekend in February. It began when the chief social worker of a transplant group received a telephone call in the midst of a dinner party, informing her that a prospective heart donor for Mr. Olaf L. had just been admitted to the University Medical Center. Over the next twenty-four hours we shared the physical and emotional demands that preparing for and performing a cadaver transplant make on medical professionals, as well as on the patient recipient, his family, and the relatives of the donor.

On a Saturday night in February, twenty-six-year-old Mark J. was brought to the emergency room of a local hospital after a serious motorcycle accident. Mark was conscious, but agitated and confused, when he entered the hospital, and he soon lapsed into a comatose state. Surgeons performed a craniotomy to try to relieve the pressure on his brain, but he did not recover consciousness. He required artificial respiration, was

1. L. K. Christopherson and D. T. Lunde, "Heart Transplant Donors and Their Families," *Seminars in Psychiatry* 3:26–35, February 1971.

unresponsive to stimuli, and showed a flat EEG tracing. All signs indicated massive brain stem damage. On Sunday night, with the permission of his next of kin, Mark was transferred to the nearby University Medical Center as a possible cadaver organ donor.

Several kidney patients were awaiting cadaver transplants at the Medical Center. In addition, the cardiac transplant team was ready to operate on Olaf L. as soon as a suitable cadaver heart became available. Miss A., the transplant team's chief social worker, was called at her home Sunday night, shortly after Mark's admission, to alert her that a prospective donor had been admitted to the hospital.

At eleven P.M. that Sunday, Mark J. was pronounced dead by a neurologist unaffiliated with the transplant team. Miss A. later told us that this neurologist "tends to be skeptical and uncomfortable about heart transplants. I think this is a positive control over the possible tendency of physicians to declare a patient dead when they know that someone is awaiting a transplant from him." As soon as Mark's brain death had been pronounced, a cardiologist member of the transplant team began a night-long vigil over his body in the intensive care unit, keeping his heart beating by mechanical means until the transplant surgeons were ready to excise it and place it in Olaf L.'s chest.

We arrived at the Medical Center at nine A.M. Monday, with Miss A. Other members of the renal and cardiac transplant teams had been there for hours, preparing for the four transplants that would take place that day. Mark J., we learned, was to be a multiple organ donor: both kidneys, as well as his heart, were to be transplanted. The renal transplant team told us that the transplant probably would not take place before eleven A.M. because Mark's organs could not be removed until the two kidney recipients had been adequately dialyzed. Although Mark's heart would be removed before his kidneys, Dr. Y. explained, the multiple transplant procedure involved "split-second timing" to ensure that the organs would retain maximum viability. As Dr. Y. and his colleagues left the nursing station we heard him ask, "Who's going to take the heart out?"

We returned to Miss A.'s office, where she began trying to reach members of Mark's family by telephone. After failing to reach Mark's stepfather, she called his sister Susan, a young single girl with whom Mark had been living before his death. Both Mark and Susan, Miss A. told us, were estranged from their family, and Mark had spent most of his time with friends in his motorcycle gang. Miss A. had a brief conversation with Susan, who was "very emotional" about her brother's death and his role as an organ donor. Moments after their talk ended, Susan called Miss A. back to ask about funeral arrangements for Mark, wondering whether she would have to make the arrangements or whether it would be handled by other family members or by his motorcycle gang.

Miss A. then took us to the intensive care room, where the potential recipients of Mark's kidneys were completing their dialyses. The husband of one recipient was standing by her bed, watching her undergo these final preparations for what was to be her second transplant. "If I'd gone through fifteen years of suffering like my wife has," he told us, "I'd rather be dead than have to face another transplant. But if there's any justice in such things, my wife should do well this time." On an adjacent bed lay the second patient. His arm was bleeding profusely, and he was thrashing agitatedly on the bed. The renal transplant team, we were told, had debated at length about accepting him as a transplant recipient, in part because he had been a heroin addict.

It was now early afternoon, and Miss A. was paged by the main reception desk. The receptionist said that a young man who identified himself as Mark's brother urgently wanted to talk to her. We accompanied her downstairs to greet Joe, a tall, lanky boy in his early twenties, with long, neatly combed hair, dressed in slacks and a colorful sports shirt. With him was another boy, similarly dressed and wearing one small gold earring and a blue stocking cap. Joe explained that he was Mark's "motorcycle-gang brother," not his sibling. He had rushed to the hospital as soon as he had learned about Mark's accident, and until Miss A. talked with him he knew nothing about Mark's being a cadaver donor. He pleaded several times to be allowed to see his brother. She gently explained that this would be impossible, since Mark was now in an operating room and that after his heart and kidneys had been removed his body would be sent to the coroner for autopsy, a legal requirement when a person dies in an accident. Joe several times requested reassurance that everything possible had been done to keep his brother alive and asked exactly when he had been pronounced dead. Miss A. explained in detail the process by which the medical team gradually and reluctantly decides that nothing more can be done for a patient like Mark. Both Joe and his companion were deeply moved and grief stricken as they talked with Miss A., although they kept their composure throughout the interview and indicated their sympathy for her difficult job of dealing with the bereaved family. During the conversation, Joe and his friend indicated that they, rather than Mark's biological family, would probably want to arrange his funeral. Saddened, stunned, but still dignified, the two young men thanked Miss A. and departed, saying they would go to Susan's house to see if they could help her.

At 3:30 P.M. Miss A. called the hospital's publicity office to inform them officially that the heart and kidney transplants were in progress. She told them that the family of the heart recipient, Olaf L., had requested as little publicity as possible, but that Mark's family wished to have the fact that they had offered his organs mentioned at least in the local paper.

Throughout the day, we repeatedly saw Mr. L.'s wife and mother, seated in the corridor outside the surgical wing waiting for news of the operation. Miss A. stopped to talk with them each time we passed by, telling them various details of what they should expect once Mr. L. returned from the operating room. Earlier in the day, before Mr. L. was taken to surgery, we had visited his room briefly and met his mother, wife, and personal physician. Mr. L. looked pale and drawn, but his manner was cheerful and expectant. Mr. L.'s physician was permitted to be in the operating room during the transplant, and at the end of the day, around five P.M., we found him sitting in the main nursing station of the intensive care unit, looking weary but relieved that Mr. L. had successfully completed surgery.

Mr. L.'s wife and mother were also waiting outside the intensive care unit where Mr. L. had been brought after surgery. Both women had carefully controlled their emotions throughout the day, although they were close to tears. They now thanked Miss A. repeatedly for her "goodness" to them during the long day, for spending so much time with them and briefing them so carefully on how Mr. L. would look when he emerged from the operating room. Mrs. L. asked whether she would be allowed to hold her husband's hand when she visited him in the intensive care unit "because," she explained, "I'm a toucher."

As the day ended, we made rounds with the kidney team and Miss A., visiting patients in their rooms on the clinical research unit and in the intensive care unit. The recipients of Mark's kidneys, recuperating from surgery in the intensive care unit, were "doing well." The almost tearful husband of the woman who had received a kidney from Mark was standing close to her bed, holding her hand tightly and now looking not at all ambivalent about his wife's transplant. The renal team was exhausted. They had done three transplants in one day and were also handling a large caseload of critically ill pre- and post-transplant patients.

We left the Medical Center about seven P.M., weary and emotionally drained. Two images continued to haunt us: Mark J. lying in the intensive care unit room attended by nurses, though officially dead; and the face of his brother Joe when he was informed that Mark was lying on the operating table having his heart removed so that a fifty-one-year-old salesman might live.

The Case of Ernie Crowfeather

RENÉE C. FOX AND JUDITH P. SWAZEY

ARTIFICIAL KIDNEY USE POSES AWESOME QUESTIONS

LAWRENCE K. ALTMAN

Seattle, Oct. 23 [1971]—Ernie Crowfeather, a bright, charming part American Indian with a history of personal instability and brushes with the law, died recently at the age of 29 after he refused further life-supporting therapy.

By what was regarded as a suicide, Ernie averted the frightening possibility that his doctors would have had to purposely turn off, for lack of funds and because of his irresponsibility, the artificial kidney that for two years had kept him alive on public money totaling $100,000.

Ernie Crowfeather and the problems associated with chronic dialysis and transplantation that he experienced and personified were introduced to a national public through these lead paragraphs of a front-page story in *The New York Times.* We had first heard of Ernie from his

From *The Courage to Fail* (Chicago: University of Chicago Press, 1974), pp. 280–315.

physicians at the University Hospital, Seattle, when we were conducting field research there in 1969. We were struck with how intensely the doctors of the dialysis and transplant teams were preoccupied with his case. Although we never met Ernie, he came to exemplify for us all the medical dilemmas and the human and moral anguish that these modes of treatment can entail.

Our study of the Seattle dialysis program, which included some facets of Ernie's case, had been completed and was being reviewed by Dr. Belding Scribner and his associates when we learned of Ernie's death in June 1971. Later that summer, Scribner urged us to include an extensive account of Ernie's story in our book. For to Scribner, still haunted by the implications of Ernie's life and death, this was a "classic case," "the epitome of all the problems," "the personification of everything at once." We expressed our interest, but indicated that we would not be able to return to Seattle to interview those who had been closely involved with Ernie. Scribner offered to make available the necessary data, including extensive interviews that Dr. Lawrence K. Altman of *The New York Times* was conducting with the principals in the case. We then consulted Dr. Altman, who felt it was appropriate that we use the materials he was collecting, and he subsequently made them available to us, with the consent of those interviewed.

Ernie Crowfeather can no longer speak for himself. But his experiences and their import live on in the testimony of the medical professionals who cared for him, his family, members of the community who rallied around him, and the journalists who wrote about him. This chapter is based on what they felt, said, and did.

Ernie Crowfeather was first admitted to the University Hospital with a renal disease of unknown origin on January 23, 1969. Thirty months later, on July 29, 1971, he died in the emergency room of the Ellensburg, Washington, hospital. For Ernie, those thirty months were a constant struggle for eligibility to receive treatment by dialysis and transplantation, the only means that offered him a chance of survival. He was also faced with painful "quality of life" problems, which finally confronted him with a classically tragic dilemma. In the words of his primary physician, "Ernie felt so miserable that he really didn't want to live . . . but he couldn't face death either. He couldn't summon up the courage, as some of our patients have, to say 'I want to stop.'"

Ernie's response to his medical situation was conditioned by his social background and his personality traits. These same factors contributed to the ways physicians and the local community became involved in his case. For everyone concerned, Ernie and his situation evoked the life and death issues, the sense of obligation to intervene actively, the problems of meaning, the uncertainties, and the feelings of guilt and failure that terminal kidney disease, chronic hemodialysis, and transplantation can trigger.

PERSONAL VIGNETTES

To understand Ernie Crowfeather's last thirty months of life, it is necessary to know something about his personal history. What we have learned about Ernie indicates that his attitudes and behavior patterns, independent of his illness, were strongly influenced by three factors: his half-Indian ancestry, his home life as a child, and his loss of a kidney during early adolescence. Similarly, it seems clear that the feelings and actions of the medical personnel and laypeople who were involved with Ernie after the onset of his terminal renal disease were due as much to his "Indian-ness," his personality, his economic situation, and his social record as to his medical condition.

Ernie Crowfeather, the son of a full-blooded Sioux father and a German-American mother, was born at Fort Yates, North Dakota, in 1942. Although Mr. Crowfeather was the only member of his family who had attained a college education, according to Ernie's mother, he had "worked on a ranch for a white guy" before joining the army in 1941. A year after Ernie's birth, his parents had their sixth child. Soon after, Mrs. Crowfeather moved her five daughters and her son to Yakima, Washington, where her own mother was living. As one of Ernie's sisters explained, "Mother didn't want to be in Fort Yates, as a white woman among Indians, while our father was in the service." Although Yakima is a predominantly white town, it is adjacent to a reservation. Thus Ernie's family lived in close proximity to an Indian community. In 1946, Mr. Crowfeather left the army and rejoined his family in Yakima. Within a year he died of a coronary thrombosis, leaving his wife with little money and six young children to raise.

When her husband died, Mrs. Crowfeather related, she "shipped his body back to the Indian reservation in North Dakota because that's where he'd always wanted to be buried." Subsequently, she had little contact with her husband's relatives, and so "the kids grew up without knowing much about their father's family and the Indian way of life. I didn't know much about this either."

Of the Crowfeather children, Ernie alone seems to have been in conflict about his Indian inheritance. His feelings about his background, as we shall see, were strikingly manifested during the fund drive that made his dialysis treatment possible. Ernie's Indian-ness was made the focal point of this effort to "save" his life, and it was the Indian community who responded most strongly to the fund appeal.

A psychiatrist who worked with Ernie at the University Hospital was struck by the fact that "Ernie simply didn't identify with Indians. Whenever I tried to involve him at all with the Indians, he cooled off completely. . . . I think it was partly a denial of this part of his ancestry, and also a certain sense of uneasiness about being identified with a group which on the whole had not been held in very high esteem."

Ernie's mother and an older sister to whom he was very close both remember vividly how from early childhood Ernie had reacted to his Indian heritage. They imply that he may have been more troubled about his ethnicity than the other children in the family because, as the only son, he felt more closely and indelibly identified with what he viewed as the largely negative status of Indian. His mother said that he "was always ashamed and resentful because 'Crowfeather' was his last name. He always felt rejected in school because he was an Indian. I know I probably spoiled him by letting him have things like the good clothes he always asked for. He always wanted to dress and look nice, because he thought that would hide the Indian part of him and make him be more like white people. I know that being Indian hurt him a lot. But near the end, after the fund drive, he used to say to me, 'If it weren't for the Indians, I wouldn't be here.'"

His sister, too, knew how sensitive Ernie was about his lineage. Although he was very close to many of his doctors at University Hospital, she noted, "Ernie still felt that some of them were rejecting him and picking on him because he was an Indian. Dr. N. [a young physician with Indian origins who helped launch the fund drive] was the only one who could call Ernie 'the chief' and get away with it." "Ernie," his sister continued, "always used to say he envied me because I could get married and change my name. I never experienced the rejection he felt he got from white people, maybe because I was never looking for it."

At the same time that he resented his half-Sioux background, Ernie's sister felt, he sought from Indians an acceptance he felt denied by the white community in which he was raised. "Ernie used to search Indians out all the time because he felt rejected by whites. He'd tell me he only felt accepted by other minority groups, like Indians and Mexicans and Negroes. Ernie just couldn't accept things. I suggested that he shorten or change his name, but he didn't feel that would help him."

Ernie, his sister believes, was also strongly affected by two features of his childhood environment: the female-dominated home and the German-Catholic religious atmosphere in which he was raised. "It was hard for him to grow up in a household of women. Ernie didn't like or see much of my mother's relatives; he felt they disliked him because he was part Indian. So he never had any strong male influence. He was just around women. And he was brought up, at home and in school, under a strong Catholic influence." "Ernie never could conform to the strict rules of Catholicism," his sister added, "but he had religious beliefs, and his family was very important to him."

When Ernie's mother and sister were asked what he was like as a child, they described a charming, handsome boy, who loved sports and reading and showed a marked artistic ability. Even as a little boy, they acknowledged, Ernie was often "hard to manage"; Catholicism was one of the many types of authority he found hard to accept. And, they remembered, Ernie often "got his own way," for he always showed a great ability to manipulate people and situations for his own ends. They also depicted an often lonely, withdrawn, and insecure boy, bothered by many things besides the name Crowfeather.

The course of his life from midteens on, they believe, was strongly influenced by two events: his mother's brief second marriage and the loss of his kidney. After these incidents, Ernie became an increasingly troubled youth, rebellious against a society he felt would not accept him, and at the same time seeking out a guidance and discipline he was unable to provide for himself. He also seems to have been deeply affected when an older sister, Bernice, died from a kidney disease in 1960. These aspects of Ernie's life, before the onset of his own kidney disorder in 1969, are captured by the following vignettes from our case materials.

University Hospital. Social Service Report
CROWFEATHER, ERNIE. 1/28/69

Background Information:

At age 14 Ernie was hurt in a fall from his bicycle injuring his kidney. His mother described his kidney as pulverized and added that the organ was removed by a Yakima physician.

The patient's mother had been married a year to a Mr. ______ at the time of the patient's bicycle injury. The step-father was angered by the patient's need for care and so vindictive that the mother took her children and left him. . . .

Ernie apparently recovered satisfactorily from his kidney surgery and resumed his interest and participation in football, basketball, etc. His doctor, however, refused to sanction his playing. In his last year of high school the patient was much interested in a white girl, whose parents restricted her from seeing the patient because he was an Indian. His mother feels that the patient had social problems from this point on and a difficult time adjusting. . . .

[Ernie's mother] spent many years working to support her children. Though she is a small person, she did much heavy work. For years she picked and packed apples.

University Hospital. Vocational Counseling Report.
CROWFEATHER, ERNEST. 4/4/69

Educational and Work History: In 1956 (9th grade) Ernie dropped out of high school. He worked at an uncle's hop ranch for something over a year. After a six month abortive attempt to stay in and finish his schooling, he was caught in an effort to rob a store (bar?). He spent 22 months in the Monroe reform school. There he worked as a kitchen worker, orderly, and library helper. On a parole violation, according to the client, he returned for another 21 months. He spent three more periods, 9 months and 6 months and 90 days, for similar violations. The reformatory also provided him with training in a clerical and supervisory capacity in a warehouse and as a barber. He completed his high school equivalency (GED) also. Prior to his hospitalization he was waiting on a Job Corps placement with the Bureau of Indian Affairs.

ERNIE'S MOTHER: Ernie was always a good kid, until he lost that kidney. He had loved sports, especially running—he was like a little deer. Then the doctors told him he couldn't run and play ball. I think he'd have had a different life if that hadn't happened.

ERNIE'S SISTER: After he lost his kidney, Ernie got more and more quiet and reserved. He never complained about pain, unless he was really suffering. The day he hurt himself in the bicycle accident, he lay in bed bleeding all day. He wouldn't tell anyone, until I came home from school and he told me.

MOTHER: Ernie read a lot. He liked medical things, and stories about what people do when they get desperate—like those books by Thomas Wolfe. He did a lot of art work, too. And he liked animals, and loved children.

SISTER: As a young boy, Ernie loved poetry. He used to write me little notes and poems and put them in my school lunch pail. He read a lot. He was always quiet within himself. He was capable of learning, but it was hard for him to stay in school, or keep a job, because he couldn't conform to everyday things.

Ernie wasn't malicious. He was a quiet boy, and did the little, everyday things he was told to do. But he couldn't cope when it was time for him to grow up and strike out on his own. He functioned best when he had someone to tell him what to do, and help him.

I think a lot of Ernie's problems about accepting responsibility came when Mother divorced her second husband, after Ernie lost his kidney. Then, Ernie wanted to be his own boss, and that's when he started getting into trouble. Mother never could handle him, although I usually could, maybe because I'm forceful.

Ernie was a terribly lonely, frightened person. He was scared to do anything on his own. But he was a con artist from the day he was born. He could make you believe he had blue eyes, when you were looking right at him and could see they were brown. When he first got into trouble, the police tried to help him, and he conned them—he talked his way right out of it.

MOTHER: Every time he did something wrong, he was sorry. He'd say he didn't know why he acted that way. He just would get to a point where he had to do something, because he felt rejected all the time. He used to do things, even like robbery, to get attention because he was so desperate to be rescued. He'd always feel bad afterward. I'd hear him cry.

SISTER: In the last few years, after he started feeling sick, he'd be out of Monroe Reformatory a while, doing fine, and then he'd get into trouble. He admitted to me he was lonely, and wanted help and supervision. He used to write beautiful letters home from the Reformatory. He was always happy in prison.

MOTHER: When my oldest daughter, Bernice, got pregnant, she discovered her kidney trouble. I don't know its origin; her husband wouldn't let them do an autopsy. She was treated at the University Hospital, too. I think her dialysis was paid for by the hospital because the treatment was so new then, and they experimented with her. She just lasted two weeks. She died in 1960, at 26, with complete kidney failure.

SISTER: As a little boy, Ernie talked a lot about religion. He was brought up in a religious atmosphere, where he thought a lot about the meaning of life and death. Later, after Bernice died [when Ernie was 17] and Ernie knew he only had one kidney left, he focused a lot of his worries on getting a kidney infection. He often said he'd never live to be an old man.

DECEMBER 1968–APRIL 1969

Soon after Ernie was paroled from the Monroe Reformatory in October 1968, his health began to decline. Around Christmastime, when he began to cough up yellow sputum and blood, Ernie became frightened enough to go to his family's physician in Yakima. He was given antibiotics, and his condition seemed to improve. On January 2, following "some heavy New Year's drinking," his face swelled markedly for twenty-four hours. Ernie then noticed that he was having difficult and painful urinations (dysuria), and that traces of blood were appearing in his urine (hematuria). He was hospitalized briefly for his condition, and told he had anemia and a urinary tract infection. Tests indicated that his remaining left kidney had no obstructive disorder, and Ernie was discharged, with medication for the infection. His course from this episode through his referral to the University Hospital on January 23, 1969, is recorded in his medical chart as follows:

> Since that time he has felt weak, fatigued and nauseated, drinking around a case of beer every other night. Two weeks prior to admission he noted the onset of frontal headaches and over the past 10 days, he has had swelling of the face, hands, and feet, gaining around 5 to 10 pounds. He then developed intractable vomiting and was hospitalized on January 19. His BUN [blood-urea-nitrogen level in the blood—an index of kidney function] was then discovered to be greater than 100 and his urine output around 150 ml/24 hours. Consequently he was transferred here for further diagnosis and treatment.

The day after his admission to the University Hospital, Ernie was started on peritoneal dialysis to alleviate his uremia, and his doctors began an exhaustive series of tests to determine the nature and cause of his renal problems. The physicians soon discovered, to their dismay, that attempts to treat Ernie by either peritoneal or hemodialysis would be fraught with difficulties. Ernie himself began to suffer a round of new and serious complications, related both to his disease and to the efforts to treat it. The extensive problems of uncertainty, both diagnostic and therapeutic, that he presented during his first two months of hospitalization are graphically documented in the following excerpts from his clinical record.

> On admission the patient was felt to have evidence of hypertensive encephalopathy [brain damage] with recent renal failure, possibly secondary to hypertension. He was initially treated with hydrazine in an effort to lower his blood pressure, which was successful. . . .
>
> A peritoneal catheter was inserted [on 1/24/69] and the patient was begun on peritoneal dialysis. Initially this procedure went smoothly with good dialysis, but the patient soon developed fever, abdominal pain, and bleeding around the site of the cannula. . . . The patient was started on steroids and intravenous heparinization. However, the patient then began to lose blood into the peritoneal fluid during peritoneal dialysis, and heparinization had to be discontinued. . . .
>
> Because of further difficulties with peritoneal dialysis, the patient was placed on hemodialysis [on 2/7/69]. There were marked difficulties with this procedure because of problems with cannula clotting [recannulations were required on 2/14, 3/3, and 3/4/69] and [artificial] kidney clotting. The patient developed a pericardial effusion on Feb. 17 and underwent a pericardiocentesis. . . . On Feb. 21 the patient was taken to surgery and had open drainage of the pericardial effusion and creation of a pericardial window, with drainage into the left pleural space. After a few days of production of large amounts of bloody drainage from the left chest tube, the patient stabilized and the chest tube was removed. . . .

> Soon thereafter the patient developed signs and symptoms of cardiac failure and because the pericardial tamponade could not be ruled out, he underwent cardiac catheterization. . . . Because of further difficulties with cannula clotting the patient was placed on peritoneal dialysis on March 5. Thereafter he has been maintained on peritoneal dialysis with no complications and having good dialyses with maintenance of adequate control of his creatinine and BUN. On March 7 a renal biopsy was performed. . . . [The biopsy showed] changes compatible with both intervascular coagulation and hypertensive nephropathy.
>
> One week after the renal biopsy the patient passed a small amount of blood in his urine and complained of left flank pain. . . . On March 12 he developed a supraventricular tachycardia with potassium elevated to 7.4 and was treated with intravenous calcium, with lowering of his potassium to 6.0. . . . After the patient had been stabilized on peritoneal dialysis, further hematologic evaluation was carried out which showed that he had a markedly abnormal platelet half-time of 2½ days and marked elevation of fibrinogen turnover time. This was felt to be evidence for continuing intravascular coagulation and hypothesis was raised that the patient's remaining kidney was responsible for continuation of this process.

The hospital record describes what Ernie's physicians called a "medical disaster." From a social service report, the physicians also learned that their new patient might provide nonmedical management problems, and that financing the costly treatment of his life-threatening illness would be difficult and probably impossible for his family.

Social Service Report: 1/28/69

> *Impression:* It appears that the patient, his mother and sister are all very much aware of the gravity of the patient's problems. They all recall vividly the demise of the eldest daughter and are saddened and frightened.
>
> This patient is on parole. . . . He is described as being fond of women and has been involved in two common-law marriages. When the first wife became pregnant, the patient left. She and her child are supported by the Welfare Department. The patient then became involved in the second relationship.
>
> The Parole Officer describes the patient as immature, irresponsible and impulsive, adding that he has always been over-protected by his mother. The mother has had "nervous breakdowns." The Parole Officer states all the other children are responsible citizens and that the step-father is a hardworking laborer who pays his bills and conducts himself very well. The Parole Officer verifies that the patient is talented artistically.

> The patient has a pleasant and winning manner but has evaded discussing himself.
>
> In checking with the Hospital Business Office, his sister made a $300 down payment on his admission and his mother and sister have signed an agreement to pay up to $2,000 at $30 per month. The patient has not lived on an Indian Reservation since he was 2 years old. . . . [The] Director of the Indian Health Office at U.S.P.H. Hospital . . . was positive that since the patient had not lived on the reservation since age 2, he had no benefits coming.

By the end of March 1969, Ernie's condition under peritoneal dialysis appeared to have stabilized. For his family and his physicians at the University Hospital, the source of funds for long-term treatment now became a central concern. The costs of any one of the three treatment options available to Ernie—transplantation, hemodialysis, or peritoneal dialysis—seemed to be beyond the limited resources of his family or of the hospital.

"We had no way to pay for his treatment," Ernie's mother stated. "We barely lived from paycheck to paycheck, and had no insurance. And Ernie couldn't get any insurance because he only had the one kidney. By the time he died, Ernie's doctor bills were over $280,000. For a family, that's an impossible cost. Unless you have a silver spoon, no one can raise that kind of money."

After his death, Ernie's mother and sister recalled their emotions during his first months of treatment. In their voices, one could still hear the anguish they felt at the pain and suffering they saw him endure, and the financial barriers that seemed to block any alleviation of his plight. The cost of a transplant, they knew, was beyond their means. And, as they understood Ernie's case, money rather than the problems he had encountered with dialysis was preventing the implantation of a permanent dialysis catheter for long-term treatment. In their words and tone, however, there seemed to be no bitterness against the University Hospital physicians, but rather a profound sorrow and amazement that a situation such as Ernie's could exist in the United States.

"You hear Apollo this and Apollo that," Ernie's sister declared, "and you suddenly realize that people are dying because they haven't any money for treatment. . . . I appreciated the efforts of the hospital, and the doctors' kindnesses to Ernie. But to have the doctors keep puncturing his stomach with those peritoneal catheters, over and over again, and say they can't implant a permanent catheter because they need $5000–6000 first or to say they won't transplant him until they know the

$20,000 cost will be paid—that's pretty hard to take. How do you weigh a life against $20,000, even though that's a lot of money?"

Ernie's mother, who had moved to Seattle after his admission to the University Hospital, also talked with distress about "how the doctors said they had no funds, so they couldn't put in a permanent dialysis catheter. I remember how he lay there and just took it. Each time they put another catheter in, the pain got a little worse, and he got more and more upset. We were all there with him as much as we could be. He and I would talk sometimes, and it was heartbreaking. I think it was the worst thing possible, next to death—to sit there and see him suffer, because you haven't got the money to take care of your child."

In early April Ernie's physicians sought to resolve his financial problems by applying for home dialysis treatment through the Northwest Kidney Center. For several reasons, neither they nor Ernie and his family were optimistic about his candidacy. His case was complex medically, especially in view of the shunt and kidney clotting problems he had experienced with hemodialysis. Dr. Henry Tenckhoff, one of Ernie's primary physicians at the University Hospital, felt that Ernie might do well on home peritoneal dialysis. But Dr. Tenckhoff had only recently developed techniques to permit long-term home peritoneal dialysis, and (in a colleague's words) he was "battling" to have the Kidney Center accept it as a mode of home treatment. In addition, the center's selection committee would consider other nonmedical facets of Ernie's case in deciding his eligibility for home dialysis treatment. "The doctors [at the University Hospital] told Mother and me," Ernie's sister recalled, "that the center would weigh Ernie's financial status and the fact that he hadn't been a very 'productive' citizen."

Ernie's application was rejected by the Kidney Center's Medical Advisory Committee. Ernie's lack of financial resources and his personal history, including an "unstable home situation with a common-law wife," entered into their deliberations. Ernie's unconventional life-style evoked a certain amount of moral disapproval from committee members. But they were also more neutrally concerned with the difficulties that his domestic situation might create for a safe and effective home dialysis regimen.

Ernie's prison record was also considered by the committee. "We knew he'd been in the Monroe Reformatory for breaking and entering, or something." However, in the words of one committee member, "it didn't sound like a major crime so it wasn't in itself a strike against him."

The committee's final judgment was stated purely in medical terms. In their opinion, Ernie's shunt-clotting problems, coagulopathy (blood clotting in the artificial kidney) and other medical factors indicated that he would not do well on home dialysis.

At least in front of his family, Ernie reacted calmly to the news of his rejection by the Kidney Center. "All he said to me," his sister recalled, "was 'Well, they told me they wouldn't accept me. Maybe I won't be around as long as I thought I would be.' Ernie even joked about it some. He had a good sense of humor about his situation until the end, when he just lost his will to live."

Ernie's family then began a desperate effort to find money for continuing his treatment. "I told him there were ways to get money, and we would," his sister related. "We first tried to get money from Welfare, asking if funds were available from the Indian Agency in North Dakota. The agency didn't even reply for a long time, and then we finally got a short note saying there were no funds. Then we wrote to a state senator, but he told us no funds had been appropriated for a case like Ernie's."

THE CLINICAL RESEARCH CENTER, APRIL–SEPTEMBER 1969

Ernie's physicians at the University Hospital shared his family's distress over his rejection by the Kidney Center and were determined to find a means for continuing his treatment. They realized that certain unusual and puzzling aspects of his renal disease might make Ernie eligible for admission to the hospital's Clinical Research Center (CRC), where he could be treated and his case studied through research grant funds. A "historical review" of Ernie's case, prepared for us by his primary physician, recognizes that his transfer to the CRC was not solely impelled by his challenging medical problems.

> Because of the rather unusual features of his renal disease, a "unique opportunity study" was formulated, applying to the Clinical Research Center for six months of dialysis support including initial nephrectomy and final renal transplantation in an effort to demonstrate whether the coagulopathy that was involved in his renal disease would abate after nephrectomy and whether transplantation could be successfully performed thereafter without recurrent disease. This became necessary because the patient was turned down for dialysis support by the Northwest Kidney Center on account of his medical history, his background including the lack of a stable home, and lack of financial support.

Ernie's rejection by the NKC, as we indicated earlier, was the primary stimulus for the formation of the University Hospital's Dialysis Utilization Committee, which has enabled a limited number of dialysis patients to receive in-hospital dialysis treatments and home training by means of research funds. When members of the Kidney Center staff were asked how they felt about the hospital treating a patient like Ernie, whom the center had rejected, they responded as follows. Dr. A.: "They've got the right as long as they don't expect us to fund them. I guess that's what it comes down to. Any private physician could do it if he wanted to, as long as he's expending funds from somewhere else." Dr. C.: "This has been the problem historically. In the earlier days a number of the patients that were rejected here were then accepted at the University Hospital on a research grant basis. When the grant money runs out, what happens to these patients? They're on dialysis, we feel a community commitment to treat all patients with chronic renal disease, and therefore we are obligated to take these people on and assume their financial burden."

The commitment Ernie's physicians felt to him was not unique. The bond between Ernie and his physicians in many ways typified the close, intense, at once personal and collegial relationship that often develops between clinical investigators and the patients they care for and study. As Belding Scribner said to us, using Ernie as an example of his own and his colleagues' involvement with their patients: "You get locked into these things and can't quit. At some point in time we become committed to these patients. We don't know exactly when that is, but once it happens, then we find it impossible to let them die."

The response of Ernie's physicians to his rejection by the Kidney Center, then, was in many ways prototypic. But at the same time, their relationship with Ernie had some special nuances and was increasingly stressful. The fact that Ernie was half-Indian, and thus belonged to a minority group whose history and present socioeconomic conditions disturb many more advantaged persons in this country, was one element in the physicians' reactions to Ernie and their relationship with him. As one physician put it, "There was a special sense of injustice about his having so many problems."

Second, and perhaps more important, were Ernie's own personal qualities. His physicians knew that he had many nonmedical problems, as evidenced by his prison record. He was often labeled by psychiatrists, social workers, and others as a sociopath.[1] The hospital staff found him "difficult" in many ways. But they all liked Ernie Crowfeather.

1. According to the most recent system of nomenclature adopted by the American Psychiatric Association, the "antisocial type" of "sociopathic personality" that was attributed to Ernie is now termed an "antisocial personality." The second edition of the

DR. SCRIBNER: Ernie wasn't that clever, but in his own uneducated way he was a very intelligent type of guy, intuitively. He was a con man in certain ways. The way he manipulated people was unbelievable. . . . I liked Ernie, but I tried to stay clear of his case because of the terrible complexities. Dr. Tenckhoff seemed willing to take the brunt of our side of it, so he was the guy who sort of carried it all.

DR. TENCKHOFF: Despite all the problems and headaches he gave us, Ernie was very much liked by his doctors, which is strange. His inability to get along with his medical regimens was extremely frustrating to us. He had many appealing qualities. He was artistic, and very verbal about his feelings. He was honest, except for self-deceptions—and then he'd deceive others, too. Ernie was always pleasant, and very apologetic about his failures. He had the appeal of a child who needed help.

DR. G. [a psychiatrist]: When I first met Ernie, I could see very quickly that he represented a chronic challenge. The nurses didn't quite know how to handle him. He would be rather uncooperative about his dialysis—moody, demanding, difficult.

Ernie's knowledge of himself was that he was a man doomed. I'm reminded of a few other young patients I have known, who knew that they were facing a life-threatening illness with a probably fatal outcome. Without a prior history of what we might call "sociopathy," they, too, decided "as long as I have to die anyway, I might as well try to get all I can out of life." Ernie really didn't seem to appreciate all the special things that were done for him; he took it all for granted. And, like every person whom one might diagnostically call sociopathic, there was really no awareness of one's death and obligations. . . . Ernie, like sociopaths generally, was very impulsive, and the immediate gratification of his wishes was a predominant concern of his. . . .

American Psychiatric Association's *Diagnostic and Statistical Manual of Mental Disorders* uses this term for "individuals who are basically unsocialized and whose behavior pattern brings them repeatedly into conflict with society" (p. 43).

The classic work on this type of personality disorder, formerly designated as "constitutional psychopathic state" or "psychopathic personality," is Dr. Hervey Cleckley's *The Mask of Sanity* (St. Louis, Mo.: C. V. Mosby Co., 2d ed., 1950, pp. 355–56). According to Cleckley, the sociopath's clinical profile has sixteen dominant characteristics: "1. Superficial charm and good 'intelligence'; 2. absence of delusions and other signs of irrational 'thinking'; 3. absence of 'nervousness' or psychoneurotic manifestations; 4. unreliability; 5. untruthfulness and insincerity; 6. lack of remorse or shame; 7. inadequately motivated antisocial behavior; 8. poor judgment and failure to learn by experience; 9. pathologic egocentricity and incapacity for love; 10. general poverty in major affective reactions; 11. specific loss of insight; 12. unresponsiveness in general interpersonal relations; 13. fantastic and uninviting behavior, with drink and sometimes without; 14. suicide rarely carried out; 15. sex life impersonal, trivial, and poorly integrated; 16. failure to follow any life plan."

> One of the unfortunate things about Ernie is that he stereotyped the prejudices or images that people have about the American Indian—unreliable, shiftless, demanding, alcoholic, somewhat potentially or actually criminal, unable to form long, intimate relationships. . . . But I was aware of the fact that I really liked Ernie in spite of it all.

On April 27, 1969, Ernie was admitted to the Clinical Research Center "for his nephrectomy, then repeat studies, and subsequently for renal transplantation." Ernie was to receive a cadaver kidney, when one became available, for "a search for a living donor was made, but no compatible donor was found."

Ernie's physicians had cause to be pleased with the outcome of their "unique opportunity study" stratagem. For the next six months, Ernie's treatment, including the cost of a transplant, would be borne by the CRC. Then, *if* the new kidney functioned well and was not rejected, the major part of Ernie's financial problems would be over. Ernie and his family, too, were relieved of a major worry. But his transfer to the CRC did create some apprehensions. "I was frightened when the doctors told me he could be treated by a research grant," Ernie's sister remembered. "I didn't want them to try things on him. One day, he called me and said 'the doctors want to put an artificial kidney in me. Maybe it will work.' I said, 'Ernie, you're kidding. You're on the top of the transplant list. Just wait.'"

The day after his admission to the CRC, Ernie's single kidney was removed, and he started peritoneal dialysis three times a week. After recovering from his nephrectomy, Ernie was allowed to leave the CRC between most dialysis sessions. In addition to receiving treatment and undergoing various studies, Ernie also was taught home peritoneal techniques, "and learned them rapidly." The CRC staff, however, like the Kidney Center, found that Ernie did not have a home situation that would be favorable to a successful home treatment program until his transplant occurred. Ernie's mother could not stay in Seattle indefinitely to help him with dialysis and manage his strict diet because she had a husband and a teen-age daughter in Yakima. Ernie's girl friend was initiating divorce proceedings against her husband and planned to marry Ernie when the divorce was final, in about three months. In the interim, she could not provide Ernie with the type of home assistance he would need. And, even assuming that Ernie could manage his own care, he had no income to provide himself with housing. Thus, "due to lack of a home," Ernie's physicians "elected to keep the patient [on dialysis] at the CRC."

Ernie's six-month course of treatment and study at the CRC was not a smooth one. "Largely due to inconsistencies in sterile techniques, he contracted a total of three peritoneal infections." Never an ideal patient, Ernie became increasingly "moody, demanding, and difficult," and uncooperative about following his medical regimen. "On one occasion," his record notes, "when he got mad at the nurses, he disconnected his dialysis catheter with his bare hands and left the hospital."

The problems that CRC personnel encountered with Ernie also involved their plans to have him train for a job that he could assume after his transplant. The week he was admitted to the CRC, Ernie was interviewed by a vocational counselor and given various intelligence and aptitude tests. His report read in part as follows:

> *Counselor's Impression:*
>
> The patient was most cooperative, congenial, and verbal in the interview. He appeared relaxed and confident and spoke frankly of his reform school experiences. At the same time he greatly oversimplified and "played down" the reasons for his several stays there. His smooth interaction with the counselor and others, his history of trouble with society's standards, his embellishment of his experiences impressed this counselor as being rather typical of the sociopath (another conjecture!).
>
> *Summary and Recommendations:*
>
> Ernie's present condition might be expected to demand 3–7 nights per week on dialysis. He appears to be mildly anxious and compulsive in his behavior, and might have some difficulty adjusting to social demands made of him. . . .
>
> The following recommendations seem to be tenable:
>
> (1) that, in spite of his social history, medical condition, and prognosis, Ernie should be considered a candidate for vocational rehabilitation,
>
> (2) that such rehabilitation, limited in scope, be sponsored and undertaken by the Division of Vocational Rehabilitation, if possible,
>
> (3) that the patient's training be directed toward a vocation allowing him considerable autonomy, and which also enables him to perform certain minimal administrative functions, e.g., warehouse dispatcher, stock clerk, sales clerk, office clerk, or worker, etc.

Ernie had some training as a barber, and following the vocational counselor's findings, his physicians "went through many procedures and problems to get him enrolled in barber school, and get special hours for him." "Multiple and persistent efforts" were made to motivate Ernie to utilize this opportunity, about which he expressed enthusiasm, but "he completely fell down on this; he barely followed through, going only to a few training sessions."

Ernie's sister was familiar with the behavior patterns he showed on the CRC—his moods, failure to accept responsibility and act on his own initiative, his difficulties in adhering to regimentation, and his "charming con man" approach to most people and situations. She had seen all these patterns in Ernie since he was a young child, but she also attributed many of his attitudes and actions while at the CRC to an increasing fear of the endless studies and dialyses. "At first, Ernie truly was a very good patient. He'd let the doctors do anything to him without complaining. But after a while, he got so frightened of pain he couldn't bear the thought of anything else being done."

To his psychiatrist, in turn, Ernie's reactions to his medical regimen represented a familiar pattern of denial, a reaction to his illness that was exacerbated by Ernie's "sociopathic personality."

> As is frequently the case with men who are sick, their illness, to them, is identified with weakness and weakness is identified with lack of masculinity. I think I would explain Ernie's almost desperate attempt to deny to himself over and over again the fact that he needed treatment two or three times a week, and just had to lie there and take it, partly on that basis. . . . I think it's likely that the sociopathy he displayed was present without his illness, and then was tremendously accentuated.

Near the end of Ernie's allotted six months on the CRC, his fiancée obtained her divorce, and they were married. With public assistance funds the couple were able to rent an apartment in Seattle. Subsequently, because Ernie's time on the CRC was running out, he was started on home peritoneal dialysis.

TRANSPLANTATION AND REJECTION: OCTOBER 1969–NOVEMBER 1970

Ernie's physicians were not optimistic about his prognosis on home dialysis. They felt it was fortunate that on October 14, 1969, just a few days after he started home treatments, a cadaver kidney was obtained and Ernie received his transplant. Ernie's new kidney, from a twenty-year-old woman, was a "C" match. The implantation went smoothly, and his post-operative course was "essentially uncomplicated." Ernie was discharged from the CRC on October 29 on an immunosuppressive therapy of prednisone, Imuran, and ALG. He was scheduled to report at regular intervals to the hospital's Renal Transplantation Clinic for post-transplant checkups.

On November 5, through a laboratory error that yielded a falsely high creatinine level, his physicians diagnosed an acute rejection crisis. Ernie had a renal biopsy, received intravenous prednisone and a radiation treatment at the graft site, and had his oral prednisone dosage increased. The following day, when his creatinine test was within normal limits, the laboratory error was discovered. Ernie's prednisone dosage was reduced to its former level, and he was discharged.

After this episode, Ernie's transplant appeared to be functioning satisfactorily, and his prednisone dosage was further reduced. There were indications, however, that Ernie would again be a management problem for his physicians. His chart, for example, notes that on December 18, Ernie "was admitted for a planned platelet survival study. However, patient leaves hospital the same evening without giving reason."

From late December through February, Ernie spent much of his time in the hospital, fighting off a rejection episode and the infections that are a constant hazard for patients on immunosuppressive therapy. When he was discharged on March 5, "essentially improved," Ernie boarded a train for his mother's home in Yakima. By now his life was further complicated by a failing marriage, and he and his wife had separated. "I know Ernie really loved his wife," his sister related. "We tried to tell her how ill he was, but she married him anyway. Ernie was very hurt when his marriage didn't work. He had hurt her a lot, but he still expected her to stand behind him."

En route to Yakima on March 5, Ernie felt a sudden pain in his chest and shoulder. The pain increased over the next few days, and he entered a hospital in Yakima with a fever and chest and shoulder pains. On March 27, Ernie was transferred back to the University Hospital. A presumptive diagnosis of splenic infarcts was made, but his physicians decided not to remove his spleen because he still had an infected wound in his abdominal wall. Ernie was discharged "improved" on March 31 to be followed weekly at the Renal Transplantation Clinic.

In the first six months after his transplant, as we have seen, Ernie experienced a series of complications—rejection reactions and infections—common to many organ recipients. These problems, as we read in the following extract from his case history, continued over the next eight months, culminating in the removal of his transplanted kidney on November 23, 1970. During this period Ernie again struck out against society or, as many feel, again appealed for help and the institutional guidance he seemed to need and desire. Ernie committed an armed robbery, immediately surrendered to the police, and then attempted suicide in his jail cell.

> Although in good physical health on the whole, the patient did not try to find employment and most of the time hung out with friends. About the middle of May, after ample alcohol ingestion, he was involved in an armed robbery in a local motel, following which he gave himself up to the police in a nearby bar. He was taken to the local jail, where he attempted suicide and was transferred to Western State [psychiatric] Hospital on 5/20/70. From there he would come to his clinic appointments under guard. . . . During this time at Western State Hospital it was noticed that his renal function was declining, and on 10/8/70 he was readmitted to the University Hospital for renal biopsy because of more rapid deterioration of renal function and duodenal ulcer.
>
> There has been some question about the consistency of his taking the prescribed immunosuppressive therapy. By 10/27/70 his renal function had deteriorated to the point at which it no longer sustained well-being and he was transferred to the medical service. He was restarted on peritoneal dialysis on 11/6/70 with the intention to retrain him for home dialysis with the possibility of a future second transplant. On 11/23/70 his renal graft was removed.

The loss of Ernie's transplant was not the only rejection he underwent in the fall of 1970. At the end of October, when it was evident that his kidney function was irreversibly failing, Ernie faced the same plight he had when first admitted to the University Hospital: how to pay for dialysis treatments. Once again, his physicians turned to the Northwest Kidney Center. On November 5, the center's patient admissions committee met to review Ernie's candidacy. The record of that session states:

> Ernie Crowfeather presented by Dr. ——— is a 28-year-old separated male who had been previously rejected by the Medical Advisory Committee in April 1969. He subsequently received a transplant . . . and is being re-presented for dialysis at this time because the transplanted kidney is failing. Careful evaluation of the medical, psychiatric, social, and rehabilitation reports revealed a long history of recidivism, and that he was again in custody for a felony at the time of his present University Hospital admission. Mr. Crowfeather has been historically uncooperative in his medical management both before and after his transplant. Medical, psychiatric, and social worker opinions reveal little hope for successful reform and indicated a highly probable inability to manage home dialysis. The consensus of the Committee was that Mr. Crowfeather would be an unsuccessful dialysis patient due to medical and emotional instability. It

was moved and seconded that Mr. Crowfeather be denied treatment. Motion passed unanimously. Rejected.

A year after Ernie's second rejection by the Kidney Center, in the course of interviews conducted by Dr. Lawrence K. Altman of *The New York Times,* several staff members discussed why Ernie was twice refused treatment by the center, and the pros and cons of those decisions. They also considered whether the center's policy had changed sufficiently in the interim that if Ernie were a candidate today he would have a better chance of acceptance.

DR. E.: I think at the present time the situation with respect to selection is a little bit different from Ernie's day. . . . [A]t the moment, I think it's fair to say that people are only rejected on . . . mainly medical grounds. You see, it's very hard to distinguish medical, social, and psychological factors at this level. I think we're very liberal now. We take patients whom we have a very good idea are going to cause us a lot of problems, cost a lot of money, and be very difficult to handle. If Ernie came back again now, and it appeared to us that he couldn't be hemodialyzed, I think we might accept him now for peritoneal dialysis.

DR. G.: We're in a position today of not having to be confronted by selection dilemmas very often. . . . We can go a long way because of our financial condition. But we still have a selection committee. And I think the thing that scares everybody here is that we might, if funds were cut, have to go back to the previous selection process, where you're using such intangible factors to select a patient because there are no absolute criteria; they just don't exist.

DR. F.: By the time Ernie was presented to us the second time, in November 1970, he had received all three types of treatment that are available, and he had failed in all three. And the possibility of getting another transplant for him just looked like a hopeless situation. In fact, the only thing in our minds that would be open to him would be in-center dialysis, which the NKC does not offer.

DR. G.: When Ernie came up the second time, he was on probation. He should have been incarcerated and treatment provided at that point. But we didn't have the facilities, and the authorities didn't want to handle the responsibility of having to take him to a hospital for dialysis under guard. I think that was one aspect of his rejection. Another aspect was the fact that we don't do in-center dialysis anymore. . . . So we take the case of Ernie Crowfeather. He was going to cost what we estimated to be $21,000 a year for in-center treatment, and that would support six people at home, at $3,500 each. We just don't have enough funds to blow them all on one patient when it's very questionable as to whether he can survive the medical and other complications. What is our obligation? How far can we go? One theory is that you spend all the money you have, take everybody in, and when you're broke, you're broke. Another view is that you've got a responsibility to the patients now on the program, that you've got to provide care and treatment for them as ongoing patients.

Dr. F.: I agree that he might be accepted today if his first candidacy came up again. But I think his second application might still be denied, because he'd gotten in so much trouble with the police, for example, and hadn't been good at looking after himself from a medical point of view.

Dr. G.: I think this is where Ernie's is a classic case, because it falls into that gray area of decision where you get into so many problems. Whether a person is or can be rehabilitated is a very subjective thing. Can this individual operate at home by himself? You can't tell about a lot of these things until you get into them, and today we can be very liberal because of available financial resources. . . . I can think of two or three people we've taken this year who had a criminal record or were accused of some crime. . . . Since Ernie, we've had another patient who got into legal trouble while he was on dialysis, I think for armed robbery. But I don't see how that alone can jeopardize a person's standing with the Kidney Center. I mean we can't turn him off. This a commitment that we make to people. Once they get on the program, there's no way that we're going to drop them. We're financially and morally committed to that guy for as long as he lives. . . .

Mr. Z.: So far, we've gotten through Russian roulette without blowing our brains out.

Dr. F.: You can outline quite a story from Ernie's side. You know, "This is my last will and testament, and this is what society has done to me." The establishment, the Kidney Center, the University Hospital, society in general couldn't have responded to his accusations. Everybody was in a defenseless position because he could have presented a very dramatic case. "I have been rejected and denied life-saving treatment because (a) I'm an Indian, (b) I've got a criminal record, (c) I have no money, (d) my wife has left me."

THE ERNIE CROWFEATHER CAMPAIGN FUND: NOVEMBER 9, 1970–FEBRUARY 1, 1971

Ernie's second rejection by the Kidney Center seemed to signal the end of his economic and medical struggle to live. With his kidney transplant no longer functioning, and without funds for dialysis, death from uremic poisoning would occur within a few weeks. "Ernie really didn't suffer through his first series of dialyses and the transplant," his primary physician believes. "But when the transplant failed, he became extremely unhappy. He really didn't want to live." His mother and sister, too, feel that Ernie began to lose hope and to abandon the will to live in November 1970. "He'd ask me, 'What are we going to do now, Mom? Am I just going to lie here and die?' "

But once again, the intense way in which those who knew Ernie became involved in his case led to another temporary financial reprieve. This time those who were determined to "save" Ernie went "outside the medical system," launching a massive public fund-raising campaign. Ernie's Indian heritage was the fulcrum of this effort. It motivated the actions of his fund raisers, was the dominant theme of their campaign, and served to rally an extensive local and national response from both Indians and whites.

Three people initiated and guided the Ernie Crowfeather Fund: Dr. N., a young physician of Indian ancestry, who had been a resident at the University Hospital and treated Ernie during his first months there, and who was working at the Indian Health Clinic in Seattle in November 1970; Mrs. J., a social worker with the Washington Indian Center in Seattle, who was herself an Indian; and Mr. D., a Seattle social worker with the American Jewish Committee.

Mr. D. and Dr. N. had met and become friends through their work with several Indian organizations in Seattle establishing the Indian Health and Dental Clinic. When Dr. N. learned of the Kidney Center's decision, Mr. D. recalled, "he came to my house that night and told me what was happening to Ernie, and that Ernie would die, and he said, 'What do you think?' And, I suppose because I'm a human being, a social worker, a Jew, and an American, I said, 'Well, we just can't let him die.' I just couldn't understand how they were going to pull the plug on this character and just let him go, no matter who he was. And I suppose the fact that he was an Indian and that he was discriminated against, which I think he was, probably added to it. So Dr. N. and Mrs. J. and I set out as a committee of three, initially, to convince the hospital to continue his treatment and from there on to raise the money."

Mrs. J. had first heard of Ernie in the spring of 1969 after his first rejection by the Kidney Center. "A friend called me and said, 'there is a twenty-seven-year-old guy who is going to die because he has no funds and a bad kidney.' We started thinking about doing something for him, but then he got picked up by a research project, and they did a transplant and the problem was solved. Then, a year later, I went to volunteer at the Indian Health Center, and Dr. N. told me there was a young man who would be dead in two to four weeks if he didn't get some funds. When he mentioned Ernie's name, I said, 'Oh, that's the same young man that had the problem last year,' and I told Dr. N. I'd like to get involved in an effort to help him. So the three of us got together with a group of the doctors, and then it was determined by the hospital board or somebody that we had to raise $20,000. It was a lot to do, and we did just about everything we could think of to get the money."

The nonprofit Ernie Crowfeather Fund Drive started on 9 November 1970. The University Hospital, after a series of meetings with Dr. N., Mrs. J., and Mr. D., had agreed to provide Ernie with dialysis treatments, *if* the fund drive could raise $10,000 by December 20 and another $10,000 by early February. Mr. D. and Mrs. J. both remember how Ernie's physicians discussed his many personal and medical problems with them, and their fears that, money or not, his prospects were dubious.

> MR. D.: When we first began to meet with the doctors at the hospital, they told us what we would be going through and they practically assured us that Ernie was not going to make it, that he was going to become antisocial, that he was manipulative. And we found out that he was. He was a wonder. And we didn't believe it. We really passed it off as being prejudice against Indians. I think if we had it to do over again, we would have gone about it differently. We wouldn't have gone out and sought public donations. I think we would have focused more on the system, on changing the system. But we didn't have time. We were facing a life and death problem, and that problem was to meet a deadline, to raise $20,000. We didn't have time to really lobby the Kidney Center and the hospital.
>
> MRS. J.: They told us at the outset Ernie was suicidal, and said it wasn't worth the effort of raising the money for him when so many others were in need. But we felt we had to do it, that Ernie was just another typical example of the plight of Indians. . . . Dr. N. said, "Knowing all these things, you must decide. He may be a sociopath, he may be suicidal, he may be wasting our time." I don't know. . . . I think Ernie was great at managing people.

Convinced that Ernie's problems in obtaining treatment were due to his being part Indian, his fund raisers focused their campaign on events that would appeal to the Indian community. On November 23, 1970, the day Ernie's transplant was removed, the *Seattle Post-Intelligence* carried a story headlined "INDIAN BROTHERHOOD KEEPS ERNIE ALIVE." The article described the Crowfeather Fund Drive's activities and featured an interview with Ernie, arranged by his fund raisers in which he talked about his illness, his feelings about being part Indian, and what the fund drive meant to him.

> "Two weeks ago," Ernie said, "my doctor noticed that my chemistries had dropped drastically, and informed me that the kidney had failed.

"I've had so many operations that this one doesn't bother me at all. I'm not afraid of the pain. I've got the best doctors I could have. There are so many scars on my abdomen I've suggested they install a zipper."

Ernie approaches most things calmly and with humor. And he acknowledges that his illness has changed the course of his life in fundamental ways.

"I wasn't raised as an Indian," he said. "My father was Sioux, my mother is German Catholic, but I had little contact with Indians as I grew up.

"All my life I was thought of by others as Indian but I found it difficult to identify with Indians. Now I feel something better than proudness—I'm reaching for some other word which would fit. It is Indians who are helping me, and I realize clearly what I have missed. . . .

"In some ways," he added, "I don't know where I stand. I saw a picture in the papers the other day and had a feeling that I was just an Indian being exhibited. I felt that it wasn't me.

"Don't put me up there on a pedestal, I think to myself, and demand that I fulfill all those obligations. Don't hang those on me like an albatross. If you do that I won't be me. In other words, it boils down to this: am I going to be a good or bad Indian? I can only be me. . . ."

Last week Indian friends gathered at the hospital, and under the leadership of Sioux medicine man, Frank White Buffalo Man, grandson of Sitting Bull, assisted in a Sioux ceremonial healing rite for Ernie, including the ancestral prayer pipe.

After today's surgery, Ernie will require a peritoneal dialysis machine to stay alive.

"That machine is pretty ugly," he said as he pointed to it. "I have—what do you call them?—ambivalent feelings about it. A love-hate relationship. But I know that that machine is my life.

"When I first learned of my disease, my reaction was that it was probably the end. . . .

"Now I believe everything is going to come through and I'm going to live to a ripe old age. I'm learning to live with a new purpose."

Mrs. J. and Mr. D. remember vividly and proudly the range of fund-raising efforts for Ernie and the generous response to these appeals.

Mrs. J.: We thought it should be an Indian thing, since it was an Indian problem. . . . I think nothing like this has ever taken place before, where we, the Indian community, all became so united. We sort of planned it that way. The Indians had to get behind this one guy. And Ernie's problems, you know, his mental problems, were such typical Indian problems. This society destroys Indians. I don't think Ernie was unusual in his problems. Some of us survive it, and he didn't.

I started by going to a meeting of the American Indian Women's Service Committee, I told them about Ernie, and said, "Well, what are you going to do about it?" We . . . set up a press conference. . . . We formed committees, and always had people going around with coffee cans, collecting nickels and dimes. Once we found a $20 bill in a can, and wondered what Indian was rich enough to stick that much in. So while the Indians didn't give a whole lot of money, they all pitched in and really became involved. The Seattle public schools put on an Indian Heritage program, one hour a week, and they'd charge a little admission money and turn it over to us. . . . Whenever there was an Indian meeting in town, I'd go and make an appeal, and they'd resolve to help however they could. . . . The first big effort we made was at a football game during half-time. We collected about $1400 that day.

We called all the national Indian figures we could think of and asked them for their help. They all got involved, and they thought of asking the Bureau of Indian Affairs to contribute. I think they gave over $1000. That December, some of our people went as delegates to a National Congress for Indian Opportunities in Washington, and set up public projects through that meeting. Then there was a big movement between school kids, who set up various projects and also elderly people who sent in dollars and dimes. We also had things like a two-day jazz and rock concert, and an arts and crafts fair. It really was a wonderful experience, and I think Ernie was delighted with it. The course of his life was changed.

When they first told us we'd have to raise $20,000, I thought we'd never do it, with the depression and all. I thought we might get $10,000, and then help Ernie to get Bureau of Indian Affairs benefits, which he was entitled to. If he went back to the reservation, we thought, he could qualify for medical care, but there just were no facilities there to keep him alive. We tried to get him funded through an Indian Public Health Service Hospital, too. The head of one of those hospitals was asked at a reservation conference, "How come you aren't helping Ernie Crowfeather?" And he said, "Oh, I could help him. But if I take $20,000 and keep Ernie alive, that means your children won't get their vaccinations." And that just took care of it right there. I really took exception to his statement because I figured there goes somebody pitting the reservation Indians against the urban Indians.

But it all turned out okay. We announced around the middle of January that we'd reached our goal, and had a public thank-you. We raised just about $23,000.

MR. D.: I think the Ernie Crowfeather campaign probably did more to solidify the urban Indian community than any other single incident I can

> remember. . . . And I think the public, in general, learned something that most of them didn't know. People were astounded to learn that for a mere $20,000 a life was going to waste. . . . We were able to put Ernie up in front of a TV camera and get ten pages on him in newspapers, telling people that here's a twenty-eight-year-old Indian who's been rejected by the whole world, and let's not let this character die. Ernie had nothing going for him, and everything going against him, which was great from a publicity standpoint. "Crowfeather" literally became a household word. People were breaking their backs to send him money.

Ernie's fund raisers omitted two facets of Ernie's case from the publicity campaign. First, Ernie's full history—including his criminal record, suicidal behavior, and difficulties in following his medical regimen—was not mentioned. To a psychiatrist who had worked closely with Ernie, the fund appeal's portrayal of him was "nauseating because it was sentimental and untrue. . . . It was almost sickening to see the sentimental appeal for saving this poor Indian boy. I'm not saying that any life is not worthwhile. But the whole thing was dramatized and romanticized through wide publicity. The Ernie Crowfeather Fund was a real tear-jerker."

Those involved with Ernie's campaign also decided not to dwell on the complex set of social and ethical issues inherent in the operation of the Kidney Center. "In the beginning," Mr. D. stated, "the papers started to play this up in terms of Ernie's rejection by the center. But we sat down with a series of newspaper people and told them that they would be doing the center and the public and those who needed the services and the University Hospital a tremendous disservice. We didn't want to hurt the Kidney Center. This wasn't our intention. Our intention was to save Ernie, and to try to change the Kidney Center. We were successful in one and not the other. I think the center has done a good job, and I think the public knows it."

The Kidney Center, as Mr. D. realized, was in a potentially vulnerable spot concerning the Crowfeather Fund. Their operation, which is dependent upon generous public support, could have been jeopardized if Ernie was portrayed as a terminally ill patient who had been twice rejected by the "white system," the center, because he belonged to a minority group. When Ernie's campaign started, one of his physicians at the University Hospital stated, "You should have seen the reaction of the people at the center. They were petrified. They didn't know where it would end. All due credit to the Indians and those helping them. They did their job with good restraint, and they didn't point a finger at the center, which they easily could have done—the white man rejecting the

Indian. . . . The whole reputation of the center was on the line. It could have been a disaster for them; they were right in the middle of a fund drive."

After Ernie's death, members of the center's staff recalled how they had reacted to the Crowfeather Fund Drive.

> Mr. Z.: We cooperated. We did that for two reasons. One was selfish—his need for funds occurred at the same time we were launching our fund drive. We had to be careful not to conflict, and we worked with his fund raisers and helped them. The whole thing resolved itself in a very nice fashion. There was no hue and cry that the center did this to us, and now we need some money. The majority of the general public didn't differentiate between the center's drive and the Crowfeather appeal. Ernie's was the first appeal that I know of for someone already rejected by the center. But in the past, center patients had to go out into the community and raise their own funds. So people are very used to this type of appeal, and it had no effect whatsoever on our drive.
>
> Dr. G.: Ernie's people raised the question whether, if they went out and raised money and gave it to the center, we would then accept Ernie. We had to say no. The decision to reject Ernie wasn't specifically a financial one. This is the framework in which we have to operate. . . . I think the publicity about Ernie's case has been very well handled from all standpoints. There were no accusations, no throwing of rocks. But everywhere I go, people ask me about Ernie. Everybody knew about him.

ERNIE'S LAST CHAPTER: DECEMBER 1970–JULY 29, 1971

On December 6, 1970, after his transplant was removed, Ernie was discharged once again. He was to return to the hospital for peritoneal dialysis treatments until enough money had been raised, and other preparations completed, for him to begin home dialysis. About Thanksgiving time, he and his wife had worked out a reconciliation and rented an apartment in Seattle so that he could obtain home care.

Ernie's family believe that he was genuinely moved by and deeply thankful for the public's response to his case. "Ernie greatly appreciated the funds raised for him," his mother affirmed. "He saved letters from people, especially schoolchildren, and tears would roll down his cheeks while he read them. He often said to me, 'Mom, if it weren't for the Indians, I wouldn't have this care.'"

Despite his professed gratitude for the funds that enabled his treatment to continue, Ernie did not adhere to the strict routine necessary for a successful dialysis program. Between January and March 1971, while he was on home peritoneal dialysis, he was frequently admitted to the University Hospital. His charts record admissions for "technical problems with dialysis, minor drug overdosage, analgesic and narcotic abuse, and abdominal pain of unknown origin," plus several sign-outs "against medical advice." Ernie's drug dependency had developed over a period of several months as he became increasingly reliant upon painkillers to blot out the discomfort that went with his many infections and various medical tests and treatment. His need for drugs, Ernie's records note, was "a major management problem throughout the remaining months of his life. He was seen on numerous occasions in the emergency room requesting pain medication; also on many occasions under false names [he] went to other hospitals requesting and receiving drugs. On 1/31/71 he was admitted for an acute barbiturate overdose."

On February 28, Ernie entered the hospital with a severe purulent infection around his peritoneal catheter site. A new catheter was inserted for an overnight dialysis, then removed the following morning when Ernie was discharged. Until the infection cleared up, his physicians decided, Ernie again would have to endure "acute catheterization," returning to the hospital every two days to have a peritoneal catheter inserted into his abdomen for an overnight dialysis.

The infection, however, did not respond to medication, and a "large area of Ernie's abdominal wall became involved with a cellulitis" (an inflammation of cellular or connective tissue). With this condition, Ernie could not undergo peritoneal dialysis. His only other treatment option was hemodialysis, a procedure that had not worked well, because of clotting problems, when Ernie first entered the hospital in January 1969.

Ernie was placed on hemodialysis at the University Hospital on March 9, 1971. Subsequently, his physicians arranged a "special contract" with the Veterans Administration Hospital, and Ernie was transferred there for home dialysis training and biweekly treatments. His records chart Ernie's downward spiral after beginning hemodialysis.

> He did not attend his dialysis treatments regularly and never showed up for the special training sessions arranged for him. In the interval, he would show up at the University Hospital with multiple physical complaints, some of which were based on medical complications. . . . In addition, he was admitted on many occasions because he had missed one or several of his regularly scheduled dialyses at the V.A. Hospital.

> This is one of many UH admissions for this 29-year-old Indian male who enters for hemodialysis. Ernie missed his dialysis time at the V.A. Hospital Kidney Center secondary to prior preoccupations with both drugs and

alcohol. He spent three days in a stuporous state, claiming that he was not going to undergo further dialysis and wanted to die.

Ernie's friends will not soon forget their ceaseless efforts to get him to utilize the home dialysis machine he was given or to report to the V.A. hospital for treatment after the machine was removed from his apartment because he failed to use it properly and regularly.

MR. D.: I know that Dr. N. was there at Ernie's house at two o'clock in the morning trying to counsel the guy and adjust the machine. I was there in the middle of the night many times, and on the phone, my God, at two, four, seven o'clock in the morning. I know how his doctors at the V.A. and University hospitals and Mrs. J. all tried to help him. If we could have a dollar an hour for what we did, we would literally have been able to stop working.

DR. A.: One of the big failures in Ernie's case, probably the thing that tipped the balance toward his death, came when he just couldn't cut it on home dialysis. He was doing fine from the medical-technical point of view. He just goofed it up.

Ernie became increasingly unresponsive to the efforts of his family and friends. He dreaded and avoided his hemodialysis treatments and, as his family saw him, began not to care whether he lived or died.

ERNIE'S MOTHER: Toward the end, Ernie said if he had it to do over again, he'd never have gone on the hemodialysis machine the first time. He said he'd never relive that suffering no matter how much money he had. . . . He had nightmares about having to go on that machine. I'd hear him crying and moaning in his sleep, and he'd tell he'd dreamt that the tubes were strangling him. It was horrible. . . . Unless you have a child of your own, you can't imagine what it was like to know that his life depended on that machine. I'd have given my life to spare him that suffering.

ERNIE'S SISTER: Though Ernie sometimes felt alone, we were with him. Those last few months, when he was so sick, one of us was always with him at the hospital, around the clock. . . . The way he suffered was terrible, day after day. A lot of it may have been self-made—Ernie could have been a lot more comfortable if he hadn't abused the gifts of the heart from so many people. But a lot of his suffering was also due to the operations and tests and dialyses. . . . His lack of responsibility was why he wouldn't learn how to run the home dialysis machine. He was afraid of it, and wanted someone else to be in charge of it. . . . He always hated to go into the dialysis room at the hospital. He'd plead with me, "Don't ever let them do that to me again. . . ." After he lost the transplant, he just started to give up.

In the second week of July a new, excruciating problem was added to the load Ernie was already finding it hard to bear. He learned that his $23,000 fund was almost depleted.

ERNIE'S SISTER: Ernie knew that this money was his last resort. People had helped him more than he ever thought possible. He was frightened beyond belief when he was told that the funds were running out. He felt maybe he wasn't worthy of a second appeal. He'd call me, and say, "I'm going to die. The doctors tell me I can only get a few more dialyses unless I raise some money."

ERNIE'S MOTHER: Ernie was supposed to be on dialysis three times a week. But he said, "I can't afford it twice a week, so what would happen if I went three times a week?" He was always worried about the money part of it. I think that's why he didn't report for dialysis a lot of times; he was trying to stretch out his treatments. . . . When he knew the money was almost gone, he'd lie in bed and say he felt like it was all over for him now, and he couldn't ask all those poor people who'd given him money to do it again. He just gave up, from the way he acted and the things he said. He was an unhappy boy. Those last two weeks, his attitude was, "I don't care. No one can help me anymore."

Ernie's physicians at the University Hospital met with his fund raisers, Mr. D. and Mrs. J., to tell them the news and to explore with them the agonizing issue the doctors now faced: given his personal and medical record, should Ernie continue to receive treatment once his funds were exhausted? Mrs. J. was bitter and angry because the physicians might now deny Ernie treatment. But slowly she and Mr. D. also began to perceive the full facts of Ernie's case and to appreciate the complex problems facing his physicians.

MRS. J.: I knew we had problems with Ernie, but I had no idea how severe they were. I was really distressed that the hospital waited until the money was about gone before they told us. In view of the fact that we went to all the trouble of raising that money, we should have been notified how fast it was being used up. In retrospect, though, I don't think it would have done any good even if we had known. I think Ernie had really become suicidal at that point. The doctors told us there would be another meeting of the hospital board to determine what their responsibility was about giving him treatment if he showed up for dialysis. . . . I said, "Well, are we to be involved in having to decide he's going to die? When I worked so hard to save his life, I don't think it's right; I don't like it."

MR. D.: When Mrs. J. and I met with the people at the hospital, we for the first time began to understand some of the painful questions that the doctors have to cope with. And I think we probably made a decision at that point that there was probably nothing more that we could do for Ernie. But it was very tough for us. We're bleeding hearts, both of us.

At their meeting with the University Hospital physicians, Mrs. J. also learned that just that day Ernie and his wife had separated again. "I called his wife," Mrs. J. related, "and I said, 'Did you know that Ernie hasn't had treatment for a week, and that he's going to be dead if he doesn't go in for dialysis?' And she said, 'Well, I don't know where he is.' She became quite upset, and I told her, 'You'd better find him, and tell him to get treatment if he wants to live, and tell him the hospital is going to decide in the next week or two whether to keep treating him.' Then I called Mr. D. and told him, 'I can't buy this, permitting Ernie to die.' I told him to call Ernie's wife, too, and also to call his mother. When he talked to the mother, she told him that at three o'clock that morning she had put Ernie and a girl friend on the train to come back to Seattle. So we located the girl friend's apartment, and went there and told Ernie to get a dialysis, which he did."

After this dialysis, Ernie again skipped his scheduled treatment at the V.A. hospital. Then, on July 18, "after heavy alcohol intake," he attempted to rob a restaurant at the Hilton Hotel, telling the cashier, "there's a bomb on every floor." He was arrested on the spot, charged with "creating a disturbance," and taken to jail. A few hours later, Ernie began complaining of abdominal pain and nausea. The police took him to a nearby hospital, and he was then sent to the University Hospital for dialysis. "The patient," his chart states, "was given one run of hemodialysis and discharged to the Police Department."

Ernie was in prison for about one week. During that time, he was taken under guard to the V.A. hospital for dialysis. His sister was with him during his last treatment. "He told me he knew he only had money for two more dialyses. He was just beaten, with no money and divorcing his wife. He said, 'I can't take take this any more. I'm not going to be dialyzed again. I'm going to go out and drink myself into oblivion. No one cares any more. The only thing that worries me are all those little kids who sent me money.' "

According to newspaper accounts, Ernie's brief tenure in jail ended when the prison authorities "allowed him to forfeit a $50.00 bond." His release, in part, was prompted by the efforts of Mrs. J. "After the Hilton robbery, I had one of the agency people go down and talk to the probation people, and tell them Ernie couldn't stay in jail for very long because he had a kidney problem. Then, they just let him out." Upon his release, Ernie disappeared.

While Ernie's friends and family searched for him, his physicians at the University Hospital met "to decide what we were going to do when Ernie came back." They spent long, soul-searching hours over what is perhaps the most complex, difficult issue they can face: the overt termination of a patient's treatment. As it applied to Ernie Crowfeather, however, their discussion was academic. Ernie did not return. He disappeared, taking with him $2000. This money included a large check for his treatment at the V.A. hospital, which he had somehow intercepted and cashed.

ERNIE'S SISTER: Ernie knew one of us would make him report for a dialysis. That's why he disappeared those last few days, so we couldn't make him do it. Before he left, one of my sisters did take him to the hospital for a treatment. She left him at a motel in Seattle, and he waited awhile and then caught a plane back to Yakima. Then he vanished. I found out that he left some money for his wife, and bought her some clothes, and paid back some of his friends, and just gave some money to other friends. He only had a few dollars left in his wallet.

He called me at my home on July 29, from a motel in Ellensburg. I'd been going out of my mind for a day and a half, because no one could find him. He told me he'd seen a doctor in Ellensburg the night before, and that day, because he was so sick from not having been dialyzed. Then he said, "I'm so alone. I can't go back to the University Hospital, because they won't help me anymore." I told him he was wrong, that Dr. B. would help him. Then I called Dr. B., and told him I'd found Ernie and could I bring him back to Seattle. Dr. B. said, "I'll be here." I got to Ernie's motel in Ellensburg as fast as I could, and took him right to the emergency room at the Ellensburg Hospital. He died there, about eleven that night.

REFLECTIONS

ERNIE'S UNIVERSITY HOSPITAL PSYCHIATRIST: When it was all over, I remember I had a certain sense of relief; this death was necessary, was the feeling. There was nothing in it for Ernie. I liked him very much, but I could not feel sad when I heard he had died. I just asked myself, "What was the meaning of his life?"

For a person like Ernie, almost no physician will have the courage to turn off the machine while he is in the hospital. Not because it wouldn't seem like the right decision, but because to explain the decision, if called upon to do so afterward, would be so complicated. . . . If Ernie had made it back here from Ellensburg, I think he would have been dialyzed again. Fortunately, doctors haven't been confronted with too many Ernie Crowfeathers, yet.

DR. G. OF THE KIDNEY CENTER: If Ernie hadn't died in Ellensburg, if he'd come back, and been presented a third time here, I think we would have rejected him again. I think that just everything Ernie did the last year he lived, after we rejected him the second time, emphasized the fact that the Kidney Center had made the right decision on this individual.

MRS. J., THE FUND RAISER: It was worth it to me, and I think to all the people who became involved. Ernie was a guy in trouble, and we did something about it.

I think in a way that Ernie had a strong will to live, and a strong will to die. . . . An Indian counselor told me that the strong message she had gotten from Ernie was that he sat by and watched life happen, but he didn't see himself as part of life. That is probably as good a description of Ernie as any.

I felt that everything was done in the system to keep Ernie from living, even the way he was. The recurring theme was that this guy wasn't worth it, why waste time on him when you could save a lot of other people. Who's entitled to say who is to live and who is to die? You know, there's no priority on who should live.

MR. D., THE FUND RAISER: Ernie really had more than his chance. There were so many of us who bent over backward. He wouldn't accept psychiatric help. He wouldn't even learn how to run the dialysis machine. . . . We couldn't have raised the money again, nor do I think we would have. Ernie didn't want to live, and I can understand that.

ERNIE'S MOTHER: I think that if Ernie had had some money, and felt more secure, he wouldn't have given up. He had a lot of fight, but he just felt like, here I am, I'm going to die. This worked on him; no one likes to die.

ERNIE'S SISTER: Ernie wasn't self-pitying, but he often said, "Why does all this have to happen to me?" I think it might have taken a person like Ernie to go through what he did. . . . Ernie did a lot of living in his life, and I think he died the way he would have wanted to. My mind might be more at ease if I really knew why Ernie abused and hurt himself and others so. I feel there's something unfinished about Ernie's life.

DR. BELDING SCRIBNER: One major thing I think I've learned from Ernie's case is that the selection system has worked, at least in Seattle, because the principals involved are willing to let it work. What is selection, basically? It's the decision by somebody on some grounds that a person will not be permitted dialysis, or a transplant, which says in effect that he must now die. And the system works because the doctor involved, or the family, or the patient himself, recognizes that his is a rational decision, a form of euthanasia, if you will.

But I also know that anybody who wants to beat the system can do it. A lot of people more deserving than Ernie get selected out because they're "dumb bunnies," too "square" to question or try to manipulate the system. Ernie went outside the system to get treated. And this posed a terrible problem for the University Hospital, because we're not supposed to touch anybody who isn't appointed by the Kidney Center. We have no mechanism for funding, and we don't know how to handle somebody who comes in with $20,000 and says, "I want to be treated." If you have money, there's no system. Nobody is going to let you die if you have money.

The selection system probably isn't going to hold up very well much longer. The public, or average guy, is going to become more and more aware of what the selection process really means, and the more awareness there is, the more difficult it's going to be to select. In the long run, it's going to be a lot simpler to put everybody on dialysis, an Ernie included, and hopefully let them kill themselves in due course if that's what they want to do. It's the only rational way to solve this selection problem. Working through this whole issue of selection, at least in this culture, is infinitely more difficult than just putting a few losers on among the 95 percent that will do reasonably well. Selection then will take the form of advising the patient and his family that we don't think this treatment is right for him, that it would be a fate worse than death to dialyze or transplant him. If the patient doesn't agree, he'll be taken regardless of the expense or the difficulty. The alternative is the route we went for two years with Ernie, which is intolerable for everybody.

When we met to discuss Ernie's case, just before his death, I felt that if anybody was to blame for the jam the University Hospital was in, it was the failure of the penal system to be able to cope with the situation. They abdicated their responsibility completely. If anybody had held up the Hilton and said there was a bomb on every floor, he would have been in a fairly precarious position legally. But they just let Ernie out in a few days, because he was so sick and they didn't want to assume the responsibility for his treatment.[2]

2. This indictment of the penal system by Dr. Scribner and some of his associates is sociologically interesting and significant. In the sociological view, both sickness and crime are forms of deviance, because they entail nonconformity to "normal" social expectations and responsibilities. One of the major distinctions between them is that whereas illness is defined as "not the fault" of the individual, and thus as semilegitimate, behavior that is considered criminal is not exempted from condemnation and incurs punishment rather than treatment. Typically, in modern Western society, serious illness is cared for in a hospital, whereas crime is dealt with in a prison. As our society moves progressively toward defining many actions that were once deemed criminal either as illness or as the consequence of social evils, and as our concept of dealing with those who have engaged in crime becomes more oriented toward personal rehabilitation and social reform, the distinctions between crime, sickness, and injustice become more blurred. The case of Ernie Crowfeather is complicated not only by these changing definitions and the ambiguities they create, but also by the fact that at the same time he was guilty of criminal acts, gravely ill, and receiving a type of extraordinary treatment not routinely available in a prison hospital. In a sense, Ernie ended up "commuting" between prison and the University and V.A. hospitals as much because of indeterminacy regarding which institution had primary responsibility for his care, as because of the complexity of his medical condition. The irony of his predicament is that had chronic dialysis and renal transplantation not yet been devised, Ernie would not have been alive either to receive treatment or to be sentenced to jail.

Why can't we figure out a way to terminate a patient when it seems reasonable to do so, when he's indicated that he wants it, too. It really isn't fair to a person to prejudge his ability to cope with dialysis. And yet we do this because we're afraid to get locked into a situation we won't know how to handle. We can't get out once we start. But for some reason, if you don't start a guy, if you don't get really involved with him, the fact you know he is going to die, and then does, doesn't seem to bother you so much. But once you've seen him on the machine, and walking around, then the thought of not dialyzing him and having him die just becomes overpowering.

When we had those last meetings about Ernie, just before he died in Ellensburg, a lot of people spent a lot of time deciding what the hell we were going to do if he came back. We finally agreed that we would literally have never pulled the plug on Ernie, or anybody else. I said at that meeting, "I really don't think we can kill Ernie. I just can't see the logic of killing Ernie Crowfeather." I know it would have probably been best for everybody, but when I thought about it in the most basic ethical way I am capable of, I said I really don't think we can let Ernie die. It's so foreign to the total effort we make that it just about undoes you to even contemplate how you would go about it. Here's Ernie walking down the street. Sure he robs banks, but he's a nice guy, and people like him. But even liking him isn't important. He's a person who's alive, and you know how you can keep him that way. And suddenly you're asked to say, "Okay, this is it. You can't be alive anymore."

If Ernie had come back again, we would have treated him. But that would have been begging the question. As long as an Ernie Crowfeather succeeds in beating the system, it indicates that we're not ready to handle the problem of priorities and selection.

PART FOUR

BELGIAN MEDICAL RESEARCH

Journal Intime Belge/ Intiem Belgisch Dagboek

I write this in the salon of my Brussels apartment, this first week of my third summer in Belgium. What is it—let me be frank—what is it that I am looking for now? I search and research, no longer just pursuing the "professional" questions that first brought me here, nor content with the scholarly way I once thought of them: "How Various Social, Cultural and Historical Factors Affect Medical Research and Research Careers in Belgium. . . ." Now I know that I must begin to understand Belgium—for itself. I must begin to look for the Belgium beneath the modern, orderly, energetic, burgher-solid and -sensual exterior . . . the Belgium hidden behind exquisitely synchronized mailmen and the trains that arrive precisely *à l'heure;* sidewalks scrubbed at least once a week with soap, water, and brush by all respectable housewives; big apartment buildings—concrete "blocs"—springing up everywhere; immaculate, new Common Market plants; raucous processions of shiny cars; Frigidaires, television sets, and transistor radios, ballpoint pens, Kleenex, Scotch tape, and all the brands of toothpaste and cigarettes in the thriving stores; basketloads of flowers for sale on every corner, in every market and square; the succulent, abundant, all-important Belgian cuisine—huge amethyst grapes, parchment-crisp French-fried potatoes, miniature sea-sweet shrimp, heaping platters of astoundingly varied cold

---

From *Columbia University Forum*, Vol. 5, No. 1 (Winter 1962), 11–18.

cuts and cheeses, whole shops of creamy chocolates and opulent pastries (freshly made each day, and arranged like precious jewels), pungent black coffee, good aromatic cigars, cheek-flushing Burgundy wine, cafés-full of every standard brew of beer, and a whole series of variations uniquely Belgian—Kriek-Lambic, for instance: beer flavored with cherries. . . .

But now I am aware that there is also a Belgium less palpable than this—older, deeper, less rational. It is that undisclosed Belgium I want to know and understand.

I think the landmark most generically Belgian on my street is the red mailbox on the wrought-iron gate . . . a shiny red mailbox with two slots: the one on the left-hand side of the box with instructions for mailing letters printed in French, the one on the right-hand side of the box with the same instructions in Flemish. (Should letters *written* in French be mailed in the French slot, those in Flemish in the Flemish slot? And what ought one to do with a letter written in English?)

This reminds me of the beginning of last summer when I stayed at the University Club here in Brussels for several weeks. My first evening there, I went to the writing room hoping to catch up on my correspondence. I sat down at one of the room's two writing desks filled with University Club stationery. The first piece of paper I pulled out was headed in Flemish—and the second, and the third. . . . A little more rifling through the desk confirmed that it was all Flemish. My eye moved speculatively toward the only other writing desk in the room, a desk in every physical detail identical to the one at which I was seated, placed at precisely the same angle, on the diametrically opposite side of the room. I crossed the room to discover that it was filled with stationery exactly the same in all respects but one: it was exclusively headed in French rather than in Flemish. For a diabolical moment I considered mixing a little bit of French and Flemish stationery in both desks, but I restrained myself.

In Belgium, not only letterheads and mailbox slots, but virtually everything is divided and replicated at least twice over. Speeches, lectures, sermons are delivered twice, once in Flemish, once in French. The street on which I live has two names, printed on a bilingual sign: "Avenue Louise—Louiselaan." I've just discovered that Mons and Bergen are the same city: Bergen is the Flemish name for Mons. Or is it vice versa? And if I were a Belgian of Flemish extraction who owned a French-manufactured Peugeot car, would I join the Royal Belgian Automobile Club or the Royal Flemish Automobile Club?

My travels this past week have taken me first to Flanders, the Flemish-speaking part of Belgium, and then to Walloonie, the French-speaking part.

Early Tuesday morning, I set off for Ghent, in Flanders. I rode west from Brussels, deep into the Flemish countryside. Through the windows of my brisk and tidy little train the flat landscape seemed infinite—misty, dream-shrouded, yearning toward an intuited sea (one senses it, but where is it?). We moved across the Flemish "prairies"—past silver rows of delicate poplars, all turned in the same direction by the wind from the somewhere ocean, past miniature cows and muscular horses grazing, the grass intensely, strangely green, past old, whitewashed farmhouses, their fervid red roofs ablaze in the fog-filtered sunlight. And soaring up out of this flat, flat land, the great towers of Flanders, fashioned by men who longed for mountains, freedom, supremacy, Heaven itself. Towers filled with bell-music-like voices, in a haunted land, where from behind every tree and door and shuttered window some shy, frightened, suspicious presence seems to be peering out at one, and the apprehension, distrust, silent fury of centuries hover like ghosts on the foggy air.

I was invited to spend the weekend at the summer home of friends in the Ardennes. So on Friday afternoon I traveled east and south from Brussels, into the *pays Wallon*—Walloonie. Through the windows of this train, gentle, rhythmic, human-sized hills, green with forests of miniature pines, as delicate and carefully arranged by Nature as the trees in Japanese paintings. Shiny, sinuous rivers—partridges and pheasants darting nervously across a field, taking to the air with a whirr—the gray stone farmhouses of Walloonie, and its gray stone Romanesque churches, hewn out of the land—a special gray, full of the mist, the rain, the melancholy, the flinty strength and lustrous piety of the peasants who built the shrines that you see at the crossroads, and decorated them with tidy nosegays of geraniums and roses from their gardens. . . .

On Monday morning, we drove back from the Ardennes into the very Walloon city of Liège. Liège comes on you all at once. No belfries and clock-towers in the distance, as when you approach a city in Flanders. You round a bend of the River Meuse, and suddenly, there is Liège. . . . The "strange capital of nuances" and of antitheses. Girdled by mines and black slag heaps, shrouded in smoke from the furnaces, mills, and factories by which it is ringed round . . . Yet built like a great balcony overlooking the gleaming River Meuse, romantically arched by bridges . . . The birthplace of the dynamo and the "Béatitudes" of César Franck . . . More French than France, and yet (perhaps from Germany on which it borders) something Teutonic in its sentimentality, its logic . . . As if the essence of Proust and of Wagner had somehow been blended with Belgian fog and energy and factory smoke . . . .

I went to visit the Free University of Brussels today, primarily to speak with its rector and its secretary-general about the progressive *dédoublement* of the courses that the university offers. Originally, all its classes were taught in French; but since World War II, various parts of the university have doubled their facilities, duplicating professors who lecture in French with those who can lecture in Flemish, so that all courses may be taught in both languages. Most recently, the medical school has been "doubled." Forty-four students are enrolled in the new Flemish section of the medical school, and with their advent, the rector and secretary-general both admit, some new problems arise. Where will the University of Brussels find enough competent professors to teach in Flemish, when the completely Flemish-speaking State University of Ghent and the Flemish section of the already doubled University of Louvain employ so many of them? When the present first class of Flemish-speaking medical students reaches the clinical stage of their training, should they be assigned exclusively to Flemish patients to prepare them for the practice of medicine in the increasingly monolinguistic Flemish part of Belgium? And how many more Flemish medical students can the University of Brussels expect to recruit in future years?

Of course, the Flemish students thus far enrolled are mostly of middle-class origins and subscribe to the "Free Thought," Masonic, anticlerical, religious-philosophical convictions on which the University of Brussels is founded. But Flemish nationalism has reached such a crescendo that most such young Flemish are too *Flamingants* in their sentiments to be happy attending a school in alien Brussels that, though increasingly populated by Flemish citizens and increasingly bilingual, is not part of the mother soil of Flanders. And so, the secretary-general feels—as do any number of others with whom I have spoken this summer—that, as "absurd" and wasteful as it may be in many respects, it is more probable that a fifth university will be created at Antwerp (Flemish-speaking on Flemish soil, non-state and Free Thought). If such a university is established, it is all but inevitable that still another university, an equivalent *French* one (French-speaking, in Walloonie, non-state and Free Thought) will immediately be founded either at Mons or Charleroi. In a sense, that will really make eight universities in Belgium, a country smaller in area than the State of New Jersey: the French and Flemish sections of both the Free University of Brussels and the Catholic University of Louvain (four), plus the two State Universities, Flemish-Ghent and French-Liège (six), plus the two contemplated new universities (eight).

Now, because each of the universities represents a different combination of these social and cultural distinctions that ride and rend every part of Belgian life, each tends to seal itself off hermetically from the others. The universities are veritable cloisters—the Belgians say so—with a very limited traffic between them. (Outside of the occasional exceptional case, one gets a faculty position, if at all, only at the university where one was a student.) An extraordinary amount of energy is expended in jealous competition with what are defined as the other *rival* universities (and rival departments in the *same* university). Some of the competition is of the positive, rather American sort. A good deal more of it is not: try to keep "the others" from having what you have, and certainly from what you haven't. . . . But the type of competition in the medical schools (at least) that is most characteristically Belgian of all is competition for identicalness. To wit—*they* have a Swedish artificial heart machine, 1960 model, color, slate gray. *We* must have an artificial heart machine, too, and one precisely like it in every detail. Not an American machine, a Swedish one; not a 1961 model, a 1960 model; not a green one, but exactly their tone of slate gray. Result (give or take a little for my provisional research so far): sixteen artificial heart machines, four artificial kidney machines, four betatrons, four cobalt bombs—some of them still in crates, standing unused in hospital or research institute corridors; 1200 separate university research institutes; an undetermined number of chairs without professors, a far greater number of competent, aspiring professors without chairs or university nominations of any sort. . . . All this crowding the landscape of a tiny country whose greatest length is about 175 miles, and greatest width about 90 miles.

Some very Belgian statistics that I've been collecting: the little country of Belgium is divided into nine provinces and 2633 communes! Here sit the very proud, highly autonomous local governments of this constitutional monarchy. The King's official title is "King of the Belgians," *not* "King of Belgium." There are over 15,000 social organizations (societies, clubs, associations, academies, etc.) formed around special interests, which, to take a somewhat extreme case, become so special as to give rise to an Association of Hammer-Handle Makers of Lower Ixelles.

I wonder—has it occurred to those who know the plays and prose of Michel de Ghelderode (the reclusive Belgian writer whose works burn so with the carnal mysticism of Breughel and Bosch, of a centuries-ago Spanish Flanders), has it occurred to the people interested in Ghelderode that he is a quite contemporary Belgian social critic? In one of his earliest tales, for example, Ghelderode describes the arrival of Kwiebe-Kwiebus, a picaresque mythical Flemish philosopher, in a city "bristling with belfries":

> . . . And in all these belfries, the bells ringing without respite made a carillon cacophony. The philosopher entered the city, which was like all

> other cities except that it was divided into one hundred very well delimited districts, each one having its belfry with its bell. Kwiebus went from district to district, noticing that the inhabitants of one district had no desire to know the inhabitants of the other. And in each public square the idlers, at the foot of the tower, exclaimed with admiration: "Isn't our bell unique; could there possibly exist another that even approaches it in accuracy, tone, size, form, the peal of its tongue! . . . The marvelous bell!" . . . "The marvelous bell, indeed!" Kwiebus exclaimed to himself. And the idlers pursued him: "Having heard our bell, you would be very foolish if you went to hear those of our neighbors. What a pity! Just so much beating of cauldrons!" . . . And Kwiebus moved on into the adjacent district, where people pursued him with the same remarks. Having scoured the town in this way and heard one hundred different bells, Kwiebus concluded that these connoisseurs of cow-bells, by dint of hearing only one bell, heard only one sound. . . .

Ghelderode is still exhausted by his grave illness this winter. And he was never inclined, even in younger days of better health, to admit strangers behind the green shutters of his ground-floor apartment in a working-class district of Brussels. Nevertheless, he and his wife asked me to visit them again today. ("But no, you are not a stranger," Ghelderode wrote me after my first visit to him. "Without ever having seen you before, I had the sense of recognizing you—but from where, when . . . ?")

I arrived at Ghelderode's front door at twilight. ("Come preferably after five o'clock," Ghelderode had written. "The light changes then. . . .") Madame Ghelderode opened the door, and once more I was ushered into—I can think of it no other way—the Ghelderodean universe.

This time he was at his work table in the salon, seated in a carved, throne-like Spanish chair, over which an antique crimson velvet cover, gold-embroidered with some kind of royal insignia, had been draped. And for the next few hours, nothing was real, nothing existed for me outside the room ("my little museum of inexpressible things, my collection of imponderables," Ghelderode calls it), the man who presides over it, and the phantoms and apparitions, romantic, mischievous, macabre, demonic, that haunt both his salon and his soul.

We talked, surrounded by masks; marionettes from the traditional puppet theatres of Brussels and Liège; seashells from the beaches of Ostende in Flanders; swords and scabbards; ancient Madonnas; crucifixes, church hangings, a Gothic stone frieze reputedly a fragment from the sculptured face of Brussels' Hôtel de Ville; discarded dress-shop dummies in various states of theatrical dress and undress; two carousel horses from a carnival or *kermesse;* and whole walls of paintings. Paintings—the graphic language of silent Flanders.

But the room was filled, too, with Ghelderode's words: his elegant, precise, elaborate, archaic French, infused somehow with the enormous, frenetic energy, the sensual joy, the terror and violence that are Flemish.

Ghelderode told me that he has me identified now—some of the heroines in the tales of Edgar Allan Poe, with their purity, phosphorescence, other worldly eyes, *not* their malignancy, he teasingly assured me, and a certain princess in a youthful work of Maeterlinck. But what I like best is when Ghelderode calls me *"cher ange maigre"* ("dear skinny angel").

Before I left today, as on every preceding visit, Madame Ghelderode served me many large cups of strong, savory coffee, and a whole platter of tastefully arranged, delicious *pâtisserie.* It must be she, the good Belgian housewife, who keeps the Ghelderodean museum so exquisitely neat, systematically arranged—and perfectly dusted!

Monseigneur Van Wayenbergh, Recteur Magnifique of the Catholic University of Louvain, paid me a tea-time visit today. Wearing his black soutane, purple sash, large black beaver hat, and amethyst bishop's ring, he drove his black Buick with its red leather seats up to my front door, and emerged from it, carrying a package of newly harvested purple grapes that he had bought for me at a roadside stand on the highway between Louvain and Brussels.

As he came up the front steps of my house, two images flashed through my mind in rapid succession: the first, a history-book rector magnificus advancing through the streets of Louvain in the Middle Ages, *un très grand personnage* dressed all in purple, preceded by five beadles carrying a silver mace and golden staffs, and followed by a phalanx of servants, before whom everyone—the citizens, magistrates, and burgomaster of the town, as well as the students and faculty of the University—bowed respectfully as they moved aside. And then, an image from my own first summer in Belgium, two years ago. Looking out my window one afternoon at the ancient, cobble-stoned street below, just as two young novitiates in white robes, with sandals on their feet and shaven heads, emerged from the radio store a few doors away carrying a transistor set. Climbing into their waiting 1959 Volkswagen, they drove noisily and speedily away. . . .

At the University Hospital in Liège today, I was taken to see a suite of "new" operating rooms. They have actually been under construction for several years, and now look almost as if they had been blitzed. All work on them has been stopped while the next stage in the sequence of required discussions, applications, agreements, and permissions is awaited. The minimal progression of steps, I was told, goes something like this: University → "Commission Mixte" (representatives of the University, Commission of Public Assistance, and Medical School) → Commission of Public Assistance → Communal Council → Permanent Deputation → Ministry of the Interior → Ministry of Finance → Court of Accounting → Ministry of Public Health → City Planning.

On the way to see these operating rooms, the young surgeon who accompanied me laughingly remarked that they had recently discovered that the local Commission of Public Assistance is in charge of painting walls *outside* the Hospital and the State is in charge of painting walls *inside* the Hospital. No one yet knows to which agency you ought to apply in order to make needed repairs on windows.

Two scenes from Ghelderode's play *The Blind Men* suddenly come to mind:

Three blind men, probing the ground with their sticks, holding the edge of each other's coats, are traveling back and forth, week after week, along the same roads in old Brabant, not far from Brussels. They travel hoping, believing, they are advancing along the road that leads to Rome, the end of a pilgrimage. Suddenly, in the distance, they hear a carillon playing a Flemish song: The bells of Rome, ringing out in our honor! they joyously conclude. "You'd think it was the carillon at Bruges where I was born," says the first blind man. "Rather the magnificent one in Ghent, my noble city," says the second blind man. "It's identical with the one at Antwerp, that city of riches where I came into the world," says the third blind man.

After seven weeks, though, the blind men begin to wonder whether they may not only be retracing their steps. They seek directions from a Voice, which has from time to time seemed to echo their own. The Voice turns out to be Lamprido, the one-eyed king of the ditch country, otherwise known as the country of the blind. In order to help the three blind men who call out to him, Lamprido descends from the tree in which he has been perched. "I see who's coming," says the first blind man. "He's a tall man with a round hat." "No," says the second blind man, "he's a little man with a square hat." "Keep still!" says the third blind man. "He's a tall man who's become little because he's hunchbacked like a crane. And his hat is only a cap with sewn-on medals. . . ."

At the University-affiliated Institute I visited today, the young research physicians entrusted me with a copy of a report they drafted last year and finally submitted to "whoever the responsible persons are who determine the policy of the Institute." The grievances and recommendations they discuss in this document are "usual," almost inevitable, for most young professionals the world over, I suppose—problems of salaries, status, equipment. . . . It's not the concrete difficulties these physicians describe that I find so striking, but rather the impalpables:

> As early as 1956, the *assistants* and *adjoints* of the Institute were feeling a certain amount of discontent. This discontent led to our establishing an association. . . . On the 16th of November, 1956, for the first time, the association sent a letter to the Scientific Director of the Institute setting forth some of our problems. Other letters were sent and interviews were held but without any real results. . . . It became clear to us that the framework within which our interviews took place was totally inadequate. In effect, they took place half-officially, half-officiously, with persons who declared that they themselves were without power of decision or even information . . . !
>
> It is remarkably difficult to know who determines the policy of the Institute. If one tries to find the responsible agent for a given situation, one finds oneself confronted by a maze of entwining organizations: the Board of Directors, the *Assistance Publique*, the University, the Faculty of Medicine, etc. . . .
>
> It cannot be denied that a serious state of crisis is developing at the Institute. . . . The future of the Institute appears uncertain.
>
> Up until now we have not been listened to. Therefore, we asked *Monsieur le Professeur* to allow us to meet the personages who *are* responsible on the Board of Directors, in such a way that it would be possible for the Board or its representatives to answer our questions and to satisfy some of our essential needs. . . .

This document—so many of the conversations I've had this summer—my own often oddly frustrated attempts to learn, to identify—make me think of K., the Land-Surveyor, moving in the strange village of Kafka's *Castle*, trying to ascertain whether in fact there is a Count who inhabits the Castle, what he looks like if he exists, whether this presumed Count actually controls what does and does not take place in the village below, and how he can be reached so that K. can discuss with him some of the problems he is experiencing because the position of Land-Surveyor that he was hired to fill does not seem to exist. . . .

This week I met and interviewed three men. The first gentleman is the vice-president, effective director, and cashier of virtually all the foundations that exist in Belgium that have anything whatsoever to do with scientific research. The second gentleman is the secretary-general of all these same foundations and secretary of each of the twenty-five scientific commissions under the aegis of the most important of these foundations. The third gentleman is, at one and the same time, the secretary-general of a government ministry and president of a fund for medical research that receives a good part of its budget from this ministry.

Could any of these men be *l'Esprit Directeur*—the "Count" in the "Castle" of Medical Science in Belgium?

Monseigneur Joseph-Ernest Van Roey, Cardinal of Belgium for thirty-five years, is dead. Over my radio this morning, first, the sound of all the bells in all the belfries of Malines, the seat of the archdiocese. Then silence, as the long funeral cortège enters the cathedral for the requiem mass: the cardinal's family, his servants, professors of the Catholic University of Louvain, seminarians, priests, bishops, foreign cardinals, burgomasters, ministers of the state, and finally the King and the Queen come to pay their last ceremonial and personal respects to a prince of the church. The Solomon-ancient, sobbing, soaring, Gregorian chants of the mass. A sentimental funeral oration (the first half in Flemish, the second half in French) by his Excellency Monseigneur Van Wayenbergh, Bishop and Recteur Magnifique of the University of Louvain. After this, in a half-emptied church, each of the four bishops of Belgium in turn singing the absolution. The last response, "*Libera me. . . . Libera me. . . . Libera me. . . . Libera me.*" . . . The great organ bellowing out the parade-like strains of the "*Brabançonne,*" the Belgian national anthem. . . . The ceremony ushering a Belgian cardinal out of this world into the next is over, as all the bells in all the belfries of Malines ring out once more.

In 1935, construction began on the University Hospital of Ghent. Twenty-six years later, the hospital is still not completed. Several departments are functioning in the parts that *are* ready for use, but most continue in a medieval hospital building that was once part of a cloister. The "old" hospital is beautiful, with its soaring, gabled roof, high, vaulted ceilings, exquisitely carved doors, tiled floors, and cathedral windows that look out on an ageing rose garden. But the wards are so enormous, several hundred feet long, that it is impossible to heat them. (And it is no longer considered quite proper, as it was in the Middle Ages, for three to six patients to share a bed, and keep warm that way.) The only laboratory space is in the hospital basement, in Gothic niches. . . .

Why has it taken more than twenty-five years to build a new hospital? Why has the work on it been delayed again and again? The explanations given are almost as various as the people you ask.

Lack of funds, some say, and disagreement about who ought to be responsible for financing the construction and the administration of the hospital. (The local Commission of Public Assistance to whom the hospital officially belongs? The university, at whose disposition the commission is required by law to put the hospital for the training of young physicians? The national government?—for after all, the University of Ghent is a state university, and wouldn't the National Ministry of Public Health, for example, or of Finance, have more funds for defraying the enormous expenses of a modern teaching hospital than a small city, or a single university?)

The primary difficulty in building the hospital, others contend, is that the professors on the medical school faculty responsible for its architecture could never make up their minds what it should look like, what equipment it should include, etc. And each time a professor came back from a foreign medical congress, he insisted that "the very latest ideas" about hospital construction, with which he had just become acquainted, should be incorporated. A number of people maintain that the war, of course, had a great deal to do with the delay.

It's mostly because the university tried not to leave the responsibility for the building of the hospital in the hands of the local Commission of Public Assistance, still others claim. The permanent members of the commission generally do not see beyond their particular interests in the particular community of the particular commune of the particular province of which they are citizens. And the elected members of the commission generally are not required to know anything about the problems of hospitals in order to qualify for nomination. They need only be Belgian and at least twenty-five years of age. For these reasons, it is said, the university bypassed Public Assistance and entrusted the building of the Hospital to the Ministries of Public Works and of Public Instruction. But these ministries had had virtually no experience in hospital building. . . .

But the "real story" of the delay in the hospital, a few persons say (lowering their voices as they recount it), revolves around a certain professor of medicine. He was the "moving spirit" behind the original project. He was also a *Flamingant*—an extreme Flemish nationalist—and after the war, he was accused of having collaborated with the Germans. Because the hospital had been so largely his idea, it fell into disrepute with those on the faculty and in the larger community who took a stand against this professor.

Which of these accounts *is* the "real" one? Could *all* of these factors have contributed to the twenty-six-year-old saga of the hospital? Or is there a story, buried deeper than any of these, which no one has chosen or dared to tell me?

Belgian newspapers and magazines are full of speculation about who will be chosen to succeed Cardinal Van Roey. The favored rumors are that *two* new cardinals will be appointed, a Flemish-speaking cardinal from Flanders and a French-speaking cardinal from Walloonie; and that Malines will no longer be the seat of the archdiocese. The archdiocese, they say, will be divided into two new dioceses, one in the Flemish city of Antwerp, the other in the Brusselois city of Brussels, and these will take their place alongside an already established third diocese, that in the Walloon city of Liège. . . .

"*Mademoiselle* . . . *Juffrouw* . . . What you know about our medical schools and hospitals . . . about Belgium . . . is remarkable! Far more than any Belgian could hope to know . . ." Everyone with whom I speak tells me this. The ludicrous, humbling thing is that I have more and more reason to think this might actually be so. . . .

"Therefore we have arrived at the conclusion that our situation here at the institute is very complicated and far from being free and clear," said the secretary-general recently. "Under the circumstances, *messieurs,* the academic authorities must begin simply by studying the possibility of changing all of this cumbersome structure. We regret that for the time being there is no more that we can do. . . ."

Medical Scientists in a Château

On Sunday afternoon, November 15, 1959, a medical scientific colloquium was held in the château at Laeken, which belongs to the royal family of Belgium. This was a meeting officially devoted to accomplishments and problems in the field of cardiac surgery. The conference was held in honor of three foreign medical scientists, A. G. Brom of Leyden University, André Cournand of Columbia, and Robert Gross of Harvard, who, through their trail-blazing experimental work, made outstanding contributions to this field. The three men had traveled to Belgium in order to personally receive the "doctor *honoris causa*" degree that each was to be awarded in the course of the following week. Along with King Baudouin of the Belgians, who was honored with the same diploma, Cournand subsequently received his honorary degree from the Free University of Brussels on the same day that Gross and Brom were awarded their degrees by the Catholic University of Louvain.

According to accounts in Belgian newspapers, among the persons invited to the medical scientific gathering in the royal château were the following: numerous members of the royal family (King Baudouin, ex-King Leopold, Princess Liliane, Prince Alexandre, Prince Albert, Princess Paola); the ambassadors of France and the United States; various ministers, present and past, of Cultural Affairs, Public Instruction, So-

From *Science*, CXXXVI (1962), 476–483.

cial Security, Public Health, and so on; the rectors and deans of each of the four major Belgian universities (Ghent and Liège, as well as Brussels and Louvain); professors of the medical faculties of each of the universities and numerous other professors; medical specialists from various university-connected centers; certain young Belgian physicians who were members of cardiac teams; mature physicians in private practice specializing in cardiology; Belgian physicians who had received some training in the United States; the director and various members of the Princess Liliane Cardiology Foundation; representatives of the Belgian Academy of Medicine and the Royal Flemish Academy of Medicine; the president of the Fund of Medical Scientific Research; the president of the Red Cross; a commissioner from EURATOM; Belgian patients with heart maladies who had undergone cardiac surgery outside of Belgium, chiefly in the United States (there were approximately forty of these); Belgian patients who had undergone cardiac surgery in Belgium (there were 400 such individuals at this time—how many of these came to the colloquium was not specified in the newspapers); some candidates for cardiac surgery; and the families of all these patients.

Before the colloquium, a tea was served in the Palm Rotunda of the château. In the midst of the reception a sudden failure in electricity extinguished all the lights of the château. Members of the palace staff had to be summoned to bring candles, and for a while the reception proceeded in the at once eerie and romantic ambience of candlelight.

After the tea (electricity restored), a speech was delivered in French by a professor of medicine of the University of Brussels, who was also Belgium's delegate to the International Council of Cardiology. Another professor then gave a complementary speech in Flemish. Prince Alexandre, the son of ex-King Leopold and Princess Liliane, who had himself undergone cardiac surgery as a patient of Gross, was the next to speak. He delivered an address, thanking modern medical science and the physicians and surgeons who are its agents for what it had done to help patients like himself. The speech was delivered first in Flemish, then in French.

Following this, the colloquium proper took place in the small and elegant theater of the château, in the presence of the royal family and their invited guests and of many of the assembled medical personages. The guests of the royal family included certain members of the nobility and a number of prominent businessmen, several of whom were believed to be important Free Masons. A professor of medicine from each of the four Belgian universities and several foreign physicians participated in the discussion. This was on a rather elementary scientific level, out of consideration for the persons in the audience who were not medically or surgically trained.

After the colloquium there was a cold supper, to which all who had been present at the meeting in the afternoon seem to have been invited, with the exception of the patients and their families. In addition, the five bishops of the Belgian Catholic Church, some more members of the nobility (counts, countesses, barons, baronesses), and various members of Parliament were cited in the newspapers as having attended the supper.

A SYMBOLIC GATHERING

Nothing could more dramatically suggest some of the ways in which various social, cultural, and historical factors affect clinical medical research[1] and research careers in Belgium than this medical colloquium that took place in a château. This is not to imply that Belgian medical congresses are usually held in such a setting, or that medical scientific work necessarily proceeds under the direct surveillance of the royal family. (In fact, in certain specific ways the "story of cardiac surgery" in Belgium is atypical, involving as it does the personal medical history of Prince Alexandre and the consequent interest of his immediate family in medical and surgical developments that bear upon his congenital heart condition.[2]) However, in several respects this medical gathering in a château may be said to be a symbolic expression of the complex social structure and cultural tradition within which a good deal of medical research in Belgium functions, and of the rather special psychological atmosphere that consequently surrounds it.[3]

1. I use the term "clinical medical research" in a relatively loose, descriptive sense to refer to medical research which has some ostensible, intended relationship to an understanding of the etiology, diagnosis, treatment, or prognosis of disease, or of the maintenance of health, in human beings. In the particular case of Belgium, almost all such research is conducted under the aegis of the medical school faculty of a university, most frequently by investigators who are graduate physicians.

2. A potential new link between medicine in Belgium and the royal family was forged in the fall of 1961 when Prince Alexandre enrolled as a first-year student in the Faculty of Medicine at the University of Louvain.

3. The medical colloquium seemed symbolic not only to me but also to a number of physicians with whom I had occasion to discuss it in each of the four Belgian universities. Several of the physicians with whom I talked had been present at the colloquium; others had merely read accounts of it in the newspapers or had spoken with colleagues who had been invited to attend.

To begin with, the extraordinarily long and sociologically encompassing list of guests present at this colloquium is representative of virtually every social institution, organization, and group that affects medical research and researchers in Belgium. The diversity and importance of extramedical influences on research and research careers is suggested by the presence at the colloquium of political and religious personages, nobles, financiers, and patients and their families, in addition to the expected array of physicians. The fact that such a range of persons was invited; that two different Belgian universities had chosen to award honorary degrees at the same time to medical scientists of French, Dutch, and American origin; that each address given by a professor from one of the four Belgian universities was paralleled by an address given by a comparable professor from at least one of the other three; that Prince Alexandre's speech was delivered in both Flemish and French—all these are outward manifestations of the continuous vying for absolute equality that characterizes the many competitive groups involved in Belgian medical research, and of the exponentially complicated attempts that are made to try to meet their rival demands.

In a more abstract and general sense, this medical colloquium held in the royal château may be viewed as symbolic of social conditions under which medical research proceeds in Belgium. Metaphorically speaking, Belgian medical scientists can be said to operate continuously in a "château." The word is used here in much the same way that it was used by Raoul Kourilsky (professor of clinical medicine at the University of Paris)—to symbolize those still-unchanged aspects of traditional social structure which tend to curtail medical scientific creativity and productivity and the possibilities for careers in medical research: "The great sacrifice has been research," Kourilsky said.[4] "We have conserved the old 'château' and its arrangements that belong to another age. . . . We have watched from afar the triumphant ascent of biology. . . ."

Here Kourilsky was referring to the predicament of medical research in present-day France, rather than to the situation in Belgium. His comments suggest, however, that it is not only in Belgium that certain aspects of the traditional social structure within which medical research is carried out are unsuited to the fullest development, exchange, and application of medical scientific talent, facilities, and knowledge. Throughout a significant part of Europe, with the notable exception of England and the Scandinavian countries, a good deal of medical re-

4. R. Kourilsky, *Leçon inaugurale* (reprint from *L'Expansion scientifique française* [1958], pp. 27–28).

search is still housed, sociologically as well as architecturally, "in ancient buildings, remnants of a glorious past."[5]

Finally, this particular medical colloquium held in a royal château symbolizes to some extent the psychological milieu within which many Belgian medical researchers feel they are forced to operate by the intricate, time-entrenched *système* of which they are a part—a highly elaborate, ceremonial, delay-ridden, often paralyzing, enigmatic kind of atmosphere.

The purpose of this article is to describe and analyze the social structure within which clinical medical research is carried out in Belgium, and to suggest some of the problems that this structure creates for Belgian medical science and scientists. Although, in concrete detail, some of the phenomena discussed may be peculiar to Belgium, I hope that perhaps there is also a more general level on which the descriptive analysis that follows is relevant to problems of medical research in other European settings as well.

SOME GENERAL CHARACTERISTICS OF BELGIAN SOCIETY

The tiny, densely populated country of Belgium, smaller in area than the state of New Jersey, is a very complex, diverse little society—in the words of one Belgian physician, a "veritable social mosaic." With every few miles one travels in Belgium one finds marked differences in landscape, architecture, language, tradition, and orientation. For, within the 11,779 square miles that comprise Belgium, its more than 9 million inhabitants distribute themselves in countless ways between two cultures, French and Flemish; two languages (each with numerous dialects); two sharply contrasting philosophical-religious attitudes toward life (traditional Catholicism and anticlerical Masonic "Free Thought"); and four political parties (Social Christian, Liberal, Socialist, and Communist). They are distributed, too, among the nine provinces and the 2633 communes[6] that make up the highly autonomous local governments of

5. D. M. Gates, *Science* **128,** 227 (1958).

6. Of these communes, 1733 have a population of less than 2000 inhabitants. The smallest Belgian commune, Zoutenaaie, has 25 citizens, who belong to five families. It has been necessary for Zoutenaaie to "borrow" two inhabitants from a neighboring commune to sit on its council, since there is a law forbidding two members of the same family to be members of the council at the same time. Symbolic of the proud, traditional insistence on local autonomy in Belgium are, on the one hand, the red, yellow, and black national flag, which represents the heraldic *émaux* (enameled colors) of the provinces of Brabant, Flanders, and Hainaut in the Middle Ages, and, on the other hand, the fact that the official title of the King is the "King of the Belgians" rather than the "King of Belgium."

the constitutional monarchy; within an elaborate hierarchy of social classes that include peasants, factory and mine workers, white-collar workers, industrial and commercial bourgeois, professionals, members of the clergy, and members of the nobility; and among more than 15,000 social organizations—societies, clubs, associations, academies—formed around special interests (which, to take an extreme case, can become so special as to give rise to an "Association of Hammer-Handle Makers of Lower Ixelles").[7]

Belgium has been described as "surely one of the most particularistic societies in the world."[8] The reference is not only to the great diversity of social and cultural groupings that exist in Belgium but also to the emotionally charged, central role that ethnic, linguistic, philosophical, religious, political, community, class, and special-interest differences play in every aspect of Belgian life. At one and the same time there is a tendency for individuals to deeply identify themselves with what they consider to be "their" groups and a tendency to regard the groups to which they do not belong with apprehension, suspicion, animosity, and competitiveness. As John L. Brown (former American cultural attaché to Belgium) has remarked, given the "rivalries and resentments that smoulder under the surface" of Belgian life, "it is sometimes hard to understand how the country holds together and functions at all."[9] These particularistic groups keep a close jealous watch over each other, devoting at least as much energy to trying to prevent opposing groups from outdistancing them as to advancing their own interests through efforts devoted to self-improvement and achievement. A very literal "it-must-be-identical-and-not-simply-equivalent" conception of equality is imposed by one group upon the other. This gives rise to a number of phenomena highly characteristic of Belgian society.

One of the consequences of these rival demands for exact equality in the distribution of material resources, status, and authority is the development of numerous social organizations that replicate each other in all respects except that of the particularistic group from which each draws its membership. Thus, for example, in Belgium there is both a Royal Belgian Academy of Science, Letters and Fine Arts and a Royal

7. J. L. Brown, in *Discovering Belgium* (Lumière, Brussels, 1960), preface.

8. The adjective "particularistic" (or "particularist") was frequently and spontaneously used by many of the Belgian physicians with whom I talked. Interestingly enough, they used the term in almost the same way that it is used by Talcott Parsons, the well-known American sociologist, though few of these physicians have had work in formal sociology, and none of them has any knowledge of Parsons' writings.

9. Brown, *Ibid.*

Flemish Academy of Science, Letters and Fine Arts; a Royal Belgian Automobile Club and a Royal Flemish Automobile Club; Boy Scout and Girl Scout organizations and a Catholic Scouts organization.

Still other consequences are suggested by the following ironic, but nonetheless telling, description[10] of the inner political life of Belgium (the phenomena depicted characterize more than just political groups): "Once in power the [political] parties are equally consecrated to impotence. The necessity to act splinters all their divisions: in the face of this kind of peril, without fail, they put off until tomorrow what they could not settle today. Thus, nothing ever comes to pass in Belgium. . . ."

What is implied here is that the continual vying for equality between groups often leads to a kind of impasse between them. Opposing groups are deliberately so evenly balanced and so unyielding in their relations with one another that it frequently becomes impossible to initiate any particular course of action. To do so would be construed as honoring and favoring one group's opinion more than another's. Futhermore, under the circumstances, when a particular group is faced with the challenge of trying to make and implement a decision, it often begins to split internally into smaller and smaller particularistic groupings. This, then, makes it unlikely that the original group will be able to maintain enough inner unity to take any kind of definitive and effective stand on behalf of what presumably were the shared interests around which it was organized in the first place. The internal factions that emerge also tend to engage in the same kind of divisive struggle for exact equality. Not infrequently, what results from this is an amoeba-like fission process through which still other evenly balanced formal organizations, offices, and so on are created; this, in turn, produces another impasse of even greater social complexity.

The King and the Parliament, of course, through the symbolic and operational executive and legislative powers invested in them by the constitutional monarchy, represent and provide a certain overarching national coherence, direction, and unity. The Council of Ministers (presided over by the Prime Minister), formally appointed by the King according to which parties predominate in Parliament, has the most effective voice in introducing and administering legislation. Each minister has a permanent official (the secretary-general) at the head of his staff and, in addition, appoints his own bureau of advisers, who retire with him. But here again the characteristic particularism of Belgian

10. R. Micha and A. de Waelhens, *Les Temps Modernes*, **4,** 432 (1949).

society and the continuing pressures to achieve and maintain a literal kind of equality between all vying groups manifest themselves, creating impasses and the proliferation and still further decentralization of ministries, ministers, and ministerial advisers. Thus, in the twentieth century most Belgian ministries have been formed by coalition, since the electoral system has rarely returned a party with a working parliamentary majority. And new kinds of ministries and ministerial posts have again and again been created in the face of impasse, conflict, and crisis; they have simply been added on to those already existing.[11]

It is partly because of the proliferation of officials, agencies, and so on, as well as because of the particularistic rivalry among them, that the formal processes by which decisions are made and actions are taken in many areas of Belgian life are typically slow-moving, often delay-ridden, and sometimes indefinitely blocked. This leads, in turn, to still another characteristic Belgian phenomenon—a widespread tendency to try to find ways around the cumbersome formal structure ("*petits chemins*"), chiefly through the use of personal, often covert, influence, in order to get things more efficiently, speedily, and assuredly done.

Intricately connected with this "mosaic" of particularistic groups that make up Belgian society, and sharing many of its characteristics, is the complex of social organizations within which most of the clinical medical research in Belgium takes place.

11. This was illustrated in recent Belgian history (September 1960), when, as a result of the Belgian public's reaction to the uprisings in the Belgian Congo, Gaston Eyskens, the (Social-Christian) Prime Minister, was obliged to reorganize his cabinet. The new cabinet with which Eyskens emerged on 3 September typified some of the processes I have been describing. The preceding government had consisted of 20 ministers, of whom 13 were members of the Social-Christian Party and seven belonged to the Liberal Party. The new cabinet was made up of 24 ministers, 15 of them Social-Christians, nine of them Liberals. Thus, two ministers from each of these political parties were added to the original number. Furthermore, four new ministerial posts were created—so-called Under-Secretaries of State; two of these posts were filled by Social-Christians and two by Liberals. Commenting on this reconstitution of the cabinet, the French newspaper *Le Monde* expressed the opinion (4–5 Sept. 1960) that there was essentially nothing "new" about it, and that "the Prime Minister will more than ever be paralyzed." The nation-wide, violence-accompanied strikes which occurred in Belgium little more than 3 months later dramatically bore out this prediction. For now a "whole nation" seemed to be "revolting against itself" as, for 27 days, "nearly everything that keeps a modern nation going—trains, busses, trams, gas and light works, garbage and mail deliveries, schools, shops, ports, steel mills, coal mines, even football teams—stopped still" [C. Sterling, *The Reporter* (16 Feb. 1961)]. The origins of these strikes, of course, were very complex. But from one point of view they may be regarded as extreme outward manifestations of some of the contending, recalcitrant forces that continually threaten the progress of Belgian society.

SOCIAL STRUCTURE OF CLINICAL MEDICAL RESEARCH IN BELGIUM

Most clinical medical research in Belgium is carried out in a department, hospital, or institute affiliated with one of the four major universities.[12] Each of these universities represents a different combination of some of the social and cultural distinctions that dominate so many sectors of Belgian life. To be more explicit: Brussels is a Free Thought (largely anticlerical, Free Mason), non-state university. Originally, all its classes were taught in French, but since World War II, various parts of the university have doubled their faculties, adding professors who give in Flemish the same courses that are given in French. Ghent is a state university, officially neither Catholic nor Free Thought, but with a great many practicing Catholics in the student body and on the faculty. Since the early 1930s all classes have been taught in Flemish. Liège is a state university, neither Catholic nor Free Thought, but with the greater number of its students and faculty nonpracticing Catholics or non-Catholics. All classes at Liège are taught in French. Louvain is a Catholic, non-state university with a "double" (completely replicated) faculty and student body, the one section of the university being Flemish, the other French.

Because each of the universities represents a particular constellation of some of the social and cultural differentials that fragment Belgian life, each tends to seal itself off from the others. As some Belgians put it, the universities are "veritable cloisters," with a very limited interchange of ideas and information and an even more restricted exchange of personnel. The faculty of each of the universities is drawn almost exclusively from its alumni.

The creation of a new, fifth university in Antwerp is presently being considered. This would be a non-state, Free Thought, Flemish-speaking university, differing from the Flemish section of the University of Brussels in that it would be located on what is considered part of the mother soil of Flanders. Given the mounting fervor of Walloon as well as Flemish nationalism during the past few years, it is predicted by many that not only will a "Flemish" university be built in Antwerp but that its Walloon equivalent will immediately be founded either in Mons or in

12. It is informally estimated that there are at least 1200 separate university research institutes in Belgium. This number includes institutes in fields other than medicine, of course. Nevertheless, it suggests the wide dispersion and the duplication of research facilities and efforts characteristic of this tiny country, in which cooperation and collaboration between different groups is so difficult to effect in any domain.

Charleroi. This anticipated sixth university would be non-state, Free Thought, French-speaking, and located on the soil of Wallonie.

The structure of the staffs of the university departments, hospitals, and institutes where medical research is carried out is, in the words of a young research physician, "like a building in which the ground and top floors have been constructed, but in which they haven't gotten around yet to putting in the floors in between." Research units are typically headed by one full professor, with all of the authority and responsibility of a *patron.* Generally, the other members of the research staff are junior to him and greatly subordinate in status. A few such junior research workers may have university positions—for example, that of *chargé de cours* or *assistant*—but usually these are not positions with tenure. The greater number of researchers hold no formal university appointment. Rather, their positions (often title-less) exist only by virtue of the fact that the *patron* has been able to raise a sufficient sum of money temporarily to pay them a salary and support their research. Usually there is no formal assurance of funds for continuing their research from one year to the next. It is only in the course of the past year that a law has been passed[13] officially creating two kinds of tenure positions in the structure of Belgian universities, in addition to that of full professor. These new positions are those of *chargé de cours associé* and *professeur associé.* In effect, they represent some of the "floors in between" the ground floor and the top floor, hitherto completely missing in the formal status system of Belgian university faculties.[14]

An integral relationship between medical research and research careers in Belgian universities and the national government is already suggested by the fact that legislation was required to create these positions. The determining influence of the government in the progress of Belgian medical research stems primarily from its important role as financier. To begin with, chiefly through the Ministry of Public Instruction, the government has the major responsibility for the support of the two state universities, Ghent and Liège, and the subsidies it has given to the "free" universities of Brussels and Louvain in the past few years have been almost as great. Above and beyond this, it is not an exaggeration to

13. This law came into being on 14 December 1960, when it was signed by the King, the Minister of Public Instruction, and the Minister of Justice.

14. Thus far, the creation of these posts has had only a token effect in increasing the number of stable, prestigious, adequately remunerated positions in Belgian society from which one can do research. For only 30 such positions have been created in each of the four universities, and these 30 must be distributed between all the departments of the university. What is more, the problem of where the funds for financing these positions will come from has not been fully resolved.

say that practically all the government ministries have some control over medical research in Belgium, through their authority to pass judgment on requests relevant to research that are submitted to them (for personnel, equipment, buildings, and so on), and, of course, ultimately through their willingness or refusal to grant the funds to meet these requests. Some of the ministries that affect medical research in Belgium are the ministries of public health and family, public works, finance, economic affairs, cultural affairs, interior, national defense, and agriculture. Perhaps more striking than the mere number of governmental bodies involved in the control and support of medical research is the fact that no one ministry or council of ministers is responsible for the overall coordination of the many agencies involved and for the development of medical scientific research as a whole. The closest approximation to such a committee is the Conseil National de la Politique Scientifique, created only two years ago by a legislative act. This National Council of Scientific Policy is made up of twenty-eight regular members drawn primarily from the four universities and from various sectors of the worlds of industry and finance. The council also has two consultant members: the secretary-generals of the ministries of public instruction and of economic affairs. The council has no executive power. Its function is purely an advisory one—that of helping to integrate and advance scientific research in Belgium through formal and informal interchange with the ministers who make up the Ministerial Committee and the Interministerial Commission of Scientific Policy, created under the legislative act that created the council. It is as yet too early to predict whether this strictly advisory council will carry enough moral weight and will remain sufficiently free of political pressures and particularistic loyalties to fulfill its hoped-for goals.

It is not only the national government that affects the execution and development of clinical medical research in Belgium. The governments of local communes in the cities of Brussels, Ghent, Liège, and Louvain also have a considerable influence. This is because, in each of these four cities in which a university is located, at least one major hospital—used by the faculty of medicine to carry out research (as well as to teach and to help care for patients)—is owned, partly financed, and administered by the local Commission de l'Assistance Publique. The commissions of public assistance in Ghent and Liège, cities which have state universities, are required by law to put their hospitals at the disposition of the faculties of medicine of those universities; the commissions of public assistance of Brussels and Louvain, although not legally obligated, have voluntarily done the same. The commissions of public assistance, which exist in every commune of Belgium, date from the era of the French

Revolution. They were originally charged with two missions: to prevent poverty and to organize hospital services. Their primary obligation was to give free care to the indigent sick of their communes in the civil hospitals that they had created, but from the very beginning they also cared for patients from the local community who were capable of paying.[15] Direction of the hospitals of the commissions of public assistance rests in the hands of a special commission, made up of five to twelve members according to the size and population of the commune. These members of the commission, elected by the communal council, hold office for six years and may have their terms renewed. Any resident of the local community who is a Belgian citizen, is twenty-five years of age or older, and has never committed a serious legal offense is eligible to be nominated for this office. Nothing else is required. The commissions of public assistance function under the "protectorship" of the government of the commune, the government of the province in which the commune is located, and the national government. They must obtain formal authorization for many of their decisions and actions from each of these governing bodies.

In addition to the various local and national governmental agencies, a number of *oeuvres nationales* (against cancer, poliomyelitis, tuberculosis, and so on) and foundations of a private or semiprivate nature (the National Fund of Scientific Research, the National Fund of Medical Scientific Research, the University Foundation, the Francqui Foundation, the Queen Elisabeth Medical Foundation, the Inter-University Institute for Nuclear Sciences, and so on) are involved in the conduct and support of Belgian medical research.

Perhaps the most important of these agencies is the Fonds National de la Recherche Scientifique (FNRS), or National Fund of Scientific Research, founded in 1928 in response to a speech made by King Albert in which he declared that a "state of crisis [existed] in the scientific institutions and laboratories of Belgium" and that something must be done to "arouse, encourage and sustain" scientists and their work. A large-scale public drive for funds resulted from this speech, and within a relatively short time enough money was raised (chiefly from banks, industry, commerce, and contributions by private individuals) to launch the FNRS. Such a drive was unprecedented in Belgium, and nothing comparable has occurred since.

The thirty-member board of directors of the FNRS is composed of

15. In 1958 a new law was passed, giving these hospitals two additional formal obligations: those of caring for patients with prepaid health insurance and of caring for all emergency cases which occur within the confines of the commune in question.

nine representatives of the institutions of higher education and research of Belgium (the rector of each of the four universities and the rectors of five other institutions); the permanent secretaries of the four major academies of Belgium (the Royal Academy of Sciences, Letters and Fine Arts; the Royal Academy of Medicine; the Royal Flemish Academy of Sciences, Letters and Fine Arts; and the Royal Flemish Academy of Medicine); fourteen members nominated by the University Foundation (eight professors, evenly distributed between the four universities; one of Belgium's most important businessmen, who is president of the FNRS board of directors; the director general of the Ministry of Public Instruction, and four other persons); the secretary-general of the FNRS; and, finally, its director and first vice-president.

Decisions about the granting of funds to the various research groups who apply to the FNRS for subsidies are made by its twenty-five scientific commissions. Each of these commissions, organized around a different subgroup of sciences, is comprised of four professors (one from each of the four universities) and a president (twenty of the presidents are university professors—five from each university—and the other five are professors at several nonuniversity institutions of higher education). All told, then, 125 different professors are members of the scientific commissions of the FNRS—virtually every university professor of science in Belgium. Since, as we have already seen, most research in Belgium is carried out in the universities in a group headed by a full professor, most of the research projects reviewed by the commissions of the FNRS are being conducted under the aegis of one or another of the commission members.

Although originally the major part of the funds distributed by the FNRS came from private sources, the organization now receives more than two-thirds of its annual income from grants made to it by the state (chiefly via the Ministry of Public Instruction). In addition, during the past few years (by virtue first of custom and now of royal decree), the FNRS has become the direct recipient of funds allocated by the national government to some of the other foundations. The FNRS passes those funds on, in turn, to the designated foundations. For example, the FNRS receives the subsidy granted to the National Foundation of Medical Scientific Research by the Ministry of Public Health. It then turns this money over to the president of that foundation (who is also secretary-general of the Ministry of Public Health).

The FNRS, the National Fund of Medical Scientific Research, the University Foundation, the Francqui Foundation, and the Inter-University Institute of Nuclear Sciences (as well as several other foundations with somewhat different functions) are all housed in the same building, the Club of the University Foundation, 11, rue d'Egmont, Brussels. The director and first vice-president of the FNRS has his office there. He is the effective director, first vice-president, and cashier of *all* the foundations at 11, rue d'Egmont, and is on the boards of directors of a number of other foundations. The secretary-general of the FNRS also has his office in this building. He is secretary of each of the twenty-five scientific commissions of the FNRS and of every one of the rue d'Egmont foundations. A close examination of the membership of the board of directors of each of these legally independent foundations reveals a considerable amount of further overlapping.

These are the outlines of the formal structure of medical research in Belgium—the empirically built, time-encrusted "château," with all its separate-but-identical "rooms" and its maze of winding, interconnecting "corridors," within which Belgian medical science and scientists function. It is a paradoxical structure characterized in some respects by extreme decentralization, in others, by what appears to be an extraordinary concentration of authority and power in the hands of a few agencies and persons. And this dualism is being perpetuated by recent, slowly implemented efforts to modify the existing structure.

SOME PROBLEMATIC CONSEQUENCES

What are some of the observable consequences of the structure of clinical medical research in Belgium—with its particularism, its pluralism, its centralization and decentralization—for the advancement of medical investigation and for the careers of researchers?

Although in the various institutes and departments of the four universities there are well-trained medical investigators of ability carrying out competent research, often this work is being done under adverse social and psychological conditions, or in spite of them.

The salaries of men engaged in research are generally so low that they cannot support themselves, much less their families, unless they supplement their incomes by doing some work in addition to research. (Typically, most medical researchers who are physicians see a number of private patients.) Everywhere researchers lack the funds, equipment, and personnel that would help them carry out their work. At the same time, one finds very expensive equipment duplicated in the four universities, rather than some sort of cooperative arrangement worked out between departments, institutes, and universities for the joint use of such equipment. (At last count there were sixteen artificial heart machines, four artificial kidney machines, four betatrons, and four cobalt bombs in Belgium—a country, it must be remembered, smaller than the state of New Jersey.)

Most of the hospitals of Belgium were built in a much earlier historical era—several of them even date back to the Middle Ages—and thus are not appropriate for medical research (or, for that matter, ideal for modern medical care). New hospitals, institutes, and laboratory buildings are obviously urgently needed, yet one university hospital started twenty-five years ago is still not completed and has only several departments functioning within it; another university hospital stood completely ready but unaccountably closed and unused for almost two years, until its doors were virtually forced open in the spring of 1961 by a threatened strike of medical students and "assistants"; and a crated betatron delivered more than a year ago can still be seen in the corridor of a third university-affiliated hospital building, which is too old and fragile to withstand the operation of such a powerful machine.

In the various university settings one finds medical researchers with only the most provisional of positions and, in private practice, any number of physicians who were forced to give up the idea of a research and teaching career because of the lack of reasonably well insured positions. At the same time, in departments of several medical schools there are professorial chairs, long vacant, for which occupants have still not been definitely chosen. Furthermore, especially in certain university milieux, such particularistic considerations as the political, ethnic, linguistic, philosophical, religious, class, and family affiliations of candidates play as important a role as their scientific competence in determining whether or not they will be named to an available university position. Indeed, this state of affairs is quasi-institutionalized in that each university represents a distinct political, ethnic, linguistic, and religious-philosophical cluster and that almost all faculty appointees are chosen from among the graduates of the university in question.

Despite the good relations that exist in a number of settings between professors of medicine who head a research unit and the younger medical investigators who work under their jurisdiction, a great gap in attitudes as well as in status often characterizes the outlook and interchanges of these two groups. Young research physicians speak of their "*patrons*" and professors of their "*jeunes*" with a degree of incomprehension that suggests a far greater lack of certain kinds of communication than generally would characterize, for example, the relations between an American professor of medicine who heads a research group and individuals of junior status who work under his supervision.

The professors of medicine who are the chiefs of research units—the *patrons*—spend a good deal of their potentially creative time and energy simply in coping with the burdensome administrative responsibilities that running a department or an institute entails, given the complicated network of university, governmental, and private agencies of which it is necessarily a part in Belgium. Above all, these professors are engaged in what they refer to as the "*chasse aux subsides*" (the "hunt for subsidies"). This "hunt" involves them in a complicated, time-consuming, neverending process of writing eloquent, inquiring, imploring, demanding, grateful letters; of making formal and informal visits to strategic officials; and of sitting on numerous commissions. For, in the words of a recent report by the Conseil National de la Politique Scientifique, since "the universities insure their Faculties of Medicine with [funds] that one would hesitate to call a 'decent standard for research,' " money must be sought largely outside the universities. The funds for any particular department or institute must be procured from a great many different agencies; it is altogether unlikely that large enough grants could be obtained from only one or from several extrauniversity sources. This is because, as we have already seen, a great deal of the money given for medical research in Belgium, even when it comes from funds and foundations, is supplied by the national government. In particularistic Belgium these agencies are under political pressure to try to allocate their resources equally between the different university groups that apply for aid. Since the research-designated funds of any ministry, foundation, or fund must be evenly distributed among a large number of the hundreds of medical research groups that exist in Belgium, the absolute amount that any one group receives will be very small. And so the professors who are chiefs of research units must apply to many different agencies in order to amass enough funds for salaries and needed equipment. Grants are usually given only on an annual basis; this makes it necessary to repeat the "hunt" for subsidies each year. In view of the limited money available for research from universities and formal extrauniversity agencies, the typical professor who heads a research unit must also spend a great deal of time skillfully cultivating and elaborately tending personal social relationships with individuals who, if astutely handled, may be willing to donate substantial private sums of money for research.

Whatever the specific nature of the problems of medical research and researchers in the various university milieux of Belgium—problems of procuring funds and equipment; of modifying, building, and opening hospitals; of utilizing facilities; of creating and establishing research positions and appointing competent, committed investigators to fill them—there is usually a long delay in trying to deal with them, and sometimes utter paralysis. It is these delays and impasses above all that erode the morale of junior and senior researchers alike—that encourage them, as one research physician put it, "to seek [their] own ways . . . licit if possible, illicit if not . . . independent and outside of the system" to speed matters on in what might otherwise be hopelessly deadlocked or infinitely delayed situations. It is only by circumventing the formal structure and engaging, if need be, in "*sous la table*" tactics that, to quote another researcher, you can "work your way out . . . put your situation on more firm grounds . . . insure your happy survival . . . and hope for the development and expansion of the research group with which you work. . . ."

Perhaps more striking than any of these concrete problems faced by Belgian medical researchers is what might be termed the psychological atmosphere or climate in which they work. In discussing their problems with us, many researchers talked of the "absurd," "ridiculous," "arbitrary," "irrational," "undecipherable," and ultimately "absolutist" ways in which, it seems to them, things come to pass or are blocked in the milieux in which they work. They frequently expressed apprehension and frustration over the "capricious, all-or-nothing, arbitrary game" of which they feel themselves a part, and which gives them the sense (as one Flemish researcher put it) that they are "tussling with phantom windmills." Even researchers relatively satisfied with their professional situations voiced a considerable amount of disquietude over the reasons for their "exceptional good luck" in having a fairly well insured position, an adequate salary, needed equipment, and a *patron* who understands, supports, and facilitates their research.[16]

The seemingly absurd, enigmatic, arbitrary qualities of the milieux in which these medical investigators conduct their work are partly a consequence of some of the characteristics of the social structure of medical research in Belgium already discussed. To begin with (as a group of young research physicians put it, in a document of grievances they drafted), in a Belgian research institute or department "one finds one's self confronted with such a maze of entwined organizations that it is remarkably difficult to know who determines policy. . . ." Formal authority to make and implement decisions is divided between so many different groups that it is especially hard for younger medical researchers to identify all the agencies and officials involved, and to trace out the long sequence of steps by which decisions are supposed to be

16. These descriptions of what many Belgian researchers find absurd, inscrutable, and arbitrary about the atmosphere in which they work forcibly reminds one of the novels of Franz Kafka—especially *The Castle* and *The Trial.* In this connection it is interesting to consider that Kafka, a Czech, was also a citizen of a small country of Continental Europe. Perhaps that accounts in part for the striking pertinence of his writings to Belgium.

made. For, unlike their *patrons,* these young investigators have not been directly involved with these agencies and officials year after year in the "hunt for subsidies."

The lack of interchange of information, ideas, and opinions between departments, institutes, and universities and, in general, between persons who belong to different particularistic groups and live in different local communities also contributes to the sense of mystery about "who determines policy" and "who really has the power of decision" that is expressed by many researchers. For this insulation of one group from another means that one cannot easily develop a view of the forces larger and more general than those originating and immediately perceivable in a given research institute or department that might be affecting its progress.[17]

The fact that so many of the decisions that affect medical researchers and the institutes and departments in which they work are made in ways that circumvent the complex, delay-ridden means that are formally prescribed also accounts for what many researchers find incomprehensible, unpredictable, and arbitrary in their professional situations. For such informal, ex officio negotiations are less "visible," less subject to control by surveillance, and more likely to be influenced by particularistic factors (as opposed to medical scientific considerations) than negotiations conducted in the formally designated ways.

Finally, many of the feelings of apprehension and indignation expressed by researchers about the apparently inscrutable or capricious forces that affect their professional activities and destinies seem to focus around certain persons in strategic positions who, it is assumed, determine, often covertly and prejudicially, what does and does not happen in the various worlds of Belgian medical research. Sometimes these "*messieurs les responsables*" are cited by position and name; sometimes they are referred to half jokingly, half fearfully as "*Esprits Directeurs*" or "*éminences grises.*" As we have seen, there is some realistic basis for attributing a great deal of authority and power to certain individuals who simultane-

17. As a sociologist from a foreign society I was accorded a privilege that no Belgian enjoys: I was permitted to move freely from one university to another and between departments and institutes within each university. As a result, I was able to directly observe and discuss many things about which Belgians themselves can only conjecture. Most striking of all was the opportunity I had to see that, irrespective of the particular university settings in which medical research groups were located, they were all faced with many of the same problems. That this is only guessed, not really known, by Belgian researchers is suggested by the fact that many of them asked me whether, without being indiscreet, I could tell them if I had observed difficulties similar to their own in other groups that I had visited.

ously hold many different offices in various of the organizations which are part of the intricate social structure of medical research in Belgium. However, the extraordinary amount of power and the nature of the power ascribed to such persons by medical researchers who discuss them; the vague and sinister allusions to still other influential, and invisible, "*messieurs*"; the remarkable lack of agreement even within a particular department or institute as to who these persons with "special powers of decision" actually are—all point to their somewhat legendary character. In part, what Belgian medical researchers seem to be doing is projecting some of their uncertainty, bewilderment, frustration, and anxiety about the social structure of which they are a part and the problems to which it subjects them onto these presumably all-powerful "*messieurs les responsables.*"

An American Sociologist in the Land of Belgian Medical Research

This is the story of a piece of research[1] that began as the summertime project of an American sociologist who voyaged to a small reputedly fathomable and friendly land known as Belgium to make a rather specialized study of how social, cultural, and historical factors affect clinical medical research and research careers[2] in a contemporary European society. It is the story of an undertaking that was destined to engage the American sociologist for more than four years in a complex search that by implication touched on many sectors of Belgian life in such a way that the publication of her first findings excited passionate responses from virtually every significant group in Belgian society. The story of this research, then, is distinctive in at least two ways.

1. The research project to which this chronicle refers was made possible by special grants from the Council for Research in the Social Sciences of Columbia University (summer 1959) and the Belgian American Educational Foundation (summers of 1960 and 1961) and by a fellowship from the John Simon Guggenheim Memorial Foundation (1962).

2. I use the term "clinical medical research" in a relatively loose, descriptive sense to refer to medical research which has some ostensible, intended relationship to an understanding of the etiology, treatment, or prognosis of disease, or of the maintenance of health in human beings.

From Phillip E. Hammond, ed., *Sociologists at Work* (New York: Harper & Row, 1964), 345–391.

(1) Although it is an account of an attempt to make a sociological study of a particular aspect of a particular institution in Belgium—medical research—it is a story that can be deciphered and understood only if it is linked to certain characteristics of the social structure and value system of Belgium that go far beyond its world of medical research.

(2) It is primarily through an analysis of Belgian reactions to the publications of the American sociologist that the largely unanticipated, more general significance of this study of medical research in Belgium emerges.

In the chronicle of research experiences that follows, it is on these aspects of my journey as an American sociologist into the land of Belgian medical research that I shall focus. But first, how did this journey begin?

The idea for a sociological study of medical research and research careers in a present-day European society grew directly out of my special interest in the sociology of medicine, medical education, and science. Since the beginning of my graduate studies in 1949, I have been involved in a series of research projects in this domain, primarily in the medical institutions of Boston and New York. These experiences brought me into contact with many European physicians, professionally engaged in academic medical research in their own countries, who had come to the United States for certain kinds of specialized post-graduate training. Some of these physicians were senior men, even professors; most were younger physicians in early stages of their aspired-to careers; all had demonstrated sufficient competence in their fields to be accepted to study and work in medical centers of the excellence of a Harvard or a Columbia.

I became interested that such physicians had come to the United States in significant numbers for specialized training. Why had they chosen American medical centers for advanced work, rather than European centers, as most such physicians would have done even as recently as the years preceding World War II? Gradually I also became aware of a problem that many of these European research physicians seemed to share. Especially the younger ones apparently felt uncertain and apprehensive about whether they would be able to pursue the career of their choice successfully in their own countries: Could they expect to find appropriate positions when they returned home? they asked themselves. Would they have anything like the working conditions, equipment, and salaries that would make the career of research physician possible and practicable for them? Could they hope to do work *à leur mesure*—in keeping with their capacity? For the most part, they were skeptical as well as anxious about their future in all these regards; but when their designated training period in the United States was over, one by one they returned to their native countries, as they put it, "to try and to see."

I became interested in learning something about the conditions and problems to which such research physicians were returning in their respective European countries. My professional contact with them raised another kind of question in my mind. I knew from my personal acquaintance with a wide range of medical publications, as well as from formal and informal opinions expressed by members of the American medical profession with whom I worked, that progressively, since World War II, a significant amount of what was considered to be the best current medical research was being produced by investigators in the United States, Canada, England, and the Scandinavian countries rather than in countries of Continental Europe, as had formerly been the case. Why, I wondered, had research on the Continent suffered this relative decline when these countries seemed to have a reservoir of talented, well-trained, committed research physicians like those whom I had been meeting in American medical centers?

I decided to devote the academic summer of 1959 to exploring these questions by visiting some of the medical milieux from which such European research physicians had come and to which most of them eventually returned. My intellectual "baggage" for this voyage consisted of little more than the observations I had made and a conceptual hunch that perhaps there were certain common, possibly traditional, features of the social structures and value systems of the countries of "Old Europe" that created problems for the development of medical research careers. With this very general hypothesis, based largely on intuition, I set sail for Europe in June; my plan was to spend most of the summer visiting medical research groups in Belgium.

"But why Belgium?" This is the question about my research perhaps most frequently asked of me. What this question usually means even when asked by Belgians is: "Why did you pick such a small, relatively inconspicuous country as Belgium?" Though I eventually chose Belgium for what I feel are good sociological reasons, I must admit that the original bases for the decision were a blend of the strictly pragmatic, the sentimental, and even the spurious.

To begin with, since all I envisioned when I left for Europe that first summer was a delimited personal exploration of the problems that had caught my attention, it seemed to me that the most rational and profitable way to proceed would be to try to attain some understanding in depth and detail of social factors that affect medical research by focusing largely on a particular European society rather than making superficial, panoramic observations on a continent-wide geographical scale. A number of elements entered into the choice of Belgium in this connection.

Through my work in the realm of the sociology of medicine and science, I had met quite a few Belgian physicians, temporarily in the United States, who I knew would be willing to help introduce me to the world of medical science in Belgium. The fact that I had made contact with a significant number of Belgian physicians was partly a consequence of something like a tradition among university-educated Belgians to seek a certain amount of their advanced training abroad. More specific to the presence of such physicians in the United States for training was the creation of the Belgian American Educational Foundation after World War I,[3] which has made it possible for two generations of selected Belgians, especially in the fields of engineering and medicine, to come to the United States on fellowships for specialized postgraduate education.

My meeting numerous Belgian physicians was also a result of working under the aegis of a well-known American professor of medicine who had played such a significant role in the training of Belgian research physicians that he had received an honorary degree from a Belgian university for his contribution to medical science in this respect. He, of course, influenced my choice of Belgium both by his personal attachment to this country and by his offer to write letters of introduction for me to some of the outstanding Belgian professors of medicine. The one foreign language that I could handle with some certainty and skill was French, and this also inclined me to locate my summer-long explorations in Belgium. I was aware that Belgium is a bilingual nation, Flemish- as well as French-speaking; but I was told by persons whom I consulted, Belgians and non-Belgians alike, that with a combination of French and English I could proceed without difficulty to interview Belgian research physicians and that, Flemish nationalism notwithstanding, even the most fervent young Fleming would excuse a foreigner like me for not being able to converse with him in his maternal language.

Given my relative facility with the French language, France perhaps would have seemed a more likely place for my exploratory research, especially because of the historical glory of the "French School of Medicine," on the one hand, and the effort that France is currently making,

3. In 1920, the Belgian American Educational Foundation created a number of Commission for Relief in Belgium Special Fellowships as part of the general purposes of the foundation, which are to promote closer relations and an exchange of intellectual ideas between Belgium and the United States and to commemorate the work of the Commission for Relief in Belgium in World War I. According to a memorandum issued by the foundation on March 18, 1964, in the past forty-three years about 1000 Belgians have studied in the United States for one or more years on such fellowships.

for the first time since the beginning of the nineteenth century, via the so-called "*Réforme Debré,*" to bring about major changes in its medical education and the organization and functioning of its hospitals. But, because I had only a summer at my disposal, a number of persons discouraged me from locating my inquiry in France and reinforced me in my tentative decision to work in Belgium. My research would advance much more quickly and get much further in Belgium than in France, they said, for the attitudes of Belgians toward America and Americans were far more receptive than those of the French.

Finally, as important as any other factor in my choice of Belgium was a conception about small countries set forth by a number of the physicians and social scientists whom I consulted, which, at the time, seemed to me both reasonable and inviting. A small country like Belgium, these persons implied, would not only be easier for a lone investigator like me to cover geographically but would also be simpler than a large country to comprehend in a sociological sense. That conception, which I easily accepted, was to prove to be so untrue, at least of the small country known as Belgium, that if I were now asked to formulate a sociological hypothesis about the relationship between the size of a country and the complexity of its social system, I would be tempted to suggest that there is an inverse relationship between the two; that is, the smaller the country, the more complex its social system!

Certain aspects of this sociological complexity and of its possible relevance to the problems of medical research that I wished to explore were manifest almost from the moment of my arrival in Louvain, where I lived that first summer. I had picked Louvain because it was the site of one of the four Belgian universities and hence of one of the medical schools in which a significant amount of medical research is carried out; because it is a town with a medieval Catholic tradition, which I felt would give me a chance, atmospherically and intuitively, to come to know something of "Old Europe"; and because, in this community, via my American contacts, I had excellent introductions to young research physicians and professors of medicine alike.

The first small thing that caught my eye when I debarked from the train was to prove to be connected with a salient characteristic of Belgian life, centrally relevant to my study. The signs on the four *quais* of the station, I noticed, were printed alternately in French and Flemish. "Louvain, Leuven, Louvain, Leuven," they read. These were indicators in miniature, I was soon to learn, of the so-called "linguistic problem" of Belgium: the vying between French-speaking and Flemish-speaking Belgians of Wallonie, Flanders, and environs for equal recognition and rights in all domains of Belgian life, a struggle symbolized by their disputes over the coexistence and the geographical distribution of their respective maternal languages.

Some of the characteristic sights and sounds of Louvain (Leuven) introduced me from the very first to still another kind of complexity of Belgian life, which I soon realized had consequences for medical research as well as other Belgian activities. On the one hand, there were the ancient, narrow, cobblestoned streets of Louvain, its Gothic town hall and baroque churches, the many priests moving about the town dressed in their cassocks,[4] the lamplighter making his rounds at dusk and at dawn, and the periodic chiming of carillon bells. On the other hand, those same venerable streets were filled with a raucous procession of shiny, fast-driven cars as well as horse-drawn wagons and *vélos;* new buildings were springing up everywhere; and the plate-glass show windows of the town's thriving shops were filled with the newest-model refrigerators, cameras, television sets, transistor radios, ballpoint pens, and typewriters. The deeply rooted traditional and the up-to-the-minute modern lived side by side in these and other ways in the town of Louvain, sometimes in harmony, sometimes in conflict, affecting medical research as well as other factors of Belgian life, I quickly discovered, on a far more than local scale.

During my first week in Louvain, largely though discussions with the physicians and their families to whom I had letters of introduction, I also came to understand more precisely where Louvain "fitted" in the social structure of Belgian medical research. Most such research in Belgium, I learned, is carried out in a department, hospital, or institute affiliated with one of the four Belgian universities (Louvain, Brussels, Ghent, and Liège). Each of these universities, it was explained to me, represents a different combination of some of the social and cultural distinctions institutionalized in many sectors of Belgian life.

Louvain is a "free" (that is, a private, nonstate) Catholic university with a double faculty and student body, the one section of the university being Flemish, the other French. Brussels is also a free university, but Free Throught, rather than Catholic, in its religious-philosophical orientation—Free Thought encompassing a set of attitudes that range from a nonconfessional, humanitarian kind of rationalism to the flagrantly anticonfessional, anti-Catholic attitudes of at least certain chap-

4. It was not until January 1, 1963, that the cardinal and bishops of the Catholic Church in Belgium passed an ordinance which made it officially acceptable for Belgian priests to wear "clergymen suits" in public.

ters of the Free Mason Lodge in Belgium.[5] Originally, all its classes were taught in French, but since World War II various parts of the university (including the medical school) have doubled their faculties, adding professors who give in Flemish the same courses that are given in French. Ghent is a state university, officially neither Catholic nor Free Thought, but with a great many practicing Catholics in the student body and on the faculty. Since the early 1930s, all classes at Ghent have been taught in Flemish. Liège is also a state university, like Ghent, neither Catholic nor Free Thought, but with the greater number of its students and faculty nonpracticing Catholics or non-Catholics. All classes at Liège are taught in French.

But the structure within which Belgian medical research is conducted "is even more complicated than that," my informants assured me; and I subsequently saw this myself, when I began to move from one university research setting to another. For one thing, the two free nonstate universities, as well as the two state universities, receive large subsidies from the Belgian government; for another, though the two state universities are presumably neutral in their overall political and religious-philosophical orientations, a majority of members of certain faculties of each of these universities, or of particular departments within the faculties, may be affiliated with one of the three major Belgian political parties (Social Christian, Liberal, and Socialist) in an active, partisan way or may be fervently Catholic, non-Catholic, or anti-Catholic.

I carried out my exploratory research that first summer in Belgium in the same general way I proceeded the three subsequent times I returned to Belgium to go on with the inquiry I had started. What I attempted to do was to divide my time as equally as possible among the various clinical

5. The religious structure of Belgian society is a rather special one. Belgium is a predominantly Catholic country, one in which the influence of the Catholic Church in many domains of Belgian life is still strong and pervasive enough for it to be described by some persons as a "clerical" country. It is also a country in which Protestantism is of minor importance, in terms both of its small number of adherents and its relative lack of influence. There are significant groups of Jews only in the communities of Antwerp and Brussels. On the whole, most Belgians who are not practicing Catholics were nonetheless baptized as Catholics. Many such Belgians belong to the religious-philosophical orientation known as Free Thought. Within this category of Free Thought, there is an indeterminate number of persons who are members of the Free Mason Lodge, which, in Belgium, as in France, was historically founded as a secret organization, with one of its primary goals that of combating the doctrine and the influence of the Catholic Church. The influence of the lodge, in general, in Belgian society, as well as in this particular anticonfessional respect, is thought by many Belgians to be considerable. It is hard to be more precise than this about the beliefs and membership of the lodge and about its impact on Belgian life since it still remains essentially a secret organization in Belgium.

medical research groups within each of the four universities and to function as a participant observer in these research milieux, as well as to conduct focused interviews with the physicians who worked in each of these settings. Because each of the universities represents a particular constellation of some of the social and cultural differentials that fragment Belgian life, each tends to seal itself off from the others. As numerous Belgians to whom I spoke in the course of this summer put it, the universities are "veritable cloisters," by which they meant that there is a limited interchange of ideas and information between them and an even more restricted exchange of personnel, for the faculty of each one is drawn almost exclusively from its own alumni. Thus, the conviction of numerous research physicians that their professional environment, satisfactions, and problems were distinctly different from those of their colleagues in other Belgian university settings was a consequence of local, particularistic pride on their part, combined with a relative lack of first-hand information about "what it was really like" in Belgian research milieux other than their own. Above and beyond how they affected the reaction to my activities, these restrictions on the exchange of information and personnel among Belgian universities obviously have implications for medical research and research careers in Belgium. Nevertheless, it is methodologically interesting that it was my own personal research experiences that first sensitized me to this important situation.

In contradiction to the sense of uniqueness that each of the groups of research physicians seemed to have regarding their own university situation, as I moved progressively from one research setting to another I was more and more impressed by the fact that certain phenomena affecting medical research and research careers seemed to occur in every one of the four Belgian universities. The differences between the several university worlds of medical research in these respects seemed to be more differences of nuance and degree than differences of kind. Some of the recurrent phenomena by which I was struck include the following.

(1) The paucity of funds available for medical research, partly as a consequence of the relatively small amount of money voted for scientific research each year by the national government, the primary source of research funds in Belgium. Difficulties in obtaining needed equipment and ancillary medical personnel—difficulties primarily, but not exclusively, financial in origin.

(2) Problems of constructing the kind of hospitals and laboratories needed for the most up-to-date, advanced medical research (and care) or, at least, of renovating hospital and laboratory buildings that were constructed years, sometimes even centuries, ago. Problems of completing, opening, and utilizing such new or rehabilitated buildings, once work on them had begun. The sound of hammering could be heard in

every one of the four universities, and research physicians eagerly and impatiently awaited the outcome of these building and rebuilding efforts. Yet, in one university, a hospital in construction for twenty-five years was still not completed; in a second, a newly constructed hospital, ready for use, stood idle and closed; in a third, a major piece of research equipment (a betatron), delivered months earlier, remained in the crate in which it had arrived, because the construction of the special kind of building in which it would have to be housed had only begun.

(3) Problems connected with obtaining an academic position in one of the four universities, primarily on the basis of professional competence, from which a physician could function as a medical researcher with some degree of stability and security. As already noted, Belgium is a country in which practically all medical research is carried out from a position within the university structure; there is virtually no other professional "place to stand," for example, in government or industry, if one wishes to do medical research. Even within the structure of universities there are relatively few formal positions open to a man who aspires to a research career. This was especially true in 1959, when I began my work in Belgium. At that time, more than now, the structure of the staffs in the university departments, hospitals, and institutes where medical research is conducted was, in the words of one physician, "like a building in which the ground and top floors have been constructed, but in which they haven't gotten around yet to putting in the floors in between." Research units were, and still are, typically headed by one full professor, with all the authority and responsibility of a *patron.* Below the rank of professor-*patron,* and greatly subordinate to it, there exist a certain number of university statuses like those of *chargé de cours* or assistant, from which one may carry out medical research (but usually with a heavy load of clinical medical responsibilities as part of one's duties).

A greater number of physicians engaged in medical research hold no such formal university appointment; rather, their positions (often titleless) exist only by virtue of the fact that the *patron* has been able to raise a sufficient sum of money temporarily to pay them a salary and support their research. It was not until 1960 that a law was passed officially creating two new kinds of tenure positions in the structure of Belgian universities in addition to that of full professor: those of *chargé de cours associé* and *professeur associé.* In effect, they represent some of the "floors in between" that were missing in the formal status system of Belgian university faculties; but, even so, the number of such positions created and of men appointed to them is still very limited.

As already mentioned, the positions open to a physician who wishes to devote himself primarily to research are further restricted by the relative infrequency with which a graduate from one Belgian university is named to a position in another. Even within his own alma mater, the chances of a physician's being appointed on the basis of scientific competence to one of the few staff or faculty positions in which sustained research is possible are curtailed by the considerable extent to which such particularistic considerations as the political, ethnic, linguistic, philosophical, religious, class, and family affiliations of candidates play a role in determining who is named and by the significant influence that the particularistically or personally based preferences of the *patron* of a given department or institute may exert in choosing the physician to whom a position is accorded. The low salaries typically paid to other than professors engaged in research, combined with this degree of uncertainty about whether one will be appointed to a relatively permanent academic position from which to carry on research, make it difficult, and in many cases impossible, for young physicians with families to support to continue to take the risk and to make the sacrifice of trying to remain primarily in the field of research.

(4) Existing side by side with these problems of medical research and research careers were two phenomena that seemed to be almost paradoxically related to them. Though in each of the universities there was a dearth of adequate positions available to competent research physicians, there were also certain university research positions and even professorial chairs that remained vacant or were not filled for long periods of time. Everywhere medical researchers lacked funds, equipment, and ancillary personnel that would facilitate their work; yet, at the same time, very expensive equipment was duplicated in the four universities for lack of some cooperative arrangement among departments, institutes, and universities for the joint use of such equipment. (For example, I counted sixteen artificial heart machines, four artificial kidney machines, four betatrons, and four cobalt bombs in Belgium, a country smaller than the state of New Jersey.)

(5) Finally, there were certain characteristics of what might be called the psychological atmosphere that seemed to be present in all the university settings. Whatever the specific nature of their problems, medical researchers were all confronted with the general, morale-eroding phenomenon of long delays in trying to deal with them, and sometimes utter paralysis. In the face of these delays and impasses, there was a tendency everywhere to try to find ways around the cumbersome formal procedures and structures that in part caused and perpetuated these blocks. *Petits chemins* ("byroads" or "detours"), even *truques* (a Belgian word for

somewhat illicit "gimmicks" or "tricks" for getting things done more speedily), were invented and used pervasively by medical researchers with frustration-born zest.

At the same time, many research physicians seemed to feel something like a sense of mystery about what they described as the absurd, enigmatic, arbitrary qualities of the conditions under which they had to conduct their work. They expressed apprehension and indignation about what they experienced as the inscrutable or capricious nature of some of the forces that affected their professional activities and destinies. These sentiments often focused on certain strategic persons who, these medical researchers implied, determined often in an invisible and prejudicial way what did and did not happen. Sometimes these presumably powerful individuals were cited by position and name; more often they were referred to, half jokingly, half fearfully, as *messieurs les responsables, Esprits Directeurs,* or *éminences grises.*

As even this brief account of my first Belgian summer makes obvious, what had begun as a June–September voyage of self-education in matters pertinent to my professional interest in the sociology of medicine and science had quickly become far more than that. Almost inadvertently, I had carried out the first stage of a potentially long-term study of medical research and medical-research careers in Belgium; it was already involving me in thinking about certain general attributes and problems of the intricate and diverse little society (in the words of one Belgian physician, the "complex social mosaic") of which these medical scientific institutions are an integral part. For in all the research situations with which I had made contact, in all the universities, the range of problems that confronted medical investigators was significantly related to and affected by rather general traits of Belgian society. These included:

(1) Various forms of particularism—the importance attached to ethnic, linguistic, philosophical, religious, political, community, social-class, special-interest, and family differences in Belgium.

(2) Some of the conflicts and strife that result from this particularism, notably disputes between Walloon and Flemish, Catholic and Free Thought groups.

(3) A very literal "it must be identical and not simply equivalent" conception of equality imposed by one group on the other, which often leads to the replication of resources, facilities, organizations, and so on and, in certain decision-making situations, to delays and impasses because the opposing groups involved are so evenly balanced and so unyielding in their relations with one another.

(4) An elaboration of ministries, agencies, and other divisions of the central government that enters all domains of life in Belgium—ministries and agencies that have numerous overlapping functions and archaic rules and regulations, which are the hard-to-change heritage of a historical past and which have grown more, rather than less, complex by virtue of some of the new functions and positions (created partly in response to pressures for greater representation on the part of vying particularistic groups).

(5) The importance of local communities in Belgian life—of the nine provinces and 2633 communes that make up the highly autonomous local governments of Belgium—with their tendency to exhibit jealous pride in their own local authority and to regard the central government with suspicion and even a certain disdain.

One or another of these factors, and sometimes virtually all of them, seemed to pervade the stories that lay behind the recurrent problems faced by Belgian medical researchers in the various university milieux. For example, a particularly striking concrete instance was the university hospital begun twenty-five years ago and still not completed. This appeared to be a consequence of a maze of factors, which included the involvement of one of the professors of medicine (a moving spirit behind the building of the hospital) in the Flemish nationalist movement and the disrepute into which the hospital fell when he was accused by persons less "Flamingant" than himself of having collaborated with the Germans in World War II; conflicts between the local Commission of Public Assistance and the ministries of Public Health and National Education of the central government over various aspects of the work; certain ineptitudes on the part of all three of these bodies in conceiving, planning, and executing the building; and their susceptibility to political, religious-philosophical, and ethnic-linguistic pressures which resulted in disputes, delays, and curtailments of funds.

By the time the summer was over, I had committed myself to making a formal study of clinical medical research in a current European society and to locating that study explicitly in Belgium for reasons that were now preeminently sociological. The apparent relationship in Belgium between the problems of medical research and numerous other sectors of the society were intriguing. Furthermore, moving in a "Rashomon-like" circle from one university to another, as I would have to do in Belgium to make such a study, had the built-in sociological attraction of enabling me to look systematically at these problems of medical research from the points of view of the different particularistic clusters that each university represented.

The study of clinical medical research in Belgium that began in this way continued for the next three years. My actual physical presence in Belgium consisted all told of three summers (June through September of 1959, 1960, and 1961) and finally a six-month stay extending from July through December of 1962. However, there were a number of respects in which, over the course of those years, I never completely left Belgium behind, even when I was residing and working in the United States. For one thing, I received a large cross-section of popular, medical, and scholarly publications of Belgium—newspapers, magazines, journals, books—in French and also in Flemish (which I progressively learned to read with the help of a dictionary and to understand when spoken). Second, I carried on a vast and vigorous correspondence with research physicians—professors as well as younger researchers—in each of the Belgian universities, who kept me closely informed of any happenings while I was away which they thought might be relevant to my study. Third, during those years almost every Belgian connected with medical research or the medical profession in any way who had occasion to be in the United States contacted me. So, too, did a certain number of Belgians outside of medicine, from the worlds of the universities, business, politics, and the Church, who passed through America at that time. This also helped to keep me in constant touch with Belgium and considerably expanded the network of Belgians with whom I was in communication.

Especially because of the light it will eventually shed on the dramatic ways (both positive and negative) in which Belgians reacted to some of the findings of my research when they were first published, it should not be taken for granted that such a sizable number of Belgians actively sought me out and remained conscientiously and enthusiastically in touch with me, even when I was not in Belgium, throughout the entire course of my study. It is easier to see now, *ex post facto,* than it was at the time that simply by the act of being engaged in this research I was already cast in a rather special role by Belgian medical researchers and by other Belgians, such as the ever-widening group of persons who wrote to me, phoned me, visited with me, both in Belgium and the United States.

In a society like that of Belgium, where particularistic sentiments and attitudes are not only deeply felt but also formally institutionalized, the relations between persons from different groups are sufficiently restricted so that many Belgians found it interesting and valuable to hear what the American sociologist, who in the course of her research was passing more freely than they could from one social universe to another in Belgium, might have to say about "what it was like" in groups other than the ones to which they themselves belonged. The research physicians of each university, for example, asked me whether conditions in medical research units of the other Belgian universities were comparable to their own. Flemings asked about the ideas, opinions, outlook of the Walloons to whom I had spoken, the Walloons about those of the Flemings. Catholics and Free Masons made inquiries about each other. *Patrons* of medicine were interested in knowing how younger research physicians (to whom they referred as *les jeunes*) felt about their professional situations; *les jeunes,* in turn, asked about the *patrons.* It would have been at once methodologically undesirable and morally dubious for me to pass on concrete information of this kind from one group to another. But, within careful and scrupulous limits, I did provide something like a general, analytic overview of the multiple worlds of Belgian medical science—an overview that, as already indicated, suggested as many similarities as differences between these supposedly diverse milieux. Constrained as they had been by their own particularistic attitudes from observing and recognizing such common features, many Belgians seemed to find my overarching perspective original and instructive.

In addition, my continuing and caring interest in things Belgian touched what was apparently a disguised love of country on the part of numerous Belgians. When they spoke about their country, generally what they said was critical, even depreciatory in nature; nevertheless, they were obviously pleased and flattered as well as surprised by the fact that a non-Belgian should be so vitally concerned with what one Belgian physician described as "the absurd and pitiful problems of our small and beautiful country." It also became increasingly apparent that one of the reasons for which Belgian research physicians from each of the universities, and certain other Belgians as well, maintained contact with me and helped with my research was that they saw in me something like a potential *dea ex machina.* As an American, rather than a Belgian, they felt, I could look into some of the problems that beset them, not only with a certain objectivity, but also with relative impunity.

In the tight, invidious, particularistic situations within which they functioned personally and professionally, in their small, tension- and apprehension-ridden country, it was perhaps the better part of wisdom, they reasoned, for them to keep silence about their problems. Partly, this was a matter of pride—personal, local, and national. Partly, it seemed to be a consequence of widespread anxiety, bordering on fear, of the kind of retaliation from a competing individual or group, or even from an all-powerful *monsieur le responsable,* that publicly speaking out might provoke. But if an American sociologist "from outside the System," as a number of persons put it, could be privately encouraged to look into these problems and eventually to make them known, the silence about them might at last be broken in a way that would not involve any specific Belgian or group of Belgians and might help to bring about needed changes. But here we are getting ahead of the story; for this aspect of my role did not really become manifest until my last journey to Belgium, after the publication of two articles.

I returned to Belgium that second summer (1960) as a Special Fellow of the Belgian American Educational Foundation and rented an apartment in Brussels. Both of these arrangements were, in part, consequences of what my first year of research there had taught me about the Belgian social system and its implications for my own work. I had applied for the fellowship with the hope of receiving some help in defraying my expenses, of course; but just as important to me was having the moral support of an organization, at once Belgian and American, highly regarded in the Belgian academic world and considered, on the whole, to transcend the divisive conflicts and rivalries of Belgium. I hoped that working with the sponsorship of the foundation would symbolize my commitment to Belgium, on the one hand, and my neutrality, on the other.

The choice of Brussels as my place of residence was also suggested, if not dictated, by the particularism of Belgium. If I had lived in Louvain again I would have been irrevocably classified as a "*Louvainiste*" and, as a probable result, not given the kind of access to the other three universities (especially the University of Brussels) that I sought and needed. Brussels, ostensibly, was the least partisan place of residence to choose. Actually, like any community in Belgium, it represents a special particularistic cluster, but I could justify living there in such terms as its being the capital city, centrally located, convenient for obtaining transportation to the other university towns, and so on. The important thing is, of course, that I even had to plan carefully where I should live in order to avoid being classified with any one group in such a way as to disqualify me for working with all the groups pertinent to my research.

So in 1960 (and again in 1961 and 1962) I located in Brussels. The view from the windows of my apartment there was not so medieval as the one I had in Louvain, but one of its landmarks especially linked my second Belgian summer with my first. On the wrought-iron gate that separated my small, private, nineteenth-century-style street from the bustling modern avenue on which it opened was a shiny red mailbox with two slots. The slot on the right-hand side of the box was labeled with the Flemish word for "letters," *brieven;* on the left-hand side was the equivalent French word, *lettres.*

The planned objectives of my research that summer were several. In addition to my very general aim of acquiring more empirical knowledge and a better analytic understanding of social aspects of clinical medical research in Belgium, one of my specific goals was to equalize my acquaintanceship with the different university settings in which medical research is conducted. Thus, in order to balance out my research experiences of the first summer, I now spent a good deal more time at the universities of Brussels, Ghent, and Liège than at the University of Louvain and, when I was at Louvain, more time in the Flemish section than in the French section of the medical school. Another of my aims that second summer, and in my subsequent research visits to Belgium as well, was to look more deeply into some of the phenomena already mentioned that seemed to be present in many different Belgian research groups and to follow through time the unfolding of certain types of happenings or clusters of events apparently connected with these phenomena. Tracing out in this way what were essentially a series of sociological case histories, I felt, would give me more precise information about how social factors affect medical research and research careers in Belgium and suggest how tenacious or how subject to change were the associated problems.

In this manner, to take one concrete example, I was able to identify and follow some of the social processes involved in the vacating of a particular professorial chair in one of the four universities; the delay of more than two years before that chair was filled (although there were at least four qualified local candidates desirous of that chair); some of the consequences of that delay for these aspiring candidates, for other physicians who worked with them, for the quality and quantity of the research produced by the department during that prolonged waiting period, and for the medical-school faculty at large; the way in which a new professor was finally chosen; and the consequences of that choice, in the context of all that had preceded it, for the new professor, for the candidates not chosen, for their associates, and for their research. Since the stories that I closely observed and followed in this way were chosen because they seemed to be exemplifications of comparable phenomena taking place in many different research groups, these case studies gave me general, as well as particular, insights into the sociodynamics of various facets of Belgian medical research.

Although in a book-length account of my research experiences in Belgium it would merit at least a whole chapter of description and analysis, I can only mention in passing here that my entire second summer of research was carried out against the larger backdrop of Belgium's "Congolese crisis"—the unexpectedly violent way in which

Belgium totally lost her former colonial possession, the Congo, one month after she had formally granted its independence. This grave event, so shocking to Belgians, also affected my research in at least two ways. In the discussions I heard about the Congo and Belgium that summer and the reading I progressively did about it, I began to see how some of the same ethnic-linguistic, religious-philosophical, and political divisions of Belgium that I was observing and analyzing in connection with medical research had been transposed to the Congo by the Belgian colonial regime, contributing to the complex pressures for independence in the Congo and the uprisings of July 1960. Being in Belgium during this summer of crisis also gave me a vivid and empathic sense of what it felt like to be a citizen of a small country, suddenly closed in upon itself by the loss of its one open frontier and condemned by the big world powers for its colonial policies. A wave of hurt indignation mounted over the fact that even the United States, with whom there had been especially warm and friendly relations since World War I, had joined those countries that severely criticized Belgium. As a consequence, throughout the summer of 1960 it was no longer especially desirable to be an American sociologist, or an American of any genre, in Belgium. Belgian sensitivity about American criticisms of their policies in the Congo evidently persisted beyond that summer. For, two years later, when my articles about medical research in Belgium were published, among the negative comments about the American sociologist that were verbalized and printed in the lay press were remarks to the effect that she had exhibited the same uncomprehending, unsympathetic attitudes toward Belgian medical research that her country had demonstrated in 1960 when Belgium was faced with its Congo crisis.

During these first two summers, as has been seen, the locus of my research was confined mainly to the four universities and my methods of inquiry were primarily those of participant observation and interviewing of physicians in the medical research groups associated with the universities. Back in the United States, as I reflected on the kind and scope of materials that I had thus far collected and as I prepared myself for a third summer of research in Belgium, I decided that what I now needed to do was to supplement and extend my data in two ways. I should now deliberately go in search of documentary and statistical materials bearing on the status and functioning of medical research in Belgium: for example, figures on how many physicians are engaged full time or part time in clinical medical research, how many different research groups there are, exactly how large or how small the research budget of various of these groups is, from what sources they obtain their funds, how they allocate them; minutes of department or faculty meetings in which matters relevant to medical research and research careers have been discussed;

documents connected with the planning and constructing of various hospitals and laboratories, the procuring of equipment, and so forth. In addition, it seemed to me that the time had come to try to make contact with various structures outside the universities that had some bearing on the functioning and financing of medical research, notably particular ministries of the national government, private foundations, and those public-assistance bodies of local communes that own and help to administer university hospitals in which medical research is conducted. Upon my return to Belgium,[6] when I actually set out to enrich and more solidly document my research in these ways, I encountered certain apprehensions and obstacles that once again proved to be related to attitudes and practices deeply rooted in Belgian tradition and social organization rather than just a passing, idiosyncratic response to a querying American sociologist.

The collection of the kinds of documentary and statistical materials that I had in mind was not easy to accomplish. Records of meetings in university, foundation, and government settings that bore on issues or events affecting medical research and researchers, and statistics other than the most gross and general sort on research personnel, grants, budgets, and salaries in some instances did not exist; in others, they existed but through polite evasions were not made available to me. There were even a few occasions on which I was given access to the materials I sought but where I had enough auxiliary information to recognize that the data were inaccurate (for example, the minutes of a medical-school faculty meeting that took such liberties with some of the exchanges between professors as to distort if not falsify them; or the annual budget for the research unit of a professor that significantly underestimated the funds he had available for medical research, since certain private donations he received were not mentioned).

The difficulties of data collection that I experienced, as indicated, were by no means unique but rather were a concrete illustration of the sorts of problems that many other individuals and groups have encountered in trying to assemble and transmit detailed and reliable data bearing on contemporary phenomena in Belgium.[7] To cite just four relevant examples: (1) it has not been possible to conduct a language

6. In the summer of 1961, I once again received a Commission for Relief Special Fellowship from the Belgian American Educational Foundation that enabled me to go on with my work, and my place of residence once more was Brussels.

7. There is perhaps a touch of historical irony in these difficulties, since one of the founding fathers of "social statistics" (out of which has been born a tradition of census-taking in many societies) as well as of certain quantitative aspects of the discipline of sociology was Lambert Adolphe Jacques Quételet (1796–1874), a Belgian astronomer, meteorologist, and statistician, originally from Ghent.

census in Belgium since 1947; (2) the Sauvy Report, a study of the demographic evolution of the Walloon and Flemish provinces of Belgium and of the *arrondissement* of Brussels, was finally published in 1962, but only after a long prehistory of attempts to discourage first the carrying out of the study on which it was based and then the diffusion of its findings; (3) one of the *raisons d'être* of an independent organization known as the Center of Socio-Political Research and Information, or CRISP (*Centre de Recherche et d'Information Socio-Politiques*), is that it enables a group of social scientists, lawyers, journalists, and the like to operate on a personal, anonymous, extraofficial basis, outside of their usual professional organizations and roles, and thereby obtain from individuals and groups data on current social, economic, and political happenings that they would not be granted otherwise; (4) most germane to my own efforts to collect certain data on Belgian medical research are the recent, as yet not very successful, attempts of the National Council of Scientific Policy (*Conseil National de la Politique Scientifique*), an advisory group created by the national government, to do a general survey of the funds, apparatus, and personnel engaged in scientific research of all sorts in Belgium.

The characteristic difficulties that lie behind all these efforts, my own included, systematically to collect and make known facts and figures about various aspects of present-day Belgian society seem to stem largely from some of the same particularistic attitudes already examined. The persons and groups approached for pertinent information tend to be latently, if not always openly, apprehensive and suspicious about one's motives for carrying out the inquiry, about the group by which one is sponsored or employed and its intentions, and about the possible consequences of revealing certain facts to groups other than their own.

As I shall subsequently show in connection with my own research project, there were some very practical, reality-based reasons for which my inquiry evoked this kind of anxiety and wariness in the worlds of medical research and even in a number of milieux outside of them; but, in addition, there were also strong nonrational elements that contributed to it.[8] Nowhere was this more apparent than when I made my first

8. It has been suggested to me by a number of Belgians, among them several former members of the underground that operated in Belgium during World War II when the country was occupied by Germany, that another origin of the lack of documents and data that I encountered—as well as the difficulty in obtaining what records and figures do exist, the falsification of certain materials, and the atmosphere of mystery and tension with which persons like myself who set out to collect such data have been confronted—is the fact that again and again over the centuries Belgium has been besieged and occupied by conquering powers (Spain, Holland, France, Germany, etc.). As a consequence (the individuals who

overtures toward accomplishing my other major research goal of that third Belgian summer: direct contact with certain persons in some of the extrauniversity organizations that affect medical research.

Perhaps the interview that most vividly illustrates the kind of anxiety about my research and the potential barriers to it that I progressively began to encounter was the one I made when I first arrived back in Belgium in the summer of 1961. I went to a certain gentleman who had greatly helped with my work during the two prior years and who occupied an administrative position that linked universities, foundations, business, and government. I sought his assistance in meeting the small list of persons I thought essential to my contact with Belgian oganizations other than the universities that had some relationship to medical research. This list included a prominent businessman, known to have been a generous donor of funds for scientific research; the vice-president/director and the secretary general of the Belgian foundation that plays the most important role in allocating funds for scientific research, the National Fund of Scientific Research (*Fonds National de la Recherche Scientifique*, or FNRS); the minister and the secretary general of the Department of Public Health and Family of the Central Government; and the president of the Commission of Public Assistance of Brussels.

Mr. X, the gentleman on whom I called for help in being introduced to these people, reacted to my request with great nervousness. The businessman I wished to interview, he said, would be of no special value to my work; though he was high on the board of administrators of several foundations connected with science, his position was "strictly honorific," and he was "just a businessman" who would not be qualified to discuss research. Then why did I feel I had to see the secretary general of the National Fund of Scientific Research if I saw its director? Would it not be sufficient just to talk with the director? As for the appointments I had requested at the Ministry of Public Health and Family, did I have to talk with the minister as well as the secretary general? Ministers generally do not know as much as their secretary generals, Mr. X assured me, for they are always being shifted from one office to another, according to the way the political winds are blowing. Mr. X also ventured the opinion that, if I continued on the path

---

offer this explanation say), Belgians have perfected techniques for making it difficult for powers who have occupied her to gain easy access to information about the country and her inhabitants; and, perhaps in a way that is not completely rational, Belgians have also had a tendency to carry such underground attitudes and sabotaging techniques over to times of relative normalcy and peace.

that I proposed, I would be moving away from my specific topic of research and from carrying it out "scientifically"; I would be collecting "opinions, rather than facts."

I politely countered each of Mr. X's comments, and then, at a certain point in our conversation when it seemed appropriate, I asked him if the real reason he was warning me that my work was getting unscientific and somewhat off the track was that he was trying to find a way to tell me, as others had begun to, "*Attention!* You had better be careful! There's danger in trying to include some of the people and some of the questions you're now broaching in your research." Mr. X breathed a sigh of relief that I had so outrightly stated this and admitted that it was so. He told me that I was now moving in a "difficult situation," and he did not want me to have undue trouble or unpleasantness. In the end, Mr. X did decide to help me because he thought my study was necessary and important, he said, and because I had shown a great deal of "courage" in discussing my determination to go on with the research. He made all the appointments for me that I had requested, with the exception of one with the prominent businessman (whom I never did meet). As I left Mr. X's office that afternoon, his last words to me were, "Be careful! What you're doing now is very risky! Move like a snake!"

Despite the admonitions that preceded my meetings with such government and foundation officials, once I was received by them they were not only cordial to me but remarkably open and free in giving me information, some of which might even be considered delicate in nature. For example, from the officers of the National Fund of Scientific Research whom I interviewed I learned the following kinds of things: The fund receives virtually all its money from the national government and allocates it to applying researchers. All research grants awarded are given to persons currently affiliated with one of the four Belgian universities. Who receives these grants is decided primarily by the twenty-five scientific commissions of which the fund is composed, each one organized around a different subgroup of sciences. Each commission consists of four professors, one from each of the four Belgian universities, and a fifth professor who acts as chairman. Chairmanships are also equally distributed among professors of the four universities (with one exception, since there are twenty-five rather than twenty-four commissions). The vice-president of the fund is also its effective director and the vice-president/director of a number of other Belgian foundations that distribute funds for scientific research. He himself has no formal training in science. The secretary general of the National Fund of Scientific Research, a physical scientist, is secretary general of a number of these other foundations as well.

My interviews with the minister and the secretary general of Public Health taught me first hand that the gentleman occupying the post of minister at that time, who admittedly was not trained or experienced in medical or scientific matters, had just assumed office, whereas the person who was secretary general, a physician, had occupied this position for years. The secretary general of Public Health, I learned from these conversations, was also president of the National Foundation of Medical Scientific Research, a body that receives from the Ministry of Public Health, via the National Fund of Scientific Research, some of the subsidies it distributes to clinical medical researchers.

From my discussions with a number of different officers of the National Council of Scientific Policy came accounts of strong resistance on the part of certain foundation officials and professors to the council's attempts to think through the complex structure within which Belgian research currently operated, to suggest possible modifications in it, and to try to institute a national plan for the development of scientific research in Belgium. My interviews with some foundation officials, on the other hand, as with some professors, had contained apprehensive and sometimes hostile statements about the extent to which they believed the council to be a political instrument of the parties currently in power, hence a far from ideally objective advisory group for national policy concerning medical research.

Certain aspects of the information I gained from meetings with executives in government and foundation positions were potentially delicate in their implications; that is, the simple descriptive facts they supplied about the social structure of the organizations affecting scientific research quite naturally raise certain kinds of questions. For example:

(1) Despite the significant degree of decentralization in the social structure of Belgian medical research suggested by the complex of social organizations within which most of it seemed to take place (four universities, various of their departments, institutes, hospitals, numerous ministries of the national government, the governments of local communes, a network of voluntary health organizations and of foundations, and so on), is there not, at the same time, an extraordinary amount of authority and power concentrated in the hands of a few agencies and persons, notably in the National Fund of Scientific Research and its vice-president/director and secretary general, who occupy these same positions in a number of other foundations as well?

(2) Since, in addition, there is a considerable overlap in the boards of directors of these various foundations that distribute funds for scientific research, and the president of one of them, the National Foundation of

Medical Scientific Research, is also secretary general of the Ministry of Public Health, exactly how independent are these foundations, of each other and the government, and how independent are they, then, of political and other particularistic influences?

(3) Does the fact that two of the key positions in the social structure of government and foundation organizations concerned with research (those of director of the National Fund of Scientific Research and of minister of Public Health) are held by men who are not scientists and do not have advanced scientific training affect the degree to which criteria other than scientific excellence enter into the distribution of research funds?

(4) It is true that the commissions of the National Fund of Scientific Research seem to be the main judges of the merits of the research projects that are submitted to the fund for consideration, and these commissions are composed of professors in various fields of science. But these 125 professors constitute a sizable proportion of the *patrons* who head research groups in the four universities. Does this mean, then, that those who allocate the research grants of the fund are often its recipients either directly or indirectly through the younger members of their various research teams who apply for grants? What implications does this have for the degree of objectivity with which funds are distributed?

(5) Since the commissions are equally divided among representatives of the four universities, might there not be some tendency in these circumstances, in a particularistic society like Belgium, to divide equally among them the total budget available for research rather than to judge primarily on its scientific merits each project submitted?

These were the questions that my interviews with foundation and government officials suggested to me. It is of some interest to note that I never openly raised them or gave voice to them in any of my interviews or in the two articles about medical research in Belgium that I subsequently published. In the second of these articles, for example, I simply described the social organization of government and foundation agencies connected with scientific research in Belgium largely as they had been explained to me by high-ranking executives within them. Yet, after this article was published, one of the questions most frequently and anxiously raised in many different settings was: Who had provided the American sociologist with her information about the government and foundation structures? Various "sinister others" were implicated even by some of the very persons, foundation and government officials among them, who had supplied me with pertinent information.

This phenomenon of "collective amnesia," and the projecting of the blame for having told the American sociologist things that were described at one and the same time as indiscreet and untrue, was one I experienced frequently during my last year of research in Belgium. In this particular context it is especially interesting, because what I published was no more than a description of the social organization and composition of several government and foundation agencies without any interpretation whatsoever. Here, and in numerous other instances, as will be seen, Belgian reactions to my findings were far more suggestive and significant than the findings themselves.

At the end of the third summer of research in Belgium, I returned to the United States once more, where I now set to work writing the aforementioned two articles based on what I had learned thus far. The first article, entitled "Journal Intime Belge/Intiem Belgisch Dagboek" ("Belgian Journal"), appeared in the winter 1962 issue of the *Columbia University Forum.*[9] As the title implies, it was written in the form of a personal diary, through which I tried to evoke an emotional as well as an intellectual understanding of some of the general sociological characteristics of Belgium already described and of certain specifically medical scientific phenomena seen against that backdrop. I used a number of literary devices and images in my attempt to convey this kind of understanding; among them, the gently ironic "doubled" title of the article, evenly balanced between Flemish and French, and a description of the American sociologist standing in front of the two-slotted mailbox on the street where she lived in Brussels, trying to decide whether she should mail a letter she had written in English in the "French slot" or the "Flemish slot." There was an immediate and rather large flurry of responses to this article, both appreciative and critical, first from Belgians in America and then from Belgians at home. These reactions took the form of letters to the editors of *Forum,* to the Belgian Government Information Center in New York, and to me and mention of the article in one of the weekly broadcasts to Belgium from its Information Center in New York.

I shall postpone any real examination and analysis of the comments that were made until the end of this chronicle, for virtually all of them were mild versions of the more heated responses that followed the publication of my second article. The one specific detail that might be noted here is that the image of the bilingual mailbox seems to have elicited more powerful reactions from Belgian readers than any other single aspect of the article. It was referred to in many of the letters I received, and it was the central focus of the Information Center's broad-

9. Renée C. Fox, "Journal Intime Belge/Intiem Belgisch Dagboek," *Columbia University Forum,* V (1962), 11–18.

cast to Belgium. Almost a year after the publication of the "Belgian Journal," toward the close of my last research visit to Belgium, a certain professor of medicine devoted a good part of my interview with him to that selfsame mailbox: at first, earnestly denying that such mailboxes even exist in Belgium, and then, after conceding that there might be *some* of this type, chastizing me in all seriousness for not having explained that, no matter which slot one uses to mail a letter, "everything ends up in the same mailbox!" Obviously, even with my first article I had touched on certain very deeply felt Belgian sensitivities. One of the more friendly critics of the "Belgian Journal" who wrote to me after it was published expressed the emotions I aroused in this way:

> In reading it, I felt a blush of shame mount on my face. We are so accustomed to living in our spiderweb, in the unbelievable cloister of our confessional, linguistic, social, and scientific quarrels, that we hardly even pay attention to them anymore. They begin to seem normal to us. To see all that, put in black and white, by a foreigner, even by one with much tact and sympathy for us, inevitably gives one a shock.

The publication of my second article, this time in *Science*, seems to have constituted a greater "shock" for the much larger Belgian public who read it. It was called "Medical Scientists in a Château,"[10] and its theme, as the editors of *Science* described it, was: "The traditional social structure creates problems for medical research and researchers in Belgium."

The image of the château, around which I built the first section of the article, was meant in part to symbolize those aspects of traditional social structure in Belgium which tend to curtail medical scientific creativity and productivity and the possibilities for careers in medical research.[11] It also referred more specifically to a medical scientific colloquium held in 1959 in Laeken, at the château of the Belgian royal family. I began the article by describing this colloquium in detail because it seemed in so many ways a ceremonial expression of how social, cultural, and historical factors affect medical research in Belgium. For example, most of the speeches

10. Renée C. Fox, "Medical Scientists in a Château," *Science,* CXXXVI (1962), 476–483.

11. The use of the image of the château in this sense was suggested to me by certain comments made by Raoul Kourilsky, professor of clinical medicine at the University of Paris, about the predicament of medical research in present-day France. In the inaugural lesson he gave after being named to his professorial chair, Kourilsky said: "The great sacrifice has been research. We have conserved the old 'château' and its arrangements that belong to another age. . . . We have watched from afar the triumphant ascent of biology." See Raoul Kourilsky, *"Leçon Inaugurale,"* reprint from *L'Expansion scientifique française*, 1958, 27–28.

or presentations made at the colloquium were delivered twice, once in Flemish and once in French. The principal guests of honor at the colloquium were three foreign medical scientists (Dutch, French, and American) who had done experimental work that contributed importantly to the field of cardiac surgery, for which they were about to receive the degree of Doctor *honoris causa* from two Belgian universities. The French scientist was scheduled to receive this degree from the Free University of Brussels on the same day that the American and Dutch scientists were to be awarded their degrees from the Catholic University of Louvain.

The other persons invited to the medical scientific gathering in the château included not only physicians, patients who had undergone cardiac surgery and their families, professors of medicine and science, the rectors of the four universities, officials of voluntary health organizations and of foundations, ministers and secretary generals of the national government, and officials of the local governments, but also numerous members of the royal family and of the nobility, university professors from fields other than medical or biological science, directors of various museums and libraries (some with no bearing on science or scientific work), bankers, businessmen (among them several gentlemen known to be especially prominent members of the Free Mason Lodge), Bishops of the Catholic Church, and others.

In short, representatives of a great many of the institutions in Belgian life had been assembled in the château for this presumably medical scientific occasion in a way that suggested the complex interrelationship of these institutions and certain of their *responsables* (as Belgians would say) and, in turn, their influence on medical research in Belgium. Finally, the image of the château in this article was meant to convey the psychological atmosphere in which many Belgian medical researchers felt they were working: an atmosphere with some of the "absurd," "arbitrary," "undecipherable" qualities reminiscent of those evoked by Franz Kafka in *The Castle*.[12]

The second section of this article described some general characteristics of Belgian society. The third dealt with the social structure of clinical medical research in Belgium, especially the respects in which it shares these general characteristics. The last section of the article traced some of the problematic consequences of this structure and its attributes for medical research and research careers.

12. It is interesting to consider that Kafka, a Czech, was a citizen of another small country of Continental Europe. Perhaps that accounts in part for the striking pertinence to Belgium of certain sociopsychological dimensions of his writings.

Almost immediately after the publication of "Medical Scientists in a Château," a series of remarkable events began to take place—events that rapidly transformed the article and its author into something approaching national *causes célèbres* in Belgium. The first Belgian reaction occurred, only a few days after the article appeared, in the form of a telephone call from an associate of the Belgian Government Information Center in New York. The comments were far from happy or calm. I was accused of having been "unscientific," "erroneous," and "hostile" in what I had said about Belgian medical research and, above all, of having implied that what I had written about it was applicable to other sectors of Belgian society as well. ("You have generalized from a particular case!" the Belgian gentleman on the other end of the line repeated several times.) He went on to say: "What if an American businessman should pick up a copy of this issue of *Science* in his dentist's office and read your article? What will he think? He will think, 'I had better invest my money in Holland, rather than in Belgium!' "

A few weeks after this telephone call, five minutes of an Information Center broadcast to Belgium were devoted to my article. The broadcaster referred to it as an indictment of Belgian medical research and said it would be more appropriate for medical researchers than for himself to pass judgment on the accuracy of its contents. He had only two comments to make, he concluded. First, there would be those who would say that its author has a love-hate complex with respect to Belgium; and second, right or wrong, love or hate, "she has courage!"

A swelling stream of personal letters now began arriving from Belgium, mainly from research physicians (more from *les jeunes* at this time than from their *patrons*), telling me that "Medical Scientists in a Château" had already become, as a physician put it, "one of the most read and discussed bundles of papers in this country." Copies of the issue of *Science* in which it had been published, and photocopies of the article itself, I was told, were being passed from person to person. Not only were they circulating among medical researchers, their families, and their friends, but they had also reached various deans of the four universities, their rectors, foundation officials, certain ministers of the central government, members of the Catholic clergy, businessmen, bankers, engineers, museum and library directors, writers, artists, and even some members of the royal family. These reports about the wide circulation of the *Science* article were confirmed by the vast number of requests for reprints that I began to receive from Belgium and by the varied sources from which they came.[13]

13. In addition to all the requests for reprints that I received from Belgium, I received many from other countries of Continental Europe (France, Germany, Italy, Holland),

The personal mail also indicated, as several of my correspondents put it, that Belgian reactions to the article were "passionate." There are those who consider it a "manifesto," wrote one research physician, and "others who wave it in the air angrily and don't like it, to say the least. . . . I wonder if your planned stay in Belgium will be safe," he added with a flash of humor. "Well, anyway, some of us will protect you!"

The stay in Belgium to which this letter referred was scheduled to begin the third week in July. I thought of it as my definitive research period in Belgium, one that would enable me to complete the data-gathering phase of my study. For I was fortunate enough to have been awarded a Guggenheim Fellowship and to have been granted a semester's leave of absence from my university teaching duties. This made it possible to spend an unbroken period of five months in Belgium from the end of July until the end of December 1962, a time span that, in addition to its duration, had the advantage of including several months of the academic year when university-based medical research activities would be at their height.

But before I set sail for Belgium toward the end of July, a series of reactions of another kind to "Medical Scientists in a Château" began to occur, contributing to the highly charged atmosphere in which I was destined to carry out the last months of my research. On June 15, 1962, an article about "Medical Scientists in a Château" appeared in *Pourquoi Pas*, a weekly French-language magazine published in Brussels. The title of the article (in relatively small print) was "Scientific Research in Belgium," and its subtitle (in much larger print), "Are We a Ridiculous Country?". In rapid succession, over the course of the next month, six more articles appeared in the Belgian press about "the article in *Science* by the American sociologist."

On July 1 and July 11, respectively, there were two articles about it in *Le Soir* (a daily French-language, Free-Thought-inclined newspaper of Brussels). The first article was entitled "Is Belgian Particularism Shackling the Progress of Medical Research: A Severe American Indictment," and the second article simply "Particularism." Some of the passage in the *Science* article about the medical scientific colloquium in the royal palace was cited in a July issue of another French-language Belgian magazine called *Europe,* devoted in that instance largely to articles on the Belgian

---

England, the Scandinavian countries of Sweden, Norway, and Denmark, two countries behind the Iron Curtain (Czechoslovakia and Poland), Canada, Latin America (Panama and Venezuela), and many regions of the United States. This attests, of course, to the vast and wide-ranging circulation of *Science.* It also suggests that my analysis of some of the problems of clinical medical research in Belgium might have their counterparts in numerous other societies as well.

royal family. A bimonthly review called *Tonus,* circulated to Belgian physicians by the Winthrop drug house, carried a summary of my article headed "Progress of Medical Research and Belgian Particularism." A signed editorial was printed in a publication called *Recipe,* a monthly magazine put out by the Medical Circle of the French section of the Medical School of the Catholic University of Louvain. This editorial, written by a Jesuit priest who was editor-in-chief of *Recipe* and chaplain of the Medical Circle, took its title from the *Pourquoi Pas* article which it attacked: "Are We a Ridiculous Country?". Still another article with the same heading subsequently appeared in *Pourquoi Pas,* this one an evaluation of my article by a physician who was a professor of medicine and the head of a clinical medical research unit of the University of Brussels Medical School.

From the beginning of August 1962, after my return to Belgium, until the end of that December, when I finally left Belgium, nine more articles about my own were published in the Belgian press. These included: an article in the August issue of the monthly journal of the College of Physicians of Brussels and environs *(Bulletin du Collège des Médecins de l'Agglomération Bruxelloise)* called "An Odious Attack against Medical Research in Belgium"; an answer to this article in the "Free Tribune" section of the October issue of the same magazine, signed by thirty-five Belgian research physicians, mainly from Brussels, and entitled "Back-Wash [*Remous*] Apropos of the Article of Renée Fox"; an article in the October 26 issue of *De Linie,* a Flemish-Jesuit Christian-Socialism-oriented weekly newspaper, entitled "Medical Research in Belgium: An American Finger in the Wound"; a long discussion of my article, especially the parts of it devoted to the colloquium in the palace, in the context of an article on "What Is Being Done to Promote Scientific Research in Belgium?" that was published in the November 11 issue of *Le Drapeau Rouge,* a French-language Communist newspaper of Brussels; an account in a November issue of *Recipe* of a talk I gave on my research at the Medical House *(Maison Médicale)* of the French section of the Medical School of Louvain; a prominent reference to my article in the introductory paragraphs of an article written by a professor of economics of Louvain University whose theme was "Dispersion: Our Economy Is the Victim of It," printed in the September 8 issue of *La Libre Belgique,* a French-language, Catholic, politically conservative newspaper; and still another reference to my article in the November 28 edition of *Le Soir,* in an article called "Magic Skin,"[14] which was largely

14. This is a reference to a novel by Balzac, *La Peau de chagrin.*

concerned with the low salaries received by members of the faculties and research staffs of the Belgian universities. Finally, just before I left Belgium in December, two small articles appeared, the first in *La Libre Belgique* and the second in *Le Peuple* (a French-language Socialist newspaper published in Brussels), both of which summarized the content of a talk that I had given on Belgian medical research to a Flemish group interested in promoting industry in Flanders, the so-called *Vereniging voor Economie.*

There are several general features of this literature that deserve mention here. For one thing, as their titles suggest, most of the articles published were written in the controversial spirit and tone of editorials, either "celebrating" or "denouncing" "Medical Scientists in a Château" and its author, as the case might be. Second, many of these articles were written by people who were not professional journalists: a professor of medicine, for example, a professor of economics, a Jesuit priest. Third, these discussions of my article appeared in publications representing (albeit not in perfect, Belgian-type equality) each of the major particularistic groups of the country: Flemish and Walloon; Catholic and Free Thought; Liberal (Conservative), Christian Socialist, Socialist, and Communist. Fourth, although the publication of some of these articles about my research was spontaneous, others appeared because they were encouraged or engineered by people who evidently wished to bring a discussion of problems of Belgian medical research before the larger public. For example, the first "Are We a Ridiculous Country?" article that appeared in *Pourquoi Pas* was the direct result of the fact that a professor of medicine at one of the Belgian universities went to the editorial office of this magazine with a copy of my article in hand and asked a journalist there to publish what he expressly hoped would be a provocative essay about it.

These aspects of the way in which my article was brought to the attention of Belgian newspapers, magazines, and journals and handled by them are indicative of certain general characteristics of the press in Belgium. The Belgian press not only reports news and attempts to reflect and influence public opinion. It also seems to provide an important channel through which individuals who represent specific social groups in Belgium, but who are not journalists by trade, can speak out, directly or from behind the scenes, on behalf of the interests of those groups. Writing for the popular press, or utilizing it by supplying professional journalists with materials, seems to be a socially acceptable and, to some extent, even prestigious activity in which Belgian physicians, lawyers, professors, priests, and the like engage, as well as politicians and journalists. Apparently it is one of the more important, legitimate, potentially effective ways in Belgium to exert enough social pressure either to foster or to deter social change in various sectors of Belgian life.

This function of the Belgian press[15]—in combination with the zealous way that some people encouraged me to write another article as soon as possible and the dismayed fashion in which others deplored all the "noise" *(bruit)* that my article had created—suggests that, using journalism as one of their principal means, advocates of change in some of the social conditions surrounding medical research were tourneying with those who were defending the *status quo* in this domain. Another characteristic of many of these articles about "Medical Scientists in a Château"—their tendency to make general references to *all* forms of scientific research in Belgium, to various intra- and interuniversity problems, to certain attributes of the Belgian economy, to the role of the royal family in the political life of Belgium, and even to positive qualities and problems of the country as a whole—also suggests that my article and its press coverage touched off an involved controversy between Belgian groups with vested interests in far more than the status of clinical medical research in Belgium. (I shall return to this point in the last pages of this chronicle.)

At any rate, the kind of coverage that was given to "Mademoiselle/ Juffrouw/Miss Fox" and her "famous [or "infamous"] article" in the lay press was one of the factors that made it almost impossible for me to carry out the last phases of my research in the discreet and private fashion that had characterized my three prior stays in Belgium. I now found myself moving in an emotional atmosphere in which I was called and considered a "heroine," a "Jeanne d'Arc," by some persons and a "viper" by others.

I was asked to discuss the content of my article and the larger study of which it was a part before a whole series of groups. The audiences ranged in size from a small dinner gathering, like that of the editorial board of a medical review, to an amphitheater filled with almost the entire faculty of one medical school; and they ranged in type from audiences entirely or primarily composed of physicians and medical scientists to those that fell completely outside the sphere of the medical profession—for example, the members of the Civil Service Executive Training Program of one university and the Economics Society already

15. This is not to imply that I believe these characteristics necessarily to be unique to the Belgian press. It is my impression, for example, that the newspapers and magazines of certain other Continental European countries that I have only visited, and therefore know less well, might have some of the same traits. France and Holland come to mind in this connection.

mentioned. None of the talks before such groups was conventional, in the sense that first the speaker gave a formal presentation of some length and then a shorter question-and-answer period followed. Instead, most of these occasions were transmuted into heated discussions with the American sociologist and between the members of the audience themselves.

At a particularly animated gathering, for example, a younger research physician, newly appointed to a university position with tenure, bitterly attacked "Medical Scientists in a Château," virtually line by line, whereas an older, full professor of medicine from the same medical school vehemently defended both the article and its author. At a certain point in this discussion, the young physician turned to the *patron* and expressed his surprise and dismay that he, a professor of distinction and accomplishment, should espouse the point of view of the American sociologist and be so severely critical of the Belgian "System," which could not have drastically mistreated him. For, after all, said the young physician, whatever difficulties he may have encountered in the course of his career, the professor had received enough support to do research of quality that was recognized internationally. The response of the professor to these remarks of the *jeune* ringingly ended the evening's debate. Oh, yes, he had received enough money and facilities with which to do research, said the professor. But when? he asked. "At the end of my career," he replied to his own question. "And what did I do before then to have the resources I needed to do research? I'll tell you what I did. I cheated [*J'ai triché*] to have what I needed! I repeat—I cheated!" Again and again, exchanges as emotional as these seemed to be unleashed by my article and by my presence before groups that had invited me to speak about it.

In addition to the public presentations that I was asked, and in a sense required, to give, I was a guest at many more private, social gatherings than during my first three stays in Belgium: luncheons, dinners, after-dinner get-togethers, and so forth. Once again, these occasions were rather out of the ordinary in several significant ways. I was usually the guest of honor or at least a focus of intense interest. In a number of instances, among the other guests who had been invited to meet me were persons prominent in sectors of Belgian life other than the medical: important political, business, or religious figures. Usually these affairs were not purely social but turned into miniature versions of the kinds of discussions and debates in which I was involved when making formal, public presentations of my work. At several of these gatherings, one of the guests privately recommended to me that before my study was finished I ought to discuss some of my observations and impressions with a member of the Belgian royal family. King Baudouin, Queen Mother Elisabeth, Princess Liliane, former King Leopold, were all mentioned in this connection; and in several cases, the persons making the suggestion offered to do what they could to obtain an audience for me—an audience, they said, with joking reference to my article, "in the château."

The excitement generated by the article and by my presence in Belgium produced still another series of extraordinary experiences. I began to receive confidences and data of a kind to which I had not previously had access. Without my actively soliciting them, I was given verbatim transcripts of several meetings highly revelatory of certain attitudes and events that significantly affected Belgian medical research; various documents that medical researchers had drafted at one time or another, individually or in groups, as attempts to analyze their professional situations, criticize or protest against them, or make recommendations for their modification; several reports written by professors of medicine who headed research groups, containing intimate details about the activities of their research teams, the sources of their research funds, and their itemized budgets. Other medical researchers talked to me directly about professional problems they themselves had experienced or about which they knew—problems they had never before discussed with me. And suddenly there also appeared on the scene (once or twice, announced only by their knocking on my front door) individuals with document-accompanied personal histories to tell about how they had been maltreated and professionally blocked by "the System" and sometimes by specific *messieurs* within it. It was hard to ascertain the authenticity of these stories. But from a certain point of view, perhaps as important as the veracity of the reports was the role that such persons imagined that I could play. They had come to tell the American sociologist "all about it," to unburden themselves, to "get the record straight." Above and beyond that, they hoped that through my personal and political influence in Belgium, which they judged to be considerable, and through future articles that I might write, I would be able to help rectify their personal situations and the more general problems of which they conceived them to be a part.

Those whom I did *not* get to see during these eventful six months in Belgium are also significant. Certain persons in the structure of the foundations with whom I tried to renew contact indicated by letter that they felt there was no special reason or value in receiving me. The appointments that people tried to make for me with several high-placed government officials did not materialize. I was received in the royal palace once, by the Chief of the King's Cabinet, but the promised audience with a member of the royal family never took place. And in the medical milieux of each of the four universities there were a certain number of researchers (among them some who had received me with cordiality and helped me with my study during the three previous summers) who now treated me coldly, kept me at a distance, or avoided any contact with me at all.

In the final analysis, how can one explain the degree and kinds of impact that my article in *Science* made on the medical scientific world of Belgium and on other sectors of the society as well? Before attempting an answer to that question, it is enlightening to examine in somewhat more detail the content of the sixteen articles about "Medical Scientists in a Château" published in the Belgian press and of the remarks made about the article at the various formal and informal gatherings to which I was invited during my stay in Belgium. Whether the comments were positive or negative, written or spoken, the majority of them were polemical in nature. On the whole, persons discussing the article were either for it or against it. Rarely were their comments accompanied by objective evidence or counterevidence to support the viewpoints they set forth.

The positive opinions tended to be general. Those well disposed toward the article called it "accurate," "insightful," "well written," and "courageous." By this they meant that they felt that the article evocatively, boldly, and precisely described the problems lived out, largely in silence, by Belgian medical researchers. As one article put it, "No Belgian could or would publish what Miss Fox has written. . . . We should render homage . . . to the foreign writer who dared to touch on these problems, without passion, with a scientific spirit, and, nevertheless, with an enormous amount of sympathy for our country."

The negative criticisms were more copious and specific. The recurrent themes that ran through them are as follows.

(1) How could "Medical Scientists in a Château" have been accepted by *Science,* an outstanding scientific publication? The article is not scientific at all. It is a subjective, impressionistic piece of journalism, a satiric, even cruel indictment of Belgian medical science and scientists. Concrete proof that the article is not scientific is that it contains no supporting statistics *("Mais, où sont les chiffres?").*

(2) This subjective, depreciatory account of medical science in Belgium will be diffused to scientists throughout the world, who will read the article and believe it because it has been published under the distinguished aegis of *Science*. This will adversely affect the way that Belgian medical research and researchers are regarded abroad. It may also jeopardize the financial support for their research that Belgian inves-

tigators can hope to receive from foreign sources, especially American ones.

(3) This image of Belgian medical research presented in the article was conceived and produced by an American. She in particular, and Americans in general, cannot hope to penetrate and understand the complexities of European culture and civilization or appreciate the richness and values of its traditions and the high place that it accords to that which is human rather than materialistic or technological. A typical American's perspective on things European is superficial, naïve, upstart, and self-satisfied. It has been perfectly portrayed in the novel *The Ugly American* and recently exemplified by the way that Americans reacted to Belgium in the Congo crisis. In her article, the American sociologist exhibits all these characteristic traits. And let it not be forgotten, either, that the United States has some of the same problems in the realm of medical research that the sociologist has attributed to Belgium. Why has Belgium been singled out for special scrutiny and criticism?

(4) The account of the medical scientific colloquium held in the royal palace at Laeken and the use of the image of the château to convey certain things about the kind of "house" in which medical research in Belgium is carried out are inappropriate, misleading, and snide. The colloquium in the palace was not so much a scientific gathering as a ceremonial and public-relations occasion, having its American counterpart in certain elaborate receptions held at the White House. Ordinarily, Belgian medical scientists do not spend their time drinking cocktails and tea at four o'clock in the afternoon in palaces and great houses, as the sociologist implies. They are hard-working, dedicated researchers. And the royal family has nothing but a symbolic relationship to scientific research in Belgium. The palace at Laeken in no way controls or affects it.

(5) The American sociologist's description of the social organization of medical research in Belgium is inaccurate and self-contradictory, as well as insinuating. There are not as many research groups and institutes in Belgium as she contends. Universities are not as "cloistered" as she maintains. Relationships between *jeunes* and *patrons* are more colleague-like than she says. The direction of Belgian foundations is not monopolized by one or two men; and the awarding of research grants by foundations like the National Fund of Scientific Research is determined exclusively by the professors of science who make up its commissions. There is nothing complicated or mysterious about the organizations concerned with medical research in Belgium or the relations between them. This misconception on the part of the American sociologist is due to her being a foreigner and probably to her contact with certain young

medical researchers who are still relatively unknowledgeable about these social organizations and with other older researchers who are particularly devious in trying to manipulate "the System." Just as one telling example of her lack of knowledge, consistency, and logic—all three—how can the American sociologist say, as she does, that the social organization of medical research in Belgium is at once highly centralized and highly decentralized?

(6) Certainly none of the observations the author claims to have made are characteristic of *this* university, or of *this* department (which university, or which department, depending on the affiliation of the critic writing or speaking). What she says may be relevant to other universities or other departments, but not to ours.

(7) As a matter of fact, from whom did the American sociologist get her information? Did she really spend an equal amount of time at each university? She seems to have been more influenced by some milieux than by others. And who were the persons who acted as her informants in the various places she visited? What she has written has the ring of aggrieved statements made by persons who have no special talent for research and yet are discontent because they have been unsuccessful in trying to obtain a university research position. It also sounds as if she were very much influenced by the *jeunes* who, like young people the world over, tend to be critical of their elders and desirous of change. In her remarks about the palace and the foundations, the sociologist must certainly have been skillfully led astray by certain vituperative *messieurs* we could name who constantly and insidiously attack these institutions out of motives of personal, economic, and political aggrandizement.

(8) What was the "real reason" that the American sociologist carried out this inquiry into Belgian medical research and then wrote what amounts to a sensationalistic exposé of it? Her motives surely were not impersonal, objective, and pure. Was she more in sympathy, if not in formal affiliation, with the Flemings or Walloons, with Catholics or Free Masons, with the Liberal, Christian Socialist, Socialist, or Communist party?

(9) Lurking behind the author's account of medical research in Belgium is the implication that what she has written is applicable to other areas of Belgian life as well. This is grossly untrue. In fact, if there is any validity at all to the picture the American sociologist paints, some of the things she describes might be uniquely true of the world of medical research and the universities.

(10) If the American sociologist's description of the conditions surrounding Belgian medical research were accurate, Belgium would be devoid of any well-trained, competent researchers and would not pro-

duce any scientific work of merit. Neither of these things is true. Belgium has even had two Nobel Prize laureates in medicine in the course of the last fifty years. In fact, if the portrait of the problems, confusions, conflicts, and impasses in Belgian society that is suggested by the sociologist's article were authentic, Belgium would be a completely paralyzed, unproductive, unviable country. We may have our family quarrels, our limitations, our faults. "We are only a small country" geographically and in some of our ways. But we are also a dynamic country, a land of work, achievement, and progress, with the courage to spring back again and again in the face of invasion, occupation, and adversity.

If we consider these reactions to the publication of "Medical Scientists in a Château" not only in relation to the actual nature of the study I conducted, the manner in which I proceeded, and the manifest content of the articles I published but also in the context of some of the characteristics of Belgian society already described, we are led to make certain interpretations about the deeper, more general significance of my explorations in the land of Belgian medical research.

Perhaps most evident of all is that by focusing attention through my study on *problems* of medical research in Belgium and (as numerous Belgian newspaper accounts put it) "diffusing" knowledge of these problems "throughout the world" via my *Science* article, I aroused strong nationalistic sentiments on the part of many Belgians, medical researchers and others. Affirmative pride of Belgians in the hard-working, hard-won, impressive accomplishments of their small country, in its history and some of its traditions, in its physical beauty, and in the kind of bravery for which Belgians have been cited since the days of Caesar all emerged in response to my article, together with a more defensive pride about the sort of denigration to which Belgians felt they had recently been subject by foreign reactions both to their Congo crisis and their linguistic problems. Now, along came an American sociologist who, especially because she wore the respected guise of scientist, could depreciate and damage the public image of Belgium still further. This Belgian *amour-propre* was admixed with certain practical considerations and concerns: namely, how the way Belgium was seen abroad, especially in the United States, might affect the money from foreign sources granted to Belgian scientists for research and, more important, the interest of foreign businessmen in Belgium as a site of Common Market investments.

Along with these overarching nationalistic sentiments, various manifestations of Belgian particularism were involved in the reactions to my study and the publication of some of its findings. It was implied by some in the medical research groups of each of the four Belgian universities that, whereas my analysis greatly misrepresented the conditions under which they themselves worked, it could possibly be more accurately descriptive of the situations of investigators in "the other" Belgian universities or in a special one of them. This sort of particularistic assumption, as already pointed out, was made all the more probable because, as a consequence of the relatively limited interchange of ideas and personnel between the universities, Belgian medical researchers do not usually have detailed, first-hand knowledge of professional milieux, other than their own.

Some of the particularistic attitudes and sentiments of Belgians partly account for another set of responses to my research activities and articles. It was often implied in private and public gatherings, and several times in print, by friendly as well as by hostile critics that the "real" covert motives of the American sociologist for investigating medical research in Belgium were not scientific, objective, or independent. Rather, she was conceived to be more identified with certain groups in Belgium than with others—possibly even in their employ—and consequently "out to get" the groups and individuals associated with them to whom she and her unseen manipulators and sponsors were opposed. The hidden ("clever," as defined by some, "sinister," as defined by others) ideologically committed role I was regarded as playing in league with certain powerful "others" was to some extent a projection onto my work and my person of the very kinds of suspicion and enmity-ridden attitudes toward members of particularistic groups other than their own and of the sorts of *messieurs les responsables* explanations of complex social events that I had described as being characteristic of many Belgians in my articles.

But the attribution of partisan and subversive motives to the American sociologist also derived from certain realities connected with Belgian social science. For in the research, teaching, and advisory activities in which they have been engaged, and in the planned social action they have initiated both in Belgium and in the Congo, at least two of the major groups of social scientists affiliated with Belgian universities have, in fact, operated primarily as ideologues. Actively and passively encouraged and sponsored by certain influential *messieurs* from outside as well as inside the universities, these Belgian social scientists have worked in an organized, systematic way to promote their particular religious-philosophical, political, and economic points of view. This was one of the implicit, unverbalized referents that certain Belgians had in mind when they speculated on what might be the "real" motives of the American sociologist and the most influential source of her information and support.

In fact, despite all their anxieties and suspicions, Belgians granted me a privilege they would not easily have accorded a compatriot, social scientist or otherwise. Precisely because I was not Belgian, and thus, at least in the earlier phases of my research, assumed to be less implicated in "the System" than any Belgian, I was allowed to pass with remarkable freedom from one university milieu and from one particularistic group to another, gathering sociologically relevant insights and information wherever I went from people who helped me and who confided in me even more than they ordinarily would have in one another. The range and depth of social contacts I was accorded in these ordinarily "boxed up" and "boxed in" Belgian milieux explain certain other features of the ultimate reactions to my work and publications.

For one thing, as already indicated, by virtue of the special opportunities given me I acquired and was able to present a detailed overview of the worlds of Belgian medical science and their relationship to certain more general Belgian characteristics—an overview not ordinarily or easily accessible to Belgians themselves. Thus, my perspective impressed and startled them in both a positive and a negative sense.

Furthermore, it might be said that, although none of my research activities would have been possible without at least the tacit consent of Belgians connected with medical research, the observations and interviews I carried out in this connection broke through certain norms of constraint and silence that usually prevailed. Medical researchers everywhere, and even the foundation and government officials whom I got to see, spoke to me with what was evidently far less inhibition than was generally characteristic of them. Not only did they tutor me in the routine things I needed to learn about the organization of medical science in Belgium and point out to me what positive advantages it had for the advancement of research and their own careers, but they were even more vocal about the many social, cultural, psychological, and material conditions under which medical science operates in Belgium and which create problems for research and the investigators who conduct it. They themselves supplied the facts for "Medical Scientists in a Château"; but what seems to have happened when it was published is that virtually all the medical researchers and foundation and government officials reacted with some degree of anxiety, and in some cases shock, when they "saw in black and white" the analysis that was a product of what each of them had told the American sociologist.

Contributing to this anxiety and shock (along with the nationalistic and particularistic sentiments already considered) were what might be described as certain "guilt feelings" experienced by each of the people who had helped me with my work, for in so doing they had violated what were apparently their strongly held beliefs that the best and wisest thing to do morally and practically was to keep quiet about one's professional difficulties, or at least discuss them only with the most trusted of intimates among family and friends. Even those who were unequivocal and fearless advocates of my work, after as well as before my article was published, admitted in public that until the American sociologist had come along they, too, had "suffered in silence" because they had not had "the courage to speak out" manifested by the sociologist.

Such allusions to the "courage" that it took to "break the silence" suggest that Belgian medical researchers felt reluctant to speak out about their problems, not only because of "principles of conscience, loyalty, and pride," as one of them put it, but also because they feared what the consequences might be for their own professional situations and futures if they raised their voices to reveal and to protest, and especially if they were identified by others as the persons who had done so. This widespread fear derived in good part from the very limited professional opportunities that exist in Belgium for a man who wishes to devote himself primarily to medical research—the same situation I described and analyzed in my article.

The apprehensions of medical researchers about their careers significantly influenced a great many of the reactions to "Medical Scientists in a Château" and to its author. Certain medical researchers, as already indicated, who had done a great deal to advance my work dissociated themselves from my findings and from any contact with me, once my article was published. Others continued to see me and support me on a private basis but publicly indicated that they were not in agreement with what I had written and published. Even those who consistently supported my work and my person, both publicly and privately, were worried to some extent about what this might mean for them professionally.

How individual medical investigators reacted in this regard was determined, in part, by their status in the field. For example, in the exchange between a young research physician and an older professor of medicine earlier described, in which the *jeune* attacked the American sociologist and her article and defended the way medical research in Belgium is currently organized and the *patron* defended the article and attacked "the System," it was the firmly established success of the professor in his career which made it just that much more possible for him to speak out with a sense of relative impunity. The younger man, newly appointed to a university position, undoubtedly felt that he would be jeopardizing his career, which was just beginning to unfold in a favorable way, if he were critical of the very organization in which he hoped progressively to succeed.

This is not to suggest that most of the younger Belgian medical researchers defended the *status quo* and attacked my analysis while their seniors generally advocated both my work and certain changes. As might be expected, a greater number of younger medical researchers than older ones regarded my study, the articles I had thus far published, the public discussion they had evoked, and what I could be expected to write in the future as what they called "catalysts" through which certain changes in the social structure of medical research in Belgium might be brought about—changes that could improve their own professional situations and open up new research possibilities to them. As the thirty-five young research physicians who wrote a signed letter to the *Bulletin of the College of Physicians of the Area of Brussels* stated in print: "We wish . . . to remark that medical research, like all human activity, is perfectible; that is why we must rejoice in commentaries, suggestions and even criticisms that are addressed to it, because it is a demonstration of the interest that the powers of public opinion take in it throughout the world. In this regard, the article of Mademoiselle Fox . . . deserves to be read with attention, and ought to be full of lessons for all those, from near and far, who are interested in medical research in our country."

In the case of some of the less easily predictable reactions to my work and publications, certain particularities of a medical researcher's local university situation sometimes exerted an implicit influence. This was one of the elements, for example, that went into the overt and almost perverse dispute that my article seemed to have provoked between the aforementioned young research physician and the professor. It was also true of an even more dramatic occasion when, at the invitation of a relatively young, newly appointed professor of medicine to come and talk with him privately, I arrived at his medical school and, without any advance warning, was whisked before an auditorium filled with members of the medical faculty whom my host had assembled. Presided over by the dean, the faculty engaged me in a two-hour discussion about my work, in the course of which the physician who had engineered all this without telling me about it turned out to be one of the most vocal of my negative critics.

As different as these two incidents were with respect to the concrete details that went into their making (details that I shall not recount here), they had one important element in common. In both these instances, the young research physician in the first case and the young professor of medicine in the second took positions and used means that were essentially what we have already indicated are called *petits chemins* or *truques* by Belgians—that is, calculated, somewhat devious methods to consolidate and further their university research careers and to cover up for other, more illicit techniques they had used in the past to get ahead. In a social system like the Belgian, in which, as we have seen, medical researchers are so often confronted with ambiguity, conflict, delay, and total impasse, the frequency with which nonlegitimate ways are used to get around "the System" is probably very high. (In this connection, we recall the words of the successful professor who, in his heated debate with the young research physician, confessed that he had "cheated" to obtain the funds and equipment he needed to do his research.) Perhaps, then, fear of being detected and exposed in such maneuvers, and guilt and shame about having had to use them, lay behind some of the apprehensive and hostile reactions to my article on the part of certain medical researchers.

Finally, there was a whole series of responses to "Medical Scientists in a Château" that, in one way or another, suggest that the analysis of how social, cultural, and historical factors affect Belgian medical research touched on far more than that. These reactions include the several instances in which my analysis was cited in discussions of characteristics of other Belgian institutions—for example, as illustrative of dispersion in the Belgian economy; the many times that I was accused of having "generalized from a particular case"; the interest that my article aroused among a wide range of persons and groups who were not connected, at least ostensibly, with Belgian medical research; the number of individuals in high-ranking political, economic, and religious positions into whose hands my article was delivered; the royalist and antiroyalist sentiments it evoked; the great houses in which I was received; and the distinguished people who refused me when I asked to see them. These reactions invite one at least to speculate on the extent to which my analysis of medical research in Belgium might be applicable to other institutions as well. They suggest that a number of Belgian institutions have the same general characteristics; that there is an intricate, almost interlocking relationship between many Belgian institutions, the medical scientific among them; and that there may indeed exist a group of *messieurs les responsables* who, in a way that perhaps is not mythical, after all, might wield enough authority and power in many different domains of Belgian life to account for some of their similarities and interconnections.

Two final incidents that occurred before I left Belgium in December 1962, just as my research was officially ending, make a fitting conclusion to this chronicle.

(1) A research physician presented me with a framed reproduction of

a primitive Flemish painting, accompanied by a note that said: "Thank you for having done more than anyone ever has for Belgian medical research and researchers, in what may turn out to be our essentially hopeless struggle. . . ."

(2) A Belgian gentleman, indirectly associated with the medical scientific world, told me that the reason I had never quite met some of the important political figures to whom he had volunteered to introduce me was that I had dined too often in the home of a certain count, regarded by these personages as someone who secretly acted as their enemy. The amusing, mysterious, and perhaps very Belgian thing about this assertion is that in the course of my four consecutive research trips to Belgium I never met the count cited or even saw him from afar.

Both of these final incidents exemplify some of the attitudes and processes that I tried to study in the land of Belgian medical research and of which I (or, at least, the projected image of the American sociologist as seen by Belgians) inadvertently but not regretfully also became the object.

Why Belgium?

"Why Belgium?" is the question that American and Belgian colleagues and friends have asked me recurrently since I began doing research in that society in 1959. Ever since then, Belgium has been one of the consistent sites of my sociological inquiry, reflection, and analysis. (Zaïre, Belgium's former colony in Central Africa, became another such site, beginning in 1962.) With a mixture of real interest, conventional politeness, perplexity, and, on the part of Belgians, a tinge of traditional irony, those who have followed my fieldwork have often wondered out loud what I was discovering and learning in that small society that could possibly preoccupy me for so many years. Through some of my publications on the sociology of Belgian medical science and research or, more accurately, on "Belgium Through the Windows of Its Medical Laboratories," I have implicitly responded to this question.[1] And I have periodically speculated on it more privately in my fieldnotes, and in letters to friends. But I have never dealt with it in an explicit, public way. This article constitutes my first formal attempt to do so.

1. Renée C. Fox, Journal Intime Belge/Intiem Belgisch Dagboek, *Columbia University Forum*, Vol. 5 (1962), 11–18; Medical Scientists in a Château, *Science*, Vol. 136 (1962), 476–483; An American Sociologist in the Land of Belgian Medical Research, in Phillip E. Hammond (ed.), *Sociologist at Work: The Craft of Social Research* (New York: Harper and Row, 1964), 345–391.

Reproduced with the permission of *Archives européennes de Sociologie,* Vol. 19 (1978), 205–228. Delivered as a Presidential Address to the Eastern Sociological Society, March, 1977.

I "chose" Belgium, or perhaps Belgium chose me, in the summer of 1959 when, as I wrote in "An American Sociologist in the Land of Belgian Medical Research," I first "voyaged to a small, reputedly fathomable and friendly land . . . to make a rather specialized study of how social, cultural and historical factors affect clinical medical research and research careers in a contemporary European society."[2] In that same essay, I went on to say that "the story of this research can be deciphered and understood only if it is linked to certain characteristics of the social structure and value system of Belgium that go far beyond its world of medical research"; and that it was "primarily through an analysis of Belgian reactions to the [presence] and publications of the American sociologist that the largely unanticipated, more general significance of the study . . . [gradually] emerge[d]."[3]

The specific subject and focus of my research grew directly out of my prior work in the sociology of medicine, in ways that I have reported in the literature and that I will not elaborate here. For the purposes at hand, it is more relevant to indicate how the kind of professional socialization that a sociologist of my generation received influenced the project that I undertook. For the "ethos" of immediately post-World War II American sociology, the period in which I did my graduate training (1949–1954) contributed to the fact and the nature of my involvement in the sociology of Belgian medical research.

It was an interdisciplinary era: a time when there was widespread interest in the interrelationships and interactions between social structural, cultural, psychological, and biological influences in social life. At Harvard, for example, in the then Department of Social Relations, I received some training in psychology (social and clinical), psychiatry, cultural anthropology, and biomedicine, as well as in sociology during my graduate years. There was a shared, underlying conviction that even a strict social-structural approach could be enhanced by the sociologist's trained "silent" awareness of the role of cultural, psychological, historical, and/or biological factors in social life. At the very least, that awareness would enable one to specify more precisely and powerfully exactly what the influence of social structure was (and was not) in the phenomena under study and analysis. Beyond that, it would enable one to cross the institutionalized boundaries and approaches of various fields in order to forge new links between them, theoretically, empirically, and methodologically.

It was a nondichotomous, relatively nondogmatic and nondoctrinaire

2. Fox, An American Sociologist in the Land of Belgian Medical Research, p. 345.
3. *Ibid.*

time. It was also a cross-cultural time. The intellectual fascination with cultures and societies other than one's own, and the moral conviction that this was a good and necessary thing was one of the major factors that drew people toward sociology and a sociological career. This shared fascination and conviction had various sources: among them, the spirit of "internationalism" and the "one world" hopes that were born out of World War II; the rich influence of the many ethnographic works on primitive societies written by anthropologists in the 1930s and 1940s, and their sense of urgency about the importance of knowing and studying these societies before they "disappeared" as a consequence of the accelerating global process of modernization; and certainly the impact of the establishment of a whole series of new, independent nation-states in Africa and Asia, in this dawning post-colonial period. We were expected to learn more about the structure and dynamics of American society through our sociological training. But it was also understood, in a Durkheimian kind of way, that because sociological analysis is inherently comparative, one could not identify distinctively American structural and cultural traits without systematic, knowledgeable reference to other societies. This was implied in the comparative institutional analysis framework in which we were educated, and facilitated by the then fashionable area and regional studies programs available to us in numerous university settings.

Looking back on my sociological training and the professional socialization process that was a part of it, my research in Belgium does not seem accidental. To be sure, there are serendipitous elements involved, both in its origins and its evolution. Furthermore, as I have written elsewhere, at least one of the basic sociological assumptions on which I launched my Belgian research proved to be patently wrong: namely that "a small country . . . would . . . be easier for a lone investigator . . . to cover geographically [and] . . . simpler than a large country to comprehend in a sociological sense." (In the light of my close to two decades of research in Belgium, "if I were now asked to formulate a sociological hypothesis about the relationship between the size of a country and the complexity of its social system, I would be tempted to suggest that there is an inverse relationship between the two; that is, the smaller the country, the more complex its social system!")[4] These qualifications notwithstanding, in retrospect it does not seem aleatory that I undertook a sociology of medicine and science study in a small, non-American society, geopolitically and culturally at the "crossroads" of Western Europe: a highly modern yet deeply traditional European society that

4. Fox, *op. cit.* p. 349.

opened onto a much larger, Central African society, the Belgian Congo—its colony, its frontier, and its dreaming space. Nor does it seem to be purely coincidental that Belgium turned out to be a land that stirs one's unconscious and evokes one's psychic imagination: a tiny land, often shrouded in mist, under a huge, continually changing, cloud- and light-filled sky, swept by westerly winds from the sea, whose inner life as well as its art is pervaded by the everyday images and strange symbols of Breughel and Bosch, Ensor and Magritte. (In that subterranean, painterly world, the commonplace and routine, human festivity, wonder and *angoisse*, sensuality and mysticism, tenderness, anger, horror, and fear meet in realistic, romantic, and surrealistic ways.) The fact that my research on a particular set of Belgian institutions progressively changed over time into a study of a total society is prefigured in the "whole society"- and "whole culture"- oriented way in which I was trained. And this transformation was catalyzed by the self-reflexive analysis of the observer effects of my early field research that my exposure to psychoanalysis and cultural anthropology had taught me to make.

Rather than reporting the concrete results of my study of Belgian medical research, I would like to try to delineate some of the more general structural and cultural features of Belgian society that I have come to understand through the medium of this study. It is primarily these attributes of Belgian society that have endowed the inquiry of medical research with its larger personal and sociological meaning for me. They also account for the fact that even after all these years in its midst as a questing, "familiar stranger," I still experience Belgium as an endlessly interesting and enigmatic country. This does not mean that I have found a "lost horizon" or "paradise" in this land. In certain regards, it represents the very *antithesis* of what is comfortably usual for me, of fundamental things in which I believe, and of aspects of "Americanness" that I particularly value. Its significance, then, is negative as well as positive.

Belgium is first of all a physically small, densely populated society (11,799 square miles in area, with a population of some 9½ million inhabitants). But what does "small" mean sociologically? Simply or primarily that, if one travels from any point in Belgium for more than two hours by car or train, in any direction, one has crossed its borders? Or that even opulent houses are built on a small, so-called "human" scale, and that under the vast, illumined skies of Flanders, cows and horses, poplar and birch trees, harvesters and bicyclists are miniaturized? Or that Belgium is no longer a colonial power? In their characteristically self-mocking way, Belgians themselves raise this sort of question when they repeatedly affirm, "Small country, small mind!" ("*Petit pays, petit esprit!*") They imply that something more is involved than geography, size, or the political economy. (I shall return to this "something more.")

Belgium is also a particularistic society: one of the most particularistic in Europe, and perhaps in the world. The family, the community, the region, the social class into which one is born, the ethnic-linguistic group to which one belongs (Flemish, Walloon, i.e., French-speaking, and that hybrid mix, *Bruxellois/Brusselaar*), the religious-philosophical tradition out of which one comes (Catholic, Free Thought, Free Mason), and the political party with which one identifies (Christian, Socialist, Liberal, and their variants) not only affect one's existence in Belgium, but determine it, in many inescapable, immutable ways. So much is this the case, that Belgians speak of the *familles* (families) that certain clusters of these variables constitute, or the *verzuiling* (pillars, columns): families from which one cannot secede, and pillars that, even with Atlas-like strength, one cannot easily budge. These particularistic categories and constellations of categories ascriptively influence the type of hospital in which one is born, the schools one attends, the occupations for which one is eligible, the jobs and positions one can hope to obtain, the sick fund, mutuality, and syndicate in which one is enrolled, the other voluntary organizations to which one belongs, the newspapers and magazines one reads, the radio stations and television channels one selects, the vacation trips one takes, the soccer team for which one roots, and the brand of beer one drinks, as well as where one lives, whom one marries, and how many children one has. The role that these social background factors play is much greater in Belgian than in American life. Their influence is more broadly encompassing, narrowly constricting, and powerfully binding. Thus, for example, practically all medical research in Belgium is carried out from a position within a university. There are very few positions within alternative structures (such as government or industry) that provide opportunities for a research career. With the exception of the new and still experimental University of Antwerp, each of the Belgian universities represents a combination or permutation of the major social and cultural variables in Belgian society already identified. Ghent is a Flemish and State university; Liège is a *francophone* and State university; and neither of them is officially associated with any particular religious or philosophical persuasion. Brussels, on the other hand, is a "Free," that is, a non-State university, with a Free Thought/Free Mason orientation, that has progressively evolved into two sub-universities, the Flemish Vrije Universiteit Brussel and the French Université Libre de Bruxelles. The Free and Catholic University of Louvain was split into two universities in 1968, becoming the French Université Catholique de Louvain (Louvain-la-Neuve), and the Katholieke Universiteit Leuven. And so on. (The fission, doubling, and multiplication processes involved in the division of the universities of Brussels and Louvain into two/four is an expression of still other societal traits that I will mention later.)

Not only are the particularistic and ascriptive categories into which one fits decisively associated with what university one attends but, by and large, the university from which one graduates is the only milieu where one will be seriously considered a candidate for an academic position. And such an academic position is prerequisite for being a medical researcher. "There are cases," Belgians will quickly and invariably tell you that do not conform to this pattern: the case of Dr. Albert Claude (Nobel Laureate in Medicine and Physiology), for example, who graduated from the University of Liège; worked for many years at the Rockefeller Institute in New York City; returned to Belgium, where he assumed the medical direction of the Institut Jules Bordet (for cancer), which is affiliated with the University of Brussels Medical School; and who is currently working in his own laboratory at the Université Catholique de Louvain. But the story of Albert Claude is virtually legendary, precisely because it constitutes a brilliant exception to the Belgian "rule" of particularism. Belgian particularism, then, provides individuals and groups with certain opportunities, and excludes them from others. And even in social settings where more universalistic considerations such as aptitude, training, and competence enter the picture, particularistic factors have already created the basic social structures within which these inevitably secondary criteria are invoked.

As the foregoing suggests, the particularism is related to another overarching characteristic of Belgian society: its cloistered fixity. By this I do not mean physical immobility, although in pre-World War II Belgium, a trip to Brussels, the capital, would have been a rare, momentous, and somewhat frightening event for farmers or workers, from Walloonie or Flanders. But in 1978, members of all groups in the population do an impressive amount of travelling back and forth over the face of the country, in automobiles and on motorcycles, via the relatively new, national highway, and in immaculate, fast-moving, and punctual Belgian railroad trains (which are important culture symbols, as the paintings, the postage stamps, and the literature of Belgium suggest). I experienced at least one, striking, first-hand indicator of this kind of mobility during my 1976–1977 stay in Belgium. From October through February, I lived in a hotel in Leuven on Maria Theresiastraat, the street that leads directly to the local railroad station. Every week, beginning on Thursday, and extending through Monday, a constant stream of university students passed under my window, en route to catch a train to their parents' house for the weekend, or returning from home, laden down with zippered valises full of clean laundry and favorite foods prepared by their mothers. The sharp, staccato click of students' fashionable shoes and boots on the Leuven pavement is related to their social as well as their geographical mobility. For these young men and women are part of the first generation of Flemish to receive a university education on a general, if not a mass basis. Exactly how much (horizontal and vertical) social mobility there is in Belgium, in what groups and regions of the country, is hard to ascertain, for at least two reasons that, once again, are connected with more general phenomena. Belgians are reluctant to speak about their social origins. And it is difficult to obtain information of many kinds in Belgium. (What I have come to think of as the "sociology of information/*renseignements*/*inlichtingen*" in Belgium will be further discussed in a while.) This apparently increased geographical and social mobility notwithstanding, as the weekly trajectory of the university students suggests, the "traveling" tends to be bounded by the particularistic groups to which one is attached, and that make strong and continuous claims upon one. (The university students may express considerable ambivalence about doing so, but they dutifully and, to a great extent, voluntarily return to their families and home communities every weekend. And to a much greater extent than in the United States, their extended families will remain their primary social group throughout all of their lives.) In this era when there is considerably more geographical, professional, intellectual, and political contact between different groups than there was in the past, strict, mutually cloistering limits are nonetheless maintained. Personal, social, or visiting relations between groups are not usually established. And professional contacts are also sharply circumscribed. For example, an interuniversity research project now exists in Belgium that entails the collaboration between groups of sociologists and physicians in each major university of the country. (It is one of a number of so-called "*projets concertés*" that have recently been established.) Yet inside the project very little intergroup collaboration actually occurs. The Flemish teams carry out their inquiries in Flanders and Flemish-speaking settings, the French sociologists in Walloonie and French-speaking settings, but the Flemish and French groups never meet to discuss ideas or data on a face-to-face basis, across ethnic-linguistic lines. (Some of the Flemish subgroups have come together from time to time: for instance, members of the Antwerp, Brussels, Ghent, and Leuven teams. However, to my knowledge, this is not equally true of Bruxelles, Liège and Louvain-la-Neuve.) A certain shyness and discomfort exists between individuals from different particularistic categories and groups, along with the anxiety-ridden distrust (*méfiance*) and competitiveness that Belgians themselves so often cite. These attitudes sharply inhibit the range and depth of intergroup contacts and knowledge. I still find it poignant that in and through my research role, I have acquired a certain envoy-like status and function in Belgium, carrying messages, insights, and information back and forth between individuals, groups and environments that do not have direct or sustained relations with one another. Paradoxically, because I am not Belgian, and as such fall outside the institutionalized "boxes" in Belgian life (by an "accident of birth," even outside the Catholic-Christian "box"), I have been given a "free pass" by Belgians of all backgrounds to enter and exit from their milieux and to learn from and about them. My mobility is both privileged and deviant, and is viewed by the very Belgians who have made it possible with a mixture of admiration, wistfulness, envy, and suspicion. In order to be permitted to continue to move so unrestrictedly in the social system, I must constantly prove and prove again that I am no more identified with one group than another. (And so I accepted two teaching assignments in 1976–1977, one at the Katholieke Universiteit Leuven, and the other at the Université d'État de Liège, thus balancing off "particularisms.") Herein lies one of the primary implications of Belgian particularism and the cloisters it creates and maintains. It is among the most fundamental and powerful social control mechanisms in the society. The various particularistic categories of Belgium are borne, and affixed to others as labels, that structure where one can go in the society, what one can do, whom one can know, and what one can learn. These labels are used more as negative, than as positive sanctions: to prevent persons who do not belong to the same particularistic groups from having access to certain opportunities and relationships, even more than to favor and benefit one's self and one's own groups.

In turn, this is consistent with three other Belgian societal patterns. The first of these is a pervasive pattern of "negative competition": recurrent attitudes and behaviors whose manifest and latent intent is to inhibit, minimize, or undercut the accomplishments of others. These attitudes and behaviors are directed against individuals or groups whose achievements are substantial enough to "put them ahead" of others. Negative competition comes most forcefully into play when members of one particularistic political, ethnic-linguistic, or philosophical-religious group feel that persons who belong to another one are unduly outdistancing them, or unjustly receiving more of something that is valued than they are. Under these circumstances, on the informal level, malicious gossip about the persons or groups who have distinguished themselves in this way is one of the first reactions that occurs. In a small society like Belgium, with its still smaller communities, the mechanism of gossip has a magnified capacity to cause psychic and social damage to the individuals or groups who are its object. This is all the more true, because the persons on whom the gossip focuses are aware of its existence and its content, as well as its effects, to a greater extent than would be the case in larger, more impersonal social settings.

The negative competition is associated with a second Belgian pattern: the expectation and exaction of a high degree of conformity in certain regards, especially around the axis of ascription-achievement. In turn, this is related to a third pattern: commitment to what might be termed a "mechanical" conception of equality, or to the notion that equality is identity, rather than equivalence. In interaction with the particularism of the society, it has led to the special version of what Belgians call "pluralism." In effect, this means the creation of multiple, "separate but equal" networks of institutions, each of which not only represents and serves a so-called particularistic "community," but also is entitled to the "same" funds, personnel, facilities, equipment, and so forth, as every other. (In this connection, the national government is the major "banker," directly and indirectly supporting these *réseaux/nets* through a maze of intricately interconnected ministries, foundations, *oeuvres, caisses*, parastatal organizations, etc.) The educational and health networks of the country are the most focal and sensitive, because they are emanations of common values of special importance in the society, and because, as such, they are also potential centers of very serious, invidious conflicts between the major particularistic groups of Belgium. The schools have played a key historic role in this regard, and the Belgian universities, hospitals, sick funds, and labor unions (syndicates) also have symbolic importance.

In the realm of my own concentrated study of Belgian medical research, since 1960, such pluralism, along with particularism, mechanical equality, and both positive and negative patterns of competition have contributed to the *dédoublement* (doubling) of the universities of Brussels and Louvain; the *splitsing* (splitting) of Louvain; the creation of new universities, notably Antwerp, and continuing pressure to establish still others, such as Hainaut; the multiplication of the *candidatures* of each university (that is, the first two years of university education), and their physical location in various regional areas of the country; the establishment of new academic statuses—*chargé de cours*, associate professor, and various chairs; the establishment of a Ministry of Science Policy and Programmation that complements the role played by the older National Foundation for Scientific Research and its affiliates, and also "evens out" the political, philosophical and linguistic balance historically struck by the Foundation; the building of numerous university and university-affiliated hospitals (there are now eight in Brussels alone); and both the rational and nonrational duplication of certain types of scientific and medical equipment. (In this latter regard, for example, two, semi-coordinated dialysis units exist in the medical faculty at a particular university, each under the aegis of a different professor of medicine.) The patterns of decentralization, splitting and replication that are exemplified by these developments are not confined to the university and scientific sectors of Belgium. They, too, are general characteristics of the society that, as the foregoing suggests, have both functional and dysfunctional consequences. For example, although they promote greater equity, as well as regional representativeness, and enlarge the range of opportunities and alternatives in the society, they also foster a multiplication, replication, and dispersion of institutions, facilities, and personnel that is not only financially expensive to the social system, but also psychically and culturally costly. For instance, the processes of decision-making on every level of the society are frequently delayed or blocked by the fact that the country's major particularistic groups are so evenly balanced and so intransigently oriented in relationship to one another. The institutionalized impasses that often result are collectively referred to by Belgians as the "immobilism" tendencies of the society.

With all this emphasis on the particularistic, cloistering, mechanically egalitarian, negatively competitive, and fissionary aspects of Belgian life, one might well ask what accounts for the viability of the society, its integration, and its overall dynamism. This brings us to another whole set of Belgian characteristics.

Belgium is also an industrious, energetic society, permeated with a cheerful, Catholicism-derived equivalent of the Protestant work ethic. It is an achievement- and burgher-oriented society, in which great value is placed on building and owning a house (Belgians teasingly characterize themselves as having been "born with a brick in [their] stomachs"), furnishing it tastefully, cultivating a fine garden, possessing original paintings, having a good car, dressing well, eating and drinking bountifully, and taking interesting vacation trips abroad (mainly towards lands where there is more sun and warmth than in rain-streaked and fog-ridden Belgium). Belgians work hard and zestfully to attain these things, which they enjoy with aesthetic gusto. The groaning banquet tables of Breughel's paintings have not disappeared, but they are now exquisitely arranged, with artistic displays of flowers, hors d'oeuvres, and pastries—and at one elegant reception that I attended, not only was champagne served, but also gorgeous Belgian chocolates *("pralines")*, arranged like jewels in huge brandy snifters, and passed among us by white-coated waiters.

(Parenthetically, it is unclear what will happen to these aspects of the society in the future. For, since the Belgian student protest movement in 1968, a generation of young women and men has appeared who, sullenly but emphatically, reject the traditional Belgian work ethic. "Our parents worked too hard," they say, in a more petulant and condemnatory tone of voice than their age-mate counterparts in the United States. At this economic juncture, they are pessimistic about their chances of getting a good job, even with a university diploma. They are inclined to blame the state of affairs on "the system," particularly on an omnipresent "power elite" whom they regard as hostile to youth and change. However, these young people do not appear to be anti-materialistic or ascetically inclined. Rather, they express a passive kind of *ressentiment* over what they already feel will be the unattainability of the status, influence and possessions they covet. Numerous of the sociology students whom I taught at the universities of Leuven and Liège, this fall and winter, exhibited this mélange of characteristics, reflecting, it would seem, some of the side-effects of their families' hard-won advance from working-class to petty bourgeois status, and of the transition of the Belgian economy [along with other Western societies], from a prolonged, post-World War II period of affluence to one of "stagflation.")

In addition to its industriousness (and the kind of vigorous, cleanly sense of order and property that have made it traditional for housewives to wash the windows and stoops of their homes and the sidewalks in front of them with soap and water every Friday [*"faire le vendredi"*]), Belgium is a society in which manipulative ingenuity prevails. In a legendary way, the wily peasant, Till Eulenspiegel, with his roguery and wit, personifies some of these aspects of Belgian culture. Belgians have invented and quasi-institutionalized a series of adroit, even trickster-like means of budging the system or getting around it. These legitimate and semi-legitimate forms of behavior seem to have developed as patterned responses to the many invasions and occupations by foreign enemies which have been endemic to Belgian history, to the overall complexity and legalism of Belgian formal organization, and to the "immobilism" with which the society is continually confronted. One of the common expressions that Belgians use to describe this aspect of their national life is *"les petits chemins."* The capacity to find, create, and/or utilize such byroads and detours is generally admired. Not only Till Eulenspiegel, but also the smuggler is a kind of culture hero in Belgium, particularly the *smokkelaar* who managed to do an undetected, profitable and life-saving business under the noses of the Germans who occupied Belgium both in World War I and World War II. (This fall, I spent a week in a small, Flemish village of some 500 inhabitants, located in the Polder region of the country on the border between Belgium and Holland which, in collaboration with five other like communities in the area, had created a special holiday to commemorate the Smokkelroute that this ensemble of villages had formed during the Second World War.) Belgians also take a certain mischievous, overtly displayed delight in contriving, falsifying, or skillfully altering documents (minutes of meetings, reports, attestations, identity cards, etc.), and works of art—or, at least, in implying that such crafty and clandestine manipulations have taken place. These allegations and stories tend to cluster around the "enemy" type-situations that the smuggler figure represents, though they are not confined to such contexts. For example, it is reported that during World War II, a perfect reproduction of the beautiful and priceless *châsse* of St. Ursula by Hans Memling, permanently on display at St. Jan's Hospital in Brugge, was made by local artists. This was exhibited at the hospital, whereas the "real *châsse*" was sequestered away in the home of one of St. Jan's physician chiefs of staff, so that if the Germans made off with the *châsse* in the hospital, it would be a false one that they had been duped into taking. This story teasingly concludes with the statement that no one knows to this day whether the *châsse* of St. Ursula currently visible in the Memling Museum section of the hospital is the original or the copy. As such tales suggest, these manipulative aspects of Belgian social structure and culture are not only expedient, entrepreneurial adaptations. They are also associated with a subterranean defiance of oppression and centralized authority, and with an actively ironic, existential outlook on human society, and on the human condition more generally. In addition, they are interconnected with two other notable attributes of Belgian life: the role of the intermediary, on the one hand, and the phenomenon of *cumul*, on the other.

For a number of reasons, in the Belgian system, it is not only convenient and helpful to have the assistance of someone who can act as a contact and a conduit for one. In many instances, it is a precondition for the relatively straightforward, efficient, undelayed accomplishment of a necessary task, or for the achievement of a desired goal. Because of the diffuse particularism and distrust (*méfiance*) in Belgian society, even in relatively modern, bureaucratized, and rationalized structures, it is often difficult, and beyond that, complicating to try to conduct one's business in an independent, universalistic way. (My own most vivid encounter with this dimension of the Belgian social system concerned my at once ingenuous and very American attempt to open a checking account in a Brussels branch of Belgium's most venerable bank [the Société Générale de Banque] on my own. Waiting for a checkbook to be issued to me, and trying to find out why it never appeared was a baroque affair that stretched on for weeks, until a Belgian colleague who was himself a client of the bank intervened for me. More than a telephone call of inquiry from him, or a letter of recommendation concerning my financial and professional status and my good character were required. A face-to-face visit to the bank on my behalf, personally to introduce me and to vouchsafe for me were implicitly required, though never overtly requested.) Belgian vocabulary is rich in words that make mockingly serious reference to the essential role played by the agent-intermediary in many areas of local and national life, with respect to everyday as well as exceptional matters. In French, allusion is often made to the *piston* one needs, or already has to back up and push forward certain activities one has undertaken. In Flemish, a more bucolic expression is used: the desirability or necessity of having a human *kruiwagen* or "wheelbarrow."

Whether these mediating persons are called *pistons* or "wheelbarrows," the facilitating role that they play is not just dependent on their capacity and willingness to use personal influence, or pressure group tactics to expedite a matter. One of the important functions that they serve is that of obtaining and "deblocking" information that their "clients" need in order to act appropriately and effectively. Here we return to my earlier comment about some of the special features of the "sociology of information/*renseignements*/*inlichtingen*" in Belgium. The particularism and localism, the vested interests and distrustful caution that accompany them, and the elaborate division of knowledge as well as of labor characteristic of many Belgian organizations all converge to control, limit or impede the existence of information in the system, its circulation, and access to it. In a study made by the Centre de Recherche et d'Information Socio-Politiques (C.R.I.S.P.—Bruxelles) on political decision-making in Belgium,[5] the authors identify the "mediocrity and superficiality of information" as one of the dominant traits of the Belgian political system (a trait that they consider a *grief,* and of which they are highly critical). They isolate three factors that contribute to this state of affairs. The first is that "often the necessary documentation [simply] does not exist." The second is that "available documentation does not circulate (the incoercible tendency of the services for *cloisonnement* [partitioning, cloistering] is practiced with particular intensity when it comes to the communication of information)." The third is that "the person responsible for the presentation of the dossier does not take [the

5. Jean Meynaud, Jean Ladrière, and François Perin, *La décision politique en Belgique: Le pouvoir et les groupes* (Paris: Armand Colin, 1965).

relevant information] into account, or does so in a superficial manner either because of lack of time, negligence, or because of [his] refusal to examine figures or papers that might challenge or oppose a point of view already agreed upon."[6] In my view (based on my research), these "communication of information" phenomena are not confined to the political sector of Belgian society, though they may be "practiced [there] with particular intensity." They represent a more widespread characteristic of the society, that, in turn, underlies the critical services that the agent-intermediary performs, as a detective, diagnostician, and conveyor of information.

However, the role of the intermediary is not a full-time specialized occupation. Rather, it is an activity in which people engage on their own behalf and for the sake of others, in conjunction with their usual professional, familial and social affairs. In fact, the extensive degree to which persons request and receive such "*piston*/wheelbarrow" services from one another makes it an important general component of interaction in the society. Who asks for and receives what from whom, under what circumstances and conditions is a complex sociological matter that surpasses the analysis I can undertake here. But as a consequence of the reciprocal, intermediary services that are exchanged, a gift relationship type of net or web is established between the numerous persons involved, with all the potentialities for what Judith P. Swazey and I called the "tyranny of the gift" in our book on organ transplantation and dialysis, as well as all the possible advantages and benefits of the gift.[7]

In some of its origins and consequences, *cumul* is closely related to the role of the intermediary. In French (and the same word is used by Flemish Belgians as well), *cumul* means "cumulation," "lumping," "the holding of several offices," and/or the "receiving of several salaries" at the same time. It is the plurality of jobs and salaries phenomenon to which people ordinarily refer when they use the term, particularly a "cumulation" that includes political or governmental positions in the "bundle." Two examples from my study of medical research in Belgium illustrate the complexity and extensiveness of the structural and financial arrangements that *cumul* can entail. In the 1959 to 1962 phase of my inquiry, the most important source of support for medical and other forms of scientific research was the Fonds National de la Recherche Scientifique (the National Fund for Scientific Research). The FNRS received more than two-thirds of its annual income from grants made to

6. Meynaud, Ladrière, and Perin, *op. cit.*, 378–380.

7. Renée C. Fox and Judith P. Swazey, *The Courage to Fail: A Social View of Organ Transplants and Dialysis* (Chicago: University of Chicago Press, 1974); see especially pp. 5–39 and 332–334.

it by the national government, chiefly via the then Ministry of Public Instruction, now renamed the Ministry of National Education. The FNRS was also the direct recipient of governmental funds allocated to certain other foundations, for example the subsidies given by the Ministry of Public Health to the Fonds National pour la Recherche Médicale (the National Fund for Medical Research). The FNRS received the monies designated for the National Fund for Medical Research and turned them over to the president of that Fund, who was also the secretary general of the Ministry of Public Health. The FNRS, the National Fund for Medical Research, the University Foundation, the Francqui Foundation, and the Inter-University Institute of Nuclear Sciences (as well as several other foundations less directly concerned with scientific research) were all housed in the same building, the Club of the Fondation Universitaire, 11, rue d'Egmont, Brussels. The director and first vice-president of the FNRS had his office there. He was the effective director, first vice-president and treasurer of *all* the rue d'Egmont foundations, and on the boards of directors of a number of other foundations as well. The secretary general of the FNRS also had his office in this building. He was the secretary of each of the twenty-five scientific commissions of the FNRS, and of every one of the rue d'Egmont foundations. Much has changed in this complex structure since 1962. The director and first vice-president of the FNRS is dead, and no one person has assumed his various statuses and roles with the impressive *cumul* that they involved. Furthermore, another important set of parallel, if not competing structures that support and fund scientific research has developed: namely, the Ministry of Science Policy and Programmation and its advisory body, the National Council for Science Policy. Here again, a *cumul* constellation has progressively evolved. The minister of Science Policy and Programmation is not only secretary general of the National Council for Science Policy as well, but also national minister of the Budget and this, in turn, means that he has fiscal policy responsibilities in all the ministries of the government.

Cumul occurs frequently enough in Belgium to have acquired a name. To a considerable degree, it can be said to be institutionalized in the Belgian social system, although what is referred to as "exaggerated *cumuls*" (*cumuls exagérés*) are disapproved, and there are periodic attempts to restrict the number and type of positions that an individual can occupy at the same time, along with the earnings that he amasses from multiple salaries. (In the winter of 1977, for example, the national government initiated legal and budgetary actions to limit the *cumuls* practiced in the universities, either by persons who are full-time professors and take on extra-university jobs, or by those with an occupational base in another structure who do part-time teaching as "extraordinary professors" in the universities.) There is a considerable amount of sociological as well as personal ambivalence in Belgian society about the desirability and dangers of *cumul*. Its status and financial advantages for those who engage in this practice are obvious to everyone, and potentially attractive to hard-working, entrepreneurial and achievement-oriented Belgians. However, it is also acknowledged that *cumul* is as conducive to negative as it is to positive competition in Belgium. And there is considerable concern about the abuses of influence, authority, and power that could result from the packaging of certain statuses and roles, their occupancy by one person, and the centralization that this implies. These apprehensions notwithstanding, on a deeper, more latent level, there is some recognition (rarely verbalized) that *cumul* serves important interpersonal, intergroup, and interstructural societal functions, analogous to those of the agent-intermediary. In a social system permeated by particularism, cloistering, segmentation, mechanical equality, negative competition, institutionalized distrust, restriction of information, and immobilism, *cumul* is an integrating mechanism. The complex status- and role-sets occupied by persons who engage in *cumul* allow them to move back and forth between the different organizations, groups, and structures to which they simultaneously and legitimately belong. In so doing, they help to link these entities, establish communication between them, set them into motion vis-à-vis each other and the issues they must mutually resolve, and create some kind of dynamic equilibrium between them. Looked at from another vantage point, *cumul* allows certain individuals to act as their own, and other persons' intermediary-agents, as they travel between the different parts of the social system in which they fit.

In previous publications, I have stated that the social structure of Belgian medical research and, by implication, of Belgian society is "paradoxical" or, at least, "dualistic": that is, highly centralized in certain respects, and decentralized in others. I was accused in print by some Belgians of being "inconsistent" and "contradictory" in asserting that both these things were true. I would still claim that these two forces are visibly at work in Belgian society, and I now see a dialectical relationship between them. *Cumul*, for example, is not only integral to the process of centralization, but it also acts as a counterweight to the trends toward decentralization, fission, and what Belgians call *morcellement* (fragmentation) present in the society. In turn, to some extent these more centrifugal forces in Belgian society counterbalance its even stronger centralizing tendencies. The recent history of the Belgian communes (whose origins date back to the Middle Ages) embodies both these processes. When I began my research in 1959, Belgium was made up of 2633 communes, each one of which had a proudly autonomous local government. During the past few years, what Belgians term a process of *fusion* has been set into motion, with the intent of consolidating the communes into larger blocks, for a whole series of reasons, including greater efficiency and economy, and the satisfaction of various ethnolinguistic, regional, and political economic interests. Accompanied all the way by discussion, controversy, and gerrymandering tactics and countertactics, the fusion process has now progressed to the point where the number of Belgian communes has been reduced to 589. Still another important politico-symbolic way in which this centralization-decentralization duality has long been exemplified and institutionalized in the society is to be found in the fact that although the country has a constitutionally recognized, central monarch, his official title is King of the *Belgians*, rather than King of *Belgium*.

Finally, as the analysis of *fusion*, *cumul*, the "intermediary," *petits chemins*, and the like suggests, in the face of its many tensions, impasses, and potentialities for schism, Belgium has developed and institutionalized a set of mechanisms and processes that continually establish and reestablish the overall unity, viability and dynamism of the society. Underlying these mechanisms and processes, and transcending the differences and blockages that they help to resolve are the "collective conscience" bases of solidarity and consensus that Belgians share. Their conceptions of particularism and pluralism notwithstanding, and despite their inclination to express their nationalistic sentiments in a scoffing, self-deriding fashion, Belgians are strongly identified with their country in certain, ultimately binding and consolidating ways. In fact, a more universalistic than particularistic notion of "solidarity" (*solidarité/solidariteit*) is a basic value in the society, as the ideological tenets both of the Christian and the Socialist *réseaux/verzuiling* indicate. And Belgians associate the great moral value that they attach to *courage* or *moed*—that is, skillful, energetic, and brave persistence in response to adversity—with their collective, as well as their personal history and survival. The values of solidarity and courage, and the Belgian way of thinking of them, are partly related to one of the most fundamental cultural facts about the society, and one of its most basic sources of identity and accord. Belgium is historically and contemporaneously a Catholic country, in which the Reformation and Protestantism have played a negligible role, and Judaism is largely confined to the semi-ghetto of Antwerp and to a community of Jews in Brussels. A detailed and nuanced consideration of the major attributes of Belgian Catholicism cannot be attempted here. But it is important to note that virtually everyone in Belgian society is significantly oriented to, and influenced by the doctrine, beliefs, and practices of Catholicism, and by the educational, health, social welfare, occupational, economic, and political institutions that it has created in Belgium. In a thesis/antithesis way, even Belgian Free Thought and Free Masonry have been shaped and structured by Catholicism, as has the separate, equal and identical network of Socialist institutions that parallel the Catholic set. Furthermore, from Belgium's inception as a nation in 1830, Catholics, as well as non-Catholics and anti-Catholics have accepted the principle of the separation of Church and State. What one sees in Belgium at the present time in this post-Vatican Council II (and for Belgians, post-*Pacte Scolaire*) era of greater secularization and laicization of Catholicism is a tension-ridden, but nonetheless agreed-upon, further elaboration of that already accepted, traditional principle.

The allusion to the *Pacte Scolaire* (the School Pact) brings us to a last, "collective conscience" and societal source of the country's integration and identity. Publicly and ritually, flavored by gallow's humor, Belgians often express doubts about the reality, existence, and survival of their own society. This bravado-tinged concern on the part of Belgians that their society might cease to be is perhaps the most forcefully and conclusively integrating mechanism in the country (the one that, in the end, makes "Belgium" out of "Belgians"). Predictably, this response is most evident when the society is confronted with issues of such importance and magnitude that Belgians regard them as constituting a potential or actual national crisis. There have been a series of such episodes in the history of twentieth-century Belgium, to which Belgians have affixed code-like and capitalized titles: the "Royal Question," the "Congo Crisis," the "School War," the "Linguistic Problem," the "Community" or "Cultural Question," the "Abortion" or "Ethical Question." In this article, I cannot examine the content of the societal crisis that each of these "Questions" or "Problems" entailed. But I can point out that every one of the crises has crystallized around fundamental questions of values and beliefs that Belgians define as crucial to the integrity and the continuance of their society. Each crisis has temporarily drawn the many subgroups and factions of Belgian society into several large, antagonistic blocks. And in each instance, when these *en bloc* conflicts and confrontations have escalated to a certain point, they have been negotiated and resolved in an extraparliamentary way, by a commission or a "conclave" in a "castle." (Belgians are semi-aware of the at once ecclesiastical, royal, and Kafkaesque significance of their "castle conclaves," and are wryly amused by it if one brings this to their attention.) In every instance, the result has been a "truce" or an "armistice" agreed upon by representatives of the principal groups involved, out of which has come a formal, contractual agreement between the parties concerned, that subsequently has been written into law. Belgians call the contractual agreement a "pact." (The two major ones since World War II have been: the School Pact that decisively granted legitimacy both to the Catholic and public educational systems in Belgium, and settled the relationship between them, as well as the terms of their financial support by the State; and the Culture Pact, that resolved some of the country's ethno-linguistic and regional questions.) A prominent Flemish journalist (Frans Verleyen) terms such pacts "noiseless" or "silent" (*geruisloose pakts*). Through this phrase he highlights their most essential properties and consequences. The pact is a societal device, invented by Belgians to arbitrate and settle a national controversy that is considered to be a grave threat to the "well-being" and subsistence of the country, using sufficiently depoliticized and privatized procedures to avoid extremism, achieve moderation, and establish harmony and peace. (In fact, the School War, resolved by the School Pact, is referred to as the School Peace.) There are numerous Belgian commentators who insist on a more "power elite" interpretation of Belgium's pact-making tendencies. They emphasize the degree of consensus and collusion that exist at the "top" of the society between persons of great influence, who have common vested interests, despite the publicly different positions that they appear to represent. To an indeterminate degree, this probably does enter into the dynamics of the Belgian pact. But even more fundamental is the general Belgian disinclination to allow the divisions, conflicts, and passions present in the country to get too far out of hand, for fear that they will ultimately lead to the dissolution of the society. The sources of this anxiety about the dangers of dissension and the survival of the society, and of the propensity for temporizing and for seeking "quiet," harmonious ways of resolving conflict are not easy to document. But Belgium's history of recurrent occupations, on the one hand, and its essentially Catholic world-view, on the other, seem to be contributing factors.

Before concluding, I would like to make some sociology of knowledge related comments on how Belgians would view the kind of analytic perspective on their society that I have presented here. By and large, although they would be intrigued by it, it would make them uncomfortable, partly because it is more culturally and psychodynamically oriented than the analyses of their society to which they are accustomed. They would probably consider my approach to be too focused on values, beliefs, symbols, and motives, and too little concerned with formal patterns of behavior, economic and political structures, the "power elite" (their "conspiracy" and their "dominance"), "pressure groups," and *verzuiling*. This might lead them to question how "scientific" my analysis is, and to define it as more "philosophical," "theological," or "literary" in certain respects, than sociological. With characteristic irony and self-satirizing wit, they might summarize their reactions by saying that they are gratified and reassured that I have discovered that Belgium is *indeed* a society, and that it *does* have a distinctive culture, their own prior, and continuing convictions to the contrary. These reactions are not hypothetical. I have heard them repeatedly during the present phase of my field research; and they are integrally related to some important Belgian culture patterns.

One of these is a strong tradition of positivism in Belgian intellectual life (that at times borders on scientism). This tradition has complex sources that I will not discuss here. But in Belgian social science, one of its effects has been to foster work that deals with overtly observable phenomena (particularly formal social organization and formal practices), and that entails the collection of many official documents, the extensive use of statistics, or the application of an experimental model of inquiry. What it has *not* encouraged is the systematic analysis of feelings, beliefs, values, and symbols, of nonrational aspects of social life, or of latent structures and processes more generally. One sees this reflected, for example, in the greater development of experimental psychology and of neuropsychiatry in Belgium than of social psychology, clinical psychology, or psychoanalysis, and in the fact that although Belgium has produced some outstanding cultural anthropologists (particularly those who have worked in ex-Belgian Africa), no chair or department of anthropology has ever existed in Belgian universities.

But the reluctance to probe too deeply into questions that directly concern feelings, beliefs and values, the symbolic, and that which lies below the surface of social and psychic life is not purely an outgrowth of positivism and scientism. In fact, one might argue that in the realm of social science at least, these propensities have been reinforced by an older, more diffuse cultural tendency to regard delving into matters of emotion and conviction as potentially unwise, and even dangerous. These reservations and apprehensions are rooted in the kinds of historical experiences and associations that have contributed to the society's pact-making. The same Belgian apprehension about the society's lacerating conflicts and enmities has also discouraged research and analysis that deal too directly or deeply with its culturodynamic and psychodynamic aspects. There appears to be a high level of latent concern that such inquiries and analyses may exacerbate the destructive and self-destructive conflicts that are prevalent in the social system, or reopen conflicts that have reached some point of settlement and stasis. (In this latter connection, for example, although I have been invited to give numerous lectures on the sociology of bioethics in various Belgian milieux, I have found that my audiences uneasily associate these issues, especially abortion and euthanasia, with the religious and ideological questions that they believe they definitively settled with the School Pact, and that they do not want to rekindle. It is interesting, too, that it has been widely predicted that the abortion question in Belgium will eventually be resolved through what some journalists and politicians call an "Ethical Pact.")

The caution and suspicion with which Belgians regard cultural and psychological probing are also connected with certain aspects of their underlying existential view: a cosmic outlook that is most clearly and brilliantly expressed in and through their paintings. Since the time of Breughel and Bosch, strange, everyday objects, curious, grotesque, often brutal crowds of people, and galleries of masks have appeared in these works of art. They evoke a sense of the human condition that emphasizes its mysteries and absurdities, its masquerades, the passions and evils behind its façades, and the discrepancies between the external behaviors demanded by society, and the internal countenances of the persons who outwardly comply. This centuries-old vision is allowed to explode into the art, the carnivals, and the *kermesses* of Belgium. But it is collectively denied in daily life, and systematically excluded from intellectual and scientific work, as if it were both improper and perilous to acknowledge it in such commonplace, orderly, and rational contexts.

Belgian sociologists have been consistently engaged in social criticism and adversary roles, as much outside the academy as within it, directing their major attention to the polity and the economy, in the broadest and most structural senses of these terms. Although many individuals and groups have been antagonized by their analyses and activities for this reason (and although quite predictably, given the ideological impact of Belgian positivism, they have been deemed "unscientific" by members of other intellectual disciplines who have not been happy with their stance), there is a real sense in which the critic-adversary role that Belgian sociologists have played is considered more legitimate and less threatening than sociological analyses that would explore and unmask the dimensions of Belgian life that are depicted in its art. And yet, as I have shown, outside of the formal confines of social science, and the at once realistic, expressionistic and surrealistic images of Belgian art, there is continual, colloquial reference to the attributes of the society that I have considered. It is compressed in all the Belgian expressions that I have cited, and in numerous others that could be added to the list: "particularism," "pluralism," *verzuiling, petits chemins, piston, kruiwagen, messieurs les responsables, méfiance, courage, splitsing, fusion,* "immobilism," *cumul,* "conclave," "castle," "silent pacts," and the like. Viewed as an ensemble, these phrases constitute a coded and, in a sense, disguised running commentary on the cardinal features of Belgian society that are only rarely explicitly analyzed by its own citizens—its sociologists included.

In the end, what is the answer to the question, "Why Belgium?" I have tried to show how my training, socialization, interest, and prior research as a sociologist led me to Belgium. I think I can now simply state that the study of Belgian medical research and progressively of Belgian society would not have been possible without an interdisciplinary base (one that drew on history, anthropology, psychology, and biomedicine, as well as sociology), a cross-cultural perspective (that both implicitly and explicitly juxtaposed North American, Western European, and Central African societies), and the use of field methods of social research. My almost 20 years of exploring Belgian society have been full of personal meaning for me, as is usually the case with intensive, absorbing work. And in some respects it has had the quality of a prolonged pilgrimage.

In addition, I have attempted to suggest something of the more impersonal and general social scientific value I have found through my continuing study of Belgian society, within the framework that I have delineated. To begin with, although Belgium ostensibly belongs to the group of societies that we as social scientists would characterize as modern, Western, European, urban, industrialized, capitalistic, democratic, and Christian, when examined systematically, over time, and in empirical detail, it has many structural and cultural attributes that do not fit these established conceptual categories. What is more, Max Weber's heritage to us notwithstanding, Belgium turns out to be a Catholic, virtually Protestant-less country, which nevertheless has a Protestant Ethic-like work ethos. For all of its modernity and dynamism, it is also highly traditional, committed to values of consensus, harmony and solidarity, and sufficiently concerned about its potentialities for inner strife and self-demolition to establish and maintain permanent "pacts" around critical societal issues. Many of Belgium's salient features (like its particularism, its negative competition, its conception of equality, the kind of conformity it exacts, its institutionalization of gossip and of distrust) remind one more of the predominantly mechanical solidarity traits of the premodern and even primitive societies in Durkheim's paradigm than of the attributes of organic solidarity that, in theory, should predominate in a modern society. And yet, one could hardly call Belgium a primitive, or archaic society. Is Belgium a bizarre, as well as an anomalous case in all these respects, or does it invite and challenge us to revise some of our notions about modernity and traditionality, societal evolution, change and non-change, conflict and consensus, "Western-ness," "European-ness," and "Christian-ness"? And how does all of this bear on one of the questions raised earlier, namely, what is the relationship between Belgium's primary social and cultural features, and the fact that it is a small society? Do societies as diverse as Holland, Switzerland, Sweden, and Israel have some of the same characteristics as Belgium (as has been suggested to me by other sociologists), principally because they, too, are small societies? And why do the key images, and the psychological and metaphysical atmosphere evoked by Franz Kafka's allegorical novels *The Trial*, and especially *The Castle* resemble those of Belgium? Is it because the small, Continental European society out of which Kafka wrote, Czechoslovakia of the 1920s, had comparable traits? Does societal "smallness" produce such characteristics, or do such attributes define and create what we mean sociologically by a society that is "small"?

I may need at least nineteen more years of involvement with Belgium, as a comparative, interdisciplinary-oriented, field working sociologist, before I can begin to answer such questions. But without the *first* nineteen Belgian years, I might never have thought to raise them.

PART FIVE

SPECIAL (OCCASIONAL) CASE STUDIES

The Case of the Floppy-Eared Rabbits: An Instance of Serendipity Gained and Serendipity Lost

BERNARD BARBER AND RENÉE C. FOX

As with so many other basic social processes, the actual process of scientific research and discovery is not well understood.[1] There has been little systematic observation of the research and discovery process as it actually occurs, and even less controlled research. Moreover, the form in which discoveries are reported by scientists to their colleagues in professional journals tends to conceal important aspects of this process. Because of certain norms that are strongly institutionalized in their professional community, scientists are expected to focus their reports on the logical structure of the methods used and the ideas discovered in research in relation to the established conceptual framework of the relevant scientific specialty. The primary function of such reports is con-

1. For an account of what is known see Bernard Barber, *Science and the Social Order* (Glencoe, Ill.: Free Press, 1952), Chap. 9, "The Social Process of Invention and Discovery," 191–206.

From *American Journal of Sociology*, Vol. 64, No. 2 (September 1958): 128–136.

ceived to be that of indicating how the new observations and ideas being advanced may require a change—by further generalization or systematization—in the conceptual structure of a given scientific field. All else that has occurred in the actual research process is considered "incidental." Thus scientists are praised for presenting their research in a way that is elegantly bare of anything that does not serve this primary function and are deterred from reporting "irrelevant" social and psychological aspects of the research process, however interesting these matters may be in other contexts. As a result of such norms and practices, the reporting of scientific research may be characterized by what has been called "retrospective falsification." By selecting only those components of the actual research process that serve their primary purpose, scientific papers leave out a great deal, of course, as many scientists have indicated in their memoirs and in their informal talks with one another. Selection, then, unwittingly distorts and, in that special sense, falsifies what has happened in research as it actually goes on in the laboratory and its environs.

Public reports to the community of scientists thus have their own function. Their dysfunctionality for the sociology of scientific discovery, which is concerned with not one but all the components of the research process as a social process, is of no immediate concern to the practicing research scientist. And yet what is lost in "retrospective falsification" may be of no small importance to him, if only indirectly. For it is not unlikely that here, as everywhere else in the world of nature, knowledge is power, in this case power to increase the fruitfulness of scientific research by enlarging our systematic knowledge of it. The sociology of scientific discovery would seem to be an especially desirable area for further theoretical and empirical development.

One component of the actual process of scientific discovery that is left out or concealed in research reports following the practice of "retrospective falsification" is the element of unforeseen development, of happy or lucky chance, of what Robert K. Merton has called "the serendipity pattern."[2] By its very nature, scientific research is a voyage into the unknown by routes that are in some measure unpredictable and unplannable. Chance or luck is therefore as inevitable in scientific research as are logic and what Pasteur called "the prepared mind." Yet little is known systematically about this inevitable serendipity component.

2. For discussions of serendipity see Walter B. Cannon, *The Way of an Investigator* (New York: W. W. Norton & Co., 1945), Chap. 6, "Gains from Serendipity," 68–78; and Robert K. Merton, *Social Theory and Social Structure* (rev. ed.; Glencoe, Ill.: Free Press, 1957), 103–108. Our colleagues, Robert K. Merton and Elinor G. Barber, have undertaken an investigation and clarification of the variety of meanings of "chance" that are lumped under the notion of serendipity by different users of that term.

For this reason it seemed to us desirable to take the opportunity recently provided by the reporting of an instance of *serendipity gained* by Dr. Lewis Thomas, now professor and chairman of the Department of Medicine in the College of Medicine of New York University and formerly professor and chairman of the Department of Pathology.[3] Then, shortly after hearing about Dr. Thomas's discovery, we learned from medical research and teaching colleagues of an instance of *serendipity lost* on the very same kind of chance occurrence: unexpected floppiness in rabbits' ears after they had been injected intravenously with the proteolytic enzyme papain. This instance of serendipity lost had occurred in the course of research by Dr. Aaron Kellner, associate professor in the Department of Pathology of Cornell University Medical College and director of its central laboratories. This opportunity for *comparative* study seemed even more promising for our further understanding of the serendipity pattern. Here were two comparable medical scientists, we reasoned, both carrying out investigations in the field of experimental pathology, affiliated with distinguished medical schools, and of approximately the same level of demonstrated research ability (so far as it was in our lay capacity to judge). In the course of their research both men had had occasion to inject rabbits intravenously with papain, and both had observed the phenomenon of ear collapse following the injection.

In spite of these similarities in their professional backgrounds and although they had both accidentally encountered the same phenomenon, one of these scientists had gone on to make a discovery based on this chance occurrence, whereas the other had not. It seemed to us that a detailed comparison of Dr. Thomas's and Dr. Kellner's experiences with the floppy-eared rabbits offered a quasi-experimental opportunity to identify some of the factors that contribute to a positive experience with serendipity in research and some of the factors conducive to a negative experience with it.

We asked for and were generously granted intensive interviews with Dr. Thomas and Dr. Kellner.[4] Each reported to us that they had experienced both "positive serendipity" and "negative serendipity" in their research. That is, each had made a number of serendipitous discoveries

3. Lewis Thomas, "Reversible Collapse of Rabbit Ears after Intravenous Papain, and Prevention of Recovery by Cortisone," *Journal of Experimental Medicine*, Vol. 104 (1956), 245–252. This case first came to our attention through a report in the *New York Times*. The pictures printed in Dr. Thomas's original article and in the *Times* will indicate why we have called this "the case of the floppy-eared rabbits."

4. These interviews lasted about two hours each. They are another instance of the "tandem interviewing" described by Harry V. Kincaid and Margaret Bright, "Interviewing the Business Elite," *American Journal of Sociology*, Vol. 63 (1957), 304–311.

based on chance occurrences in their planned experiments, and on other occasions each had missed the significance of like occurrences that other researchers had later transformed into discoveries. Apparently, both positive and negative serendipity are common experiences for scientific researchers. Indeed, we shall see that one of the chief reasons why Dr. Kellner experienced serendipity lost with respect to the discovery that Dr. Thomas made was that he was experiencing serendipity gained with respect to some other aspects of the very same experimental situation. Conversely, Dr. Thomas had reached a stalemate on some of his other research, and this gave him added incentive to pursue intensively the phenomenon of ear collapse. Partly as a consequence of these experiences, in what were similar experimental situations, the two researchers each saw something and missed something else.

On the basis of our focused interviews with these two scientists, we can describe some of the recurring elements in their experiences with serendipity.[5] We think that these patterns may also be relevant to instances of serendipity experienced by other investigators.

SERENDIPITY GAINED

Dr. Thomas

Observing the established norms for reporting scientific research, in his article in the *Journal of Experimental Medicine,* Dr. Thomas did not mention his experience with serendipity. In the manner typical of such reports he began his article with the statement, "For reasons not relevant to the present discussion rabbits were injected intravenously with a solution of crude papain." (By contrast, though not called by this term, serendipity was featured in the accounts of this research that appeared in *The New York Times* and *The New York Herald Tribune*. "An accidental sidelight of one research project had the startling effect of wilting the ears of the rabbit," said the *Times* article. "This bizarre phenomenon, accidentally discovered . . ." was the way the *Herald Tribune* described the same phenomenon. The prominence accorded the "accidental" nature of the discovery in the press is related to the fact that these articles were written by journalists for a lay audience. The kind of interest in scientific research that is characteristic of science reporters and the audience for

5. In this paper we shall concentrate on the instances of serendipity gained by Dr. Thomas and lost by Dr. Kellner and give somewhat less attention to elements of negative serendipity in Dr. Thomas's experiments and elements of positive serendipity in those of Dr. Kellner.

whom they write and their conceptions of the form in which information about research ought to be communicated differ from those of professional scientists.[6])

Although Dr. Thomas did not mention serendipity in his article for the *Journal of Experimental Medicine*, in his interview he reported both his general acquaintance with the serendipity pattern ("Serendipity is a familiar term. . . . I first heard about it in Dr. Cannon's class. . . .") and his awareness of the chance occurrence of floppy-eared rabbits in his own research. Dr. Thomas first noticed the reversible collapse of rabbit ears after intravenous papain about seven years ago, when he was working on the effects of proteolytic enzymes as a class:

> I was trying to explore the notion that the cardiac and blood vessel lesions in certain hypersensitivity states may be due to release of proteolytic enzymes. It's an attractive idea on which there's little evidence. And it's been picked up at some time or another by almost everyone working on hypersensitivity. For this investigation I used trypsin, because it was the most available enzyme around the laboratory, and I got nothing. We also happened to have papain; I don't know where it had come from; but because it was there, I tried it. I also tried a third enzyme, ficin. It comes from figs, and it's commonly used. It has catholic tastes and so it's quite useful in the laboratory. So I had these three enzymes. The other two didn't produce lesions. Nor did papain. But what the papain did was always produce these bizarre cosmetic changes. . . . It was one of the most uniform reactions I'd ever seen in biology. It always happened. And it looked as if something important must have happened to cause this reaction.

Some of the elements of serendipitous discovery are clearly illustrated in this account by Dr. Thomas. The scientific researcher, while in pursuit of some other specific goals, accidentally ("we also happened to have papain . . .") produces an unusual, recurrent, and sometimes striking ("bizarre") effect. Only the element of creative imagination, which is necessary to complete an instance of serendipity by supplying an explanation of the unusual effect, is not yet present. Indeed, the explanation was to elude Dr. Thomas, as it eluded Dr. Kellner, and probably others

6. Further discussion of this point lies beyond the scope of this paper. But in a society like ours, in which science has become "front-page news," some of the characteristics and special problems of science reporting merit serious study. A recently published work on this topic that has come to our attention is entitled *When Doctors Meet Reporters* (New York: New York University Press, 1957). This is a discussion by science writers and physicians of the controversy between the press and the medical profession, compiled from the record of a series of conferences sponsored by the Josiah Macy, Jr., Foundation.

as well, for several years. This was not for lack of trying by Dr. Thomas. He immediately did seek an explanation:

> I chased it like crazy. But I didn't do the right thing. . . . I did the expected things. I had sections cut, and I had them stained by all the techniques available at the time. And I studied what I believed to be the constituents of a rabbit's ear. I looked at all the sections, but I couldn't see anything the matter. The connective tissue was intact. There was no change in the amount of elastic tissue. There was no inflammation, no tissue damage. I expected to find a great deal, because I thought we had destroyed something.

Dr. Thomas also studied the cartilage of the rabbit's ear, and judged it to be "normal" (". . . The cells were healthy-looking and there were nice nuclei. I decided there was no damage to the cartilage. And that was that. . . ."). However, he admitted that at the time his consideration of the cartilage was routine and relatively casual, because he did not seriously entertain the idea that the phenomenon of ear collapse might be associated with changes in this tissue:

> I hadn't thought of cartilage. You're not likely to, because it's not considered interesting. . . . I know my own idea has always been that cartilage is a quiet, inactive tissue.

Dr. Thomas's preconceptions about the methods appropriate for studying the ear-collapsing effect of papain, his expectation that it would probably be associated with damage in the connective or elastic tissues, and the conviction he shared with colleagues that cartilage is "inert and relatively uninteresting"—these guided his initial inquiries into this phenomenon. But the same preconceptions, expectations, and convictions also blinded him to physical and chemical changes in the ear cartilage matrix, which, a number of years later, were to seem "obvious" to him as the alterations underlying the collapsing ears. Here again, another general aspect of the research process comes into the clear. Because the methods and assumptions on which a systematic investigation is built selectively focus the researcher's attention, to a certain extent they sometimes constrict his imagination and bias his observations.

Although he was "very chagrined" about his failure, Dr. Thomas finally had to turn away from his floppy-eared rabbits because he was "terribly busy working on another problem at the time," with which he was "making progress." Also, Dr. Thomas reported, "I had already used all the rabbits I could afford. So I was able to persuade myself to abandon this other research." The gratifications of research success elsewhere and the lack of adequate resources to continue with his rabbit experiments combined to make Dr. Thomas accept failure, at least temporarily. As is usually the case in the reporting of scientific research, these experiments and their negative outcome were not written up for professional journals. (There is too much failure of this sort in research to permit of its publication, except occasionally, even though it might be instructive for some other scientists in carrying out their research. Since there is no way of determining what might be instructive failures and since space in professional journals is at a premium, generally only accounts of successful experiments are submitted to such journals and published by them.)

Despite his decision to turn his attention to other, more productive research, Dr. Thomas did not completely forget the floppy-eared rabbits. His interest was kept alive by a number of things. As he explained, the collapse of the rabbit ears and their subsequent reversal "was one of the most uniform reactions I'd ever seen in biology." The "unfailing regularity" with which it occurred is not often observed in scientific research. Thus the apparent invariance of this phenomenon never ceased to intrigue Dr. Thomas, who continued to feel that an important and powerful biological happening might be responsible. The effect of papain on rabbit ears had two additional qualities that helped to sustain Dr. Thomas's interest in it. The spectacle of rabbits with "ears collapsed limply at either side of the head, rather like the ears of spaniels,"[7] was both dramatic and entertaining.

In the intervening years Dr. Thomas described this phenomenon to a number of colleagues in pathology, biochemistry, and clinical investigation, who were equally intrigued and of the opinion that a significant amount of demonstrable tissue damage must be associated with such a striking and uniform reaction. Dr. Thomas also reported that twice he "put the experiment on" for some of his more skeptical colleagues. ("They didn't believe me when I told them what happened. They didn't really believe that you can get that much change and not a trace of anything having happened when you look in the microscope.") As so often happens in science, an unsolved puzzle was kept in mind for eventual solution through informal exchanges between scientists, rather than through the formal medium of published communications.

A few years ago Dr. Thomas once again accidentally came upon the floppy-eared rabbits in the course of another investigation:

> I was looking for a way . . . to reduce the level of fibrinogen in the blood of rabbits. I had been studying a form of fibrinoid which occurs inside blood

7. Thomas, *op. cit.*, p. 245.

vessels in the generalized Schwartzman reaction and which seems to be derived from fibrinogen. My working hypothesis was that, if I depleted the fibrinogen and, as a result, fibrinoid did not occur, this would help. It had been reported that if you inject proteolytic enzyme, this will deplete fibrinogen. So I tried to inhibit the Schwartzman reaction by injecting papain intravenously into the rabbits. It didn't work with respect to fibrinogen. . . . But the same damned thing happened again to the rabbits' ears!

This time, however, Dr. Thomas was to solve the puzzle of the collapsed rabbit ears and realize a complete instance of serendipitous discovery. He describes what subsequently happened:

I was teaching second-year medical students in pathology. We have these small seminars with them: two-hour sessions in the morning, twice a week, with six to eight students. These are seminars devoted to experimental pathology and the theoretical aspects of the mechanism of disease. The students have a chance to see what we, the faculty, are up to in the laboratory. I happened to have a session with the students at the same time that this thing with the rabbits' ears happened again. I thought it would be an entertaining thing to show them . . . a spectacular thing. The students were very interested in it. I explained to them that we couldn't really explain what the hell was going on here. I did this experiment on purpose for them, to see what they would think. . . . Besides which, I was in irons on my other experiments. There was not much doing on those. I was not being brilliant on these other problems. . . . Well, this time I did what I didn't do before. I simultaneously cut sections of the ears of rabbits after I'd given them papain *and* sections of normal ears. This is the part of the story I'm most ashamed of. It still makes me writhe to think of it. There was no damage to the tissue in the sense of a lesion. But what had taken place was a quantitative change in the matrix of the cartilage. The only way you could make sense of this change was simultaneously to compare sections taken from the ears of rabbits which had been injected with papain with comparable sections from the ears of rabbits of the same age and size which had not received papain. . . . Before this I had always been so struck by the enormity of the change that when I didn't see something obvious, I concluded there was nothing. . . . Also, I didn't have a lot of rabbits to work with before.

Judging from Dr. Thomas's account, it appears that a number of factors contributed to his reported experimental success. First, his teaching duties played a creative role in this regard. They impelled him to run the experiment with papain again and kept his attention focused on its implications for basic science rather than on its potentialities for practical application. Dr. Thomas said that he used the experiment to "convey to students what experimental pathology is like." Second, because he had reached an impasse in some of his other research, Dr. Thomas had more time and further inclination to study the ear-collapsing effect of papain than he had had a few years earlier, when the progress he was making on other research helped to "persuade" him to "abandon" the problem of the floppy-eared rabbits. Third, Dr. Thomas had more laboratory resources at his command than previously, notably a larger supply of rabbits. (In this regard it is interesting to note that, according to Dr. Thomas's article in the *Journal of Experimental Medicine*, 250 rabbits, all told, were used in the experiments reported.) Finally, the fact that he now had more laboratory animals with which to work and that he wanted to present the phenomenon of reversible ear collapse to students in a way that would make it an effective teaching exercise led Dr. Thomas to modify his method for examining rabbit tissues. In his earlier experiments, Dr. Thomas had compared histological sections made of the ears of rabbits who had received an injection of papain with his own mental image of normal rabbit-ear tissue. This time, however, he actually made sections from the ear tissue of rabbits which did *not* receive papain, as well as from those which did, and simultaneously examined the two. As he reported, this comparison enabled him to see for the first time that "drastic" quantitative changes had occurred in the cartilaginous tissue obtained from the ears of the rabbits injected with papain. In the words of the *Journal* article,

> The ear cartilage showed loss of a major portion of the intercellular matrix, and complete absence of basophilia from the small amount of remaining matrix. The cartilage cells appeared somewhat larger, and rounder than normal, and lay in close contact with each other. . . .

Immediately thereafter, Dr. Thomas and his associates found that these changes occur not only in ear cartilage but in all other cartilaginous tissues as well.

How significant or useful Dr. Thomas's serendipitous discovery will be cannot yet be specified. The serendipity pattern characterizes small discoveries as well as great. Dr. Thomas and his associates are currently investigating some of the questions raised by the phenomenon of papain-collapsed ears and the alterations in cartilage now known to underlie it. In addition, Dr. Thomas reported that some of his "biochemist and clinical friends" have become interested enough in certain of his findings to "go to work with papain, too." Two of the major problems under study in Dr. Thomas's laboratory are biochemical: the one concerning the nature of the change in cartilage; the other, the nature of the factor in papain that causes collapse of rabbits' ears and lysis of cartilage matrix in all tissues. Attempts are also being made to identify the antibody that causes rabbits to become immune to the factor responsible for ear collapse after two weeks of injection. The way in which cortisone prolongs the reaction to papain and the possible effect that papain may have on the joints as well as the cartilage are also being considered. Though at the time he was interviewed Dr. Thomas could not predict whether his findings (to date) would prove "important" or not, there was some evidence to suggest that certain basic discoveries about the constituents and properties of cartilaginous tissue might be forthcoming and that the experiments thus far conducted might have "practical usefulness" for studies of the postulated role of cortisone in the metabolism of sulfated mucopolysaccharides and of the relationship between cartilage and the electrolyte imbalance associated with congestive heart failure.

In the research on reversible ear collapse that Dr. Thomas has conducted since his initial serendipitous discovery, the planned and the unplanned, the foreseen and the accidental, the logical and the lucky have continued to interact. For example, Dr. Thomas's discovery that cortisone prevents or greatly delays the "return of papain-collapsed ears to their normal shape and rigidity" came about as a result of a carefully planned experiment that he undertook to test the effect of cortisone on the reaction to papain. On the other hand, his discovery that "repeated injections of papain, over a period of two or three weeks, bring about immunity to the phenomenon of ear collapse" was an unanticipated consequence of the fact that he used the same rabbit to demonstrate the floppy ears to several different groups of medical students:

> I was so completely sold on the uniformity of this thing that I used the same rabbit [for each seminar]. . . . The third time it didn't work. I was appalled by it. The students were there, and the rabbit's ears were still in place. . . . At first I thought that perhaps the technician had given him the wrong stuff. But then when I checked on that and gave the same stuff to the other rabbits and it *did* work I realized that the rabbit had become immune. This is a potentially hot finding. . . .

SERENDIPITY LOST

Dr. Kellner

In our interview with Dr. Thomas we told him that we had heard about another medical scientist who had noticed the reversible collapse of rabbits' ears when he had injected them intravenously with papain. Dr. Thomas was not at all surprised. "That must be Kellner," he said. "He must have seen it. He was doomed to see it." Dr. Thomas was acquainted with the reports that Dr. Kellner and his associates had published on "Selective Necrosis of Cardiac and Skeletal Muscle Induced Experimentally by Means of Proteolytic Enzyme Solutions Given Intravenously" and on "Blood Coagulation Defect Induced in Rabbits by Papain Solutions Injected Intravenously."[8] He took it for granted that, in the course of these reported experiments, which had entailed papain solution given intravenously to rabbits, a competent scientist like Dr. Kellner had also seen the resulting collapse of rabbits' ears, with its "unfailing regularity" and its "flamboyant" character. And, indeed, our interview with Dr. Kellner revealed that he had observed the floppiness, apparently at about the same time as Dr. Thomas:

> We called them the floppy-eared rabbits. . . . Five or six years ago we published our first article on the work we were doing with papain; that was in 1951 and our definitive article was published in 1954. . . . We gave papain to the animals and we had done it thirty or forty times before we noticed these changes in the rabbits' ears.

Thus Dr. Kellner's observation of what he and his colleagues dubbed "the floppy-eared rabbits" represents, when taken together with Dr. Thomas's experience, an instance of independent multiple observation, which often occurs in science and frequently leads to independent multiple invention and discovery.

Once he had noticed the phenomenon of ear collapse, Dr. Kellner did what Dr. Thomas and any research scientist would have done in the presence of such an unexpected and striking regularity: he looked for an answer to the puzzle it represented. "I was a little curious about it at the time, and followed it up to the extent of making sections of the rabbits' ears." However, for one of those trivial reasons that sometimes affect the course of research—the obviously amusing quality of floppiness in rabbits' ears—Dr. Kellner did not take the phenomenon as seriously as he took other aspects of the experimental situation involving the injection of papain.

In effect, Dr. Kellner and his associates closed out their interest in the

8. See Aaron Kellner and Theodore Robertson, "Selective Necrosis of Cardiac and Skeletal Muscle Induced Experimentally by Means of Proteolytic Enzyme Solutions Given Intravenously," *Journal of Experimental Medicine,* Vol. 99 (1954), 387–404; and Aaron Kellner, Theodore Robertson, and Howard O. Mott, "Blood Coagulation Defect Induced in Rabbits by Papain Solutions Injected Intravenously," abstract in *Federation Proceedings*, Vol. 10 (1951), No. 1.

phenomenon of the reversible collapse of rabbits' ears following intravenous injection of papain by using it as an assay test for the potency and amount of papain to be injected. "Every laboratory technician we've had since 1951," he told us in the interview, "has known about these floppy ears because we've used them to assay papain, to tell us if it's potent and how potent." If the injected rabbit died from the dose of papain he received, the researchers knew that the papain injection was too potent; if there was no change in the rabbit's ears, the papain was not potent enough, but "if the rabbit lived and his ears drooped, it was just right." Although "we knew all about it, and used it that way . . . as a rule of thumb," Dr. Kellner commented, "I didn't write it up." Nor did he ever have "any intention of publishing it as a method of assaying papain." He knew that an applied technological discovery of this sort would not be suitable for publication in the basic-science-oriented professional journals to which he and his colleagues submit reports of experimental work.

However, two factors apparently were much more important in leading Dr. Kellner away from investigating this phenomenon. First, like Dr. Thomas, Dr. Kellner thought of cartilage as relatively inert tissue. Second, because of his pre-established special research interests, Dr. Kellner's attention was predominantly trained on muscle tissue:

> Since I was primarily interested in research questions having to do with the muscles of the heart, I was thinking in terms of muscle. That blinded me, so that changes in the cartilage didn't occur to me as a possibility. I was looking for muscles in the sections, and I never dreamed it was cartilage.

Like Dr. Thomas at the beginning of his research and like all scientists at some stages in their research, Dr. Kellner was "misled" by his preconceptions.

However, as we already know, in keeping with his special research interests, Dr. Kellner noticed and intensively followed up two other serendipitous results that occur when papain is injected intravenously into rabbits: focal necrosis of cardiac and skeletal muscle and a blood coagulation defect, which in certain respects resembles that of hemophilia.[9]

It was the selective necrosis of cardiac and skeletal muscle that Dr. Kellner studied with the greatest degree of seriousness and interest. Dr. Kellner told us that he is "particularly interested in cardio-vascular disease," and so the lesions in the myocardium was the chance observation that he particularly "chose to follow . . . the one closest to me." Not

9. See Kellner and Robertson, *op. cit.*, and Kellner, Robertson, and Mott, *op. cit.*

only did Dr. Kellner himself have a special interest in the necrosis of cardiac muscle, but also his "laboratory and the people associated with me," he said, provided "the physical and intellectual tools to cope with this phenomenon." Dr. Kellner and his colleagues also did a certain amount of "work tracking down the cause of the blood coagulation defect"; but, because this line of inquiry "led [them] far afield" from investigative work in which they were especially interested and competent, they eventually "let that go" as they had let go the phenomenon of floppiness in rabbits' ears. Dr. Kellner indicated in his interview that the potential usefulness of his work with the selective necrosis of cardiac and skeletal muscle cannot yet be precisely ascertained. However, in his article in the *Journal of Experimental Medicine* he suggested that this serendipitous finding "has interesting implications for the pathogenesis of the morphological changes in rheumatic fever, periarteritis nodosa, and other hypersensitivity states."

Thus Dr. Kellner did not have the experience of serendipity gained with respect to the significance of floppiness in rabbits' ears after intravenous injection of papain for a variety of reasons, some trivial apparently, others important. The most important reasons, it seems, were his research preconceptions and the occurrence of other serendipitous phenomena in the same experimental situation.

In summary, although the ultimate outcome of their respective laboratory encounters with floppiness in rabbits' ears was quite different, there are some interesting similarities between the serendipity-gained experience of Dr. Thomas and the serendipity-lost experience of Dr. Kellner. Initially, the attention of both men was caught by the striking uniformity with which the collapse of rabbit ears occurred after intravenous papain and by the "bizarre," entertaining qualities of this cosmetic effect. In their subsequent investigations of this phenomenon, both were to some extent misled by certain of their interests and preconceptions. Lack of progress in accounting for ear collapse, combined with success in other research in which they were engaged at the time, eventually led both Dr. Thomas and Dr. Kellner to discontinue their work with the floppy-eared rabbits.

However, there were also some significant differences in the two experiences. Dr. Thomas seems to have been more impressed with the regularity of this particular phenomenon than Dr. Kellner and somewhat less amused by it. Unlike Dr. Kellner, Dr. Thomas never lost interest in the floppy-eared rabbits. When he came upon this reaction again at a time when he was "blocked" on other research, he began actively to reconsider the problem of what might have caused it. Eventual success was more likely to result from this continuing concern on Dr.

Thomas's part. And Dr. Kellner, of course, was drawn off in other research directions by seeing other serendipitous phenomena in the same situation and by his success in following up those other leads.

These differences between Dr. Thomas and Dr. Kellner seem to account at least in part for the serendipity-gained outcome of the case of the floppy-eared rabbits for the one, and the serendipity-lost outcome for the other.

Experiences with both serendipity gained and serendipity lost are probably frequent occurrences for many scientific researchers. For, as Dr. Kellner pointed out in our interview with him, scientific investigations often entail "doing something that no one has done before, [so] you don't always know how to do it or exactly what to do":

> Should you boil or freeze, filter or centrifuge? These are the kinds of crossroads you come to all the time. . . . It's always possible to do four, five, or six things, and you have to choose between them. . . . How do you decide?

In this comparative study of one instance of serendipity gained and serendipity lost, we have tried to make inferences about some of the factors that led one investigator down the path to a successful and potentially important discovery and another to follow a somewhat different, though eventually perhaps a no less fruitful, trail of research. A large enough series of such case studies could suggest how often and in what ways these factors (and others that might prove relevant) influence the paths that open up to investigators in the course of their research, the choices they make between them, and the experimental findings that result from such choices. Case studies of this kind might also contribute a good deal to the detailed, systematic study of "the ways in which scientists actually . . . think, feel and act," which Robert K. Merton says could perhaps teach us more "in a comparatively few years, about the psychology and sociology of science than in all the years that have gone before."[10]

10. See his Foreword to *Science and the Social Order* by Bernard Barber, p. xxii.

The Clinical Moratorium

JUDITH P. SWAZEY AND RENÉE C. FOX

The purpose of this paper is to identify and analyze a particular phenomenon that recurs in the development of new medical and surgical procedures, most commonly during the early phases of their clinical trial. What we shall call "the clinical moratorium" is an event that we consider generic to the process of therapeutic innovation. Its significance lies not only in the frequency with which it occurs, but also in its relationship to some fundamental conceptual, technical, social, and ethical properties of clinical investigation.

Our interest in the clinical moratorium was stimulated by certain observations we made in the context of a socio-historical study of organ transplantation that we are currently conducting.[1] Since the announcement of the world's first human heart transplant, performed by Dr. Christiaan Barnard in December 1967, this procedure has been widely discussed within the medical profession and also by lay people. These

1. The work that, in part, formed the basis of that study has been published as *The Courage to Fail.*

From Paul A. Freund, ed., *Experimentation with Human Subjects* (New York: Braziller, 1970), 315–357.

debates have been chronicled and to some extent amplified by the lay press, which has covered the 151 cardiac transplants done through September 25, 1969.[2] Both in professional and lay press contexts, there have been continuing discussions concerning whether or not a moratorium on heart transplants should be called. These exchanges reached a crescendo in Winter 1969, when the Montreal Heart Institute announced that it was halting cardiac transplants.[3] Hospital spokesmen stated that the Institute would not resume the operation until the high mortality rate accompanying the procedure could be reduced through better control of the immunological processes which cause a recipient's body to reject a transplanted organ.

As we followed the cardiac transplantation debate,[4] it became apparent that there is some confusion over the precise meaning of a clinical moratorium, both semantically and operationally. Partly for this reason, controversy over whether it is justifiable to continue heart transplantation on patients at this stage in its development has repeatedly been accompanied by the question of whether a moratorium on this procedure has already occurred.

The word moratorium is derived from the Latin *moratorius*—"serving to delay"—and is defined in the *Oxford English Dictionary* as "a legal authorization to a debtor to postpone payment for a certain time." In press accounts of cardiac transplantation, often quoting physicians, the following words and phrases have appeared synonymously with

2. Data supplied by the National Heart Institute. It is interesting that the "box score" reporting on cardiac transplantation has virtually ignored the chimpanzee-to-human heart transplantation performed by Dr. James Hardy at the University of Mississippi Medical Center on January 23, 1964. The recipient, a sixty-eight-year-old male, died some two hours after surgery, because the implanted heart was too small to pump an adequate supply of blood.

3. We would have predicted that the death of Dr. Philip Blaiberg on August 17, 1969, the first patient to survive a heart transplantation for almost two years, would cause an increase in calls for a moratorium on this procedure. However, our survey of major professional and lay press publications indicates that this did not occur. Although Blaiberg's death was prominently and extensively covered by the press, for example, most statements about its implications for cardiac transplantation went no further than to advocate "moving ahead . . . with a renewed sense of caution." The only article we found that asked for an *in memoriam* stoppage of heart transplants appeared in the London *Times*, and was written by its medical correspondent (August 18, 1969): "What is certain . . . is that Dr. Blaiberg must not be allowed to have died in vain. The heart surgeons of the world must show their respect for this gallant soul by vowing to carry out no more heart transplantations until the full lessons of those already done have been absorbed."

4. In addition to covering professional publications, we have been following national and local American press coverage of organ transplantations via articles provided by a national press clipping service.

moratorium: *halt, diminish, stop, stop entirely, slow the tide, set aside for the time being, cease, boycott, suspend, defer, slow down, languish, decline, abandon, pause, quit.* As this range of terms suggests, both medical professionals and laymen seem unclear as to whether only the total cessation of trials of a new procedure on human subjects constitutes a moratorium or if a slowdown or temporary halt in its clinical application might also be considered kinds of moratoria. What the press and dictionary definitions have in common is that both turn around the seeking of legitimation for postponing or halting an activity which is felt to be morally binding.[5]

Our interest in cardiac transplantation led us to explore instances of clinical moratoria in recent medical history. This paper will focus upon a case study of the moratorium phenomenon in the development of surgery on the heart's mitral valve over the period 1902 to 1949.[6] We have chosen this case for two principal reasons. First, it represents an earlier innovative period in cardiac surgery. Second, the cessation of mitral valve surgery that extended from 1928 to 1945 is an unusually clearcut as well as prolonged instance of the clinical moratorium.

Based on this study and on our wider acquaintance with medical sociology and history, we will use the word moratorium to mean a *suspension* of the use of a still experimental procedure on patients, a suspension which may last for weeks, months, or years depending upon the particular case.

The first section of our paper will examine critical events in the history

5. It is interesting that the word "moratorium," which originally had a very specific legally defined debtor-creditor referent, is now applied to a number of different kinds of situations, in which the delay or stoppage involved is normatively, rather than juridically, invoked and authorized. In clinical investigation, a research physician or group calling for a moratorium implicitly or explicitly appeals to colleagues for the right, at least temporarily, to withdraw from participation in the ongoing stream of medical research. The moral commitment involved is that of contributing to the general process of clinical research, rather than to a particular procedure, such as cardiac transplantation. We will discuss this point at greater length in the final section of the paper.

6. Three other instances of clinical moratoria, which we would like to study in more detail, have occurred in the development of brain surgery and of kidney and liver transplantation. In the latter case, for example, we find that when human whole liver transplantation was first attempted in 1963, four out of five patients survived surgery, but died of various complications within six to twenty-three days. In the face of these results there occurred what Dr. Francis Moore has termed a "spontaneous moratorium" in liver transplantation until Spring 1967. A few isolated operations were attempted, but "most authorities were in agreement by this time that major improvements [in immunosuppression, organ preservation, and tissue typing] would be necessary before further clinical trials were justified." (F. D. Moore, quoted in the *Boston Globe*, February 8, 1969, p. 1; *Status of Transplantation, 1968*. A Report by the Surgery Training Committee of the National Institute of General Medical Sciences, National Institutes of Health, p. 36.)

of mitral valve surgery. In the light of this analysis, we will then identify numerous of the factors responsible for the halting and resumption of an innovative clinical procedure. Finally, we will attempt to more precisely define the core attributes and patterned variations in the various types of clinical moratoria that can occur.

MITRAL VALVE SURGERY: 1902–1949

> On looking at the contracted mitral orifice . . . one is impressed by the hopelessness of ever finding a remedy which will enable the auricle to drive the blood in a sufficient stream through the small mitral orifice, and the wish unconsciously arises that one could divide the constriction as easily during life as one can after death. The risk which such an operation would entail naturally makes one shrink from it, but in some cases it might be well worthwhile for the patients to balance the risk of a shortened life against the certainty of a prolonged period of existence which could hardly be called life.[7]

With this introduction, in 1902, Sir Lauder Brunton, a Fellow of the Royal Society and one of England's leading cardiologists, proposed a surgical technique for correcting stenosis (narrowing) of the heart's mitral valve.[8] At the time of his short note in *Lancet* Brunton had been working out his procedure on animals, recognizing that "no one would be justified in attempting such a dangerous operation as dividing a mitral stenosis on a fellow creature without having first tested its practicability and perfected its technique by previous trials on animals." As other work was keeping him from further experiments, he continued, he felt he should make his preliminary findings available to the surgeons who might someday perform such an operation on a patient.

Although a growing body of work on mitral stenosis had been conducted in the animal laboratory since the turn of the century, the first operation on a patient suffering from mitral stenosis waited until 1923, twenty-one years after Brunton's proposal. A total of ten operations were carried out between 1923 and 1928; two patients survived (see Table 1). The operation then lay fallow until 1945.

7. L. Brunton, "Preliminary Note on the Possibility of Treating Mitral Stenosis by Surgical Methods," *Lancet* (February 8, 1902), p. 352.

8. Oxygenated blood flows from the left auricle into the left ventricle through the mitral valve. Mitral stenosis is a narrowing of the valve, caused by an inflammation following a severe attack of rheumatic fever. As the valve progressively constricts, a reservoir of blood builds up in the auricle, putting an extra strain on the heart and causing an increasing back pressure, which may eventually clog the lungs and leak through the lung tissue to cause dangerous, perhaps fatal congestion.

Table 1. *Surgery for Chronic Valvular Disease, 1912–1928**

Case	Date	Surgeon	Diagnosis	Procedure	Outcome
1.	1912	Tuffier	Aortic stenosis	Finger dilatation	Recovery, improved
2.	1913	Doyen	Pulmonary stenosis	Tenotome	Died, few hours postoperatively
3.	5/20/23	Cutler	Mitral stenosis	Tenotome	Died, 4 yrs. 6 mo. postoperatively
4.	8/7/23	Allen & Graham	Mitral stenosis	Cardioscope	Operative death
5.	10/7/23	Cutler	Mitral stenosis	Tenotome	Died, 10 hrs. postoperatively
6.	1/12/24	Cutler	Mitral stenosis	Tenotome	Died, 20 hrs. postoperatively
7.	2/25/24	Cutler	Mitral stenosis	Cardiovalvulotome	Died, 6 days postoperatively
8.	6/11/24	Cutler	Mitral stenosis	Cardiovalvulotome	Died, 3 days postoperatively
9.	5/6/25	Souttar	Mitral stenosis	Finger dilatation	Recovery, improved
10.	11/14/25	Pribram	Mitral stenosis	Cardiovalvulotome	Died, 6 days postoperatively
11.	12/8/26	Cutler	Mitral stenosis	Cardiovalvulotome	Died, 15 hrs. postoperatively
12.	4/15/28	Cutler	Mitral stenosis	Cardiovalvulotome	Died, 3 hrs. postoperatively

* Adapted from E. Cutler and C. Beck, "The Present Status of the Surgical Procedures in Chronic Valvular Disease of the Heart," *Archives of Surgery,* Vol. 18 (1929), p. 413.

It was not until 1948 that successful surgery for mitral stenosis was accomplished, drew wide attention, and began to be accepted by surgeons and internists despite an initially high mortality rate.

Sir Lauder was "emboldened" to propose intracardiac surgery by the "good results" recently obtained in suturing wounds of the heart. Attempts to treat injured heart muscle, in animals and man, had been the major thrust of cardiovascular surgery in the nineteenth century, but it was only in 1896 that a patient, operated on by Dr. Ludwig Rehn of Frankfurt, survived suturing of a stab wound.[9] A modern heart surgeon

9. For detailed histories of cardiac surgery see L. A. Hochberg, *Thoracic Surgery Before the Twentieth Century* (New York, 1960), and R. A. Meade, *A History of Thoracic Surgery* (Springfield, Ill., 1961).

has epitomized Rehn's operation as "a victory of the doers over the doubters,"[10] for the prevalent view since antiquity had been that wounds of the heart were necessarily fatal and that the beating heart could not withstand manipulation. (Aristotle himself had declared that "the heart alone of all the viscera cannot stand serious injury.") The reigning dogma was challenged in 1882 when M. H. Bloch of Danzig successfully sutured heart wounds in animals and demonstrated that the heart rate could be slowed to the stage of cardiac arrest during surgery without necessarily causing death. But Bloch's work was received skeptically at best, and one year later the authoritative German physician Dr. Theodor Billroth declared that "any surgeon who should ever attempt to stitch a wound of the heart can be certain of losing the respect of all his colleagues forever."[11] And in 1896, shortly before Rehn's surgery, the prominent British surgeon Stephen Paget affirmed: "Surgery of the heart has probably reached the limit set by Nature to all surgery: no new method, and no new discovery, can overcome the natural difficulties that attend a wound of the heart."[12]

By 1900, despite caveats such as the above, at least seventeen attempts had been made to suture heart wounds with seven survivors—indeed a "good result" considering the general state of thoracic surgery. But when it came to taking the next step, to risk operating within the heart itself, the animus of Billroth and Paget prevailed. A week after Brunton's note appeared, his "sufficiently heroic therapeutic suggestion" was roundly criticized in a leading article in *Lancet*.[13] Brunton's critic (one of the editors of *Lancet*) first faulted him for advising others to try a dangerous operation he himself had not perfected in animals, much less tried clinically. More serious charges concerned "the difficulty of the operation and the doubt as to its efficacy, even if successfully carried out." For example, it seemed possible that the surgically divided valve would quickly heal in its old, narrowed form, or that—a point debated through the 1940s—the stenosis would be converted into a possibly more serious mitral regurgitation (backflow of blood from the ventricle into the auricle).

Criticism of Brunton continued in the next two issues of *Lancet*. This did not preclude the publication of two claims for priority in having suggested mitral valve surgery, presumably in case the operation should be successfully tried. Thus, another leading cardiologist, Dr. Lauriston Shaw, wrote that he had discussed surgery for mitral stenosis at least

10. Dr. Dwight E. Harken, personal communication.
11. Quoted in T. Simon, *The Heart Explorers* (New York, 1966), p. 3.
12. S. Paget, *The Surgery of the Chest* (Bristol, 1896), p. 121.
13. "Surgical Operation for Mitral Stenosis," *Lancet* (February 15, 1902), 461–62.

twelve years ago, but had decided it was not "a justifiable therapeutic procedure." Sir Lauder's "chief task," charged his fellow cardiologist, "is not to show his surgical colleagues that it is possible to enlarge the stenosed mitral orifice, but to persuade his medical colleagues that such a procedure is useful."[14] There appears to have been no further published discussion between Brunton and his colleagues on surgery for mitral stenosis, nor did Sir Lauder ever continue his experiments. He later stated that he developed blood poisoning and had to give up the work,[15] though one may wonder why, given his large subsequent contribution to medical literature, it was this particular endeavor that had to be abandoned.

The twenty-one year hiatus between Brunton's proposal and the first clinical operation for mitral stenosis was marked by a considerable body of experimental work in Europe and the United States, and by two operations on patients with chronic valvular disease.[16] In 1912, Dr. T. Tuffier did a finger dilatation for aortic stenosis, and his patient survived. In 1913, Dr. E. Doyen unsuccessfully operated for pulmonary stenosis. Doyen apparently had also worked out a technique for mitral stenosis, but his death in 1916, during World War I, cut short his career and a possible clinical trial of the procedure.

Experimental study of the anatomy and physiology of mitral stenosis and of its surgical correction was hampered by the inability of investigators to create a stenosis in the laboratory animal. The best that could be done with the various techniques that were developed was to produce defects and a resulting regurgitation or insufficiency. The most successful of these methods was to cut or tear out the valve cusps by the insertion of a valvulotome (knife-hook) into the aorta or base of the left auricle. However, a series of significant findings did emerge from the laboratory, and these data helped to resolve many of the issues raised by Brunton's critics. From 1907 to 1909 Dr. W. G. MacCallum and his colleagues at Johns Hopkins showed that the normal animal could withstand experimentally produced mitral regurgitation. In a 1914 summary of their work in experimental heart surgery, Drs. Alexis Carrell and Tuffier pointed out that in pure mitral stenosis the myocardium (heart muscle) is not damaged. They also succinctly reviewed the dangers involved in cardiac surgery, such as injury to the coronary vessels,

14. Letter to the editor, *Lancet* (March 1, 1902), p. 619. See also *Lancet* (February 22, 1902) for letters by Brunton, Lane, Fisher, and Samways.

15. Meade, *Thoracic Surgery*, p. 433.

16. For a review of clinical and laboratory work up to 1923, see E. C. Cutler, S. A. Levine, and C. S. Beck, "The Surgical Treatment of Mitral Stenosis: Experimental and Clinical Studies," *Archives of Surgery*, Vol. 9 (1924), 690–821.

hemorrhage, air embolism, thrombosis, and so forth. These problems would be encountered by surgeons repeatedly in the next decades. Another important aspect of Carrell and Tuffier's work, as well as that of other researchers, was that it demonstrated how much physical manipulation and trauma the heart would tolerate. In 1922, Allen and Graham, using their newly developed cardioscope, with which they could both see the valve and incise its leaflets, found that the cut ends of the mitral valves in experimental dogs did not heal. This suggested that stenosis might not recur in man following surgical division.

On May 20, 1923, after more than two years of laboratory work, the first human case of mitral valve surgery was undertaken by Dr. Elliot C. Cutler, then an associate in surgery at Boston's Peter Bent Brigham Hospital, in collaboration with the cardiologist Dr. Samuel A. Levine. Cutler and his research associate, Dr. Claude S. Beck, had learned much of value in their animal work, despite the inability to create a stenosis, but felt they "had reached a point where . . . further knowledge could only be gained by an attempt in an actual case, and much as we feared the difficulties, our experimental work gave us the courage to carry out what must appear as a hazardous trial."[17]

Cutler chose to operate with the valvulotome rather than the cardioscope, feeling that the latter technique was too intricate and time consuming. His account of the operation vividly illustrates the problems of working blindly within the heart, as was generally necessary until the development of open-heart methods in the 1950s.

> . . . rolling the heart out and to the right . . . the valvulotome . . . was plunged into the left ventricle. . . . The knife was pushed upwards about 2½ inches, until it encountered what seemed to us must be the mitral orifice. It was then turned mesially, and a cut made in what we thought was the aortic leaflet, the resistance encountered being very considerable.[18]

Cutler and Levine's patient, a twelve-year-old girl, survived the surgery and four days later was presented to the staff of the Brigham during the hospital's decennial celebration, an index of the importance Cutler attached to the operation. In their first published report of the case, appearing five weeks after the operation, they concluded:

> At this stage of our observations we cannot with accuracy define just what has occurred nor what benefits may have accrued, if any. . . . The experi-

17. E. C. Cutler and S. A. Levine, "Cardiotomy and Valvulotomy for Mitral Stenosis. Experimental Observations and Clinical Notes Concerning an Operated Case with Recovery," *Boston Medical and Surgical Journal,* Vol. 138 (1923), 1023–27.

18. *Ibid.,* p. 1025.

ence with this case, however, is of importance in that it does show that surgical intervention in cases of mitral stenosis bears no special risk, and should give us further courage and support in our desire to attempt to alleviate a chronic condition, for which there is now not only no treatment, but one which carries a terrible prognosis.[19]

Cutler and Levine's paper was quickly hailed as a "milestone" in a publication as prestigious as the *British Medical Journal,*[20] and within a year their work had attracted enough attention to have started the priority bandwagon rolling again.[21]

In November 1924, in the best nineteenth-century tradition, Cutler, Levine, and Beck published a paper of over one hundred pages in which they detailed the historical background, experimental work, and protocols of their first four cases of mitral valve surgery. In discussing their "rationale for operative intervention," Cutler and his associates lamented the fact that cardiac surgery had for so long been "practically restricted to wounds of the heart." They acknowledged that the field has many dangers, but affirmed that "since the dangers are chiefly those of technic, they should be surmountable."[22] They went on to emphasize their conviction that there are cases of mitral stenosis in which "mechanical obstruction" of the valve plays the dominant role. Thus, they challenged the prevailing wisdom that weakness of the myocardium, not valvular obstruction, was chiefly responsible for producing the symptoms of cardiac failure seen in mitral stenosis. Despite data such as Carrell and Tuffier's, attention had been focused for many years on the myocardium, chiefly due to the teaching of one of the world's leading cardiologists, Britain's Sir James MacKenzie.[23]

Cutler, like the next generation of surgeons who sought to correct

19. *Ibid.,* p. 1027.

20. "Operative Treatment of Mitral Stenosis," *British Medical Journal* (September 22, 1923), 530–31. The article notes that "Sir Lauder Brunton's suggestion appears to have inspired too much apprehension to be followed except by Doyen, whose patient did not survive the operation."

21. For example, see J. S. Goodall and L. Rogers, "Some Surgical Problems of Cardiology. Technic of Mitralotomy," *American Journal of Surgery,* Vol. 38 (1924), 108–12. Commenting on Cutler's operation, and describing the technique for mitral surgery that they have designed (but not tried clinically), Goodall and Rogers stated: "It was about [1913] that one of the writers [at Middlesex Hospital, England] was working at the possibility of introducing surgery for relief of mitral obstruction."

22. Cutler, *Archives of Surgery,* Vol. 9, p. 691.

23. J. MacKenzie, *Diseases of the Heart,* 3rd ed. (London, 1918). It is interesting to note that one of Brunton's critics in 1902 had suggested that the prognosis in mitral stenosis probably depends as much on the condition of the myocardium as on the degree of stenosis.

intracardiac defects, was occupied with the critical importance of accurate anatomical diagnosis and the criteria for patient selection. After enumerating the diagnostic criteria he employed, Cutler predicted that "the difficulties of the future will be encountered in the attempt to distinguish the cases of pure mitral stenosis from those in which there is, in addition, tricuspid and aortic valve disease." It would be preferable, he continued, to choose patients who are older than twenty for surgery, for beyond this age repeated infections of rheumatic fever are unlikely to occur. They should also have a "quite marked" valvular obstruction and be individuals in whom "the muscular wall might be expected to be in fair condition."[24]

Though Cutler tried to follow the above precepts, and despite all that had been learned through animal experimentation, only one of his four cases, the young girl on whom he had operated first, survived. The other three patients had survived surgery for ten hours, twenty hours, and six days postoperatively. However, Cutler's faith in his surgical procedures still seemed strong, as he reflected in his comments on these cases.

> From such a limited experience no final deduction can be drawn either for or against the proposal or the procedure. We feel, however, that much has been learned that should be of value in the consideration of such cases and in subsequent operations. Certainly, there can be no doubt that the method of exposure used is satisfactory, simple in execution, and that it apparently produced no especially harmful effect on our patients. The fact that there were no operative deaths or any indication that the procedure per se was a factor in the subsequent fatalities is comforting.
>
> A mortality of 75 per cent is alarming, but to those who will analyze the full reports of the separate cases it may not appear so disastrous. . . .
>
> Indeed there are so many questions, obviously unanswered, before the first and even after the last operation, that we feel that our mortality rate should be judged, if one wishes to use this as a criterion, only in comparison with figures obtained in the early surgery of other parts of the body, when similar important questions were still unanswered. May we recall the mortality figures in the early surgery of such a relatively simple field as that of the stomach, collected by Dr. W. W. Keen for his Cartwright lectures. Of the first twenty-eight gastrostomies, collected in 1875, all the patients died, and in a series of thirty-five gastroenterostomies in 1885 the operative mortality was 65.7 per cent. Moreover, it took years for these figures to improve. In 1884 the mortality for gastrostomy was still 81.6 per cent.[25]

24. Cutler, *Archives of Surgery,* Vol. 9, 696, 698.
25. *Ibid.,* p. 812.

In 1929, Cutler and Beck reviewed the total of twelve operations reported for chronic valvular disease of the heart through 1928. The subtitle of the paper was significant: "Final Report of all Surgical Cases." For, by then, Cutler had privately, if not publicly, revised his belief in the simplicity and efficacy of mitral valve surgery. As the word "final" suggests, he was calling a personal halt to further trials. A glance at Table 1 quickly suggests why Cutler, in the words of a colleague, was "just devastated"[26] by the outcome of his pioneering efforts. Of the three valvulotomies and four valvulectomies[27] Cutler and his associates had performed, all patients are listed as "died"—though the first patient had lived a creditable four and a half years after surgery. Out of a total of ten operations only one patient was cited as both "living" and "improved." Not only was the mortality rate 90 percent, but "eight of the ten patients died so soon after operation that the changes brought about in the mechanics of the circulation could not be adequately studied."

The one "successful" case of mitral valve surgery in the 1920s deserves notice. In May 1925, Dr. Henry S. Souttar, director of surgery at London Hospital, operated on a nineteen-year-old girl first hospitalized in 1921 for mitral stenosis. After exposing the heart, Souttar reported, he incised the left auricle and began to explore its interior with his left forefinger. He found that he was able to pass his finger into the ventricle through the mitral valve, and "as the stenosis was of such moderate degree . . . it was decided not to carry out the valve section which had been arranged, but to limit intervention to such dilatation as could be carried out by the finger."[28] The patient made an uninterrupted recovery, and all present during surgery were "struck by the facility and safety of the procedure." To the best of his knowledge, Souttar wrote, this was the first time the mitral valve had been reached by the auricular route, or that the interior of the heart had been subjected to digital examination. Comparing his procedure with Cutler's, Souttar commented that

26. D. Harken, personal communication.

27. The various kinds of surgical techniques used to open a stenotic heart valve have included: (1) a simple incision of a valve cusp, also called valve section or valvulotomy, (2) excision of the valvular ring, or valvulectomy, (3) finger dilatation, (4) commissurotomy (Dr. Charles Bailey's term for a combination of finger dilatation and use of a knife to partially excise the valve), and (5) valvuloplasty (the term used by Dr. Dwight Harken to indicate his goal of restoration of valvular function). Harken first used a partial valvulectomy technique, and then employed a method of finger dilatation he called "finger-fracture valvuloplasty." As one reads the literature on mitral valve surgery, one has the impression that innovators in the field have been anxious to gain credit for coining a new term as well as perfecting a new technique.

28. H. S. Souttar, "The Surgical Treatment of Mitral Stenosis," *British Medical Journal* (October 3, 1925), 603–06.

although one cannot judge a method on a single case, "it appears to me that the method of digital exploration through the auricular appendage cannot be surpassed for simplicity and directness."

Despite some favorable press from colleagues,[29] Souttar himself never repeated his finger dilatation procedure, and no other surgeon tried to use what then seemed the only successful technique for alleviating mitral stenosis until 1948. We will later explore the reasons for the 1925 to 1948 moratorium. For the present, let us record that Souttar failed to repeat his surgery because, in Meade's words, "he had no more patients referred to him for operation . . . [MacKenzie's] opposition [to surgery for mitral stenosis] prevented Souttar from continuing his work."[30]

Cutler's seventh operation for mitral stenosis, and the last one known to have been performed until 1945, was in April 1928. The conclusion of his "Final Report" reflects the professional outward optimism of the surgeon rather than the inward "devastation" of the innovator who has realized that, for a combination of reasons, his is not a good procedure.

> It may seem that the information obtained from the twelve cases of chronic valvular disease in which operation was performed is so meager that further attempts are not justified. However, in view of the preceding discussion, we feel that a few more attempts are necessary in order to answer certain questions already mentioned. Should it be possible to produce experimental stenosis, these questions could be answered in the laboratory. Unfortunately, our own attempts for seven years along this line have been as unsuccessful as the attempts of other and more experienced investigators.
>
> It is our conclusion that the mortality figures alone should not deter further investigation both clinical and experimental, since they are to be expected in the opening up of any new field for surgical endeavor.[31]

The seventeen-year moratorium on the clinical use of mitral valve surgery ended on November 14, 1945, when Dr. Charles P. Bailey, in Philadelphia, attempted a valvulotomy. However, as can be seen in Table 2, this did not precipitate a rapid resurgence of mitral valve surgery. By 1948 only three other surgeons had performed such operations: Dr.

29. For example, four letters, generally favorable in tone toward the Souttar operation, appeared in the *British Medical Journal* (October 17, 1925), p. 722; (October 31, 1925), p. 818. Although there is no indication that they tried finger dilatation, Cutler and Beck felt that, "The method may be worthy of trial." E. Cutler and C. Beck, "The Present Status of the Surgical Procedures in Chronic Valvular Disease of the Heart," *Archives of Surgery*, Vol. 18 (1929), p. 415.

30. Meade, *Thoracic Surgery*, p. 447.

31. Cutler and Beck, *Archives of Surgery*, Vol. 18, p. 416.

Dwight E. Harken in Boston, Dr. Horace G. Smithy in South Carolina, and Dr. Russell Brock in England. The revival of mitral valve surgery demonstrates that several kinds of priority are involved and may be claimed in therapeutic innovation.[32] For, whereas Bailey resumed mitral valve surgery sixteen months prior to Harken, his first successful result came only six days before Harken's and, in turn, Harken published on the surgical treatment of mitral stenosis five months before Bailey.

A series of medical and surgical advances facilitated the resumption of mitral valve surgery. A major breakthrough toward resolving the problems that had plagued surgeons in the 1920s came in 1930–32, when methods to create mitral stenosis in the dog were finally worked out. That Elliot Cutler had not lost his interest in the disease and its correction is indicated by the fact that the first man to create stenosis in the dog was one of his residents, Dr. John Powers. Powers went on to study the dog's responses to resection of the mitral valve, the technique Cutler had used in his last four cases, hoping definitively to answer the question of whether an insufficiency could be tolerated. But the dogs, like Cutler's patients, all died after valvulectomy, and on the basis of physiologic studies before and after surgery Powell concluded that the valvulectomy operation was "unphysiologic and should not be used. He suggested that dilatation of the valve . . . might be effective, or that small bits of the stenosed valve might be removed in stages."[33]

Apart from diagnostic and operative problems specific to mitral valve surgery, intrathoracic and intracardiac surgery in general, in the words of Dr. Francis D. Moore, was "still in its infancy" in the 1920s. "Application of [animal work] to the human was still held back by lack of established principles for intrathoracic anaesthesia. There was no good way of following the physiologic progress of the patient."[34] Limitations in diagnostic tools and the dangers of death from hemorrhage during surgery or post-operative death from infection constituted other critical impediments. By the mid-1940s, largely in response to the medical and surgical demands created by World War II, this cluster of problems had been greatly reduced. Major advances included: cardiac catheterization;

32. The basic study of priority disputes in science is by Robert K. Merton, "Priorities in Scientific Discovery: A Chapter in the Sociology of Science," *American Sociological Review*, Vol. 22 (1957), 635–59. As Merton did not deal with clinical medicine, however, his analysis of priority disputes does not cover cases such as credit for performing a certain operation for the first time versus credit for performing that operation successfully for the first time.

33. Meade, *Thoracic Surgery*, p. 440.

34. F. D. Moore, "Report of the Surgeon-in-Chief," Peter Bent Brigham Hospital, Boston, *Thirty-seventh Annual Report*, for the year 1950, p. 55.

Table 2. *Mitral Valve Surgery, 1945–1949. Results of the First Series by Bailey, Harken, and Smithy**

Case	Date	Procedure	Outcome
Dr. Charles P. Bailey			
1.	11/14/45	Valvulotomy	Operative death
2.	6/12/46	Finger dilatation	Death, 60 hrs. postoperatively, thrombosis at valve
3.	3/22/48	Commissurotomy	Death, 6 days, "technical difficulty"
4.	6/10/48	Exploratory	Operative death
5.	6/10/48	Commissurotomy	Living, "excellent result"
6.	6/27/48	Commissurotomy	Living, "excellent result"
7.	7/13/48	Commissurotomy	Death, 7 days, cerebral embolus
8.	8/2/48	Valve section (cusp incision)	Death, 3 mo., mitral regurgitation
9.	9/2/48	Valve section	Death, 24 hrs., mitral regurgitation
10.	9/2/48	Commissurotomy	Death, 24 hrs., hemorrhage
11.	9/10/48	Interauricular shunt	Death, 60 hrs., diminished cardiac output
12.	9/16/48	Dilatation	Living, "greatly improved"
13.	2/1/49	Dilatation	Death, 60 hrs., cardiac failure
14.	2/2/49	Commissurotomy	Living, "excellent result"
15.	3/23/49	Commissurotomy	Living, "excellent result"
Dr. Dwight E. Harken			
1.	3/22/47	Partial valvulectomy (valvuloplasty)	Death, 24 hrs., pulmonary edema
2.	6/16/48	Valvuloplasty	Living, little improvement
3.	no date	Interatrial septal defect created	Living
4.	no date	Septal defect created	Living
5.	no date	Cardiac denervation	Living
6.	1/6/49	Valvuloplasty	Living, improvement
7.	3/4/49	Valvuloplasty	Operative death
8.	3/18/49	Valvuloplasty	Death, 5 days, pulmonary edema

Table 2. *Continued.*

Case	Date	Procedure	Outcome
Dr. Horace G. Smithy			
1.	1/30/48	Partial valvulectomy	Death, 10 mo., congestive heart failure
2.	3/1/48	Partial valvulectomy	Death, 10 hrs., acute cardiac insufficiency
3.	3/8/48	Partial valvulectomy	Death, 48 hrs., pneumonia
4.	4/20/48	Partial valvulectomy	Living, "excellent condition"
5.	5/3/48	Partial valvulectomy	Living, improved, but persisting auricular fibrillation
6.	6/4/48	Partial valvulectomy	Living, improved, limited in activity
7. & 8.	May & June '48	2 operations on 1 patient	Living, improved, but systolic murmur

* Data compiled from: Bailey, *Diseases of the Chest*, Vol. 15 (1949) and *Journal of Thoracic Surgery*, Vol. 19 (1950); D. Harken, *New England Journal of Medicine*, Vol. 239 (1948), and *Journal of Thoracic Surgery*, Vol. 19 (1950); H. Smithy, J. Boone, J. Stallworth, "Surgical Treatment of Constrictive Valvular Disease of the Heart," *Surgery, Gynecology and Obstetrics*, Vol. 90 (1950), 175–92 (Dr. Smithy died prior to the publication of this paper). The first eight operations by Brock in England, beginning in September 1948, were not included in Table 2 as specific data on them were not available.

the improvement of anesthetic techniques for intrathoracic surgery, particularly the institution of endotracheal anaesthesia; the development of methods permitting rapid blood transfusion; and the discovery and synthesis of antibacterial and antibiotic agents.

Another major technical and psychological stimulus for the relaunching of mitral valve surgery came from the successful initiation of surgery for congenital defects of the heart's great vessels, surgery which also had been proposed but not executed years earlier. In 1907, Dr. John Munro of Boston detailed a method for ligation of patent ductus arteriosus. Ligation was finally attempted, unsuccessfully, by Dr. John Streider of Boston in March 1937, and his presentation of the case at the American Association of Thoracic Surgery meetings two months later drew little notice. Thus, many would date the era of modern heart surgery from 1938, when Dr. Robert Gross of Children's Hospital, Boston, unaware of Streider's earlier attempt, successfully ligated the ductus in a young patient.[35] A second milestone came in 1944 with the implementation of the Blalock-Taussig operation (anastomosing the systemic and pulmonary arteries) to correct the cluster of congenital defects known as the tetralogy of Fallot (which came to be called the "blue baby operation").[36]

If we now look at how Bailey and Harken revived mitral valve surgery, independently, though with awareness of each other's work, we begin to see the confluence of scientific, personal, and historical factors in ending the moratorium.

In 1940 Harken began his residency at Boston City Hospital after a year of work in England with Mr. Tudor Edwards. Studying the heart at autopsies, Harken became absorbed with the challenge of devising a method to enter the heart and remove the vegetations of bacterial endocarditis. For "endocarditis was one disease of the heart that could be absolutely diagnosed and that we knew absolutely was fatal. And I reasoned that, if it was fatal, I had the right to try any operation that might possibly be expected to work."[37] In devising a method to enter the heart through the auricular appendage and remove the vegetations with the visual aid of a cardioscope, Harken made a discovery that we can now appreciate as a fundamental advance for mitral valve surgery. The mitral valve's two leaflets have different functions, and if the major

35. The nonpursuit of ideas proposed or techniques tried is a common occurrence in the history of science, medicine, and technology. We have several examples of these kinds of discontinuity in the development of cardiac surgery which provide insight into some of the bases of this phenomenon. These include: the unresponsiveness of Streider's colleagues to his technique for ligation of a patent ductus; Gross's unawareness of Streider's previous attempt at ligation; the deterring effect of collegial criticism on Brunton's proposal to move from the animal to the human level in surgery for mitral stenosis.

36. For a fuller discussion and references to these developments see Meade, *Thoracic Surgery,* Chapters XVII, XIX.

37. D. Harken, personal communication. The account of Harken's work is also drawn from: D. Harken, "Foreign Bodies in, and in Relation to, the Thoracic Blood Vessels and Heart, I. Techniques for Approaching and Removing Foreign Bodies from the Chambers of the Heart," *Surgery, Gynecology and Obstetrics,* Vol. 83 (1946), 117–25; D. Harken and P. M. Zoll, "Foreign Bodies . . . III. Indications for the Removal of Intracardiac Foreign Bodies and the Behavior of the Heart During Manipulation," *American Heart Journal,* Vol. 32 (1946), 1–19; D. Harken, L. Ellis, et al., "The Surgical Treatment of Mitral Stenosis, I. Valvuloplasty," *New England Journal of Medicine,* Vol. 239 (November 25, 1948), 801–09; D. Harken, L. Ellis, and L. Norman, "The Surgical Treatment of Mitral Stenosis, II. Progress in Developing a Controlled Valvuloplastic Technique," *Journal of Thoracic Surgery,* Vol. 19 (1950), 1–15; D. Harken, L. Dexter, et al., "The Surgical Treatment of Mitral Stenosis, III. Finger-fracture Valvuloplasty," *Annals of Surgery,* Vol. 134 (1951), 722–42; D. Harken, L. Ellis, et al., "The Responsibility of the Physician in the Selection of Patients with Mitral Stenosis for Surgical Treatment," *Circulation,* Vol. 5 (1952), 349–62; Moore, *Annual Report,* 1950, 54–61; Meade, *Thoracic Surgery,* Chapter XXVII.

or aortic leaflet is destroyed, the experimental animal soon dies of regurgitation; conversely, regurgitation is not the necessary price of relieving stenosis as long as the aortic leaflet is not destroyed. Bailey was to reach independently the same conclusion, and in their early papers on the subject both surgeons stressed their conviction that it is neither desirable nor necessary to exchange stenosis for regurgitation.

World War II intervened before Harken could try his approach to bacterial endocarditis on a patient, and soon the availability of penicillin removed the fatal threat of the disease. He persuaded Cutler (then in England) and Edwards to use their influence to establish the army's first thoracic surgery specialty unit in England. Subsequently, Harken was named the unit's chief. In that setting he soon had ample opportunity to apply his techniques for intracardiac surgery to new problems. In doing the first elective intracardiac surgery, Harken and his team removed shell fragments and bullets from the heart and great vessels of one hundred and thirty-four wounded soldiers, in one hundred and thirty-nine operations, without a single fatality. One of the "elementary rules" of cardiac surgery that emerged from this work was that the heart does not readily tolerate dislocation from its position of optimal function in the chest. Such dislocation causes sudden, potentially fatal arrhythmias. As Moore has observed, here "was a guiding principle for further work and . . . an explanation for some of Dr. Cutler's difficulties twenty years before . . . ."[38]

In a 1945 lecture in London, Harken paid tribute to his predecessors who had made a new era in intracardiac surgery possible.

> The brilliant work and writing on heart surgery by Doyen, Duval, Tuffier, Carrell, Graham, Beck, and Cutler mark the evolution from dreams to experiment and from experiment to bold human adventure. Today it is fair to expect certain simple intracardiac maneuvers to be successful. The door has been opened by modern anaesthesia and the technique of rapid blood replacement.[39]

"Intracardiac maneuvers" for mitral stenosis were in fact attempted that very year, but not successfully. After five years of laboratory study at Philadelphia's Hahnemann Hospital, Bailey felt he understood why earlier mitral valve surgery had not succeeded. He attributed its failure to using a poor route (ventricular) into the valve and to causing a sudden and large regurgitation by damaging the major leaflet. The method

38. Moore, *Annual Report, 1950,* p. 56.
39. Harken, *American Heart Journal,* Vol. 32.

which Bailey worked out included an auricular approach and palpation of the valve with the finger prior to actual valvulotomy.[40]

As previously mentioned, on November 14, 1945 Bailey attempted his first clinical case, but before he could enter the heart, the auricle was torn and the patient bled to death. (See Table Two for a resumé of Bailey's and Harken's first operations.) He performed a second operation in June 1946: "since [the patient] was deemed hopeless," Bailey reported, "her physicians felt that she might be subjected to valvulotomy."[41] During surgery, as Bailey later wrote to Meade, Souttar's operation was unexpectedly revived when the stenosis was found to be so severe that the knife would not cut the valve.

> In desperation, remembering Souttar's report, I inserted my finger through the auricular appendage, palpated the valve and pushed my finger through the diminished slit . . . both commissures split well. . . . For about twenty-four hours post-operatively, the patient's condition improved remarkably and steadily. There was no clinical evidence of regurgitation. However, one day later, she suddenly collapsed and died.[42]

Bailey operated on a third terminal case of mitral stenosis in March 1948; the patient died six days later of hemorrhage from the chest wall.

Bailey's three operations had been performed at three different hospitals in the Philadelphia area, and he was informed that further intracardiac surgery would not be permitted at those institutions. Nevertheless, he scheduled two more cases of mitral surgery for June 10, 1948, at the last two Philadelphia hospitals where he still had operating privileges. Case four died during surgery in the morning, of cardiac arrest judged by Bailey to be unrelated to an attempted finger dilatation. Success finally came that afternoon, at Episcopal Hospital, when a twenty-four-year-old housewife withstood her surgery so well that one week later, "she was transported without incident in a train to a medical convention a thousand miles away for presentation in person."[43]

Six days after Bailey's first success, Harken did a valvuloplasty operation on a twenty-seven-year-old man at Boston City Hospital. The pa-

40. The account of Bailey's work is drawn from: C. Bailey, "The Surgical Treatment of Mitral Stenosis (Mitral Commissurotomy)," *Diseases of the Chest,* Vol. 15 (1949), 377–93; C. Bailey, R. Glover, and T. O'Neill, "The Surgery of Mitral Stenosis," *Journal of Thoracic Surgery,* Vol. 19 (1950), 16–45; T. Simon, *The Heart Explorers;* Meade, *Thoracic Surgery,* chapter XXVII; L. Engel, "Heart Surgery: A New Attack on our Number 1 Killer," *Harper's Magazine,* 1957; "Surgery's New Frontier," *Time,* March 25, 1957, 66–77.

41. Bailey, *Diseases of the Chest,* Vol. 15, p. 85.

42. Meade, *Thoracic Surgery,* 440–41.

43. Bailey, *Diseases of the Chest,* Vol. 15, p. 390.

tient survived surgery and five months postoperatively was reported symptomatically improved. Harken's first case, like Bailey's, had ended in failure: the patient died twenty-four hours after his valvuloplasty in March, 1947, in respiratory collapse and pulmonary edema. From his knowledge of Cutler's work and from his own laboratory experiments and clinical experience in the war, Harken ventured into mitral valve surgery with four basic premises:

> (1) to approach the mitral valve from above rather than through the ventricle, (2) to operate on the heart without dislocating it from its normal position, (3) to remove only portions of the lesser leaflets . . . thus avoiding regurgitation, and (4) to use the superior pulmonary vein as the port of entry.[44]

By the time he had completed his first five operations for mitral stenosis, Harken had developed a threefold "preliminary classification" of patients and the indicated surgery according to their degree of stenotic incapacitation: (A) low fixed cardiac output: mitral valvuloplasty; (B) normal cardiac output: artificial interatrial shunt; (C) uncontrollable tachycardia or anginal pain: cardiac denervation.[45]

While Harken's only fatality in these cases had been with the first valvuloplasty, it was this procedure, designed to help the most critically ill class of patients, upon which he concentrated. His first paper on mitral valve surgery, for example, is devoted largely to presenting four "basic principles" for valvuloplasty. But like his predecessor, Cutler, and his contemporary, Bailey, Harken soon found that a background of experimental animal surgery, the use of carefully designed instruments, criteria of patient selection, and operative guidelines could not alone ensure the success of mitral valve surgery. In the winter of 1948–49, six out of Harken's first nine patients died, during or shortly after valvulotome surgery.

> At this point I went home depressed and said "I quit." Some people suggested I should try my technique on better-risk patients, in order to help me get better results, so I wouldn't "ruin the reputation of cardiac surgery." But I wouldn't do that. After I lost my sixth patient, I had a call from Dr. Laurence Ellis [then President of the New England Cardiovascular Society]. I told him I wouldn't kill any more patients [through mitral

44. Moore, *Annual Report, 1950,* 356–57.

45. Harken, *New England Journal of Medicine,* Vol. 239, p. 802. Harken next evolved a fourfold classification: benign, handicapped, hazardous, terminal.

> valve surgery], and that no respectable referring physician would send me any more patients anyhow. Ellis asked me what I meant: didn't I realize that these patients surely would die if I didn't operate? He said he would still refer patients to me, and didn't I think he was a good cardiologist? This talk with Ellis was a turning point. I went back and operated and my patients suddenly started doing better. But I almost called a moratorium.[46]

Early in 1949, Dr. Harken realized that he "couldn't do an operation successfully with the [valvulotome] and have the patient survive in a substantial number of cases."[47] As he studied postmortem specimens of mitral stenosis, seeking to improve his procedure, he became convinced that the best way to open up the fused bridges of the valve's leaflets, without unduly damaging the valves themselves, was the simple technique Souttar had pioneered: finger dilatation through an auricular entry. After a few cases it "became apparent" that this method, which Harken aptly named finger-fracture valvuloplasty, "had made possible an entirely new evaluation of valvular surgery because it was done with a new order of accuracy."[48]

Apart from some technical refinements, the operation done today for most cases of mitral stenosis differs little from that done by Souttar in 1925. By the early 1950s, with the reports of successful mitral valve surgery by Bailey, Harken, Smithy, Brock, and others, surgical intervention for mitral stenosis became generally accepted by surgeons and cardiologists. Overall mortality rates began to decline as experience was gained and as patients not in the last stages of the disease were referred and accepted for surgery. For critically ill patients (Harken's Class IV), the mortality rate took longer to decline. In Harken's first eighty cases there were twenty-nine deaths (twenty-five of them surgical), a 35 per cent mortality rate. "Why do we keep operating in that situation, with such an overwhelming mortality rate?" Harken asked rhetorically in a talk at the Brigham. "Because if we don't, we think these people would die in the normal course of their disease. And if we do, people look like some of the patients you see here. . . ."[49]

46. Harken, personal communication.

47. From a speech by Harken at the Peter Bent Brigham Hospital, quoted in R. C. Fox, *Experiment Perilous* (Glencoe, Ill., 1959), p. 24.

48. Moore, *Annual Report, 1950*, p. 58. Harken's first finger-fracture valvuloplasty was covered widely and, historically, somewhat inaccurately, by the lay press. Accompanied by a photo of the patient as she prepared to leave the hospital, stories on March 2, 1950, had headlines such as "First Restoration of Heart Valve by Surgery Reported," and "Radical Operation Inside the Heart Hailed as a 'Startling Success.' "

49. Harken, quoted in Fox, *Experiment Perilous,* p. 58.

THE CLINICAL MORATORIUM: CONTRIBUTORY FACTORS

Study of the development of surgery for mitral stenosis has served as a starting point for defining the parameters of what we believe to be a common occurrence in the process of therapeutic innovation, the calling of a moratorium on the use of a new medical or surgical procedure. From the history of mitral valve surgery, and that of cardiac transplantation, we have been able to identify a number of factors that contribute to a clinical moratorium. Depending upon specifiable circumstances, the interplay of these factors may either help to induce, deter, or terminate a moratorium. They include: the stage of medical knowledge and practice (state of the art factors); the experiment-therapy dilemma inherent in clinical research; facets of the dual role of physician-investigator; certain social structural characteristics of relations between the physician, his colleagues, and the hospital in which he carries out his investigative work; the impact of media of mass communication and lay opinion on the medical profession; the influence of cultural conceptions and beliefs, such as attitudes toward the human heart.

State of the Art Factors

Virtually every medical and surgical procedure, even the most established, carries with it a certain modicum of uncertainty as to its efficacy and safety. Gaps in knowledge, technical inadequacies, and the problems of uncertainty that stem from them are inherent to medical research and practice. These problems occur in a dramatic form during a period of therapeutic innovation, creating intensive strains for research physicians and their patients alike. This is one reason why a moratorium is likely to occur during the early phases of clinical trial, error, and evaluation. The investigator continually weighs the known and probable risks and the benefits of a new procedure for the patients on whom he is conducting clinical trials. On the basis of this dynamic calculus, decisions are made and remade concerning the circumstances under which a new treatment may justifiably be used, and on what categories of patients.

The most immediate and manifest reason for suspending a therapeutic procedure is that the mortality rate associated with it is judged to be "too high." However, as we will see in the next section, there is no simple definition of therapeutic "success" and "failure," and no ready answer to the question of what constitutes an "acceptable" mortality rate at different points along the experiment-to-therapy spectrum, and with various kinds of patients.

We have seen in the development of mitral valve surgery that numerous state of the art factors may influence the decision to initiate, suspend, or resume use of a given procedure on patients. The levels of development of the following elements play determining roles: relevant basic science knowledge; an animal model (an animal in which one can reproduce or simulate a human disease state and test therapies); knowledge about the specific applicability of the procedure to given disease states and individual patients; the degree of relevant technical proficiency (in surgery, for example, anaesthesia, transfusion, and other areas of operative management, and in medicine, the control of a drug's unanticipated side effects).

Our case study of mitral stenosis provides numerous examples of the role that state of the art factors can play in the "stops" and "starts" associated with moratoria. A major reason why American surgeons did not adopt Souttar's finger dilatation method, despite the success of his one case, was expressed by Dr. Evarts Graham. As he wrote to Meade, Graham was "much interested" in Souttar's operation, "but felt that his procedure would never amount to very much because it lacked precision and was a blind one."[50] When next we look at the resumption of mitral valve surgery in 1945–48, we find that Smithy revived the valvulectomy operation used by Cutler, knowing that six of Cutler's seven patients and all of Power's experimental dogs had died. In Smithy's case, with the major strides in intrathoracic surgery and anaesthesia since the 1920s and his own work on a partial valvulectomy technique in dogs, beginning with aortic valve surgery, five of his first seven patients survived surgery and the immediate postoperative period. (Of those five, one died ten months later; three showed slight improvement, and one great improvement in the course of the first year.)[51] The importance of instrumentation and technique in the mitral valve surgery done by Bailey and Harken, in turn, has been well summarized by Meade.[52]

> It is generally agreed that for a satisfactory result the commissures must be opened all the way to the myocardium. Souttar had planned to use a tenotome, as Cutler had used in his first and only successful case. Until Bailey demonstrated the correctness of Souttar's ideas, everyone working on the valves of the heart had devised and used instruments with which segments of the valve leaflets could be excised. Indeed it was with such an instrument that Bailey had planned to attack the valve which he was forced

50. Meade, *Thoracic Surgery,* p. 448.

51. H. G. Smithy, J. Boone, and J. Stallworth, "Surgical Treatment of Constrictive Valvular Disease of the Heart," *Surgery, Gynecology and Obstetrics,* Vol. 90 (1950), 175–92.

52. Meade, *Thoracic Surgery,* 445–46.

> to treat by finger dilatation. Bailey's first successful case was treated by finger fracture. Harken, six days later, used an instrument with which he cut through the commissures. He and Bailey then devised knives with which the commissures could be cut without resecting segments of the valves. Since then a great variety of knives have been made. It is interesting that Harken, who first used a knife, became one of the chief advocates of the finger fracture method, and Bailey came to feel that more of the valves needed to be enlarged by the use of knives.

Partly as a consequence of these and other technical advances, by the mid-1940s the medically prevalent view of the heart as an organ too vital and fragile to withstand manipulation or surgical trauma changed. Gradually, the heart came to be seen as a strong, resilient, and fairly simple muscular pump. In turn, this conceptual shift facilitated the work that opened the modern era of intracardiac surgery.

The Experiment-Therapy Dilemma[53]

One of the most fundamental problems shared by all physicians trying out new treatments on sick patients is that of determining how experimental and/or therapeutic that treatment is. Such an evaluation depends heavily on the state of the art factors discussed above, and as earlier mentioned is a primary criterion for deciding on whom and under what circumstances the new procedure may justifiably be used. The usual discussions of this calculus, under the rubric of the "ethics of human experimentation," are too often couched in dichotomous terms of "experiment" or "therapy."[54] In practice, however, one sees a *process* of therapeutic innovation which generally progresses from animal experiments to clinical trials with terminally ill patients beyond conventional therapeutic help, to the use of the treatment on less and less critically ill patients.

In the evolution of surgery for mitral stenosis, as in all clinical research and innovation, there were no clear guideposts telling physician-investigators that the time had arrived to move from one stage to another. Rather, physicians had continually to assess the state of the art, their own capabilities, the probable risks and benefits to their patients,

53. Material in this and the following section is partly drawn from R. Fox, *Annals* of the New York Academy of Sciences, and *Experiment Perilous*, Chapters 2 and 3.

54. The difficulties of either-or decisions emerge clearly if one tries to categorize a procedure such as kidney transplantation. Although twenty-five years have passed since the first human trial, the operation is neither manifestly experimental, nor conventional therapy, and those involved in the field have trouble articulating its status.

the possible yield in knowledge that might help other patients,[55] and the proper allocation of scarce resources (manpower, equipment, facilities, funds).

As illustrated by the responses to Brunton's proposal in 1902 and by the short-lived course of valve surgery in the 1920s, the transition from animal experimentation to clinical use, for any procedure, is one "which is inherently 'premature' [particularly in the absence of an animal model], and for that reason is often judged to be controversial, and, sometimes, 'immoral.' It typically involves a stressful and discouraging period. . . . For, as a combined consequence of the many unknown and uncontrolled factors in this stage of experimentation, and of the drastic, complicated illness of the patients who undergo the clinical trials, successful outcomes are rare and ephemeral. Failure and death rates are high."[56]

In order to evaluate what constitutes the justifiable use of a new procedure and to appraise "success" and "failure," physicians characteristically make what Joseph Fletcher has termed "mathematicated decisions" based upon a "statistical morality."[57] They estimate and express in terms of probabilities and percentages the differential diagnosis of a disease, and its course under different circumstances, especially its prognosis in response to alternative treatments. This way of reasoning is not peculiar to the clinical investigator; rather, it is inherent in all medical practice.

We have noted that after his first four valvulectomies Cutler acknowledged that a 75 percent mortality rate is "alarming," but maintained that in terms of each case it is not "disastrous," and affirmed that his results must be judged in comparison with other pioneering surgical efforts—mortality rates of 65 to 81 percent were long common in surgery "of such a relatively simple field as that of the stomach." Similarly, in his "Final Report" of 1929, Cutler insisted that "the mortality figures [90 per cent] alone should not deter further investigation . . . since they are to be expected in the opening up of any new field for surgical endeavor." Another form that "statistical morality" reasoning may take is that the

55. A statement attributed to the pioneer neurosurgeon, Victor Horsley, epitomizes this element of benefit to other patients. When his colleague Dr. Charles Beevor said, "But Victor, if you operate on this man for a brain tumor, he will surely die," Horsley responded, "Of course he will die, but if I don't operate on him, those who follow me won't know how to perform these operations." E. Thomson, *Harvey Cushing. Surgeon, Author, Artist* (New York, 1950), p. 134.

56. R. Fox, *Annals* of the New York Academy of Sciences.

57. J. Fletcher, "Our Shameful Waste of Human Tissue," in *The Religious Situation: 1969* (Boston, 1969), 223–52.

critically ill patient, beyond the help of conventional therapy, will most probably die if the new therapy is not tried. For example, Brunton argued that "the risk of a shortened life" with heart surgery should be balanced against "the certainty of a prolonged period of existence which could hardly be called life" without surgery. Harken explained that this is why he kept operating on class IV mitral stenotics despite an "overwhelming" mortality rate of 35 percent. Similarly, Moore in 1950 emphasized that Harken's decision to operate initially only on severely ill patients was "realistic," for "of sixteen patients selected for operation but who were not operated upon, fourteen are now dead, eleven within six months of the time when surgery was advised."[58]

Cutler's argument, that surgery for mitral stenosis must go on despite high mortality, expressed the research physician's moral commitment to the continuing perfection of new clinical methods. Beyond this, Cutler was the kind of "first pioneer" who, as Moore has put it, is likely to have "a certain amount of inspirational vision. . . . He is driven by this to do something that his own insight tells him can be accomplished. This may be done, and either he or others may be lost in the process. But he points the way."[59]

Despite this kind of drive and commitment, the stresses Cutler experienced in losing his valvulectomy patients seem to have impelled him to call a personal halt to this operation. It is significant to note that it is only through the ambiguous subtitle of his 1929 paper—"Final Report of All Surgical Cases"—that Cutler publicly signaled his moratorium, and that in his paper he desisted from urging other surgeons to do likewise. Nevertheless, as we have seen, no mitral valve surgery was performed for the next seventeen years. This moratorium is associated with a classical phase in trailblazing scientific advances. "There is . . . a gap or pause or moratorium before others—ordinary mortals—can undertake it. They usually have to wait for collateral and technological developments to occur so that the visionary adventure becomes a pathway taken by other people."[60]

The criteria for the kind of surgical failure that Cutler experienced seem easier to define than those for success. Using failure as synonymous with death, Moore has pointed out that failures in surgery of mitral stenosis, like all surgical failures, fall into at least three categories: the disease was too far advanced to stand the stress of surgery; postoperative complications occurred; or technical methods were not adequate to the

58. Moore, *Annual Report, 1950,* .p. 58.
59. Moore, personal communication.
60. *Ibid.*

problems encountered.[61] One might also include in the category "failure" cases in which no improvement is effected, and those in which the procedure results in another serious problem, such as mitral regurgitation. On the other hand, as was true for Souttar's patient, Cutler's first case, and for mitral valve surgery patients in the 1940s, merely to survive a radical new surgical procedure and the postoperative hospitalization may be rated as a success. Thus, the meaning of a surgical success, depending on the nature of the operation and its stage of development, may range from survival to palliation through correction of a condition. Another criterion for success is the decision that a therapy can be employed on other than terminally ill patients. When this occurs, a new treatment moves into a less experimental phase of its development. For example, in 1950, Moore judged that:

> The surgery of mitral stenosis has now been through its "dark days," days when the surgeon, his medical colleagues and those with whom he sought counsel were tried as to whether or not the effort should be maintained through such difficulties. It is through those dark days and into a phase where its scope should be broadened. Recently a group of six patients who were *not* in the last stages of the disease have been operated upon. All of them have done well and showed a gratifying return to normal heart function.[62]

The Dual Role of the Physician-Investigator

In any historical era, a significant number of the patients for whom a research physician cares are ill with diseases that are not well understood and can only be imperfectly treated. The institutionalized role of such a clinical investigator is dualistic. On the one hand, like all physicians, he is responsible for the diagnosis, treatment, and mitigation of his patient's suffering. On the other hand, he is obligated to conduct research that bears directly or indirectly upon the maladies of his patients, using some of them as his subjects.

For all of its intellectual, professional, and humanitarian gratifications, the role of research physician is accompanied by characteristic problems and stresses. We have already discussed some of the problems of uncertainty such a physician encounters, resulting from limitations in medical knowledge and practice at a given time. To these may be added those uncertainties that are artifacts of the inability of any physician personally

61. Moore, *Annual Report, 1950,* p. 59.
62. *Ibid.*, p. 58.

to command all available medical knowledge and skill. Furthermore, the research physician deliberately works in the realm of the uncertain, focusing on those questions which medicine still has not answered, seeking to make some headway with their solution.

Given the fundamental nature of his orientation and activities, the clinical investigator is confronted with more numerous and grave problems of therapeutic limitation than are other types of physicians. He seldom can help to effect the total recovery of his patients; more often, he can only ameliorate or palliate their conditions; and frequently, he can do nothing more than postpone their imminent death.

Under optimal conditions, the research and clinical responsibilities of such a physician are complementary. His investigative work bears directly on the diagnosis and treatment of his patients' conditions, which in some sense it benefits, and conversely, his clinical activities on behalf of his patients also advance his research. However, the clinical and investigative responsibilities of the research physician are not always perfectly reconcilable, and they may openly conflict. Some of the procedures he conducts on research patients may help future generations of persons ill with similar disorders or contribute to general medical knowledge rather than to his subjects' own immediate welfare. What the research physician does to aid or protect his patients may undermine an experiment he ideally would have liked to bring to its logical conclusion. And the research in which he asks patients to participate often exposes them to discomfort or risk.

These attributes of their double-edged role cause stress for most physician-investigators. The strains that they experience are intensified by their typically close and continuous relations with the patients who are also their subjects; by colleagues' scientific and ethical judgments of their work; and by a certain vested interest not only in protecting their professional reputations, but also, in advancing them through recognition for being eminently successful with breakthroughs in knowledge or technique.

When the role strains associated with clinical experimentation become acute and especially burdensome, one of the options open to research physicians is that of calling a moratorium. Physician-investigators also have other patterned ways of coming to terms with their professional stresses, which may either push them toward a moratorium or pull them away from it. From a certain point of view, their research constitutes one of their primary intellectual and moral mechanisms for coping with the problems of uncertainty and the unknown. For research activities provide investigators with a way of trying to do something about the hiatuses in knowledge and therapeutic limitations that currently exist. Through this medium they can express their hope and belief that medical advances eventually will come through their efforts. Partly for this reason, unless other factors intervene, a medical investigator tends to continue a particular line of research in what from the outside may seem a self-propelling way.

A good deal of contemporaneous medical research is organized and carried out in a group. Membership in such a team may provide investigators with a way of sharing responsibility, and with the kind of day-by-day collegial counsel, support, and tension release that helps them continue their research despite its concomitant strains and frustrations. However, the fact that by and large the solo investigator pattern has given way to a team model also means that research physicians are more immediately subject to being criticized, contradicted, or overruled by their collaborators. Thus, the sense of the group may be a powerful factor in compelling an investigator to call a moratorium on clinical trials which his colleagues believe ought to be discontinued.

The nature of the relationship between a team of research physicians and their patient-subjects is one of the cardinal factors that may lead them to feel they cannot go on with certain of their experimental procedures. Such physicians and patients are typically drawn closer together by the inexorability of the patients' illnesses, the tragic outcome that awaits many of them, the prolonged contact of patients with physicians over the course of their repeated hospitalizations and periodic follow-ups, and by the collegial relations between patients and physicians that develop as a consequence of their mutual participation in clinical research.[63] Thus, when it seems to research physicians that their clinical trials are exposing patient-subjects to too much discomfort or risk, are not benefitting them in any ostensible way, or are accompanied by an excessive mortality rate, they may decide to call a halt to the trials. Under these circumstances, the pressure to invoke a moratorium comes as much from physicians' subjective reactions to the fate of their patients as from their responsiveness to more impersonal ethical constraints.

Several of these "push-pull" factors, emanating from the stresses of the physician-investigator's dual role and the ways he may respond to them, were encountered in our case study of mitral valve surgery. For example, we can infer that the strong criticism which Brunton's 1902 proposal met was largely responsible for his not undertaking clinical

63. For further discussion of the properties of the relationship between research physicians and their patient-subjects, see: R. C. Fox, *Experiment Perilous,* especially 85–109, and "Some Social and Cultural Factors in American Society Conducive to Medical Research on Human Subjects," *Clinical Pharmacology and Therapeutics,* Vol. 1 (1960), 423–43.

trials of his technique for mitral valve surgery. When such trials were attempted two decades later, Cutler was "pushed" into calling a moratorium because he could not personally tolerate the high mortality rate encountered with valvulectomy and related procedures such as anaesthesia and postoperative management. We do not know the role that the opinion of his colleagues played in Cutler's decision. But we do know that when mitral valve surgery was next attempted, in the 1940s, Harken was deterred from calling a halt in the face of repeated failures by the strong personal and professional encouragement he received from Ellis, an eminent colleague.

The Research Physician, His Colleagues, and the Hospital

As the case of Harken and Ellis suggests, relations with colleagues that are more occasional and distant than those with members of his own research team may also be key elements in determining whether or not an investigator pursues a line of experimentation on which he has embarked. If such "outside" or remote colleagues enjoy high professional status and prestige, their influence on a research physician's course of action may be all the greater. For the opinion that a high-ranking physician may have of his work can affect an investigator's own professional reputation and, as a consequence, both the facilities put at his disposal and his state of morale. The impact that Ellis's opinion had on Harken, for example, was enhanced by the fact that Ellis was a respected cardiologist and president of the New England Cardiovascular Society.

An authority figure can also exert a deterring influence on clinical trials. This is exemplified by the role played by Sir James MacKenzie in mitral valve surgery during the 1920s. MacKenzie, one of England's and the world's leading cardiologists, believed that a diseased heart muscle was the major feature of mitral stenosis, and thus he opposed valvular surgery as an essentially useless measure. In the face of MacKenzie's influence on other cardiologists in England, Souttar had no more patients referred to him for mitral valve surgery. This was in spite of the fact that he was one of England's leading surgeons (Director of Surgery at London Hospital) and that his first patient to undergo valvular surgery survived and seemed to show improvement. The impact of MacKenzie's opinions was also felt in America. This impact, however, was less strong in the United States than in England, partly due to the geographical distance and professional insulation that working in another society provided. Thus, as Meade records, in Boston, Dr. Samuel Levine, a leading American cardiologist, "stood out in opposition to Sir James and was responsible for Cutler being able to operate."[64]

The particular "social circles"[65] within the medical profession to which a research physician belongs may also act as a stimulus for his undertaking and continuing certain forms of clinical investigation or may lead him to abandon them. There is good circumstantial evidence for assuming that Cutler's decision in 1928 to call a personal moratorium on mitral valve surgery was instrumental in its nonresumption by the profession at large for almost two decades. In this respect, he may be said to be an authority figure who, like MacKenzie, exercised a profession-wide deterring effect on valvular surgery, albeit for different reasons and in a more latent and general fashion. However, despite his moratorium, Cutler continued to exert a positive influence, in his social circle, on surgery for mitral stenosis. Younger physicians of the Peter Bent Brigham Hospital who had contact with him conducted relevant animal experiments. And it seems more than coincidental that Harken, one of the two surgeons who ended the moratorium in the 1940s, had significant contact with Cutler both in Boston and England during the period when Harken was working out his valvuloplasty procedure. Although Harken, Bailey, Smithy, and Brock were not close friends, they all knew each other and followed the course of each other's laboratory and clinical work.[66]

64. Meade, *Thoracic Surgery*, p. 447. The history of mitral valve surgery suggests that it might be fruitful to explore more generally the relative impact that different kinds of medical specialists have on the occurrence or nonoccurrence of a moratorium. For example, MacKenzie, the cardiologist, blocked Souttar, the surgeon; and conversely, it was two cardiologists, Levine and Ellis, who encouraged Cutler and Harken to perform mitral valve surgery. Historically, surgeons and physicians have more frequently than not represented different, sometimes complementary and more often conflicting, points of view. We hypothesize that the encouragement that Cutler and Harken received from Levine and Ellis was all the more forceful and effective precisely because it came from colleagues belonging to a medical specialty from which they, as surgeons, would not ordinarily have expected such firm support.

65. The best recent statement by a sociologist of the concept of social circles and appropriate methods for studying their influence is: C. Kadushin, "Power, Influence, and Social Circles. A New Methodology for Studying Opinion Makers," *American Sociological Review*, Vol. 33 (1968), 685–99.

66. The influence of social circles in the development of cardiac transplantation seems to have been much greater than in mitral valve surgery. As Diana Crane has documented, ten out of twenty-three surgeons in the United States and Canada (no information on five other surgeons) who had performed heart transplants by May 1969, had been associated as teacher or student with two universities, Johns Hopkins or Minnesota (D. Crane and D. Matthews, "Heart Transplant Operations: Diffusion of a Medical Innovation," presented at the 64th Annual Meeting of the American Sociological Association, San Francisco, Cal., September 4, 1969).

Since the turn of the century, most clinical medical research has been conducted in a hospital setting. A significant proportion of such investigative work now takes place in university-connected hospitals committed to the advancement of medical knowledge as well as to the care of patients, the training of medical professionals, and, in recent years, more generalized community-oriented health functions. Affiliation with a hospital that can provide a research physician with a site for his investigations, the complex facilities, highly trained personnel, and kinds of patients necessary for his work is indispensable to him.

The hospital as an institution can not only do a great deal to foster a physician's research, it can also impede or terminate it by refusing to grant him affiliation, or by withdrawing certain rights and privileges from him once association has been accorded. In the 1940s, three hospitals in the Philadelphia area used the second kind of social control over Bailey by forbidding him to do any more operations after he had lost a mitral commissurotomy patient in each institution. This could easily have brought his early attempts to perform a successful commissurotomy to an involuntary close. Were it not for the boldly manipulative ways in which he utilized the surgical amphitheaters of the two Philadelphia hospitals still open to him, Bailey might have gone down in medical history as a surgeon on whom a moratorium was imposed.[67]

Mass Media and Lay Opinion

Advances in medicine are of great interest and concern to the lay public in many contemporary societies. News of the latest basic and applied biomedical developments is continually conveyed to the public through the various media of mass communication. The media not only accord a good deal of space and time to such reporting, but frequently they also assign it the prominent status of "front-page news." As we have suggested elsewhere, the great amount of popular attention accorded to medical science is "indicative of a high cultural value attached to health, longevity, relief of suffering, and the 'conquest of disease.' "[68] It is also associated with the role that medical research and those who conduct it

67. By 1957, Bailey's own professional status and that of cardiac surgery had changed radically, as witnessed by the following passage from a story in *Harper's Magazine:* "In 1957 the Prince of the operating room, the man the big league hospital can't afford to be without, is the heart surgeon. . . . In the Philadelphia area, there are several hospitals where Bailey is now a power and, within limits, can do very nearly anything he wants." L. Engel, *Harper's* (1957), 38, 41.

68. Fox, *Annals* of the New York Academy of Sciences.

or collaborate in it are presumed to play in the achievement of these goals. To an ever increasing extent, the media have the power to reflect and shape lay attitudes toward medical research and innovation, in ways that may help to facilitate or impede it.

We have not made a systematic study of the role that the mass media played throughout the history of mitral valve surgery. But, as far as we know, this surgery was not extensively covered until the early 1950s. At this time, the operation had developed to the point where it was technically successful and had begun to benefit numerous patients in a still restricted number of hospitals. The content of all the news articles that we have examined from this period is highly positive and even triumphant in tone. Valvular surgery is presented as a harbinger of a new era of open heart surgery, and emphasis is placed on the "new life" that such operations can make possible for former cardiac invalids.

The treatment of organ transplantation, especially human heart transplants, by the press and other media has been much more copious and extensive than the coverage of mitral valve surgery. Dr. Irvine H. Page has characterized it as "instant reporting," and contended that "there has never been anything like it in medical annals."[69] The same kinds of positive themes run through the press treatments of heart transplantation as those of surgery for mitral stenosis. The surgeons who have performed this trailblazing procedure have been presented as heroes, along with the heart recipients, donors, and their respective families. Those who have survived surgery and shown improvement have been depicted as undertaking activities that not only surpass what they were able to do preoperatively, but that also demonstrate unusual "physical prowess or endurance."[70] It may be assumed that these aspects of reporting have helped to encourage many of the sixty surgeons who have thus far conducted heart transplants to perform them. Such presentations have given them public support, recognition, and, in some cases, fame. Publicity about heart transplants has also facilitated their work by emphasizing the need for donors as well as the promise this operation holds for desperately ill recipients.

However, certain themes that the mass media have emphasized may have undermined rather than reinforced the continuance of heart transplantation. Medical spokesmen have stated their feeling that a "too optimistic" impression of the present state of cardiac transplantation has

69. I. Page, "The Ethics of Heart Transplantation," *Journal of the American Medical Association*, Vol. 207 (1969), 109–13. We realize that this increase in coverage is partly a consequence of the general growth of the mass media in the past two decades, and of their increasing reportage of developments in the life sciences.

70. *Ibid.*

been given and that this has had some boomerang effects on the lay public. This has been made all the more likely by the fact that newspapers have kept a "box score" on all heart transplants done and their outcome, demonstrating the typically high mortality rate for a therapeutic innovation in this very early stage of development. Furthermore, as some physicians have pointed out, the "transplanter" has often been presented as a taker of organs, rather than as a healer and the patient's guardian. Debates about the pros and cons of cardiac transplantation have taken place as much on the pages of daily newspapers as within the confines of the medical profession. And, to some extent, the spectacular, "circus trappings and glitter"[71] way in which some of the heart transplant surgeons have been presented to the public has subjected them to collegial criticism rather than increasing their professional standing, because such publicity violates professional norms of privacy, modesty, and disinterestedness.

Cultural Conceptions and Beliefs

Both the evolution of mitral valve surgery and cardiac transplantation demonstrate that concepts, ideas, and beliefs deriving from the cultural tradition of a society may latently affect the occurrence or nonoccurrence of a moratorium. The fact that in Western society the heart was considered to be a delicate, vital organ by physicians as well as laymen was long an impediment to cardiac surgery. The Judeo-Christian conception of the heart as a mystical organ, where the soul and the most noble motives and sentiments of man reside, has also forestalled and slowed down attempts to manipulate it.

These underlying ways of thinking about the human heart surfaced during the period of early clinical trials of mitral valve surgery and receded once the operative technique had been sufficiently perfected to demonstrate its viability and therapeutic benefit. In the more recent era of cardiac transplantation, these same conceptions have again manifested themselves, indicating that they have not been dispelled. These notions about the heart have been especially visible in the attempt by some members of the medical profession to redefine death as cessation of brain activity rather than of cardiorespiratory function and to have their new criteria accepted by physicians and laymen alike.[72]

71. *Ibid.*

72. See, for example, "A Definition of Irreversible Coma. Report of the *Ad Hoc* Committee of the Harvard Medical School to Examine the Definition of Brain Death," *Journal of the American Medical Association*, Vol. 205 (1968), 337–40.

ATTRIBUTES OF THE CLINICAL MORATORIUM

Clinical moratoria rarely occur in as total and clearcut a form as the moratorium on mitral valve surgery that began in 1928 with Cutler's last operation and ended in 1945 with Bailey's first. Slowdowns or suspensions in the experimental use of new therapeutic measures on patients are more commonly of shorter duration. The moratorium period is usually one of reflection, re-evaluation, and study for the research physicians formerly conducting clinical trials. During this time, they often return to laboratory experiments in an attempt to solve certain of the problems that led them temporarily to cease human trials.

As the foregoing implies, a moratorium does not mean a permanent abandonment of a therapeutic innovation, either because it has proved to be unfruitful or noxious, or because, in the natural flow of medical scientific advance, it has been superseded by a better one. Nor, according to our definition of the phenomenon, does the failure to move from the level of animal to human trials constitute a clinical moratorium. Thus, for example, we do not define as a moratorium the period 1902 through 1922 when no one tried Brunton's technique "for dividing a mitral stenosis on a fellow creature."

The two major subtypes of clinical moratoria that we have identified, then, are total cessations and slowdowns of the use of a new clinical procedure on human subjects.

Slowdowns may occur for a number of reasons, singly or in combination: After a certain number of clinical trials, some physicians may cease to use an experimental procedure; other physicians may try it once or twice and then stop; physicians working in a particular institution may collectively withdraw from further clinical trials; all or most of a group of pioneer physicians may continue with their trials, but at a decelerated pace.

We have not studied a sufficient number of moratoria to generalize about their average duration. And we do not have enough data to determine whether it is more common for a short-lived moratorium (lasting weeks or months) to take the form of total cessation or of a slowdown.

In the previous section of this paper, we discussed various factors that bear upon a moratorium. When these factors converge to push toward a moratorium, they do so either by virtue of "internal" or "external" pressures. By internal pressures toward a moratorium, we mean those that originate primarily with the research physician who feels that he ought to discontinue clinical trials. A classical example is Cutler's conviction that he should terminate mitral valve surgery in the face of a mortality rate that was "devastating" to him. External pressures conducive to a moratorium are generated by the opinions of colleagues or lay persons that trials should not proceed, and by the actions they may take to implement their judgment. This type of pressure is illustrated by the fact that after Souttar had attempted one mitral valve operation, patients with mitral stenosis no longer consulted him, partly because colleagues did not refer such patients to him. Another example is seen in cardiac transplantation. Dr. Denton Cooley, the surgeon who has performed the greatest number of these operations, attributed the decline in heart transplants from December 1968 through February 1969 to the fact that "the stream of heart donors . . . dried up" because critics among the lay public and in the medical profession had become "faint hearted . . . in the face of a few initial defeats."[73]

Moratorium pressures may also be "formal" or "informal" in nature. When three Philadelphia hospitals withdrew operating privileges from Bailey, they exercised a formal constraint over his ability to conduct more mitral valve surgery. In contrast, when Harken's colleagues suggested that he would damage the reputation of cardiac surgery if he continued to operate with such a high mortality rate, they exerted informal pressures upon him. A research physician may or may not consent to arrest trials in response to external pressures. If he does not agree, as the case of Bailey shows, those generating the pressures may decide to use formal sanctions to ensure his compliance.

The actual moratorium may be formally or informally declared. For example, when Dr. Pierre Grondin of the Montreal Heart Institute decided to halt cardiac transplants in Winter 1969, his decision was formally made public through press announcements issued by the Institute. A moratorium may be formally proclaimed not only through the mass media, but also in a professional publication or in a presentation at a medical meeting. Cutler's halt occurred in a more informal way. Although he published a final report on his valvular surgery attempts, he "signed off" in this article without explicitly declaring that he was doing so. The more usual informal manner of declaring a moratorium is through face-to-face exchanges with colleagues.

To summarize, the pressures toward calling a moratorium can logically and empirically take the following three forms: internal, external-formal, and external-informal. The actual declaration of a moratorium,

73. Cooley's statement, delivered during an interview at the annual meeting of the American College of Cardiology in New York City, was carried in newspapers across the country on February 28, 1969.

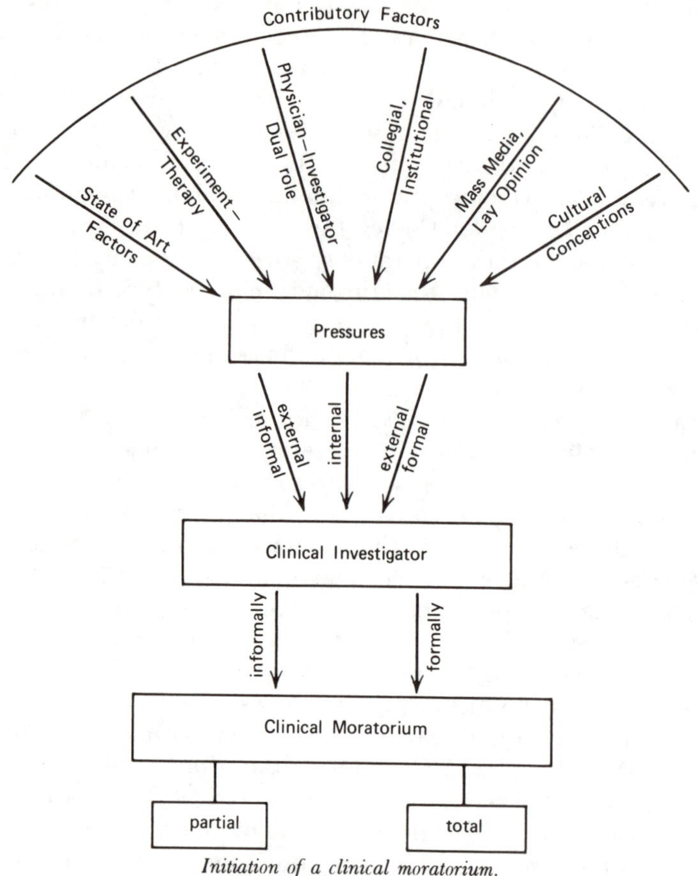

Initiation of a clinical moratorium.

in turn, can be made through formal or informal channels.[74] Our view of the process through which a moratorium comes to be called can be schematized as shown above.

APPENDIX

As pointed out at the beginning of this paper, our analysis of the clinical moratorium grew out of our study of cardiac transplantation. We feel that we have established the moratorium as a normal, recurring phe-

74. Thus, we would redefine the slowdown in liver transplantation termed by Moore, a "spontaneous moratorium" (see note 6) as an informally declared moratorium generated by internal pressures.

nomenon in clinical investigation, and have identified the key factors contributing to its occurrence, and its essential attributes. Methodologically, working with both an historical medical development (mitral valve surgery) and a contemporary one (heart transplantation) has taught us what kinds of data are needed to ascertain whether or not a moratorium has occurred. For example, the graph on page 362, in and of itself, does not tell us whether cardiac transplantation through September 1969 has undergone suspensions or slowdowns that meet the criteria of moratoria. The facts that no transplants were done in March 1968 or that there was a dramatic drop in the number carried out from November to December 1968 might both constitute moratoria. But it might also be true that during these months there were no facilities or personnel free to care for new heart recipients or that the surgeons who have performed the majority of transplants were meeting other professional responsibilities, such as attending medical congresses.

Ideally, one needs personal interviews with the relevant clinical investigators and their close colleagues, study of what they and other physicians are writing and saying about cardiac transplantation in both professional and lay contexts, and a survey of mass media coverage of transplantations during this period. The absence of such systematic data accounts for the fact that physicians as well as laymen are not sure whether moratoria on cardiac transplantation have taken place.

Clinical moratoria only take place when the pressures on the research physician to desist from certain trials on patients are stronger than those counterpressures generated by what would ordinarily be his scientific and therapeutic obligations to continue. Here we return to an essential attribute of the clinical moratorium referred to earlier in this paper. The physician who commits himself to the career of clinical investigator incurs the obligation to conduct research with patients. His goal is to advance medical science and practice in ways that he hopes will benefit his subjects and other patients with similar or related medical problems. Within the limits of what the ethics of human experimentation permit him to do, the research physician has an obligation to contribute to an ongoing investigative process. In and through these research activities, he is bound to bring the latest developments in knowledge and technique to bear upon diseases that cannot otherwise be adequately prevented or treated. If for some reason an investigator wishes to interrupt or roll back this process, as is the case when a physician would call a clinical moratorium on his own or colleagues' work, there is a sense in which the burden of proof falls on him.[75] In some form, he must explain

75. A similar burden of proof falls on the non-physician (for example, clergyman, lawyer, journalist) who advocates the calling of a clinical moratorium.

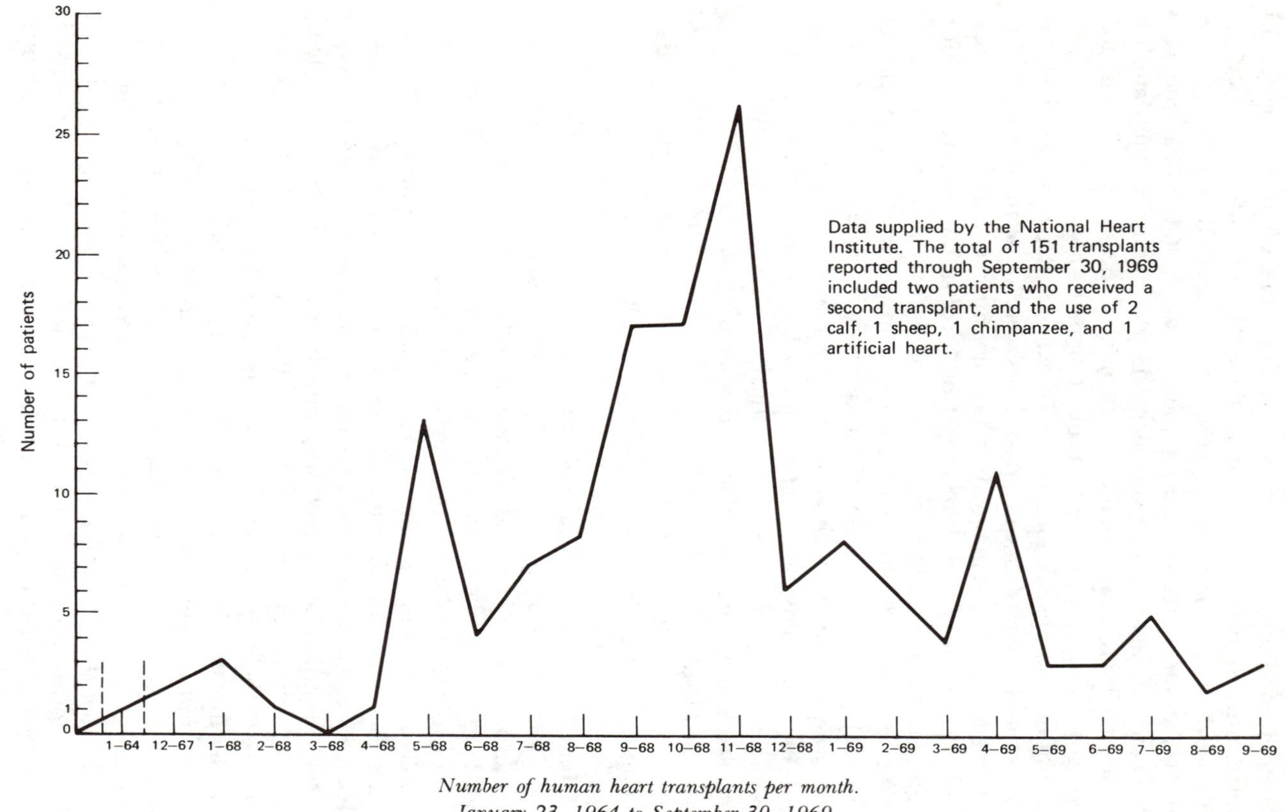

Number of human heart transplants per month.
January 23, 1964 to September 30, 1969

to colleagues and patients why he feels this step ought to be taken. For, when he invokes a moratorium, he challenges institutionalized values that work to keep the process of clinical research ongoing: "We have made a beginning; now it is time to proceed. . . . Why do we continue? Because if we don't, these people will die, and if we do, some will improve." A call for a clinical moratorium, then, entails the seeking of legitimation from significant others temporarily to bring a halt to an otherwise obligatory research activity, on the grounds that this suspension will ultimately serve the values of clinical investigation better than continuing the trials in question.

The Case of the Medical Assistants of Zaïre

WILLY DE CRAEMER AND RENÉE C. FOX

This essay is excerpted from *The Emerging Physician,* a monograph coauthored with Willy De Craemer, that presents our historical and ethnographic study of the Medical Assistants and the first modern, African physicians of ex-Belgian Congo, now Zaïre. The essay, derived from the introduction and conclusion sections of the monograph, constitutes a synthesis as well as a summary of the major empirical and conceptual findings of our study. The body of the monograph consists of first-hand field materials on the social backgrounds of the Medical Assistants; why and how they became interested in medicine and decided to embark on medical careers; their education and professional socialization; their professional experiences in the colonial era; the historical circumstances that made it possible for some of them to become physicians right after independence was granted to the Congo; their interlude in France where they attended medical school; and what awaited them in the independent Democratic Republic of the Congo when they returned to their country as ex-medical assistant physicians.

From *The Emerging Physician* (Stanford, Ca.: Hoover Institution Press, 1968), 1–5, 76–78.

INTRODUCTION AND METHODS OF RESEARCH

At ten o'clock in the morning on June 29, 1963, fourteen Congolese men just graduated from the School of Medical Assistants of Kisantu gathered in the dormitory room of one of their members. They had met to drink a farewell glass of beer together before completing their packing and boarding the afternoon train to Kinshasa, the capital of the Congo.[1] There, at the Ministry of National Education, they would receive their diplomas and, at the Ministry of Public Health, their first professional assignments. Here in the dormitory room, garnished with books, family photographs, religious pictures, "pin-ups," and a spray of purple bougainvillea blossoms in a soda bottle, the young men discussed their present professional status and their aspirations for the future. All were firmly resolved to begin whatever steps were necessary to go to medical school and become physicians after completing their one obligatory year of employment by the government.

> What is a medical assistant, anyway? A medical assistant is neither a nurse nor a doctor. He is something intermediary . . . a hybrid . . . and a creature of colonialism. The status of medical assistant does not even exist in countries like Belgium, France or the United States. And here in the Congo, it is already *dépassé*. . . . We are the last group of medical assistants that Kisantu will graduate, and among the last medical assistants of the Congo. . . . This is a new, young, independent country. . . . From now on, every Congolese man interested in medicine who has ambition and ability will want to become a doctor in medicine.[2]

Seven months later, a group of fifty-six ex-medical assistant physicians held their first formal meeting under the palm trees of the Zoo Restaurant in Kinshasa. Representatives of the local press were invited to be present at the gathering. These ex-medical assistants were men who had been sent overseas by the World Health Organization to various French universities (Bordeaux, Lyon, Montpellier, Nantes, and Rennes) to complete their medical training. They had just returned to the Congo as

1. In June 1966, in honor of the sixth anniversary of independence of the Congo, the names of some of its cities were changed from European to African titles. Coquilhatville became Mbandaka; Elisabethville, Lubumbashi; Jadotville, Likasi; Leopoldville, Kinshasa; and Stanleyville, Kisangani. Their present African names will be used in this text, except when the former name of one of these cities is cited in a verbatim quotation, or when it is part of an official title (e.g., "School of Medical Assistants of Leopoldville").

2. From here on, unless otherwise stated, all quotes cited in the body of this text are verbatim excerpts from interviews carried out with medical assistants and Congolese physicians.

newly graduated physicians.[3] In the words of their spokesman, the purpose of the meeting was to "throw some needed light on various points relative to our situation, first as medical assistants and then as the physicians that we have subsequently become":

> Yesterday, medical assistants in a colonized country, the Belgian Congo; today, doctors in medicine in an independent country, the Republic of the Congo. The physician, formerly a medical assistant, appears here as an indisputably positive result of the irreversible process of liberation of our dear country. . . .[4]

Behind this press conference of physicians and the farewell party of medical assistants lay almost thirty years of entwined social and medical developments in the ex-Belgian Congo. In 1935, the first school to train *assistants médicaux indigènes* (native medical assistants) was established in Leopoldville (now Kinshasa) by the colonial government. One year later, a second school was opened at the Mission of Kisantu by Jesuit Fathers in collaboration with a group of medical school professors from Louvain University. A third school was founded in Kalenda (Kasai) in 1950 by Scheut Fathers working with the medical staff of Louvain.

Congolese men who attended these schools say, "We were trained in the image of the doctor" to serve as "auxiliary collaborators" of European physicians in the diagnosis, treatment, and prevention of disease.[5]

3. The first two Congolese physicians were graduated from the University of Lovanium in Kimwenza (Kinshasa) in 1961; the third, also from Lovanium, in 1962; and the fourth Congolese physician received his doctorate in medicine in June 1963, from the University of Paris.

4. *Le Courrier d'Afrique* (Kinshasa, Democratic Republic of the Congo), January 29, 1964, p. 3.

5. A school to train medical assistants was also created by the Belgian colonial administration in Astrida, Rwanda. It was not attended by Congolese students, but by Banya-Rwanda and BaRundi.

The institution of such medical assistants or assistant doctors is not unique to ex-Belgian Africa. For example, colonial French Africa trained comparable medical auxiliaries, known as *médecins africains*, at schools created for that purpose in Dakar and Tananarive. In the late 1920s, the colonial government of Nigeria founded the Yaba Medical School for the education of medical assistants. Schools to prepare medical assistants for service in country districts exist in Tanganyika, Kenya, Uganda and the Sudan. In Suva, in the Fiji Island group, the Fiji School of Medicine to train what are now called "assistant medical officers," has existed since 1878. The *officiers de santé* of Indo-China, the *behdar* of Iran, the *practicante* of Spain and the *Feldscher Therapeute* of the Soviet Union are all middle-level medical auxiliaries similar to the medical assistants of the Congo.

In Lord Hailey's *An African Survey,* reference is made to a survey of auxiliary medical personnel in tropical Africa that was conducted in 1952 by Dr. C. C. Chesterman. This study followed upon a meeting of the World Health Organization in 1951, where it was

In certain remote areas of the bush country where there was no physician, or where the services of a physician were only infrequently available, the Congolese medical assistant acted as a substitute for the doctor and helped to make the medical system of the Belgian Congo one of the best organized and most effective on the continent of Africa. The importance of his role can be better understood when one considers that in this vast country (905,381 square miles) with its sizable, rapidly increasing native population (13,864,421 in 1959) subject to the whole array of endemic and epidemic diseases characteristic of a tropical country—and to diseases introduced by Europeans as well—there was never more than one physician available for each 18,000 inhabitants.[6]

Up until July 1959,[7] a graduate of a school of medical assistants generally had at least six years of primary school education and three or four of secondary education, before he began the six-year program of classroom studies and clinical work that constituted the core of the medical assistant's training.[8] Thus, with some sixteen years of formal education and their status as high-ranking medical auxiliaries, medical assistants had attained a so-called "summit position" for Congolese men in the colonial era. As such, they belonged to a small elite class of Congolese called *évolués*. They were regarded as having "evolved" intel-

decided that such personnel were necessary for adequate health services in underdeveloped areas at the present time. But at this same meeting it was also urged that some categories, particularly that of assistant to registered doctors (the equivalent of Congolese medical assistants) be replaced as soon as possible by fully qualified persons. (See Lord Hailey, *An African Survey*, revised 1956. London: Oxford University Press, 1957, 1099–1102.)

6. Ratio cited in "Rapport Annuel 1959 Direction Générale des Services Médicaux." At the end of 1959, there were 761 physicians working in the Congo, whose population at that time came close to 14 million inhabitants. Compare this ratio, for example, with the number of physicians per inhabitants in the United States in 1961: one physician per 780 inhabitants. (See Bruce M. Russett, et al., eds., *World Handbook of Political and Social Indicators*, New Haven and London: Yale University Press, 1965, p. 206. According to latest figures available, in 1965 there were just 532 physicians—Congolese and foreign—in the Congo, and 206 of these were working in Kinshasa. (See *Annuaire de la République Démocratique du Congo*, 1965, edited by l'Agence Nationale de Publicité Congolaise, Kinshasa, p. 94.)

7. On July 2, 1959, an ordinance was passed by the government (Ordonnance no. 75/355 Hyg.) reducing the professional training of medical assistants from six to three years. In actual practice, the operating schools of medical assistants never abided by this ordinance. The only concession that they made was to reduce the training of medical assistants from six to five years.

8. The School of Medical Assistants of Kisantu required, in addition, two preparatory years of general education with special emphasis on science, after the four years of secondary studies, before a young man was admitted to the six-year course for medical assistants. Thus, graduates of Kisantu had received at least 18 years of formal education.

lectually, morally, and socially beyond the "mentality," "way of life," and material standing of the Congolese "masses."

At the end of 1959, on the threshold of independence for the Congo, there were 136 graduate medical assistants practicing in the country. Only two of these were to succeed in finding a way to study for their doctorates in medicine.[9]

The first university in the Congo, the Catholic University of Lovanium, opened its doors in 1954, and started a program of medical studies leading to a doctor's degree. Among the students in the first medical school class of the University were three Congolese men. Two of them were graduated in 1961, the third in the following year, thus becoming the first Congolese physicians in the country. By 1963, four more Congolese had graduated from Lovanium as physicians. None of these seven men had ever been medical assistants. The Official University of the Congo in Elisabethville (now Lubumbashi), a state university and the second university to be established in the Congo, began to function in 1955.[10] Its first group of physicians was graduated in 1963, a class of five men, among whom three were Congolese who had previously been medical assistants.

Thus, in June 1960, when independence had come to the Congo, there was as yet no Congolese physician. The first months of independence saw much disorganization and some violence. Many Europeans, including numerous physicians, left the country. By October 1960 there were only 120 physicians in the Congo.[11] This scarcity of medical personnel occasioned an acute emergency. Its long-range consequences were equally serious, since no more than a handful of Congolese physicians could be expected to graduate from the Congolese universities for at least a decade to come.

Hence, in 1960, the World Health Organization stepped in and, with authorization of the Congolese government, provided the country with

9. One of them was the Congolese physician who was graduated from the Faculty of Medicine of the University of Paris in June 1963.

10. There is now a third university in the Congo, the Free University of the Congo in Kisangani, a university of Protestant inspiration, which began operating in 1963. During the academic years of 1964–1965 and 1965–1966, it conducted most of its classes on the campus of Lovanium University. Only a small pre-university unit was based in Kisangani in 1965–1966. This is because the city of Kisangani had still not sufficiently emerged from the rebellion of 1964 to make the resumption of university classes there prudent or practical.

11. *Le Courier d'Afrique*, October 10, 1960, p. 1. This statistic was cited in a press conference given by M. Mackenzie Pollock, representative of the World Health Organization in the Congo. Aside from these hundred-odd physicians, there were, by this time, approximately 140 medical assistants, 1200 Congolese *infirmiers* and approximately 3500 *aides-infirmiers*.

the services of foreign physicians. As a result, 168 physicians were working as members of the W.H.O. emergency medical team in the Congo by December 1963. W.H.O. also offered a plan and a series of scholarships whereby Congolese medical assistants could go on with their studies and become physicians. Various European countries were approached for help. The French government responded first; it agreed to extend to Congolese medical assistants the same rights accorded to their professional counterparts in French Africa. These men were called "*médecins africains*" and had graduated from the schools of Dakar and Tananarive. By French government decree,[12] medical assistants, like African physicians, were given access to an accelerated program of studies that would lead to the university degree of Doctor in Medicine. French medical school training ordinarily takes six years. But because of their past medical education and clinical experience medical assistants were permitted to enter the fourth year of medical school and thus to graduate in a little more than three years.

By newspaper and by radio a call went out to the medical assistants of the Congo appealing to them to come to Kinshasa and present their credentials. For the sake of the health and welfare of their independent country, they were asked to go abroad and complete their training. In the fall of 1960, sixty-one of the medical assistants who had responded to this appeal began training in the faculties of medicine of the five designated French universities.

At the same time, the Belgian universities of Brussels, Liège, and Louvain opened their faculties of medicine to a smaller number of medical assistants from the Congo. Fifteen men were awarded Belgian government grants and were admitted to the fourth year in the seven-year training program that characterizes Belgian medical schools.[13] Back home, three medical assistants were admitted on scholarship to the Official University of the Congo, entering the fourth year of a seven-year medical school course modeled after that of Belgian universities.

Annually, since 1961, successive groups of Congolese medical assistants have gone to France, Belgium, and Switzerland,[14] as well as to Lubumbashi in the Congo. In addition, the French government has

12. The particular decrees involved here were those of October 17 and November 30, 1960.

13. In July 1966, eight Congolese—six of them former medical assistants—received their degrees of doctor in medicine at Belgian universities. For the year 1966–1967, thirteen Congolese students were enrolled in the final year of medical school in the Belgian university system, and all but one of these were ex-medical assistants.

14. Only six Congolese medical assistants have gone to Switzerland to study. These were men sent to the universities of Geneva and Lausanne in 1961 on W.H.O. scholarships.

offered scholarships for French medical schools to Congolese men who have graduated from schools of medical assistants since 1960. All told, by August 1966, 115 medical assistants had become physicians.

In 1960, Kalenda, one of the three schools in the Congo training medical assistants, closed down. Four years later, the school of Kisantu graduated its last class of medical assistants. In 1965, the School of Medical Assistants of Kinshasa awarded diplomas to its final class of students, and the era of the medical assistants of the Congo came to an end. But to the ranks of the 136 medical assistants who were practicing in the Congo when independence came had been added 189 more before this kind of training ceased. As a result of the political and social processes that brought independence to their country, most of these 325 men will have had the opportunity to become doctors. And so the long journey from medical assistant to physician, made by the pioneers of the Congolese medical profession, has ostensibly come to its desired end.

"We are no longer medical assistants. . . . We are *ex*-medical assistants," these Congolese physicians affirm. "Our former status is now submerged in that of Doctor of Medicine,[15] the first national doctors of medicine of the Congo. . . . Before us lies the responsibility of establishing the Congolese medical profession on the best possible scientific, ethical and organizational bases, so that the health and welfare of the population of this new nation can be optimally served. . . . As physicians, we are unified in the art of healing which transcends ethnic, racial, political, and ideological factors." Yet, as these ex-medical assistants have discovered during their first years of practice as physicians, in the Congo, their struggle for recognition and for the establishment of a Congolese medical profession has not been completely won either by their medical diploma or by the political independence accorded to their country. . . .

GENERAL SOCIOLOGICAL CONCLUSIONS

. . . The genesis and growth of a modern medical profession in the Congo is integrally tied into the larger processes of change through

15. The unanimous, strongly felt and formally expressed desire of medical assistants who became physicians to shed their prior professional status is an interesting case to examine in the context of Robert K. Merton's current reflections on "status-sequence." Merton, a professor of sociology at Columbia University, New York City, is exploring the social, cultural, psychological and situational factors that contribute to the retention and/or elimination of a status in a status-sequence. In the pages that follow, the reasons why the first Congolese physicians wished to be considered *ex*-medical assistant doctors rather than medical assistants *and* doctors will be revealed.

which the Congo has moved in passing from traditional, to modern colonial, to modern independent society. This history of the medical assistants and first Congolese physicians, therefore, affords an opportunity to examine in substance and detail certain factors that have facilitated change and others that have impeded it, as well as some of the continuities and discontinuities that this process of change has involved.

The modern Congolese medical profession . . . has its origins and roots in traditional Congolese society. Its members were deeply concerned, religiously, magically, scientifically, and socio-psychologically, with health and illness. They attached a high positive value to well being and good health. And they reserved a place of special honor, prestige, and even sacredness to their healers and medicine men. The medical assistants and first Congolese physicians were progeny of this tradition in two senses: they were born and grew up in it; and in a number of instances they were descendants of traditional healers. There exist, too, significant points of continuity in attitudes, values, and social structure between medicine in traditional Congolese society, and modern Western European medicine brought to the Congo by Christian missionaries and by the Belgian colonial administration. These undoubtedly contributed to the general receptivity of the Congolese population to European medicine and to its practitioners. In the case of the BaKongo and the BaLuba tribes from which many medical assistants and physicians were recruited, certain more specific factors seem to have heightened their responsiveness to European medicine, and to European civilization in general. The relevant factors . . . include early and long-standing contact with Europeans; particularly intense and concentrated efforts by the missions and by the colonial government to develop medical, educational, and religious facilities in the regions of the BaKongo and the BaLuba; and the deliverance European medicine was able to effect of the BaKongo population in the Madimba Territory from epidemics of sleeping sickness and yaws disease.

The presence of European medicine in the Congo also brought in its wake certain changes in the attitudes, values, and conduct of the people it treated. For one thing, its approach to the cause, diagnosis, treatment, and prognosis of disease, unlike the traditional Congolese system, was based on the idea that illness is a natural rather than a supernatural phenomenon. It proceeded on the premise that disease can and ought to be approached in a rational empirical, purely scientific way. For another, the European medical services that were offered to the Congolese were intermeshed with a whole range of other institutions the Europeans had brought with them and established in the Congo, notably, systems of religion, education, economy, occupations, and government. Sometimes, as was the case with the earlier Catholic missionaries, these new European facilities, functions, forms, and ideas were all combined in the same person. Because of the interrelationship between them, the acceptance by Congolese of one of these institutions predisposed them to accept the others.

Almost all the medical assistants and Congolese physicians . . . were educated in Catholic primary schools, usually in a mission setting. Many of them also received their secondary education and all or a part of their training as medical assistants in a Catholic institution—a *collège*, a seminary, and the schools of medical assistants of Kisantu and Kalenda. It would seem that it was primarily through the socialization process they underwent in the course of their education in these settings that medical assistants deeply internalized new attitudes and values that we have referred to as the "moral virtues of the *évolués*." These attitudes and values . . . were essentially European and Christian in nature, and in certain particulars, specifically Belgian-Catholic middle class. Our contention that they made a deep impression seems to be borne out by the fact that, throughout their entire professional history, medical assistants have been motivated by their commitment to those values. . . . They include: education, science and technology, work, courage, unity and universalism, love of country, a *savoir vivre* style of life, and commitment to the new generation. This does not necessarily imply that medical assistants totally relinquished or repudiated traditional Congolese values assimilated earlier in life in family, tribal, and village settings. In some respects . . . there was enough consistency between European and Congolese cultures to make for a natural compatibility between them. In other regards, the medical assistants themselves effected a blend between the two traditions of which they were a part. Such was the case in the areas of modern medicine that especially attracted ex-medical assistant physicians. Their interest in pediatrics, in obstetrics and gynecology, and in social and psychological medicine . . . was influenced by both Bantu and European traditions.

Following these men through their entire career as medical assistants, on to medical school, and from there through their first year in practice gives us some insight into the kinds of socio-psychological experiences and conditions that could bring them to behave in ways that run counter to the beliefs and values, Congolese and European, that they profess. Here, we refer specifically to the fact that many of the ex-medical assistant physicians now in the Congo have begun to see patients on a private basis, and that a number of them are seriously contemplating the possibility of running for political office in the next elections. Neither private practice nor politics is in keeping with the universalistic frame of reference that has been characteristic of this professional group over the years. What is more, they still do not basically approve of such behavior, which they consider more self-interested and partisan than is ideally appropriate for a doctor, particularly for one who is practicing in a society in such a stage of development as the Congo. The most obvious factor propelling these physicians toward private practice and political office is the financial situation in which they currently find themselves. Mature married men, in their thirties and forties, fathers of many children, as the practitioners of a high-ranking liberal profession, they feel that they do not earn enough money to house, feed, clothe, and educate their families properly. Neither can they provide any degree of security for the future.

But these material considerations are not the only factors or even the most important ones drawing physicians into private practice, and certain of them toward politics. A combination of elements is at work. They have experienced a discouraging repetition of certain problems that they knew as medical assistants, such as the questioning of the equal status of their diploma, and the persistent frustration of certain of their high-priority values, notably the education of their children, which they will not be able to provide without a certain level of income. All these factors have begun to influence Congolese physicians in the direction of withdrawing some of their energies from responsibility for public medicine. Other physicians have responded with more active civic concern, but in a way that carries them, at least in intention, beyond the sphere of medicine per se into the arena of politics.

At least one other possible kind of reaction to the problems and frustrations that the ex-medical assistant physicians share comes to mind—a militant, insurgent response which could make these doctors an elite source of revolution. This is an option the first Congolese physicians have not taken. But will the younger generation of physicians who will come after them, those who have become doctors in the conventional way, as well as ex-medical assistant physicians, respond in as peaceable a fashion to their professional problems?

In the colonial Congo, the status and role of medical assistant were both expressions and instruments of social change. Here was one of a small, experimental group of elite categories for Congolese that formally recognized the evolution toward European knowledge, ideas, attitudes, values, and behavior a man had already made. It rewarded him for it and encouraged him to move further in the same general direction. It both invited and obliged him to take a special part in the development of the Congo. If we look upon the status and role of the medical assistant in this light, it is interesting to reflect briefly on the different attitudes toward medical assistants demonstrated by various groups in the colonial period. This allows us to identify certain structural sources of receptivity and resistance to change.

In Congolese circles, as we have seen, medical assistants held the highest social, moral, intellectual, and material status. They represented, literally and symbolically, the summit of what modern, "civilized" Congolese could hope to attain. On the whole, the Belgian physicians who supervised the medical assistants also respected and appreciated them. Secure in their own professional competence and status, and by and large genuinely devoted to the task of developing preventive and curative medicine in the Congo, the Belgian physicians gave full credit to medical assistants for the important role they were playing. They also were aware of the knowledge, skills, and experience these Congolese men possessed for their task. In many instances, such physicians went further: they encouraged the medical assistants with whom they had the closest association to continue on if possible to become doctors like themselves.

European sanitary agents, on the other hand, had a more negatively competitive attitude toward medical assistants, a general tendency to look down on them and to depreciate their worth. From the point of view of class origins, most sanitary agents began life on a relatively humble social plane, closer to that of the medical assistants than that of the European physicians who worked in the Congo. Sanitary agents had far less formal education and professional training than physicians, and generally less than medical assistants. Their rank in the medical status hierarchy was much lower than that of a physician; it was also lower than that of the medical assistant, although their salary was higher than his. In short, sanitary agents were more like medical assistants in social origin than like physicians, but they were less like physicians in terms of professional training, competence, and status than medical assistants. Furthermore, in the authority structure of the medical team, sanitary agents were subordinate not only to physicians, who in principle were their chiefs, but also to the medical assistant, who was "doctor in miniature" and the "right arm of the physician." Sanitary agents did not question the qualifications or authority of the physician. But with the medical assistant, an African rather than a European, who occupied the status just below that of the physician and just above their own, they seem to have felt threatened enough to need to express their hostility and assert their so-called "racial superiority." For the sanitary agents, the medical assistant was not just a rival who might take away their jobs; he was also an invidiously felt challenge to their own sense of social status and social esteem. The insecurity they felt was rooted more in social structure than in either material considerations or individual personality traits.

Religious sister nurses, it would seem, also tended to react to medical assistants with certain kinds of reservation and resistance. But the origins of their hesitant and only partial acceptance of the medical assistants were, in some ways, quite different from those that motivated sanitary agents. Perhaps there were elements of status sensitivity on the part of some sisters. As members of religious orders, Europeans, and nurses they may have had difficulty in accepting medical assistants—Congolese laymen—as superior to themselves in education, medical competence, and professional authority. However, a far more characteristic source of the sisters' attitudes seems to have been their kind of religious commitment, meliorism, and perfectionism. In effect, what they tended to ask of medical assistants was nothing less than absolute and ultimate performance as "good Congolese" and "good Christians," as well as good medical auxiliaries.

As members of religious orders in a missionary setting, the sisters felt they had to teach, help, and oblige Congolese lay persons to live up to certain standards of religious, familial, personal, and professional excellence. They felt this would come about partly through the example that they themselves set, and partly through the demands they made upon the Congolese with whom they had continuing contact. The expectations of the sisters regarding the medical assistants were especially high, for these were, presumably, Congolese elite—models for other Congolese evolving toward Christian and European values—and the men were charged, like the sisters themselves, with the delicate and important moral as well as medical responsibility of caring for patients. Their outlook and behavior, then, the sisters felt, should be particularly exemplary. Their acceptance of a medical assistant tended to be contingent on the degree to which he lived up to all these things they required of him. It is significant to note in this regard that, unlike Belgian physicians who encouraged the most gifted and upright of the medical assistants with whom they worked to try to become physicians, the top level to which the sisters tried to bring medical assistants was excellence within their present category.

So, in the persons of sanitary agents and religious sister nurses and their attitudes toward Congolese medical assistants in the colonial era, we have seen two different kinds of vested interest at work—one centered on status and the other on value. The sanitary agents wanted to defend their own social status, and the sisters were interested in guarding the ultimate values to which they were committed and seeing that they were realized in specific, rather rigidly defined ways. However different may have been the motivation of the sanitary agents and the sisters, both groups constituted sources of tension for medical assistants and barriers to their full acceptance.

In independent Congolese society, ex-medical assistant physicians have encountered at least two kinds of resistance to their total recognition and appropriate remuneration as physicians that bear some resemblance to those they experienced as medical assistants in the colonial era. One has been the reluctance of certain administrators in the government to define them formally as equal to physicians who have been trained by the normal route, rather than by passing from medical assistant to physician. Nor have such administrators been eager to augment the salary scale of Congolese physicians. These attitudes of administrators regarding Congolese physicians, ex-medical assistants or otherwise, do not seem to be directed toward this group alone. Rather, they are extended to all Congolese men in the post-colonial Congo whom such administrators define as intellectuals because they have had at least a university education or its equivalent. Administrators of this type are not quick to favor such individuals, better educated than themselves, who comprise a new elite in a new society. They see them not so much as potential usurpers of their own positions in the literal sense, but as men who, by their very presence on the Congolese scene, their qualifications, their questioning, and their potential achievements could challenge the social status and prestige of an administrator. Thus, as was the case with sanitary agents and medical assistants the administrators feel threatened by Congolese physicians and like intellectuals in the domain of social standing and esteem. This reaction is potentially heightened by their finding themselves confronted with doctors who only a few years ago worked side by side with them in the administration as civil servants. At that time, the doctors-to-be had not much more education and no more professional prestige than they themselves.

The other major source of resistance to the acceptance of ex-medical assistant physicians as fully qualified physicians has come from certain members of the administration and faculty of Lovanium University. Here, it seems, the vested interests involved are rather close in nature to those that kept many religious sister nurses from a complete acceptance of medical assistants. The spokesmen for Lovanium believe there are certain standards of intellectual and moral excellence on which any university and any profession worthy of its name, its tradition, and its special function are necessarily based. Any attempt to manipulate these standards, or to modify the program of required studies, they contend, must be scrutinized carefully and undertaken guardedly, for it may lead to a dangerous lowering of standards. In principle, their concept of

"Africanization," a process to which they subscribe, includes a sensitive adjustment of the university curriculum and professional training to certain historical, cultural, sociological, and psychological characteristics of the present-day Congo. Thus, their purism about academic and professional traditions and requisites limits what they feel they can legitimately modify. It also makes them less able to recognize which aspects of the model of a university and of a profession they are upholding are bound to European culture and are not universally applicable. For members of the administration and faculty of Lovanium with this perspective, the special arrangements made to exempt medical assistants from the first half of medical school training, and the conferring upon them, nonetheless, of the diploma of doctor in medicine at the end of their studies, represented a deviation from standards that should not have been allowed. They felt it should not go without comment lest it become a precedent in Congolese society. Thus it may be said that the academic authorities of Lovanium in the independent Congo, like the religious sisters in the colonial Congo, saw themselves as the guardians of certain values, principles, and standards, and of particular ways of implementing them. As a consequence, then, they refused to concede that the ex-medical assistant physicians were the equivalent of fully trained doctors. Such vested interests can be potent agents of social change, under some circumstances. Under other circumstances, they can reinforce the status quo.

Finally, our study of the medical assistants and first Congolese physicians allows us to speculate on the social, psychological, and historical conditions under which a marginal status like that of medical assistant, or "graduate in medicine" is tenable. As the medical assistants themselves have testified, even in the colonial era the intermediary nature of their status, training, responsibilities, authority, and rights was a source of strain for them. Not only did they want a clearer and more just definition of what it was to be a medical assistant; they also yearned to advance toward becoming doctors, even though this seemed unrealistic in the colonial era.

Nevertheless, under the particular circumstances of colonialism, the status of medical assistant was not only tolerable for a Congolese man, but it also carried with it many satisfactions. It did represent, after all, a peak of education, responsibility, standing, and honor for a Congolese man in the colonial society. And though he may have aspired to rise higher and go farther, he was part of a tightly structured and regulated social order, with established "ceilings" in opportunities for Congolese. These he was obliged to accept if he were to adjust himself to the colonial regime and advance in its prescribed limits.

In the independent Congo, however, the status of medical assistant or its functional equivalent is no longer acceptable either to ex-medical assistant physicians, or to a new generation of young Congolese with a vocation for medicine. The in-between status of medical assistant is for them an artificial and anomalous category, historically and psychologically associated with colonialism. As they see it and feel it, such a status limits a man with the talent, competence, and drive to qualify for a higher medical level to a nebulous position somewhere below that of physician. In the new, developing society, with its need of trained personnel on every level, nothing less than the sky is now the limit on the aspirations of an ambitious Congolese man, and on what he can hope to achieve. Opportunity is a reality, not just a daydream, and there is now no need to halt on the social scale somewhere between a nurse and a doctor.

Certain older medical assistants who have not become physicians, Congolese physicians who were never medical assistants, local and national administrators, and European physicians . . . have advised that personnel like medical assistants be continued. They have also worked to re-establish such a status in the new form of "graduates in medicine." They recognize the contribution made by medical assistants in the colonial era, especially in the remote inland areas of the country, and they do not wish to see the rural populations of the independent Congo totally deprived of adequate medical care. Nevertheless, this point of view fails to take into account some of the most deep-rooted social and psychological consequences of the story of "the emerging physician" . . . , and of the evolution of the Congo from a colonial to an independent society of which this history is a part.

PART SIX

BIOETHICS

Ethical and Existential Developments in Contemporaneous American Medicine: Their Implications for Culture and Society

Contemporaneous Western medicine is often depicted as a vast body of scientific knowledge, technical skills, medicaments, and machinery wielded by physician-led teams of hospital-based professionals and paraprofessionals, garbed in uniforms of starched white, surgical green, and auxiliary pink or blue. Underlying this image is the conception that medicine is shaped primarily by scientific and technological advances, and that its major impetus derives from a highly organized collective effort vigorously to preserve life, by attaining a progressive mastery over illness and preventable death.

However commonplace and accurate this notion of modern medicine may be in some regards, it is distorted and obsolete in others. It does not take into account a new and important set of developments in present-day medicine that seems to be gaining momentum. Over the course of

From The Milbank Memorial Fund Quarterly: *Health and Society,* Fall 1974, 445–483. Presented at the Conference on Medical Sociology, sponsored by the Polish Academy of Sciences, Warsaw (Jablonna), Poland, August 1973.

the past fifteen years, in a number of European and American societies, concerned interest in ethical and existential issues related to biomedical progress and to the delivery of medical care has become both more manifest and legitimate in medical circles and in other professional and organized lay groups as well. This is a phenomenon that merits sociological attention, for it suggests that a serious re-examination of certain basic cultural assumptions on which modern medicine is premised may be taking place.

This paper will identify some of the forms in which these moral and metaphysical problems are currently being raised in the medical sector of American society. It will also essay an interpretive analysis of the broader socio-cultural implications of the more general re-evaluative process that I believe is occurring in this fashion.

> Recent advances in biology and medicine make it increasingly clear that we are rapidly acquiring greater powers to modify and perhaps control the capacities and activities of men by direct intervention into and manipulation of their bodies and minds. Certain means are already in use or at hand—for example, organ transplantation, prenatal diagnosis of genetic defects, and electrical stimulation of the brain. Others await the solution of relatively minor technical problems . . . still others depend upon further basic research. . . .
>
> While holding forth the promise of continued improvement in medicine's abilities to cure disease and alleviate suffering, these developments also pose profound questions and troublesome problems. There are questions about who shall benefit from and who shall pay for the use of new technologies. . . . There will be questions about our duties to future generations and about the limits on what we can and cannot do to the unborn. . . . We shall face questions concerning the desirable limits of the voluntary manipulation of our own bodies and minds. . . . We shall face questions about the impact of biomedical technology on our social institutions. . . . We shall face serious questions of law and legal institutions . . . [and] problems of public policy. . . .
>
> . . . [A]s serious and vexing as these practical problems may be, there is yet another matter more profound. The biomedical technologies work directly on man's biological nature, including those aspects long regarded [as] most distinctively human. . . . The impact on our ideas of free will, birth, and death, and the good life is likely to be even more staggering than any actual manipulation performed with the new technologies. These are matters of great moment and we urgently need to take counsel from some of our best minds. . . .

The statement quoted above was not made by a physician, a scientist, or a philosopher. It was delivered by the Honorable Walter F. Mondale of Minnesota, a member of the United States Senate. He made these remarks from the floor of the Senate in 1971, as he introduced a bill to establish a National Advisory Commission on Health, Science and Society. The measure was intended to provide for "study and evaluation of the ethical, social and legal implications of advances in biomedical research and technology." What is particularly significant about the Mondale proposal is that it demonstrates that involvement with the issues it cites is not confined to medical and academic milieux. Rather, these matters have entered political and public domains in American society.

The specific advances in biology and medicine to which Mondale alludes are those most generally invoked in the various contexts where such ethical, existential, and social questions are pondered. Actual and anticipated developments in genetic engineering and counseling, life support systems, birth technology, population control, the implantation of human, animal, and artificial organs, as well as in the modification and control of human thought and behavior, are principal foci of concern. Within this framework, special attention is concentrated on the implications of amniocentesis (a procedure for detecting certain genetic disorders *in utero*),[1] *in vitro* fertilization, the prospect of cloning (the asexual reproduction of an unlimited number of genetically identical individuals from a single parent), organ transplantation, the use of the artificial kidney machine, the development of an artificial heart, the modalities of the intensive care unit, the practice of psychosurgery, and the introduction of psychotropic drugs. Cross-cutting the consideration being given to these general and concrete areas of biomedical development, there is marked preoccupation with the ethicality of human experimentation under various conditions, with the proper definition of death and the human treatment of the dying, and with the presumed right of every individual and group to health and adequate health care. Certain moral and metaphysical themes recur in the discussions of all these aspects of the so-called new biology and medicine. Problems of uncertainty, meaning, of the quality of life and death, of scarcity, equity, and distributive justice, of freedom and coercion, dignity and degradation, solidarity and societal community, and of the vigor with which one ought to intervene in the human condition are repeatedly mentioned.

The media and agencies through which these concerns are expressed

1. This technique involves the insertion of a hollow needle through the abdominal and uterine walls of a pregnant woman into the amniotic sac, and withdrawing fluid and cells shed by the fetus.

are manifold. Articles and editorials on these topics not only appear frequently in medical and scientific journals,[2] but also in popular magazines and daily newspapers. In the course of the week of July 8 to July 15, 1973,[3] for example, *The New York Times* published the following relevant items: two bulletin-type articles on the performance of two new heart transplants; two articles on recent cases of "euthanasia" or "mercy killing" that raise questions about the "right to die" and "death with dignity"; a long article reporting and analyzing a decision rendered by the Wayne County Circuit Court in Michigan that experimental psychosurgery may not be performed on persons confined against their will in state institutions, even when such a person's consent for this surgery is formally obtained; two feature articles with photographs, and an editorial on the ethical and legal implications of a case under investigation by three federal agencies and a Senate subcommittee, in which it is alleged that two mentally retarded black girls, ages twelve and fourteen, were sterilized by a federally funded family planning clinic in Montgomery, Alabama, without either their informed consent or that of their parents; another article with byline, announcing that based on comparable cases, the American Civil Liberties Union was filing a suit in federal district court, seeking to void as unconstitutional a North Carolina law allowing sterilization of "mentally defective" persons; a substantial article summarizing a report published in a journal of biomedical ethics concerning five experiments on human beings funded by grants from divisions of the Public Health Service that raise "disturbing ethical questions"; an article by one of the paper's medical writers on the "complex and not always obvious issues of medical research ethics" that have surfaced in a "recent spate" of stories of "abuse, real or potential," evoking "newly critical looks at medical ethics [by] Government and private citizens and new proposals for more effective controls"; and, finally, an article by the same writer on the redesigning of a national blood policy that is now under way in the United States with the goal of achieving an all-volunteer donor system in the next two years.

The numbers of books that have been published on such subjects and

2. In *Research on Human Subjects,* Barber, *et al.* (1973: 2), comment that, "the recent increase of concern in the biomedical research community . . . [about] the possible or actual abuse of the subjects of medical experimentation and medical innovation . . . can be seen perhaps most clearly in the dramatic rise of medical journal articles devoted to facets of this problem." Barber, et al. (1973: 2–3), report that, in a survey they made of articles listed in *Index Medicus* over the period 1950 to 1969, those that dealt with the ethics of biomedical research on human subjects increased "in both the absolute number and the proportion of articles in this area. . . . The figure begins to get large in 1966."

3. This is the week when I happened to be writing this section of my paper. In that sense, it was chosen randomly.

themes in the past ten years is impressive.[4] Leading the list, in saliency and frequency, is a group of books on death and dying. (For some major works on this subject, see Reference Note A.) The most famous of these, written by a psychiatrist, Dr. Elizabeth Kübler-Ross, and published in 1969, had sold over 100,000 copies in the paperback edition alone by the end of 1972. Presenting first-hand case materials based on her intensive work with incurably ill and dying patients, Dr. Kübler-Ross delineates what she considers to be the five psychological stages through which a dying person characteristically evolves. She both explicitly and implicitly affirms that persons passing through these "final stages of life," can be our "teacher[s]," helping medical professionals, and all of us, not to "shy away from the 'hopelessly' sick," as she feels we are inclined to do in American society. Those who "get closer" to the dying, she asserts, will not only "help them during their final hours . . . they will learn much about the functioning of the human mind, the unique human aspects of our existence, and will emerge from the experience enriched . . . perhaps with fewer anxieties about their own finality."[5] Less directly, Dr. Kübler-Ross's book also evokes questions about the rationality and humanity of our medical and cultural propensity to do everything possible to "save" and prolong life. If there is a phenomenon akin to a "death and dying movement" occurring in the United States, as we believe there may be, then Elizabeth Kübler-Ross is one of its charismatic leaders.[6]

Another important collection of books that has appeared in the last few years is devoted to the ethics and legal aspects of biomedical research on human subjects. (For prominent recent books in this area, see Reference Note B.) In all these books, the problem of the rights and adequate protection of subjects looms large, as does the question of how best to establish surveillance and social control over the activities of investigators, without unduly impeding research. A great deal of consideration is given to the necessity and difficulties of obtaining truly informed and voluntary consent from subjects. Special attention is focused on candidates for research who are already subject to particular kinds of dependence, disability, or constraint, such as children, persons who are mentally retarded or mentally ill, prisoners, the poor, and the minimally educated. The question of what constitutes the most just allocation of

4. For an excellent review-essay of the scope and content of the burgeoning literature on ethical and existential aspects of medicine published during the decade 1960–1970, see J. R. Elkinton (1970).

5. Elizabeth Kübler-Ross (1969: Preface, no page given).

6. Professor Diana Crane (who is also a member of the Department of Sociology of the University of Pennsylvania) and I are planning a paper on this phenomenon, tentatively entitled, "The Death and Dying Movement: A New Kind of Social Movement?"

limited and costly experimental therapies is debated in these works, along with the issue of when a society may expose some of its members to risk or harm, in order to seek benefits for them, for others, or for the society as a whole. Each of these volumes cites and examines problematic instances of human experimentation that are known to have taken place.

Two other types of relevant books are being published in significant numbers: those dealing with ethical and existential aspects of specific biomedical developments, and those that treat a broad range of such moral and metaphysical issues as they apply to numerous medical phenomena. (For examples of these two types of works, see Reference Note C.)

A number of social patterns applicable to this flow of articles and books are worthy of note. To begin with, the authors of these works come from a broad spectrum of fields, including journalism, politics, the law, the clergy, philosophy, ethics, theology, social science, social work, nursing, and psychiatry, as well as medicine and biology. Second, a considerable amount of the research and reflection on which these writings are based has been sponsored or supported by established private foundations like the Ford, Robert Wood Johnson, Joseph P. Kennedy, Jr., Rockefeller, and Russell Sage Foundations, by scholarly bodies, such as the American Academy of Arts and Sciences, the New York Academy of Sciences, the United States National Academy of Sciences, and by some government agencies, notably, several branches of the National Institutes of Health and the National Endowment for the Humanities.

What is perhaps more striking is the fact that the interest and work that these publications reflect have brought into being a network of new organizations whose principal *raison d'être* is to deal with these matters. Among the most prominent in the United States are the Institute of Society, Ethics and the Life Sciences in Hastings-on-the-Hudson, New York; the Society for Health and Human Values in Philadelphia; the Foundation of Thanatology in New York City; the Euthanasia Society of America and the Euthanasia Educational Fund, both in New York City; the Committee on the Life Sciences and Social Policy of the National Research Council, a division of the National Academy of Sciences in Washington, D.C.; and the Joseph and Rose Kennedy Institute for the Study of Human Reproduction and Bioethics, located at Georgetown University in Washington. With the exception of the two euthanasia societies, these groups, and others like them, have all been founded since 1969.[7]

7. In the international sphere, there are some comparable developments. For example, the Council for International Organizations of Medical Science (CIOMS), a non-governmental agency created in 1949 by the World Health Organization and Unesco to

Mention has been made of the National Advisory Commission on Health, Science and Society proposed by Senator Walter Mondale. In addition, the health subcommittees both of the Senate and the House of Representatives have been transformed by their respective chairmen, Senator Edward M. Kennedy of Massachusetts and Representative Paul G. Rogers of Florida, into groups that are actively engaged in conducting investigations and hearings on medical issues of social, ethical, and existential import, in raising public consciousness about these matters, and in proposing legislation and other control mechanisms bearing upon them. It is of some consequence to observe that the medico-moral concerns to which Mondale, Kennedy, and Rogers are addressing themselves have sufficient public resonance to enhance the political following and prestige of these men in the eyes of their local and national constituencies. The most important piece of legislation that has thus far resulted from their activities is the National Research Act (H.R. 7724) passed by both houses of Congress, and signed into law by President Nixon on July 12, 1974. Title II of this act established a temporary two-year National Commission for the Protection of Human Subjects of Biomedical and Behavioral Research. The commission, an advisory body to the Department of Health, Education, and Welfare (HEW), is composed of eleven members who were named by HEW Secretary Caspar Weinberger on September 10, 1974. Their task is to study a number of ethical issues set forth in the law. These include fetal research, the problem of obtaining informed voluntary consent for investigations in which children, prisoners, or persons who are mentally ill or retarded are asked to participate as subjects, and the ethics of psychosurgery. When the two-year life span of the commission is ended, a permanent council to deal with these matters will come into being.[8]

Their growing numbers and diverse backgrounds notwithstanding, the scholars, scientists, medical and legal practitioners, authors, foundation officials, organization members, and legislators seriously involved in considering ethical and existential aspects of biomedicine can be said to constitute a closely knit "social circle." Not only do they belong to overlapping groups and read each other's work attentively, but they partici-

---

re-establish scientific communications after World War II, has now turned its primary attention to interdisciplinary conferences and publications on topics such as the "protection of human rights in the light of scientific and technological progress in biology and medicine" (Round Table Conference scheduled to be held in Geneva, November 14–16, 1973). Furthermore, the CIOMS has recommended that a new international entity be established to explore the "moral and social issues" raised by new and forthcoming developments in biomedicine.

8. For a competent and critical account of the history of the National Research Act, its development and its provisions, see Culliton (1974a).

pate in many of the same formal meetings, meet informally, communicate with one another through correspondence and by telephone, call upon one another as consultants, and recommend each other for relevant assignments and honors.[9]

The new institutional forms that are being summoned forth by these developments in contemporaneous medicine extend beyond the establishment of pertinent contemplative and action-oriented groups. Another kind of emergent phenomenon is the gradual formation of "bioethics," an incipient new discipline. Its contours are still not clear. In the words of Daniel Callahan (1973: 68), "Most of its practitioners have wandered into the field from somewhere else, more or less inventing it as they go. Its vague and problematic status in philosophy and theology is matched by its even more shaky standing in the life sciences." Callahan (1973: 73) goes on to advocate that if bioethics is to develop into a full and accepted field, it should be interdisciplinary and problem- and case-focused in the following regard:

> . . . so designed, and its practitioners so trained that it will directly—at whatever cost to disciplinary elegance—serve those physicians and biologists whose position demands that they make practical decisions. This requires, ideally, a number of ingredients as part of the training . . . of the bioethicist: sociological understanding of the medical and biological communities; psychological understanding of the kinds of needs felt by researchers and clinicians, patients and physicians, and the varieties of pressures to which they are subject; historical understanding of the sources of regnant value theories and common practices; requisite scientific training; awareness of and facility with the usual methods of ethical analysis as understood in the philosophical and theological communities . . . and personal exposure to the kinds of ethical problems which arise in medicine and biology.

Although bioethics is still a tentative field, and its definition and legitimacy are under discussion, a comprehensive *Encyclopedia of Bioethics* already is in preparation. Its editor (Warren T. Reich, a former theology professor at Catholic University) and his staff are based at the Kennedy Institute of Georgetown University. Their advisory editors are drawn from multiple university, foundation, and government milieux. And the project is financed by the Kennedy Foundation and the National Endowment for the Humanities.[10]

9. A systematic study of the sociometry of this circle, its patterns of communication, and their consequences for intellectual growth and policy formation in this area, such as Diana Crane carried out in two scientific communities, would be illuminating. See Crane (1972).

10. An interesting history and sociology of science kind of question that might be posed here is whether there is any precedent or principle that would lead one to assume that the

Quite apart from the prognosis for bioethics as a discipline, a new conception of medical ethics seems to be unfolding in the medical profession. Increasingly, medical ethics is being viewed less exclusively as a code of professional etiquette. It is coming to be regarded as a component virtually of all medical decision making and to include the questions of how such decisions should be made and who should participate in them, as well as what ideally ought to be done in given cases. Even the conservative American Medical Association has expanded its ethical program to encompass these broader considerations, along with the dilemmas posed by recent biomedical advances.

But it is in medical schools that one sees the most significant activity in this regard. In 1970, for example, under the aegis of Drs. Robert M. Veatch and Willard Gaylin, both members of the Institute of Society, Ethics and the Life Sciences, the Columbia College of Physicians and Surgeons launched an experimental Medical Ethics Program (see Veatch and Gaylin, 1972). This Program included lectures, seminars, clinical case conferences, dinner-discussion meetings and intensive workshops for students in every stage of medical school training. An internship in medical ethics for several fourth-year students was also created; an interdisciplinary seminar on "the new biology and the law" that brought medical students together with students from Columbia Law School and the Union Theological Seminary was organized; and sessions on medical ethics for interested faculty and clinical staff were arranged. This Program has had wide repercussions. Its staff has made a survey of the teaching of medical ethics in medical schools throughout the country, has developed bibliographies and case studies that are available upon request, has acted as consultants to other medical schools, and, in June 1972, organized a National Conference on the Teaching of Medical Ethics. Although their survey revealed that in the curricula of most medical schools medical ethical issues are presented largely on an informal and somewhat *ad hoc* basis, institutional response to the Medical Ethics Program staff "suggests a rapidly developing interest in the [formal] teaching of medical ethics" (Veatch and Gaylin, 1972: 785). By October 1971, the program's staff already had been consulted by 29 American medical schools, in addition to faculty in biology, philosophy, religion, law, and social science departments; and about 150 representatives from medical school faculties attended the National Conference on the Teaching of Medical Ethics.

---

preparation of such an encyclopedia will help to establish a field that only potentially exists. For, normally, one would expect an encyclopedia to appear when a field is firmly rooted and recognized, with a sufficiently well-defined body of theory, methodology, and empirical data to be articulated.

In my view, one of the most significant patterns that Veatch and Gaylin (1972: 783) report is that their whole undertaking was initiated by medical students:

> Early in 1970 a group of students, upon hearing a lecture pointing out the ethical implications of the judgments made in the practice of psychiatry, approached the curriculum committee of the school and members of the Institute of Society, Ethics and the Life Sciences and asked that a full program be established, one which would make ethical and social perspectives an integral part of their medical education. . . .

This is consistent with what I believe to be a fundamental shift in the outlook of American medical students. It has been remarked that medical students of the late 1960s and early 1970s appear to be more socially concerned than their predecessors. They are especially outspoken about the inadequacies and inequities in the nation's system of health care delivery, about the responsibility that they feel the established medical profession bears for the existence of these deficiencies and injustices, and about their own determination to play an active role as physicians in eliminating them. How deep these concerns and commitments of the "new" medical student go, and how enduring they will prove to be is a matter of some debate not only among medical educators, but also among students themselves (who are inclined to be self-critical in this, as well as in other matters). Whatever their long-term import, these medical student tendencies are sufficiently notable to have elicited continuing discussion about whether or not they will persist under the impact of students' medical educational experiences and the demands that their subsequent medical careers will make upon them.[11] Accompanying the

11. Studies of the social backgrounds of men and women currently entering medical school, of the attitudes, values, sentiments and life experiences that led them to opt for medicine, and of the socio-psychological as well as cognitive learning that they undergo in the course of medical school, house officer training, and their early years of practice are very much needed. Whereas several such major studies of medical socialization were carried out in the 1950s, for reasons that merit investigation, no such studies that are comparable in depth and scope have been attempted more recently.

My own comments about medical student attitudes and interests set forth in this paper are based upon the data I gathered as chief field worker for a study of the education and socialization of medical students conducted in the mid-1950s by the Columbia University Bureau of Applied Social Research. *The Student-Physician* (Merton, et al., 1975) was a product of that investigation. My observations on medical students in the late 1960s and early 1970s are less extensive and systematic. They grow out of my role as a sociologist in the Departments of Psychiatry and Medicine of the University of Pennsylvania, and from the numerous opportunities that I have to visit other medical schools as a consequence of my continuing research and teaching in the sociology of medicine.

ostensible social consciousness of present-day medical students, and integrally related to it, is their manifest interest in ethical and existential aspects of medicine. Along with their concern about a more just allocation of material and immaterial medical resources in American society, one of the areas in which students' moral and metaphysical interests are most apparent is that of "death and dying." Their orientation is distinctly different from the attitudes toward death and the ambiance surrounding it that predominated in American medical schools twenty years ago. In a recent article, I have portrayed the contrast as follows (Parsons, *et al.*, 1972: 367–415):

> . . . In the medical school climate of the 1950's . . . faculty virtually never raised questions with students like "what is death?" "why death?" or "in what deeper senses, if any, does death differ from life?" Even in situations conducive to such querying—notably, the anatomy laboratory, the autopsy, or in the face of students' early confrontation with terminally ill patients—instructors rarely initiated such discussions. And if a student made a timorous effort to do so, he was likely to be silenced by classmates and faculty alike with the quip, "that's too philosophical." Decoded, this meant "the matters of which you speak are not sufficiently rational, objective, scientific or pragmatic to fall within the proper domain of medicine, or of truly professional behavior." It was also characteristic of this decade that [medical students and their teachers] were more inclined to speak euphemistically about the death of a patient—"he [she] expired," "passed on," or "was transferred to Ward X"—than straightforwardly to state that death had occurred. In sharp contrast to such medical attitudes in the 1950's (at least in academic milieux where new physicians were being trained and scientific research emphasized), the late 1960's and early 1970's appear very "philosophical." . . .

In addition to new organizations, new intellectual disciplines and new perspectives on the part of medical students and educators, certain spokesmen for medical practitioners, some legislators and sectors of the lay public, the ethical and existential refocusing of medicine has been accompanied by three other institutional responses. These consist of new guidelines, or codes, several moratoria, and a number of legal decisions and statutes.

Perhaps the most momentous guideline issued thus far is the new criterion for judging a person dead that was formulated and proposed by Harvard Medical School's Ad Hoc Committee to Examine the Definition of Brain Death (1968), chaired by Dr. Henry K. Beecher, and consisting of nine physicians, a lawyer, a historian of science, and a theologian. The Harvard report opened with the statement that the

Committee's "primary purpose [was] to define irreversible coma as a new criterion for death," and that there were two reasons why there was "a need for a definition":

> (1) Improvements in resuscitative and supportive measures have led to increased efforts to save those who are desperately injured. Sometimes these efforts have only partial success so that the result is an individual whose heart continues to beat but whose brain is irreversibly damaged. The burden is great on patients who suffer permanent loss of intellect, on their families, on the hospitals, and on those in need of hospital beds already occupied by these comatose patients. (2) Obsolete criteria for the definition of death can lead to controversy in obtaining organs for transplantation.

The report went on to identify and describe in detail the major characteristics of a state of irreversible coma, which indicates a "*permanently* [italicized in the report] nonfunctioning brain." These are: "unreceptivity and unresponsivity [to] externally applied stimuli and inner needs," "no spontaneous muscular movements or spontaneous respiration," and "the absence of elicitable responses." A flat or isoelectric electroencephalogram is held to be "of great confirmatory value." Furthermore, it is advocated that all the tests involved in these various determinations (which not only assess higher brain functions, but brain stem and spinal cord activity and spontaneous respiration, as well) should be "repeated at least 24 hours later with no change." In effect, the committee has recommended that the traditional method used by physicians for ascertaining and pronouncing death—the total cessation of all vital signs, that is, heart beat and respiration—be replaced by criteria for "cerebral death" or "brain death." Although this proposal has evoked a certain amount of commentary and some disquietude both in lay and professional circles, by and large, it has been well received, particularly in the medical community. "It is remarkable," Dr. David D. Rutstein of Harvard Medical School has observed with concern (1970: 386) that "a revolution in our cultural concept of death . . . this major ethical change . . . has occurred right before our eyes, and that this change is more and more widely accepted with little public discussion of its significance. This new definition . . . raises more questions than it answers."

A second important set of guidelines that has been set forth is that "relating to moral and ethical aspects of clinical investigation." A policy statement formulated in 1966 by the National Institutes of Health (NIH) and Public Health Service (PHS) (see Curran, 1970: 402–454) mandated that all clinical research involving human subjects supported by the NIH or PHS should be submitted to peer review by a committee of colleagues from the principal investigator's institution. That review should address itself to the rights and welfare of the human subjects involved, to the appropriateness of methods used to secure their informed consent, and to the risk-benefit ratio that the research entails. In 1971, these requirements were extended to all research on human subjects supported by any agency of the Department of Health, Education, and Welfare (HEW), the parent organization of the NIH and PHS. It is expected that over the next two years, the federal commission on ethics created by the National Research Act will supplement these general guidelines with more specific recommendations concerning psychosurgery, as well as clinical research on the fetus, the abortus, children, prisoners, and on the institutionalized mentally disabled. In principle, the commission has no regulatory authority, and its guidelines apply only to research funded by HEW. But its *de facto* influence on HEW and also on other agencies is expected to be considerable. For, the act requires that whenever the commission submits a recommendation to the Secretary of HEW, within 60 days, he must publish it in the *Federal Register* for comment. No more than 180 days later, the Secretary must act upon the recommendation, and if he decides to reject it, he must give his reasons for doing so, in writing. Although legally, the commission's deliberations are only relevant to research funded by HEW, many members of Congress are eager to have guidelines developed that are broadly applicable to other governmental organizations. And the commission has been asked to devise a mechanism to make the rules pertaining to human experimentation uniform.

A third type of policy statement has been set forth. This concerns a formal determination of where, on the experiment-therapy spectrum, a therapeutic innovation can be said to fall at a given phase in its development, and how and when, in the light of its status, it ought (or ought not) to be utilized. The best example of this sort of guideline is the statements on human cardiac transplantation issued by several different medical associations and government-affiliated medical groups (see Reference Note D). The over-all judgment on heart transplants that emerges from these position papers is that "the procedure of total cardiac replacement is so formidable, and uncertainties about the duration of life after replacement are so great, that physicians may be expected to be conservative about recommending it for an individual patient." Replacement cannot "as yet be regarded as an accepted form of therapy, or even an heroic one. It must be clearly viewed for what it is, a scientific exploration of the unknown, only the very first step of which is the actual feat of transplanting an organ." For this reason, "it may be reasonably assumed that imminent death will be the basic criterion for total cardiac replacement, at least in the near future." The "primary justification" for heart transplants at this time is deemed to be the "new knowledge of benefit to others in our society" that may come from it. In light of this view, and in recognition of the fact that "theologians, lawyers and other public-spirited persons, as well as physicians are discussing with deep concern the many new questions raised by the transplantation of vital organs," specific recommendations are made about the proper treatment of donors and recipients, the types of medical center qualified to undertake the operation, and the appropriate reporting of a transplantation both in medical journals and the mass media.

This period of "deep concern" about the issues raised by human experimentation and by biomedical advances like the increasing ability to maintain certain signs of life artificially, or to transplant human organs has also generated moratoria of several kinds. The first of these is what Judith P. Swazey and I have called clinical moratoria: the suspension of the use of a still experimental medical or surgical procedure on patients. This type of moratorium usually occurs in the stage of development of a new treatment when the uncertainties and risks associated with it are very high and become starkly apparent. Often, the patient mortality rate seems unbearable or unjustifiable. Pressure for such a moratorium can come from physician-investigators' own reactions to the situation and/or from "external" sources (from their colleagues, the institution in which they work, patients and their families, organizations sponsoring their research, and, less frequently, from the courts).

One important instance of such a moratorium (that we have personally had an opportunity to study) is the virtual cessation of human heart transplants (see Fox and Swazey, 1974: 122–148). As compared with 1968, for example, which was heralded by the mass media as the "Year of the Transplant," because 105 cardiac transplantations were performed throughout the world in that year alone, 1974 is a time when only an occasional heart transplant is done. The very high mortality rate of the persons who have undergone this procedure and their relatively short period of survival have been primary factors in the demise of the operation. The pressures that resulted in this moratorium came principally from within the medical profession itself, from prospective donors, recipients and their families, and from the mass media's continual publishing of heart transplant "box scores."

I have already identified another, more recent moratorium that was enacted into state law in July 1973 in a Michigan circuit court. Here, three judges rendered a unanimous opinion against the experimental performance of psychosurgery on persons involuntarily confined to state institutions. The judges based their opinion on the fact that brain surgery to attempt the correction of behavioral abnormalities like murderous aggression is "clearly experimental, poses substantial danger to research subjects, and carries substantial unknown risks," such as the blunting of emotions, the deadening of memory, the reduction of affect, and limitation of ability to generate new ideas. Furthermore, the judges reasoned, there is "no persuasive showing" that, in its present stage of development, this neurosurgical procedure would have its intended beneficial effects. In addition to the "unfavorable risk-benefit ratio" involved, it was concluded that the procedure ought not to be performed in the kind of case under consideration, because an involuntarily confined mental patient, living in an "inherently coercive atmosphere," has been intrinsically deprived of the basic conditions that are requisite to voluntary consent.[12]

This ruling is related to another type of moratorium that is being considered: the halting of medical experimentation on certain categories of persons. In this case, what is being contemplated is calling a moratorium on research conducted on "captives" of the state—prisoners, as well as involuntarily committed mental patients—in order to provide optimal conditions for re-evaluating the circumstances, if any, under which such research might be justified. The major impetus for this moratorium has been coming from the Senate Health Subcommittee, while a serious review of research on prisoners, mentally ill and mentally retarded persons, and on children is under way at the National Institutes of Health as part of their general inquiry into ethical guidelines for clinical research.[13] The federal commission on ethics

12. As already indicated, the ethics of psychosurgery is one of the major questions that the National Commission for the Protection of Human Subjects of Biomedical and Behavioral Research, created by the National Research Act, has been asked to study. Until their deliberations are completed, HEW is maintaining the position that psychosurgery is a highly experimental procedure, which should be done only under the most rigorously defined and controlled circumstances.

13. Concern over the conditions under which serious medical procedures ought to be carried out on persons whose ability to give informed voluntary consent may be constrained by institutional pressures to which they are subject, has spread beyond the realm of human experimentation. For example, this issue is being vigorously debated in connection with the controversy over the way in which sterilization has been carried out on girls and women in HEW-sponsored welfare programs. Earlier in this article, mention was made of the case of two mentally retarded, teenaged black, Alabama girls whose family was on relief, and who were sterilized without their own or their parents' understanding of the procedure or its consequences. Since the disclosure of that case, numerous others like it have been revealed. The American Civil Liberties Union, Ralph Nader's Health Research Group, the Mental Health Law Project, and at least fourteen other women's and civil rights groups, as well as some state legislators and the Senate Health Committee have all entered this arena of dispute. In response to the growing argument, the HEW has been trying to draft a set of acceptable regulations that would permit federal funds to be used for nontherapeutic sterilization, without violating informed voluntary consent or other civil and client rights. A number of lawsuits involving sterilization are in process. For a useful summary of the sterilization controversy, see Coburn (1974).

created by the National Research Act has also been asked to examine this question.

Two other moratoria which have developed are concerned with embryonic human life, in both the literal and figurative senses of the term. The first of these moratoria, a ban on fetal research, was officially declared by Title II of the National Research Act. The act charges the National Commission for the Protection of Human Subjects of Biomedical and Behavioral Research with the task of studying the nature, extent, and purposes of research involving living fetuses, as well as alternative ways of achieving these purposes. The commission has been given four months to complete this study, and to make recommendations to the Secretary of HEW. Until regulations are issued governing fetal research, HEW has decreed that its health agencies, grantees, and contractors "may not conduct or support research in the United States or abroad on a living human fetus, before or after the induced abortion of such fetus, unless such research is done for the purpose of assuring the survival of such a fetus."

This moratorium grows partly out of the fact that many more abortions are now being legally performed by reputable physicians, as a consequence of a recent United States Supreme Court decision (Roe *v.* Wade, 1973) in which it was stated that there exists "no compelling State interest" to warrant intervention in abortion decisions during the first two trimesters of pregnancy. The purpose of the moratorium is to give relevant experts the time and responsibility systematically to reflect on how to deal with the complex ethical and existential questions that increasing opportunities to conduct experiments on, or manipulate human fetuses have begun to raise. When does life begin? When does a living human embryo acquire "protectable humanity" (Kass, 1972: 32)? Is there any morally viable way in which proper consent for experimentation on human fetuses can be obtained? From whom should such consent be sought: from the would-have-been mother and/or father, for example? To whom does the aborted fetus "belong," or, at least, to whom should it be entrusted?

Certain states and cities have taken local measures to enforce a moratorium on fetal research. A law passed in California in 1973 forbids scientific experiments on human fetuses. Cleveland, Ohio, now has an ordinance that prohibits research on products of aborted human conception, or the medical use of these products. And on April 11, 1974, in Boston, Massachusetts, four physicians at Boston City Hospital were indicted by a county grand jury who accused them of violating an 1814 Massachusetts grave-robbing law, because they had studied the effect of two antibiotics on aborted fetuses, as well as on the women who had been pregnant with them.[14]

There is a second moratorium associated with the issues raised by fetal research, which has been developing. This is an incipient moratorium, rather than one that has already been formally declared, and it applies to *in vitro* fertilization: the implantation into a woman's uterine cavity of human egg cells that have been fertilized by human sperm in the test tube.

Various biologists, physicians, theologians, and philosophers, as well as members of the right to life movement have actively worked to deter this line of biomedical research. The *Journal of the American Medical Association* has gone so far as to publish a statement advocating a complete "moratorium on experiments that would attempt to implant an in vitro-conceptus into a woman's womb." Such individuals and groups have asserted that a ban on embryo implants ought to be enacted in order to avert the social, moral, and metaphysical problems that they anticipate would ensue from the successful application of a "new method for making babies" (Kass, 1972: 19). Among the objections to *in vitro* fertilization that have been raised, two are especially prominent. It has been contended that reproduction is human, personal, and moral only when conception results from so-called ordinary, heterosexual inter-

14. For a detailed account of the Boston "grave-robbing" case, see Culliton (1974b). Among the factors that brought it to the attention of the district attorney's office, the public, and the court were the political activities of a local branch of the National Right to Life Committee. This is an organized antiabortion movement, headed by the Reverend Warren A. Schaller, Jr., an Episcopal priest. The committee was incorporated as a non-profit organization in 1973, after several years of formal affiliation with the United States Catholic Conference. The 1973 Supreme Court decision on abortion added momentum to the right to life movement. It has been particularly vigorous and influential in Boston, in political and Roman Catholic milieux.

Another medical area in which ethical and existential issues closely associated with some of those raised by experimentation with human fetuses has been surfacing concerns the decisions made in special-care nurseries about whether or not to treat infants born with severe genetic defects. In an article entitled "Moral and ethical dilemmas in the special care nursery," which has attracted a great deal of professional and public attention, Dr. Raymond S. Duff and Dr. A.G.M. Campbell (1973) confront the question, "who decides for a child":

> . . . It may be acceptable for a person to reject treatment and bring about his own death. But it is a quite different situation when others are doing this for him. We do not know how often families and their physicians will make just decisions for severely handicapped children. Clearly, this issue is central in evaluation of the process of decision making that we have described. But we also ask, if these parties cannot make such decisions justly, who can? . . .

course (preferably within the confines of marriage). It has also been argued that because it is an "artificial," "engineered" mode of reproduction, *in vitro* fertilization may be conducive to the development of fetal anomalies and aberrations that could be difficult to prevent, remedy, or eliminate.[15]

One other genre of moratorium on biomedical research that has recently been invoked is perhaps the rarest of them all. Unlike the other moratoria, it does not concern clinical research that is conducted on human subjects. Rather, it addresses itself to certain kinds of experiments that involve the genetic manipulation of living cells and viruses, which a group of distinguished molecular biologists feel could have unpredictably hazardous "bioconsequences" for man. These scientists form the Committee on Recombinant DNA Molecules of the Assembly of Life Sciences of the National Research Council, which is under the aegis of the National Academy of Sciences. They have asked "scientists throughout the world" to join them in "voluntarily deferring" research which would insert either new bacterial or viral genetic material into

15. Some writers, like Leon Kass, who take this point of view also believe that because a "test-tube" embryo is so willfully created and "wanted," it may be more immoral to resort to abortion to destroy such a fetus (if, for example, it is seriously defective), than it would be if the fetus were conceived through sexual intercourse.

It should be mentioned here that in July of this year, at the annual scientific meeting of the British Medical Association at Hull, in Yorkshire, Dr. Douglas Bevis, a professor of gynecology and obstetrics at Leeds University, handed out a press release in which he announced that human embryos, conceived *in vitro* had been successfully implanted in the wombs of three women, who had given birth to normal babies. According to his report, the women had been infertile due to diseased, blocked, or missing Fallopian tubes. Eggs had been surgically removed from the women, fertilized in test tubes with their husbands' sperm, and subsequently reimplanted in the women's wombs. Dr. Bevis said that out of the thirty such attempts he had made, these were the only successful ones. The babies were said to range in age from twelve to eighteen months, and to be developing normally. By and large, medical scientists and physicians in Britain and abroad responded to this report with a mixture of skepticism and criticism. The fact that Dr. Bevis had worked in secret, had never published his findings in a medical scientific paper, and refused to reveal the identities or whereabouts of the infants and their parents, in the name of safeguarding their privacy, contributed to the disbelief and disapproval of the medical scientific community. The frustrated competitive ambitions of some clinical researchers who had aspired to be "first" in this area may also have been involved in the adverse reaction. But the apprehension that physicians and scientists expressed over the biological and moral consequences that might ensue from such an accomplishment, whenever it might occur, sounded genuine. In a later news report, Dr. Bevis was quoted as expressing chagrin over the reaction that his original press release had evoked. He affirmed that because of it, he was seriously considering calling a halt to this aspect of his work. If, in fact, he has now done so, his act can be thought of as a personally imposed moratorium, brought about by the disapproving attitudes of the medical profession, conveyed to Dr. Bevis largely through the media of mass communication.

bacteria (such as *Escherichia coli,* which commonly resides in the human intestinal tract), that could infect human beings. Their appeal was issued in the form of a cosigned statement that was published in July 1974 in *Science*, and also in *Nature* (Berg, *et al.*, 1974: 303). They have appealed to all investigators working in this area temporarily to halt these types of research "until attempts have been made to evaluate the hazards and some resolution of the outstanding questions has been achieved." They have also recommended that experiments that entail inserting animal genes into bacteria "should not be undertaken lightly." According to *Science,* this is "apparently the first time that biologists have publicly called attention to the possible public hazards of their own research" since 1969, and that they "have ever suggested that their own line of investigation should be halted" (Wade, 1974: 332).

A final indicator of the degree to which not only the American medical profession but the society at large has been deliberating ethical and existential issues associated with biomedicine is some of the legislation concerned with life and death matters that has been drafted in the last few years. The Kansas Death Statute, the Uniform Anatomical Gift Act and the United States Supreme Court decision on the Texas abortion case of Roe *v.* Wade represent three such major pieces of legislation.

In 1970, the state of Kansas (1970) adopted "An Act relating to and defining death," which was the first attempt legislatively to reformulate the standards for determining death. The Kansas statute sets forth and grants equal validity to two "alternative definitions of death": the traditional notion that a person is "medically and legally dead" if a physician determines "there is the absence of spontaneous respiratory and cardiac function and . . . attempts at resuscitation are considered hopeless"; and the new, irreversible coma criterion of death, which turns on the absence of spontaneous brain function if during "reasonable attempts" either to maintain or restore spontaneous circulatory or respiratory function, "it appears that further attempts at resuscitation or supportive maintenance will not succeed." The statute has received a great deal of attention. It has served as a model for similar legislation enacted in the state of Maryland in 1972, as well as for statutes now under consideration in a number of other jurisdictions. It has also been vigorously criticized for its dualistic approach to death, for the fact that it implies that a special definition of death, "brain death," has been developed to facilitate cadaveric organ transplantation, and because it mixes the question "When is the patient dead?" with "When may the doctor turn off the respirator?" and "When may a patient be allowed to die?" (see Capron and Kass, 1972: 104–111).

The Uniform Anatomical Gift Act is a statute designed to insure the provision of a more adequate supply of cadaver organs for transplantation than has been possible under traditional American law.[16] In this common law heritage, courts have ruled that in order for the next of kin adequately to discharge his (her) responsibility for proper burial of the deceased, that relative has the right to receive the body in the same condition as it was at the time that death occurred. Furthermore, in keeping with Judeo-Christian views on the sacredness of the body and respect for the dead, the body of a deceased person is not to be regarded as an item of commerce, to be bought, sold, or used to pay off debts. Courts expressed these premises by stating that there are no "property rights" in the body of the deceased. From this, there developed the ruling that a person could not direct the manner of his burial, because the body is not property and therefore not part of his estate.

In recent years, partly as a consequence of advances in the transplantation of corneal and other tissues, these views have come under increasing criticism. In the 1950s, donation statutes were enacted in several states which allowed an individual to determine what was to be done with his remains and to authorize donation for medical purposes. However, "most statutes failed to recognize the unique time requirements for organ and tissue removal and frequently viewed the act of donation as merely an extension of the testamentary disposition of property" (Sadler and Sadler, 1973: 16). The Uniform Anatomical Gift Act is the product of a three-year investigation into the matter of cadaver organ procurement that was conducted by a Special Committee of the National Conference of Commissioners on Uniform State Laws. The study was initiated in 1965. On July 30, 1968, the act was approved by the commission. It was endorsed by the American Bar Association on August 7 of the same year, and subsequently received support from virtually every relevant medical organization.

Blair and Alfred Sadler (1973: 25), who played a major role in drafting the Uniform Anatomical Gift Act, summarize its key provisions as follows:

> Under the Uniform Act, a person of sound mind and 18 years of age or more may give all or part of his body for any purpose later specified in the Act, the gift to take effect after death. In the absence of a contrary statement by the deceased before death, the next of kin (in a specified order of priority) are authorized to donate all or part of the body of the

16. For the account of the legal background of the Uniform Anatomical Gift Act and its provisions that follows, I am indebted to the writings of Blair L. Sadler and Alfred M. Sadler, Jr., especially their co-authored article, "Providing cadaver organs: three legal alternatives," 1973.

> deceased. The individual's interests are paramount to the next of kin's. Consequently, if a physician obtains adequate consent from an individual via the card mechanism [a donor card], he need not consult the next of kin for this purpose. The consent mechanism is greatly simplified under the Act and includes any written instrument such as a card carried on the donor's person, signed by the donor, and witnessed by two people. Consent by the next of kin can be obtained by an unwitnessed document or by recorded telegraphic or telephonic message.

The act forms the basis of new laws that have now been adopted in 51 jurisdictions, including the District of Columbia. It has "enjoyed unprecedented success," for, "never in the 78-year history of the National Conference of Commissioners on Uniform State Laws has a uniform act been so widely adopted during the first three years of consideration by state legislatures" (Sadler and Sadler, 1973: 25). When one considers the existentially fundamental and sacrosanct nature of what this act has legislatively influenced or altered, the ease and rapidity with which it has been widely accepted is all the more remarkable. Like the Kansas statute, it represents a basic change in conceptions of death and of the human body. It also places the desires and commitments of the individual with respect to his body at death above those held by members of his family (including inhibiting traditional religious sentiments that his relatives may hold in this connection). The act not only makes it easily possible for many individuals to make a sacrificial gift of life-in-death, but it also implicitly encourages them to do so. And it legally sanctions a new and ultimate way of expressing the Judeo-Christian injunction to be "our brothers' [and our] strangers' keepers" (Titmuss, 1971).

The Supreme Court abortion decision handed down on January 22, 1973, has been called one of the most controversial decisions of this century. Its core rulings are as follows:

> 1. A state criminal abortion statute of the current Texas type, that excepts from criminality only a *life saving* [italics in text] procedure on behalf of the mother without regard to pregnancy stage and without recognition of the other interests involved, is violative of the Due Process Clause of the Fourteenth Amendment.
> (a) For the stage prior to approximately the end of the first trimester, the abortion decision and its effectuation must be left to the medical judgment of the pregnant woman's attending physician.
> (b) For the stage subsequent to approximately the end of the first trimester, the State, in promoting its interest in the health of the mother, may, if it chooses, regulate the abortion procedure in ways that are reasonably related to maternal health.

> (c) For the stage subsequent to viability the State, in promoting its interest in the potentiality of human life, may, if it chooses, regulate, and even proscribe, abortion except where it is necessary, in appropriate medical judgment, for the preservation of the life or health of the mother.

The full legal and moral implications of this decision are too complex to discuss here. But several aspects of the ruling should at least be singled out, because they bear so directly on the matters we are considering. To begin with, although ostensibly the Court's decision grants a woman what it deems a "right" to abortion, it not only regulates this right, but also equivocates about it. For, while affirming the right, throughout its exposition, the Court recurrently declares that abortion is "inherently and primarily, a medical decision" to be "left to the medical judgment of the pregnant woman's attending physician." Furthermore, after the first six months of pregnancy, the life of the fetus, termed here "the potentiality of human life," is given precedence over all other considerations short of "the preservation of the life or health of the mother" herself. In these ways, the Court has adhered to the conviction about the sanctity of life and the importance of safeguarding it, that is so strongly upheld in the traditional legal as well as value system of American society.

The definition of health developed by the Court is a broad one. It has been extended to include "the stigma of unwed motherhood," "the distress for all concerned associated with the unwanted child," and an unspecified complex of conditions referred to as "the full setting of the case." The fact that such psychological and social considerations have been incorporated into this legal conception of health can be expected to have influence that extends beyond the abortion situation.

From our perspective, the dimension of the Court's decision that is the most significant and debatable is its implicitly expressed point of view on when human life begins. In his majority opinion, Associate Justice Harry A. Blackmun disclaims that the Court has done so. "We need not resolve the difficult question of when life begins," he states. "When those trained in the respective disciplines of medicine, philosophy, and theology are unable to arrive at any consensus, the judiciary, at this point in the development of man's knowledge, is not in a position to speculate as to the answer." However, in fact, the Court's decision does more than speculate. It says by implication that life does not begin during the first two trimesters. And it suggests that it begins in "the stage subsequent to viability" when it mandates the state, "if it chooses," not only to regulate, but to "even proscribe" abortion thereafter. The Court's position on the point at which personhood comes into being is more blurred. It reaffirms that "the word 'person,'" as used in the Fourteenth Amendment, does not include "the unborn"; but it does not distinguish the commencement of human life from the inception of personhood.

What emerges from the overview sketched out in these pages is a picture of a contemporaneous system of medicine that has reached a stage of development characterized by diffuse ethical and existential self-consciousness. This state of awareness involves the searching out of ways in which certain moral principles and metaphysical assumptions on which American society is traditionally based have been imperfectly realized, or violated. It also entails a reaffirmation of these premises and the initiation of various forms of social action intended to modify the medical system, so that it will more fully actualize its stated ideals. Among the major values and beliefs that are being reasserted are the right of every individual to some modicum of integrity, dignity, autonomy, and fulfillment; the right of all men, women, and children, independently of their personal endowment or social status, to have equal access to conditions, like the alleviation of illness-induced suffering, that are indispensable to their personal and collective humanity; and the right freely to give of one's self to others in life-enhancing ways.

In other regards, this ethical and existential *prise de conscience* in American medicine is accompanied by what appear to be major shifts in fundamental conceptions about health and illness, life and death. Increasingly, health is being defined as a universal human right, rather than as a privilege, a sign of grace, or an aleatory consequence of good fortune. Both health and illness are coming to be viewed in a more societal and less individualistic framework. Along with the absence of adequate medical care, lack of good health and affliction with illness are now more frequently attributed to society-borne stresses, deprivations, and injustices than they were in the past. A discernible modification is also occurring in the absolute nature of the cultural commandment to preserve life. While the sacredness of human life and its preservation continue to be affirmed, the new operational definition of death, the assertion, however qualified, of the right to abortion and the mounting insistence both on "the right to die" and on "death with dignity" all suggest that medicine is moving from an ethic based on the unconditional "sanctity of life" to one premised on the "quality of life."[17] Furthermore, the reconceptualization of death as "brain death" and the

17. This opinion was offered by the ethical scholar, Joseph Fletcher, in the course of a keynote address that he delivered at the National Conference on the Teaching of Medical Ethics, held at the Tarrytown Conference Center, Tarrytown, New York, on June 1–3, 1972. The conference was co-sponsored by the Institute of Society, Ethics and the Life Sciences and the Columbia University College of Physicians and Surgeons.

Supreme Court decision on abortion are important crystallized expressions of the point that American society has now reached, in what seems to be a gradual movement toward revised definitions of viable life, personhood, and "humanness."

Finally, numerous of the phenomena that I have identified and discussed suggest that there is a peaking of doubt over the unconditional virtue of still another important value-component of American medicine. The debates over how much ought to be done to maintain the life of terminally ill or dying patients, for example, the proposed moratorium on experimentation with *in vitro* fertilization, the apprehension about what the consequences of prospective developments in genetic engineering and behavior control may prove to be, all constitute challenges to the energetic, often aggressive meliorism for which American medicine is known. This blend of activism and meliorism rests on the assumption that out of unrestrictedly vigorous efforts to advance and apply biomedical knowledge and technique will come indisputable gains in human capacities, health and longevity, and in the alleviation of suffering. That conviction is now being thrown into question by many biologists and physicians, as well as by members of other professions, of government agencies, and of the general public. There is palpable skepticism about whether we have the "ultimate wisdom," to deal with the fact that "recent advances in biology and medicine suggest . . . we may be rapidly acquiring the power to modify and control the capacities and activities of men by direct intervention and manipulation of their bodies and minds" (Kass, 1971: 779, 786):

> If we can recognize that biomedical advances carry significant social costs, we may be willing to adopt a less permissive, more critical stance toward new developments. We need to reexamine our prejudice not only that all biomedical innovation is progress, but also that it is inevitable. Precedent certainly favors the view that what can be done will be done, but is this necessarily so? Ought we not to be suspicious when technologists speak of coming developments as automatic, not subject to human control? Is there not something contradictory in the notion that we have the power to control all the untoward consequences of a technology, but lack the power to determine whether it should be developed in the first place? . . .

Although the danger of excessively deterring medical progress is continuously reiterated, as the various moratoria cited suggest, the present trend is clearly in the direction of greater regulation of actual and incipient biomedical developments. The origins of this tendency are complex, but one of the important factors contributing to it is the growing belief that heroic medical scientific and technical efforts to improve "man's estate" are not unequivocally admirable or good, and that some of their consequences may be seriously harmful to collective as well as individual human existence.

The data presented suggest that modern American medicine is entering a new evolutionary stage. Organized concern about ethical and existential matters has become one of its salient features. The prominence and legitimacy of medicine's interest in these issues, and the involvement of many nonmedical groups in them indicate that a new rapprochement is taking place in the profession and the society. The overweening emphasis on scientific and technological phenomena that has characterized modern medicine, and its insistence on separating these so-called objective considerations from more "subjective" and "philosophical" orientations toward health and illness, life and death, seem to be giving way to a closer integration between the two dimensions. Some of the ethical and existential issues under consideration in medicine entail reaffirmations of ultimate values in American culture and society. Others involve either a modulation or a broader generalization of such basic values. In two critical respects, the ethical and existential reorientation that is occurring implies a sharper break with cultural tradition, and seems to presage more radical sociocultural change. We refer here to the major shifts away from some of the principles on which are founded the ethic of the sanctity of life and the ethic of progress.

It is tempting to assume that these value shifts and changes are predominantly, if not exclusively, caused by recent biomedical developments. And, indeed, this allegation is frequently made in the relevant literature. However, such an interpretation does not take note of the fact that in many other domains of American society, there is increasing preoccupation with the same questions of values, beliefs, and meaning that have been raised in the medical sector. Concern about the quality, dignity, and meaningfulness of life, about "assaults" on nature and the human condition, about distributive justice, equity, universalism, solidarity, community, and the "theme of the gift" (Mauss, 1954: 66) also have been prominent, for example, in the civil rights, peace, antipoverty, ecology, and population control movements visible on the American scene.[18] From my perspective, these are but some of the phenomena

18. Many of the participants in these social movements have been young people, relatively affluent and well-educated. Once again, this raises the question whether or not the "new" youth will prove to be effective agents of change. It also suggests the intriguing hypothesis that one of the prerequisites for widespread collective involvement in the kinds of moral and metaphysical issues dealt with here is a sufficient level of prosperity and fulfillment to free whole groups in a society from primordial anxieties about food, shelter, employment, and the like.

which suggest that the ethical and existential developments in contemporaneous medicine examined in this paper may be part of a broader process of change that is carrying American society into a new stage of modernity.

REFERENCES

Ad Hoc Committee of the Harvard Medical School to Examine the Definition of Brain Death—1968. "A definition of irreversible coma." Journal of the American Medical Association 205, No. 6 (August 25): 85–88.

Alsop, Stewart—1973. Stay of Execution, Philadelphia: J. B. Lippincott.

American College of Cardiology's Fifth Bethesda Conference—1968. "Cardiac and other organ transplantation in the setting of transplant science as a national effort." American Journal of Cardiology 22 (December): 896–912.

American Medical Association Judicial Council—1968. "Ethical guidelines for organ transplantation." Journal of the American Medical Association 205 (No. 6, August 5): 341–342.

Bailey, Herbert—1958. A Matter of Life and Death. New York: G. P. Putnam's Sons.

Barber, Bernard, *et al.*—1973. Research on Human Subjects. New York: Russell Sage Foundation.

Beecher, Henry K.—1970. Research and the Individual. Boston: Little, Brown and Company.

Berg, Paul, *et al.*—1974. "Letter to the editor—potential biohazards of recombinant DNA molecules." Science 185 (July 26): 303.

Brim, Orville G., Jr., *et al.* (eds.)—1970. The Dying Patient. New York: Russell Sage Foundation.

Cadbury, H. J., *et al.* (eds.)—1970. Who Shall Live? (for the American Friends' Service Committee). New York: Hill and Wang.

Callahan, Daniel—1970. Abortion. New York: The Macmillan Company.

———1973. "Bioethics as a discipline." The Hastings Center Studies 1, No. 1: 66–73.

Capron, Alexander Morgan, and Leon R. Kass—1972. "A statutory definition of the standards for determining human death: an appraisal and a proposal." University of Pennsylvania Law Review 121, No. 1 (November): 87–118.

Coburn, Judith—1974. "Sterilization regulations: debate not quelled by HEW document." Science 183 (March 8): 935–939.

Cooper, I. S.—1973. The Victim Is Always the Same. New York: Harper and Row.

Crane, Diana—1972. Invisible Colleges. Chicago: University of Chicago Press.

Culliton, Barbara J.—1974a. "National Research Act: restores training, bans fetal research." Science 185 (August 2): 426–427.

———1974b. "Grave-Robbing: the charge against four from Boston City Hospital." Science 186 (November 1): 420–423.

Curran, William J.—1970. "Governmental regulation of the use of human subjects in medical research." In Freund, Paul A. (ed.), Experimentation with Human Subjects. New York: George Braziller.

Cutler, Donald R. (ed.)—1968. Updating Life and Death. Boston: Beacon Press.

Delgado, José—1969. Physical Control of the Mind. New York: Harper and Row.

Dobzhansky, Theodosius—1962. Mankind Evolving. New Haven, Connecticut: Yale University Press.

Dubos, René—1972. A God Within. New York: Charles Scribner's Sons.

Duff, Raymond S., and A. G. M. Campbell—1973. "Moral and ethical dilemmas in the special-care nursery." The New England Journal of Medicine (October 25): 890–894.

Ehrenreich, Barbara, and John Ehrenreich—1970. The American Health Empire (a report from the Health Policy Advisory Center). New York: Random House.

Elkinton, J. R.—1970. "The literature of ethical problems in medicine" (Parts 1, 2, and 3). Annals of Internal Medicine 73: 3, 4, and 5 (November): 495–498, 662–666, 863–870.

Etzioni, Amitai—1973. Genetic Fix. New York: Macmillan Publishing Company, Inc.

Fletcher, Joseph—1967. Moral Responsibility. Philadelphia: The Westminster Press.

———. 1974. The Ethics of Genetic Control: Ending Reproductive Roulette. Garden City, New York: Anchor Press/Doubleday.

Fox, Renée C., and Judith P. Swazey—1974. The Courage to Fail: A Social View of Organ Transplants and Dialysis. Chicago: The University of Chicago Press.

Freund, Paul A. (ed.)—1970. Experimentation with Human Subjects. New York: George Braziller.

Fulton, Robert (ed.)—1965. Death and Identity. New York: John Wiley and Sons, Inc.

Glaser, Barney G., and Anselm L. Strauss—1965. Awareness of Dying. Chicago: Aldine Publishing Company.

———. 1968. Time for Dying. Chicago: Aldine Publishing Company.

Handler, Philip—1970. Biology and the Future of Man. New York: Oxford University Press.

Hendin, David—1973. Death as a Fact of Life. New York: W. W. Norton and Company, Inc.

Hinton, John—1967. Dying. Baltimore: Penguin Books.

Kansas—1970. Law of Mar. 17, 1970, ch. 378 [1970] Kan. Laws 994 (codified at KAN. STAT. ANN. § 77-202) (Supp. 1971).

Kass, Leon R.—1971. "The new biology: what price relieving man's estate?" Science 174, No. 4011 (November 19): 779–788.

———. 1972. "Making babies—the new biology and the 'old' morality." The Public Interest 26 (Winter): 18–56.

Katz, Jay, with the assistance of Alexander M. Capron—1972. Experimentation with Human Beings. New York: Russell Sage Foundation.

Kennedy, Edward M.—1972. In Critical Condition. New York: Simon and Schuster.

Kübler-Ross, Elizabeth—1969. On Death and Dying. New York: The Macmillan Company.

Ladimer, Irving (ed.)—1970. New Dimensions in Legal and Ethical Concepts for Human Research. Annals of the New York Academy of Sciences 169.

Ladimer, Irving, and Roger W. Newman (eds.)—1963. Clinical Investigation in Medicine. Boston: Boston University Law-Medicine Research Institute.

Lasagna, Louis—1968. Life, Death and the Doctor. New York: Alfred A. Knopf.
Lepp, Ignace—1968. Death and Its Mysteries. New York: The Macmillan Company.
London, Perry—1969. Behavior Control. New York: Harper and Row.
Mack, Arien (ed.)—1973. Death in American Experience. New York: Schocken Books.
Mannes, Marya—1973. Last Rights: A Call for the Good Death. New York: William Morrow and Company, Inc.
Mauss, Marcel—1954. The Gift. Translated by Ian Cunnison. Glencoe, Illinois: The Free Press.
Mendelsohn, Everett, Judith P. Swazey, and Irene Taviss (eds.)—1971. Human Aspects of Biomedical Innovation. Cambridge, Massachusetts: Harvard University Press.
Merton, Robert K., *et al.* (eds.)—1957. The Student-Physician. Cambridge, Massachusetts: Harvard University Press.
Monod, Jacques—1971. Chance and Necessity. New York: Alfred A. Knopf.
Moore, Francis D.—1965. Give and Take. Garden City, New York: Doubleday Anchor Books.
———. 1972. Transplant: The Give and Take of Tissue Transplantation (later edition of above title). New York: Simon and Schuster.
National Academy of Sciences—1968. "Cardiac transplantation in man: statement prepared by the Board of Medicine of the National Academy of Sciences." Journal of the American Medical Association 24 (No. 9, May 27): 805–806.
National Heart Institute—1969. Cardiac Replacement. A Report by the Ad Hoc Task Force, National Heart Institute. Washington, D.C.: U.S. Government Printing Office.
Noonan, John T., Jr.—1965. Contraception. Cambridge, Massachusetts: The Belknap Press of Harvard University.
Papworth, M. H.—1967. Human Guinea Pigs. London: Routledge and Kegan Paul; Boston: Beacon Press.
Parsons, Talcott, Renée C. Fox, and Victor M. Lidz—1972. "The 'gift of life' and its reciprocation." Social Research 39, No. 3 (Autumn): 367–415.
Pearson, Leonard (ed.)—1969. Death and Dying. Cleveland: The Press of Case Western Reserve University.
Peterson, Virginia—1961. A Matter of Life and Death. New York: Atheneum Press.
Ramsey, Paul—1970. Fabricated Man. New Haven, Connecticut: Yale University Press.
———. 1970. The Patient as a Person. New Haven, Connecticut: Yale University Press.
Rutstein, David D.—1970. "The ethical design of human experiments." In Freund, Paul A. (ed.), Experimentation with Human Subjects. New York: George Braziller.
Sadler, Blair L., and Alfred M. Sadler—1973. "Providing cadaver organs: three legal alternatives." The Hastings Center Studies 1, No. 1: 14–26.
Schneidman, Edwin S. (ed.)—1967. Essays in Self-Destruction. New York: Science House.
——. 1972. Death and the College Student. New York: Behavioral Publication.
Schoenberg, Bernard, *et al.*—1970. Loss and Grief: Psychological Management in Medical Practice. New York: Columbia University Press.

Sudnow, David—1967. Passing On. Englewood Cliffs, New Jersey: Prentice-Hall.

Supreme Court of the United States—1973. Roe *et al. v.* Wade. District Attorney of Dallas County, Appeal from the United States District Court for the Northern District of Texas, No. 70-18. Argued December 13, 1971; reargued October 11, 1972; decided January 22, 1973.

Swazey, Judith P., and Renée C. Fox—1970. "The clinical moratorium: a case study of mitral valve surgery." In Freund, Paul A. (ed.), Experimentation with Human Subjects. New York: George Braziller.

Taylor, Gordon—1968. The Biological Time Bomb. Cleveland: World Publishing Co.

Titmuss, Richard M.—1971. The Gift Relationship: From Human Blood to Social Policy. New York: Pantheon Books.

Torrey, E. Fuller (ed.)—1968. Ethical Issues in Medicine. Boston: Little, Brown and Co.

Veatch, Robert M., and Willard Gaylin—1972. "Teaching medical ethics: an experimental program." The Journal of Medical Education 47, No. 10 (October): 779–785.

Wade, Nicholas—1974. "Genetic manipulation: temporary embargo proposed on research." Science 185 (July 26): 332–334.

Williams, Robert H. (ed.)—1973. To Live and to Die. New York: Springer-Verlag.

Wolfenstein, Martha, and Gilbert Kliman (eds.)—1965. Children and the Death of a President. New York: Doubleday and Company, Inc.

Wolstenholme, G. E. W., and M. O. Connor (eds.)—1966. Ethics in Medical Progress. Boston: Little, Brown and Company.

REFERENCE NOTES

Reference Note A

Among major works on death and dying:

Stewart Alsop, *Stay of Execution.* Philadelphia: J. B. Lippincott, 1973.

Herbert Bailey, *A Matter of Life and Death.* New York: G. P. Putnam's Sons. 1958.

Orville G. Brim, Jr., *et al.* (eds.), *The Dying Patient.* New York: Russell Sage Foundation, 1970.

Robert Fulton (ed.), *Death and Identity.* New York: John Wiley and Sons, Inc., 1965.

Barney G. Glaser and Anselm L. Strauss, *Awareness of Dying.* Chicago: Aldine Publishing Company, 1965.

Barney G. Glaser and Anselm L. Strauss, *Time for Dying.* Chicago: Aldine Publishing Company, 1968.

David Hendin, *Death as a Fact of Life.* New York: W. W. Norton and Company, Inc., 1973.

John Hinton, *Dying.* Baltimore: Penguin Books, 1967.

Elizabeth Kübler-Ross, *On Death and Dying.* New York: The Macmillan Company, 1969.

Ignace Lepp, *Death and Its Mysteries.* New York: The Macmillan Company, 1968.
Arien Mack (ed.), *Death in American Experience.* New York: Schocken Books, 1973.
Marya Mannes, *Last Rights: A Call for the Good Death.* New York: William Morrow and Company, Inc., 1973.
Leonard Pearson (ed.), *Death and Dying.* Cleveland: The Press of Case Western Reserve University, 1969.
Virginia Peterson, *A Matter of Life and Death.* New York: Atheneum Press, 1961.
Edwin S. Schneidman (ed.), *Essays in Self-Destruction.* New York: Science House, 1967.
Edwin S. Schneidman (ed.), *Death and the College Student.* New York: Behavioral Publication, 1972.
Bernard Schoenberg, *et al., Loss and Grief: Psychological Management in Medical Practice.* New York: Columbia University Press, 1970.
David Sudnow, *Passing On.* Englewood Cliffs, New Jersey: Prentice-Hall, 1967.
Robert H. Williams (ed.), *To Live and To Die.* New York: Springer-Verlag, 1973.
Martha Wolfenstein and Gilbert Kliman (eds.), *Children and the Death of a President.* New York: Doubleday and Company, Inc., 1965.

Reference Note B

Recent works on human experimentation include:

Bernard Barber, *et al., Research on Human Subjects.* New York: Russell Sage Foundation, 1973.
Henry K. Beecher, *Research and the Individual.* Boston: Little, Brown and Company, 1970.
Paul A. Freund (ed.), *Experimentation with Human Subjects.* New York: George Braziller, 1970.
Jay Katz, with the assistance of Alexander M. Capron, *Experimentation with Human Beings.* New York: Russell Sage Foundation, 1972.
Irving Ladimer and Roger W. Newman (eds.), *Clinical Investigation in Medicine.* Boston: Boston University Law-Medicine Research Institute, 1963.
Irving Ladimer (ed.), *New Dimensions in Legal and Ethical Concepts for Human Research.* Annals of the New York Academy of Sciences 169, 1970.
M. H. Papworth, *Human Guinea Pigs.* London: Routledge and Kegan Paul; Boston: Beacon Press, 1967.
G. E. W. Wolstenholme and M. O. Connor (eds.), *Ethics in Medical Progress.* Boston: Little, Brown and Company, 1966.

Reference Note C

1. Among books dealing with ethical and existential aspects of specific biomedical development are:

Daniel Callahan, *Abortion.* New York: The Macmillan Company, 1970.
I. S. Cooper, *The Victim Is Always the Same.* New York: Harper and Row, 1973.
José Delgado, *Physical Control of the Mind.* New York: Harper and Row, 1969.
Theodosius Dobzhansky, *Mankind Evolving.* New Haven: Yale University Press, 1962.

Amitai Etzioni, *Genetic Fix*. New York: Macmillan Publishing Company, Inc., 1973.

Joseph Fletcher, *The Ethics of Genetic Control: Ending Reproductive Roulette*. Garden City, New York: Anchor Press/Doubleday, 1974.

Renée C. Fox and Judith P. Swazey, *The Courage to Fail: A Social View of Organ Transplants and Dialysis*. Chicago: The University of Chicago Press, 1974.

Perry London, *Behavior Control*. New York: Harper and Row, 1969.

Francis D. Moore, *Give and Take*. Garden City, New York: Doubleday Anchor Books, 1965.

Francis D. Moore, *Transplant: The Give and Take of Tissue Transplantation*. New York: Simon and Schuster, 1972 (later edition of work cited above).

John T. Noonan, Jr., *Contraception*. Cambridge, Massachusetts: The Belknap Press of Harvard University, 1965.

Richard M. Titmuss, *The Gift Relationship: From Human Blood to Social Policy*. New York: Pantheon Books, 1971.

2. Books treating a broader range of medical issues include:

H. J. Cadbury, *et al.* (eds.), *Who Shall Live?* (for the American Friends' Service Committee). New York: Hill and Wang, 1970.

Donald R. Cutler (ed.), *Updating Life and Death*. Boston: Beacon Press, 1968.

René Dubos, *A God Within*. New York: Charles Scribner's Sons, 1972.

Barbara and John Ehrenreich, *The American Health Empire* (a report from the Health Policy Advisory Center). New York: Random House, 1970.

Joseph Fletcher, *Moral Responsibility*. Philadelphia: The Westminster Press, 1967.

Philip Handler, *Biology and the Future of Man*. New York: Oxford University Press, 1970.

Edward M. Kennedy, *In Critical Condition*. New York: Simon and Schuster, 1972.

Louis Lasagna, *Life, Death and the Doctor*. New York: Alfred A. Knopf, 1968.

Everett Mendelsohn, Judith P. Swazey, and Irene Taviss (eds.), *Human Aspects of Biomedical Innovation*. Cambridge, Massachusetts: Harvard University Press, 1971.

Jacques Monod, *Chance and Necessity*. New York: Alfred A. Knopf, 1971.

Paul Ramsey, *Fabricated Man*. New Haven, Connecticut: Yale University Press, 1970.

Paul Ramsey, *The Patient as a Person*. New Haven, Connecticut: Yale University Press, 1970.

Gordon Taylor, *The Biological Time Bomb*. Cleveland: World Publishing Co., 1968.

E. Fuller Torrey (ed.), *Ethical Issues in Medicine*. Boston: Little, Brown and Co., 1968.

Reference Note D

Statements on human cardiac transplantation include:

National Academy of Sciences, "Cardiac transplantation in man: statement prepared by the Board of Medicine of the National Academy of Sciences." *Journal of the American Medical Association* 24 (No. 9, May 27, 1968): 805–806.

American College of Cardiology's Fifth Bethesda Conference, September

28–29, 1968, "Cardiac and other organ transplantation in the setting of transplant science as a national effort." *American Journal of Cardiology* 22 (December 1968): 896–912.

National Heart Institute, *Cardiac Replacement.* A Report by the Ad Hoc Task Force, National Heart Institute. Washington, D.C.: U.S. Government Printing Office, October 1969.

American Medical Association Judicial Council, "Ethical guidelines for organ transplantation." *Journal of the American Medical Association* 205 (No. 6, August 5, 1968): 341–342.

For a fuller discussion of these statements, see:

Renée C. Fox and Judith P. Swazey, *The Courage to Fail: A Social View of Organ Transplants and Dialysis.* Chicago: The University of Chicago Press, 1974, particularly pages 78–83.

Advanced Medical Technology—Social and Ethical Implications

INTRODUCTION

During the past decade, from the mid-1960s to the present, there has been a progressive outpouring of publications on the social, ethical, theological, and legal implications of developments in biomedical research and technology. The appearance of this now vast literature has coincided with the emergence of a new area of inquiry and action that has come to be known as bioethics.[1] In the words of Daniel Callahan (1973e), a philosopher-ethicist who has pioneered in this field, "Bioethics is not yet a full discipline. Most of its practitioners have wandered into the field from somewhere else, more or less inventing it as they go. . . . It is not yet a genuine discipline as that concept is usually understood in the academic and scientific communities."

1. It is unclear who coined the term bioethics. Van Rensselaer Potter, a biologist who has conducted cancer research throughout his career, claims to have invented this new word and the field that goes with it (Potter 1970, 1971). Potter views bioethics as a "science of survival . . . built on the science of biology and enlarged beyond the traditional boundaries to include the most essential elements of the social sciences and the humanities with emphasis on philosophy in the strict sense, meaning 'love of wisdom' " (Potter 1971: 1–2).

From *Annual Review of Sociology* 2 (1976): 231–268.

From its inception, bioethics has been multidimensional and cross-disciplinary in orientation and content. Formal statements about the primary participants in the discussion, research, and writing that it has entailed are likely to cite sociologists along with "physicians, biologists, psychologists . . . lawyers, historians and philosophical and religious ethicists" (Walters 1975). However, an examination of the literature on bioethical issues associated with advances in medical science, technology, and therapy reveals a remarkable paucity of work by sociologists or by other social scientists in this area. The relative absence of sociological articles and books concerned with these aspects of biomedical knowledge and techniques is surprising; many of the questions of value and belief with which the bioethics literature is concerned are appropriate foci for social research as well as for philosophical, theological, medical, and legal inquiry. Furthermore, the growth of intellectual, professional, and public interest in ethical and existential issues that this literature reflects is an important sociocultural happening that merits sociological study.

This review identifies some of the ways in which the new bioethical concern has been manifesting itself on the American scene during the past ten years. It then proceeds to examine certain attributes of the literature associated with this concern. Attention is focused on the sparse contribution sociologists have made to the literature. In this connection, some observations on the phenomena, concepts, and issues with which sociologists of medicine have more characteristically dealt are presented. Finally, the relatively few books and articles on socioethical implications of biomedical research, therapeutic innovation, or technology written by sociologists are discussed, both from the point of view of the questions that they treat and the social circle that their authors constitute.

MANIFESTATIONS OF BIOETHICAL CONCERN

The bioethical concern that has surfaced in recent years has crystallized around particular biomedical advances and cultural themes (Fox 1974b):

> . . . Actual and anticipated developments in genetic engineering and counseling, life support systems, birth technology, population control, the implantation of human, animal, and artificial organs, as well as in the modification and control of human thought and behavior are principal foci of concern. Within this framework, special attention is concentrated on the implications of amniocentesis (a procedure for detecting certain genetic disorders *in utero*), *in vitro* fertilization, the prospect of cloning (the asexual reproduction of an unlimited number of genetically identical individuals from a single parent), organ transplantation, the use of the artifi-

> cial kidney machine, the development of an artificial heart, the modalities of the intensive care unit, the practice of psychosurgery, and the introduction of psychotropic drugs. Cross-cutting the consideration being given to these general and concrete areas of biomedical development, there is marked preoccupation with the ethicality of human experimentation under various conditions, with the proper definition of death and the human treatment of the dying, and with the presumed right of every individual and group to health and adequate health care. Certain moral and metaphysical themes recur in the discussions of all these aspects of the . . . new biology and medicine. Problems of uncertainty, meaning, of the quality of life and death, of scarcity, equity, and distributive justice, of freedom and coercion, dignity and degradation, solidarity and societal community, and of the vigor with which one ought to intervene in the human condition are repeatedly mentioned.

Since the mid-1960s, a number of new centers and programs have been established whose primary reason for existence is to deal with these matters. Among the most preeminent are the Institute of Society, Ethics and the Life Sciences in Hastings-on-Hudson, New York; the Joseph and Rose Kennedy Institute for the Study of Human Reproduction and Bioethics, located at Georgetown University in Washington, D.C.; the Society for Health and Human Values in Philadelphia; the Foundation of Thanatology in New York City; the Department of Humanities program at the Pennsylvania State University College of Medicine in Hershey; the Institute for the Medical Humanities at the University of Texas Medical Branch in Galveston; the Harvard University Program on Technology and Society[2]; and the Harvard Interfaculty Program in Medical Ethics. In addition, organizations such as the Euthanasia Society of America and the Euthanasia Education Fund, both in New York City, which were founded in an earlier era, have acquired greater visibility during the bioethics decade. These organizations and programs and others like them have received sponsorship or support from an impressive array of private foundations, scholarly bodies, and government agencies, such as the Ford, Robert Wood Johnson, Joseph P. Kennedy, Jr., Andrew W. Mellon, Rockefeller, and Russell Sage foundations; the National Academy of Sciences, the National Institute of Medicine; the American Academy of Sciences; the New York Academy of Sciences; the National Endowment for the Humanities; and the National Institutes of Health (Branson 1975, Fox 1974b).

2. The Harvard Program on Technology and Society, founded in 1964, terminated in 1972. As its name implies, it was not only concerned with the consequences and implications of biomedical developments, but of scientific advance and technology more generally.

During the same period, a number of new guidelines and codes relevant to bioethical issues have been developed. These include the "definition of irreversible coma as the new criterion of death," proposed by the Harvard Medical School's Ad Hoc Committee to Examine the Definition of Brain Death (1968), the "Patient's Bill of Rights" presented by the American Hospital Association (1972), and the institutional guidelines for human research adopted by the Food and Drug Administration, on the one hand, and the Department of Health, Education, and Welfare-National Institutes of Health-Public Health Service complex, on the other (U.S. Dept. Health, Educ., Welfare, Publ. Health Serv. and Natl. Inst. Health 1971, U.S. Dept. Health, Educ., Welfare, Natl. Inst. Health 1974, U.S. Dept. Health, Educ., Welfare 1974, Curran 1970, Frankel 1972).

In addition, a series of legislative and judicial actions with bioethical import have been occurring. A number of public hearings on "ethical, social and legal implications of advances in biomedical research and technology"[3] have been held by the U.S. Congress, among which the 1972 investigation into the Tuskegee syphilis study, which was partly funded by federal agencies, evoked the greatest amount of political, public, and symbolic attention (U.S. Cong., Senate Comm. on Labor, Publ. Welfare 1973; U.S. Dept. Health, Educ., Welfare, Publ. Health Serv. 1973). On July 12, 1974, Public Law 93-348, Title II, brought into being a temporary two-year National Commission for the Protection of Human Subjects of Biomedical and Behavioral Research. This is an eleven-person group of professionals drawn from medicine, psychophysiology, the law, theology, and philosophy, whose task is to study a designated set of bioethical issues. These include fetal research; the problem of obtaining informed voluntary consent for investigations in which children, prisoners, or persons who are mentally ill or retarded are asked to participate as subjects; and the ethics of psychosurgery. In the fall of 1975, a bill to establish the commission as a permanent body, and to extend its membership and jurisdiction was introduced into the Senate. A Uniform Anatomical Gift Act has been adopted in fifty-one jurisdictions, which permits persons to donate all or parts of their bodies to be used for medical purposes after their death (Sadler, Sadler & Stason 1968; Sadler & Sadler 1973). Beginning with the Kansas Death

3. From a speech delivered in 1971 by U. S. Senator Walter F. Mondale of Minnesota on the floor of the Senate, as he introduced a bill to establish a National Commission on Health, Science and Society. Along with Senator Mondale, other members of the United States Congress who have been consistently involved in bioethical issues include Senators James Buckley, Edward Kennedy, and Jacob Javits; and Congressmen Emilio Daddario and Paul Rogers.

Statute of 1970, eight states have passed legislation that places the new "irreversible coma" criterion of brain death on an equal legal footing with the traditional pronouncement of death on the basis of cessation of respiratory and cardiac function (Curran 1971, Kennedy 1971, Capron & Kass 1972, Capron 1973). Through its 1973 ruling on the case of Roe *v*. Wade, the United States Supreme Court granted the pregnant woman and the attending physician greater rights to determine whether or not an abortion will be performed. Also, in its decision on Doe *v*. Bolton, handed down in the same year, the Court stated that private hospitals may be barred from adopting restrictions on abortion eligibility that are more severe than those imposed by state law. During the past decade the Supreme Court has also arrived at several decisions that have advanced the "right to treatment" concept. In Rouse *v*. Cameron (1966), the Court ruled that an involuntarily committed patient has such a right to treatment, that the court has the responsibility to determine whether or not he (she) is receiving it, and if not, why. In the case of Wyatt *v*. Stickney (1971), the Court decided that programs of treatment in state mental hospitals were scientifically and medically inadequate and thus deprived patients of their constitutional rights. Defendants were given six months to implement satisfactory treatment programs. Most recently, in the case of Donaldson *v*. O'Connor (1974), the Court ruled against the involuntary, purely custodial confinement of untreated, mentally ill persons who are not dangerous to themselves or others, and who can live in the community with the help of family or friends. The plaintiff in this case was not judged to have been deprived of a constitutional right to receive treatment, but he was released from the hospital and awarded damages for the fourteen and a half years in which he had been institutionalized with little or no psychiatric care or therapy. Finally, in 1975–1976 the New Jersey courts were asked for a decision in the unprecedented case of Karen Ann Quinlan, whose parents petitioned for authorization to turn off a respirator that had helped to keep her alive in a "persistent vegetative state" for almost a year. The Superior Court denied this request on the ground that it would take life from a "person who is not brain dead by present known medical criteria," and who has the constitutional "right to live," but not the "right to die" (Superior Court of New Jersey 1975). The case was appealed to the State Supreme Court, which rendered a "declaratory relief" judgment, grounded in the "right of privacy." Mr. Quinlan was named his daughter's guardian and empowered to discontinue the life-support apparatus, if attending physicians and the hospital ethics committee agreed that there was "no reasonable possibility" that she would return to a "cognitive, sapient state" (Supreme Court of New Jersey 1976).

Many of these developments have been accompanied by wide media coverage, generating a huge body of newspaper and magazine articles on the biomedical advances, ethical and existential issues, cultural themes, new institutions and guidelines, and legislative and judicial actions involved. In addition, an impressive number of scholarly articles and books on these matters have been published during the same ten-year period. This literature is too extensive to review systematically or to summarize,[4] but various bibliographies have been published that provide useful maps to it. For example, there is the *Hastings Center Bibliography of Society, Ethics and the Life Sciences* (Sollitto & Veatch 1973; Sollitto, Veatch & Fenner 1975); the Kennedy Institute *Bibliography of Bioethics* (Walters 1975); and the report and annotated bibliography on *Ethical Issues in Health Services,* published by the Department of Health, Education, and Welfare (Carmody 1974). There is an array of National Library of Medicine bibliographies on particular bioethical subjects, assembled by its Literature Search Program (human experimentation, informed consent, death, psychosurgery, genetic counseling, genetic engineering, transplantation, and hemodialysis, among others).[5] There are bibliographies on special bioethical topics such as abortion, genetics, hemodialysis, organ transplantation, and death and dying, compiled by authors working intensively in these areas, among which the death and dying bibliographies are the most conspicuous (Clouser & Zucker 1974, Sorenson 1973, Fox & Swazey 1974a, Kübler-Ross 1969, Kutscher 1969, Kalish 1970, Smith & Penry 1972, McCormick 1973, Crane 1975a).

INTELLECTUAL AND SOCIAL ATTRIBUTES OF THE BIOETHICAL LITERATURE

Philosophical and theological ethicists, physicians (particularly psychiatrists), biologists, and lawyers are the most prolific and prominent contributors to the literature. The ethicist authors predominate, in number and in their intellectual and public policy influence. Some of the major authors in each of these clusters are:

1. In the philosopher-theologian group: Sissela Bok, Daniel Callahan, K. Danner Clouser, Arthur J. Dyck, John C. Fletcher, Joseph

4. This review article represents a responsibly comprehensive, but by no means exhaustive survey of the literature.

5. These are available from the Literature Search Program, National Library of Medicine, Bethesda, Maryland 20014.

Fletcher, James M. Gustafson, Albert R. Jonsen, Richard A. McCormick, Paul Ramsey, Kenneth Vaux, and Robert M. Veatch.

2. In the physician-biologist group: Henry K. Beecher, Eric J. Cassell, Theodosius Dobzhansky, Raymond S. Duff, H. Tristram Engelhardt, Jr., Willard Gaylin, Leon R. Kass, Jay Katz, Elizabeth Kübler-Ross, Marc Lappé, Robert C. Morison, Robert F. Murray, Jr., Edmund Pellegrino, Jonas B. Robitscher, and Laurence R. Tancredi. (H. Tristram Engelhardt, Jr., is a physician-philosopher, with a Ph.D. in philosophy, as well as a doctorate in medicine. Jonas B. Robitscher is a psychiatrist-lawyer, with a doctorate in jurisprudence, as well as a doctorate in medicine.)
3. In the lawyer group: Alexander Morgan Capron, William J. Curran, and Charles Fried.[6]

6. In the philosopher-theologian group: Sissela Bok (1970, 1973, 1974a, 1974b, 1975; Bok & Behnke 1975); Daniel Callahan (1969a,b, 1970a,b, 1971a,b, 1972, 1973a,b,c,d,e,f,g, 1974a,b, 1975; Callahan & Gaylin 1974); K. Danner Clouser (1973a,b,c,d, 1975a,b; Clouser & Zucker 1974); Arthur J. Dyck (1969, 1971a,b, 1972, 1973a,b,c,d, 1975; Dyck & Richardson 1967); John C. Fletcher (1967, 1971, 1972, 1973a,b,c, 1974, 1975a,b); Joseph Fletcher (1954, 1967, 1968, 1969, 1971, 1973a,b, 1974a,b); James M. Gustafson (1970, 1973a,b,c, 1975a,b,c; Lappé, Roblin & Gustafson 1974; Gustafson & Pizzulli 1975); Hans Jonas (1970, 1973, 1974); Albert R. Jonsen (1973, 1974, Jonsen et al. 1975a,b); Richard A. McCormick (1972, 1973a,b,c, 1974a,b,c, 1975); Paul Ramsey (1950, 1967, 1968, 1970a,b,c, 1971, 1972, 1973a,b,c,d, 1974, 1975); Kenneth Vaux (1970, 1974); and Robert M. Veatch (1971a,b,c, 1972a,b,c,d,e,f, 1973, 1974a,b, 1975a,b; Veatch & Draper 1971; Veatch & Gaylin 1972; Veatch & Clouser 1973; Veatch, Gaylin & Morgan 1973; Veatch & Sollitto 1973; Veatch & Steinfels 1974).

In the physician-biologist group: Henry K. Beecher (1959a,b, 1966a,b,c, 1968, 1969a,b,c, 1970a,b,c; Curran & Beecher 1969); Eric J. Cassell (1969, 1970, 1973a,b,c); Theodosius Dobzhansky (1962, 1967a,b, 1970, 1973a,b); Raymond S. Duff (Duff & Campbell 1973); H. Tristram Engelhardt, Jr. (1973a,b,c,d, 1974, 1975a,b); Willard Gaylin (1965, 1972a,b,c, 1973a,b,c,d, 1974a,b; Veatch & Gaylin 1972; Veatch, Gaylin & Morgan 1973; Gaylin et al. 1973; Gaylin & Callahan 1974; Gaylin & Lappé 1975); Leon R. Kass (1971a,b,c, 1972, 1973, 1975; Capron & Kass 1972); Jay Katz (1969, 1970; Katz, Goldstein & Dershowitz 1967; Katz, Capron & Glass 1972; Katz & Capron 1975); Elizabeth Kübler-Ross (1969, 1974, 1975); Marc Lappé (1971, 1973a,b,c,d,e, 1974, 1975; Lappé, Roblin & Gustafson 1974); Robert S. Morison (1971, 1973a,b, 1974; Morison & Twiss 1973); Robert F. Murray, Jr. (1972, 1973, 1974; Murray & Sable 1974); Edmund Pellegrino (1969a,b, 1971a,b, 1972, 1973a,b, 1974a,b, 1975); Jonas B. Robitscher (1966, 1967, 1972a,b, 1973, 1975); and Laurence R. Tancredi (1975; Tancredi & Clark 1972; Tancredi & Barsky 1974).

In the lawyer group: Alexander Morgan Capron (1972, 1973a,b,c,d, 1975a,b,c,d; Katz, Capron & Glass 1972; Capron & Kass 1972; Capron & Green 1974; Katz & Capron 1975); William J. Curran (1959, 1966, 1970, 1971a,b,c, 1972a,b, 1973a,b,c, 1974, 1975a,b; Curran & Beecher 1969; Curran et al. 1973); and Charles Fried (1970, 1973a,b, 1974).

A majority of the authors who have made important contributions to the bioethics literature are active members either of the Hastings Institute of Society, Ethics and the Life Sciences, or of the Center for Bioethics of the Kennedy Institute. Some of them are members of both. Many of these authors received their professional education in the same schools—Yale, Johns Hopkins, Harvard, and Columbia—and those who are academics are clustered in certain universities, for example, Boston University, Cornell, Georgetown, Princeton, and the University of Pennsylvania, as well as the ones already cited.

Intellectuals of Catholic and Protestant background are more numerous and salient in the bioethics literature than intellectuals of Jewish origin. This is especially noticeable in the philosophical and theological ethicist subgroup, and the least true of the biomedical subgroup. A significant number of ethicist authors belong to the tradition of Christian ethics. Their training and orientation are more philosophical than theological. Even the theologians in this group of authors tend to develop their analyses in a philosophical rather than a theological framework.

The paucity of Jewish ethicists who have contributed to bioethics up to now may be related to the fact that the tradition of religious ethics has been predominant; religiously oriented Jewish ethicists are not as numerous as Christian ethicists. Several rabbis have suggested that this may be associated with the legalistic definition of good and bad in orthodox Jewish tradition, which has also influenced modern, liberal Judaism. There is a vast body of laws (*mitzvot*) for behavior in Jewish tradition, all of which are believed to have been commanded by God. In this framework one does something not because it is right or wrong, but because God commands it. Following the commandment is "the good," and not following it invites divine punishment.[7]

Although philosophers in the tradition of religious, particularly Christian, ethics have thus far had the greatest influence on the development of bioethics, this may be changing. During the past few years, the more general field of philosophical ethics has begun to pay a significant amount of attention to medical ethics. A Committee on Philosophy and Medicine has been formed within the American Philosophical Association. Its chairman is John Ladd of Brown University. The other members of the committee are H. Tristram Engelhardt, Jr. (University of Texas Medical Branch, Galveston), Holly Goldman (University

7. Personal communication, Rabbi Martin P. Beifield, Jr., Congregation Rodeph Shalom, Philadelphia, December 16, 1975.

of Michigan), Samuel Gorovitz (University of Maryland), David Mayo (University of Minnesota), and William Ruddick (New York University).

The increasing importance of medical ethics for philosophers is partly related to certain developments in American philosophical ethics since 1950. During the first half of the twentieth century, in the United States as in other English-speaking and -writing countries, metaethics, especially the analysis of ethical language, dominated the field. In the past twenty-five years, however, although work in metaethics has continued, an emphasis on normative ethics has been reintroduced into the discipline. According to Carl Wellman (1972),[8] race relations and civil rights were among the first specific moral issues on which professional philosophers focused their attention when this trend toward normative ethics began to manifest itself. Philosophers next began to deal with questions of the just war, civil disobedience, and violence. Their recent work in medical ethics is a continuation and extension of this development.

The philosopher, biomedical, and jurist authors cited have written about the whole gamut of bioethical concerns, but have devoted particular attention to several issues: human experimentation (especially questions of informed consent, notably problems of experimenting with fetuses); abortion (where again, the biological, legal, ethical, and human status of the fetus is one of the central questions pursued); genetic screening and counseling; and death and dying (problems of defining death, of making decisions about life-saving treatment, and of euthanasia, as well as of caring for dying patients). The bioethics literature on death and dying intersects with a much larger body of more popular writings on this subject that have been published in the last ten years. Exhortative, emotional, filled with personal testimony, often religious in tone, and sometimes cultic, these writings suggest that there is a phenomenon akin to a death and dying movement occurring in the United States, and that Elizabeth Kübler-Ross is one of its principal charismatic leaders[9] (Fox 1974b).

By and large, the bioethical literature is based on the assumption that the ethical and existential concern that has arisen in the biomedical

8. The analysis of "Ethics Since 1950" by Carl Wellman (Department of Philosophy, Washington University, St. Louis, Missouri) contained in his article was supplemented by a personal communication, dated December 8, 1975, that I received from him.

9. In her most recent talks and writings, Dr. Kübler-Ross has been presenting what she considers to be scientific evidence of a life after death, based on her interviews with many patients who "died" (showed no vital signs or brain waves), and then were "brought back to life" through heroic medical means (Kübler-Ross 1975).

sector of the society has been caused by biological and medical advances. Roy Branson (1975) states this widely held view in the following way: "In the late sixties, with the arrival of spectacular developments in medicine and biology such as heart and kidney transplants, and possibilities for genetic engineering, a wider public became interested in ethical issues raised by medicine and biology. A new era in the ethical reflection on medicine had begun." Partly because of their biomedical and technological determinism, few authors take note of the fact that some of the questions of value, belief, and meaning that have crystallized around biological and medical developments have also been central to a variety of nonmedical issues that have surfaced in American society over the past ten to fifteen years. (A number of the same cultural preoccupations and themes, for example, have appeared in the civil rights, peace, antipoverty, ecology, and women's movements). Nonetheless, the bioethics literature is focused on American society and culture in ways that most authors seem to take for granted. They mention the extensive public as well as professional bioethical interest in the United States, without observing that these concerns are more manifest and pervasive here than in any other society. They do not ask why this is so, or whether the questions being pondered in and through bioethics have some distinctively American features. Thus, the literature does not deal with the possibility that the florescence of bioethics in the United States may be as much an expression of metamedical, collective conscience issues with which American society is grappling, as it is a consequence of spectacular developments in medicine and biology.

Another general intellectual characteristic of the bioethical literature is the tendency of its contributing authors to call the religious, as well as the philosophical issues associated with biomedical research and advance, ethical. Problems of meaning (such as "what is life?," "what is death?," "what is a life of quality or a death with dignity?," and "why do suffering, injustice, and inequity persist?") that Max Weber and other social theorists consider to be the essence of religion are not distinguished from questions of normative ethics or moral philosophy. In part, this grows out of the predominance of philosophical ethics in the cognitive framework that has come to be shared by the interdisciplinary group of authors who have written about bioethical matters. It may also reflect their latent conviction that presenting these issues in the relatively secularized language of ethics facilitates communication between them because it transcends whatever their religious as well as disciplinary differences may be.

These attributes of the bioethics literature—its social circles and social movement aspects, on the one hand, and some of its intellectual premises on the other—merit further investigation. Not only are they of interest from a sociology of knowledge point of view; they also have social policy implications. The authors, books, and articles identified are influencing congressional hearings on various bioethical issues, the court's opinion in cases like that of Karen Ann Quinlan, the deliberations of bodies like the National Commission for the Protection of Human Subjects of Biomedical and Behavioral Research, and the passage of legislation such as death statutes and the Uniform Anatomical Gift Act.

SOCIOLOGISTS' LIMITED CONTRIBUTIONS TO BIOETHICS

The limited contribution that sociologists have made to bioethics[10] emanates largely from the prevailing intellectual orientation and the *Weltanschauung* of present-day American sociology. Most sociologists have not chosen to concentrate on the kinds of problems with which bioethics is concerned and are unaware either that bioethics exists, or of its potential sociocultural import. This is related to sociologists' greater propensity to work in a social structural or social organizational frame of analysis than in a cultural one. In part, this preference is an artifact of the traditional conceptual emphasis of sociology, especially as it distinguishes itself from social or cultural anthropology. It is also connected with the ideological conviction held by many sociologists who espouse a critical, change-oriented, or radical approach to the field that focusing on questions of supposedly entrenched values and beliefs is inherently more conservative than being interested in what are assumed to be modifiable social structures. Along with these factors that have curtailed sociologists' involvement in bioethical phenomena and issues, the lack of

10. I have not included the considerable sociological literature on population control issues and policies in what I have defined as the bioethical writings of sociologists. (The one exception I have made to this is the study of ethical aspects of population control that Donald Warwick is currently conducting under the aegis of the Institute of Society, Ethics and the Life Sciences.) Sociologists like Bernard Berelson, Judith Blake, and Kingsley Davis who have written extensively on population matters are not cited or discussed in this review article. Some readers may consider my decision arbitrary, but I feel that it is justified on several grounds. It is true that this sociologically oriented population literature deals with certain problems treated in the bioethics literature, and that some of the work of bioethical writers like Daniel Callahan and Donald Warwick has been funded by the Population Council, of which Bernard Berelson is president. However, most of the population literature by sociologists grows out of another intellectual and social policy tradition, whose origins antedate those of bioethics, and its major authors belong to a demography-population social circle and social movement, rather than to the bioethics subculture.

relevant interdisciplinary competence in the sociological community has been another deterrent. Some ability to handle the relationship between sociological variables, on the one hand, and biological, biomedical, philosophical, theological, and/or legal variables on the other, is requisite. Not many sociologists have this trained competence or seem willing to acquire it.

It should also be said that the emerging field of bioethics has not been enthusiastically welcoming to social scientists. One of the inadvertent consequences of the skewing of the field in the direction of philosophical and theological ethics is a tendency on the part of influential members of the bioethics circle to regard social science and its practitioners as insufficiently humanistic. A C. P. Snow-like "two cultures" split exists between the intellectual self-conceptions of the gatekeepers of bioethics and their tendency to view most social scientists, particularly sociologists, as excessively scientistic. Lawyers, biologists, and physicians in the bioethics group, as well as philosophers and theologians, share this perspective, which is institutionalized across the disciplines making the primary input to the bioethical debate and literature. Thus, the ethos of bioethics converges with that of sociology in a way that reinforces the tendency of sociologists to hold themselves aloof from this area of intellectual, moral, and politico-legal concern.

The branch of sociology that one would expect to have the most affinity for an analysis of social and ethical implications of biomedical advance and technology is the sociology of medicine. And indeed, as will be seen, a number of the sociologist authors who have contributed to the bioethics literature are known for their work on medicine. However, taken as a whole, the sociology of medicine has paid little attention to topics of direct relevance to bioethics, such as the sociology of medical science; research and therapeutic innovation; the interplay between medicine, medical science, religion, and magic in an advanced modern society; or the relationships between medicine and law in such a society. Rather, research and writing have been mainly devoted to the sociology of illness, medical care, the hospital, and the profession of medicine. Sociologists have published more about the patient than about the physician, the nurse, or other medical and paramedical professionals, and more about mental illness and its treatment than about physical illness. During these past ten years, when bioethics has been developing, sociologists of medicine have been most concerned with the sick role, its formulation by Talcott Parsons (1948, 1951, 1958, 1975; Parsons & Fox 1952), and its phenomenology—the "labeling" of illness (Scheff 1966, 1975), the "medicalization of deviance" (Pitts 1968), and with the "professional dominance" and "organized autonomy" of physicians (Freidson

1970a, b). The literature of the past decade is a curious genre. Although it has roots in important theoretical and empirical works such as those of Parsons, Freidson, Scheff, and Goffman (1961), a good deal of what has been written in the sociology of medicine since the 1960s is social criticism rather than social science. In contrast to the literature of the 1950s, for example, which presented a rich array of conceptual insights and first-hand empirical studies, many of the more recent publications are neither based on first-hand research, nor present original theoretical ideas. Rather, they repeatedly fault Parsons's notion of the sick role, decry the extension of the social stigmata and controls of illness to an increasing number of conditions and behaviors, denounce the monopolistic, self-regulating comportment of physicians, and deplore the attributes of American society that permit and encourage progressive medicalization.

THE SOCIOLOGICAL-BIOETHICAL LITERATURE AND ITS AUTHORS

The handful of sociologists who have written bioethics-relevant articles and books are not uncritical of the health-illness-medicine complex as it is currently institutionalized in American society. However, in most cases, whatever criticisms they offer or recommendations they make grow out of the implications of empirical research that they or others have conducted.

The number of sociologist authors who have published works that deal with the social, ethical, and existential concomitants of biomedical knowledge, technology, and their advance is so small that a nearly exhaustive list of them can easily be made. In alphabetical order, they are Bernard Barber (and with him, as coauthors, John J. Lally, Julia Loughlin Makarushka, and Daniel F. Sullivan [Barber 1970, 1973; Barber et al. 1973; Lally & Barber 1974]); Daniel Bell (1973); Diana Crane (1969, 1975a,b,c; Crane & Matthews 1969); Amitai Etzioni (1968, 1973a,b,c,d,e); Renée C. Fox (1957, 1959, 1960, 1970, 1974b,c; Fox & Lief 1963; Fox & Swazey 1974; Swazey & Fox 1970; Parsons, Fox & Lidz 1972); Barney G. Glaser & Anselm Strauss (1965, 1968); Bradford H. Gray (1975a,b); Talcott Parsons (alone, and with Renée Fox and Victor M. Lidz [Parsons 1970; Parsons & Lidz 1967; Parsons, Fox & Lidz 1972]); Roberta G. Simmons (Simmons, Fulton & Fulton 1970; Simmons & Najarian 1970; Simmons, Hickey, Kjellstrand & Simmons 1971a,b; Simmons & Simmons 1971; Simmons, Klein & Thornton 1972); James R. Sorenson (1971, 1973a,b,c, 1974a,b); David Sudnow (1967); Judith P.

Swazey[11] (1971, 1974a,b; Swazey & Fox 1970; Swazey & Bessman 1971; Fox & Swazey 1974); Richard M. Titmuss (1971); and Donald P. Warwick (1968, 1973, 1974a,b, 1975a,b,c; Warwick & Kelman 1973).

These authors are interconnected in various ways. Many of them received their graduate training at Columbia or Harvard, and/or have held teaching or research positions at these universities (Barber, Lally, Makarushka, Sullivan, Bell, Crane, Etzioni, Fox, Parsons, Lidz, Simmons, Swazey, and Warwick). In many instances, they were present on the same campus at overlapping times. Several of the authors are currently faculty members at the same colleges or universities (Barber and Makarushka at Barnard College; Barber and Etzioni at Columbia University; Crane, Fox, and Lidz at the University of Pennsylvania, where Parsons is currently a visiting professor); Parsons and Bell at Harvard University; Glaser and Strauss at the University of California Medical Center, San Francisco; and Sorenson and Swazey at Boston University. As their acknowledgments to one another in book prefaces, dedications and footnotes, as well as their coauthorships indicate, formal and informal collaboration between different authors in this group has been extensive. In some instances, the work in progress or already done by certain authors engendered and facilitated a project undertaken by another. To cite one such instance, Gray's book on *Human Subjects in Medical Experimentation* is a revised version of his doctoral dissertation written at Yale. As he states in the preface to his book, his "original interest in this area was stimulated by Diana Crane in her seminar in sociology of science at Yale." While planning the study on which his thesis and book are based, Gray spent time with the Research Group on Human Experimentation at Columbia University, composed of Barber, Lally, Makarushka, and Sullivan. They were gathering the data for their own book, *Research on Human Subjects,* and gave him the benefit of their experience to that point. Subsequently, Barber urged Gray to prepare his dissertation for publication and wrote the foreword to his book. There are also a number of teacher-student chains in this group, like the Crane-Barber-Gray one. For instance, Parsons taught Barber, Fox, and Lidz when each was a graduate student and Barber taught Fox when she was an undergraduate. Fox, Swazey, Sorenson, and Warwick are all active members of the Hastings Institute of Society, Ethics and the Life Sciences, which provides them with face-to-face, as well as scholarly, contact. Both Barber and his colleagues, and Crane worked closely with

11. Although Judith P. Swazey is an historian of science and a biologist, a significant amount of her research and writing has been done in a sociological framework, and she is a faculty member in the Department of Socio-Medical Sciences at Boston University Medical School, which is sociological and anthropological in outlook.

the Russell Sage Foundation in the conception and execution of their respective books, particularly with Orville G. Brim, Jr., and Howard E. Freeman. The Foundation published, as well as funded, their research. And finally, as might be expected, a considerable number of the authors in this group are known principally for their work in the sociology of medicine and/or science (Barber, Sullivan, Crane, Fox, Glaser, Strauss, Simmons, Sorenson, and Swazey).[12]

This is not to imply that all the authors in this group are intellectually and interpersonally linked to one another in these ways. For example, Titmuss belongs to the British rather than to the American sociological tradition. Glaser and Strauss were trained at Chicago, Gray at Yale, Sorenson at Princeton, Sudnow at Berkeley, and Warwick at Michigan, rather than at Columbia or Harvard, and Bell has never written about medicine. But even on a surface level of analysis, there are enough similarities and interrelationships between sociologists who have contributed to the bioethics literature to suggest that they are not a randomized cross-section of the profession. The kind of a social circle they constitute and the influence this has had on their work need further study.

Unlike the bioethical articles and books of philosophers, theologians, physicians, biologists, and lawyers, most of the sociological writings in this area are based on empirical research. They present and analyze systematically collected primary as well as secondary data. Many of these sociological publications grow out of first-hand inquiries the authors themselves conducted, using survey, historical, or field methods of research. The literature they have produced is rather evenly distributed between so-called qualitative and quantitative approaches, and several studies have utilized both.

The chief substantive topics on which the sociologist authors have concentrated are human experimentation, death and dying, organ transplantation and dialysis, and genetic screening and counseling. These are subjects that have evoked high public as well as professional interest in recent years and that, in contrast to the anticipated but still futuristic biomedical developments that have been causing concern, (such as genetic engineering and behavior control), can be observed here and now. Sociologists have studied how human subjects and medical investigators, patients and their families, physicians and other medical professionals think, feel, and act in situations relevant to the illness-dying-research-therapy phenomena on which they have focused. They

12. Talcott Parsons is a special case in this regard. He is, of course, principally renowned as a theorist, but he is also one of the founders of the sociology of medicine.

have described and analyzed the actual behavior of the participants in these settings, its collective patterns, the origins of these patterns, and how these behaviors are like and unlike what is generally believed to occur and what is considered to be ideal. In these respects, the sociological sector of the bioethical literature reflects the orientation and ethos of social research. It invites commentary only because it is strikingly dissimilar to the speculative, albeit systematic, nature of most of the nonsociological bioethical writings, their greater attention to ideal than to actual patterns of behavior, and their heavy reliance on individual, rather than on institutional or aggregate case studies.

DEATH AND DYING

The writings on death and dying include some of the earliest sociological explorations of a bioethically relevant field. They foreshadow what now seems to be a generalized American interest in how death is defined and experienced in this society, in the human as well as the technical features of the modern hospital (which, along with the nursing home, is the principal setting where death occurs), and in the degree and kind of control that the dying person, the family, and the medical team exert over the "dying trajectory" (Glaser & Strauss 1968).

A number of the sociological works that deal with death and dying provide detailed ethnographic accounts of what Glaser & Strauss and Sudnow call the "social organization of death work" (Glaser & Strauss 1968, Sudnow 1967), and the way it is structured by different services in various types of urban hospitals. Somewhat more material is presented on attitudes and behaviors of hospital staff members, particularly doctors and nurses, than on patients and their families; however, the stages of dying and mourning through which terminally ill patients and their relatives pass, their states of awareness (Glaser & Strauss 1965), and their ways of coming to terms with their conditions (Fox 1959, Fox & Swazey 1974) are not neglected.

A common assumption in much popular and professional writing on death and dying by nonsociologists is that the denial of death is basic to American national character and culture. Given the frequency and conviction with which this point of view is stated, it is notable that none of the sociologist authors under review support this premise. Parsons & Lidz explicitly argue against it (1967). However, all the authors cited report on a number of conditions surrounding death in the hospital that create the impression of denial: the routinization and ritualization of the practices and procedures of hospital personnel; their outward display of efficiency, equanimity, and "do something" care; and the mutual pretext of unawareness that is often enacted by patient, family, and medical staff in the face of the uncertainties and anxieties of the dying process.

These works are sensitive to the fact that the nurses and physicians who care for dying patients need special defenses and supports to help them maintain "detached concern" (Fox & Lief 1963) in situations that normally arouse the deepest kind of anxiety and questioning about human suffering and mortality. Several authors give accounts of critical, symbolic cases—the dying child or youth; the suicidal, alcoholic, or "criminal" patient—that bring such questions of meaning and moral worth so acutely to the surface that institutionalized ways of dealing with death temporarily break down, and with them the usual capacity of medical personnel to manage their feelings (Fox 1959, Sudnow 1967). However, all the authors seem to agree that, by and large, the professional socialization process that nurses and physicians undergo and the social organization of the hospital and its daily round generate more detached than concerned care. Certain aspects of the socialization process and of the social structure of medical work are identified as particularly conducive to this process of emotional distancing and to the noncommunication and miscommunication of the staff with colleagues, as well as with dying patients and their kin, that can result. Implicit in the conceptual framework of the sociological literature on death and dying is the assumption that, if anything is to be done substantially to improve the ambience of terminal care in the hospital, exhortation and consciousness raising will not be sufficient, and could even have unanticipated negative side effects. Rather, the medical socialization process will have to be altered in ways that affect latent as well as manifest attitudes and behavior patterns, and new organizational arrangements and mechanisms will have to be devised and implemented. These are among the major recommendations that Glaser and Strauss explicitly make (1968). They also advocate that "medical and nursing personnel should encourage public discussion of issues that transcend professional responsibilities for terminal care," especially the question of the circumstances under which various kinds of procedures for prolonging life should be initiated, and how long and vigorously they should be maintained (1968:258–259).

With this last issue, the sociological literature opens into a consideration of the most basic cultural premises about life and death in American society. These premises, derived from the Judeo-Christian tradition, constitute a fundamental, "civil religion" substratum in the society. As formulated by Parsons, Fox & Lidz (1972), this set of beliefs and values emphasizes that, because human life is divinely given, it is inherently sacred and important, has absolute, inestimable worth and meaning, and should be protected and sustained. At the same time, these authors contend, this "gift of life" tradition implies that the death of the individual is not only inevitable but, "especially in the fullness of a complete life," is an obligatory way of reciprocating the original gift received (1972:371). This obligation to reciprocate notwithstanding, the Parsons, Fox & Lidz article, as well as the writings of Crane (1975a,b,c), Fox & Swazey (Fox & Swazey 1974, Fox 1974), and Glaser & Strauss all indicate that in recent years, the unqualified commandment to support and sustain life has become increasingly problematic in American society, particularly in the medical sector. The sanctity of life ethic has helped to push physicians, nurses and other medical professionals into a pugilistic tendency to combat death at any cost, and to define its occurrence as a personal and professional defeat. This heroically aggressive, "courage to fail" stance (Fox & Swazey 1974) has been reinforced by the development of more powerfully effective forms of medical technology that increase the medical team's ability to save and maintain life. However, some of the consequences of doing everything possible to keep all chronically afflicted and terminally ill patients indefinitely alive have come to be questioned. The material and psychic costs; the suffering that prolonging life under certain conditions may entail for the dying person, his (her) family and the medical team; and the allocation of scarce resources problems that such massive efforts pose for the entire society are now often discussed and debated. Affirmations about the right to die as well as the right to live, and about death with dignity, are recurrently heard, along with queries about the quality of life of persons being maintained on artificial support systems or by other extraordinary means. A new operational definition of death (irreversible brain coma) has been proposed and is progressively being institutionalized. It codifies the position that, although the heart may beat and respiration continue (either naturally or by artificial means), without neocortical activity and the cerebration it makes possible, essential human life does not exist. The corpus of sociological articles and books on death and dying suggests that these are all signs that a transition is taking place in American society from an absolutist ethic based on the unconditional sanctity of life, to a more relativized ethic or what Weber would have called an ethic of responsibility premised on a socially as well as biologically defined conception of quality of life (Parsons, Fox & Lidz 1972:402–409; Fox & Swazey 1974:320–326).

Diana Crane's study of what physicians do when they are faced with the treatment of critically ill patients documents this inference. She reports that a disparity has developed between the traditional medical ethic that advocates that treatment "be continued as long as life, defined in physiological terms, can be preserved" and the actual behavior of physicians (1975a:204). Based on extensive interviews that she conducted with physicians in several medical specialties, a total of 3189 questionnaires completed by samples of internists, pediatricians, neurosurgeons, and pediatric heart surgeons, and on studies of the records of hospital patients, Crane concludes (1975a:199–200) that:

> . . . physicians respond to the chronically ill or terminally ill patient not simply in terms of physiological definitions of illness but also in terms of the extent to which he is capable of interacting with others. The treatable patient is one who can interact or has the potential to interact in a meaningful way with others in his environment. The physically damaged salvageable patient whose life can be maintained for a considerable period of time is more likely to be actively treated than the severely brain-damaged patient or the patient who is in the last stages of terminal illness. The brain-damaged infant is also not defined as treatable by many physicians, since he lacks the potential to establish social relationships with others. The unsalvageable infant is less likely to be treated than the salvageable infant, even if the latter is physically or mentally damaged. Consistent with the interpretation that physicians are using a social definition of life are the findings from this study which show that the family's attitude toward the brain-damaged child is an important influence upon the physician's decision to treat the child. . . . Although the data are not entirely consistent or conclusive on this point, it appears that social capacity rather than social value is the more important factor in the physician's decision to treat these patients. In other words, the patient's capacity or potential capacity to engage in social interaction is a more important factor in the decision to treat him than his social status or prestige.

Like the other sociological authors, Crane feels that the implications of her study and of "new developments in related areas" ramify beyond the medical sector; that in changing its definition of life and death American society is undergoing a "fundamental (cultural) shift" (1975a:206). However, she is concerned about some of the immediate consequences of the current stage of transition, with its "disparity between formal and informal norms" regarding the treatment of critically ill patients. In her opinion, this normative discrepancy could create a reaction-formation response in the medical profession. It could lead physicians to "overstress . . . the preservation of life at all costs," in an attempt to deny and control the degree of deviance from this injunction that already exists in medical practice. Crane's recommendation for what she considers to be this undesirable state of affairs is to "alter the formal norms" by developing medico-ethical "guidelines for the withdrawal of treatment with respect to certain specifically defined conditions" (1975a:204). What she advocates, then, as a controlled way of relaxing and qualifying the physician's absolute obligation to sustain life is not a general ethical code, but rather, concrete sets of guidelines such as those that define the condition under which irreversible coma and brain death (and thus the death of the person) can be said to have occurred.

MEDICAL RESEARCH ON HUMAN SUBJECTS

Experiment Perilous by Renée Fox bridges the sociological literature on death and on human experimentation. It also spans two quite different time periods in American sociology, the 1950s and the 1970s. It was first published in 1959 and was reissued in 1974 in a paperback edition. On the one hand, this participant-observation-based study of Ward F-Second, a clinical research unit in a renowned university hospital, is one of a number of pioneering ethnographic studies of hospitals and hospital wards as social systems that were carried out in the 1950s. On the other hand, as Fox writes in her introduction to the paperback edition, there are several senses in which this work is "more contemporaneous now than it was at the time of its initial publication" (1959/1974:11). For, in contradistinction to the decade 1966–1976, in the period when the fieldwork for *Experiment Perilous* was done (1951–1954), "no first-hand sociological study of terminal illness, medical experimentation with human subjects, or the psychosocial dynamics of therapeutic innovation had ever been made. Not only was there no precedent for such an inquiry, but its legitimacy was questionable" (1959/1974:10). Furthermore, some of the medical research and therapeutic developments that took place on Ward F-Second twenty-five years ago—notably, very early clinical trials with cardiac surgery, hemodialysis, and organ transplantation—are now in the forefront of bioethical discussion and of the contributions that sociologists are making to it.

Experiment Perilous is essentially a study of the entwined problems of the patients and physicians of Ward F-Second, of their reciprocal stresses, and of the socially patterned ways that they evolved for coming to terms with these problems and stresses. Out of their common predicament of chronic and terminal illness, high medical uncertainty and risk, severe therapeutic limitation, and constant closeness to death; and in response to their dual, often conflicting roles of physician-investigators and patient-subjects, the men of F-Second created a tragicomic community in which doctor and patient were collegially committed to medical research. In their more recent book *Research on Human Subjects* (1973), Barber, Lally, Makarushka & Sullivan assert that, in the universe of American institutional settings in which medical research with human subjects is carried out, the attributes of Ward F-Second are relatively rare. (Lally & Barber's article, "The Compassionate Physician" [1974], makes this claim in more explicit detail.) Their conclusions are based on a nationally representative questionnaire survey of 239 biomedical research institutions, and on a more intensive, comparative study (via 331 personal interviews) conducted in a university hospital and research center on the one hand, and a community and teaching hospital on the other.

Barber, Lally, and their colleagues found that in research situations where the procedures being tried are dramatically innovative, dangerous, or painful; where there is a continuing relationship between researchers and their subjects; and where the physician-investigators are responsible for caring for their subjects, who are also their patients, a Ward F-Second-type situation was likely to prevail. Under such circumstances, medical researchers do tend to be keenly aware of the risks and suffering to which they are exposing their subjects, humanly and personally concerned about them, and anguished by the research-therapy conflicts involved. It is in this kind of situation, too, that research physicians are most likely to live up to the highest ethical standards of human experimentation by treating their subjects as collaborators and co-adventurers, explaining the risks and benefits of the procedures that they ask them to undergo in scrupulous detail, making it clear to them that they can withdraw from the experiment at any time, and thereby obtaining from their subjects the most fully informed voluntary consent possible.

But while acknowledging this special situation, Barber, Lally, Makarushka & Sullivan contend that such "concern-producing factors" occur relatively infrequently in biomedical research (1973:113):

> In most research projects . . . the investigator is not faced with a decision about serious, life-threatening procedures for his patient-subjects. . . . [T]here is . . . evidence . . . that there are mechanisms which protect investigators from emotional involvement in research by limiting their contact with their subjects. . . . Much research is brief, involving simple measurements on large numbers of subjects. Much research could be, and some is, conducted without the knowledge and cooperation of the subjects. The patients' involvement is not necessarily conscious, long-term or painful. . . . [Thus]only a minority of research projects have the characteristics of risk and patient contact which seem to make researchers aware of research ethics. . . .

There is considerable agreement among the sociologists writing about medical experimentation that the values, attitudes, and behavior patterns of investigators and subjects are not only shaped by the interaction structures and ambience of the groups within which the research is conducted, but also by the patterned characteristics of what Fox and Swazey have called the process of "therapeutic innovation" (Fox & Swazey 1974, Swazey 1974a). The three sets of phenomena that sociologist authors have identified as most strategic in this regard are problems of uncertainty and of the unknown that are inherent to medical research; the experiment-therapy or science and therapy dilemma that it entails; and the socially structured competition and system of differential rewards that are involved both in the making of medical scientific discoveries and in the advancement of medical scientific careers.

Bradford Gray (1975a) and Bernard Barber and his associates have focused their attention on the ways in which these and other aspects of the medical research context and role contribute to lax, even deviant standards and practices in investigators' conduct with human subjects. Gray was especially impressed with the pervasive inadequacies in the process of obtaining informed, voluntary consent from subjects that characterized the fifty-four projects at "Eastern University" Medical Center that he examined. In the labor-induction drug study, one of the two projects that he analyzed most intensively, out of the fifty-one patients involved as subjects, at the time that they began receiving an experimental drug, as many as twenty patients were unaware that they were participants in research. On this project and on others that he explored, Gray found that the researchers had obtained many of the subjects' signatures on consent forms in a routinized, largely ritualistic way. Only "cursory, euphemistic, verbal" explanations were given to the subjects (1975a:221). A considerable number of them did not understand the procedures they had ostensibly agreed to undergo or the possible risks they entailed, or that they had had the option not to sign the consent form when they were asked to do so. In the labor-induction study, as in others, some subjects were not only persuaded but pressured to participate in the research project by young physicians on the house staff, acting on behalf of senior physicians conducting research whom they were eager to please. And the quality of consent obtained from subjects who were relatively uneducated, of lower class status, clinic patients, and/or black was often dubious. In fact, persons with these social characteristics were most likely to fall into what Gray calls the category of "unaware subjects" (1975a:128–139), and to be involved in projects where the risks were relatively high in proportion to the therapeutic benefits for the subjects themselves or for other patients. Barber and his coauthors arrived at a similar finding in their study.

Ward and clinic patients, they report, are more likely than private patients to be subjects of studies where the risks exceed the benefits. Furthermore, they add, "it is not at all clear from our data that . . . the sacrifice these patients make [provides] important scientific benefits," or that when researchers launched their high-risk studies and engaged subjects in them, they had such an intent or hope in mind (Barber, et al., 1973:55–57).

Gray, Barber, and coauthors were especially interested in studying how various social control structures and processes affect medical researchers' sensitivity to issues of informed, voluntary consent and of the proper balance between benefit and risk, their ethical concern about their human subjects in these and other regards, and the way that they plan and actually conduct their experiments. The three major types of control that Gray, Barber, et al., consider are the professional socialization relevant to ethical research that physicians undergo; the patterns of informal interaction that characterize the collaborative groups and teams within which physicians generally carry out their research; and the peer group review of research with human subjects that has been made mandatory by numerous governmental and nongovernmental funding agencies during the past ten years. In many respects, Gray, Barber, *et al.*, find each of these social control mechanisms inadequate, or in serious need of improvement, or of more far-reaching changes, which they discuss in detail in the final chapters of their books.

As this makes apparent, these books by Barber and Gray (and by Crane as well) all represent attempts to "achieve two different but interrelated purposes" (Barber, et al., 1973:185): "First . . . we hoped to make a contribution to sociological theory and understanding. And second, we hoped that the theory and understanding arrived at through our research would result directly in specific and useful suggestions for policy change and reform."

POLICY AND METHODOLOGY CONCERNS

The explicit commitment that these sociologists have made to the formulation of social criticism and policy merits comment, for this is a general, though not universal, characteristic of the recent, bioethically relevant publications of sociologists. While cleaving to the conviction that their primary responsibility is to advance the theory, methodology, and knowledge base of sociology, a significant number of the sociologist authors who have been writing about bioethical topics seem to feel that they have the intellectual and social obligation to make policy suggestions based on their findings and analyses. This applied, critical, action- and change-oriented dimension of their work appears to have several sources: the social relevance ethos that gained momentum in sociology in the 1960s and has continued into the 1970s; the degree to which bioethical issues like research with human subjects and death and dying have become matters of public interest and concern; the financial support and publishing outlet that organizations such as the Russell Sage Foundation have been providing for this sort of policy-directed research (Barber, et al., 1973; Crane 1975a; Katz, Capron & Glass 1972; Katz & Capron 1975); and these authors' shared preoccupation with the power of professions in American society and the importance of insuring that they use it in a socially responsible way. Sociologists writing about the socioethical ramifications of biomedical progress have tended to see medicine as the quintessential case of such a powerful profession and of the problems of social control it presents. As Bernard Barber and coauthors (1973:188) have put it:

> . . . medicine is too important to be left to the doctors, science is too important to be left to the scientists, and biomedical research is too important to be left to the biomedical researchers. Because the consequences of professional power are too important to be left to the professionals, outsiders ask the kind of control that comes at least from having the professionals make a reasonable effort to give a reasonable account of what they are doing. Immersed in their own special culture and activities, professionals often not only do not take the initiative in offering such accounts but are resistant to the requests of their clients that accounts be given. . . .

Based on their conviction that as informed outsiders they have probing insights to offer that grow out of their research findings, and out of their pre-research commitment to social-system-oriented analysis and to particular paradigms such as Robert Merton's "social structure and anomie" typology, Gray, Barber, et al., offer their policy suggestions about medical socialization, scientific competition, research collaboration, and peer-group review.[13] Both of their books end with exhortations to the medical profession to work as hard on ethical problems as they have on medical scientific ones, even if that shift in priorities means slowing the tempo of biomedical advance.

13. Bradford Gray is currently carrying out a major research project in a context that is explicitly addressed to policy analysis, recommendations, and change. He is a member of the staff of the National Commission for the Protection of Human Subjects of Biomedical and Behavioral Research, where he is conducting a national survey of the way that medical and nonmedical institutions review research conducted with human subjects. None of the Commissioners are sociologists and Gray is the only sociologist staff member.

The Courage to Fail, by Fox & Swazey (1974), deals with many of the same phenomena that concern Gray, and Barber and his coauthors, but it is a different genre of work in methodology, style, and analytic intent. It deals with medical research on human subjects in the framework of a larger interest in the process of therapeutic innovation. The book is built around an exploration of transplantation and dialysis, which are viewed as paradigmatic of the range of medical and social phenomena that accompany biomedical research and its clinical application. Transplantation and dialysis are also seen as both empirically and symbolically associated with a number of the metamedical "collective conscience" issues, with which American society seems to be grappling and which are central to the bioethics movement. Because the authors are especially interested in the sociology of medical science, they concentrate somewhat more attention on research physicians engaged in the transplantation and dialysis enterprise than on patient-subjects and their families. However, first-hand data on transplant and dialysis patients are presented throughout the book, and Chapter 1 ("Gift Exchange and Gate Keeping," pp. 5–39) and Chapter 10 ("Ernie Crowfeather," pp. 280–315) are built on patient and family case materials. The entire book is composed of cases ranging in size and scope from those of individual patients, physicians, nurses, relatives, etc., to whole medical centers. These data were gathered over a period of four years, through field research (participant observation, face-to-face interviews, analysis of documents, etc.), in dialysis and transplant centers located in various regions of the country. Two centers were studied more continuously and intensively than the others during this time.

Fox & Swazey present what Clifford Geertz has called a "thick" analytic and interpretive description of these many-faceted dialysis/transplantation, human experimentation, therapeutic innovation phenomena, and of the social milieux in which they occur. Both because the work is ethnographic and because it is cultural as well as social structural in its theoretical orientation, it sets forth to a greater extent than the Barber, Crane, and Gray books the tapestry of dilemmas and ambivalences that clinical medical research and human experimentation entail. And although in certain regards it is as piercingly critical of the comportment of the medical profession in particular kinds of situations (see, for example, Chapter 7, "The Case of the Artificial Heart," pp. 149–211), it suggests that there may be some irreducible elements in those situations that cannot easily be changed by enlightened good will, a reformed medical socialization process, or even by new social structural arrangements.

It is of some "sociology of sociology" interest to note that a work with these methodological and conceptual-interpretive attributes is more likely to be regarded by reviewers as a biased and politically conservative work that has "uncritically . . . adopt[ed] the medical perspective," presenting research physicians as romantic, ethically sensitive "heroes,"[14] than the type of study that the Barber, Crane, and Gray books represent. In addition, it has qualities that evoke another, more subtle set of allegations[15]:

> . . . viewing the terrain of illness from the seemingly heroic stance of the research physician doing battle at the furthermost frontiers of clinical practice obscures the pained everyday world of the patients. . . . Rather, the physician-borne perspective does not encourage [the authors] to conceptually chart and amplify this underworld of frustration, embitterment, dismemberment, and, on occasion, even triumph. . . .

Theoretical, methodological, schools-of-sociology, and even world-view issues and differences are involved here that clearly go beyond the scope of this review.

TRANSPLANTATION AND DIALYSIS

The Courage to Fail is the one book-length sociological work about dialysis and transplantation that has thus far been published. The book on kidney transplantation that Roberta Simmons is writing is not yet available,* but its perspective is prefigured in her numerous coauthored articles (Simmons, et al., 1970, 1971, 1971a,b, 1972). She is particularly interested in the role that the family and the physician play in the complex, often poignant process of decision making that the selection of a kidney donor and recipient entails. She also tried to trace out the long-range as well as the immediate psychosocial consequences of this extraordinary exchange for donors, recipients, their families, and the transplantation team. In addition to her microdynamic analysis of these phenomena, like Fox and Swazey she has systematically reflected on some of the larger societal problems that transplantation poses.

In their writings about the phenomena associated with transplantation and dialysis, Simmons, Swazey, and Fox (Swazey & Fox 1970, Fox 1970, Fox & Swazey 1974, Swazey 1974a, Fox 1974b) highlight several interrelated socioethical issues integral to these extraordinary modes of

14. Marcia Millman, 1975. Review of *The Courage to Fail, Cont. Sociol.* 4:617–19.
15. Fred Davis, 1975. Review of *The Courage to Fail, Am. J. Sociol.* 81:417–20.
* Since the writing of this article, the book has been published as *The Gift of Life.*

treatment: "gift of life," quality of life, and allocation of scarce resources concerns.

The "gift-exchange" aspects of organ transplantation, Simmons, Swazey, and Fox agree, constitute its most distinctive feature. A vital organ is donated by one individual in order to give life to another person who is terminally ill. Like other forms of gift exchange, organ donation is structured by a set of norms that shape the feelings and behavior of both donors and recipients. These are the norms that Marcel Mauss identified and analyzed in his classic monograph *The Gift* (1954): the obligations to give, to receive, and to repay. Failure to live up to any of these expectations produces social strains that affect the giver, the receiver, and those associated with them.

As Simmons, Swazey, and Fox show, because a live as well as a cadaveric organ donation is an option in the case of renal transplantation, the dynamics of the gift exchange involved can be especially intricate.[16] When a live renal transplant is contemplated, the members of the prospective recipient's family face strong normative pressure to offer a gift of a kidney. A live transplant from a donor who is genetically related to the recipient and is a "good tissue match" has a better medical prognosis than a cadaveric transplant.[17] In addition, the integrity, closeness, and generosity of the family and each of its members are symbolically involved in the willingness of kin to give of themselves to their dying relative in this ultimate, life-maintaining way. Under these circumstances, the possibility of a coerced or self-coerced gift of a kidney by a family member is sufficiently great for medical teams to have felt obliged to devise gatekeeping mechanisms that help them eliminate relatives from donorship who are subject to an inordinate amount of inner or outer pressure to give a kidney. The terminally ill patient who is offered the gift of a live kidney from a candidate-donor is under complementary normative pressure to accept it. To refuse to do so is not only life-denying in the biomedical sense, but also implies a rejection of the

16. Because the kidneys are paired vital organs and one kidney can safely do the work of two, the loss of one kidney is not life-threatening. It is for this reason that the medical profession and the larger society of which it is part permit live as well as cadaveric kidney transplants to take place. The live transplantation of any other vital organ is forbidden, since its removal would cause the death of the donor. It is interesting that the desire to donate a singular vital organ is defined as unacceptably self-destructive or suicidal, rather than as a noble act of sacrifice.

17. The prognosis with a live kidney transplant that is a good tissue match is better than with a cadaveric transplant because there is less likelihood that a rejection reaction will occur rapidly and with a severity that jeopardizes the functioning of the implanted organ. However, with the exception of the case of a transplant between identical twins, the eventual rejection of the transplanted organ is inevitable.

person who offered the live kidney and of the family unit to which the donor and recipient both belong. If the live transplant does take place, then in keeping with Mauss's paradigm there is a sense in which the donor-recipient relationship takes on what Fox and Swazey have called a "tyrannical" dimension. The donor has made a priceless gift; the recipient has received and accepted an inherently unreciprocable gift from the donor. The transcendent meaning of what has been interchanged can unite them in ways that reinforce their solidarity and enhance their mutual self-esteem without jeopardizing their autonomy. But it is also possible that because of the unrepayable nature of the gift that binds them one to the other, the giver and the receiver may find themselves locked in a creditor-debtor vise that constricts their independence and their ability to relate to others.

Swazey and Fox attach more importance to the "tyranny of the gift" concomitants of transplantation than does Simmons, and to the psychosocial suffering that they can involve for donors, recipients, and their families. In their view, these occur frequently, in heart and liver, as well as kidney transplants, and regardless of whether the organ donated is a live or a cadaveric one. (In the latter case, a comparable bond is forged between the family of the deceased donor, the recipient, and his or her relatives.[18]) Fox and Swazey are also more impressed than Simmons with the anthropomorphic phenomena that accompany transplantation. However animistic it may appear to be, they report, the transfer of a vital organ from one person to another often evokes the at once apprehensive and hopeful belief on the part of the recipient that along with the organ, he (she) is receiving some of the physical, social, and psychic qualities of the person who donated it. This sense that part of the donor's self has been transmitted to the recipient appears to be most pronounced with cardiac transplants, perhaps because of the special symbolic and religious meaning of the human heart in Western Judeo-Christian tradition. Simmons does not seem to have observed many examples of these "tyrannical" and anthropomorphic attributes of transplantation. This may be because her field research has been confined to one medical center (Minnesota) and because she has been exclusively concerned with kidney transplants. It may also be an artifact of her greater interest in the sociodynamics of transplantation than in its psychodynamics, or its cultural symbolism and meaning.

18. Out of their gradual recognition that the identification of the family of a deceased donor, the recipient, and his or her family may be psychologically injurious to them all, most transplant teams in the United States now keep the identity of the donor and the recipient anonymous.

Fox and Swazey analyze hemodialysis as well as transplantation in a gift-exchange framework. Whether dialysis (the use of the artificial kidney machine) is conducted in a medical center or at home, they explain, it entails the continuous exchange of life for death through the donation of time, energy, skill, and concern by persons who help run the kidney machine and attend the dialysis patient. In the case of home dialysis, this exchange is all the more remarkable because it requires and permits a lay person (usually the patient's spouse) to assume an unprecedented amount of responsibility for operating a complex life-support system. As a consequence, home dialysis in particular confronts patients with the problem of receiving and reciprocating a recurrent gift of life.

The biomedical as well as the phychosocial side effects and sequellae of transplantation and dialysis raise a series of quality-of-life questions to which Simmons alludes, and which Fox and Swazey discuss in detail. Underlying these questions is the immutable fact that, no matter how well a patient seems to be adjusting to life with dialysis or transplantation, he is chronically dying.

The gift-exchange phenomena and the quality-of-life issues related to dialysis and transplantation have implications for the third set of socioethical issues treated by Simmons, Swazey, and Fox: the allocation of scarce resources problems that these treatments present. On the most microscopic level, questions arise about whether the net balance of suffering, reprieve, and well-being for individual dialysis and transplant patients and their families justifies the investment and expenditure of money, equipment, technical competence, personnel, time, hospital space, vital organs, and human concern that these particular ways of keeping terminally ill persons alive entail. On the more macroscopic level, two clusters of issues emerge. First, what proportion of such inherently scarce, precious resources should be allotted to dialysis and transplantation, as compared to other medical therapies, the treatment of other diseases, preventive medical procedures, medical research, or medical education? And second, how much should the society invest in the health-illness-medicine sector as a whole, relative to other needed and valued activities? The case of hemodialysis and kidney transplantation suggests that, even if it were possible to provide the funds, matériel, professional skill, and human care to make such treatments available to all who need them, this would still not resolve many of the scarce resource problems associated with such quasi-experimental, psychically and fiscally expensive, life-sustaining, but not curative modes of treatment. In 1972, Public Law 92-603 was passed, which extended financial coverage under Medicare to the treatment costs of dialysis and kidney transplants. This legislation has not solved the resources problems that existed prior to its implementation. And it has opened up new, largely unanticipated scarce resources, quality-of-life and gift-exchange questions. Fox and Swazey (1974:326–327, 336–337) and other social scientists are only beginning to study their implications.[19]

Laced through the writings of sociologists on death and dying, therapeutic innovation, human experimentation, hemodialysis, and transplantation is the ever-present question of who should have the responsibility and authority to make the kinds of decisions that each of these biomedical situations entails. As Katz & Capron point out (1975: 1–2), these decisions "exemplify the 'tragic choices'" that not only face individuals, but the society as a whole, in "many areas . . . besides medical care." The roles that the physician-investigator, the patient-subject, the family, the professions, and the state can and should play in this momentous decision making are currently being debated and reformulated in American society. The literature under review in this article both reflects and contributes to that process.

Another overall characteristic of at least the sociological sector of this literature is that a particular set of concepts has played a major role in the analyses developed by the authors who have written on these biomedical and bioethical subjects. The principal concepts that they have used (in addition to values, norms, statuses, roles, institutions, socialization, and the like that are the building blocks of any sociological analysis) are uncertainty, detached concern, the gift and gift exchange, the experiment-therapy dilemma, and structures and processes of social control. The repetition of these concepts in the literature derives from several sources: their applicability to certain phenomena and patterns that recur in the empirical data under examination; the current state and orientation of sociological theory; the training that this group of sociologist authors received in the limited circle of graduate departments of sociology cited earlier; and the formal and informal influence that these writers have had on one another.

APPLIED HUMAN GENETICS

The final substantive area to which sociologists dealing with biomedical advance and its implications have turned their attention is applied human genetics. This is still a sketchily developed field of sociological

19. I discussed the post-Public Law 92–603 dialysis and kidney transplant situation in some detail last year, at a Clinicosociologic Conference held at the Washington University School of Medicine in St. Louis. These remarks have been published in "Long-Term Dialysis" 1975. *Am. J. Med.* 59:702–12.

reflection and inquiry. James Sorenson has been attempting to delineate its parameters (1971, 1973a,b) and has written the only articles on sociological aspects of genetic screening and genetic counseling that have thus far been published (1973a, 1974a,b). Judith Swazey (who is now doing collaborative research with Sorenson on screening and counseling) has written a case study of the passage of laws in forty-one states that mandate testing newborn infants for phenylketonuria (PKU), a hereditary metabolic disorder that may cause severe mental retardation (Swazey & Bessman 1971a, Swazey 1971b). Amitai Etzioni has published a book entitled *Genetic Fix*, which is not easy to classify. In his preface to it, he explains its form and intent in this way (1973a:9–12):

> . . . This book is not primarily a chronicle of new scientific developments; rather, it focuses on your right to know of opportunities and their consequences, your right to be in on the decisions thrust upon us, your right to decide if you want to administer the genetic fix to yourself, your next child, and—with other fellow citizens—to a nation's biological inheritance and future. . . . To highlight that we are in the initial phase of the age of genetic *engineering*, I refer to a genetic "fix"; we can *now* tamper with our biological inheritance, both fix it where it went wrong, and improve it [author's italics]. . . . This somewhat personal volume deals chiefly with what I learned and felt when I participated in an international meeting of experts that reviewed the new scientific breakthroughs, the foundations of tomorrow's technology. It also deals with what I have tried to do about all this and how far I have gotten (not very far, let me tell you right away).

Despite the disparate nature of the sociological work thus far done on human genetics and its still fragmentary state, the three social scientists who have written in this area have all focused on certain features of the current genetics situation. This is a dynamic area of frontier research (Taviss 1971:25) in biomedicine, they emphasize, that has the powerful potential to "alter man's role in evolution. . . . Man is no longer limited to passive acceptance of all inherited characteristics but is rapidly expanding his technological capacity to include the active treatment, selection and elimination of many individual genetic attributes" (Sorenson 1971:1). At the same time, the field of genetics is so fraught with uncertainty that even geneticists disagree about how advanced their research is now or is likely to be in the future, and about what dangers and benefits may ensue from some of the research procedures they are using or contemplating, as well as from the new knowledge and techniques that these may eventually bring forth. Against this state-of-the-art background, Etzioni, Sorenson, and Swazey have been concerned with three types of social control problems: controls to help implement already existing genetic knowledge and techniques; controls to regulate their human application; and what Taviss has called "anticipatory social controls" (1971:26) to forestall developments in genetic research and engineering that might have noxious, even perilous biological, psychological, social, and cultural consequences. As the foregoing implies, the area of genetics (like that of behavior control) tends to evoke deep apprehensions about the potentialities that developments in this field may have for "dangerous" tampering with the natural order, and for "sinister" politico-biological manipulation of the population by government and/or scientific groups. Etzioni, Sorenson, and Swazey are mindful of these possibilities and of the specters they arouse. At the same time they are concerned that controls instituted over genetic research, treatment, and engineering not be unduly hasty or subversive of the potential benefits that may come from advances in basic and applied genetics. Primary among the social control mechanisms that these authors consider is what Etzioni calls a "health ethics commission"—an interdisciplinary body whose job would be to study and make binding recommendations about the social and ethical, as well as the biological and medical implications of genetic and other forms of biomedical advance,[20] biomedical legislation, such as the PKU laws, which Swazey judges to be "premature . . . given the state of our knowledge about the nature and management of inherited metabolic disorders" (1971b:927–928); and the calling of a moratorium on certain types of genetic research or experimental clinical procedures whose consequences are considered to be too unpredictable or hazardous (Swazey & Fox 1970; Fox 1974b:459–465).[21]

GENETIC SCREENING AND COUNSELING

The second set of phenomena with which the small body of sociological writings on human genetics deals is genetic screening and counseling.

20. Since the publication of Etzioni's book *Genetic Fix*, the kind of commission he enthusiastically advocates has found at least one exemplification in the establishment of the National Commission for the Protection of Human Subjects of Biomedical and Behavioral Research that was created under the National Research Act of July 1974.

21. A rather remarkable moratorium deferring research that entails inserting either new bacterial or viral material into bacteria (particularly *Escherichia coli*, a common inhabitant of the human intestines and throat) that could infect human beings was called by molecular biologists (members of the Committee on Recombinant DNA Molecules of the Assembly of Life Sciences of the National Research Council) in July 1974. They feared the unpredictably hazardous bioconsequences for humans. In May 1976, this self-imposed moratorium was still in effect, while the biological community was trying to work out guidelines for containing experiments with recombinant DNA.

Sorenson is the principal author here. He has begun to ask some preliminary, sociologically framed questions about the contours and consequences of the two new roles involved in this area, those of genetic counselor and counselee. Sorenson has been interested in the personal and professional backgrounds of counselors, their value orientations, and their attitudes; the social contexts within which counseling is done; the processes by which clients are referred or self-referred to counselors; the experiences and expectations that they bring to the counseling process; the structure and dynamics of the counselor-counselee relationship—its cognitive and attitudinal content, and the ways that it is like and unlike the traditional medical professional-patient relationship; and in the marriage, reproductive, parenting, and family decisions that counselees eventually make—how they feel about these decisions, and what role the counseling transaction has played both in the formulation of these decisions and the meaning they have for counselees. As Sorenson appreciates, the counseling process takes place in a situation of high uncertainty concerning the exact nature of the roles involved, and the reliability and validity of the genetic predictions made. In the present state of genetic knowledge, in most cases the only kind of scientific and technical information that the counselor has available for counselees are probability statements about the chances of having a child with a specific genetic disorder, or probability-risk appraisals of the implications of already having given birth to a child with such a condition. Out of these systematically tentative estimates and the way they are conveyed to counselees come decisions as momentous as whether or not a couple will try to have children, whether a fetus will be brought to term or an abortion sought, and whether a family will care for and raise a child born with a severe genetic disorder or defect or will place him (her) in an institution. The consequences of these awesome decisions for individuals, couples, children, families, particular groups in the population, medicine and the medical profession, the "gene pool," and for the social structure and value system of the entire society has only begun to be explored.

SOCIETAL SIGNIFICANCE OF BIOMEDICAL AND BIOETHICAL DEVELOPMENTS

Finally, what is the overall societal significance of these various biomedical developments, their effects, and the concerned interest that they have evoked? Sociologists have offered three sorts of answers to these questions.

Daniel Bell (1973) would say that American society has entered its "post-industrial" phase, in which the "majority of the labor force is no longer engaged in agriculture or manufacturing but in services, which are defined, residually, as trade, finance, transport, health, recreation, research, education, and government"; the "professional and technical class" has become "preeminent"; "theoretical knowledge" is the "source of innovation and of policy formation for the society"; increasingly, "technological growth" is planned, assessed, and controlled; and a new "intellectual technology" has developed (1973:12–33). In such a post-industrial, essentially "technocratic society," Bell writes, "the disjunction of culture and social structure is bound to widen" (1973:480):

> The historic justifications of bourgeois society—in the realms of religion and character—are gone. The traditional legitimacies of property and work become subordinated to bureaucratic enterprises that can justify privilege because they can turn out material goods more efficiently than other modes of production. But a technocratic society is not ennobling. Material goods provide only transient satisfaction or an individual superiority over those with less. Yet one of the deepest human impulses is to *sanctify* their institutions and beliefs in order to find a meaningful purpose in their lives and to deny the meaninglessness of death. A post-industrial society cannot provide a transcendent ethic—except for the few who devote themselves to the temple of science. And the antinomian attitude plunges one into a radical autism which, in the end, dirempts the cords of community and the sharing with others. The lack of a rooted moral belief is the cultural contradiction of the society, the deepest challenge to its survival.

Richard Titmuss's analysis and societal vision are quite different. The starting point of his book, *The Gift Relationship* (1971), is human blood. It is a study of the "characteristics of those who give, supply or sell blood, and [it] analyzes in comparative terms blood transfusion and donor systems and national statistics of supply, demand, and distribution particularly in Britain and the United States." Using human blood and its mode of donation and receipt as both symbolic and indicative of larger questions of value, belief, and social policy, Titmuss argues against the "end of ideology" outlook of writers like Bell. "This study, in one small sector of human affairs," he states, "disputes both the death of ideology and the philistine resurrection of economic man in social policy. It is thus concerned with the values we accord to people for what they give to strangers; not what they get out of society" (1971:13–14). For Titmuss, the development of advanced biomedical procedures like blood transfusion demonstrates the practical necessity as well as the ethical imperative that the "freedom" and "right to give" in material and nonmaterial terms, to one's "stranger" as well as to one's "brother" be fostered by social policy. "Freedom from disability is inseparable from altruism," he concludes (1971:237–246). He also implies that certain forms of biomedical advance provide new potentialities for such altruism and freedom.

Like Bell, Fox & Swazey (1974) believe that American medicine and American society may be entering a new stage of modernity, but their study of organ transplantation and dialysis and their analysis of the larger biomedical and bioethical developments of which these are a part lead them to a societal interpretation that is closer to Titmuss's than to Bell's (1974:334):

> "The theme of the gift, of freedom and obligation in the gift, of generosity and self-interest in giving reappear in our society like the resurrection of a motif long forgotten," Marcel Mauss wrote. Organ transplantation is one recent development that has again brought such issues of gift exchange and social solidarity prominently into view. Transplantation and hemodialysis also center on problems of uncertainty, meaning, life and death, scarcity, and intervention in the human condition. This is where the ultimate significance of these therapeutic innovations . . . is to be found. And these questions, with which the "new biology" and medicine more generally are preoccupied, are a part of changing modern society that is increasingly concerned with such ethical and existential matters in many different domains.

LITERATURE CITED

American Hospital Association.—1972. Statement on a patient's bill of rights.

Barber, B.—1970. Some new men of power: The case of biomedical research scientists. In *New Dimensions in Legal and Ethical Concepts for Human Research*, ed. I. Ladimer, pp. 519–22. *Ann. NY Acad. Sci.*

Barber, B.—1973. Research on research on human subjects: Problems of access to a power profession. *Soc. Probl.* 2:103–12

Barber, B., Lally, J. J., Makarushka, J. M. L., Sullivan, D.—1973. *Research on Human Subjects: Problems of Social Control in Medical Experimentation*. New York: Russell Sage

Beecher, H. K.—1959a. *Experimentation in Man*. Springfield, Ill: Thomas

Beecher, H. K.—1959b. Experimentation in man. *J. Am. Med. Assoc.* 169:461–78

Beecher, H. K.—1966a. Consent in clinical experimentation: Myth and reality. *J. Am. Med. Assoc.* 195:34–35

Beecher, H. K.—1966b. Some guiding principles for clinical investigation. *J. Am. Med. Assoc.* 195:157–58

Beecher, H. K.—1966c. Ethics and clinical research. *N. Engl. J. Med.* 274: 1354–60

Beecher, H. K.—1968. Ethical problems created by the hopelessly unconscious patient. *N. Engl. J. Med.* 278:1425–30

Beecher, H. K.—1969a. After the definition of irreversible coma. *N. Engl. J. Med.* 281:1070–71

Beecher, H. K.—1969b. Procedures for the appropriate management of patients who may have supportive measures withdrawn. *J. Am. Med. Assoc.* 209:405

Beecher, H. K.—1970a. *Research and the Individual: Human Studies.* Boston: Little, Brown

Beecher, H. K.—1970b. Scarce resources and medical advancement. In *Experimentation with Human Subjects*, ed. P. A. Freund, pp. 66–104. New York: Braziller

Beecher, H. K.—1970c. Definitions of life and death for medical science and practice. *Ann. NY Acad. Sci.* 169:471–74

Bell, D.—1973. *The Coming of Post-Industrial Society: A Venture in Social Forecasting.* New York: Basic

Bok, S.—1970. *Voluntary euthanasia.* PhD thesis. Harvard Univ., Cambridge, Mass.

Bok, S.—1973. Euthanasia and the care of the dying. *BioScience* 23:461–78

Bok, S.—1974a. Ethical problems of abortion. *Hastings Center Studies* 2:33–52

Bok, S.—1974b. The ethics of giving placebos. *Sci. Am.* 231:17–23

Bok, S., Behnke, J. A., eds.—1975a. *The Dilemmas of Euthanasia.* New York: Doubleday/Anchor

Bok, S.—1975b. *Fetal Research and the Value of Life.* Natl. Comm. Prot. Hum. Subj. Biomed. Behav. Res.

Bok, S., Lappé, M.—1974. Case studies in bioethics: The treatment of hemophilia. *Hastings Cent. Rep.* 4:8–10

Branson, R.—1975. Bioethics as individual *and* social: The scope of a consulting profession *and* academic discipline. *JRE* 3:111–39

Callahan, D., ed.—1969a. *The Catholic Case for Contraception.* New York: Macmillan

Callahan, D.—1969b. The sanctity of life. In *Updating Life and Death: Essays in Ethics and Medicine*, ed. D. Cutler. Boston: Beacon

Callahan, D.—1970a. *Abortion: Law, Choice and Morality.* New York: Macmillan

Callahan, D.—1970b. Contraception and abortion: American Catholic response. *Ann. Am. Acad. Polit. Soc. Sci.* 387:109–17

Callahan, D., ed.—1971a. *The American Population Debate.* New York: Doubleday

Callahan, D.—1971b. What obligation do we have to future generations? *Am. Ecclesiastical Rev.* 164:265–80

Callahan, D.—1972. Ethics and population limitation. *Science* 175:487–94

Callahan, D.—1973a. *The Tyranny of Survival.* New York: Macmillan

Callahan, D.—1973b. Abortion: Some ethical issues. In *Abortion, Society, and the Law,* ed. D. F. Walbert, J. D. Butler, pp. 89–101. Cleveland: Case West. Reserve Univ. Press

Callahan, D.—1973c. The meaning and significance of genetic disease: Philosophical perspectives. In *Ethical Issues in Human Genetics: Genetic Counseling and the Use of Genetic Knowledge,* ed. B. Hilton, *et al.,* pp. 83–100. New York: Plenum

Callahan, D.—1973d. Abortion: Thinking and experiencing. *Christ. Crisis* 32:287–88

Callahan, D.—1973e. Bioethics as a discipline. *Hastings Cent. Stud.* 1:66–73

Callahan, D.—1973f. Science, limitations and prohibitions. *Hastings Cent. Rep.* 3:5–7

Callahan, D.—1973g. Human rights: Biogenetic frontier and beyond. *Hosp. Prog.* 54:80–84

Callahan, D.—1974a. Medicine's new ethics: A challenge to your decisions. *Prism* 2:43–46

Callahan, D.—1974b. Doing well by doing good. *Hastings Cent. Rep.* 4:1–4

Callahan, D.—1975. The ethics backlash. *Hastings Cent. Rep.* 5:18

Callahan, D., Gaylin, W.—1974. The psychiatrist as double agent. *Hastings Cent. Rep.* 4:11–14

Capron, A. M.—1972. The law of genetic therapy. In *The New Genetics and the Future of Man,* ed. M. Hamilton, pp. 133–56. Grand Rapids, Mich: Eerdmans

Capron, A. M.—1973a. Legal aspects of genetic control. In *Medicine and Society, 1972,* ed. W. Bell, pp. 118–27. Philadelphia: Am. Phil. Soc. Libr.

Capron, A. M.—1973b. Legal rights and moral rights. In *Ethical Issues in Human Genetics: Genetic Counseling and the Use of Genetic Knowledge,* ed. B. Hilton *et al.*, pp. 221–44. New York: Plenum

Capron, A. M.—1973c. Legal considerations affecting clinical pharmacological studies in children. *Clin. Res.* 21:141–50

Capron, A. M.—1973d. Determining death: Do we need a statute? *Hastings Cent. Rep.* 2:1–3

Capron, A. M.—1975a. *Genetic Screening: Programs, Principles, and Research.* Washington DC: Natl. Acad. Sci.

Capron, A. M.—1975b. Legal considerations. In *Gynecology and Obstetrics: The Health Care of Women,* ed. S. Romney *et al.*, pp. 49–51. New York: McGraw Hill

Capron, A. M.—1975c. Social policy experimentation and the law. In *Ethical and Legal Issues of Social Experimentation,* ed. A. Rivlin, M. Timpani, pp. 127–63. Washington DC: Brookings Inst.

Capron, A. M.—1975d. At what moment is life over? *Stud. Lawyer* 3:16

Capron, A. M., Green, H. P.—1974. Issues of law and public policy in genetic screening. In *Ethical, Social and Legal Dimensions of Screening for Human Genetic Disease,* ed. D. Bergsma, pp. 57–84. Natl. Found. Birth Defects Orig. Artic. Ser., Vol. 10. New York: Natl. Found.

Capron, A. M., Kass, L. R.—1972. A statutory definition of the standards for determining human death: An appraisal and a proposal. *Univ. Pa. Law Rev.* 121:87–118

Carmody, J.—1974. *Ethical Issues in Health Services: A Report and Annotated Bibliography.* Washington DC: US Dept. HEW

Cassell, E. J.—1969. Death and the physician. *Commentary* 48:73–79

Cassell, E. J.—1970. In sickness and in health. *Commentary* 49:59–66

Cassell, E. J.—1973a. Permission to die. *BioScience* 23:475–78

Cassell, E. J.—1973b. Making and escaping moral decisions. *Hastings Cent. Stud.* 1:53–62

Cassell, E. J.—1973c. Learning to die. *Bull. NY Acad. Sci.* 49:1110–18

Clouser, K. D.—1973a. The sanctity of life: An analysis of a concept. *Ann. Intern. Med.* 78:119–23

Clouser, K. D.—1973b. Some things medical ethics is not. *J. Am. Med. Assoc.* 223:787–89

Clouser, K. D.—1973c. Medical ethics courses: Some realistic expectations. *J. Med. Educ.* 48:373–74

Clouser, K. D.—1973d. Medical ethics and related disciplines. In *The Teaching of Medical Ethics,* ed. R. M. Veatch, W. Gaylin, M. Councilman, pp. 38–46. Hastings-on-Hudson, NY: Inst. Soc., Ethics, Life Sci.

Clouser, K. D.—1975a. Medical ethics: Some uses, abuses, and limitations. *N. Engl. J. Med.* 293:384–87

Clouser, K. D.—1975b. *Philosophy and Medicine: The Clinical Management of a Mixed Marriage.* Philadelphia: Soc. Health Hum. Values

Clouser, K. D., Zucker, A.—1974. *Abortion and Euthanasia: An Annotated Bibliography.* Philadelphia: Soc. Health, Hum. Values

Crane, D.—1969. *The Social Aspects of the Prolongation of Life.* Social Sci. Front. New York: Russell Sage

Crane, D.—1975a. *The Sanctity of Social Life: Physicians' Treatment of Critically Ill Patients.* New York: Russell Sage

Crane, D.—1975b. Decisions to treat critically ill patients: A comparison of the social versus medical considerations. *Milbank Mem. Fund Q., Health Soc.* 53:1–33

Crane, D.—1975c. Physicians' attitude towards the treatment of critically ill patients. In *The Dilemmas of Euthanasia,* ed. J. A. Behnke, S. Bok, pp. 107–20. Garden City, NY:Doubleday/Anchor

Crane, D., Matthews, D.—1969. *Heart transplant operations: Diffusion of a medical innovation.* Presented at Ann. Meet. Am. Sociol. Assoc., San Francisco

Curran, W. J.—1959. A problem of consent: Kidney transplantation in identical twin minors. *NYU Law Rev.* 34:891ff

Curran, W. J.—1966. The law and human experimentation. *N. Engl. J. Med.* 275:323–25

Curran, W. J.—1970. Governmental regulation of the use of human subjects in medical research. In *Experimentation With Human Subjects,* ed. P. A. Freund, pp. 402–54. New York: Braziller

Curran, W. J.—1971a. Legal and medical death: Kansas takes the first step. *N. Engl. J. Med.* 284:260–61

Curran, W. J.—1971b. The right to health in national and international law. *N. Engl. J. Med.* 284:1258

Curran, W. J.—1971c. Birth of a healthy child due to negligent failure of pill: Benefit or loss? *N. Engl. J. Med.* 285:1063–64

Curran, W. J.—1972a. The class-action approach to protecting health-care consumers: The right to psychiatric treatment. *N. Engl. J. Med.* 286:26

Curran, W. J.—1972b. Kidney transplantation in identical twin minors. *N. Engl. J. Med.* 287:26–27

Curran, W. J.—1973a. The abortion decisions: The Supreme Court as moralist, scientist, historian, and legislator. *N. Engl. J. Med.* 288:950–51

Curran, W. J.—1973b. The Tuskegee syphilis study. *N. Engl. J. Med.* 289:730–31

Curran, W. J. *et al.*—1973. Protection of privacy and confidentiality. *Science* 182:797–802

Curran, W. J.—1974. The patient's bill of rights becomes law. *N. Engl. J. Med.* 290:32–33

Curran, W. J.—1975a. Experimentation becomes a crime: Fetal research in Massachusetts. *N. Engl. J. Med.* 292:300–1

Curran, W. J.—1975b. Confidentiality and the prediction of dangerousness in psychiatry. *N. Engl. J. Med.* 293:285–86

Curran, W. J., Beecher, H. K.—1969. Experimentation in children. *J. Am. Med. Assoc.* 210:77–83
Dobzhansky, T.—1962. *Mankind Evolving.* New Haven: Yale Univ. Press
Dobzhansky, T.—1967a. *The Biology of Ultimate Concern.* New York: New Am. Libr.
Dobzhansky, T.—1967b. Changing man. *Science* 155:409–14
Dobzhansky, T.—1970. *Genetics and the Evolutionary Process.* New York: Columbia Univ. Press
Dobzhansky, T.—1973a. *Genetic Diversity and Human Equality.* New York: Basic
Dobzhansky, T.—1973b. Ethics and values in biological and cultural evolution. *Zygon* 8:261–81
Duff, R. S., Campbell, A. G. M.—1973. Moral and ethical dilemmas in the special-care nursery. *N. Engl. J. Med.* 289:890–94
Dyck, A. J.—1969. Religious factors in the population problem. In *Updating Life and Death: Essays in Ethics and Medicine*, ed. D. R. Cutler. Boston: Beacon
Dyck, A. J.—1971a. Population problems and ethical acceptability. In *Rapid Population Growth: Consequences and Policy Implications*. Baltimore: Johns Hopkins Press
Dyck, A. J.—1971b. Ethical issues in community and research medicine. *N. Engl. J. Med.* 284:725–28
Dyck, A. J.—1972. Perplexities of the would-be liberal in abortion. *J. Reprod. Med.* 8:251–54
Dyck, A. J.—1973a. An alternative to the ethic of euthanasia. In *To Live and To Die: When, Why, and How*, ed. R. H. Williams, pp. 98–112. New York: Springer
Dyck, A. J.—1973b. Procreative rights and population policy. *Hastings Cent. Stud.* 1:74–82
Dyck, A. J.—1973c. Ethics and medicine. *Linacre Q.* 40:132–200
Dyck, A. J.—1973d. Population, abortion, and human welfare. *Perkins J.* 27:41–49
Dyck, A. J.—1975. American global population policy: An ethical analysis. *Linacre Q.* 42:54–63
Dyck, A. J., Richardson, H. W.—1967. The moral justification for research using human subjects. In *Use of Human Subjects in Safety Evaluation of Food Chemicals*, pp. 229–47. Washington DC: Natl. Acad. Sci. and Natl. Res. Counc.
Engelhardt, H. T. Jr.—1973a. The philosophy of medicine: A new endeavor. *Rep. Biol. Med.* 31:443–52
Engelhardt, H. T. Jr.—1973b. The beginnings of personhood: Philosophical considerations. *Perkins J.* 27:20–27
Engelhardt, H. T. Jr.—1973c. Viability, abortion, and the difference between a fetus and an infant. *Am. J. Obstet. Gynecol.* 116:429–34
Engelhardt, H. T. Jr.—1973d. Euthanasia and children: The injury of continued existence. *J. Pediatr.* 83:170–71
Engelhardt, H. T. Jr.—1974. The ontology of abortion. *Ethics* 84:217–34
Engelhardt, H. T. Jr.—1975a. The counsels of finitude. *Hastings Cent. Rep.* 5:29–36
Engelhardt, H. T. Jr.—1975b. Bioethics and the process of embodiment. *Perspect. Biol. Med.* 18:486–500
Etzioni, A.—1968. Sex control, science and society. *Science* 161:1107–12
Etzioni, A.—1973a. *Genetic Fix.* New York: Macmillan
Etzioni, A.—1973b. The fetus: Whose property? *Commonweal* 98:493

Etzioni, A.—1973c. The government of our body: A resolution. *Soc. Policy* September/October:46–48

Etzioni, A.—1973d. Genetic fix: Should we dare, who shall decide? *Mod. Med.* 41:48D–48H

Etzioni, A.—1973e. Doctors know more than they're telling about genetic defects. *Psychol. Today* 7:26–36

Fletcher, J. C.—1967. Human experimentation: Ethics in the consent situation. *Law Contemp. Probl.* 32:620–49

Fletcher, J. C.—1971. Dialogue between medicine and theology: Death and transplantation. In *Should Doctors Play God?,* ed. C. A. Frazier, pp. 150–63. Nashville, Tenn: Broadman

Fletcher, J. C.—1972. Moral problems in genetic counseling. *Pastoral Psychol.* 23:47–60

Fletcher, J. C.—1973a. Parents in genetic counseling: The moral shape of decision-making. In *Ethical Issues in Human Genetics: Genetic Counseling and the Use of Genetic Knowledge,* ed. B. Hilton *et al.,* pp. 301–27. New York: Plenum

Fletcher, J. C.—1973b. Realities of patient consent to medical research. *Hastings Cent. Stud.* 1:39–49

Fletcher, J. C.—1973c. Who should teach medical ethics? *Hastings Cent. Rep.* 3:4–6

Fletcher, J. C.—1974. Attitudes towards defective newborns. *Hastings Cent. Stud.* 2:21–32

Fletcher, J. C.—1975a. Abortion, euthanasia, and care of defective newborns. *N. Engl. J. Med.* 292:75–78

Fletcher, J. C.—1975b. Choices of life or death in the care of defective newborns. In *Social Responsibility: Journalism, Law, Medicine,* pp. 62–78. Lexington, Va: Washington & Lee Univ. Prog. Soc. Prof.: Stud. Appl. Ethics

Fletcher, J.—1954. *Morals and Medicine*. Boston: Beacon

Fletcher, J.—1967. *Moral Responsibility*. Philadelphia: Westminster

Fletcher, J.—1968. Elective death. In *Ethical Issues in Modern Medicine,* ed. E. F. Torrey, pp. 139–57. Boston: Little, Brown

Fletcher, J.—1969. Our shameful waste of human tissue: An ethical problem for the living and the dead. In *The Religious Situation 1969*, ed. D. R. Cutler, pp. 223–52. Boston: Beacon

Fletcher, J.—1971. Ethical aspects of genetic controls. *N. Engl. J. Med.* 285:776–83

Fletcher, J.—1973a. Ethics and euthanasia. In *To Live and To Die: When, Why and How,* ed. R. H. Williams, pp. 113–22. New York: Springer

Fletcher, J.—1973b. Medicine and the nature of man. In *The Teaching of Medical Ethics*, ed. R. M. Veatch, W. Gaylin, C. Morgan, pp. 47–58. Hastings-on-Hudson, NY: Inst. Soc. Ethics. Life Sci.

Fletcher, J.—1974a. *The Ethics of Genetic Control: End of Reproductive Roulette.* Garden City, NY: Doubleday

Fletcher, J.—1974b. New definitions of death. *Prism* 2:13ff

Fox, R. C.—1957. Training for uncertainty. In *The Student-Physician*, ed. R. K. Merton, G. Reader, P. Kendall, pp. 207–41. Cambridge, Mass: Harvard Univ. Press

Fox, R. C.—1974. *Experiment Perilous: Physicians and Patients Facing the Unknown.* Philadelphia: Univ. Pa. Press. Originally published in 1959 by Free Press

Fox, R. C.—1960. Some social and cultural factors in American society conducive to medical research on human subjects. *J. Clin. Pharmacol. Ther.* 1:433–43

Fox, R. C.—1970. A sociological perspective on organ transplantation and hemodialysis. *Ann. NY Acad. Sci.* 1969:406–28

Fox, R. C.—1974a. Ethical and existential developments in contemporaneous American medicine. Their implications for culture and society. *Milbank Mem. Fund Q., Health Soc.* Fall:445–83

Fox, R. C.—1974b. The process of professional socialization. Is there a new medical student? A comparative view of medical socialization in the 1950's and the 1970's. In *Ethics of Health Care,* ed. L. R. Tancredi, pp. 197–227. Washington DC: Natl. Acad. Sci.

Fox, R. C., Lief, H. I.—1963. Training for detached concern in medical students. In *The Psychological Basis of Medical Practice,* ed. H. I. Lief *et al.*, pp. 12–35. New York: Harper & Row

Fox, R. C., Swazey, J. P.—1974. *The Courage To Fail: A Social View of Organ Transplants and Dialysis.* Chicago: Univ. Chicago Press

Frankel, M. S.—1972. The public health service guidelines governing research involving human subjects: An analysis of the policymaking process. George Washington Univ. Progr. Policy Stud. Sci. Technol. Monogr. #10

Freidson, E.—1970a. *Profession of Medicine: A Study of the Sociology of Applied Knowledge.* New York: Dodd, Mead

Freidson, E.—1970b. *Professional Dominance: The Social Structure of Medical Care.* Chicago: Aldine

Fried, C.—1970. *An Anatomy of Values: Problems of Personal and Social Choice.* Cambridge, Mass: Harvard Univ. Press

Fried, C.—1973a. The need for a philosophical anthropology. In *Ethical Issues in Human Genetics: Genetic Counseling and the Use of Genetic Knowledge,* ed. B. Hilton *et al.*, pp. 261–65. New York: Plenum

Fried, C.—1973b. Ethical issues in existing and emerging techniques for improving human fertility. In *Law and Ethics of A.I.D. and Embryo Transfer,* CIBA Found. Symp. pp. 41–45. New York: Elsevier.

Fried, C.—1974. *Medical Experimentation: Personal Integrity and Social Policy.* In *Clinical Studies,* ed. A. G. Bearn, D. A. K. Black, H. H. Hiatt, vol 5. New York: Am. Elsevier

Gaylin, W.—1965. Psychiatry and the law: Partners in crime. *Columbia Forum* Spring: 23–27

Gaylin, W.—1972a. We have the awful knowledge to make copies of human beings. *NY Times Mag.* March 6:10ff

Gaylin, W.—1972b. What's an FBI poster doing in a nice journal like that? *Hastings Cent. Rep.* 2:1–3

Gaylin, W.—1972c. Genetic screening: The ethics of knowing. *N. Engl. J. Med.* 286:1361–62

Gaylin, W.—1973a. The patient's bill of rights. *Saturday Rev. Sci* 1:22

Gaylin, W.—1973b. Skinner redux. *Harper's Mag.* 48–56

Gaylin, W.—1973c. What's normal? *NY Times Mag.* April:14ff

Gaylin, W.—1974a. On the borders of persuasion: A psychoanalytic look at coercion. *Psychiatry* February:1–9

Gaylin, W.—1974b. Harvesting the dead. *Harper's Mag.* September:23–30

Gaylin, W. *et al.*—1973. The law and the biological revolution. *Columbia J. Law Soc. Probl.* 10:47–76

Gaylin, W., Callahan, D.—1974. The psychiatrist as double agent. *Hastings Cent. Rep.* 4:11–14

Gaylin, W., Lappé, M.—1975. Fetal politics: The debate on experimenting with the unborn. *Atlantic Month.* 235:66–73

Glaser, B. G., Strauss, A. S.—1965. *Awareness of Dying.* Chicago: Aldine

Glaser, B. G., Strauss, A. S.—1968. *Time For Dying.* Chicago: Aldine

Goffman, E.—1961. *Asylums.* New York: Doubleday/Anchor

Gray, B. H.—1975a. *Human Subjects in Medical Experimentation: A Sociological Study of the Conduct and Regulation of Clinical Research.* New York: Wiley

Gray, B. H.—1975b. An assessment of institutional review committees in human experimentation. *Med. Care* 13:318–28

Gustafson, J. M.—1970. Basic ethical issues in the bio-medical fields. *Soundings* 53:151–80

Gustafson, J. M.—1973a. Genetic engineering and the normative view of the human. In *Ethical Issues in Biology and Medicine,* ed. P. N. Williams, pp. 46–58. Cambridge, Mass: Schenkman

Gustafson, J. M.—1973b. Genetic counseling and the uses of genetic knowledge: An ethical overview. In *Ethical Issues in Human Genetics: Genetic Counseling and the Uses of Genetic Knowledge,* ed. B. Hilton *et al.*, pp. 101–19. New York: Plenum

Gustafson, J. M.—1973c. Mongolism, parental desires, and the right to life. *Perspect. Biol. Med.* 16:529–57

Gustafson, J. M.—1975a. *Can Ethics Be Christian?* Chicago: Univ. Chicago Press

Gustafson, J. M.—1975b. *The contributions of theology to medical ethics.* Père Marquette Theol. Lect. Milwaukee: Marquette Univ. Theol. Dept.

Gustafson, J. M., Pizzulli, F. C.—1975. Case studies in bioethics: Ain't nobody gonna cut my head. *Hastings Cent. Rep.* 5:49–51

Harvard Med. School, Ad Hoc Comm. to Examine the Definition of Brain Death.—1968. A definition of irreversible coma. *J. Am. Med. Assoc.* 205:337–40

Jonas, H.—1970. Philosophical reflections on experimenting with human subjects. In *Experimentation With Human Subjects,* ed. P. A. Freund, pp. 1–31. New York: Braziller

Jonas, H.—1973. Technology and responsibility: Reflections on the new task of ethics. *Soc. Res.* 40:31–54

Jonas, H.—1974. *Philosophical Essays: From Ancient Creed to Technological Man.* Englewood Cliffs, NJ: Prentice-Hall

Jonsen, A. R.—1973. The totally implantable artificial heart. *Hastings Cent. Rep.* 3:1–4

Jonsen, A. R.—1974. A new ethic for medicine? *West. J. Med.* 120:169–73

Jonsen, A. R., Phibbs, R. H., Tooley, W. H., Garland, M. J.—1975. Critical issues in newborn intensive care: A conference report and policy proposal. *Pediatrics* 55:756–68

Jonsen, A. R., Butler, L. H.—1975. Public ethics and policy making. *Hastings Cent. Rep.* 5:19–31

Kalish, R. A.—1970. Death and dying: A briefly annotated bibliography. In *The Dying Patient,* ed. O. G. Brim Jr. *et al.*, pp. 323–80. New York: Russell Sage Found.

Kass, L. R.—1971a. Babies by means of *in vitro* fertilization: Unethical experiments on the unborn? *N. Engl. J. Med.* 285:1174–78

Kass, L. R.—1971b. The new biology: What price relieving man's estate? *Science* 174:779–788

Kass, L. R.—1971c. Death—process or event? *Science* 173:694–702

Kass, L. R.—1972. Making babies: The new biology and old morality. *Publ. Interest* 26:18–56

Kass, L. R.—1973. Implications of prenatal diagnosis for the human right to life. In *Ethical Issues in Human Genetics: Genetic Counseling and the Use of Genetic Knowledge,* ed. B. Hilton *et al.,* pp. 185–99. New York: Plenum

Kass, L. R.—1975. Regarding the end of medicine and the pursuit of health. *Publ. Interest* Summer:11–42

Katz, J.—1969. The right to treatment—an enchanting legal fiction? *Univ. Chicago Law Rev.* 36:755–83

Katz, J.—1970. The education of the physician-investigator. In *Experimentation With Human Subjects: The Authority of the Investigator, Subject, Professions, and State in the Human Experimentation Process,* ed. P. A. Freund, pp. 293–314. New York: Braziller

Katz, J., Capron, A. M., Glass, E. S.—1972. *Experimentation with Human Beings.* New York: Russell Sage

Katz, J., Capron, A. M.—1975. *Catastrophic Diseases: Who Decides What?* New York: Russell Sage Found.

Katz, J., Goldstein, J., Dershowitz, A. M.—1967. *Psychoanalysis, Psychiatry and Law.* New York: Free Press

Kennedy, I. McC.—1971. The Kansas Statute on death: An appraisal. *N. Engl. J. Med.* 285:946–50

Kübler-Ross, E.—1969. *On Death and Dying.* New York: Macmillan

Kübler-Ross, E.—1974. *Questions and Answers on Death and Dying.* New York: Collier

Kübler-Ross, E.—1975. *Death: The Final Stages of Growth.* Englewood Cliffs, NJ: Prentice-Hall

Kutscher, A.—1969. *A Bibliography of Books on Death, Bereavement, Loss and Grief: 1955–68.* New York: Health Sci. Publ.

Lally, J. J., Barber, B.—1974. The compassionate physician: Frequency and social determinants of physician-investigator concern for human subjects. *Soc. Forces* 53:289–96

Lappé, M.—1971. The genetic counselor: Responsible to whom? *Hastings Cent. Rep.* 1:6–11

Lappé, M.—1973a. How much do we want to know about the unborn? *Hastings Cent. Rep.* 3:8–9

Lappé, M.—1973b. Allegiances of human geneticists: A preliminary typology. *Hastings Cent. Stud.* 1:63–78

Lappé, M.—1973c. The danger of compulsion. Osmundsen, J. A. We are all mutants. *Med. Dimensions* February:5ff

Lappé, M.—1973d. Human genetics. *Ann. NY Acad. Sci.* 216:152–59

Lappé, M.—1973e. The institute at Hastings: An overview. *Fed. Proc.* 32:1556–57

Lappé, M.—1974. Censoring the hereditarians. *Commonweal* April:183–85

Lappé, M., Roblin, R. O., Gustafson, J. M.—1974. *Ethical, Social and Legal*

Dimensions of Screening for Human Genetic Disease. Birth Defects Orig. Artic. Ser., ed. Daniel Bergsma, Vol. 10. Miami: Symp. Spec.

Lappé, M.—1975. The moral claims on the wanted fetus. *Hastings Cent. Rep.* 5:11–13

Mauss, M.—1954. *The Gift,* transl. I. Cunnison. Glencoe, Ill: Free Press

McCormick, R. A.—1972. Genetic medicine: Notes on moral literature. *Theol. Stud.* 33:531–52

McCormick, R. A.—1973a. Notes on moral theology. *Theol. Stud.* 34:53–103

McCormick, R. A.—1973b. The new medicine and morality. *Theol. Dig.* 21:308–21

McCormick, R. A.—1973c. Medical ethics program. In *The Teaching of Medical Ethics,* ed. R. M. Veatch, W. Gaylin, C. Morgan, pp. 103–21. Hastings-on-the-Hudson, NY: Inst. Soc., Ethics, Life Sci.

McCormick, R. A.—1974a. Moral notes: Abortion dossier. *Theol. Stud.* 35: 312–59

McCormick, R. A.—1974b. To save or let die: The dilemma of modern medicine. *J. Am. Med. Assoc.* 229:172–76

McCormick, R. A.—1974c. Proxy consent in the experimentation situation. *Perspect. Biol. Med.* 18:2–20

McCormick, R. A.—1975. Fetal research, morality, and public policy. *Hastings Cent. Rep.* 5:26–31

Morison, R. S.—1971. Death—process or event? *Science* 173:694–702

Morison, R. S.—1973a. Implications of prenatal diagnosis for the quality of, and right to, human life: Society as a standard. In *Ethical Issues in Human Genetics: Genetic Counseling and the Use of Genetic Knowledge,* ed. B. Hilton *et al.,* pp. 201–20. New York: Plenum

Morison, R. S.—1973b. Dying. *Sci. Am.* September:55–62

Morison, R. S.—1974. Rights and responsibilities: Redressing the uneasy balance. *Hastings Cent. Rep.* 4:1–4

Morison, R. S., Twiss, S. B. Jr.—1973. Case studies in bioethics: The human fetus as useful research material. *Hastings Cent. Rep.* 5:8–10

Murray, R. F. Jr.—1972. Problems behind the promise: Ethical issues in mass genetic screening. *Hastings Cent. Rep.* 2:11–13

Murray, R. F. Jr.—1973. Teaching the ethics of genetic counseling in the framework of a medical genetics curriculum. In *The Teaching of Medical Ethics,* ed. R. M. Veatch, W. Gaylin, C. Morgan, pp. 124–28. Hastings-on-Hudson, NY: Inst. Soc., Ethics, Life Sci.

Murray, R. F. Jr.—1974. Genetic disease and human health . . . : A clinical perspective. *Hastings Cent. Rep.* 4:4–7

Murray, R. F. Jr., Sable, A.—1974. Case studies in bioethics: Drug treatment or drug addiction? *Hastings Cent. Rep.* 4:11–12

Parsons, T.—1948. Illness and the role of the physician. In *Personality in Nature, Society and Culture,* ed. H. A. Murray, C. Kluckhohn, pp. 609–17. New York: Knopf

Parsons, T.—1951. Social structure and dynamic process: The case of modern medical practice. In *The Social System,* chap. 10, pp. 428–79. Glencoe, Ill: Free Press

Parsons, T.—1958. Definitions of health and illness in the light of American values and social structure. In *Patients, Physicians and Illness: Sourcebook in*

Behavioral Science and Medicine, ed. E. G. Jaco, pp. 165–87. Glencoe, Ill: Free Press

Parsons, T.—1970. Research with human subjects and the professional complex. In *Experimentation with Human Subjects,* ed. P. A. Freund, pp. 116–51. New York: Braziller

Parsons, T.—1975. The sick role and the role of the physician reconsidered. *Milbank Mem. Fund Q., Health Soc.* Summer:257–77

Parsons, T., Fox, R. C. 1952. Illness, therapy, and the modern urban American family. *J. Soc. Issues* 8:31–44

Parsons, T., Fox, R. C., Lidz, V. M.—1972. The gift of life and its reciprocation. *Soc. Res.* 39:367–415

Parsons, T., Lidz, V. M.—1967. Death in American society. In *Essays in Self-Destruction,* ed. E. Schneidman. New York: Science House

Pellegrino, E. D.—1969a. Humanism in medicine: A version for today. *Pharos* 32:6–9

Pellegrino, E. D.—1969b. The necessity, promise and dangers of human experimentation. In *Experiments with Man*, pp. 31–56. World Counc. Stud., No. 6. New York: World Counc. Churches, Geneva, Friendship Press

Pellegrino, E. D.—1971a. Physician, patients and society: Some new tensions in medical ethics. In *Human Aspects of Biomedical Innovation,* ed. E. Mendelsohn, J. P. Swazey, I. Taviss, pp. 77–97, 219–20. Cambridge, Mass: Harvard Univ. Press

Pellegrino, E. D.—1971b. Reflections, refractions, and prospectives. *Proc. Sess. Inst. Hum. Values in Med., 1st,* pp. 99–115. Philadelphia: Soc. Health Hum. Values

Pellegrino, E. D.—1972. Introduction to the second institute. *Proc. Sess. Inst. on Hum. Values in Med., 2nd* pp. 28–41. Philadelphia: Soc. Health Hum Values

Pellegrino, E. D.—1973a. Toward an expanding medical ethic: The Hippocratic ethic revisited. In *Hippocrates Revisited,* ed. R. J. Bulger, pp. 133–47. New York: Medcom

Pellegrino, E. D.—1973b. Reform and innovation in medical education: The role of ethics. In *The Teaching of Medical Ethics,* ed. R. M. Veatch, W. Gaylin, C. Morgan, pp. 150–65. Hastings-on-Hudson, NY Inst. Soc., Ethics, Life Sci.

Pellegrino, E. D.—1974a. *Medicine and philosophy: Some notes on the flirtations of Minerva and Aesculapius.* Ann. Oration, Soc. Health Hum. Values. Philadelphia: Soc. Health Hum. Values

Pellegrino, E. D.—1974b. Humanism in human experimentation: Some notes on the investigator's fiduciary role. *Tex. Rep. Biol. Med.* 32:311–25

Pellegrino, E. D.—1975. The medical uses of philosophy: Roundtable discussion. In *Explanation in the Biomedical Sciences,* pp. 228–34. Dordrecht, Holland: Reidy

Pitts, J. R.—1968. Social control: The concept. In *Encyclopedia of the Social Sciences,* 14:381–96. New York: Macmillan & Free Press

Potter, V. R.—1970. Bioethics: The science of survival. *Perspect. Biol. Med.* 14:120–53

Potter, V. R.—1971. *Bioethics: Bridge to the Future.* Englewood Cliffs, NJ: Prentice-Hall

Potter, V. R.—1972. Bioethics for whom?; and General discussion II. *Ann. NY Acad. Sci.* 196:200–205, 243–246

Ramsey, P.—1950. *Basic Christian Ethics.* New York: Scribner's
Ramsey, P.—1967. The sanctity of life. *Dublin Rev.* 241:3–21
Ramsey, P.—1968. The morality of abortion. *Life or Death: Ethics and Options,* ed. D. H. Labby. Seattle, Wash: Univ. Wash. Press
Ramsey, P.—1970a. *The Patient as Person.* New Haven: Yale Univ. Press
Ramsey, P.—1970b. *Fabricated Man: The Ethics of Genetic Control.* New Haven: Yale Univ. Press
Ramsey, P.—1970c. Feticide/infanticide upon request. *Relig. in Life* 39:170–86
Ramsey, P.—1971. The ethics of a cottage industry in an age of community and research medicine. *N. Engl. J. Med.* 284:700–6
Ramsey, P.—1972. Genetic engineering. *Bull. At. Sci.* December:14–17
Ramsey, P.—1973a. Medical progress and canons of loyalty to experimental subjects. In *Biological Evolution—Theological Impact,* pp. 51–77. St. Louis, Mo.: Inst. Theol. Encounter with Sci. Technol.
Ramsey, P.—1973b. Screening: An ethicist's view. In *Ethical Issues in Human Genetics: Genetic Counseling and the Use of Genetic Knowledge,* ed. B. Hilton *et al.,* pp. 147–67. New York: Plenum
Ramsey, P.—1973c. The nature of radical ethics. In *The Teaching of Medical Ethics,* ed. R. M. Veatch, W. Gaylin, C. Morgan, pp. 14–28. Hastings-on-Hudson, NY: Inst. Soc., Ethics, Life Sci.
Ramsey, P.—1973d. Abortion: A review article. *Thomist* 37:174–226
Ramsey, P.—1974. Death's pedagogy. *Commonweal* September:497–502
Ramsey, P.—1975. *The Ethics of Fetal Research.* New Haven: Yale Univ. Press
Robitscher, J. B.—1966. *Pursuit of Agreement: Psychiatry and the Law.* Philadelphia: Lippincott
Robitscher, J. B.—1967. Public life and private information. *J. Am. Med. Assoc.* 202:398–400
Robitscher, J. B.—1972a. The right to psychiatric treatment: A social-legal approach to the plight of the state hospital patient. *Villanova Law Rev.* 18:11–36
Robitscher, J. B.—1972b. The right to die. *Hastings Cent. Rep.* 2:11–14
Robitscher, J. B., ed.—1973. *Eugenic Sterilization.* Springfield, Ill: Thomas
Robitscher, J. B.—1975. The impact of new legal standards on psychiatry, or who are David Bazelon and Thomas Szasz and why are they saying such terrible things about us? or authoritarianism versus nihilism in legal psychiatry. *J. Psychiatry Law* Summer:15–74
Sadler, A. M., Sadler, B. L., Stason, E. B.—1968. The uniform anatomical gift act: A model for reform. *J. Am. Med. Assoc.* 206:2501–6
Sadler, B. L., Sadler, A. M.—1973. Providing cadaver organs for transplantation. *Hastings Cent. Stud.* 1:14–26
Scheff, T. J.—1966. *Being Mentally Ill: A Sociological Theory.* Chicago: Aldine
Scheff, T. J., ed.—1975. *Labeling Madness.* Englewood Cliffs, NJ: Prentice-Hall
Simmons, R. G., Fulton, J., Fulton, R.—1970. The prospective organ transplant donor: Problems and prospects of medical innovation. Presented at Int. Conf. Soc. Sci. Med., 2nd, Aberdeen, Scotland, Sept. 1970
Simmons, R. G., Klein, S., Thornton, T.—1972. Family decision-making and the selection of a kidney transplant donor. Presented at Ann. Meet. Am. Sociol. Assoc., 63rd, New Orleans, August 1972
Simmons, R. G., Hickey, K., Kjellstrand, C. M., Simmons, R. L.—1971a. Donors

and non-donors: The role of the family and the physician in kidney transplantation. *Semin. Psychiatry* 3:102–15

Simmons, R. G., Hickey, K., Kjellstrand, C. M. , Simmons, R. L.—1971b. Family tension in the search for a kidney donor. *J. Am. Med. Assoc.* 215:909–12

Simmons, R. G., Najarian, J.—1970. Reply to Starzl. *N. Engl. J. Med.* 283:934–35

Simmons, R. G. Simmons, R. L.—1971. Organ transplantation: A societal problem. *Soc. Probl.* 19:36–57

Smith, A. J. K., Penry, J. D., eds.—1972. *Brain Death: A Bibliography with Key-Word and Author Indexes.* Washington DC: US Dept. HEW, Publ. Health Serv., Natl. Inst. Neurolog. Dis. Stroke, Appl. Neurolog. Res. Branch, Dept. HEW Publ. No. NIH 73–347

Sollitto, S., Veatch, R. M., eds.—1973, *Bibliography of Society, Ethics and the Life Sciences.* Hastings-on-Hudson, NY: Inst. Soc., Ethics, Life Sci.

Sollitto, S. Veatch, R. M., Fenner, D., eds.—1975. *Bibliography of Society, Ethics and the Life Sciences.* Hastings-on-Hudson, NY: Inst. Soc., Ethics, Life Sci.

Sorenson, J. R.—1971. *Social Aspects of Applied Human Genetics.* New York: Russell Sage Found.

Sorenson, J. R.—1973a. *Social Aspects of Human Genetics: A Bibliography.* Washington DC: Fogarty Int. Cent., Natl. Inst. Health, Dept. HEW Publ. No. NIH 73–412

Sorenson, J. R.—1973b. Social and psychological factors in applied human genetics. In *Proc. Conf. Ethical Issues Genet. Couns. Use Genet. Knowl.*, pp. 283–300

Sorenson, J. R.—1973c. Counselors: A self-portrait. *Genet. Counsel.* 1:29–34

Sorenson, J. R.—1974a. Some social and psychological issues in genetic screening: Public and professional adaptation to biomedical innovation. In *Ethical, Social and Legal Dimensions of Screening for Human Genetic Disease,* ed. D. Bergsma, pp. 165–84. Natl. Found. Birth Defects Orig. Artic. Ser., Vol. 10, New York: Natl. Found.

Sorenson, J. R.—1974b. Biomedical innovation, uncertainty and doctor-patient interaction. *J. Health Soc. Behav.* 15:366–74

Sudnow, D.—1967. *Passing On: The Social Organization of Dying.* Englewood Cliffs, NJ: Prentice-Hall

Superior Court of New Jersey.—1975. Opinion in the matter of Karen Quinlan, an alleged incompetent. Chancery Div., Morris Cty., NJ: Docket No. C–201–75

Supreme Court of New Jersey—1976. In the name of Karen Quinlan, an alleged incompetent. A-116. Sep. Term 1975. Argued Jan. 26, 1976—Decided Mar. 31, 1976

Swazey, J. P.—1971. Phenylketonuria: A case study in biomedical legislation. *J. Urban Law* 48:883–931

Swazey, J. P.—1974a. *Chlorpromazine in Psychiatry: A Study of Therapeutic Innovation.* Cambridge, Mass: MIT Press

Swazey, J. P.—1974b. *The Scribner Dialysis Shunt: Ramifications of a Clinical-Technological Innovation.* Presented at Symp. Manage. Technol. Health Organ., Cambridge, Mass: Harvard Bus. Sch., Apr. 30–May 1

Swazey, J. P., Bessman, S. P.—1971. Phenylketonuria: A study of biomedical legislation. In *Human Aspects of Biomedical Innovation,* ed. E. Mendelsohn, J. P. Swazey, I. Taviss, pp. 49–76. Cambridge, Mass: Harvard Univ. Press

Swazey, J. P. Fox, R. C.—1970. The clinical moratorium: A case study of mitral valve surgery. In *Experimentation with Human Subjects,* ed. P. A. Freund, pp. 315–57. New York: Braziller

Tancredi, L. R., ed.—1975. Ethics of Health Care. Washington DC: *Natl. Acad. Sci.*

Tancredi, L. R., Clark, D.—1972. Psychiatry and the legal rights of patients. *Am. J. Psychiatry* 129:318–20

Tancredi, L. R., Barsky, A. J.—1974. Technology and health care decision-making: Conceptualizing the process for societal informed consent. *Med. Care* 12:845–59

Taviss, I.—1971. Problems in the social control of biomedical science and technology. In *Human Aspects of Biomedical Innovation,* ed. E. Mendelsohn, J. P. Swazey, I. Taviss, pp. 3–45. Cambridge, Mass: Harvard Univ. Press

Titmuss, R. M.—1971. *The Gift Relationship: From Human Blood to Social Policy.* New York: Pantheon

US Congress, Senate Comm. on Labor and Public Welfare.—1973. *Quality of Health Care—Human Experimentation.* Washington DC: GPO

US Department of Health, Education, and Welfare, Public Health Service and National Institutes of Health.—1971. *The Institutional Guide to DHEW Policy on Protection of Human Subjects.* Dept. HEW Publ. No. NIH 72–102. Washington DC: GPO

US Department of Health, Education, and Welfare, Public Health Service.—1973. *Final Report of the Tuskegee Syphilis Study, Ad Hoc Advisory Panel.* Atlanta, Ga: Cent. Dis. Control Inf. Off.

US Department of Health, Education, and Welfare, National Institutes of Health.—May 30, 1974. Protection of human subjects. *Fed. Regist.* 39:Part II

US Department of Health, Education, and Welfare.—August 23, 1974. Protection of human subjects: Proposed policy. *Fed. Regist.* 39:Part III

Vaux, K.—1970. *Who Shall Live?* Philadelphia: Fortress

Vaux, K.—1974. *Biomedical Ethics: Morality for the New Medicine.* New York: Harper & Row

Veatch, R. M.—1971a. Experimental pregnancy: The ethical complexities of experimentation with oral contraceptives. *Hastings Cent. Rep.* 1:2–3

Veatch, R. M.—1971b. *A Proposal For Taxing Childbearing: Can It Be Just?* Work. Pap. Ser., Insti. Soc., Ethics, Life Sci. Hastings-on-Hudson, NY

Veatch, R. M.—1971c. Doing what comes naturally. *Hastings Cent. Rep.* 1:1–2

Veatch, R. M.—1972a. Medical ethics: Professional or universal? *Harvard Theol. Rev.* 65:531–59

Veatch, R. M.—1972b. The unexpected chromosome . . . : A counselor's dilemma. *Hastings Cent. Rep.* 2:8–9

Veatch, R. M.—1972c. Ethics, population policy and population education. *Soc. Educ.* April: 363–400

Veatch, R. M.—1972d. Models for ethical medicine in a revolutionary age. *Hastings Cent. Rep.* 2:5–7

Veatch, R. M.—1972e. Brain death: Welcome definition or dangerous judgment? *Hastings Cent. Rep.* 2:10–13

Veatch, R. M.—1972f. Choosing not to prolong dying. *Med. Dimensions* December: 8–10ff

Veatch, R. M.—1973. Generalization of expertise. *Hastings Cent. Stud.* 1:29–40

Veatch, R. M.—1974a. Drugs and competing drug ethics. *Hastings Cent. Stud.* 2:68–80
Veatch, R. M.—1974b. Human experimentation: The crucial choices ahead. *Prism* 2:58ff
Veatch, R. M.—1975a. The whole-brain-oriented concept of death: An outmoded philosophical formulation. *J. Thanatol.* 3:13–30
Veatch, R. M.—1975b. Human experimentation committees: Professional or representative? *Hastings Cent. Rep.* 5:31–40
Veatch, R. M., Draper, T. F.—1971. *Population Policy and Values of Physicians.* Hastings-on-Hudson, NY: Hastings Cent. Doc. Stud. #16
Veatch, R. M., Clouser, K. D.—1973. New mix in the medical curriculum. *Prism* 1:62–66
Veatch, R. M., Gaylin, W.—1972. Teaching medical ethics: An experimental program. *J. Med. Educ.* 47:779–85
Veatch, R. M., Gaylin, W., Morgan, C., eds.—1973. *The Teaching of Medical Ethics.* Hastings-on-Hudson, NY: Inst. Soc., Ethics, Life Sci.
Veatch, R. M., Sollitto, S.—1973. Human experimentation: The ethical questions persist. *Hastings Cent. Rep.* 3:1–3
Veatch, R. M., Steinfels, P.—1974. Case studies in bioethics: Who should pay for smokers' medical care? *Hastings Cent. Rep.* 4:8–10
Walters, L. R., ed. 1975. *Bibliography of Bioethics,* Vol. 1. Detroit: Gale Res. Co. Book Tower
Warwick, D. P.—1968. Human freedom and national development. *Cross Curr.* 18:495–517
Warwick, D. P.—1973. Tearoom trade: Means and ends in social research. *Hastings Cent. Stud.* 1:27–38
Warwick, D. P., Kelman, H. C.—1973. Ethical issues in social intervention. In *Processes and Phenomena of Social Change,* ed. G. Zaltman. New York: Wiley
Warwick, D. P.—1974a. Ethics and population control in developing countries. *Hastings Cent. Rep.* 4:1–4
Warwick, D. P.—1974b. The moral message of Bucharest. *Hastings Cent. Rep.* 4:8–9
Warwick, D. P.—1975a. Social scientists ought to stop lying. *Psychol. Today* 8:38ff
Warwick, D. P.—1975b. Contraceptives in the Third World. *Hastings Cent. Rep.* 5:9–12
Warwick, D. P.—1975c. Bullying birth control. *Commonweal* 102:392–94
Wellman, C.—1972. Ethics since 1950. *J. Value Inquiry* 6:83–90

PART SEVEN

SOCIETAL AND CULTURAL OVERVIEW

The Medicalization and Demedicalization of American Society

The statement that American society has become "medicalized" is increasingly heard these days. During the past decade or so, the allegation has been made by social scientists, jurists, politicians, social critics, medical scientists, and physicians. In many instances, it has been accompanied by the claim that the society is now "overmedicalized," and that some degree of "demedicalization" would be desirable. There are those who not only espouse "demedicalizing the society," but who also predict that, in fact, it will progressively come to pass.

One of the most extreme statements of this kind is Ivan Illich's monograph *Medical Nemesis*, which opens with the assertion that "the medical establishment has become a threat to health," and goes on to develop the many damaging ways in which the author considers modern medicine to be responsible for "social" as well as "clinical" and "structural iatrogenesis":

> The technical and non-technical consequences of institutional medicine coalesce and generate a new kind of suffering: anesthetized, impotent and solitary survival in a world turned into a hospital ward. . . . The need for specialized, professional health care beyond a certain point can be

From *Daedalus* 106, 1 (Winter 1977): 9–22. Also in John H. Knowles, ed., *Doing Better and Feeling Worse* (New York: Norton, 1977), 9–22.

> taken as an indication of the unhealthy goals pursued by society. . . . The level of public health corresponds to the degree to which the means and responsibility for coping with illness are distributed amongst the total population. This ability to cope can be enhanced but never replaced by medical intervention in the lives of people or by the hygienic characteristics of the environment. The society which can reduce professional intervention to the minimum will provide the best conditions for health. . . . Healthy people are those who live in healthy homes on a healthy diet; in an environment equally fit for birth, growth, work, healing and dying: sustained by a culture which enhances the conscious acceptance of limits to population, of aging, of incomplete recovery and ever imminent death. . . . Man's consciously lived fragility, individuality and relatedness make the experience of pain, of sickness and of death an integral part of his life. The ability to cope with this trio autonomously is fundamental to his health. As he becomes dependent on the management of his intimacy, he renounces his autonomy and his health *must* decline. The true miracle of modern medicine is diabolical. It consists not only of making individuals but whole populations survive on inhumanly low levels of personal health. That health should decline with increasing health service delivery is unforeseen only by the health managers, precisely because their strategies are the result of their blindness to the inalienability of life.[1]

There are numerous grounds on which Illich's thesis can be criticized. He minimizes the advances in the prevention, diagnosis, and treatment of disease that have been made since the advent of the bacteriological era in medicine, and he attributes totally to nonmedical agencies all progress in health that has ensued. He implies that modern Western, urban, industrialized, capitalist societies, of which the United States is the prototype, are more preoccupied with pain, sickness, and death, and less able to come to terms with these integral parts of a human life, than other types of society. Although his volume appears to be well documented, a disturbing discrepancy exists between the data presented in many of the works that Illich cites in his copious footnotes and the interpretive liberties that he takes with them. Perhaps most insidious of all is the sophistry that Illich uses in presenting a traditional, orthodox, Christian Catholic point of view in the guise of a vulgar Marxist argument. For he repeatedly claims that, "when dependence on the professional management of pain, sickness and death grows beyond a certain point, the healing power in sickness, patience in suffering, and fortitude in the face of death must decline."[2] In Illich's view, this state is not only morally dubious, but also spiritually dangerous. Because it entails the

1. Ivan Illich, *Medical Nemesis: The Expropriation of Health* (London, 1975), 165–169.
2. Illich, *Medical Nemesis, passim.*

"hubris" of what he deems arrogant and excessive medical intervention, it invites "nemesis": the retribution of the gods.

But whatever its shortcomings, Illich's essay is a kind of lightning rod, picking up and conducting the twin themes of medicalization and demedicalization that have become prominent in the United States and a number of other modern Western societies. These themes will concern us here. We shall begin by identifying the constellation of factors ininvolved in what has been termed "medicalization," offer an interpretation of these phenomena, and consider and evaluate certain signs of demedicalization. Finally, some speculative predictions about the probable evolution of the medicalization-demedicalization process in American society will be offered.

One indication of the scope that the "health-illness-medicine complex" has acquired in American society is the diffuse definition of health that has increasingly come to be advocated: "a state of complete physical, mental, and social well-being," to borrow the World Health Organization's phrase. This conception of health extends beyond biological and psychological phenomena relevant to the functioning, equilibrium, and fulfillment of individuals, to include social and cultural conditions of communal as well as personal import. Such an inclusive perspective on health is reflected in the range of difficulties that persons now bring to physicians for their consideration and help. As Leon Kass picturesquely phrased it, "All kinds of problems now roll to the doctor's door, from sagging anatomies to suicides, from unwanted childlessness to unwanted pregnancy, from marital difficulties to learning difficulties, from genetic counseling to drug addiction, from laziness to crime. . . ."[3] A new term has even been coined by medical practitioners to refer to those clients who seem to have some legitimate need of their therapeutic services, but who technically cannot be considered to be ill. With discernible ambivalence, such people are often called "the worried well."

Accompanying the increasingly comprehensive idea of what constitutes health and what is appropriate for medical professionals to deal with is the growing conviction that health and health care are rights rather than privileges, signs of grace, or lucky, chance happenings. In turn, these developments are connected with higher expectations on the part of the public about what medicine ideally ought to be able to accomplish and to prevent. To some extent, for example, the rise in the number of malpractice suits in the United States seems not only to be a

3. Leon R. Kass, "Regarding the End of Medicine and the Pursuit of Health," *The Public Interest*, 40 (Summer, 1975), p. 11.

reaction to the errors and abuses that physicians can commit, but also a reflection of the degree to which the professional is being held personally responsible for the scientific and technical uncertainties and limitations of their discipline. The vision of an "iatrogenesis"-free furthering of health, which social critics such as Illich hold forth, is also an indicator of such rising expectations.

One significant form that the process of medicalization has taken is the increase in the numbers and kinds of attitudes and behaviors that have come to be defined as illnesses and treatment of which is regarded as belonging within the jurisdiction of medicine and its practitioners. In an earlier, more religiously oriented era of a modern Western society like our own, some of these same kinds of attitudes and behaviors were considered sinful rather than sick, and they fell under the aegis of religious authorities for a different kind of diagnosis, treatment, and control. In a more secular, but less scientifically and medically oriented, stage of the society than the current one, certain of these ways of thinking, feeling, and behaving were viewed and dealt with as criminal. Although sin, crime, and sickness are not related in a simple, invariant way, there has been a general tendency in the society to move from sin to crime to sickness in categorizing a number of aberrant or deviant states to the degree that the concept of the "medicalization of deviance" has taken root in social science writings. The sin-to-crime-to-sickness evolution has been most apparent with respect to the conditions that are now considered to be mental illnesses, or associated with serious psychological and/or social disturbances.[4] These include, for example, states of hallucination and delusion that once would have been interpreted as signs of possession by the Devil, certain forms of physical violence, such as the type of child abuse that results in what is termed the "battered child syndrome," the set of behaviors in children which are alternatively called hyperactivity, hyperkinesis, or minimal brain dysfunction, and so-called "addictive disorders," such as alcoholism, drug addiction, compulsive overeating, and compulsive gambling.

This "continuing process of divestment"[5] away from sin and crime as

4. In his novel *Erewhon*, written in 1872, Samuel Butler satirized this evolution, and the degree to which what is defined as illness is contingent on social factors. In Erewhon (the fictitious country that Butler created by imagining late nineteenth- and early twentieth-century England stood on its head), persons afflicted with what physicians would call tuberculosis are found guilty in a court of law and sentenced to life imprisonment, whereas persons who forge checks, set houses on fire, steal, and commit acts of violence are diagnosed as suffering from a "severe fit of immorality" and are cared for at public expense in hospitals.

5. Nicholas N. Kittrie, *The Right To Be Different: Deviance and Enforced Therapy* (Baltimore, 1971). See especially chapter 1, "The Divestment of Criminal Justice and the Coming of the Therapeutic State," 1–49.

categories for abnormality, dysfunction, and deviance and toward illness as the explanatory concept has entailed what Peter Sedgwick calls "the progressive annexation of not-illness into illness." "The future belongs to illness," he proclaims, predicting that "we . . . are going to get more and more diseases, since our expectations of health are going to become more expansive and sophisticated."[6] If we include into what is considered to be sickness or, at least, non-health in the United States, disorders manifested by subjective symptoms that are not brought to the medical profession for diagnosis and treatment, but that do not differ significantly from those that are, then almost everyone in the society can be regarded as in some way "sick."

> At least two . . . studies have noted that as much as 90 percent of their apparently healthy sample had some physical aberration or clinical disorder. . . . It seems that the more intensive the investigation, the higher the prevalence of clinically serious but previously undiagnosed and untreated disorders. Such data as these give an unexpected statistical picture of illness. Instead of it being a relatively infrequent or abnormal phenomenon, the empirical reality may be that illness, defined as the presence of clinically serious symptoms, is the statistical *norm*.[7]

Such a global conception of illness sharply raises the question of the extent to which illness is an objective reality, a subjective state, or a societal construct that exists chiefly in the minds of its social "beholders," a question that will be considered in greater detail below.

The great "power" that the American medical profession, particularly the physician, is assumed to possess and jealously and effectively to guard is another component of the society's medicalization. In the many allusions to this medical "power" that are currently made, the organized "autonomy" and "dominance" of the profession are frequently cited, and, in some of the more critical statements about the physician, these attributes are described as constituting a virtual "monopoly" or "expropriation" of health and illness. The "mystique" that surrounds the medical profession is part of what is felt to be its power: a mystique that is not only spontaneously conferred on its practitioners by the public but, as some observers contend, is also cultivated by physicians themselves through their claim that they command knowledge and skills that are too esoteric to be freely and fully shared with lay persons.

6. Peter Sedgwick, "Illness—Mental and Otherwise," *The Hastings Center Studies,* 1:3 (1973), p. 37.

7. Irving Kenneth Zola, "Culture and Symptoms—An Analysis of Patients' Presenting Complaints," *American Sociological Review,* 31:5 (October, 1966), 615–616.

However, it is to the biotechnological capacities of modern medicine that its greatest power is usually attributed: both its huge battery of established drugs and procedures and its new and continually increasing medical and surgical techniques. Among the actual or incipient developments that are most frequently mentioned are the implantation of cadaveric, live, or mechanical organs, genetic and other microcellular forms of "engineering," and *in vitro* fertilization, as well as various chemical, surgical, and psychophysiological methods of thought and behavior control. The potentials of medicine not only to prevent and to heal, but also to subjugate, modify, and harm are implicated in such references.

The high and rapidly growing cost of medical and health care is still another measure in increased medicalization. In 1975, Americans spent $547 per person for health care and related activities such as medical education and research. This represented 8.3 percent of the GNP. In 1950, 4.6 percent and in 1970, 7.2 percent of the GNP was spent. From 1963 to the present, health expenditures have risen at a rate exceeding 10 percent annually while the rest of the economy as reflected in the GNP has been growing at a rate between 6 and 7 percent.

In addition to allocating an ever-increasing proportion of society's economic resources for health care, greater amounts of political and legal energy are also being invested in health, illness, and medical concerns. The pros and cons of national health insurance, which continue to be vigorously debated in various arenas, are as much political, ideological, and legal issues, as they are economic ones. The volume of legislation relevant to health care has grown impressively. In 1974, for example, more than 1300 health-care bills were introduced in the Congress, and more than 900 such bills in the state legislature in New York alone. The health subcommittees of the Senate and the House of Representatives are particularly active, and they have become prestigious as well. Furthermore, partly as a consequence of various congressional investigations and hearings, the federal government is now significantly involved in bioethical questions (especially those bearing on human experimentation) in addition to their more traditional interests in medical economic and health-care-delivery problems.

During the past few years, a number of medico-legal decisions have been made that are of far-reaching cultural importance, affecting the society's fundamental conceptions of life, death, the body, individuality, and humanity. These include: the Supreme Court's decisions in favor of the legal right of women to decide upon and undergo abortion; the Court's ruling against the involuntary, purely custodial confinement of untreated mentally ill persons; the Uniform Anatomical Gift Act, adopted in fifty-one jurisdictions, which permits people to donate all or parts of their bodies to be used for medical purposes after their death; death statutes passed in various states that add the new, "irreversible coma" criterion of "brain death" to the traditional criteria for pronouncing death, based on the cessation of respiratory and cardiac function; and, in the case of Karen Ann Quinlan, the New Jersey Supreme Court's extension of "the individual's right of privacy" to encompass a patient's decision to decline or terminate life-saving treatment, under certain circumstances.

One other, quite different, way in which medical phenomena have acquired central importance in the legal system is through the dramatic escalation of malpractice suits against physicians. An estimated 20,000 or more malpractice claims are brought against doctors each year, and the number seems to be rising steadily. In New York, for example, the number of suits filed against physicians rose from 564 in 1970 to 1200 in 1974; in the past decade, the average award for a malpractice claim grew from $6000 to $23,400, with far more very large awards being made than in the past.[8]

Increasing preoccupation with bioethical issues seems also to be a concomitant of the medicalization process. Basic societal questions concerning values, beliefs, and meaning are being debated principally in terms of the dilemmas and dangers associated with biomedical advances. Consideration of particular medical developments such as genetic engineering, life-support systems, birth technology, organ implants, and population and behavior control have opened up far-reaching ethical and existential concerns. Problems of life, death, chance, "necessity," scarcity, equity, individuality, community, the "gift relationship," and the "heroic" world view are being widely discussed in medical, scientific, political, legal, journalistic, philosophical, and religious circles. A bioethics "subculture" with certain characteristics of a social movement has crystallized around such issues.

The unprecedented number of young people who are attempting to embark on medical careers is also contributing to the medicalization process. In this country, on the average, more than three persons apply for each medical-school place available to entering first-year students, and there is as yet no sign of leveling off. Paradoxically, this is happening during a period when medicine and the medical profession are being subjected to increased scrutiny and criticism.

Complex, and by no means consistent, the process of medicalization is not an easy one to analyze. Several preliminary *caveats* seem in order. In part, they are prompted by two sorts of assumptions made by critics of

8. These figures were cited in the June 9, 1976 issue of *Newsweek*, p. 59.

medicalization in America: one is that the central and pervasive position of health, illness, and medicine in present-day American society is historically and culturally unique, and the other, that it is primarily a result of the self-interested maneuvers of the medical profession. Neither of these assumptions is true without qualification.

To begin with, in all societies, health, illness, and medicine constitute a nexus of great symbolic as well as structural importance, involving and interconnecting biological, social, psychological, and cultural systems of action. In every society, health, illness, and medicine are related to the physical and psychic integrity of individuals, their ability to establish and maintain solidary relations with others, their capacities to perform social roles, their birth, survival, and death, and to the ultimate kinds of "human condition" questions that are associated with these concerns. As such, health, illness, and medicine also involve and affect every major institution of a society, and its basic cultural grounding. The family, for example, is profoundly involved in the health and illness of its members, and, especially in nonmodern societies, the kinship system is as responsible for health and illness as are specialized medical practitioners. The institutions of science, magic, and religion are the major media through which the "hows" and "whys" of health and illness, life and death are addressed in a society, and through which culturally appropriate action for dealing with them is taken. The economy is also involved in several ways: the allocation of resources that health, illness, and medicine entail; the occupational division of labor relevant to diagnosis and therapy; and the bearing of health and illness on the individual's capacity and motivation for work. The deviance and social-control aspects of illness have important implications for the polity, which, in turn, is responsible for the organized enforcement of health measures that pertains to the community or public welfare. And in all societies, the influence, power, and prestige that accrue to medical practitioners implicate the magico-religious and stratification systems as well as the polity.[9]

As the foregoing implies, there are certain respects in which health, illness, and medicine are imbued with a more diffuse and sacred kind of significance in nonmodern than in modern societies. For example, in traditional and neo-traditional Central African societies, the meaning of health and illness, the diagnosis and treatment of sickness, and the wisdom, efficacy, and power of medical practioners are not only more closely linked with the institutions of kinship, religion, and magic than in

9. These ideas are presented in more detail in the monograph I am currently writing on "Medical Sociology" which will appear as a volume in the Prentice-Hall *Foundations of Modern Sociology* series.

American society; they are also more closely connected with the overarching cosmic view through which the whole society defines and orients itself. One indication of the larger matrix into which health, illness, and medicine fit in such a society is that in numerous Central African languages the same words can mean medicine, magico-religious charms, and metaphysically important qualities such as strength, fecundity, and invulnerability, which are believed to be supernaturally conferred.

In the light of the multi-institutional and the cultural significance of health, illness, and medicine in all societies, it is both illogical and unlikely to believe that the current process of medicalization in American society has been engineered and maintained primarily by one group, namely, the physicians. What the manifestations of medicalization that we have identified do suggest, however, is that the health-illness-medical sector has progressively acquired a more general cultural meaning in American society than it had in the past.[10]

Within this framework, the medicalization process entails the assertion of various individual and collective rights, to which members of the society feel entitled and which they express as "health," "quality of life," and "quality of death." The process also involves heightened awareness of a whole range of imperfections, injustices, dangers, and afflictions that are perceived to exist in the society, a protest against them, and a resolve to take action that is more therapeutic than punitive. Medicalization represents an exploration and affirmation of values and beliefs that not only pertain to the ultimate grounding of the society, but also to the human condition, more encompassingly and existentially conceived.

Thus, in American society, health and illness have come to symbolize many positively and negatively valued biological, physical, social, cultural, and metaphysical phenomena. Increasingly, health has become a coded way of referring to an individually, socially, or cosmically ideal state of affairs. Conversely, the concept of illness has increasingly been applied to modes of thinking, feeling, and behaving that are considered undesirably variant or deviant, as well as to more forms of suffering and disability. In turn, this medicalization of deviance and suffering has had a network of consequences.

Talcott Parsons's well-known formulation of the "sick role" provides important insights into what these effects have been. According to him,[11]

10. See John H. Knowles, "The Responsibility of the Individual."

11. Talcott Parsons's formulation of the sick role is the most important single concept in the field of the sociology of medicine. For his own elaboration of this concept, see, especially, Talcott Parsons, *The Social System* (Glencoe, Illinois), 428–79, and "The Sick Role and the Role of the Physician Reconsidered," *Milbank Memorial Fund Quarterly, Health and Society* (Summer, 1975), 257–77.

the sick role consists of two interrelated sets of exemptions and obligations. A person who is defined as ill is exonerated from certain kinds of responsibility for his illness. He is not held morally accountable for the fact that he is sick (it is not considered to be his "fault"), and he is not expected to make himself better by "good motivation" or high resolve without the help of others. In addition, he is viewed as someone whose capacity to function normally is impaired, and who is therefore relieved of some of his usual familial, occupational, and civic activities and responsibilities. In exchange for these exemptions, which are conditionally granted, the sick individual is expected to define the state of being ill as aberrant and undesirable, and to do everything possible to facilitate his recovery from it. In the case of illness of any moment, the responsibility to try to get well also entails the obligation to seek professionally competent help. In a modern Western society, such as the United States, this obligation involves a willingness to confer with a medically trained person, usually a physician, and to undergo the modes of diagnosis and treatment that are recommended, including the ministrations of other medical professionals and hospitalization. Upon entering this relationship with institutionalized medicine and its professional practitioners, an individual with a health problem becomes a patient. By cooperating and collaborating with the medical professionals caring for him, the patient is expected to work toward recovery, or at least, toward the more effective management of his illness.

Because the exemptions and the obligations of sickness have been extended to people with a widening arc of attitudes, experiences, and behaviors in American society, what is regarded as "conditionally legitimate deviance" has increased. Although illness is defined as deviance from the desirable and the normal, it is not viewed as reprehensible in the way that either sin or crime is. The sick person is neither blamed nor punished as those considered sinful or criminal are. So long as he does not abandon himself to illness or eagerly embrace it, but works actively on his own and with medical professionals to improve his condition, he is considered to be responding appropriately, even admirably, to an unfortunate occurrence. Under these conditions, illness is accepted as legitimate deviance. But this also implies that medical professionals have acquired an increasingly important social-control function in the society. They are the principal agents responsible for certifying, diagnosing, treating, and preventing illness. Because a greater proportion of deviance in American society is now seen as illness, the medical profession plays a vastly more important role than it once did in defining and regulating deviance and in trying to forestall and remedy it.

The economic, political, and legal indicators of a progressive medicalization cited above also have complex origins and implications. For example, the fact that activities connected with health, illness, and medicine represent a rising percentage of the gross national product in the United States is a consequence of the fee-for-service system under which American health-care delivery is organized; the central importance of the modern hospital in medical care; the mounting personnel, equipment, and maintenance costs that the operation of the hospital entails; and the development of new medical and surgical procedures and of new drugs, most of which are as expensive as they are efficacious. Some of this increase in costs results from the desire for profits that medical professionals, hospital administrators, and members of the pharmaceutical industry share to varying degrees. But how much is difficult to ascertain, though radical ideological criticisms and defensive conservative statements on the point are both rife at present.

In addition to such political and economic factors, the heightened commitment to health as a right and the medicalization of deviance have also contributed to the growth of health expenditures. Because health is both more coveted and more inclusively defined, and because a greater amount of medical therapeutic activity is applied to deviance-defined-as-illness, increasing economic resources are being invested in the health-illness-medicine sector of the society.

The political and legal prominence of questions of health care and medicine in American society at the present time reflects in part a widespread national discontent with the way medical care is organized, financed, and delivered, and with some of the attitudes and behaviors of physicians. The inequities that exist in access to care, and in its technical and interpersonal excellence, are among the primary foci of political and legal activities. Another major area of current political and legal action concerns the internal and external regulation of the medical profession better to insure that it uses its knowledge and skill in a socially as well as medically responsible way, and that it is adequately accountable both to patients and to the public at large. Various new measures, which represent a mixture of controls from within the medical profession and from outside it, have been set into motion. For example, in 1972, the Professional Standards Review Organization was established through the passage of amendments to the Social Security Act, which were designed to provide quality assessment and assurance, utilization review, and cost control, primarily for Medicare and Medicaid patients. Over the course of the years 1966 through 1971, a series of government regulations were passed which mandate peer review for all biomedical research involving human subjects, supported by the Department of Health, Education, and Welfare (and its subunits, the National Institutes of Health and the

Public Health Service), as well as by the Food and Drug Administration. In 1975, the American College of Surgeons and the American Surgical Association set forth a plan for systematically decreasing the number of newly graduated doctors entering surgical training. In part, this plan represented an organized, intraprofessional attempt to deal with what appears to be an oversupply of surgeons in the United States, and thereby to reduce the possibility that federal health manpower legislation would have to be passed to remedy this maldistribution.

The extraordinary number of young people opting for careers in health, particularly as physicians, is the final concomitant of medicalization previously mentioned. Reliable and valid data are not available to explain the mounting wave of young persons who have been attracted to medicine since the 1960s. We do not know as much as we should about how they resemble their predecessors, or differ from them. We are aware that more women, blacks, and members of other minority groups are being admitted to medical school than in the past, partly because of "affirmative action" legislation. But we do not have overall information about the characteristics of those who are accepted as compared with those who are not. Only sketchy materials are available on the impact of those changes in medical-school curricula during the past decade that were designed to make students more aware of the social and ethical dimensions of their commitment to medicine. We do not know whether their attitudes, their professional decisions, or their medical practice actually changed. More data are needed before we can interpret the short- and long-term implications of the rush of college youth toward medicine. As pre-medical and medical students themselves are first to testify, the prestige, authority, "power," autonomy, and financial rewards of medicine attract them and their peers to medicine, along with scientific interests, clinical impulses, and humanitarian concerns. But there is also evidence to suggest that even among those who readily contend that their reasons for choosing medicine are self-interested, a "new" medical-student orientation has been emerging. In fact, the very candor that medical students exhibit—and in some cases flaunt—when they insist that, regrettably, like their predecessors, their competitiveness, desire for achievement, and need for security have drawn them into medicine is part of this new orientation. Activist and meditative, as well as critical and self-critical, the "new medical student" not only wants to bring about change in the medical profession, but to do so in a way that affects other aspects of the society as well. The structural and symbolic meaning acquired by health, illness, and medicine has led such students to hope that their influence will be far-reaching as well as meliorative. How many students with this ostensibly "new" orientation will maintain it throughout their medical training and whether their entrance into the profession will significantly alter the future course of medicalization in American society remain to be seen.[12]

Along with progressive medicalization, a process of demedicalization seems also to be taking place in the society. To some extent the signs of demedicalization are reactions to what is felt by various individuals and groups to be a state of "*over*medicalization." One of the most significant manifestations of this countertrend is the mounting concern over implications that have arisen from the continuously expanding conception of "sickness" in the society. Commentators on this process would not necessarily agree with Peter Sedgwick that it will continue to "the point where everybody has become so luxuriantly ill" that perhaps sickness will no longer be "in" and a "backlash" will be set in motion[13]; they may not envision such an engulfing state of societally defined illness. But many observers from diverse professional backgrounds have published works in which they express concern about the "coercive" aspects of the "label" illness and the treatment of illness by medical professionals in medical institutions.[14] The admonitory perspectives on the enlarged domain of illness and medicine that these works of social science and social criticism represent appear to have gained the attention of young physicians- and nurses-in-training interested in change, and various consumer and civil-rights groups interested in health care.

This emerging view emphasizes the degree to which what is defined as health and illness, normality and abnormality, sanity and insanity varies from one society, culture, and historical period to another. Thus, it is contended, medical diagnostic categories such as "sick," "abnormal," and "insane" are not universal, objective, or necessarily reliable. Rather, they are culture, class, and time bound, often ethnocentric, and as much artifacts of the preconceptions of socially biased observers as they are valid summaries of the characteristics of the observed. In this view,

12. See Renée C. Fox, "The Process of Professional Socialization: Is There a 'New' Medical Student? A Comparative View of Medical Socialization in the 1950's and the 1970's," in Laurence R. Tancredi, ed., *Ethics in Health Care* (Washington, D. C., 1974), 197–227.

13. Sedgwick, "Illness—Mental and Otherwise," p. 37.

14. In addition to Illich, *Medical Nemesis,* and Kittrie, *The Right To Be Different*, see, for example, Rick J. Carlson, *The End of Medicine* (New York, 1975); Michel Foucault, *Madness and Civilization* (New York, 1967); Eliot Freidson, *Professional Dominance* (Chicago, 1970); Erving Goffman, *Asylums* (New York, 1961); R. D. Laing, *The Politics of Experience* (New York, 1967); Thomas J. Scheff, *Being Mentally Ill* (Chicago, 1966); Thomas S. Szasz, *The Myth of Mental Illness* (New York, 1961); and Howard D. Waitzkin and Barbara Waterman, *The Exploitation of Illness in Capitalist Society* (Indianapolis, 1974).

illness (especially mental illness) is largely a mythical construct, created and enforced by the society. The hospitals to which seriously ill persons are confined are portrayed as "total institutions": segregated, encompassing, depersonalizing organizations, "dominated" by physicians who are disinclined to convey information to patients about their conditions, or to encourage paramedical personnel to do so. These "oppressive" and "countertherapeutic" attributes of the hospital environment are seen as emanating from the professional ideology of physicians and the kind of hierarchical relationships that they establish with patients and other medical professionals partly as a consequence of this ideology, as well as from the bureaucratic and technological features of the hospital itself. Whatever their source, the argument continues, the characteristics of the hospital and of the doctor-patient relationship increase the "powerlessness" of the sick person, "maintain his uncertainty," and systematically "mortify" and "curtail" the "self" with which he enters the sick role and arrives at the hospital door.

This critical perspective links the labeling of illness, the "imperialist" outlook and capitalist behavior of physicians, the "stigmatizing" and "dehumanizing" experiences of patients, and the problems of the health-care system more generally to imperfections and injustices in the society as a whole. Thus, for example, the various forms of social inequality, prejudice, discrimination, and acquisitive self-interest that persist in capitalistic American society are held responsible for causing illness, as well as for contributing to the undesirable attitudes and actions of physicians and other medical professionals. Casting persons in the sick role is regarded as a powerful, latent way for the society to exact conformity and maintain the status quo. For it allows a semi-approved form of deviance to occur, which siphons off potential for insurgent protest and which can be controlled through the supervision or, in some cases, the "enforced therapy" of the medical profession. Thus, however permissive and merciful it may be to expand the category of illness, these observers point out, there is always the danger that the society will become a "therapeutic state" that excessively restricts the "right to be different" and the right to dissent. They feel that this danger may already have reached serious proportions in this society through its progressive medicalization.

The criticism of medicalization and the advocacy of demedicalization have not been confined to rhetoric. Concrete steps have been taken to declassify certain conditions as illness. Most notable among these is the American Psychiatric Association's decision to remove homosexuality from its official catalogue ("Nomenclature") of mental disorders. In addition, serious efforts have been made to heighten physicians' awareness that, because they share certain prejudiced, often unconscious assumptions about women, they tend to overattribute psychological difficulties to their female patients. Thus, for example, distinguished medical publications such as the *New England Journal of Medicine* have featured articles and editorials on the excessive readiness with which medical specialists and textbook authors accept the undocumented belief that dysmenorrhea, nausea of pregnancy, pain in labor, and infantile colic are all psychogenic disorders, caused or aggravated by women's emotional problems. Another related development is feminist protest against what is felt to be a too great tendency to define pregnancy as an illness, and childbirth as a "technologized" medical-surgical event, prevailed over by the obstetrician-gynecologist. These sentiments have contributed to the preference that many middle-class couples have shown for natural childbirth in recent years, and to the revival of midwifery. The last example also illustrates an allied movement, namely a growing tendency to shift some responsibility for medical care and authority over it from the physician, the medical team, and hospital to the patient, the family, and the home.

A number of attempts to "destratify" the doctor's relationships with patients and with other medical professionals and to make them more open and egalitarian have developed. "Patients' rights" are being asserted, codified and, in some states, drafted into law. Greater emphasis is being placed, for example, on the patient's "right to treatment," right to information (relevant to diagnosis, therapy, prognosis, or the giving of knowledgeable consent for any procedure), right to privacy and confidentiality, and right to be "allowed to die," rather than being "kept alive by artificial means or heroic measures . . . if the situation should arise in which there is no reasonable expectation of . . . recovery from physical or mental disability."[15]

In some medical milieux (for example, community health centers and health maintenance organizations), and in critical and self-consciously progressive writings about medicine, the term "client" or "consumer" is being substituted for "patient." This change in terminology is intended to underline the importance of preventing illness while stressing the desirability of a nonsupine, nonsubordinate relationship for those who seek care to those who provide it. The emergence of nurse-practitioners and physician's assistants on the American scene is perhaps the most significant sign that some blurring of the physician's supremacy vis-à-vis

15. This particular way of requesting that one be allowed to die is excerpted from the "Living Will" (revised April, 1974, version), prepared and promoted by the Euthanasia Educational Council.

other medical professionals may also be taking place. For some of the responsibilities for diagnosis, treatment, and patient management that were formerly prerogatives of physicians have been incorporated into these new, essentially marginal roles.[16]

Enjoinders to patients to care for themselves rather than to rely so heavily on the services of medical professionals and institutions are more frequently heard. Much attention is being given to studies, such as the one conducted by Lester Breslow and his colleagues at the University of California at Los Angeles, which suggest that good health and longevity are as much related to a self-enforced regimen of sufficient sleep, regular, well-balanced meals, moderate exercise and weight, no smoking, and little or no drinking, as they are to professionally administered medical care. Groups such as those involved in the Women's Liberation Movement are advocating the social and psychic as well as the medical value of knowing, examining, and caring for one's own body. Self-therapy techniques and programs have been developed for conditions as complicated and grave as terminal renal disease and hemophilia A and B. Proponents of such regimens affirm that many aspects of managing even serious chronic illnesses can be handled safely at home by the patient and his family, who will, in turn, benefit both financially and emotionally. In addition, they claim that in many cases the biomedical results obtained seem superior to those of the traditional physician-administered, health-care-delivery system.

The underlying assumption in these instances is that, if self-care is collectivized and reinforced by mutual aid, not only will persons with a medical problem be freed from some of the exigencies of the sick role, but both personal and public health will thereby improve, all with considerable savings in cost. This point of view is based on the moral supposition that greater autonomy from the medical profession coupled with greater responsibility for self and others in the realm of health and illness is an ethically and societally superior state.

> We have the medicine we deserve. We freely choose to live the way we do. We choose to live recklessly, to abuse our bodies with what we consume, to expose ourselves to environmental insults, to rush frantically from place to place, and to sit on our spreading bottoms and watch paid professionals exercise for us. . . . Today few patients have the confidence to care for themselves. The inexorable professionalization of medicine, together with reverence for the scientific method, have invested practitioners with sacrosanct powers, and correspondingly vitiated the responsibility of the rest of us for health. . . . What is tragic is not what has happened to the revered

16. See David Rogers, "The Challenge of Primary Care."

> professions, but what has happened to us as a result of professional dominance. In times of inordinate complexity and stress we have been made a profoundly dependent people. Most of us have lost the ability to care for ourselves. . . . I have tried to demonstrate three propositions. First, medical care has less impact on health than is generally assumed. Second, medical care has less impact on health than have social and environmental factors. And third, given the way in which society is evolving and the evolutionary imperatives of the medical care system, medical care in the future will have even less impact on health than it has now. . . . We have not understood what health is. But in the next few decades our understanding will deepen. The pursuit of health and of well-being will then be possible, but only if our environment is made safe for us to live in and our social order is transformed to foster health, rather than suppress joy. If not, we shall remain a sick and dependent people. . . . The end of medicine is not the end of health but the beginning. . . .[17]

The foregoing passage (excerpted from Rick Carlson's book *The End of Medicine*) touches upon many of the demedicalization themes that have been discussed. It proclaims the desirability of demedicalizing American society, predicting that, if we do so, we can overcome the "harm" that excessive medicalization has brought in its wake and progress beyond the "limits" that it has set. Like most critics of medicalization on the American scene, Carlson inveighs against the way that medical care is currently organized and implemented, but he attaches exceptional importance to the health-illness-medical sector of the society. In common with other commentators, he views health, illness, and medicine as inextricably associated with values and beliefs of American tradition that are both critical and desirable. It is primarily for this reason that in spite of the numerous signs that certain *structural* changes in the delivery of care will have occurred by the time we reach the year 2000, American society is not likely to undergo a significant process of *cultural* demedicalization.

Dissatisfaction with the distribution of professional medical care in the United States, its costs, and its accessibility has become sufficiently acute and generalized to make the enactment of a national health insurance system in the foreseeable future likely. Exactly what form that system should take still evokes heated debate about free enterprise and socialism, public and private regulation, national and local government, tax rates, deductibles and co-insurance, the right to health care, the equality principle, and the principle of distributive justice. But the in-

17. Carlson, *The End of Medicine,* 44, 141, and 203–31.

stitutionalization of a national system that will provide more extensive and equitable health insurance protection now seems necessary as well as inevitable even to those who do not approve of it.

There is still another change in the health-illness-medicine area of the society that seems to be forthcoming and that, like national health insurance, would alter the structure within which care is delivered. This is the movement toward effecting greater equality, collegiality, and accountability in the relationship of physicians to patients and their families, to other medical professionals, and to the lay public. Attempts to reduce the hierarchical dimension in the physician's role, as well as the increased insistence on patients' rights, self-therapy, mutual medical aid, community medical services, and care by nonphysician health professionals, and the growth of legislative and judicial participation in health and medicine by both federal and local government, are all part of this movement. There is reason to believe that, as a consequence of pressure from both outside and inside the medical profession, the doctor will become less "dominant" and "autonomous," and will be subject to more controls.

This evolution in the direction of greater egalitarianism and regulation notwithstanding, it seems unlikely that all elements of hierarchy and autonomy will, or even can, be eliminated from the physician's role. For that to occur, the medical knowledge, skill, experience, and responsibility of patients and paramedical professionals would have to equal, if not replicate, the physician's. In addition, the social and psychic meaning of health and illness would have to become trivial in order to remove all vestiges of institutionalized charisma from the physician's role. Health, illness, and medicine have never been viewed casually in any society and, as indicated, they seem to be gaining rather than losing importance in American society.

It is significant that often the discussions and developments relevant to the destratification and control of the physician's role and to the enactment of national health insurance are accompanied by reaffirmations of traditional American values: equality, independence, self-reliance, universalism, distributive justice, solidarity, reciprocity, and individual and community responsibility. What seems to be involved here is not so much a change in values as the initiation of action intended to modify certain structural features of American medicine, so that it will more fully realize long-standing societal values.

In contrast, the new emphasis on health as a right, along with the emerging perspective on illness as medically and socially engendered, seems to entail major conceptual rather than structural shifts in the health-illness-medical matrix of the society. These shifts are indicative of a less fatalistic and individualistic attitude toward illness, increased personal and communal espousal of health, and a spreading conviction that health is as much a consequence of the good life and the good society as it is of professional medical care. The strongest impetus for demedicalization comes from this altered point of view. It will probably contribute to the decategorization of certain conditions as illness, greater appreciation and utilization of nonphysician medical professionals, the institutionalization of more preventive medicine and personal and public health measures, and, perhaps, to the undertaking of nonmedical reforms (such as full employment, improved transportation, or adequate recreation) in the name of the ultimate goal of health.

However, none of these trends implies that what we have called *cultural* demedicalization will take place. The shifts in emphasis from illness to health, from therapeutic to preventive medicine, and from the dominance and autonomy of the doctor to patients' rights and greater control of the medical profession do not alter the fact that health, illness, and medicine are central preoccupations in the society that have diffuse symbolic as well as practical meaning. All signs suggest that they will maintain the social, ethical, and existential significance they have acquired, even though by the year 2000 some structural aspects of the way that medicine and care are organized and delivered may have changed. In fact, if the issues now being considered under the rubric of bioethics are predictive of what lies ahead, we can expect that in the future, health, illness, and medicine will acquire even greater importance as one of the primary symbolic media through which American society will grapple with fundamental questions of value and belief. What social mechanisms we will develop to come to terms with these "collective conscience" issues, and exactly what role physicians, health professionals, biologists, jurists, politicians, philosophers, theologians, social scientists, and the public at large will play in their resolution remains to be seen. But it is a distinctive characteristic of an advanced modern society like our own that scientific, technical, clinical, social, ethical, and religious concerns should be joined in this way.

The Sociology of Modern Medical Research

Medicine as an institution turns around the relationship between health and illness, and the physical and psychic capacity of individuals to perform in their social roles. Medicine is concerned with the ultimate conditions of man's existence and the problems of meaning associated with them.[1] It is linked with birth, life, pain, suffering, anxiety, mortality, and death. Medical research is a way of inquiring into and striving to control the body, mind, psyche, and environment as they bear upon health and illness.

Medical research occupies a strategic place in modern society. Like modern science, of which it is an important part, it is accorded strong and extensive value. It is a symbolic as well as concrete expression of the social structure and cultural tradition. And it epitomizes some archetypically modern forms of competence, achievement, and yearning.

This paper will consider medical research in a cross-cultural and evolutionary framework. Medical research has flourished more in modern than in pre-modern societies, and it is more firmly and centrally institutionalized in some Western societies than in others. I will not take

1. "Ultimate conditions" is a phrase of Robert N. Bellah (1964:359). "Problems of meaning" is a concept of Max Weber that has been further developed by Talcott Parsons.

From Charles Leslie, ed., *Asian Medical Systems: A Comparative Study* (Berkeley, Ca.: University of California Press, 1976), 102–114.

these facts for granted, or consider them accidental. As the distinctive features of modern medical research are identified, I will suggest the implications that variations in them have for ongoing scientific inquiry. Finally, I will comment on nascent trends visible in the current historical phase of modern medical research.

COGNITIVE ASSUMPTIONS AND MODE OF THOUGHT

The mode of thought on which modern medical research is based is an emergent, eclectic product of the biological and behavioral sciences. In its ideal form, it applies logico-rational thought to phenomena that are related to health and illness. Through observation, interviewing, and experimental techniques, information is amassed and refined. Instruments that enhance observation and increase the control of data range in power and complexity from the stethoscope to the electron microscope. The data collected are ordered by conceptual schemes, the highly generalized and systematic sets of ideas that constitute the framework for scientific thought (Conant 1951:25 and *passim*). They provide investigators with insight-provoking ways of formulating questions and seeking answers about an otherwise intricate and confusing empirical reality.

At the same time, conceptual schemes bind the investigator to a particular way of conceiving reality, so that he tends to find what he looks for. Other characteristics of medical scientific thought help curtail this penchant. Great methodological and ethical value is attached to null hypothesis reasoning, the rigorous attempt to systematically disprove or rule out the premises on which a piece of research is founded. The medical researcher is expected to be a specialist in uncertainty who is engaged by the tentativeness and incompleteness of medical knowledge. He advances knowledge by laying bare these uncertainties, as well as by mitigating or dispelling them.

The highest prestige in modern medical research accrues to contributions that constitute a "breakthrough" in knowledge. This is a primary factor in the numerous disputes over priority that have occurred in the history of scientific research (Merton 1957). In medical research such breakthroughs have the added cogency of promising relief or cure to suffering patients. Clinical investigators in the dual role of caring for and conducting experiments upon patients with conditions outside of current medical competence nourish this hope in themselves and their patients.

The value system in which modern medical research is rooted is associated with transcendent assumptions about the nature of man and the universe. Nevertheless, the problems and questions with which it deals are sharply distinguished from religious concerns: it addresses itself to the mechanisms of health and illness, life and death, rather than to the meaning of their occurrence. Although it is ethically self-conscious, and respects the subjects it investigates, its outlook is disenchanted, in Max Weber's sense of the term. It does not consider the sacred to be located in any of the spheres it explores, or to constrain inquiry into them. Modern medical research also tries to detach itself from what it regards as the biasing effects that the ideas of specific religious traditions would impose on investigation. The relationship between modern medical science and a religious view of the world might best be characterized as a state of "creative tension," rather than one of reciprocal repudiation (Bellah 1965:194). On the other hand, modern medical thought is resolutely antimagical in intent, if not always in fact.

A comparison of these cognitive traits of modern medical research with a different tradition throws into relief what is distinctive about them. Traditional Bantu African medical thought, like that of modern medical science, seeks an explanatory theory in a causal context and is concerned with classification and taxonomy.[2] But in contrast to modern medical science, it exhibits an "imperious, uncompromising demand . . . for determinism" (Lévi-Strauss 1966:11). Health and illness are determined primarily by supernatural, psychic, and interpersonal forces within a closed system of thought and belief, whose logic is that of the "self-fulfilling prophecy" (Merton 1949). Explanations for illness are limited in range, and fixed. When evidence contrary to traditional interpretations is encountered, there is a tendency to develop "secondary elaborations" that excuse or explain it away (Evans-Pritchard 1937). No room exists for the concept of probability or the formal acknowledgment of uncertainty. Objective and subjective reality, ideas and empirical happenings are not dissociated from one another. Health signifies that one's life force is intact, and that one is sufficiently in harmony with the social, physical, and supernatural environment to enjoy what is positively valued in life, and to ward off misfortunes and evils. Illness is the antithesis of health, prototypical of the most negative, tragic life experiences that beset man. It is also unnatural. It ought not and would not occur without the intervention of transhuman forces, mediated by human agents. With limited exceptions, illness is believed to be caused by the evil thoughts,

2. My analysis of Bantu medical thought is based on field work in the Democratic Republic of the Congo (now renamed Zaïre) during the period 1962–1967, and on English, French, and Belgian anthropological monographs on other Bantu African societies.

feelings, or motives of other people, through the medium of sorcery or witchcraft.

Traditional Bantu medical thought is consonant with the concepts and beliefs of a primitive or archaic religious system (Bellah 1964). It forecloses the kind of systematic, sacred-free questioning that lies at the heart of modern medical research. At the same time, it provides answers to problems of meaning associated with health and illness that modern medical science circumvents and, in some ways, increases.

VALUE ORIENTATIONS AND SOME VARIANTS

The cognitive assumptions and mode of thought of modern medical science are interrelated with the value orientations on which it is premised.[3] The value of rationality provides the raison d'être for all forms of modern scientific inquiry, and a strongly felt commitment to progress in rationally understanding health and illness is institutionalized in medical research. The pursuit of logical, orderly, generalized but open-ended knowledge is valued for its own sake, and as an expression of man's higher intellectual and moral faculties. But this pattern of rationality derives even more sustenance from the supposition that it is the primary means through which diseases will be vanquished and adventitious death overcome. Thus, rationality intersects with a dynamic, melioristic value complex that Talcott Parsons has called "instrumental activism" (Parsons 1967:225–226).

The role that affect is supposed to play in this rationality is shaped by a value conception of detached concern.[4] The medical investigator is supposed to be emotionally involved in the search he conducts, to care about the knowledge it may bring forth and the practical fruits of that knowledge. At the same time, he is to maintain a detachment that blends objectivity with organized doubting. The truth that he seeks is concepts, facts, and techniques that transcend those he would achieve if he were influenced by unexamined and unbridled sentiments.

This value orientation shades into universalism. Judgments of the reliability, validity, and import of the findings of medical investigators, along with eligibility for the status of researcher, are supposed to be dissociated from particularistic considerations. Scientific competence

3. My discussion of the value-orientations of modern medical science is based on Talcott Parsons (1951:326–383), Robert K. Merton (1949:295–316), and Bernard Barber (1952:60–83).

4. I formulated this concept in a paper that I co-authored with Miriam Massey Johnson in 1950–51, but it was not until 1963 that I used it in a publication (Fox 1963:12–35).

and excellence are considered to be the only appropriate criteria for these judgments, and the scientist's personal qualities or the social attributes of sex, age, race, nationality, class, religion, and political persuasion are believed to be irrelevant.

Finally, modern medical research is poised between individualism and collectivity orientation. The investigator is enjoined to follow the paths of knowledge that scientific inquiry opens up to him, no matter how lonely or heterodox they seem to be. But he is also expected to recognize that the knowledge he utilizes and that he helps to create does not belong to him. It is the property of a community that extends far beyond social groupings of which he is a member, and beyond his own historical time. The medical scientist is expected to be aware of the social consequences of his research, though the content and scope of these responsibilities are not clearly designated.

Rationality, instrumental activism, detached concern, universalism, individualism, and collectivism describe the ethos of science as it has developed in modern Western societies. They have not been perfectly realized in any society. Within the social systems that are both modern and Western, considerable variability exists in the form and in the degree to which they are institutionalized. For example, medical research in Belgium is conducted by institutions affiliated with the country's four major universities (Fox 1962, 1964). Each university represents a different combination of the social and cultural distinctions of Belgian life. Brussels is a Free Thought, preponderantly anticlerical, private university, with separate French and Flemish sections. Ghent is a state university, officially neither Catholic nor Free Thought, but with a sizable number of practicing Catholics in the student body and on the faculty. Since the early 1930s, all its teaching is done in Flemish. Liège is a state university, neither Catholic nor Free Thought, but with at least a plurality of its students and faculty non-practicing Catholics or non-Catholics. All classes at Liège are taught in French. Since 1969, Louvain, Belgium's venerable, private, Catholic university has split into two separate universities, a French one and a Flemish one (Leuven).

Thus, to a significant degree, the Belgian university settings in which medical research is conducted are particularistic. A person's linguistic, ethnic, and religious-philosophical affiliations, along with his related social class membership and political persuasion, are as much determinants of his appointment to a faculty position in which he can do research as are his scientific talent, training, and achievement. Furthermore, each university tends to recruit its faculty from its alumni. All this reinforces the tendency of the universities to seal themselves off from each other. In the opinion of many Belgian medical researchers, the result is cloistered academic milieux that curtail the interchange of ideas between colleagues, the mobility of personnel, and a sharing of facilities that would enhance medical research. This entrenched and pervasive particularism is a pre-modern value orientation and feature of the social structure. Although it is not totally incompatible with viable, modern medical research, it constrains its volume and originality.

SCIENTIFIC MAGIC

As a traditional element, particularism is analytically different from another pattern in modern medical research that is ostensibly pre-modern and incongruous with scientific rationality. I refer to various forms of what I have called "scientific magic" (Fox 1959). The particularistic retention exemplified in Belgian medicine impedes the full development of research, but scientific magic helps to further it.

Precisely because he approaches matters related to life and death in a scientific way, the modern medical investigator lives with the problems of uncertainty and the therapeutic limitations of medical science. He also confronts the unanswered why's of illness that fall outside the boundaries of science. These challenges help to trigger and shape the search for more adequate medical knowledge; but they are also a source of considerable strain. One of the coping mechanisms investigators develop is essentially magical, though it may be disguised to some extent in research procedures. Scientific magic tends to be more elaborate in groups of medical researchers with physicianly responsibilities to care for patients who are also their subjects. Scientific uncertainty, the limitation of therapy, and problems of meaning are compounded for these physicians, who make and use more scientific magic than their colleagues whose investigations are confined to the laboratory.

A pattern of scientific magic that characterizes all genres of modern medical researchers consists of investigators making levity-accompanied wagers with each other about what the results of particularly important and/or risky experiments will be. This ironic ritual symbolically comments on the apparent lack of order, predictability, and sense in the phenomena they are exploring. In it they express self-mocking chagrin over their inability to understand, know, predict, and control; and they protest against what seem to be existentially absurd processes or entities associated with illness, and with the efforts to comprehend it. Finally, this game of chance is an affirmative petition for success. The investigators who engage in it pit their own intelligent guesses against the unknown in ways that mimic the more speculative aspects of scientific research. They hope that their projections will have a positive relationship to the answers they seek.

Scientific magic seems to grow directly out of the limitations of rationality in modern medical research, and the strains that this imposes on investigators. Although scientific magic parodies the basic value premises of rationality and of instrumental activism, it is a latently institutionalized pattern in modern medical research. It ritualizes the optimism of medical investigators concerning the meaningfulness of their activities (Malinowski 1948:70). It appears to be a necessary condition enabling investigators to further knowledge and technique according to the cognitive and moral canons of modern science.

SOCIAL STRUCTURE AND ORGANIZATION

A mural at the Institut Jules Bordet in Brussels honors the distinguished medical scientist after whom the institute is named.[5] Though perhaps not intended by the artist to do so, the mural romanticizes the premodern conditions under which medical research was conducted in Western universities in the nineteenth century. These are not the conditions most conducive to innovation and productivity in twentieth-century, modern medical research; yet they are perpetuated in many European societies to this day.

The mural depicts Bordet as an elderly man, white haired and white mustached, lean, erect, dignified, and elegant; clad in a dark suit, his vest properly buttoned over a white shirt and dark tie, white handkerchief neatly arranged in his jacket pocket, a small ribbon rosette of honor affixed to his buttonhole. He stands with hands in his trouser pockets, a solitary figure in the midst of the laboratory where so much of his work was done. The laboratory is a cluttered, but orderly and austere, white-tiled room, lit from overhead by three gas lamps. The tables, shelves, cupboards of the laboratory are filled with test tubes, glass beakers and

5. The artist who painted the mural is P. Delvaux. Jules Bordet was awarded the Nobel Prize for medicine and physiology in 1919. His early studies showed that anti-microbic sera include two active substances, one existing before immunization (alexine), the other a specific antibody created by vaccination. Bordet introduced the method of diagnosing microbes by sera. In 1898 he discovered hemolytic sera and showed that they act on foreign blood by a mechanism comparable to that by which an anti-microbic serum acts on microbes. He also demonstrated that the reactions of all these sera are colloidal in nature. Bordet threw light on the process of formation of coagulin. He studied the formation of analyphylactic poisons. And, with Gengou, he cultivated *B. pertussis*, and laid the basis for the generally accepted opinion that this organism is the cause of whooping cough.

bottles of various sizes and shapes, syringes and pipettes. On a side counter there is a Bunsen burner on which a large white casserole with a tipsy black lid has been placed. The windowsill at one end of the laboratory contains two simple microscopes under bell jars, and another assortment of pipettes and test tubes in beakers. It is late evening. The shades of the windows have been raised, so that one sees the first sliver of a new moon rising over the tiled, gabled rooftops and tidy chimneys of traditional Belgian architecture. In short, the mural is a portrait of a scientist of gentlemanly origins and demeanor, a solo investigator, working in his laboratory at night in the anatomo-pathological and bacteriological era of medicine, and equipped only with his sense of vocation, his personal genius, and simple instruments.

Modern medical research differs from this Bordet image in fundamental respects. More than the style of the buildings, the haberdashery of its investigators, and the equipment it employs have changed. Modern research is characterized by a progressive division of labor, increasing specialization and professionalization. Biochemistry, rather than anatomy, pathology, or bacteriology, is the reigning basic medical science. The lone researcher is a relatively rare phenomenon. Increased knowledge, specialization, and the intricacy and expense of medical technology require that research be conducted by teams of investigators as a cooperative enterprise. The commitment to teamwork, however, is more than a rational recognition of the most practical way to proceed. Collaboration is considered to be morally as well as intellectually superior to an aloof, aristocratic individualism. Established, prestigious, comfortably remunerated status-roles and careers exist. These are primarily in the university, but also in government and industry. They are not the prerogative of amateur gentlemen scholars. Rather, they are open to persons from wide-ranging social class backgrounds, primarily on the basis of their training and accomplishments.

The greater part of modern medical research is carried out within the framework of large, formal organizations that are essentially bureaucratic. These structures accommodate the changing configurations of medical science, including the rise of new disciplines and subfields, and shifts in the content or scope of basic and applied goals. Furthermore, medical researchers are linked to one another by informal scientific and collegial exchanges, mutually read publications, and membership in loosely organized professional societies. These ties go beyond their formal affiliation with a particular university, government office, or firm. Thus, modern medical research is not coordinated and controlled by one centralized political or economic body. Its florescence is encouraged by the steadfast, enterprising support of government agencies, business firms, universities, and professional associations.

It is a historical fact, rather than a chauvinistic assertion by an American scholar, that these social structural conditions were more fully realized in the United States in the 1950s and early 1960s than in any other society in the world. Medical research, along with other scientific investigation, was regarded "as a resource to be developed according to its immanent possibilities and to be marketed as widely and imaginatively as possible" (Ben-David 1968:55). An "entrepreneurial . . . system of research and higher education" prevailed, "characterized by a large number of autonomous and competing organizations, the internal structures of which were flexibly adjusted to the changing requirements of scientific collaboration and division of labor" (*ibid.*:45–46). The volume and variety of support for scientific research that these organizational arrangements helped to generate, and the bold idealism, as well as pragmatism, that underlay them, attracted many talented researchers from other countries. This further enhanced scientific creativity and productivity in American society during that period.

EXPERIMENTATION WITH HUMAN SUBJECTS

A final key attribute of modern medical research is the extensive participation of human subjects in its inquiries and experiments. The furtherance of medical knowledge and skill, most particularly therapeutic innovation, involves a sequence of steps that weave back and forth between the laboratory and the clinic (Fox 1970:5–6). In the earliest stages of testing a concept, procedure, or drug, where uncertainty and risk are at a maximum, investigators work in the laboratory with animal subjects. These preliminary laboratory trials provide new information and understanding, but they are not perfectly applicable to man. Because limitations and difficulties always exist in extrapolating from animal models to the human being, researchers must engage in experimentation with human subjects. These subjects are selected because they are normal and healthy in specified ways, or because they are afflicted with medical conditions that concern the investigators. Adequate laboratory work with animals is an ethical as well as technical prerequisite for human trials. But no neat guideposts are established along the experimental road to signal that the time has indubitably come to move from animal to human experimentation. This transition in clinical research is inherently controversial.

When patients are used as subjects for new forms of therapy, the usual procedure is to advance from work with animals to clinical trials with terminally ill patients, and from there to testing with persons in progressively earlier, more benign phases of the malady. This pattern expresses the conviction that only desperately sick persons for whom established therapy offers no hope should serve as subjects in early human trials. They have little to lose, it is felt, and much to gain from the admittedly outside chance that they may benefit from the new therapy they help to test. Through these initial human experiments, investigators achieve what they consider sufficient knowledge and skill to try the new treatment legitimately on patients less drastically ill.

Human experimentation has increased in magnitude, complexity, and potential peril, and has been accompanied by increasing concern for the ethical and legal character of medical research. Systematic study of these matters was given tragic impetus by the crimes of physicians in Nazi Germany. Out of the Nuremberg trials and the thought they evoked, several codes for human experimentation have been promulgated.[6] These have attempted to define the principles and conditions for research with human subjects, while reaffirming the importance of applying "the results of laboratory experiments . . . to human beings to further scientific knowledge and help suffering humanity" (Wolstenholme and O'Connor 1966:219).

Certain medical and surgical developments have quickened concern about the increasingly dangerous and subtle abuses that could result from them. The outbreak of infantile limb deformity (phocomelia) in Western Europe in 1961 and 1962 caused by the drug Thalidomide was one such potent occurrence. In the United States, for example, it precipitated passage of the Drug Amendments Act of 1962, which legally empowered the Food and Drug Administration to exercise specific kinds of controls over the clinical testing of new drugs on human subjects.

More recently, organ transplantation has come to be a paradigmatic case of the problems that have classically accompanied clinical medical research and of new phenomena, premonitory of intricate ethical issues, that future investigators and their human subjects will encounter.[7] Con-

6. The best-known are the Nuremberg Code and the 1964 Declaration of Helsinki of the World Medical Association, which sets forth a Code of Ethics for Human Experimentation. In the United States, a Public Health Service document dated May 1, 1969, and entitled "Protection of the Individual as Research Subject" sets forth the regulations that must be followed in investigations with human subjects, if a project is to be funded by the National Institutes of the Public Health Service. This agency funds approximately 35 percent of all biomedical research conducted in the United States.

7. These insights, contained in my essay, "A Sociological Perspective on Organ Transplantation and Hemodialysis" (1970), constitute the basic premises of the book on the sociology of organ transplants and dialysis that I coauthored with Judith P. Swazey, a historian of medicine (Fox and Swazey 1974). In the last few years, at least three important published symposia on human experimentation and therapeutic innovation have focused on the case of organ transplantation (Wolstenholme and O'Connor 1966; Ladimer 1970; and Freund 1970).

cern about the ethics of human experimentation has focused on the difficulty of obtaining truly informed, voluntary consent from the subject, of striking a proper balance between the potential benefits and risks to him, and of protecting his integrity and privacy. Organ transplantation has added new dimensions to these questions. Obtaining consent for a transplant involves complex interactions between the medical team, potential donors and their kin, and the candidate recipient and his relatives. Transplantation has also brought other issues into prominence, including the justification for inflicting a major surgical injury on a live donor in order to help a dying recipient; the symbolic meaning of the human heart and other vital organs; the allocation of scarce organs; the transcendent meaning of the gift-exchange between the donor and the recipient, versus the mutual tyranny it can impose on them; the appropriate definition of death; the distinction between the extension of life and the prolongation of death; and the existential and social implications of the physicianly commitment to do everything medically possible for terminally ill persons.

The fact that in a modern society many persons are willing to act as research subjects—and, in numerous instances, are even eager to do so—needs explanation. Since this form of participation in medical research achieved a greater degree of acceptance in American society than in any other, identifying the factors that have contributed to its support is instructive (Fox 1960). The institutionalization of the role of research subject involves a widespread belief in the practical importance and moral excellence of scientific research, and medical research in particular. Contributing to it by taking the role of a research subject is thought to be a humanitarian and potentially heroic act. These individuals demonstrate their readiness to endure the discomforts and hazards of pioneering experiments partly for the self-surpassing goals of collective health and well-being. Thus, the motivation of patients who serve as human subjects often has two facets. It expresses their hope that new insights or treatments may be developed that could directly benefit them; it testifies to their disinterested conviction that, as one patient-subject put it, it will be "for the good of medical science and the humane benefit of others in the future" (Fox 1959:150).

Characteristically, the relationship of the physician-investigator to his human subject is both collegial and collectivity oriented. The participants are bound to one another by an enterprise that they consider highly significant. They are committed to the values on which the enterprise is based. And the norm of informed, voluntary consent reduces the discrepancy in medical knowledge that ordinarily exists between a physician and a layman. Yet, however close, collaborative, and egalitarian in their orientation a research physician and a human subject may become, there is always enough of a competence gap and sufficient ambivalence between them, so that their relationship depends on the institutionalization of uncontingent solidarity and confidence (Parsons 1970). In this regard, the relationship is a fiduciary one, drawing upon and contributing to the sense of trust that binds social relationships throughout the society.

"ADVANCED MODERN" OR "POST-MODERN" MEDICAL RESEARCH?

A few comments on some shifts in orientation that medical research is undergoing in American society will provide an epilogue to this sociological overview. These emerging patterns appear to be micro-dynamic expressions of changes in the society at large, and they raise vital questions about the magnitude and significance of these changes. Do these trends constitute "advanced modern" developments—that is, are they further extensions of the value system and social structure underlying modern scientific research? Or will they prove to be "post-modern" in the sense of being sufficiently discontinuous and incompatible with the social and cultural attributes of modern science to represent a break with them? Although it is too early to formulate definitive answers to these questions, it is important to ask them.[8]

Two developing patterns are especially notable.[9] The first is the tendency for modern medicine to become more social in outlook. Greater emphasis is being placed on the extent to which society is responsible for health and illness. Good health and medical care are coming to be viewed as basic human rights. Social arrangements are increasingly referred to in explaining the persistence of certain illnesses and the emergence of others, as well as to account for injustices in the delivery of medical care. And the belief that illness, along with poverty, pollution, overpopulation, and war, can be brought under control by the organized implementation of public conscience is gaining momentum.

One of the consequences of this new orientation for medical research is an augmenting pressure on investigators to address themselves to "relevant" matters. The definition of what is relevant is veering toward

8. I have greatly benefited from several personal exchanges with Talcott Parsons on these questions, most particularly from a letter I received from him dated March 24, 1971.

9. The discussion that follows draws upon a paper entitled "Medical Evolution," which I contributed to a *Festschrift* for Talcott Parsons, edited by Jan Loubser, Victor M. Lidz, Andrew Effrat, et al. (See next essay.)

massive efforts to eliminate certain diseases. In this respect, cancer has become symbolic of the most recalcitrant, painful, and lethal medical disorder in modern society to be overcome. But even more pronounced is the demand for solutions to social and economic problems that adversely affect health and its care. This development seems to call into question some of the commitments that have given modern medical inquiry moral and material support. After a decade of steady expansion in funds allocated by the United States government for medical research, the growth rate in federal support has leveled off and is now beginning to decline. In addition, particularly among younger people, a crescendo of doubt is being expressed about the intellectual and ethical values of scientific research and its pertinence to social issues.

The second major alteration through which modern medicine seems to be passing is a shift toward greater interest in the moral enigmas and existential questions that confront physicians. The sources of this new awareness are complex. In part, it grows out of the stage in knowledge and technique that modern medicine has reached. Understanding and control of disease and death have been impressively advanced. The potential human life span has been greatly extended. And yet people still fall ill and die. The juxtaposition of these accomplishments and limitations has reawakened reflection on philosophical and religious questions. Are disease and death inalterably a part of the human condition? If so, why? What does this tell us about the nature of man and the purpose of his existence?

Resuscitative techniques and organ transplantation have contributed to the fact that the cessation of breathing and heartbeat are being superseded by irreversible coma, or the so-called brain-death syndrome, as the criterion of death. The discussion that has surrounded this process has increased physician's consciousness of the fact that codified notions of death are approximate and arbitrary, and do not solve philosophical or religious questions about what death really is. The debate about heart and lung death versus brain death has also brought physicians to consider in a new way the ambiguities concerning where the prolongation of life ends and the prolongation of death begins.

Participation in organ transplantation in the role of medical professional, donor, or recipient has increased cognizance of widespread, essentially mystic conceptions about the human body, even in a science-oriented society. Furthermore, participation in the network of giving and receiving established by transplantation can be a religious experience. Many report that it has enhanced their self-understanding and self-worth and given them a sense of commitment and oneness with humanity unlike any they have known before.

In addition, physicians and biological scientists, in collaboration with lawyers, theologians, philosophers, and social scientists, are trying to foresee the moral and spiritual implications of possible biomedical developments.[10] Notable among the futuristic biomedical phenomena with which they are concerned are the widespread transplantation of all human organs, including the brain; the implantation of various kinds of artificial organs; genetic engineering, including cloning (the asexual reproduction of genetic carbon copies of an adult); and behavior control through neurophysiological or pharmacological manipulation of specific areas of the brain.

The entwined existential and social orientation that seems to be emerging in modern medical research is probably not an ephemeral happening. The best indicator of this is that the young men and women who have entered American medical schools over the past few years are increasingly engaged by this perspective. Their commitment is born out of their protest over what they consider to be the deficiencies of the medicine they have inherited and out of their belief in what it could become. Whether or not we are moving from the modern to a post-modern phase of medical research will be ascertained in the course of their generation.

LITERATURE CITED

Barber, Bernard.—1952. *Science and the Social Order.* Glencoe, Ill.: Free Press.

Bellah, Robert N.—1964. "Religious Evolution." *Am. Sociol. Rev.* 29:359.

———. 1965. "Epilogue," in Robert N. Bellah, ed., *Religion and Progress in Modern Asia.* New York: Free Press.

Ben-David, Joseph.—1968. *Fundamental Research and the Universities.* Paris: Organization for Economic Cooperation and Development.

Conant, James B.—1951. *Science and Common Sense.* New Haven: Yale University Press.

Evans-Pritchard, E. E.—1937. *Witchcraft, Oracles, and Magic Among the Azande.* Oxford: Oxford University Press.

Fox, Renée C.—1959. *Experiment Perilous.* Glencoe, Ill.: Free Press.

———. 1960. "Some Social and Cultural Factors in American Society Conducive to Medical Research on Human Subjects." *Clinical Pharmacology and Therapeutics* 1:423–443.

———. 1962. "Medical Scientists in a Château." *Science* 136:476–483.

———. 1964. "An American Sociologist in the Land of Belgian Medical Research," in Phillip E. Hammond, ed., *Sociologists at Work,* 345–391. New York: Basic Books.

10. I belong to a group concerned with these problems, the Institute of Society, Ethics and the Life Sciences, of Hastings-on-Hudson, N.Y.

———. 1970. "A Sociological Perspective on Organ Transplantation and Hemodialysis," in Irving Ladimer, ed., *New Dimensions in Legal and Ethical Concepts for Human Research. Annals N. Y. Acad. Sciences* 169.

Fox, Renée C., and Harold I. Lief.—1963. "Training for 'Detached Concern' in Medical Students," in Harold, Victor and Nina Lief, eds., *The Psychological Basis of Medical Practice,* 12–35. New York: Harper and Row, Hoeber Medical Division.

Fox, Renée C., and Judith P. Swazey.—1974. *The Courage to Fail: A Social View of Organ Transplants and Dialysis.* Chicago: The University of Chicago Press.

Freund, Paul A., ed.—1970. *Experimentation with Human Subjects.* New York: Braziller.

Ladimer, Irving, ed.—1970. *New Dimensions in Legal and Ethical Concepts for Human Research. Annals N. Y. Acad. Sciences* 169.

Lévi-Strauss, Claude.—1966. *The Savage Mind.* Chicago: University of Chicago Press.

Malinowski, Bronislaw.—1948. *Magic, Science, and Religion and Other Essays.* Glencoe, Ill.: Free Press.

Merton, Robert K.—1949. "The Self-Fulfilling Prophecy," in *Social Theory and Social Structure.* Glencoe, Ill.: Free Press, 179–195.

———. 1957. "Priorities in Scientific Discovery: A Chapter in the Sociology of Science." *Am. Sociol. Rev.* 22: 635–659.

Parsons, Talcott.—1951. *The Social System.* Glencoe, Ill.: Free Press.

———. 1967. *Sociological Theory and Modern Society.* New York: Free Press.

———. 1970. "Research with Human Experiments and the 'Professional Complex' ", in Paul A. Freund, ed., *Experimentation with Human Subjects,* 127–128. New York: Braziller.

Wolstenholme, G. E. W., and Maeve O'Connor, eds.—1966. *Ethics in Medical Progress.* Boston: Little, Brown.

Medical Evolution

Through his analysis of modern medical practice, Talcott Parsons has made a pioneering conceptual contribution to the specialized field of medical sociology that at the same time, has general significance for behavioral science theory. This essay will explore those aspects of his writings that bear on health, illness, and medicine.[1] Its theoretical goal is

1. For this essay we have drawn upon the following works, Parsons's principal sociology of medicine writings: Talcott Parsons, "Illness and the Role of the Physician: A Sociological Perspective," in Clyde Kluckhohn, Henry A. Murray and David M. Schneider (eds.), *Personality in Nature, Society and Culture,* 2nd rev. ed. (New York: Alfred Knopf, 1953), 609–617; "The Professions and Social Structure" and "The Motivation of Economic Activities" in T. Parsons, *Essays in Sociological Theory,* rev. ed. (Glencoe, Ill.: The Free Press, 1954), 34–49, 50–68; "Social Structure and Dynamic Process: The Case of Modern Medical Practice," in T. Parsons, *The Social System* (Glencoe, Ill.: The Free Press, 1951), 428–479; T. Parsons and Renée C. Fox, "Illness, Therapy, and the Modern Urban American Family," in E. Gartly Jaco (ed.), *Patients, Physicians and Illness: Sourcebook in Behavioral Science and Medicine* (Glencoe, Ill.: The Free Press, 1958), 234–245 [first published in the *Journal of Social Issues,* 8 (1952)]; T. Parsons, "Definitions of Health and Illness in the Light of American Values and Social Structure," in Jaco (ed.), *op. cit.,* 165–187; "Some Trends of Change in American Society: Their Bearing on Medical Education," in T. Parsons, *Structure and Process in Modern Societies* (Glencoe, Ill.: The Free Press, 1960), 280–294; "Some

From Jan J. Loubser, Rainer C. Baum, Andrew Effrat, and Victor M. Lidz, eds., *Explorations in General Theory in Social Science,* Vol. 2 (New York: Free Press, 1976), 773–787.

a two-fold one: to synthesize rather than merely summarize this sector of Parsons's work and to set it down in the broad evolutionary perspective on the structure and dynamics of total societies that has been central to his thinking over the last ten years.[2]

Parsons's analysis of modern medical practice turns around three interrelated ideas. The first is a view of the physician (for Parsons, the ideal-typical medical practitioner) as cast in a role that belongs to the "professional complex,"[3] which he considers a distinctively important characteristic of modern society. The second notion is a breakthrough insight into the fact that illness is not just a biological and/or psychological condition, but that it also constitutes a social role complementary to that of the physician, what Parsons calls "the sick role." The third idea links the other two. In spite of the "competence gap"[4] that exists between physician and patient, because one is a trained expert in matters of health and illness and the other is not, they are seen as bound to one another in a semicollegial relationship. In Parsons's perspective, they form a collectivity based on their joint commitment to the recovery of the sick person and on the solidarity and mutual trust that are both prerequisite to their pursuit of this common goal and a consequence of it.

Parsons regards "the case of modern medical practice" as a particularly vivid exemplification of the interplay of the four subsystems of action—social, cultural, personality, and physical-organic—as they converge on a strategic area in modern society:

> To be sick [is] not only to be in a biological state . . . but requires exemptions from obligations, conditional legitimation, and motivation to

---

Reflections on the Problem of Psychosomatic Relationships in Health and Illness," and "Health and Illness," in T. Parsons, *Social Structure and Personality* (Glencoe, Ill.: The Free Press, 1964), 112–126 and 255–358; T. Parsons and Victor M. Lidz, "Death in American Society" in E. Shneidman (ed.), *Essays in Self-Destruction* (New York: Science House, 1967); T. Parsons, "Research with Human Subjects and the 'Professional Complex,' " in *Ethical Aspects of Experimentation with Human Subjects, Daedalus,* 98 (Spring 1969), 325–360; T. Parsons, Renée C. Fox, and Victor M. Lidz, "The 'Gift of Life' and Its Reciprocation," *Social Research,* 39 (1972), 367–415.

2. The published works in which Parsons's thinking on evolution is elaborated are: T. Parsons, "Evolutionary Universals in Society," *American Sociological Review,* 29 (June 1964), 339–357; Robert N. Bellah, "Religious Evolution," *American Sociological Review,* 29 (June 1964), 358–374; S. N. Eisenstadt, "Social Change, Differentiation and Evolution," *American Sociological Review,* 29 (June 1964), 375–386; T. Parsons, *Societies: Evolutionary and Comparative Perspectives* (Englewood Cliffs, N. J.: Prentice-Hall, 1966); T. Parsons, *The System of Modern Societies* (Englewood Cliffs, N. J.: Prentice-Hall, 1971).

3. Parsons, "Research with Human Subjects and the 'Professional Complex,' " *op. cit.,* 330–335.

4. *Ibid.,* p. 336.

> accept therapeutic help. It [can] thus, in part, at least, be classed as a type of deviant behavior . . . socially categorized in a kind of role.[5]
>
> The fact that the relevance of illness is not confined to the non-motivated purely situational aspect of social action greatly increases its significance for the social system. It becomes not merely an "external" danger to be "warded off" but an integral part of the social equilibrium itself. . . . Medical practice . . . is a "mechanism" in the social system for coping with the illness of its members. It involves a set of institutionalized roles . . . "professional" roles, a sub-class of the larger group of occupational role. . . . [It] also involves a specialized relation to certain aspects of the general cultural tradition of modern society. Modern medical practice is organized around the application of scientific knowledge to the problems of illness and health, to the control of "disease." Science is of course a very special kind of cultural phenomenon and a really highly developed scientific level in any field is rare among known cultures, with the modern West in a completely unique position. . . .[6]

The kinds of functional significance that Parsons accords to the health-illness-medical practice complex qualifies it to be defined as one of the major institutions of a modern society, although he himself never conceptualizes it in this way. The overarching societal importance that he assigns to what we would term "the institution of medicine" is of two general sorts. The first is primarily social structural and motivational in nature. For Parsons, illness is an "impairment of the individual's capacity for effective performance of social roles and those tasks which are organized subject to role-expectations."[7] It is a form of partially and conditionally legitimated deviance, which, when aggregated, can have seriously disruptive consequences for the ongoing of a society. As he points out, the effect of great numbers of persons in a society taking to their beds could, in its passive way, disturb the usual functioning of that social system as much as an insurgent refusal on the part of those same individuals to tend to their daily activities and responsibilities.[8] (Here, he anticipates the "sick-in" as a form of social protest.) Furthermore, he suggests, the exemption, withdrawal, and dependence that illness characteristically entails is an especially strategic and threatening form of deviance in the kind of modern industrialized society that emphasizes value orientations like instrumental activism, achievement, personal responsibility, and independence.[9]

5. Parsons, *Social Structure and Personality,* p. 332.
6. Parsons, *The Social System,* 431–432.
7. Parsons, *Social Structure and Personality*, p. 112.
8. Renée C. Fox, "Illness" in David L. Sills (ed.), *International Encyclopedia of the Social Sciences* (New York: Macmillan and The Free Press, 1968), Vol. 7, p. 92.
9. Parsons, *Social Structure and Personality,* 277–291.

In Parsons's analysis, the second source of medicine's macro-significance lies in its cultural and, one might say, existential import. Health, illness, and medical practice are integrally associated with what he has variously called "the environment above action," "ultimate reality," and "problems of meaning."[10] Both the experience of illness and the act of caring for the sick, then, are related to the "ultimate conditions" of man's existence that Robert Bellah considers to be the immutable core of religion.[11] Notably, illness and medical practice evoke questions about the "why's" of pain, suffering, the limits of human life and death, and (latently, in a modern society) about their relationship to evil, sin, and injustice.

In this connection, Parsons is keenly aware of the special poignancy of the uncertainty dimension in modern medical practice. As he indicates, the fact that a powerful battery of scientific knowledge and technique is applied to illness and the "deepest human concerns" it arouses does not eliminate uncertainty from medicine. To begin with, by its very nature, science is an open, searching mode of thought, as much an organized way of raising systematic questions and doubts about what are assumed to be established concepts, facts, and methods, as of furthering knowledge and skill. Although medical scientific advance may solve certain problems, it also helps to create and maintain two basic types of uncertainty that affect both medical practitioner and patient.[12] The first kind of uncertainty derives from the hiatuses, limitations, and errors that characterize medical knowledge at any given point in time. The second type of uncertainty results from the paradoxical fact that despite its inadequacies, medical science is so vast and highly developed that no one can totally encompass or perfectly master it.

Parsons's insights into these cultural aspects of medicine are among the most original of his medical sociology formulations. And they are consistent with the critical place that he assigns to the cultural system in his general theory of action. "In the cybernetic sense," he writes, the cultural system "is the highest within the action system" and, as such, a major source of societal evolution and "large-scale change."[13]

The fact that Parsons considers modern medical practice a "case" implies that he views it in a comparative evolutionary framework, as the

10. Parsons, *Societies*, p. 8. "Problems of meaning" is a term that Parsons adopted from Max Weber's writings.

11. Bellah, *op. cit.*, p. 359.

12. Renée C. Fox, "Training for Uncertainty" in Robert K. Merton, George Reader, and Patricia L. Kendall (eds.), *The Student-Physician* (Cambridge: Harvard University Press, 1957), 207–241.

13. Parsons, *Societies*, 9–10.

crystallization of a certain stage of medical development and institutionalization. Occasionally he makes this evolutionary outlook more explicit, either by contrasting some of the attributes of modern medicine with those of earlier phases or by offering analytic speculations on what the health-illness-medicine complex will look like in the future. Thus, for example, he reminds us that:

> . . . the treatment of illness as a problem for applied science [should not] be taken for granted as "common sense." The comparative evidence is overwhelming that illness . . . has been interpreted in supernatural terms, and magical treatment has been considered to be the appropriate method of coping with it. In non-literate societies there is an element of empirical lore which may be considered as proto-scientific. . . . But the prominence of magic in this field is overwhelmingly great. This, however, is by no means confined to non-literate cultures. The examples of traditional China and our own Middle Ages suffice. . . .[14]

In a theoretically based attempt to forecast the direction in which modern medicine can be expected to move, Parsons predicts its growing differentiation in several respects. These include: its progressive "involvement in the nexus of formal [collectivity-oriented] organization"; the continuing "upgrading of the level of science involved in medicine, and with it the . . . increasing participation of scientists who are not themselves medical men"; and "extension of the focus of ultimate [fiduciary] responsibility for the health problems of the society," with the consequence that it will be less exclusively carried by the medical profession. In addition, Parsons foresees a continuing "generalization of the value complex involving health problems [so that] the basic concepts of health, and hence illness [will be applied] to higher levels and broader ranges in the organization of human action systems."[15] In effect, what he has done here is apply his paradigm of evolutionary change by sketching out how he thinks the broader processes of increasing differentiation, complexity, inclusiveness, and integration of organization, normative upgrading, and generalization of the value system are affecting the "present complex and rapidly changing situation" of modern medicine.[16]

Taking these statements as clues and jumping-off points, I shall first discuss more fully the key features that Parsons identifies as characteristic of modern medicine. I shall then move back to an earlier stage on the evolutionary spectrum to consider medicine in what Parsons and Bellah

14. Parsons, *The Social System,* p. 432.
15. Parsons, *Social Structure and Personality,* 342–358.
16. Parsons, *Societies,* 21–24.

would term an "advanced primitive" or "archaic" society. I have chosen to consider this phase of medical development not only because it is theoretically suggestive but also because I have had first-hand experience doing research in a developing Central African society which, despite its progressive modernization, still retains many of the sociocultural attributes of the archaic type of society from which it is evolving. My discussion of advanced primitive medicine, then, will be largely drawn from field work I conducted in Zaïre over the period from 1962 to 1967, supplemented by wide reading of English, French, and Belgian anthropological monographs on various African societies.[17] Finally, I shall try to imagine and formulate what the essential features of medicine might be in what we will call a post-modern society.[18] In this context, "post-modern" is merely a descriptive label referring to an evolutionary stage of society that at some historical juncture may develop from a modern type of society. My major empirical referents will be, on the one hand, what I know about the attitudes and values of the "new" medical student now training to be a physician in American medical schools and, on the other, what I consider to be the sociological implications of organ transplantation, taken as an ideal typical example both of present and future clinical medical advance.[19] Whether the medical trends that I discern will actually be institutionalized is not yet clear, and it is still too early to ascertain how continuous and compatible with modern medicine these developments may prove to be.

MODERN MEDICINE

The general framework within which illness is defined and explained in modern society is more ideological than cosmological. Illness is believed

17. The most general sociological statement that I have written on the basis of that field work and anthropological reading is an essay entitled, "The Intelligence Behind the Mask: Beliefs and Development in Contemporary Congo," The Eighteenth Conference on Science, Philosophy and Religion, Jewish Theological Seminary of America, New York, N. Y., 1968, unpublished paper.

18. The term "post-modern society" is influenced by Daniel Bell's phrase "post-industrial society," which he coined in his role as Chairman of the Commission on the Year 2000 of the American Academy of Arts and Sciences.

19. I have recently completed a sociological study of organ transplantation and hemodialysis with Judith P. Swazey which has been published as a coauthored book: *The Courage to Fail* (Chicago: The University of Chicago Press, 1974). In my capacity as Professor of Sociology in the Department of Medicine and the Department of Psychiatry, as well as in the Department of Sociology at the University of Pennsylvania, I am also engaged in exploratory research into the socialization of medical students in the 1970s. I bring to these explorations a comparative, historical perspective, for, in the mid-1950s, I was one of the chief field workers associated with the Columbia University Bureau of Applied Social Research studies in the sociology of medical education.

to be a "natural" rather than a supernatural happening: a state of disease and dysfunction "impersonally" caused by microorganisms, inborn metabolic disturbances, or physical or psychic stress. No mythical beings, spirits, or gods are assumed to be at work bringing sickness to bear on particular individuals; nor are people considered to be motivated or able to use arcane powers to do so. Furthermore, as Parsons indicated, one of the attributes of the sick role in modern society is that the person who falls ill is not supposed to have caused his condition by displeasing the gods, the ancestors, or "significant others" in his social milieu who, as a consequence, magico-religiously afflict him. Rather, he is regarded as being in a state attributable to factors that not only lie outside his personal control but also outside his moral and religious responsibility. Illness, then, is thought to be a natural part of the human condition, though not in a resigned or even passively accepting sense. It is considered a state that is, but that ideally ought not to be: one that should be interpreted, investigated, treated, controlled, cured, and, beyond that, eliminated.

In the opinion of microbiologist René Dubos, "Complete and lasting freedom from disease . . . is almost incompatible with living . . . a dream remembered from the imaginings of a Garden of Eden."[20] However mythical or utopian it may be, it is nonetheless a fervently espoused goal in modern society, one that is believed possible, as well as desirable, through the advance and application of scientific knowledge and medical technology. Modern medicine is also surrounded by the pervasive conviction that largely as a consequence of medical scientists' research and discoveries, members of the society enjoy a level of health superior to that known to men in bygone eras. Dubos challenges this, deeming it an "illusion" to contend either that general health has improved to this extent, or that the "laboratory scientist's labors" and the "scientific management of . . . body and soul" are that exclusively responsible for whatever progress has been made in this respect.[21] The fact that such assumptions of modern scientific medicine are subject to debate demonstrates, to use Parsonian terms, that the type of orientation it represents contains important evaluative as well as cognitive elements.

Phrased more sociologically and less subjectively, what Dubos calls an illusion can be taken to be an indicator of the fact that the conceptions and beliefs about illness institutionalized by modern medicine are supported by strongly felt cultural commitments to them. Other telling indicators of this at once evaluative and affective commitment can be cited. For example, in modern society, a person's conviction that his

20. René Dubos, *Mirage of Health: Utopias, Progress, and Biological Change* (New York: Harper and Brothers, 1959), 1–2.

21. *Ibid.*, 17–21.

illness was caused by evildoers, in the form of supernatural entities or human enemies would not be granted objective credibility, as it would in a primitive society. Rather, it would be more likely to be viewed as a paranoic symptom of mental illness. An individual persuaded that sickness is a visitation of God, an expression of His will that cannot and ought not be dealt with by other than religious means, would be considered an extreme "fundamentalist" and "fatalist," bordering on religious "fanaticism." He would not be judged to be piously exemplary, except by members of a few religious sects, as he might have been in certain kinds of theistically oriented intermediate societies. The labels "mentally ill," "fundamentalist," and "fatalist" invoked in this context imply aberrations from the normatively expected ways of thinking about illness in modern society of sufficient magnitude and import to be classified as deviant.

The modern view of illness as a "natural phenomenon," in Parsons's words, does not mean that, "like the vagaries of the weather," it is regarded as independent of the "motivated interaction of human beings."[22] Rather, influenced by personality psychology and psychiatry, the modern perspective on illness includes the underlying premise that there is "a component of motivatedness in almost all illness":[23] its etiology, meaning, impact, and/or outcome. In this respect, "the most completely 'mental' of mental illnesses . . . various ranges of psychosomatic phenomena . . . [and the most] completely 'somatic' illnesses may be said to form a continuum."[24]

The dissociation of modern conceptions of illness from the machinations of spirits, gods, ancestors, or living relatives is not only a consequence of the degree to which they are shaped by science; it is also correlated with the extent to which medicine is differentiated from kinship, religion, and magic in modern society. As already indicated, the primary agents who define, diagnose, certify, and treat illness in modern society are not magical or religious practitioners or family members. Rather, they are medical professionals, trained to be technically competent in the secular and specialized, though vast, body of scientific knowledge and technique considered appropriate, meaningful, and effective in matters of health and illness. One of the attributes of the medical professional role (which it shares with other professional roles) is the value orientation that Parsons has formulated as the pattern variable, affective neutrality, which I have renamed "detached concern."[25] The

22. Parsons, *The Social System,* p. 430.

23. Parsons, *Social Structure and Personality*, p. 331.

24. *Loc. cit.*

25. I first formulated this concept in a paper that I coauthored with Miriam Massey Johnson in the academic year 1950–1951, when I was still a graduate student in the

physician and other medical professionals are enjoined to relate to the patient by blending empathy for his person, background, condition, and feelings with sufficient objectivity and dispassion to insure that their clinical judgment will not be distorted or their efficacy impeded by too much emotional involvement with the patient. Physicians recognize that, in spite of the professional socialization they have undergone, an optimum balance of detachment and concern would be very difficult to attain were they to care for members of their family, most especially their spouse, children, parents, or siblings. An informal norm has grown up around this insight in the profession, impelling most physicians to refer close family to other colleagues. A tandem arrangement is thus established, whereby physicians care for other physicians' relatives.[26]

This convention suggests other, more general ways in which family and medical roles are differentiated and, to a certain extent, insulated from one another in modern society. The physical and psychic intimacies that a patient entrusts to a physician differ in significant respects from those he would ordinarily share with members of his family. As Parsons has emphasized, the kind of access to the patient's body granted the physician is a privileged one. "Indeed, some of his contacts, as in the case of a rectal or vaginal examination, would not be permitted to any other person,"[27] even to a husband or wife. The physician also has entrée to confidential information about those aspects of a patient's private life and feelings that are pertinent to his medical condition, information that he would not necessarily disclose to relatives. It would seem that the structure of the medical professional role, as compared with that of a kinship role—most especially, its functional specificity and detached concern—makes it psychologically easier for patients to permit the physician these health-related intimacies. Being treated by a physician

---

Department of Social Relations at Harvard University. The paper was written for a seminar conducted by Talcott Parsons, on some of the theoretical ideas with which he was preoccupied in the course of writing *The Social System.* Miriam Johnson and I applied the concept to the medical case. Many years later, I published an essay on the role of training for detached concern in the socialization of medical students. See Harold I. Lief and Renée C. Fox, "Training for Detached Concern in Medical Students," in Harold I. Lief, Victor F. Lief and Nina R. Lief (eds.), *The Psychological Basis of Medical Practice* (New York: Harper and Row, 1963), 12–35.

26. It is interesting to note that in this situation a kinship-like courtesy is institutionalized. Generally, physicians do not charge very close relatives of doctors for their medical services. This custom seems to be an extension of another informal professional norm: that of physicians waiving a fee when they take care of each other. The latent function of this professional courtesy seems to be an at-once instrumental and expressive acknowledgment that a physician treating the members of a colleague's family is acting in lieu of their doctor-relative.

27. Parsons, *The Social System,* 451–452.

who was also a relative would introduce a modicum of diffuseness and affectivity associated with family roles into the doctor-patient relationship. This would be likely either to inhibit the privileged communication between patient and physician or to push it beyond the bounds of what is emotionally tolerable for both parties, as well as medically functional. The fact that the patient is willing to bare himself to a medical practitioner who is not a kinsman or a personal friend is not only related to his confidence in the physician's medical scientific capacities, but also to his impersonal trust in the doctor's commitment to professional norms of privacy and confidentiality.

The degree of segregation between sick and medical professional roles, on the one hand, and kinship roles, on the other, that is institutionalized in modern society is partly related to the structural properties of a modern family. As Parsons and Fox have indicated,[28] this small, conjugal, relatively isolated, close knit, emotionally intense type of family is prone to certain difficulties in dealing with illness. In contrast to the more far-reaching kinship relationships characteristic of an extended family system, emotional attachments to kin in a modern family are almost totally confined to the few relatives who make up the nuclear family. Partly as a consequence, the emotional importance and intensity of these relationships are likely to be so high that the illness of any one of this narrow circle of kin will powerfully affect and, in the psychological sense of the term, threaten all the other members of the family. Individually and collectively, they may easily be thrown into a state of disequilibrium. Under these circumstances, it is probable that a sick person's relatives will overreact to his illness, with the kind of excessive sympathy or inordinate severity that will sociopsychologically impede rather than facilitate his recovery.

The relative differentiation of medicine from kinship in modern society also seems to have the latent function of preventing the psychologically induced spread of illness within a family unit. To the extent that illness may be said to have a motivational component, the modern family would be particularly vulnerable to this kind of contagion, by virtue of the relatively exclusive and strongly affective way in which its members identify with each other. Furthermore, the sick role, constituting as it does a semilegitimate channel of withdrawal from normal social responsibilities and a basis of eligibility for care by others, is inviting to various family members in patterned, often unconsciously motivated ways. The psychological "temptations" in this regard are systematically related to the structural strains associated with various role constellations in the modern family:

28. Parsons and Fox, *op. cit.*, 234–245.

> To the wife-mother, [illness] offers an institutionalized way of reacting to her heavy affective-expressive responsibilities in the family and a compulsively feministic way of [responding] to her exclusion from certain prerogatives and opportunities open to the man. For the husband-father, illness legitimizes respite from the discipline, effort, and dualistic demands of interdependence and autonomy that his occupation [requires] of him. For the child, being moved by the process of socialization along the tension-ridden path toward adulthood, illness provides an escape from increasingly exacting obligations to behave as a mature person. And for the elderly individual, retired from the occupational system, widowed, and with no traditionally assured place in the families established by his children, illness may serve as an opportunity to solicit forcibly their concern and care.[29]

The striking degree to which sickness is cared for in a hospital rather than in the home in modern society is a complex phenomenon, to which numerous factors have contributed. Not the least of these is the need to localize and integrate the complex professional teams and technological facilities that scientific medicine brings to bear on the diagnosis and treatment of illness. In addition, in the light of the susceptibilities and strains of the modern family already discussed, hospitalization has an important social control function. It places the sick person in an extrafamilial setting, where he is less likely to be emotionally reinforced in illness and where the detached concern, specificity, and universalism of the medical staff can provide some motivational leverage for progressively moving him out of the sick role and toward recovery. At the same time, isolating the sick person from members of his family mitigates the emotional strain they are likely to experience in the face of his illness and thus helps them to resist the contagious temptation to take to their own beds in response to the situation.

In modern society, then, illness is significantly disunited structurally, as well as conceptually, from religion, magic, and kinship. It is also differentiated from other types of deviance, such as crime and certain forms of sin, that incur blame or punishment, because the individual engaged in them is judged to have willfully violated important values, norms, or role obligations. In addition, modern ideas about illness distinguish it from other sorts of human malaise, adversity, or misfortune. (A notable exception to this is death, which is closely linked with the sick role because it is so often preceded by illness.)

Although, as we shall see, these modern conceptions liberate individuals and groups from some of the basic existential and psychological anxieties about the significance of illness to which, for example, mem-

29. Fox, "Illness," *op. cit.*, p. 93.

bers of a primitive society are subject, they nonetheless generate a characteristic form of disquietude of their own. We have said that in all societies health and illness are related to what Parsons has termed "ultimate reality." "But who of us really believes that his own bodily infirmities and the approaching death is a purely natural occurrence, just an insignificant event in the infinite chain of causes?" Bronislaw Malinowski has written. "To the most rational of civilized men health, disease and the threat of death, float in a hazy emotional mist, which seems to become denser and more impenetrable as the fateful forms approach."[30] By disclaiming that the cause and meaning of illness have anything to do with the supernatural or the inherently mysterious, modern medicine provides no legitimation for the occurrence of such problems of meaning and no institutionalized way of dealing with them. Precisely because of its essentially scientific orientation, it only offers explanations for the "how's" of illness; but it does not explicitly recognize, dispel, or answer the questions of "why" that inevitably arise. This phenomenon, a source of structural strain, has considerable significance; for, in modern society, there is a progressive tendency for attitudes and behavior patterns once defined as sinful or criminal to be reclassified as sickness.

Paradoxically, the fact that these questions of meaning triggered by the experience of illness fall outside the purview of modern medicine contributes to the development of new forms of magic. Along with the problems of uncertainty and the therapeutic limitations that still characterize the field of medicine, the unanswered "why's" of illness find expression and some degree of symbolic resolution in what might be termed scientific magic. In effect, these are magical attitudes and behaviors, patterned in ostensibly medical scientific ways, that help to explain illness and to increase confidence in its positive outcome. Parsons has pointed out that what he calls these "functional equivalents of magic"[31] or "pseudoscientific elements"[32] are observable among medical professionals, as well as patients and the lay public at large. On the medical practitioners' side of the interaction, he specifically mentioned their inclination to favor the most demonstrably vigorous of alternative ways to treat patients, their accentuate-the-positive tendency to be optimistic about the success of their active intervention, and their nonimmunity to jumping on the bandwagon of "fashion change" in medical

30. Bronislaw Malinowski, "Magic, Science, and Religion" in *Magic, Science and Religion and Other Essays* (Glencoe, Ill.: The Free Press, 1948), p. 15.

31. Parsons, *The Social System*, p. 469.

32. *Ibid.*, p. 466.

conceptions and therapies when it occurs.[33] With respect to medicomagical orientations of the public, Parsons cites various forms of health faddism, a continuing, widespread belief in patent medicines and home remedies, and the development and recruitment power of numerous health cults.[34]

In my own sociological observation of modern American medical practice and research over the years, I have been struck by three other scientific magic constellations through which both physicians and patients try to deal with the problems of meaning, uncertainty, and limitation that grave illness and the proximity of death pose for them.[35] The first of these is medical humor, a form of gallows humor, at once counterphobic, impious, defiant, and cathartic. The second is a "game of chance" orientation in the same spirit of blasphemous hilarity: making wagers on the diagnosis of an illness, the impact of therapy on it, its prognosis, and, most audacious of all, whether a patient will live or die. The third pattern might be called a celebration syndrome. It consists of the giving of *rites de passage* parties, in honor of the birthday of a patient or a member of the medical team, to mark the anniversary of an operation or to fete sheer survival. All three of these configurations make ironic commentary on the apparent lack of order, predictability, and sense in the shared predicament of those who fall ill and those who try to care for them. All express protest against what seems capricious, arbitrary, and existentially absurd in this situation. And all make affirmative petitions that the day will come when the illness and death of human beings are more fathomablc and more effectively dealt with by the science and practice of medicine.

In an essay on "Death in American Society,"[36] Parsons and Lidz emphasize the extent to which the "enhanced capacity to save and prolong lives . . . achieved by modern medicine" has made it possible to "differentiate the death complex" into two components. The aspects of death "inevitably grounded in the human condition" are distinguished from those which are considered "adventitious" because they are "potentially subject to some kind of human control." Parsons and Lidz contend that the ultimate reality and necessity of death are not handled with "denial" in this type of society, as some would claim. For, death "coming at the completion of a normal life cycle" is not only regarded as natural and

33. *Ibid.,* 466–469.

34. *Ibid.,* 432–433.

35. Renée C. Fox, *Experiment Perilous* (Glencoe, Ill.: The Free Press, 1959), 69–113, 139–190, 242–247, and 250–254; and also Renée C. Fox and Judith P. Swazey, *op. cit.,* 62, 87, 100–104, 268, 318, and 320–321.

36. Parsons and Lidz, *op. cit.*

inescapable, but also as positively functional in certain biological and sociocultural ways. The nonresignation constituent in the modern cultural orientation toward death, the authors argue, is quite specific. It involves an institutionalized commitment to doing all that can be done to prevent or postpone as many adventitious deaths as possible. This is in keeping with the general pattern of instrumental activism that characterizes modern Western (and particularly American) society.

My own sociology of medicine studies have sensitized me to some of the distinctive ways in which such a cultural perspective may affect the attitudes of physicians and patients toward death. To begin with, partly as a consequence of this orientation and the far-reaching medical scientific advances associated with it, death from illness in childhood, youth, or otherwise prior to old age has been dramatically reduced, in comparison with a pre-modern society. Furthermore, for the reasons I have already analyzed, most serious illness is cared for in a hospital, which is commonly the site where death takes place, rather than in the patient's home. Partly as a result of these social situational factors, the young men and women in a modern society who choose medical careers are likely never to have viewed or even personally experienced the death of a human being. Yet, more than most occupations, the field they have chosen entails the ushering out as well as the ushering in of life and, in the case of physicians, the unique right and responsibility officially to "pronounce" death. In addition, medical students often begin their medical training with such intensive dedication to "combatting" and "winning out" over illness and death that, as one of them put it, "In a way, it's a shock for us to realize that some of our patients are going to die." What is implied here is that a desocialization-resocialization process has to take place for this "realization" to occur, for the medical professional to distinguish between deaths that can and cannot be forestalled, and for him to learn when it is and when it is not appropriate to make "heroic" efforts to "save" a patient. The acceptance of life-threatening illness and all deaths, except those that occur among the elderly, comes hard in a modern society, for medical professionals as well as lay people. From what I have observed, I would say that even at the end of a long process of professional training many physicians still regard the death of any but their aged patients as a "failure," for which they as doctors are both medically and personally accountable.[37]

If anything, this tendency is reinforced by patients and their families,

37. In their medical scientific publications, it is not uncommon for physicians to use the noun "failure" as synonymous with the death of a patient.

whose belief in the capacity of modern medicine to combat death and to cure is generally high and who do not have sufficient medical knowledge to be as cognizant of the field's uncertainties and limitations as are medical professionals. This same kind of faith in the actual and incipient powers of medicine, combined with a zealous disinclination to be passive in the face of illness, contributes to the widespread willingness of patients whose diseases elude the present knowledge and skill of modern medicine to serve as human research subjects.[38] Their motivation for doing so has two facets. It actively expresses their hope that through their participation in medical experimentation new insights or treatments may be developed that could directly benefit them. It is also a testimony to their disinterested conviction that, in the words of one patient-subject, it will be "for the good of medical science and the humane benefit of others in the future."[39] The phenomenon of gravely ill patients who seek promise and meaning in the role of medical research subject is so common that, in the opinion of Dr. Francis D. Moore, "the posture of 'informed consent' in therapeutic innovation" that the physician ideally ought to assume not only involves "trying safely and sanely to explain to a volunteer what is going to be done," but also "the much more difficult task of explaining alternatives to a worried patient who wishes, above all else, to have the experiment carried out on him."[40]

In some respects, it is in this physician-investigator, patient-subject relationship, one of the unique institutionalized characteristics of modern medicine, that Parsons sees the quintessence of the collectivity orientation both of the sick role and the doctor's role. He attaches great analytic importance to this institutional pattern. In all his writings on medicine in modern society, Parsons has emphasized that this is one of two core characteristics that distinguish professional from nonprofessional occupational roles. (The other singular attribute of a profession that he has stressed is the fact that it entails "high-level and specialized competence" acquired through prolonged training, "grounded in mastery of some part of society's generalized (intellectual) cultural tradition." This training, he points out, is "increasingly . . . acquired in the

38. This is especially characteristic of modern American society. See Renée C. Fox, "Some Social and Cultural Factors in American Society Conducive to Medical Research on Human Subjects," *Journal of Clinical Pharmacology and Therapeutics,* 1 (July–August 1960), 433–443.

39. Fox, *Experiment Perilous,* p. 150.

40. Francis D. Moore, "Therapeutic Innovation: Ethical Boundaries in the Initial Clinical Trials of New Drugs and Surgical Procedures," in *Ethical Aspects of Experimentation with Human Subjects, Daedalus,* 98 (Spring 1969), p. 510.

university, whatever special provisions for *practicum* experience there may also be."[41]) Parsons's formulation of what he means by collectivity orientation (one of five pattern-variable pairs), how it is institutionalized in the medical case, and what he considers to be its general societal import has evolved over the years. At first, it referred to a type of obligation built into a genre of social roles: concretely, the responsibility of incumbents of professional roles to put the welfare of the client and disinterested service to him before such self-interested goals as maximizing profit, striving for recognition, advancement, and the like. Progressively, however, Parsons has extended his notion, so that it has become more interactive and inclusive. Collectivity orientation now also refers to certain aspects of the client's relationship to the professional as well as to the collegial dimension of the relationship to one another.

Parsons maintains that professionals and clients are bindingly interlinked in somewhat the same way that fellow professionals are: by virtue of their joint membership in what he calls a "common solidary collectivity." By this he means that they are mutually engaged in an enterprise that is of high functional significance not only for the particular individuals involved but also for the society at large. And they are reciprocally committed to the values and goals on which this enterprise is based. In turn, especially because there is a competence gap between professionals and lay persons, both the mutuality of their commitment and the viability of their relationship are contingent on the institutionalization of some degree of impersonal as well as personal trust between them. In these several respects, in addition to being collectivity oriented, the professional-client relationship is a fiduciary one.

Applying these theoretical insights to the case of modern medicine, it can be said that physicians and patients not only work together to ease birth, facilitate normal growth and development, and promote health but also to prevent or relieve illness, deformity, and physical and psychological suffering, and to forestall "needless" death. Although the patient is not a full and equal colleague of the physician, Parsons concedes, his active collaboration and trust are necessary to the successful outcome of their common undertaking. Seen in comparative evolutionary perspective, physicians and patients in modern society have a relatively high degree of confidence in each other's commitment, integrity, and competence. At one and the same time, this "draws upon" and contributes to a reservoir of trust in medicine as an institution and, beyond that, a more generalized societal pool of trust. As I shall show,

41. Parsons, "Research with Human Subjects and the 'Professional Complex,' " *op. cit.*, p. 122.

the fiduciary matrix in which modern medicine is dynamically embedded differs considerably from what is characteristic of an advanced primitive or archaic society, where a high level of nontrust is broadly institutionalized.

Parsons does not imply that the situation of modern medicine is so utopian that physicians and patients perfectly live up to their respective role obligations and collectively enjoy a relationship devoid of strain, suspicion, and resentment. In fact, he emphasizes that one of the reasons the institutionalization of a modicum of solidarity and trust in the physician-patient relationship is important is that a "persistent ambivalence . . . exists in public attitudes" toward the professions in general and medicine in particular.[42] As Robert K. Merton and Elinor Barber have suggested, this characteristic ambivalence is both sociological and psychological in nature.[43] It is generated as much by the normatively structured expectations that patients and physicians have of one another and the patterned conditions under which people obtain medical care as by physicianly deviance or malpractice.

Parsons does not gloss over what he regards as retrogressive traits in the social organization of modern American medicine. There are two sets of these tendencies that he considers strategic: some of the ways in which the medical profession "jealously guards" its independence and autonomy against what it terms lay control,[44] and its tenacious adherence to a solo-practice, fee-for-service model. In effect, Parsons predicts that these patterns, which are already incompatible with basic structural and cultural features of a modern society, will prove nonviable in a post-modern society:

> Essentially, we may say, the classical private physician was—and to some degree still is—a kind of "aristocrat" of the occupational world. His *technical* functions had become specialized around the application of scientific knowledge, but his *social status* was a typically diffuse *fiduciary status*. In terms of the general process of structural differentiation which must be regarded as central to the development of industrial societies, this classical private physician must be regarded as a special, probably transitional, role-type. It seems inconceivable that this structural type could resist the pressures to further differentiation which have operated throughout the society.[45]

42. *Ibid.*, 129–130.

43. Robert K. Merton and Elinor Barber, "Sociological Ambivalence," in Edward A. Tiryakian (ed.), *Sociological Theory, Values and Sociocultural Change: Essays in Honor of Pitirim Sorokin* (New York: The Free Press, 1963), 91–120.

44. Parsons, *The Social System*, p. 470.

45. Parsons, *Social Structure and Personality*, p. 342.

ARCHAIC MEDICINE

By and large, post-primitive or archaic societies attach general and often central symbolic significance to health and illness. This is related to the fact that the health-illness-medicine complex is tightly interlocked with the predominant institutions of an archaic society—kinship, religion, and magic—which are themselves closely interwebbed. The relative nondifferentiation of archaic medicine, religion, and magic, for example, is nicely illustrated by the fact that in the cultural tradition of numerous Central African societies, no semantic distinction is made between the term for medicines or medications, magicoreligious charms and supernaturally conferred powers such as strength, fecundity, and invulnerability.[46]

In contrast to archaic medicine, modern medicine has its closest links with the institution of science, on the one hand, and the occupational sector of the economy (specifically, the applied professions), on the other. From a comparative evolutionary point of view, it is important to note both that, in archaic society, medicine's most intimate bonds are with different institutions than in modern society and that this relationship is less independent and specialized than in the modern case.

This is not to imply that archaic medicine is devoid of scientific lore and technique. But the characteristic way of thought on which it is premised is more magicoreligious than scientific. It shares with scientific thought at least two fundamental attributes: the quest for an explanatory theory in a causal context and an interest in classification and taxonomy. However, in a number of crucial respects, archaic medical thought is nonscientific and, in certain regards, incompatible with scientific reasoning.

An "imperious, uncompromising demand for . . . determinism," to use a phrase coined by Claude Lévi-Strauss,[47] is one of the most fundamental characteristics of the cognitive precepts and existential beliefs on which archaic medicine is based. This is consonant with a more general cultural orientation, distinctive to members of this type of society. They are inclined to seek and to find explanations for all that befalls them, awake or asleep, in the realms of the conscious and the unconscious, in life and in death. Most happenings—illness figuring prominently among them—are interpreted either as adverse or felicitous; relatively few ex-

46. For example, in Swahili, the word *dawa* means medicament, charm, and magicoreligious powers; in KiKongo and Lingala, the word *nkisi* has these three meanings.

47. Claude Lévi-Strauss, *The Savage Mind*, George Weidenfeld (tr.), (Chicago: University of Chicago Press, 1966), p. 11.

periences are regarded as neutral or without meaning; and virtually none are considered to be fortuitous. They are viewed as being determinatively caused, primarily by supernatural, psychic, and interpersonal forces, within a closed system of thought and belief, whose inner logic is cogent, self-confirming and self-fulfilling. Explanations for events like illness are pre-established, limited in range, and fixed. When evidence contrary to traditional interpretations presents itself, there is a tendency to develop what Evans-Pritchard has termed "secondary elaborations,"[48] that "excuse" or explain away the untoward occurrence and thereby protest established premises. There is no room for the concept of probability in this way of thought, nor for the formal acknowledgment of an ultimate, irreducible degree of uncertainty as an inherent property of man's attempts systematically to understand, explain, and predict physical, biological, social, cultural, and psychological phenomena. Archaic thought and belief is also monistic in nature. It does not distinguish between objective and subjective reality or dissociate ideas from empirical happenings and occasions. Reality is that which is thought and believed, and ideas are "bound to the particular occasions that evoke them."[49]

Essentially, the archaic medical perspective on health and illness is metaphysical. It is the prototypical expression of the "primal world view"[50] that pervades an archaic society, blending supernatural and anthropocentric notions in a particular kind of way. Health signifies that one's life force is intact and that one is sufficiently in harmony with intersecting social, physical, and supernatural environments both to receive and enjoy the positive values of life and to ward off its dangers, misfortunes, and evils. Illness is the antithesis of health. It is one of the principal negative, discordant, depleting, and potentially tragic experiences of life. In this respect, its dynamics and meaning are not sharply distinguished from those of other major forms of adversity, such as sterility, failure, interpersonal mischance, and death.

In the archaic view, illness is "unnatural." Ideally, it ought not occur, and empirically, it would not, without the intervention of transhuman forces, mediated by human agents who are either intentional or unintentional evildoers. Illness is presumed to be caused by the evil thoughts, feelings, or motives of a significant other person. It may result from feelings of envy, jealousy, resentment, hatred, aggression, destructive-

48. E. E. Evans-Pritchard, *Witchcraft, Oracles and Magic Among the Azande* (Oxford: Oxford University Press, 1937), *passim.*

49. Robin Horton, "African Traditional Thought and Western Science," *Africa,* 37 (April 1967), p. 161.

50. John V. Taylor, *The Primal Vision* (London: SCM Press, 1965), p. 192.

ness, or the like on the part of an individual who is not necessarily aware of the fact that he harbors these emotions or that he is deliberately intent on harming the person who is his "victim." (Anthropologists generally use the term "witchcraft" to refer to this kind of secret, unconsciously motivated psychic act.) But it is also possible that illness is due to the conscious and overt malevolent thoughts, feelings, and motives of an individual who has used symbolic, ritualistic means to cause the harm which has occurred. (Anthropologists would call this "sorcery," as distinguished from witchcraft.) In either case, the thoughts and feelings of the malefactor have the capacity to harm, because they are believed to harness the power of one of the numerous kinds of spirits that move back and forth between the spheres of the dead and the living, filling the cosmic space between the Supreme Being or Creator and Man.[51]

In this cosmic outlook, the Supreme Being, the shades of the ancestors, and certain of the spirits are "good." Along with the living members of the kinship descent group to which one belongs, they are primary sources of well-being, protection, and aid. At the same time, it is also true that the universe throbs with dangerous and evil counterpresences. Among the persons in one's entourage most able and likely to cause one harm through their malignant thoughts and feelings are very close kin. "Bewitched" is one of the first anxious hypotheses entertained when things do not go well, in general, and in matters of health, in particular.

Some illnesses, like some deaths, are considered to be independently and nonvindictively caused by the Supreme Being, without the intervention either of spirits or of human beings. For example, the illness and death of very elderly persons, white-haired and toothless, would be likely to be interpreted in this beneficent way, partly because they are not considered unduly premature. But, by and large, illness is regarded as an event that, like a bad and frightening dream, carries a negative message of import that must be deciphered and acted upon, if it is to be healed. In contradistinction to modern medicine, then, archaic medicine is focally concerned with explaining the "why's" as well as the "how's" of illness; and it equates the diagnosed meaning of illness with its etiology and ultimate cure.

51. In an essay on ethnomedicine, Charles C. Hughes points out that "widespread throughout the world are five basic categories of events or situations which, in folk etiology, are believed responsible for illness: (1) sorcery; (2) breach of taboo; (3) intrusion of a disease-object; (4) intrusion of a disease-causing spirit; and (5) loss of soul." He goes on to say that groups and societies differ in the extent to which they focus on one or a combination of these causes. In many African societies, he states, "the malevolence of sorcerers or witches is especially emphasized." See C. C. Hughes, "Medical Care: Ethnomedicine" in Sills (ed.), *op. cit.,* Vol. 10, p. 88.

As already suggested, a person's kinsmen and tribesmen—those to whom he is related proximately or distantly by blood—are considered to be a fundamental source of both his physical and psychic well-being. Each individual is a member of a lineage made up of dead ancestors and of their living decendants. The living and dead of the same lineage constitute a mystic as well as a biological collectivity, on which the health and, beyond that, the very existence of the individual depends. More directly and immediately than the Supreme Being, kinsmen and especially the shades of the ancestors are believed to control all the positive values of life. Thus, the individual protects himself against illness (and other forms of misfortune and evil), and maximizes the degree of health he can expect to enjoy by maintaining good relations with his ancestors (caring for their graves, remembering them, observing ancestral norms) and also with his living kin.

Diffuse anxiety about the intentional or inadvertent harm the thoughts and feelings of others may cause, along with the bivalent conception of kinsmen as key sources of danger as well as defense, contributes to the high level of distrust and vigilance implicit in all relationships and activities. However smilingly it may be masked, or politely and skillfully dissembled, this psychocultural state of suspicion and watchfulness is omnipresent in an archaic society. It is fraught with the kind of tension that is generative of psychosomatic, sociosomatic, and psychological disorders that might not otherwise exist. In this sense, it may be said that the cosmic outlook of an archaic society is culturally conducive to the development of certain types of illness.

In an archaic society, as in a modern one, when illness occurs, it is shaped into what might be termed a sick role. However, some of the structural attributes of the archaic sick role systematically differ from those that characterize its modern counterpart. To begin with, an afflicted person in an archaic society more easily claims and is granted exemption from normally required activities and responsibilities than in the modern case. He is not under obligation to try "to carry on" his usual duties in the face of illness, to be emotionally forbearing about it, or to handle it in a relatively individualistic and personalized way. Rather, he is permitted and even expected to react to his state of illness with strong feelings of anxiety and depression, patently and forcibly to express those feelings, and actively to solicit the attention, support, and care of numerous family members, neighbors, and kin-like friends.

This patterned behavior has several functions. It enables the sick person to give vent to emotions that, if hidden, through the medium of witchcraft could not only be injurious to himself, but also to others associated with him. It rallies a group of persons around the patient, whose solidary presence helps to shield him against whatever harmful supernatural forces are at work, at the same time that it provides him with sympathy and succor. Finally, the way that his kin and others with whom he has a close relationship respond to his predicament gives the ill person some indicators to judge whether any of them might be responsible for the fact that this adversity has befallen him. In fact, the failure of a significant member of the solidary group to visit a seriously ill person and to give him both moral and material support would expose him to the suspicion that he is the agent who has caused the sickness.

Given the causal conception of illness in an archaic society, it follows sociologically that the reason for a sickness of any consequence must be personified. In contradistinction to the "it is not his fault" exemption-from-responsibility facet of the sick role as institutionalized in modern society, the etiology and meaning of illness in archaic society must ultimately be explained in terms of "who" invoked it and why. The sick person himself may be "blamed" for causing his illness, usually because he has broken important magicoreligious taboos or failed to live up to certain norms considered crucial by the kinship system or its extended expression in the larger community. Just as frequently, if not more so, culpability for illness is projected onto significant others in the entourage of the patient. This is a specific manifestation of a more general cultural trait. The supernatural and psychic determinism of an archaic society leads to an at once fatalistic and self-protective "it is not my fault" conception of responsibility, coupled with a tendency to reproach designated others for what goes wrong.

When a member of an archaic society feels that he is sick, he is expected to consult an expert in matters of health. He is likely to do so without delay and with a sense of urgency, for the existential and psychosocial anxieties that illness evokes in him are not easy for him to withstand. The role of medical practitioner in archaic society is a differentiated one.[52] Its incumbents possess more empirical knowledge about particular diseases than "lay people" and a greater command of medication assumed to heal. But the functions of a medicine man (or woman)

52. How differentiated and specialized the role of an archaic medical practitioner is, varies from society to society. As Charles C. Hughes points out:

> Sometimes the specialist's role is a full-time activity, but more frequently it is combined with other principal roles appropriate for the practitioner. In some societies there are more complex social organizations involved than the simple dyadic relationship between healer and patient. Even as the kin and covillagers of the patient may be explicitly involved in the curative process, so too there may be a society of healers, or several societies of healers devoted to diagnosis and cure of various diseases [Hughes, *op. cit.*, p. 91].

are never completely dissociated from those of a magicoreligious specialist. This is because the comprehensive diagnosis and effective cure of an illness always includes the use of mystic rites and charms to identify who has called forth illness, his motives for doing so, and the means that he has used; to exorcise the noxious spirits at work; and to restore the patient to a state of inner and interpersonal harmony consonant with health.

One of the most common and strategic rites enacted in this context is a ceremonial palaver. Typically, not only the patient and the medical practitioner, but also the patient's family and his close acquaintances are involved in such a curative parley. A vigorous, protracted, but highly stylized and tightly structured process of inquiry takes place. This is followed by a confession of wrongdoing, bad feelings, or evil intentions on the part of the patient, the other participants, or both. The ceremony terminates in conciliative and expiatory acts that are supposed to bring about healing. Thus, the way that the sick role is patterned in an archaic society does not only require the patient's active cooperation with the practitioner. It also mobilizes his relatives, neighbors, and friends, obliging them to physically, psychically, and socially participate in a collective effort to make him better. This curative rite classically expresses the interpenetration of health and illness, kinship, religion, and magic characteristic of an archaic society. It is also an important social control mechanism. For it enunciates primary values, taboos and norms of the societal community; it dramatizes the harm that deviating from them can cause; and it brings the patient, his relatives, and close associates together in a renewed state of concord.

When a person's illness does not seem to respond to the medications, charms, and ministrations of a particular practitioner, he will quickly seek the aid of other specialists or remedies presumed to be medically and magically more potent. He is not expected or likely to exhibit the same kind of loyal, trusting commitment to a given medical practitioner that is institutionalized in a modern society. Nor is the practitioner under the same obligation to maintain a continuing fiduciary relation with the patient as in the modern case.

What the sick person typically expects to receive from the practitioner's treatment is an immediate and total cure. This is consistent with at least two attributes of the value and cognitive systems of an archaic society that we have already cited. First, it is believed that because thoughts and feelings have the power to create and transmute reality, a fervently desired state like health ought to and can be made imminently accessible. Second, the cosmic outlook is an absolute, polarized one, an "all or nothing" perspective. There is extreme badness (illness) on the one hand and extreme goodness (health) on the other. The two antitheses are symbiotically linked, but there is no mixed zone in between. Thus, it is expected that dispelling the source of evil will automatically induce a wholly beneficent state.

Be this as it may, some illness does prove intractable. When this occurs, the "secondary elaborations" to which we referred earlier are invoked. It is assumed that the malefactor at work causing the sickness is especially powerful, has feigned good will and active collaboration in the healing process, and/or is chronically evil. If he cannot be magically vanquished by the supernatural forces of the practitioners consulted, then in order to preserve the sanctity and safety of the entire community, the most drastic form of punishment will be exercised against him. His physical or social death (ostracism) will be brought about by prescribed magico-religious means.

One final, additional word might be said about the "death complex," which in an archaic society, as in all societies, is associated with illness. I have shown that in this type of society, as Parsons and Lidz phrase it, "a concept of 'natural death' seems to be virtually absent," and that "deaths are always thought to be *imposed* by human action, by effects of the sacred 'souls', or by both through the mediation of black magic."[53] I have also indicated that life and death are coterminous, mediated and prevailed over by the ancestors around whom a cultic set of religious observances is organized. Death, then, is no more than a transposition from a village of living kin to one of deceased kin, with whom one has never ceased to communicate. In this respect, it is neither a traumatic nor a transcendental journey. Yet, death is also considered to be one of life's most dreaded, unnatural occurrences. For it brings one into continuing face-to-face contact with the ancestors: sacred, superkin who have a far greater power to do one harm, as well as good, than any relative in the community of the living. And so, death in an archaic society does not release one from the primal world view. It is carried to the grave and to the village of the ancestors that lies just beyond it.

POST-MODERN MEDICINE

Any attempt to depict what post-modern medicine will "look like" is a speculative enterprise. Nevertheless, it seems to us that the evolutionary trends suggested by our delineation of archaic and modern stages of medicine, when combined with reflection on strategic changes that

53. Parsons and Lidz, *op. cit.,* p. 12.

contemporaneous medicine is now undergoing, provide reasonable guidelines for venturing certain predictions. As might be expected, various social and cultural attributes of post-modern medicine that we see coming into view appear to be extensions of the evolutionary changes that the comparison of archaic with modern medicine has identified.[54] At the same time, there are indications that other characteristics of post-modern medicine may prove to be discontinuous with certain traits of modern medicine out of which they have grown. Some of these ostensible breaks with modern tendencies are structured reactions against trends that are considered neither desirable nor inevitable. Others might be called unanticipated consequences of the further development of orientations institutionalized in modern medicine. Although it would be inaccurate to label these two types of discontinuity a "return" to prior stages of medical evolution, in some respects they resemble characteristics of pre-modern medicine.

In post-modern medicine, the causes of illness are considered to be

54. In the body of the text, I shall not describe and analyze the attributes of medicine in the stage of societal evolution that Parsons terms "advanced intermediate." The main characteristics of a society of this type, as he sees it, are "full upper-class literacy and, on the cultural side, what Bellah calls an *historic* religion, one which has broken through to *philosophical* levels of generalization and systematization." Parsons, *Societies*, p. 5 (italics Parsons's own). Within the evolutionary framework that Parsons has elaborated, advanced intermediate society is post-archaic and pre-modern. As traditional China and India are two intermediate societies that he cites, it is interesting to consider the cognitive, social, and cultural traits that Ralph C. Croizier, an expert on medicine in these societies, considers their distinguishing features. In a way that is consistent with Parsons's evolutionary paradigm, Croizier emphasizes the differences between these medical systems and "primitive or folk medicine," as well as "modern scientific medicine," situating Chinese and Indian medicine somewhere between the two. "First," Croizier writes, traditional Chinese and Indian medicine have a

> complex and predominantly rational theoretical basis. Second, it is contained in a large corpus of medical "classics" of great antiquity. Third, the theoretical principles are intimately related to the dominant cosmological concepts of the society and its cultural values. Fourth, there exists a class of secular medical practitioners who are guardians of the classic medical tradition. This class of physicians stands apart from the common folk medicine practitioners of the society whose practices are often distorted reflections of the high medical tradition. Moreover, in his command of a literary tradition, the physician has pretensions to scholarly standing but suffers from the artisan, or tradesman, associations of practicing medicine as a profession. . . . As for their theoretical principles, both [traditions] may be said to have basically a homeostatic concept of health and disease. Health consists of maintaining a harmony or equilibrium within the human organism and disease is the result of physical or psychic (this allows for moral factors) disturbance of such equilibrium. . . . [R. C. Croizier, "Medicine, Modernization, and Cultural Crisis in China and India," *Comparative Studies in Society and History,* 12 (July 1970), 277–278.]

biological, psychological, and social, rather than religious or magical. In this sense, disease is regarded as a natural phenomenon. However, health and illness are also interpreted in a highly ideological way. The conviction prevails that good health and excellent medical care for all are basic human rights. By and large, anything less than optimal health and care is viewed as a form of deprivation that, ideally, should neither exist nor be tolerated. The fact that such conditions have not been totally eliminated is linked to the various ways in which the society falls short of realizing its ultimate values. Social inequities, injustices, and evils are invoked to explain the persistence of certain types of illness and the emergence of new disorders, as well as to account for imperfections in the system of delivery of medical care. In effect, society is "blamed" for helping to nurture or trigger all but the irreducible minimum of sickness. The same kind of projective mechanism is involved here as in the accusatory singling out of witches and sorcerers such as occurs in an archaic society. What is significantly different is that in a post-modern society an impersonal, collective, secular entity is held causally responsible for illness, whereas in a post-primitive society, specific individuals are identified as magicoreligious vectors of disease.

As in a modern society, illness is differentiated from other forms of misfortune and adversity. At the same time, it is associated with a cluster of what are defined as society-borne evils that are within human capacity to control, reduce, and even to eliminate. Along with poverty, pollution, overpopulation and war, it is believed, illness will yield to a massive quickening of public concern and conscience about the social conditions that foster it, if accompanied by organizational reforms of those political, economic, and professional structures that bear upon it. Thus, in a post-modern society, health and illness are viewed in a conceptual framework that not only invokes generalized social analysis and social criticism but also actively mobilizes energies for purposive, far-reaching social action and change.

Progress in medical scientific knowledge and technique, in tandem with the evolution of social scientific, ethical, and religious thought, make increasingly clear "the distinction between conditions that are really ultimate and those that are alterable."[55] Post-modern medicine has significantly advanced the understanding and control of disease, life, and death. Certain illnesses, like cardiovascular disorders, cancer, and schizophrenia, that virtually came to symbolize the uncertainties and limitations of modern medicine, the inevitable degree of suffering that illness imposes on man, and his ineluctable mortality have been illumi-

55. Bellah, *op. cit.*, p. 374.

nated and subdued by post-modern medicine. Man's life span has also been greatly prolonged. And yet, neither disease nor death has been abolished.

The furtherance of clarification, knowledge, and control, however, has not brought about a serene acceptance of the ultimacy of disease and death. Not only has the development of a more sociologically oriented theory of health and illness increased social activism in this domain, but also age-old philosophical and religious questions are revitalized by what is felt to be the mystery-laden relationship between what now seems to be alterable and what not. Who and what is man? What are the meaning and purpose of his existence? What is life, what is death, and wherein lies the essence of the distinction between them? Why do men fall ill and suffer and die? How should we understand these experiences and behave toward them? This sort of querying is characteristic of post-modern medicine and its practitioners, as well as of its patients. If one accepts the sociological view that preoccupation with such questions of meaning constitutes a religious act, then one might say that in this sense post-modern medicine is less secular and more sacral than modern medicine.

The sources of this post-modern existential awareness and emphasis are complex. Although the advancement of science and technology has not dispelled all medical uncertainties and limitations, it has increased the sense that human knowledge in this domain (and others) is finite and that mankind may be approaching the outer boundaries of what is knowable. The definition of death institutionalized in post-modern medicine is brain death. Historically, it emerged from a reexamination of what should be considered the most accurate and proper operational criteria of death, precipitated by developments in resuscitative techniques, organ transplantation, and the implantation of artificial organs. The controversy and debate that surrounded this issue not only helped to modify modern medicine's working definition of death as the cessation of breathing and heartbeat; it also fostered an enduring consciousness among medical professionals and lay people alike that any codified definition of death is to some degree approximate, relative, and arbitrary. The progress in preventing and curing illness and in extending life that characterizes post-modern medicine, viewed within its distinctive societal perspective, has been generative of still other religio-philosophical deliberations. Systematic conjectures regarding the functions of sickness and death have eventuated in teleological notions about the necessary and desirable role that these otherwise tragic experiences play in insuring biological, social, and spiritual renewal.

There is also a general reflectiveness about whether the quality of life to which a suffering, debilitated, or old person will be subject, if reprieved from death by the prowess of post-modern medicine, constitutes an existence that is sufficiently human and meaningful to justify heroic efforts to sustain him. Finally, the participation of many persons in organ transplantation, as donors or recipients, that post-modern medicine has brought to pass has increased awed awareness of how widespread essentially mystic conceptions about the human body and its parts are, and how fundamental. And for all of its sociopsychological complications, the network of giving and receiving that transplantation has established has involved a significant number of people in an act that they experience as transcendent, because they feel that it furthers their self-knowledge, enhances their self-worth, gives them a sense of totality, belief, and commitment, and augments their sense of oneness with humanity.

What I have designated as the entwined existential and societal outlooks of post-modern medicine are also reflected in the structure of the sick role. I have implied that the way of thought about sickness largely exempts the individual from responsibility for having fallen ill. In a nonsick or presick role, he has some obligation to do all that he can to prevent the onslaught of illness. Nonetheless, should he actually become sick, responsibility for his condition will be collectively defined, principally in biosocial and biocosmic terms. The process of getting better does not only entail an active, mutually trusting and collaborative effort *à deux* by physician and patient. If the illness is of any consequence, it mobilizes a group of different kinds of medical and health care personnel, who combine specialized knowledge, skills and duties with supple teamwork that is neither hierarchically fixed nor rigidly predetermined.

The physician retains ultimate responsibility and authority in the care of the patient. His singularity in this respect is based on the more extensive medical training he has received than other team members, his executive-managerial skills and functions, and the institutionalized charisma attributed to him by patients, who continue to see him as the symbolic personification of medicine's capacity to help and heal them. But the physician's relationship with his patients and with the various categories of medical personnel who comprise the health team is more egalitarian, elastic, and responsive than is generally true of modern medicine. It is also more affective. Detached concern still is one of the physician's basic role orientations and obligations, particularly with regard to his patients. But in comparison with the physicianly stance institutionalized in modern medicine, the overall balance between these counterattitudes has shifted somewhat, so that the physician is now enjoined to be more concerned and less detached in his feeling and behavior toward the patient. This is consonant with other reciprocally open and communicative aspects of the post-modern doctor-patient relationship.

A fee-for-service, private physician pattern of practice exists. However, it is not as predominant as variously structured prepaid group practices, on the one hand, and neighborhood health centers, on the other. The hospital looms large on the landscape of post-modern medicine, serving the triple functions of care, teaching, and research. But the prepayment groups and local centers, along with the sociomedical emphasis on prevention of illness, help to provide the facilities and finances as well as the motivation and knowhow to treat many nonsick, presick, and ambulatory sick persons outside the walls of the hospital. In turn, physically and emotionally, this involves the family more in the dynamics of health and illness than in a modern society and insulates them less. Finally, although peer review and control are the chief modes of regulation to which the medical profession is subject, informal and organized lay opinion as well as government pressure and statutes exert significant influence upon it.

CONCLUSION

This schematic presentation of archaic, modern, and post-modern medicine is compatible with the evolutionary perspective shared by Parsons, Bellah, and Eisenstadt: a macrosocietal view of progressive specialization, differentiation, "organic" integration, in the Durkheimian sense of the term, and adaptation. It also parallels Bellah's proposition that at each stage of religious evolution "freedom of personality and society is increased relative to the environing conditions . . . because at each successive stage the relation of man to the conditions of his existence is conceived as more complex, more open, and more subject to change and development."[56] At the same time, my account of the patterned unfolding of medicine highlights the importance of a particular cultural dimension of analysis for a general theory of social evolution. Specifically, I refer here to the complex interrelationships between three aspects of culture that our profile of medical evolution has identified: scientific knowledge and technique, cosmic view, and societal outlook.

Relative to modern and post-modern medicine, archaic medicine is less scientifically developed and more empirical in nature. It is embedded in a general magicoreligious way of thought that is deterministic, closed, monistic, and conducive to existential anxiety, suspicion, and

56. *Loc. cit.*

distrust. Illness and death are thought to be products of supernatural powers and evil human intent working in tandem. Although they are apprehensively expected, they are defined as not inevitable. Kinship is regarded as the primary basis of solidarity and safety, in the face of ever-present dangers like sickness. It is also considered a source of individual and collective peril, partly because physical, psychic, and spiritual security are so exclusively dependent upon it.

Modern medicine is scientifically oriented, to the point of formally excluding magical and religious explanations of health, illness, life, and death from its orbit. Questions of meaning generated by the predicament and experience of illness are either silently ignored, latently rather than manifestly acknowledged, or siphoned off to religious specialists. A confident and energetic rationality prevails. It is felt that disease and premature death, like numerous other problems that beset man, will progressively give way to scientific searching, robust, targeted action, and informed, organized care. Impersonal as well as personal trust is institutionalized in many nonkinship relations, albeit accompanied both by social and psychological ambivalence. The doctor-patient relationship is one of the prototypes of this more general societal characteristic. The nonpersonified way in which the causes of illness are conceptualized and their definition as not the fault of the patient, his kin, or those closest to him are consistent with this orientation.

Post-modern medicine is even more advanced scientifically and technologically. Partly as a consequence, it has reached the point where it is equally conscious of its accomplishments and its limitations and defines particular aspects of what it does not know and cannot effectively do as irreducible. This leaves more room for mystery and awe in post-modern medicine than in either archaic or modern medicine. It also means that post-modern medicine is centrally and explicitly concerned with the complex existential as well as ethical issues that develop when a highly evolved science is brought to bear on health and illness, life and death. Post-modern medicine, like archaic medicine, then, has an existential focus, but it is more religious than archaic medicine and less magical. For it is not so exclusively directed toward the achievement of concrete empirical goals like good health and longevity. Furthermore, the cosmic view that underlies it is less fearful and more trusting. Post-modern medicine is also societally oriented in a sense that differs both from archaic and modern medicine. In contradistinction to modern medicine, post-modern medicine emphasizes the extent to which society is both positively and negatively responsible for health and illness. In comparison with archaic medicine, post-modern medicine makes reference to a broader, more universalistic community than an extended kinship system. It formally recognizes the relationship between the imperfections of society and some illnesses and deaths, and it inveighs against them. But it does so with less apprehension than archaic medicine and with more confidence that a positive equilibrium can be established, in which beneficent forces will outbalance noxious ones. Yet, unlike archaic medicine, it does not have a millenarian vision of ultimate deliverance from disease and death.

The evolutionary relationship among medicine, religion, magic, and ideology, then, is not a simple linear progression. It has its own kind of social and cultural logic and coherence. But it develops in patterned ways that are more complex than a steady advance "from sacred to secular."

PART EIGHT

NEW ESSAYS

The Evolution of Medical Uncertainty

Uncertainty has been central to my work in the sociology of medicine since its inception. The importance of uncertainty in modern medical practice as a theoretical concept, an empirical phenomenon, and a human experience was first impressed on me by my teacher, Talcott Parsons (Parsons, 1951). He also conveyed to me the paradox and poignancy—for both physician and patient—of the fact that our great twentieth-century progress in medical science and technology has helped to reveal how ignorant, bewildered, and mistaken we still are in many ways about health and illness, life and death.

When I subsequently moved from his classroom into the field to study patients and physicians on a research ward, I became a participant observer in a tragicomic hospital world of men facing the unknown, where uncertainty and death were the only certainties. From Ward F-Second, one could catch a glimpse of a white, Greek temple-style medical school building, into whose stone facade had been chiseled the famous aphorism of Hippocrates:

This essay is based on the Merrimon Lecture delivered at the School of Medicine, University of North Carolina at Chapel Hill, on October 25, 1979. Originally published in and copyrighted (©1980) by *Milbank Memorial Fund Quarterly/Health and Society,* Vol. 58, No. 1 (Winter 1980), pp. 1-49. Reprinted with permission.

Life is short
And the art long;
The occasion instant,
Experiment perilous,
Decision difficult.

Experiment Perilous became the title of the book I wrote about that ward (Fox, 1959, 1974a) and the aphorism a kind of motto for me, personally and professionally. Ever since then, whether I have been exploring the process of clinical investigation, the making of a physician, or the development of a new form of therapy, in the United States, Europe, or Africa, the theme of uncertainty has appeared and reappeared as a motif in my research, teaching, and writing.

I shall not try to explain why this is so. A complete answer could not be given in purely intellectual terms; and it would carry me more deeply into my biography, and how I see and feel the world, than would be appropriate here. But it can be said that various factors in my person and life have made me unusually aware of the uncertainty dimension in medicine, and preoccupied with it, so that for thirty years, as a sociologist, I have been a watcher, chronicler, and analyst of uncertainty in numerous medical settings. It now seems to me that over these past three decades, and particularly during the last ten years, while I have been absorbed in studying problems of uncertainty in various medical contexts, a more pervasive interest in these problems and a greater concern about them have grown up around me. Something has been progressively happening in American medicine and in the larger society that has led Lewis Thomas to write:

> The only solid piece of scientific truth about which I feel totally confident is that we are profoundly ignorant about nature. I regard this as the major discovery of the past hundred years of biology . . . . It is this sudden confrontation with the depth and scope of ignorance that represents the most significant contribution of twentieth-century science to the human intellect . . . . Because of this, these are hard times for the human intellect. (Thomas, 1979:73-74)
>
> All sorts of things seem to be turning out wrong, and the century seems to be slipping through our fingers here at the end, with almost all our promises unfulfilled. I cannot begin to guess at all the causes of our cultural sadness . . . but I can think of one thing that is wrong with us and eats away at us: we do not know enough about ourselves. We are ignorant about how we work, about where we fit in, and most of all about the enormous, imponderable system of life in which we are embedded as working parts . . . . This is, in a certain sense, a health problem after all. For as long as we are bewildered by the mystery of ourselves, and confused by the strangeness of our uncomfortable connection to all the rest of life, and dumbfounded by the inscrutability of our own minds, we cannot be said to be healthy animals in today's world. (Thomas, 1979:174-175)

> As a people, we have become obsessed with Health . . . . We do not seem to be seeking more exuberance in living as much as staving off failure, putting off dying. We have lost all confidence in the human body. The new consensus is that we are badly designed, intrinsically fallible, vulnerable to a host of hostile influences inside and around us, and only precariously alive . . . . The new danger to our well-being . . . is in becoming a nation of healthy hypochondriacs, living gingerly, worrying ourselves half to death . . . . Indeed, we should be worrying that our preoccupation with personal health may be a symptom of copping out, an excuse for running upstairs to recline on a couch, sniffing the air for contaminants, spraying the room with deodorants, while just outside, the whole of society is coming undone. (Thomas, 1979:47-50)

Health, illness, and medicine appear to be epicenters of the increased malaise about uncertainty, and the anxiety about danger and risk that have surfaced in our society. This uneasiness has risen to the point where cautionary articles on the possible harmful side-effects of measures taken to forestall harm are being published:

> Informed Consent May be Hazardous to Health
>
> A considerable body of psychological evidence indicates that humans are highly susceptible . . . . This alone would lead one to suspect that adverse reactions might result from the information given during an informed consent discussion.
>
> An examination of the medical evidence demonstrates that there is . . . a dark side to the placebo effect. Not only can positive therapeutic effects be achieved by suggestion, but negative side effects and complications can similarly result.
>
> If protection of the subject is the reason for obtaining informed consent, the possibility of iatrogenic harm to the subject as a result of the consent ritual must be considered. This clear cost must be weighed against the potential benefit of giving some people an increased sense of freedom of choice about the use of their bodies. (Loftus and Freis, 1979)

Other authors, disturbed by the potentially damaging consequences of "uncertainty-of-uncertainty," "risk-of-risk," and "danger-of-danger" admonitions are responding to them with such counterbalancing notions as "necessary risks" (Jarvik, 1979) and "risk acceptance" (Comar, 1979).

This escalation of concern (and counterconcern) is as perplexing as it is striking. Like Lewis Thomas, I cannot begin to guess what all the causes of it may be, or where it is taking us. But it also seems to me that it has something to do with urgent problems that we are facing in the whole society and what he calls our "cultural sadness," as well as with advances in science and technology, and the so-called biomedical revolution that they have brought forth.

I would like to devote my Merrimon Lecture to an examination of the evolution of medical uncertainty taking place in our society: what it is, and what it means. I will begin with an overview account of some of the insights that have emerged from my own microcosmic inquiries into medical uncertainty. From there, I will move on to consider that more macroscopic ways in which the problem of medical uncertainty (and its concomitants—risk, hazard, error, and limitation) is manifesting itself at the present time. Finally, by linking up the two planes of observation and levels of analysis, I hope to offer a tentative interpretation of what appears to be the more-than-medical uncertainty crisis through which we are now passing.

MY RESEARCH ON MEDICAL UNCERTAINTY

It was through my involvement in studying the education and socialization of medical students in the 1950s that I first had a chance to observe the "training for uncertainty" that they undergo as part of the process of becoming a doctor (Fox, 1957). These observations were made in the context of the Columbia University Medical School Project: a research team, under the aegis of Columbia's Sociology Department and Bureau of Applied Social Research, that studied the socialization of medical students as it occurred in the 1950s, in the medical schools of Cornell University, the University of Pennsylvania, the University of Colorado, and Western Reserve University (Merton, 1975b). As the chief fieldworker at Cornell University Medical College, where I spent the years 1953 to 1958 in the role of participant observer, I identified, shared, and subsequently analyzed the training-for-uncertainty sequence experienced by medical students (Fox, 1957).

The research physicians of Ward F-Second, I retrospectively realized, had all known such training in their medical school days. It had not only introduced them to the uncertainty that they later faced as clinicians and investigators, but had also taught them ways of thinking about, and coping with it. The four-year-long process of training for uncertainty in medical school centered around three basic types of uncertainty:

> The first results from incomplete or imperfect mastery of available knowledge. No one can have at his command all skills and all knowledge of the lore of medicine. The second depends upon limitations in current medical knowledge. There are innumerable questions to which no physician, however well trained, can as yet provide answers. A third source of uncertainty derives from the first two. This consists of difficulty in distinguishing between personal ignorance or ineptitude and the limitations of present medical knowledge. (Fox, 1957:208-209)

This exposure to the worlds of "experiment perilous" and of "the student-physician'' also furthered my appreciation of the emotional, moral, and existential implications of these types of medical uncertainty for physicians and their patients. To be puzzled, ignorant, unable to understand; to lack needed knowledge or relevant skill; to err, falter, or fail, without always being sure whether it is ''your fault'' or ''the fault of the field'' (as one medical student put it), is especially painful and serious when the work that you do is medical. For, however familiar and routine it may be, or seemingly unthreatening and nontragic, no medical action or interaction that involves a patient is trivial or completely ordinary. Below their medical scientific surface, medical acts and events intersect with the human condition of patients, their relatives, and of medical professionals themselves—their most profound aspirations, hopes, and fulfillments, their deepest worries, anxieties, and fears.

Talcott Parsons and Ward F-Second had made me keenly aware that health, illness, and medical care in our society, as in all others, are integrally connected with some of the most elemental and basic, and some of the most transcendent and ultimate aspects of the human condition. The conception of human beings, their birth, survival, and growth, their physical, emotional, and intellectual capacities and development, their sexuality, aging, mortality, and death, I recognized, are core foci of health, illness, and medicine, as are the quality of their lives and some of the significant forms of pain, suffering, accident, and *angst* that human beings experience. In this sense, our ''coming in,'' our ''staying in,'' and our ''going out'' are continuously linked with our health, and with the medical care that we seek and receive. The experience of illness and the practice of medicine also summon up critical problems of meaning—fundamental questions about the ''whys'' of pain, suffering, the limits of human life, and death, and about their relations to evil, sin, and injustice. My participant observation in the medical school acquainted me with the forms in which physicians-in-training first encounter these aspects of their future work and their initial reaction to them.

This kind of experience, I felt, was epitomized in the anatomy laboratory and in the autopsy (of which I made special studies) (Fox and Lief, 1963; Fox, 1979). Here, I saw medical students learning about the structure and pathology of the human body by cutting into and dissecting it, and meeting the mystery of life and the enigma of death in the form of a naked, fellow human being laid out on a stainless steel table. Dissecting a cadaver and participating in an autopsy initiated students into the life-death-nudity-probing-cutting nature of medical work. I knew that, later, they would have little to do with cutting and dissecting the human body, unless they decided on anatomy, pathology, or surgery as their special field. But virtually all physicians take medical histories, do physical examinations, and carry out diagnostic, therapeutic, and prognostic procedures. These more everyday facets of their work oblige and allow them to see, peer into, touch, manipulate, explore, and penetrate the bodies of their patients, handle and analyze their urine, feces, mucus, blood, and other bodily substances and secretions, and inquire into their personal lives and intimate feelings in analogous ways. Observing rigorous norms of asepsis and noncontamination, dressed in professional starched white or astringent green, they enter orifices and inner chambers of the human body physiologically and symbolically associated with its highest and lowest functions, to extract and deal with substances like human blood, considered culturally to be both sacred and profane, dirty and pure. In clinical pathology, physical diagnosis, and on their various clinical clerkships, I watched medical students learning not only to master the techniques that these examinations involve, but also to manage their emotional reactions. What students found particularly "disquieting" (to use their own word) were those medical situations in which problems of uncertainty and problems of meaning were joined—when they attended an autopsy, for example, from which no definitive explanation of the cause of the patient's death emerged; or, when they had contact with a patient who was incurably and painfully ill with cancer, suffering from the severe side-effects of physicians' therapy.

Some of the collective ways of coming to terms with uncertainty that medical students progressively developed were junior versions of the coping mechanisms that the physicians of Ward F-Second employed. These mechanisms included achieving as much cognitive command of the situation as possible, through the acquisition of greater medical knowledge and technical skill, and the increasing mastery of the probability-reasoning logic with which modern medicine approaches the uncertainties of differential diagnosis, treatment decisions, and prognosis-setting (" . . . learning to conjure possibilities and probabilities," as one student put it). Students gradually evolved what they referred to as a more "affirmative attitude" toward medical uncertainty. They became more able to accept uncertainty as inherent in medicine, to sort out their own limitations from those of the field, meet uncertainty with candor, and to take a "positive, philosophy-of-doubting" approach. In clinical situations, they were more prone to feel and display sufficient "certitude" to make decisions and reassure patients. At the same time, the fact that students made numerous jokes about uncertainty, like Ward F-Second's physicians, indicated that this continued to be a source of stress. Counterphobic, ironic, medical humor, laced through with impiety and self-mockery, helped students to deal with uncertainty, although they never went so far as to engage in the "game-of-chance" behavior of their F-Second seniors. Confronted with extraordinary and often tragic uncertainty, the research physicians of Ward F-Second took laughter-accompanied bets on such serious matters as the diagnosis of a patient's illness, the impact of their therapy, its prognosis, the outcome of a particularly important or risky experiment that they conducted on a patient-subject and, most audacious of all, whether one of their patients would live or die.

One of the interesting consequences of the publication of my "Training For Uncertainty" essay (Fox, 1957) was the unexpected amount of appreciative response that it evoked from faculty and students in nursing, social work, law, divinity, and business schools, as well as from medical faculty and students. I received many invitations to be a guest lecturer in those settings, as well as requests for permission to reproduce the essay so that it could be distributed to large numbers of students and teachers. The response suggested that the problems of uncertainty and training for uncertainty were applicable to more than medicine, and were considered to be especially relevant in preparing for and undertaking particular kinds of professional work. I will return to these reactions when I consider the changed atmosphere in which problems of uncertainty and training for it are currently taking place.

Through the writings of physiologist Walter B. Cannon (1945:68-78), and of sociologists Talcott Parsons (1951) and Robert K. Merton (1957a:103-108), and my first-hand observation of how the research physicians of Ward F-Second thought and worked, I had become interested in the "serendipity pattern" in medical science: the role that happy (and not-so-happy) "chance" or "luck" played in the process of discovery. A chance happening that occurred in the course of my own research activities at Cornell Medical School gave me the opportunity to study "an instance of serendipity gained and serendipity lost." Lewis Thomas, then professor and chairman of medicine at the College of Medicine of New York University, and Aaron Kellner, associate professor of pathology at Cornell University Medical College, had each intravenously injected rabbits with the proteolytic enzyme papain, as part of their laboratory investigations. Both had observed unexpected "floppiness" in the rabbits' ears after the papain had been administered. But whereas Thomas had eventually gone on from there to make a discovery based on this "accidental" collapse of the rabbits' ears, Kellner had not.

A sociologist colleague, Bernard Barber, and I decided to make a comparative case study of the factors that had led one investigator down the path to discovering that the injection of papain had significantly altered the rabbits' cartilaginous tissues, and the other to follow a trail away from that discovery. The results of our inquiry into "the case of the floppy-eared rabbits" have been published and need not be discussed here (Barber and Fox, 1958). However, there is one set of observations about Kellner's and Thomas's shared outlook on medical uncertainty that I now feel we did not sufficiently emphasize. It is worth underscoring because their attitudes toward uncertainty in the mid-1950s when this case happened stand in sharp contrast to some of those that have become salient in the altered perspective on uncertainty of the 1970s. Kellner and Thomas viewed errors and mistakes, as well as uncertainty and chance, as perennial parts of the biological, medical, and human condition. Both investigators were as familiar with negative as with positive serendipity, preferring the latter, but were also convinced that mistakes were not inevitably unfortunate or dangerous. Quite to the contrary; in nature, in the laboratory, and in man's scientific and nonscientific activities, they believed mistakes could lead to unexpectedly felicitous—even wonderful—knowledge, capacities, developments, or change.

Until the end of the 1950s, my sociological studies of medical research, medical education and socialization, and chronic and terminal illness were all located in American laboratory, hospital, and medical school settings. In 1959, I began an investigation of how social, cultural, and historical factors affect medical research and research careers in a contemporaneous European society. Belgium became the primary site of this study, and since then has been one of the major loci of my sociological research (Fox, 1978). Belgium, in turn, led me to Zaire (the ex-Belgian Congo) where, from 1962 to 1967, I was affiliated with the Centre de Recherches Sociologiques in Kinshasa, and became involved in more wide-ranging research, which included studies concerned with the sociology of health, illness, and medicine phenomena (De Craemer and Fox, 1968). It took these foreign field experiences to make me realize gradually that my studies of uncertainty and ways of coming to terms with it on Ward F-Second, at Cornell Medical School, and in Thomas's and Kellner's laboratories had inadvertently been ethnocentric and culture-bound. My analyses had failed to recognize that the problems of uncertainty I had identified were distinctively modern, Western, and, perhaps, uniquely American in a number of ways. I had not even considered the possibility, for example, that the *concepts* of uncertainty, probability, and chance might not exist in some cultural traditions, or that our type of scientific reasoning about them might be incompatible with the cognitive assumptions and modes of thought of other societies and cultures. It was, above all, certain nonmodern, non-Western, Central African, aspects of Zaire's system of thought that brought me to this realization:

> Most happenings—illness figuring prominently among them— are interpreted either as adverse or felicitous, relatively few experiences are regarded as neutral or without meaning, and virtually none are considered to be fortuitous. They are viewed as being determinatively caused, primarily by supernatural, psychic, and interpersonal forces, within a closed system of thought and belief, whose inner logic is cogent, self-confirming and self-fulfilling. Explanations for

> events like illness are pre-established, limited in range, and fixed. When evidence contrary to traditional interpretations presents itself, there is a tendency to develop what Evans-Pritchard has termed "secondary elaborations," that "excuse" or explain away the untoward occurrences and thereby protect established premises. There is no room for the concept of probability in this way of thought, nor for the formal acknowledgment of an ultimate, irreducible degree of uncertainty as an inherent property of man's attempts systematically to understand, explain, and predict physical, biological, social, cultural, and psychological phenomena. (Fox, 1967b:780).

In our studies of characteristic features of the many religious movements that have developed in Zaire throughout its known history, colleagues and I found this same deterministic, fortune-misfortune-oriented way of thought to dominate and focus on the most highly valued goals of the society, including health. Among the other paramount goals with which these movements were centrally concerned was the attainment of a risk- and chance-free state of invulnerability (De Craemer, Vansina, and Fox, 1976).

I mention the new perspective on uncertainty I gained from Zaire because it throws into bas-relief the latent bias I originally brought to the study of uncertainty: a bias that is not purely personal, but built into the society and culture of which I am native. This bears on a hypothesis I will venture later in this lecture: namely, that the degree and kinds of ferment over error, risk, hazard, and the like that are now occurring in our society may be indicators that we are in the midst of questioning and altering some of our fundamental, cultural ways of thinking about, and dealing with, uncertainty. For the capacity even to speculate on such a possibility, I am especially indebted to the first-hand opportunity that Zaire gave me to explore a world view radically different from my own.

The next major piece of research I undertook involved a return both to an American context and to an old subject. In 1968, in collaboration with Judith P. Swazey, a biologist and historian of science, I began a study of organ transplantation and hemodialysis in a representative cross-section of the main American medical centers where these modes of treating patients with end-stage renal, cardiac, and liver diseases were being carried out and further developed. (Our study later came to include bone marrow transplantation as well, but in 1968 this form of organ transplantation was not yet being clinically tried on a sufficient number of patients to incorporate it into our research.) In the years 1951 to 1954, as a participant observer on Ward F-Second, I had been introduced to dialysis and transplantation at the stage when they were totally experimental therapies. During that period, the physicians of Ward F-Second (the metabolic research ward of the Peter Bent Brigham Hospital in Boston) had conducted pioneering work on the artificial kidney machine and performed the world's first kidney transplants. Some fifteen years later, coming back to these therapeutic innovations gave me a chance to study the phase movements through which they had passed, and to look at them in a broader social as well as time perspective.

Judith Swazey and I thought of transplantation and dialysis as constituting a paradigmatic case exemplifying the attributes and process of therapeutic innovation, and emblematic of the "collective conscience" issues with which the "new biology," medicine, bioethics, and American society more generally had begun to be preoccupied in the 1960s. Problems of uncertainty comprised one of the major themes around which our research and later our book (Fox and Swazey, 1974) on organ transplants and dialysis, *The Courage to Fail,* were structured. We focused our attention on the research physicians working with these therapeutic innovations, in their socially shaped professional roles as "specialists in uncertainty." We described and analyzed the diverse range of phenomena that the uncertainties associated with transplantation and dialysis posed for them: "the biological mysteries of the rejection reaction, the ambiguities of the relationship between clinical experimentation and therapy, the problematic aspects of the clinical moratorium, and the dilemmas involved in allocating various kinds of scarce resources" (Fox and Swazey, 1978:xiii-xiv).

The year 1968, when we began our study, was heralded by the mass media as the "Year of the Transplant." Over a hundred human heart transplants were performed worldwide, accompanied by much ballyhoo concerning the astronaut-like daring adventure it represented. However, at the year's end, the number of heart implants per month took a sudden, deep plunge, reached a plateau during 1969 and 1970, and decelerated so greatly that a moratorium on the procedure was said to have been called.

This sequence of events led us to identify what we termed "the clinical moratorium," to define it as the temporary cessation or marked slowdown in the use of a still-experimental form of therapy on patients, which could last for weeks, months, or years. We recognized that such moratoriums have taken place repeatedly in the development of therapeutic innovations, and set out to make a detailed study of the origins and consequences of particular moratoriums in recent medical history (Fox and Swazey, 1978:108-134; Swazey and Fox, 1970; Swazey, Sorenson, and Wong, 1978). From our inquiries, we learned that the moratorium is a recurrent, quasi-institutionalized event, most likely to take place during the early, "black-years" period of the use of a new drug, device, or procedure with patient-subjects, when problems of uncertainty are especially salient and acute for physician-investigators, and when the risks and mortality rate are so high they are judged to outweigh the possible benefits. The shared conviction that to continue the clinical trials is neither bearable nor justifiable, and the collective pressure to desist, we observed, could come from the reactions of the physician-investigators themselves to the situation, from their colleagues, the institution in which they work, or from patients and their families. These sentiments and sanctions could be expressed and enforced in informal or formal ways. Quite unexpectedly, our interest in and exploration of the phenomenon of the moratorium acquired more general significance. For, as the 1970s unfolded, and the concerned cultural mood about uncertainty, risk, and biohazards associated with health, medical practice, and medical research escalated, this kind of professional and societal response to medical uncertainty increased in prominence, frequency, and scope.

Finally, there are two additional areas of inquiry in which I have been involved since the mid-1960s; like the study of clinical moratoriums, they have given me a strategic vantage point from which to watch the evolution of medical uncertainty during the past decade. Both grow out of my earlier work.

The first is my role as participant and observer in the field of bioethics that has developed in the last fifteen years. This interdisciplinary sphere of research and action has brought biologists, physicians, philosophers, theologians, jurists, legislators, and social scientists together in various contexts and organizations to consider a cluster of issues connected with certain biomedical advances and practices—especially those involving research with human subjects. Such issues are considered empirically and symbolically to be part of the "biological revolution" of the twentieth century. Ward F-Second and *Experiment Perilous,* organ transplantation, dialysis and *The Courage to Fail,* and my analyses of medical and "human-condition" uncertainty in hospital, laboratory, and medical school settings cast me in the role of a pioneer member of bioethics. Uncertainty and the principle of risk-benefit analysis figure centrally in bioethical discussions and deliberations. They are analyzed and weighed in relation to other cultural issues and precepts that are brought to bear upon the main concern of bioethics: what ought we, and what ought we not, be doing biomedically in our society at the present time?

My involvement has enabled me to study the cultural linkages that are currently being made between uncertainty and other value and belief themes that have preoccupied us medically and societally since the 1960s: individualism and individuality, social reciprocity and solidarity, universalism and particularism, allocation and scarcity, the quality of life and of death, and the necessity and hubris of our vigorous interventions in the physical, biological, and social universe (Fox, 1974b; 1976a). I have been allowed to study, from within, what amounts to a social movement that has grown up, significantly influencing the ways that Americans are currently thinking and deciding about these questions.

The one other observation post from which I have been viewing the uncertainty problem has been from inside the medical schools of the 1970s, as much through my role as a teacher and adviser of medical students, as in the capacity of a researcher. Whether or not the content and process of medical education and socialization, and the background and attitudes of the men and women who undergo medical training, are very different from those I studied in the 1950s is a controversy that swirls around the American medical school at the present time. This debate, stimulated by the widespread criticism to which the medical profession and delivery of care are now subject, focuses on changes that supposedly have and have not occurred in the medical school, and their implications for improving the health care system. Sufficient reliable and valid data to evaluate how *new* the medical school and the medical students of the 1970s really are, do not yet exist. There is, however, tentative evidence to suggest that students of the seventies do not experience and react to some of the core aspects of the physician's role—the uncertainty dimension among them—in the same ways as their predecessors.

With regard to current training for uncertainty, I have been struck by the way today's medical students tend to be "late deciders." Compared with the students of the fifties, they take a long time to make up their minds about medicine as a career, and they come to it via a complicated, often circuitous route. They "Hamletize" about medicine and their commitment, audibly and continuously: about the rightness of their decision to become a physician, about all that doctorhood asks, and whether or not they will have the motivation and stamina to resist being molded by the medical school, the hospital, and the profession into replicating sentiments and behaviors of their predecessors of which they disapprove. Insofar as they are "new," medical students appear to be more involved in thinking about the sorts of questions with which bioethics deals, convinced that physicians ought to be doing the same, and more inclined to consider the problem of medical uncertainty in this framework, than were their counterparts of twenty years ago. In this regard, they are highly concerned that virtually all medical and surgical interventions, no matter how beneficial, have harmful side-effects, about the relations between these iatrogenic properties, the dramatic increase in malpractice suits, and their own vulnerability as practicing physicians. Doubting, self-doubting, and philosophizing notwithstanding, many of today's medical students tend to account for problems of medical uncertainty, and other problems, by invoking explanations that are more economically and politically deterministic, accusatory of outside forces and persons, and, therefore, more self-exonerating than was generally characteristic of pre-1960 medical students (Fox, 1974c).

In any case, regardless of how different these future physicians do, or do not, turn out to be, the "uncertainty scene" in medicine they are facing has changed considerably. It is to that situation that I now want to turn.

RECENT INCREASE IN AWARENESS OF MEDICAL UNCERTAINTY

The amount of concerned attention that has been fixed on uncertainty and medicine in the past decade, by a variety of scientific, professional, and business organizations and journals, health associations, legislative and judicial bodies, regulatory agencies, consumer and self-help groups, publishing houses, and the mass media, is striking. A newspaper editorial dealing with the national absorption in the problems of medical uncertainty today might aptly begin: "The American public is being swept by a medical epidemic characterized by doubt of certitude, recognition of error, and discovery of hazard" (Cournand, 1977:700).

This preoccupation with medical uncertainty is multiform. Awareness of the "long list of formidable human diseases whose underlying mechanisms are not at all clear, and [that] are presently unapproachable by such precisely targeted techniques as the use of penicillin against streptococci" (Thomas, 1977) has grown. Cancer leads this list. Consciousness of "the frail basis" (Miké and Good, 1977:678) on which many medical decisions still have to be made appears to have increased both inside and outside the medical profession. The fact that problems that are not only unprecedented but also "entirely unpredicted" continue to arise in medicine is frequently discussed with a mixture of amazement and alarm (Talk of the Town, 1979a). What is regarded as the high technical and human fallibility and error that persist in medical research and practice, in the laboratory and in the clinic, evokes an exceptional amount of troubled commentary. The phrase "biological revolution" or "biomedical revolution" is continually applied to the scientific and technological advances in understanding disease, and to the advances in diagnosis, treatment, and prevention that have been made in the last sixty years. However, the potential hazards and serious side-effects of these discoveries and developments—the capacity of the drugs, devices, and procedures they have made possible, and of the human agents who wield them to do harm—are emphasized far more than the problems they have solved or the benefits they have brought. The many allusions that are constantly made to the "power" of medicine usually refer to its scientific and moral dangers—

dangers that are described as potentially "catastrophic," rather than just "serious," when such phenomena as "human carcinogens" or "DNA damage" are discussed. The ability to cure disease is seldom mentioned. In those rare instances when it is, the term "cure" is either used ironically, or (as in recent, more hopeful reports on the outcome of therapy for childhood leukemia) with tentativeness and caution. Given the current state of medical knowledge, "an objective definition of cure is not yet possible . . . . The state of complete remission based on our current ability to detect residual disease is not distinguishable from a true disease-free state" (George et al., 1979:272). Controversies about the basic methodology of medicine and its underlying way of thought are repeatedly aired: the pros and cons of randomized clinical trials, for example, of clinical decision analysis, and, above all, of various approaches to risk assessment and containment. The need for reducing uncertainty and regulating risk is affirmed and reaffirmed, accompanied by a cacophony of opinions about who should do it, and how. The problems of uncertainty that lie on the borderline between medicine, public policy, and ethics, which are felt to touch on the "ultimate conditions [and] reality" of man's existence (Bellah, 1974:359)—for example, the uncertainties of genetic engineering—have elicited the greatest attention, the "most severe chills" (Callahan, 1979:9), and the deepest "Orwellian shadow[s]."[1]

Both collective awareness of problems of medical uncertainty and uneasiness about them seem to have grown significantly since the 1950s when I wrote the "Training For Uncertainty" essay. At that time, it was primarily through the professional education and socialization process they underwent that medical students came to recognize these problems, formulate them as such, and attach to them considerable importance. They generally did not arrive in medical school with the insight that uncertainty was generic to medicine and the role of physician, or with a social kind of concern about the subject. Whatever common anxiety they experienced in this regard was focused primarily on the individualistic question of how competent and composed each of them could learn to be in the face of this uncertainty. It is true that the publication of "Training For Uncertainty" evoked a response from more readers than I had expected, but this came from a limited range of professional and educational milieux: from those who were training persons to be nurses, social workers, lawyers, clergymen, and business executives, as well as physicians, who felt there was a special relation among these roles, the knowledge, skill, responsibility, and human relations concerns they entailed,

1. Phrase used in the opinion rendered by the Court of Appeals of New York State on the consolidated cases of *Becker v. Schwartz* No. 599, and *Park v. Chessin* No. 560, December 27, 1978. Both these cases concerned issues relevant to genetic counseling and amniocentesis.

and the uncertainty dimension. They expressed more pride than worry in the uncertainty component and the challenge of these roles, and they were appreciative of an article that acknowledged and analyzed them. Nothing like the outpouring of popular and professional discussion and writings on uncertainty that characterized the 1970s existed at that time. In fact, if anything distinguished the appearance of "Training For Uncertainty" in the 1950s, it was its singularity.

The amplification of professional and public interest in medical uncertainty, and the accompanying apprehension since then, result, in part, from the organized way in which uncertainty, error, and risk and their implications for health have been continually highlighted by the mass media, environmentalist and bioethics groups, the courts, the legislatures, and various federal government bodies, such as the Food and Drug Administration, the Department of Health, Education, and Welfare, the Occupational Safety and Health Administration, the Environmental Protection Agency, and the Nuclear Regulatory Commission. Whatever contributing role these and other agencies may have played, why have they become intensively involved in dealing with the phenomenon of medical uncertainty in the last decade, and emphasized its perilous aspects? Why is there a reservoir of general interest and disquietude in this area?

The heightened preoccupation with uncertainty, as mentioned earlier, is associated partly with the scientific and technological transformation medicine has undergone in this century. Some of the most fundamental and impressive advances in biomedical knowledge and successes in diagnosing, treating, and preventing disease have occurred quite recently, since the 1940s. One of the consequences is that the stakes have become very much higher in medicine than in the past. The modes of investigating and treating diseases are now much more powerful. They are also potentially a great deal more dangerous. As knowledge of disease and therapy has grown (as in the case of therapy for childhood leukemia cited earlier), the difficulties of sorting out what physicians call "natural" remissions and reversals of disease and transient placebo effects of treatment, from the enduring biological impact of a regimen of therapy, have become greater. The research procedures and designs that have been devised to try to cut through this type of uncertainty so that clinical results can be more accurately evaluated have become more complex, both methodologically and ethically, and in many cases, more risky. Uncertainty and risk, and awareness of them, have been increased by medical progress in both these regards. Medical advance also seems to have created a rise in expectations about health and well-being, longevity, and elimination of disease, which has had a boomerang effect on attitudes toward uncertainty. Public tolerance of medical uncertainty appears to have diminished, and indignation about its persistence has grown.

The development of scientific medicine, then, has both uncovered and created uncertainties and risks that were not previously known or experienced. Some of these problems are so new, and raise such intricate and important questions of fact, technique, judgment, authority, and values, that they cannot be quickly or neatly resolved. The indeterminateness of these perplexing issues has contributed to the sense of uncertainty about uncertainty, and augmented the sense of risk about risk. For example, in mid-1978, the World Health Organization declared that smallpox, an epidemic viral disease that has killed millions of persons over the course of human existence, is now on the verge of being eliminated from the earth:

> These events cast in sharp relief a difficult problem that science and mankind never has [*sic*] had to face before: If an ancient, deadly and historically feared disease is at last eradicated through the marvels of modern medicine, should the laboratory stocks of the virus that caused it be kept for important related research? Nine laboratories, three in the United States, are known to have retained smallpox virus. What steps are being taken so that none will escape again in the distant future, as it did in Birmingham, conceivably causing a major epidemic in a population that by then may have lost its immunity, a population treated by doctors who may have all but forgotten the disease? And how reliable are these precautions? (Stockton, 1979:36)

The Birmingham (England) case, referred to above, involved two tragic deaths: that of Janet Parker, a 40-year-old medical photographer at the Medical School of Birmingham University, who contracted a fatal case of smallpox in late August 1978 from a laboratory situated on the floor below her darkroom in the medical school; and the death by suicide (on September 1, 1978, five days before Janet Parker's) of 49-year-old Dr. Henry Bedson, the virologist who ran the laboratory. The laboratory specialized in smallpox research and, it was later revealed, failed to meet the standards of precaution and safety recommended for the handling of dangerous pathogens. Although these two interconnected deaths did not lead to a general outbreak of smallpox, they became causes célèbres, because they were felt to epitomize some of the potential uncertainties, dangers, and damage that medical progress has brought and the many unsolved problems of how to deter, contain, and control them (Hawkes, 1979).

To a much greater and more sustained extent than the intrinsic and laboratory-borne hazards of work with smallpox virus, research with recombinant DNA (the compound deoxyribonucleic acid) has become a center of deep worry and impassioned controversy over the uncertainties of new and contemplated biomedical developments. The questions concern the potential benefits of these developments and the postulated risks; whether, how, and by whom these hypothesized benefits and risks can be proved and/or disproved; and the issue of whether, why, how, and by whom such research can or should be controlled.

DNA is the molecule in which encoded genetic information is stored, and the material vehicle of the instructions by which hereditary traits are passed from one generation of organisms to the next. So-called recombinant DNA is the new technology that enables scientists to take DNA from one organism and splice it onto DNA from another, using a recently discovered class of ordinary enzymes (the restriction enzymes). This process allows the genetic information in DNA molecules to be specifically rearranged, so that new living molecules and genes—in effect, new forms of biological life—are created. Usually, the recipient organism is a bacterium that will replicate the "foreign" DNA along with its own genes, distributing both to "daughter" cells during cell division. Since bacteria divide rapidly, large amounts of the DNA segment can be synthesized by this means. This is considered a major breakthrough in genetic research, with great potential benefits. On a basic research level, because recombinant DNA technology makes it possible to obtain many copies of genes from higher organisms, it provides a valuable medium and resource for working out the detailed structure of the chromosomes and the dynamics of gene action in these organisms. Scientists believe that such advances in knowledge could, in turn, further our understanding of the fundamental mechanisms involved in immunological responses, resistance to antibiotics, the growth and spread of cancer cells, and other crucial medical phenomena. Scientists also hope that the recombinant DNA techniques may enable them to select segments of DNA that are templates for valuable therapeutic products, such as human insulin and the antiviral agent interferon, which might be multiplied and produced in copious amounts by inserting these segments into cultures of *Escherichia coli (E. coli)* or some other bacteria. Still another benefit envisioned is the prospect of extending the climatic range of food crops by equipping plants to secure their nitrogen supply from the air.

With the development of this new technology, however, and as these promising lines of research have opened up, concern about the possible biohazards of recombinant DNA has grown and become more audible, along with assertions about its advantages. The voiced concern started within the scientific community itself, coming at first from those scientists most directly connected with the research, and it has progressively come to include representatives of the government, lawyers, social scientists, private citizens, public-interest groups, and the media. The stormy debates triggered by these expressed apprehensions (debates that still continue) have been focused not only on specific and proximate technical risks of recombinant DNA research, but also on their broader, more long-term evolutionary and ecological dangers:

> Simultaneously . . . with the arrival of this new technology, some of us [began] to wonder whether it might also have unexpectedly bad consequences, such as through the creation of new types of organisms never yet subjected to the pressures of evolution and which might have disease-causing potentials that we do not now have to face. In particular, we worried about the creation of bacteria selectively tailored to be resistant to all known antibiotics or the insertion of the genes of tumor viruses into bacteria known to multiply in humans. (Watson, 1976:3)

And if such alterations inadvertently did occur, what would happen if they escaped from the laboratory into the environment? It has been urgently asked whether their effects would be malignant or toxic, and their spread irreversible.

This is not the place to chronicle the long history and vast implications of the recombinant DNA research controversy (Swazey, Sorenson, and Wong, 1978). (An archive of documents, interviews, and audio and video tapes on the history of recombinant DNA and the issues associated with it has been created as part of the Oral History Project of the Massachusetts Institute of Technology.) But I do want to identify some of the ways in which this important case of actual and incipient biomedical developments both involves and illuminates the new societal and cultural uneasiness about medical uncertainty that I am exploring.

To begin with, however vehement the statements and counterstatements about the potential benefits and biohazards of recombinant DNA techniques, the fact remains that both are largely a matter of conjecture. Most forms of recombinant DNA research are so new that there is little in the way of a laboratory past to guide scientists. Although probability reasoning and risk-benefit logic can be and have been applied to the problem of assessing, comparing, and evaluating the likelihood and magnitude of the various risks and benefits recombinant DNA research may entail, the unknowns are too great for essentially qualitative judgments to be more quantitatively, precisely, reliably, or conclusively expressed. To scientifically prove or disprove the risk-benefit appraisals that have been made would require much more laboratory, genetic, metabolic, and ecological information than is currently available.

Partly for this reason, the perspectives of scientists as well as nonscientists on the uncertainties of recombinant DNA, and the positions that have been taken by various individuals and groups on its possible benefits and hazards, have been based as much on personal and social sentiments, values, and beliefs, as on scientific concepts, facts, and methods. A powerful sentiment that has been repeatedly expressed in the discussions about DNA is awe: a mixture of wonder, reverence, and fear over how fundamental this molecule is to all forms of life. This sense of awe underlies some of the almost messianic hopes about the benefits to humanity that recombinant DNA may bring, along with "facts that may be necessary to the [very] survival of our . . . advanced societies" (Watson, 1976:15). This same conviction about the relation between DNA and the essence and continuation of life has also contributed to the even more conspicuous sense of foreboding and potential catastrophe that the capacity to manipulate genes has helped to arouse. This research has been referred to as a "manipulation of life" that constitutes an "ultimate experiment" in "man-made evolution" (Wade, 1977), an intervention that might "counteract, irreversibly, the evolutionary wisdom of millions of years" (Chargaff, 1976) by crossing a supposed "natural barrier" between species.

Thomas observes:

> The recombinant line of research is . . . upsetting, not because of the dangers now being argued about but because it is disturbing in a fundamental way to face the fact that genetic machinery in control of the planet's life can be fooled around with so easily. We do not like the idea that anything so fixed and stable as a species line can be changed. The notion that genes can be taken out of one genome and inserted in another is unnerving. Classical mythology is peopled with mixed beings—part man, part animal or plant— and most of them associated with tragic stories. Recombinant DNA is a reminder of bad dreams. (Thomas, 1979:71)

And indeed, the huge body of scientific and popular literature that has been published on recombinant DNA is full of such mythic and "bad-dreams" imagery, including Frankensteinian allusions to the production of new, uncontrollable, destructive creatures (Gaylin, 1977).

The interweaving of "deliverance" and "disaster" metaphors in the discussions of recombinant DNA, and the ambivalence expressed about whether "disturbing the universe" in this way (Dyson, 1979), or desisting from doing so, is the more dangerous, are related to another set of attitudes and beliefs around which these debates have turned: differing conceptions and philosophies about errors and mistakes, and the role they play in the physical universe, the biosphere, and human affairs. One of the premises on which some of the more sanguine and serene opinions about the potentialities of recombinant DNA is based is the notion that to err is neither exclusively human nor primarily regrettable. Rather, it is a basic life process: "Errors are made by nature . . . replication is not perfect [and] evolution is built up by the perpetuation of errors" (Thomas, 1979:28-30). In this view, DNA itself shows this "capacity to blunder"—this "driving force in evolution" (Cohen, cited in Powledge, 1977:19). The making of mistakes, and the exploration of them, are also considered to be central to imaginative, creative human thought and discovery, in science as in art.

Along with the celebration of error, a skeptical, anxious, and vigilant outlook on "natural" and "human" mistakes has been forcefully expressed throughout the debates on recombinant DNA. "The evolutionary wisdom of nature has given us bubonic plague and cancer,"[2] is the wry comment made by a professor of medicine, involved in the recombinant DNA controversy, on the supposedly benign and beneficent properties of errors in and by nature. What many observers and commentators assume are the less predictable and controllable consequences of human error have elicited still greater apprehension. These consequences, above all, have brought forth feelings of cosmic dread and primal sin, as in the following poem, "Original Synthesis," on "the Man-Made Gene," by a microbiologist:

One can't help but admire the craftsmanship.
Half a dozen years for assembly, forty synthetic
fragments joined end to overlapping end.
Larger than life it sits there,
the 126 ribs all in place.
You can almost hear it rattling its terminator.
If only it didn't look so much
like a goddamned serpent! Archetypes
crowd in, insistent as base-pairs.
Even now, in some bounteously
equipped laboratory,
a tyrosine suppressor transfer-DNA template
sidles up to an unwary investigator,
slyly whispering in vitro, *"Eritis sicut Deus,*
scientes bonum et malum.
Take the apple
and improve on it.
Be fruitful and replicate."
Or Hermes—unerring messenger—
tires of the scene, suppresses
a yawn,
unwinds his doubly-snaked staff and transfers

2. Statement by Stanley Cohen, professor of medicine at Stanford University School of Medicine, and a signatory to the 1974 letter calling for a moratorium on certain types of recombinant DNA research that was drafted by researchers working on it, and published both in *Science* and in *Nature* in July 1974. Cohen's remark is quoted in Powledge (1977:19).

to future generations
the gene for winged feet.
Deoxyribonucleic acid sounded once
strange as Quetzalcoatl and as remote.
High on the stepped pyramid
we encounter
now
the unmasked visage of the twofold god:
We look upon the bringer of maize.
We look upon the Feathered Serpent. (Isaacs, 1977)

This shuddering sense of metaphysical danger is premised not only on the belief that human error is unnatural, ungovernable, and peculiarly difficult to rectify or reverse; but also on the belief that it is made more lethal by the moral and spiritual weaknesses and imperfections of human beings and human societies—above all, by the evils that result from their self-centeredness and their temptation to play God. This latent conception of human fallibility seems to have been brought to the surface and made more acute by biological and medical developments, such as recombinant DNA, and by the risks involved in the use of nuclear power, such as the accident at Three Mile Island—widely regarded as potentially generative of unique events that could menace life as we know it on a worldwide basis:

> One characteristic of the new class of disaster is simple magnitude; for some reason, we seem to tolerate losses more easily when, as in highway accidents, they occur separately, and to recoil when a large number occur at once. Another, perhaps more significant characteristic is peril to some large and irreparable or irreplaceable piece of nature—such as a species, or the ozone in the upper atmosphere, or the birds in the spring—or to some large piece of human civilization, such as New York City, or to a particular tribe or people.
>
> In attempts to prevent one-time catastrophes, the usual tools of prediction are useless. (Talk of the Town, 1979b)

In addition to these scientific and suprascientific questions about the uncertainties and hazards of recombinant DNA research, another cluster of concerns has been prominent in the controversy. The "limits" of scientific inquiry and its "regulation" are the key words that have been used most frequently to refer to these issues, along with the reiterative question: "Who decides who decides?" The development of recombinant DNA has not only precipitated impassioned discussion about whether, when, to what extent, in what ways, and by whom decisions and actions should be taken to constrain risk-fraught scientific work. This research has also constituted a dynamic, widely publicized, in vivo experiment in the application and appraisal of a wide gamut of controls intended to govern it responsibly.

Over the course of the past six years of its complex and turbulent history, recombinant DNA has been the object of several moratoriums in certain types of potentially troublesome experiments, invoked nationally and internationally by molecular biologists themselves; by the formulation and issuance of guidelines by the National Institutes of Health, specifying physical and biological containment levels and procedures, and proscribing particular experiments; a whole series of local controversies and actions involving universities and research institutes, citizens' groups, and city and state governments in at least a dozen different American localities; congressional hearings; the introduction of regulatory bills in the United States Senate and House of Representatives; lobbying and counterlobbying on the part of numerous scientific, community, and special interest groups; and by the consequent, perhaps temporary, forestalling of national legislation to control work with recombinant DNA.

The attitudes toward uncertainty and risk that have been expressed in the context of these DNA deliberations have been far from olympian. They have included a detailed and sometimes impassioned consideration of the "possible scenarios of misfortune" and fortune that might result from work with recombinant DNA (Sinsheimer, 1978: 27-28). They have also been punctuated by attempts to assign responsibility, exact accountability, and affix blame to particular individuals, groups, and forces in the society for the handling or mishandling of uncertainty, the biohazards, medical risks, and adverse health effects that could result. A line of distinction between fault-accompanied and fault-free uncertainty has not been maintained. Nor has the concept of no-fault been considered acceptable, in this context, any more than it has in other areas of medical uncertainty and risk.

Throughout these debates, the issue of whether to regulate or not to regulate, and how, has brought a wide variety of concerns to the surface. These have ranged from freedom of inquiry anxieties and affirmations, to holocaust- and civil-rights-movement-associated protests against "genetic engineering" and trying to "perfect the human race" ("We shall not be cloned . . . "),[3] to philosophical uneasiness about the extent to which our scientific and technological endeavors continue to rest on "our faith in the resilience, even the benevolence of nature . . . . Ought we to step more cau-

3. Such allusions to the "superior race" eugenics of Adolph Hitler and to "We Shall Overcome," the hymn of protest and affirmation of the civil rights movement, were made in the course of public meetings about recombinant DNA research and its potential dangers that took place in Cambridge, Massachusetts, in the last half of 1977. See Swazey, Sorenson, and Wong (1978:1071).

tiously as we explore the deeper levels of matter and life?'' (Sinsheimer, 1978:24). The ''risk-regulation'' question has not only increased these uncertainties and made them more manifest, but has also generated new forms of methodological and moral uncertainty specifically associated with the regulation process:

> Risk regulation itself carries risks . . . . [T]here are two different kinds of uncertainty that plague risk regulation. Some uncertainty is inherent in regulating activities on the frontiers of scientific progress [where we] simply do not know enough . . . . In the face of such uncertainty society must decide whether or not to take a chance—to wait for more information before going ahead . . . . or to go forward and gamble that solutions will be found.
>
> The other kind of uncertainty that infects risk regulation comes from a refusal to face the hard questions created by lack of knowledge. It is uncertainty produced by scientists and regulators who assure the public that there are no risks, but know that the answers are not at hand. Perhaps more important, it is a false sense of security because the hard questions have never been asked in the first place. (Bazelon, 1979:279)

In the case of recombinant DNA, the hard questions *have* been asked, repeatedly, often dramatically, and on a wide local, national, and international scale. In fact, recombinant DNA constitutes a particularly important and conspicuous set of scientific and technological developments around which many of the cultural themes and social issues associated with the growing significance of medical uncertainty and its broader implications have clustered. This is only one such instance. Even more than the supposed dangers of recombinant DNA, for example, the accident that occurred last March at the Three Mile Island nuclear plant in Pennsylvania has brought forth anguished alarm and indignation over the potentially disastrous cosmic significance of experimenting and tampering with nature in basic ways; of error, particularly in its human form; and of too much scientific audacity and technological pride. These fears are clearly reflected in comments that appeared in *The New Yorker:*

> A recent headline in the Washington *Post* concerning the afflicted nuclear power plant on Three Mile Island, in Pennsylvania, read, ''Aides Wonder If Contamination May Close Plant Forever.'' . . . The appearance in news stories of words like ''forever'' is one more clear signal, if we still need it, that with the discovery of nuclear energy events of a new order of magnitude, belonging to a new dimension of time, have broken into the stream of history. In unleashing nuclear chain reactions, we have brought a cosmic force, virtually never found in terrestrial nature, onto the earth—a force that, both in its visible, violent form of nuclear explosions and in its invisible, impalpable form of radiation, is alien and dangerous to earthly life, and can, through damage to life's genetic

> foundation, break the very frame on which the generations of man are molded . . . .
>
> Another headline that caught our attention was one in the *News* which read, "Human Error Probed in Leak." The concept of "human error" has cropped up often during the Pennsylvania crisis . . . . The main thing that planners concerned with nuclear power left out of their scenarios was not the correct workings of some valve or control panel. It was the thing that no scenario can ever take into account: simple human fallibility per se—an ineradicable ingredient in the actions not only of power-plant operators but also of power-plant designers, of government officials, and of the general public as well . . . . At the deepest level, then, the human error in our nuclear program may be the old Socratic flaw of thinking that we know what we don't know and can't know. The Faustian proposal that the experts make to us is to let them lay their fallible human hands on eternity, and it is unacceptable. (Talk of the Town, 1979a)

> Experimentation, in which the consequences of certain kinds of catastrophes can sometimes be gauged, is also sharply limited. Just as one cannot remove the ozone layer in order to find out how important it is to the earth's environment, one cannot release large amounts of radiation into the atmosphere in order to discover its effects on human society. Lacking these experiments, the earth itself becomes the laboratory: it is on the earth that the effects of a particular one-time catastrophe must originally become known. First, by accident, we release the radiation; then, twenty years later, we find out how many cancer deaths have been caused. In the last analysis, therefore, the limit that restrains our nuclear pioneering is the singularity of the earth. Because there is only one earth, and one mankind living on it, all our experiments with nuclear devices and other lethal substances and machines are at the same time actions taken in real life. Of course, science is capable of many wonders, including, for example, the cloning of a frog. Maybe one day, in some other solar system, our scientists will succeed in cloning the earth itself . . . . Until then, though, they would do well to leave our present earth—the parent of us all and our only home—alone. (Talk of the Town, 1979b)

Whereas such apprehensions about the advertent and inadvertent consequences of nuclear energy and recombinant DNA are indicative of the apocalyptic modes of response that are occurring to some of the ways in which we have "probed . . . dissected [and] rearranged [the] components of nature . . . bend[ing] its forms and divert[ing] its forces to human purposes" (Sinsheimer, 1978:24), the increased concern about potential hazards of natural and man-made chemicals is more closely associated with a cluster of cognitive, procedural, and value problems to which the mounting preoccupation with risk, its assessment and its regulation has contributed. A particularly telling indicator of the magnitude of this concern about chemicals can be found in the area of drug development. The Center for the Study of Drug Development in the Department of Pharmacology and Toxicology of the University of Rochester School of Medicine and Dentistry conducted searches for me in their vast computer files of literature on drugs. Eileen Thomas, the research assistant who made the searches, found that a major part of the drug development literature was concerned with the topics of risk assessment and risk benefit. She identified 2,212 articles on these topics in the center's files that have been published during the past five years in medical and in lay literature.

There is a sense in which the concern about the noxious effects of chemicals on the environment and human health, like the disquietude about recombinant DNA and nuclear energy, involves anxiety about possible (individual and collective, short- and long-term) disaster. For it is especially focused on the dangerous possibility that many chemicals may be human carcinogens and/or mutagens—major causes of cancer and of genetic birth defects in the population. To an even greater extent, the concern highlights the difficulties and dilemmas of finding scientifically adequate, culturally appropriate, and socially effective ways of appraising and governing risk, now that it has become defined as such a central and far-reaching problem.

To begin with, the sheer number of chemicals that could be carcinogenic or mutagenic is overwhelming. And the resources available for assessing them are inherently limited:

> The American Chemical Society estimates that there are 4 million chemicals in existence, with some 6,000 new ones emerging every week. Some 44,000 of these chemicals are believed to be in common use in the United States. (Staff Paper, 1979:1)

> A key method for detecting carcinogens is the animal bioassay . . . . The utility of animal cancer tests for cancer prevention, however, is limited by several important factors. Animal cancer tests are too expensive (currently about $350,000 per chemical for a thorough test) and take too long (about 3 years) to be used for the testing of the many thousands of chemicals to which humans are exposed . . . . There are not enough pathologists to read the slides even if it was decided to test only the thousand or so new chemicals introduced into commerce each year, not to mention the 50,000 untested commercial chemicals already in use and the even greater number of chemicals in the natural world . . . . An environmental carcinogen causing cancer in 1 percent of 100 million people would result in a million cases of cancer. Detection of a chemical causing cancer in only 1 percent of the test animals would require the use of 10,000 rats or mice and would be extraordinarily expensive. A test group of only fifty mice or rats of each sex at each of two doses is the usual size of the most thorough cancer experiments. This limitation is somewhat overcome, though not entirely satisfactorily, by exposing the animals to as high a dose as possible (the "maximum tolerated dose") which, by increasing the tumor incidence, partially offsets the statistical problems inherent in the small sample size. (Ames, 1979:587-589)

As the foregoing suggests, the procedures that are utilized to identify, evaluate, and control the human risks associated with chemicals that could cause mutations or cancer pose various methodological uncertainties of their own. Primary among these are two issues. What role should human epidemiological studies, on the one hand, and animal bioassays and short-term in vitro laboratory tests, on the other, play in assessing the riskiness of chemicals? There is the problem of deciding in what ways and to what extent the findings extrapolated from animal studies can and ought to be applied to the human level, especially when high-dose testing is used on laboratory animals as a means of dealing with some of the difficulties of sampling, cost, and scarcity inherent in such inquiries. What does the finding of cancer in animals at such high doses, for example, imply for the carcinogenic potency and hazard of these same substances for human beings?

Despite these major uncertainties, quantitative risk assessment is widely employed. However, its adoption has been accompanied by a great deal of heated public, as well as professional, discussion over the quality and meaning of the numbers it produces:

> The qualitative phase of risk assessment is followed by the quantitative phase, and here the science is highly speculative and replete with uncertainty. From the carcinogenic response data obtained at the high dose levels administered in the laboratory it is, of course, necessary to extrapolate downward to arrive at an estimate of the tumor incidence in very low doses expected in the environment. Then, another leap of faith is necessary if this extrapolation of the carcinogenic response from high dose to low dose is to be accepted as even a crude approximation of human risk. The susceptibility of the highly heterogeneous human population that would be exposed to the carcinogen could differ greatly from the susceptibility found in the small number of relatively homogeneous laboratory animals tested. Also, because humans are exposed to countless pollutants, additive or synergistic effects are always possible . . . . [W]hatever the advantages of risk quantification, to reach firm conclusions as to the comparative response of laboratory animals and humans to a given carcinogen is still impossible. (Carter, 1979:813)

When the potential uncertainties and errors of the methods and techniques of risk assessment and of the reasoning underlying them are so great that, according to Arthur C. Upton, director of the National Cancer Institute, "an estimated risk of 4.2 cancers . . . per 220 million people, as calculated by extrapolation from mouse or rat data, might turn out in reality to be as low as no human cancer, or as high as 420,000 cancers" (quoted in Carter, 1979:813), what is the worth of a quantitative analysis? How should it be interpreted and utilized?

The debate about these kinds of methodological and procedural matters has been intensified by their relation to the progressively expanding role of government in evaluating and regulating risks to public health and safety, and to still another category of uncertainty that this role has engendered:

> Federal decision-making in the control of carcinogens is a hot subject that seems to invite more controversy all the time. Disagreement exists within the government itself over "cancer policy" and especially over whether the science of quantifying cancer risks is far enough advanced to be safely used by regulatory agencies in setting standards for human exposure to carcinogens.
>
> The director of the National Cancer Institute, Arthur C. Upton, has recently circulated a memorandum warning that the misuse of risk quantification could lead to public health catastrophes. Although citing no specific instances of misuse, Upton has told *Science* that he is worried lest regulatory officials make the mistake of minimizing cancer risks on the basis of estimates that fail to reflect the underlying uncertainties in the mathematical modeling.
>
> On the other side of the risk assessment issue are the government officials and scientists, including some at the White House Office of Science and Technology Policy, who are afraid that risk quantification will either be neglected by some agencies or misused to overestimate risks in support of exposure standards that are too strict and costly. (Carter, 1979:811)

Within this framework, how does one determine whether particular chemical substances pose low, moderate, or high human risks; whether these risks have been accurately characterized, underestimated, or overestimated; and, in the light of these assessments, whether they are being appropriately regulated, underregulated, or overregulated? Here the uncertainties of scientific knowledge and political governance intersect with the uncertainties of value and belief. For, as Judge David L. Bazelon has stated, virtually all risk regulation decisions entail an intricate mix of fact and value questions:

> In determining questions of fact, such as the magnitude of risk from an activity, we as a society must rely on those with the appropriate expertise. Judges and politicians have no special insights into this area. Where questions of risk regulation involve value choices such as how much risk is acceptable, we must turn to the political process.
>
> But even this formulation leaves many problems unanswered. There is no bright line between questions of value and of fact. Even when a problem is appropriately characterized as one of scientific fact, consensus and certainty may very often be impossible even in the scientific community. Many problems of scientific inference lie in the realm of "trans-science" and cannot be resolved by scientific method and experimentation . . . .
>
> The growing use of analytic tools such as cost-benefit analysis magnifies the chance that unrecognized value judgments will creep into apparently objective assessments. Even the most conscientious efforts by experts not to exceed their sphere of competence may be inadequate to safeguard the validity of the decisionmaking process. (Bazelon, 1979:278-279)

FROM MEDICAL TO METAMEDICAL UNCERTAINTY

Dealing with medical uncertainty and risk in ways that do not go beyond the boundaries of competence has become increasingly difficult, partly because many of the questions that uncertainty and risk now pose do not easily fit into established disciplinary, professional, or institutional frameworks of analysis or decision-making. Four relevant cases that have occurred in the course of the past year, and received a considerable amount of public attention, are illustrative of the kinds of metaquestions currently arising out of the matrix of medical uncertainty. (These are questions that would have been far less likely to present themselves in the 1950s when I first began my medical uncertainty-watching, or to be brought before a court of law, as they were in 1978 and 1979.)

The first case is associated with the potentialities, uncertainties, and risks of organ transplantation, and with what Judith Swazey and I have called its "gift-exchange" aspects (Fox and Swazey, 1978:5-39, 381-384). Robert McFall, an unmarried asbestos worker suffering from a terminal case of aplastic anemia, filed suit in a Pittsburgh court seeking an injunction to compel the unwilling David Shimp, his cousin, to become donor in a bone marrow transplant that might save his life. The issues with which the judge in this case had to wrestle included the question of whether we are obliged to be "our cousin's keeper"; whether we have a duty to try to "rescue" another person and, if so, when; and whether there is such a thing as a "compulsory donation"—a mandatory and coercible gift of self or life (Meisel and Roth, 1978).

The second case is one that "presents a perplexing problem spawned by modern nuclear warfare" and by "the dangers of radiation from nuclear detonation," the case of "Stanley Jaffee and Sharon Blinn Jaffee, individually, and Stanley Jaffee, on behalf of others similarly situated *v.* United States of America."[4] This case turned around Jaffee's avowal that, in 1953, when he was serving in the United States Army, he and other soldiers were ordered to stand in an open field near the test explosion of a nuclear device at Camp Desert Rock, Nevada, without any protection from radiation and without their knowledge and consent, despite the fact that the government knew of the "grave risks of injury from such exposure." Jaffee further alleged that he developed inoperable cancer because of his exposure to this radiation. In reviewing the way the district court ruled on this case, the United States Court of Appeals for the Third Circuit found itself face to face with the question of whether "under the extraordinary facts of this case, in

4. *Jaffee v. United States of America* No. 78-2041, United States Court of Appeals for the Third Circuit, argued November 17, 1978. (Opinion filed February 9, 1979).

which it is alleged that many soldiers have been exposed to nuclear radiation," the "sovereign immunity" of the United States from suit could and should be waived by the judiciary or by Congress; and, whether the United States should be directed to provide "warning relief" to Jaffee "and all members of the class about the medical risks facing them," and/or relief in the form of subsidized medical care.

The third case, a composite one, concerns genetic counseling, amniocentesis, and new concepts of genetic predictability. Two cases, those of Dolores Becker and of Hetty and Steven Park, were consolidated by the State of New York Court of Appeals. Dolores Becker, at the age of thirty-seven, became pregnant and gave birth to a child with Down's Syndrome. Mrs. Becker alleged that she was never advised of the increased risk of Down's Syndrome in children born to women over age thirty-five, or of the availability of amniocentesis to detect the condition in utero, during the period she was under the care of her obstetrician. She would have had an abortion, she contended, if the test had indicated her fetus was affected.

Mr. and Mrs. Park claimed that they consulted the obstetricians who had cared for Mrs. Park during her first pregnancy about the likelihood of their having a second child with polycystic disease. They were informed that the chances of another child's being born with this condition were "practically nil" since the disease was not hereditary. Based on this information, the couple decided to have a second child, a child they would not have chosen to conceive, they contended, if they had been "correctly informed on the true risk of reoccurence of this disease." Hetty and Steven Park, whose first child, afflicted with polycystic disease, died five hours after birth, had a second child, born with the same disease, who lived for two-and-a-half years.

Both the Beckers and the Parks sued for physical injuries, for psychiatric and emotional distress to themselves, for medical costs, and for institutional expenses in caring for the children born with genetic defects. They also sought damages on behalf of these children for "wrongful life." In rendering its decision on the companion cases, the court affirmed that "seeking compensation for the wrongful causation of life itself cast an almost Orwellian shadow . . . of genetic predictability," and this question would have to be resolved in a way that "transcends the mechanical application of legal principles":

> Whether it is better never to have been born at all than to have been born with even gross deficiencies is a mystery more properly to be left to the philosophers and the theologians. Surely the law can assert no competence to resolve the issue, particularly in view of the very nearly uniform high value which the law and mankind has placed on human life, rather than its absence. Not only is there to be found no predicate at common law or in statutory enactment for

judicial recognition of the birth of a defective child as an injury to the child; the implications of any such proposition are staggering. Would claims be honored, assuming the breach of an identifiable duty, for less than a perfect birth? And by what standard or by whom would perfection be defined? . . .

Simply put, a cause of action brought on behalf of an infant seeking recovery for wrongful life demands a calculation of damages dependent upon a comparison between the Hobson's choice of life in an impaired state and nonexistence. This comparison the law is not equipped to make . . . .

Who then can say, as it was essential to the parents' causes of action that they say for themselves, that had it been possible to make the risk known to the children-to-be—in their cellular or fetal state or, let us say, in the mind's eye of their future parents—that the children too would have preferred that they not be born at all? To ordinary mortals, the answer to the question, obviously, is "no one." Certainly, the answer does not lie in the exercise by the children, if their mental conditions permit, of subjective judgments long after their births. Therefore, whatever be the metaphysical or philosophical answer—speculative, perhaps debatable, but hardly resolvable—and, however desirable it may be for society to otherwise treat with these problems with sensitivity, I am compelled to conclude that the matter is just not justiciable.[5]

The fourth case is the one that has received the most coverage from the media. Chad Green,[6] a two-year-old boy with acute lymphocytic leukemia, received the antileukemic chemotherapy regimen at present considered to be the treatment of choice. In the second phase of this program, bone marrow tests indicated the boy's leukemia was in complete remission. However, his parents, Gerald and Diana Green, were reluctant to have their son continue chemotherapy, because of their deep concern about what they felt were the emotional and behavioral, as well as physical, side-effects Chad had suffered as a result of the treatment. They were skeptical about the cause-and-effect relation that is assumed to exist between chemotherapy and remission. In their opinion, none of the data or evidence they had seen "prove[d] that chemotherapy cures leukemia" (*New York Times,* 1978). As one of the parents said, "Chemotherapy does not give anybody any hope as far as I am concerned. They cannot prove to me that chemotherapy works . . . . Half of the children are still dying when they are on these drugs . . . . In my opinion, chemotherapy isn't so good that it should be forced down anybody's throat" (Steinmann, 1978:172). Without telling their physicians, the Greens withdrew their son from the maintenance chemotherapy schedule he was expected to follow at home for two or three years. Instead, they treated him with the

5. *Becker v. Schwartz* No. 558, and *Park v. Chessin* No. 560, State of New York Court of Appeals, December 27, 1978.

6. See the Direct Appellate Review of this case ("Custody of A Minor"), ordered by the Supreme Judicial Court of Massachusetts, Plymouth, Mass. Adv. Sh. (1978) 2002, July 10, 1978.

diet of distilled water, vegetarian foods, and high doses of vitamins they had initiated while he was receiving chemotherapy, one they believed to be more beneficent than chemotherapy. They prayed, and began to give the boy laetrile, the controversial substance derived from apricot pits that many cancer patients in this country have been taking, illicitly because it has not been recognized or approved by the medical profession, the National Cancer Institute, or the Food and Drug Administration.[7]

In February 1978, Chad Green's physician went to court to seek the appointment of a temporary guardian for the child so that his chemotherapy could be resumed. The judge so ruled, and the Greens appealed the decision. Subsequently, the Greens, the physician, and the hospital where Chad was treated moved through a series of Massachusetts courts, in legal confrontation over such questions as whether parents have the right to refuse and terminate certain forms of medically prescribed treatment for a child with a life-threatening illness, to opt for alternative forms of treatment that are not regarded as "consistent with good medical practice," to choose what they define as a "full life" rather than a long life for the child. However, there is an even more basic sense in which the case of Chad Green involved an examination of the medical profession's probabilistic way of thinking about uncertainty, benefit, and risk. In this regard, the case could aptly be considered one in which probability reasoning itself went on trial, with the Greens alleging that the quality of the (physician's) numbers was strained. What the court called the Greens' "pessimism" concerning the child's chance of cure by chemotherapy not only constituted a rejection of chemotherapy per se, but of the probability-based logic on which medical diagnosis, evaluation of therapy, and prognosis-setting are premised. In weighing the Greens' perspective on their son's prognosis, the court considered and, in the end, supported the medical opinion that "there is a substantial chance for cure and a normal life for the child if he undergoes chemotherapy treatment." The court did so in a way that set forth the analytic framework within which medical experts had reasoned, as well as the facts and opinions they had stated:

> According to the experience of medical experts in this case, the effect of this type of treatment on the long-term survival of leukemic children has been gratifying. After one year of treatment, 90 percent of the children are found to

7. On September 27, 1978, in an attempt to clear up the twenty-year-old laetrile controversy, Arthur C. Upton, director of the National Cancer Institute (NCI), called for an NCI clinical trial of laetrile. In order to carry out such a trial, the NCI must apply for an Investigational New Drug permit from the Food and Drug Administration (FDA). Once this application is made, the FDA evaluates it, and decides whether or not to approve the clinical trial. At this writing, that decision is still pending.

> be disease free. In the second year of treatment, 70 percent are in a state of remission. At the end of the third year, 65 percent are still in remission. In the fourth year the survival rate curve flattens to show a steady survival pattern of approximately 50 percent.
>
> Two other factors are relevant. First, it has been shown that survival rates vary according to the type of leukemic cells found in the child. Because in this case the child is afflicted with a "null-cell" type of leukemia, his chances of survival with chemotherapy are slightly higher than 50 percent. Second, because the child falls within an age group which has a higher probability of potential cure and long-term survival, the chances for successful treatment in his case are stronger.[8]

Thus, in affirming that "acute lymphocytic leukemia in children is fatal if untreated, chemotherapy is the only available medical treatment offering a hope for cure, the risks of the treatment are minimal," and the chances for cure are "substantial," the court upheld probability reasoning as well.

In January 1979, Diana and Gerald Green petitioned the court to reopen the case. They sought to show that laetrile treatments should replace chemotherapy treatments. When the judge ruled that chemotherapy should be continued, and that laetrile should be stopped, on the grounds that it was slowly causing cyanide poisoning in the boy, the Greens moved to Mexico with their son. There, under the supervision of a clinic in Tijuana, the boy allegedly received a combined regimen of chemotherapy and laetrile. On October 12, 1979, three-year-old Chad Green died in the rented apartment near the clinic where he and his parents resided.

Central to the problems posed by all these cases are the uncertainties connected with relatively recent scientific and technical advances (human organ transplantation, the use of nuclear energy and power, genetic screening and counseling, chemotherapy for leukemia and other types of cancer), their potential risks in comparison with their possible benefits, and, especially, the hazardous consequences they may have for health, survival, and the quality of life. The fact that they were deliberated in court is indicative of the great proliferation of law and lawsuits that has taken place in American society during the past decade, and the accelerating degree to which judicial and legislative bodies are being asked to make decisions about such complex scientific and technical matters:

> Multiplying even more quickly than lawyers are laws and lawsuits. In 1977, the legislative bodies at the federal, state and local levels enacted approximately 150,000 new laws and each of these new laws, on the average, required the issuance of ten new regulations. Between 1969 and 1972, the case load of the

8. Verbatim quote from the Supreme Judicial Court of Massachusetts' review of the case, Mass. Adv. Sh. (1978) 2002, July 10, 1978.

> federal courts (corrected for the increase in population) rose by half. If the federal appellate case load, which accounts for only 10 percent of all federal cases, continues to grow as it has in the past decade, over one million federal appellate cases a year will flood the courts by the year 2010. And four times as many suits are filed each year in the state courts of California alone as in the entire federal system. (Tribe, 1979:25)

> Courts are often thrust into the role of authoritative decision-makers. But in recent years there has been growing concern about the ability of the judiciary to cope with the complex scientific and technical issues that come before our court. Critics note, quite correctly, that judges have little or no training to understand and resolve problems on the frontiers of nuclear physics, toxicology, hydrology, and a myriad of other specialities. And the problem is growing. Hardly a sitting in our court [United States Court of Appeals for the District of Columbia Circuit, Washington, D.C.] goes by without a case from the Environmental Protection Agency, the Occupational Safety and Health Administration, or the Nuclear Regulatory Commission. These cases often present questions that experts have grappled with for years, without coming to any consensus.
>
> But the problem . . . is not confined to the judicial branch. Legislators are daily faced with the same perplexing questions. They, too, lack the expertise to penetrate the deepest scientific mysteries at the core of important issues of public concern. (Bazelon, 1979:278)

The McFall, Jaffee, Becker-Park, and Green cases described are characteristic of the uncertainty- and risk-associated scientific and technological cases that are increasingly coming before the courts and legislatures, although many of the questions they raise surpass a judge's, lawyer's, or legislator's domain of professional competence. What is more, the perplexing questions each of these cases entails extend far beyond scientific and technical issues, or even the deepest scientific mysteries. In every instance, they open onto questions fundamental to the polity, the societal community, and the human condition itself. The issues with which all the participants in these cases have been asked to cope, and that the judges have been asked to judge, include problems of nonexistence, birth, life, survival, and death; identity, individuality, integrity, and autonomy; humanness, fulfillment, and meaning; equality and sovereignty; solidarity and reciprocity; responsibility, accountability, and immunity; impairment and imperfection; injury and suffering; solace and relief; rescue and deliverance; compassion; and causality and chance. As the judge in the Becker-Park case recognized, many of these questions are essentially moral and philosophical; some of them are metaphysical. They cannot easily be resolved or even properly addressed through the law or under it. ("They are just not justiciable.") Certain of the questions—such as "the wrongful causation of life itself"—are what philosopher Simone Weil (1970:335) called "insoluble problems in all their insolubility."

Others are "telic" questions, ones no "ordinary mortal" (in the words of the judge) can answer: What is the fetus? How are we to regard its being?

As can be seen in these cases, when questions of this order and magnitude emerge from a consideration of problems of biomedical uncertainty, risk, and predictability, there is a marked tendency to draw back from them. This drawing back is occurring repeatedly in American society at the present time. Awed recognition of what is ethically and existentially involved and at stake frequently causes even the most experienced and poised experts to shrink from the essential nature of the inquiry. One of the characteristic ways in which physicians, scientists, lawyers, legislators, and judges deal with these mysteries is by declaring them to lie outside of their own trained and legitimate sphere of competence, affirming that they are more properly to be left to the philosophers and theologians. But when confronted with such ultimate perplexities, philosophers and theologians draw a similar line and make analogous disclaimers. In the end, what generally happens is that the questions are recast in more narrowly disciplinary and practically manageable ways. The issues are operationalized and reduced so they can be analyzed and decided upon within the framework of existing scientific, technological, legal, and ethical theory, knowledge, and procedures.

An instructive example of the way in which such difficult ethical and religious questions are acknowledged but set aside can be seen in the conclusion of the Ethics Advisory Board, appointed by the secretary of the Department of Health, Education, and Welfare, that "it is acceptable from an ethical standpoint to undertake research involving human *in vitro* fertilization and embryo transfer," provided that certain conditions are met (Final Report, Ethics Advisory Board, 1979). As Margaret O'Brien Steinfels (1979) points out, in the end, the board paid relatively little attention to the issue that it cited as one of the major questions it had to face: namely, what is the moral status of the fertilized human egg, and the embryo and fetus that develop from it? Nor did they give much attention to the kinds of "soft ethical issues" brought before them by Leon R. Kass, in his testimony to the board at its Boston meeting on October 13–14, 1978, questions such as "the meaning and worth of one's body"; "the meaning of the bond among sexuality, love and procreation"; "lineage, identity and self-identity, respect and self-respect"; "the *idea* of the *humanness* of our human life and the meaning of our embodiment, our sexual being, and our relations to ancestors and descendants" (Kass, 1979). Rather, the board focused more narrowly on ethical issues of special concern to researchers, particularly the problem of risk, and on a range of questions of immediate, practical importance to the Department of Health, Education, and Welfare. "Although never phrased in these words, the Board's dominant question . . . became: how can determined couples be protected from unknown risks in undertaking in vitro fertilization without recommending public funds for research and clinical trials? Proceeding in the manner of a body that hopes to reach a consensus, the Board both acknowledged and finessed the issues on which it could not agree by careful attention to the wording of its conclusions" (Steinfels, 1979:5).

At the same time, however, new institutional arrangements for handling such questions are being developed and tried: bioethics institutes, for example, science courts, institutional review boards, ethics advisory boards, mixed scientist and public-interest groups, national and presidential commissions for the protection of human subjects and the study of ethical problems in medicine, biomedical and behavioral research, and an unprecedented array of moratoriums both on basic and clinical types of medical inquiry. The creation of these groups and mechanisms indicates there is, at least, a latent collective awareness that our established political, legal, and professional institutions cannot totally encompass or adequately resolve the deepest meaning of the moral and metaphysical questions about health- and medicine-relevant uncertainty.

What *is* the deeper and larger significance of the way that medical uncertainty has evolved in American society? The phenomena we have explored in examining the development of medical uncertainty suggest a macrointerpretation I would like to offer as a speculative conclusion.

The increased professional and public preoccupation with medical uncertainty notable throughout the 1960s and 1970s has been centered on problems of error and risk, hazard and harm, as well as probability and predictability. Although they encompass a wide spectrum of health-, illness-, and medicine-associated matters, these uncertainty concerns have been especially focused on matters pertaining to molecular biology, genetics, and human reproduction; the transplantation and implantation of tissues, organs, and organisms; the use of chemicals and nuclear energy; and both innate and environmental factors that might play a role in the development of birth defects, genetic mutations, and cancer.

Central to these concerns, then, are particular advances and particular limitations in biomedical knowledge, therapy, and technology considered to have extraordinarily powerful and fundamental implications for human life, normalcy, health, mortality, and death. In this connection, for example, recombinant DNA technology is viewed not only as a recent development in biology, but also as a prototype and portent of genetic engineering, the emerging capacity of mankind to lay its hands on the evolution of all forms of life on this planet, including, and especially, on its own. Cancer is regarded not only as a set of malignant diseases with which biology and medicine are still unable to deal knowledgeably and effectively, but also, in the minds of many, as the most pernicious, invasive, and lethal type of suffering to which human beings are subject.

The increased interest in medical uncertainty and its consequences is accompanied by a highly ambivalent outlook on various modes of intervening in the universe and the human condition, in order to discover new knowledge, achieve new certainty, and make progress by enhancing the quality and prolonging the length of human life. There is a curious inconsistency, if not paradox, in the fact that indignation over the continuing incapacity of medical science and technology in dealing with unsolved problems of health and well-being coexists with anxiety about medical "hubris" and the "nemesis"-borne side-effects of medical attempts to master these problems (Illich, 1976). Conviction about the need for more energetic steps to deter or limit scientific and technological interventions that are hazardous to health and, beyond that, to the world of life, go hand-in-hand with concern about the adverse consequences of exercising and imposing such restraint.

There is an "uncertainty-about-uncertainty," "ambivalence-about-ambivalence" quality to this process of worrying, prescribing, and worrying about the prescription we noted earlier. Its boundless irresolution suggests that something more culturally disorienting is happening besides the reexamination of such social values as vigorous meliorism and unbridled inquiry. The very axes of our way of thinking about uncertainty seem to be involved. Debates and deliberations, which raise systematic doubts about the intellectual appropriateness and moral adequacy of our scientific and legal logic for dealing with the kinds of problems of uncertainty that are now before us, are continually occurring. Probability reasoning, qualitative and quantitative modes of risk assessment, and the application of legal principles have all been thrown into question.

"These are hard times for the . . . intellect," Lewis Thomas (1979:74) has observed. Within the framework of an advanced, secularized, modern society, we are being asked not only to consider collectively whether our Chad Greens have a "substantial chance for cure," but also whether we are "our cousin's keepers," and if there is such a thing as the "wrongful causation of life." Furthermore, we are called upon to do so at a stage in our societal evolution when certain aspects of our world-view seem to be shifting. Our sense of the beneficence and "resilience of both natural and man-made phenomena" (Sinsheimer, 1978:25) has somehow been shaken in ways that heighten our sense of ignorance, mystery, fallibility, frailty, vulnerability "to a host of hostile influences inside and around us" (Thomas, 1979:47), danger, capacity to harm, and potential catastrophe. We are not sure how to think lucidly and responsibly about a kind of unease and bewilderment that cannot be resolved in our laboratories, field stations, and clinics, or dispelled by the principle-based reasoning of the moral philosophers whom we are consulting increasingly. In our nontheocratic society, there is no official church that can deal with such matters on behalf of us all.

This is where the broadest significance of the evolution of medical uncertainty in American society lies. Leon Kass comes close to articulating it:

> How should we think about the ethical issues, here and in general? There are many possible ways, and it is not altogether clear which way is best. For some people ethical issues are immediately matters of right and wrong, of purity and sin, of good and evil. For others, the critical terms are benefits and harms, risks and promises, gains and costs. (Kass, 1979:34)

Our current preoccupation with medical uncertainty, error, risk, and harm is a symbolic language through which we are communicating some of our deepest questions about the cognitive, moral, and the metaphysical foundations of our cultural tradition and outlook. It is also a primary medium through which fundamental aspects of our social, cultural, and cosmic way of thinking, feeling, and believing about ourselves, our society, this planet, and the universe are gradually being altered.

REFERENCES

Ames, B.N. 1979. Identifying Environmental Chemicals Causing Mutations and Cancer. *Science* 204:587-592.

Barber, B., and Fox, R.C. 1958. The Case of the Floppy-Eared Rabbits: An Instance of Serendipity Gained and Serendipity Lost. *American Journal of Sociology* 64:128-136.

Bazelon, D.L. 1979. Risk and Responsibility. *Science* 205:277-280.

Bellah, R.N. 1974. Religious Evolution. *American Sociological Review* 29:358-374.

Callahan, D. 1979. The Moral Career of Genetic Engineering. *Hastings Center Report* 9 (April):9.

Cannon, W.B. 1945. *The Way of an Investigator.* New York: Norton.

Carter, L.J. 1979. How to Assess Cancer Risks. *Science* 204:811-816.

Chargaff, E. 1976. Letter to the Editor, *Science* 192:938-940.

Comar, C.L. 1979. Risk: A Pragmatic De Minimis Approach. *Science* 203:319.

Cournand, A. 1977. The Code of the Scientist and Its Relationship to Ethics. *Science* 198:699-705.

De Craemer, W., and Fox, R.C. 1968. *The Emerging Physician: A Sociological Approach to the Development of the Congolese Medical Profession.* Stanford, Calif.: Hoover Institution Press.

_______, Vansina, J., and Fox, R.C. 1976. Religious Movements in Central Africa. *Comparative Studies in Society and History* 18:458-475.

Dyson, F. 1979. *Disturbing the Universe.* New York: Harper and Row.

Final Report, Ethics Advisory Board. 1979. *Federal Register,* June 17.

Fox, R.C. 1957. Training for Uncertainty. In Merton, R.K., Reader, G., and Kendall, P.L., eds., *The Student-Physician,* 207-241. Cambridge, Mass.: Harvard University Press.

______. 1959. *Experiment Perilous: Physicians and Patients Facing the Unknown.* Glencoe, Ill.: Free Press.

______. 1974a.______ Paperback edition. Philadelphia: University of Pennsylvania Press.

______. 1974b. Ethical and Existential Developments in Contemporaneous American Medicine: Their Implications for Culture and Society. *Millbank Memorial Fund Quarterly/Health and Society* 52 (Fall):445-483.

______. 1974c. The Process of Professional Socialization: Is There a "New" Medical Student? A Comparative View of Medical Socialization in the 1950s and the 1970s. In Tancredi, L.R., ed., *Ethics of Medical Care,* 197-227. Washington, D.C.: National Academy of Sciences.

______. 1976a. Advanced Medical Technology: Social and Ethical Implications. *Annual Review of Sociology* 2:231-268.

______. 1976b. Medical Evolution. In Loubser, J.J., Baum, R.C., Effrat, A., and Lidz, V.M., eds., *Explorations in General Theory in Social Science* 2:773-787. New York: Free Press.

______. 1978. Why Belgium? *Archives Europėennes de Sociologie* 19:205-228.

______. 1979. The Autopsy: Its Place in the Attitude-Learning of Second-Year Medical Students. In *Essays in Medical Sociology: Journeys into the Field,* 51-77. New York: Wiley.

______, and Lief, H.I. 1963. Training for "Detached Concern" in Medical Students. In Lief, H.I., Lief, V.F., and Lief, N., eds., *The Psychological Basis of Medical Practice,* 12-35. New York: Harper and Row.

______, and Swazey, J.P. 1974. *The Courage to Fail: A Social View of Organ Transplants and Dialysis.* Chicago: University of Chicago Press.

______. 1978. 2nd edition, revised. Chicago: University of Chicago Press.

Gaylin, W. 1977. The Frankenstein Factor. *New England Journal of Medicine* 297:665-667.

George, S.L., Aur, R.J.A., Mauer, A.M., and Simone, J.V. 1979. A Reappraisal of the Results of Stopping Therapy in Childhood Leukemia. *New England Journal of Medicine* 300:269-273.

Hawkes, N. 1979. Science in Europe: Smallpox Death in Britain Challenges Presumption of Laboratory Safety. *Science* 203:855-856.

Illich, I. 1976. *Medical Nemesis: The Expropriation of Health.* New York: Pantheon.

Isaacs, L. 1977. Original Synthesis. *Hastings Center Report* 7 (April):24.

Jarvik, M.E. 1979. Necessary Risks. *New England Journal of Medicine* 300:1130.

Kass, L.R. 1979. "Making Babies" Revisited. *The Public Interest* (Winter):32-60.

Loftus, E.F., and Freis, J.F. 1979. Informed Consent May Be Hazardous to Your Health. *Science* 204:11.

Meisel, A., and Roth, L.H. 1978. Must a Man Be His Cousin's Keeper? *Hastings Center Report* 8 (October):5-6.

Merton, R.K. 1957a. *Social Theory and Social Structure.* Glencoe, Ill.: Free Press.

______. 1957b. Some Preliminaries to a Sociology of Medical Education. In Merton, R.K., Reader, G., and Kendall, P.L., eds., *The Student-Physician,* 3-79. Cambridge, Mass.: Harvard University Press.

Miké, V., and Good, R.A. 1977. Old Problems, New Challenges. *Science* 198:677-678.

New York Times. 1978. Boy with Leukemia Focus of Court Fight. April 6.

Parsons, T. 1951. Social Structure and Dynamic Process: The Case of Modern Medical Practice. *The Social System,* chapter 10, 428-479. Glencoe, Ill.: Free Press.

Powledge, T.M. 1977. Recombinant DNA: The Argument Shifts. *Hastings Center Report* 7 (April):18-19.

Sinsheimer, R.L. 1978. The Presumptions of Science. *Daedalus* 107 (Spring):23-25.

Staff Paper, 1979. Office of Science and Technology Policy, Executive Office of the President. February 1.

Steinfels, M.O. 1979. In Vitro Fertilization: "Ethically Acceptable" Research. *Hastings Center Report* 9 (June):5-8.

Steinmann, M. 1978. A Child's Fight for Life: Parents vs. Doctors. *New York Times Magazine,* December 10.

Stockton, W. 1979. Smallpox Is Not Dead. *New York Times Magazine,* February 4.

Swazey, J.P., and Fox, R.C. 1970. The Clinical Moratorium: A Case Study of Mitral Valve Surgery. In Freund, P.A., ed., *Experimentation with Human Subjects,* 315-357. New York: George Braziller.

______, Sorenson, J.R., and Wong, C.B. 1978. Risks and Benefits, Rights and Responsibilities: A History of the Recombinant DNA Research Controversy. *Southern California Law Review* 51:1019-1078.

Talk of the Town, Notes and Comment. 1979a. *The New Yorker,* April 16:27-28.

______. 1979b. *The New Yorker,* June 25:21-22.

Thomas, L. 1977. Biostatistics in Medicine. *Science* 198:675.

______. 1979. *The Medusa and the Snail.* New York: Viking.

Tribe, L.H. 1979. Too Much Law, Too Little Justice. *Atlantic Monthly* (July):25-30.

Wade, N. 1977. *The Ultimate Experiment: Man-Made Evolution.* New York: Walker.

Watson, J.D. 1976. In Defense of DNA. *Annual Report,* 1976, Cold Spring Harbor Symposium.

Weil, S. 1970. *First and Last Notebooks.* London: Oxford University Press.

The Human Condition of Health Professionals

"The Human Condition of Health Professionals" may seem a lofty title, yet it aptly expresses the everyday essence and deeper meaning of medical work and its impact on the men and women who have chosen it. The distinctive nature of medical work places demands and stresses on health professionals, who, in response, tend to develop certain coping mechanisms. Such ways of coming to terms may be helpful to the professionals who use them, but the origins of these mechanisms (and some of the behavior they entail) are not generally understood or appreciated by others. For, galvanized by the individualistic, egalitarian, and anti-hierarchy sentiments that have become prominent in American society since the 1960s, and by mounting criticism of the medical profession, commentators from a variety of fields have been insisting that there is nothing special about medical work. There is nothing different, harder, or more important about it than any other kind of work, they contend, and there is no reason for health professionals to act as if there were.

Without engaging in passion-filled debate, I want to respond to that point of view by identifying some features of the work and role of health professionals that, in my opinion, *do* distinguish them from most occupations. I shall focus on physicians and nurses chiefly because, through my sociological research, I have come to know their professional situations especially well in a first-hand way. The aspects of their work that I shall single out, however, are ones that, with some variation, are characteristic of the health professions more generally.

THE SACRED AND THE PROFANE

Health, illness, and medical care are integrally connected with some of the most basic and the most transcendent aspects of the human condition. The conception of human beings; their birth, survival, and growth; their physical, emotional, and intellectual capacities and development; sexuality; aging, mortality, and death—the very quality of their lives—are core foci of health, illness, and medicine. Our "coming in," our "staying in," and our "going out" are continuously linked with our health and illness concerns and with the medical care that we seek and receive. One of the most profound, symbolic expressions of these existential dimensions of medicine is the fact that in our society it is the physician who has the exclusive right and responsibility to "pronounce" death, and that until this at once medical, technical, legal, and priestly pronouncement is made in the name of the medical profession and the society, a person is not officially dead.

The experience of illness and the practice of medicine also summon up critical problems of meaning—fundamental questions about the "whys" of pain; suffering, accident, and *angst*; the limits of human life; and death; and about their relationship to evil, sin, and injustice. Irrespective of whether or not the particular nurses, physicians, and patients are consciously or sensitively attuned to these dimensions, they are inescapably a part of the concerns about health, being ill, seeking care, receiving it, or delivering it.

From the inception of their training and throughout their careers, nurses and physicians are confronted with the human implications of diagnosing, treating, and making prognoses about illness. Many of their encounters with patients entail primal physical activities that allow and oblige them to violate strong, even sacred, cultural taboos. This kind of experience is epitomized in the anatomy laboratory and the autopsy room where medical and nursing students learn about the structure and pathology of the human body by cutting into it and dissecting it. There they meet the mystery of life and the enigma of death in the form of a naked fellow human being who is laid out on a stainless steel table.

Dissecting a cadaver and participating in an autopsy are powerfully symbolic events in the making of a doctor and nurse because they play a cardinal, and somewhat macabre, role in initiating men and women preparing for medical careers into the life-death-nudity-probing-cutting nature of medical work. Even in taking a medical history; doing a physical examination; carrying out diagnostic, therapeutic, and prognostic procedures; and in everyday hospital care, nurses and physicians continually see, peer into, touch, manipulate, explore, and penetrate the bodies of their patients. They handle and analyze patients' urine, feces, mucus, blood, and other bodily substances and secretions, and inquire into their personal lives and intimate feelings in ways that nonmedical persons are neither asked nor permitted to do.

A paradoxical and potentially disturbing mix of the sacred and the profane is part of their work. Observing rigorous norms of asepsis and noncontamination, dressed in starched white or astringent green, they enter orifices and inner chambers of the human body that are physiologically and symbolically associated with its highest and its lowest functions, and they extract and deal with substances, such as human blood, that are considered culturally to be both dirty and preciously sacrosanct.

Physicians and nurses do not come to their training, however, with ready-made attitudes of detachment and composure toward these viscerally, emotionally, and metaphysically perturbing features of medical care. They progressively learn to deal with them and the feelings that they evoke in so-called professional ways.

Medical work, then, is morally and existentially serious. However familiar and routine it may be, or seemingly unthreatening and nontragic, no medical action that involves a patient is trivial or completely ordinary. Below their scientific surface, medical acts and events intersect with the human condition of patients and their relatives, and of medical professionals themselves—with some of their most profound aspirations, hopes, and fulfillments; their deepest worries, anxieties, and fears. Even an annual check-up is a solemn inquiry into the patient's mortality, as well as his or her state of health.

LIVING WITH URGENCY AND UNCERTAINTY

Partly because of the seriousness of health, illness, and medicine, the principle of "continuous coverage" has been institutionalized in the medical profession, particularly in the modern hospital. As sociologist Eviatar Zerubavel perceptively points out in his book *Patterns of Time in Hospital Life,* continuous coverage is a "moral imperative" that involves a "strong belief in the indispensability of ever-available medical and nursing coverage of services,'' and emphasizes the emergency aspects of responsible care.[1] This ceaseless cycle is organized so that individual physicians and nurses are not ''on duty'' or ''on call'' all day, every day, though the hospital or the practice with which they are affiliated may never close its doors or turn off its telephone answering service. But the continuous coverage, on-call, emergency ethos of medicine, along with the day-and-night, unpredictably scheduled, anxiety-accompanied way in which patients' needs for medical care occur, places nurses and (to a greater degree) physicians under great moral and psychological pressure to define their work as limitless in time and potential urgency.

Along with its seriousness and relentlessness, the work of nurses and physicians also involves an intricate, frequently troubling, relationship to uncertainty:

> . . . the fact that a powerful battery of scientific knowledge and technique is applied to illness and the ''deepest human concerns'' it arouses does not eliminate uncertainty from medicine. To begin with, by its very nature, science is an open, searching mode of thought, as much an organized way of raising systematic questions and doubts about what are assumed to be established concepts, facts, and methods, as of furthering knowledge and skill. Although medical scientific advance may solve certain problems, it also helps to create and maintain two types of uncertainty. The first kind of uncertainty derives from the hiatuses, limitations, and errors that characterize medical knowledge at any point in time. The second type of uncertainty results from the paradoxical fact that despite its inadequacies, medical science is so vast and highly developed that no one can totally encompass or perfectly master it.[2]

Thus, what physicians and nurses do for patients is always accompanied by uncertainties that stem from both how much and how little they know and how much is or is not known in the field of medicine. The logic of modern, Western medical thought—the probability reasoning on which differential diagnosis, treatment decisions, and prognosis setting are based—is a codified expression of the uncertainty factor in medicine. In the words of a medical student, it is a systematic way of ''conjuring possibilities and probabilities'' in the face of perennially imperfect knowledge in situations vital to patients' welfare. Furthermore, the ''there is an X percent chance that . . . '' statements that this mode of reasoning enables medical practitioners to make

1. Eviatar Zerubavel, *Patterns of Time in Hospital Life: A Sociological Perspective* (Chicago: University of Chicago Press, 1979), pp. 37-42.
2. Renée C. Fox, ''Medical Evolution,'' in Jan J. Loubser, Rainer C. Baum, Andrew Effrat, and Victor M. Lidz, eds., *Explorations in General Theory in Social Science* (New York: The Free Press, 1976), 2: 773-787. See also, Renée C. Fox, ''Training for Uncertainty,'' in Robert K. Merton, George Reader, and Patricia L. Kendall, eds., *The Student-Physician* (Cambridge, Mass.: Harvard University Press, 1957), pp. 204-241.

about the problems of their particular patients are based on aggregate statistics that apply more accurately to large populations of patients than to individual cases. In this sense, all medical acts are approximations. They are also subject to mistakes of various kinds, some of which are calculable and avoidable, many of which are not.

In addition, no matter how "appropriate" or "indicated" a medical or surgical intervention may be, how "tested," "conventional," and "standard," how relatively safe or potentially beneficial, it always carries with it a degree of risk and some unwanted side-effects. This is systematically acknowledged in the "benefit/risk ratio" calculations and judgments about diagnosis, therapy, and outcome that medical professionals are enjoined and trained to make on behalf of their patients. These uncertainty-ignorance-error-risk factors add poignancy to nursing and doctoring. In recent years, this source of stress for nurses and, above all, for physicians has greatly increased as a consequence of the growing extent to which medical professionals are being held morally, legally, and economically responsible for what they do and fail to do in the care of patients. The grounds on which they are being made accountable do not always clearly distinguish between the current state of the field of medicine, the competence or fallibility and malfeasance of individual practitioners, and the abilities and abuses of the medical profession as an organized, collective entity.

Perhaps the most dramatic and significant expression of this development is the virtual epidemic of malpractice suits during the past decade. It is a complex happening, about which we know too little. But among the numerous factors that seem to be contributing to it are: an intensified preoccupation with health and illness in our society; raised public consciousness about the uncertainties, risks, and dangers in medicine and medical practice, accompanied by greater anxiety and indignation about them and less willingness to accept or submit to them; and an increased public tendency to blame physicians, the health care system, and the larger society for imperfect health, disease, illness, limited life expectancy, and undignified and unfulfilling deaths. In turn, these may be manifestations of broader cultural concerns and changes for which health, illness, and medicine have progressively become "primary symbolic media" through which we are grappling with fundamental questions of value and belief.[3]

3. Renée C. Fox, "The Medicalization and Demedicalization of American Society," *Daedalus* 106, no. 1 (winter 1977), 9-22. Also in John H. Knowles, ed., *Doing Better and Feeling Worse* (New York: Norton, 1977), pp. 9-22. See also, Renée C. Fox, "The Evolution of Medical Uncertainty," *Milbank Memorial Fund Quarterly/Health and Society* 58, no. 1 (winter 1980), 1-49 (also reprinted within this book).

THE SEARCH FOR DETACHED CONCERN

These are some of the principal ways in which the work of physicians and nurses is not "just like any other." They cannot go "naked" into it. Because of what it asks them to do emotionally, morally, and spiritually, as well as intellectually and physically, doctors and nurses need ways to meet these stressful aspects of their work with equanimity as well as efficiency. What means of coming to terms do physicians and nurses develop? As a partial answer to that question, I will identify several of the coping mechanisms shared by medical professionals that I have noticed over the course of my many years of doctor- and nurse-watching in the role of participant observer.

The first, and perhaps the most obvious of these mechanisms, is a cognitive one. Involvement in the intellectual subject matter of medicine can help medical professionals handle the stresses of their work with vigor and poise. Two vignettes are instructive in this regard. Often, the cases that physicians and nurses refer to as "interesting" are those that are not only scientifically and clinically intriguing and challenging, but also perplexing and frustrating—cases that present diagnostic and treatment problems that are not easily or satisfactorily solved by medicine in its present state. There is an ironic, *double entendre* connotation to the way that medical professionals use the term "interesting." It implies that, on latent levels at least, they recognize both the strains that they experience in taking care of patients whose medical conditions present such problems and the way in which their own intellectual engrossment in these problems enables them to cope with uncertainty and its potentially negative consequences for their patients.

Or, to take a second example: in the deliberations around the issue of whether it is justifiable to do research on human fetuses, profoundly stirring biological, ethical, and existential questions have arisen that cannot be simply and summarily resolved. What is the fetus? How ought we to think of it, morally as well as medically? What is life? What is a human life? And when does human life begin? Faced with such questions, medical professionals, in collaboration with philosophers, theologians, and jurists, have operationalized them by invoking the medical scientific concept of the "viable fetus" and by defining "viable" in measurable terms, such as determining how many grams the fetus weighs and how the weight is related predictively to the probability that it would be able to develop into a normal, full-term baby. This scientific reductionism enables medical professionals and their consultants to deal intellectually, emotionally, and practically with what would otherwise be an overwhelming and paralyzing problem for them.

Both these examples indicate that "detachment" is another mechanism that medical professionals use to deal with the more stressful aspects of their work. The process by which such detachment is achieved (or more ideally, what I have called "detached concern" in my writings[4]), is ill understood, but in any case, it is not strictly a consequence of the kind of intellectualizing just described. Here again, a few concrete observations are suggestive. A particularly insightful medical student once made the following comment on how he and his classmates were coming to deal with the illnesses about which they were learning in clinical pathology and were seeing in hospital patients, without feeling continually and shakily susceptible to illness themselves. Referring to what he perceived as the collective, hypochondriacal stage that he and his second-year classmates were passing through, he commented: "We are now in the process of contracting the diseases we are studying in order to develop emotional immunity to them." The possibility of developing so much immunity that the medical professional comes to feel too invulnerable to empathize with the patient is real, as is a state of "emotional numbness" described by some physicians and nurses.

But, more commonly, what nurses and doctors seem to do with their strong feelings about emotionally upsetting aspects of their work is to push them just below the surface of their consciousness. That these feelings are not deeply buried is suggested by how easily they can be aroused under certain circumstances. For example, in a sociology seminar for medical practitioners, a surgeon once explained that he was not normally conscious of the organic, "autopsy smell" that was always present in the operating room when a surgeon was cutting into the live flesh of a patient; but when he was particularly tired or anxious, he became acutely aware of the odor. The degree to which managing emotional reactions in this way is contextually specific, and depends on defining the situation as a medical one, is illustrated by the behavior of a group of nurses at a weekend conference at a lakeside center, where I was present as a speaker. When we were eating dinner together one evening, a mouse was suddenly sighted scampering across the dining room. The nurses at my table (as did I) reacted to it with overtly expressed fright. They themselves laughingly remarked that if they had to work with the mouse in a medical laboratory, they could do so with professional composure, but in the extra-professional setting of Lake Bluff, they responded to the mouse's presence in an emotional, non-nurse way.

It is of some interest to note that the same surgeon who reported on the autopsy smell in the operating room interpreted his awareness of this odor as a sign that his deeper feelings about what performing surgery "really" en-

4. See, for example, "Training for 'Detached Concern' in Medical Students" (with Harold I. Lief), in Harold I. Lief *et al.*, eds., *The Psychological Basis of Medical Practice* (New York: Harper & Row, 1963), pp. 12-35.

tailed had surfaced in a way that could adversely affect his equanimity, judgment, and technical skill. Under these circumstances, which he regarded as potentially dangerous to the outcome of the operation and to the patient's welfare, he monitored himself more closely and consciously than usual. For, in his view, the learned defense mechanisms, and the various props in the surgical situation on which he usually relied, were not working adequately to protect him and his patient.

An example of such a contextual prop in the operating room is the routine procedure of draping the patient on the table—covering all parts of the patient's body except the specific area on which the surgeon works. Draping, of course, has an important relationship to aseptic technique and also to respecting the dignity of the anesthetized patient. In addition, it seems to have the latent function of reducing the surgeon's awareness of the patient as a whole person, while the surgeon is engaged in cutting into, "wounding," repairing, and sewing up a fellow human being.

The characteristic features of a medical examination room have similar, prop-like implications for the capacity of health professionals (and their patients) to keep certain feelings that might otherwise be aroused below the surface of their consciousness. This generally white or green room, with its stone floor; its stainless steel and leatherette examining table fitted out with white or green crepe paper sheeting; its medical cabinet, through whose glass doors instruments, bandages, and medications are visible; its sink, over which hang special soap and paper towel dispensers; and its occasional calendar or set of medical instructions, printed by a pharmaceutical company, pinned up on its otherwise undecorated walls; announces to the physician, nurse, and patient that this is a scientific, medical setting, where, however intimate they may be, professionally relevant and competent examinations are carried out with appropriate decorum. Health professionals, like their patients, depend to a considerable degree on these attributes of the examination room to define the situation for them in this way. To the extent that they do, fundamental changes in the interior decorating of this room, particularly alterations that might make it look more personal and homey, could easily disturb the examining physician's or nurse's habitual professional poise.

PROTECTIVE HUMOR

The laughter of the nurses on that mouse-ridden evening at Lake Bluff is associated with another coping mechanism used a great deal by medical professionals: a characteristic form of humor. Counterphobic and ironic, infused with bravado and self-mockery, often impious, defiant, and macabre, it closely resembles what Freud termed "gallows-humor," and the front-lines-of-the-battlefield humor of a Bill Mauldin "Willie and Joe" cartoon, or the TV drama *M*A*S*H*. It occurs most frequently and floridly in situations where medical professionals are under an unusual or extreme amount of stress, and it most characteristically centers on medical uncertainty, the limitations of medical knowledge, medical errors, and the side effects of medical and surgical interventions, the failure to cure, sex and sexuality, and, above all, death. It is epitomized, for example, in the names that oncologists have given to some of the chemotherapy protocols that they use to treat cancer: SCARY, CRAB, CURE, POMP. It would appear that surgeons, obstetrician-gynecologists, oncologists, and clinical researchers make use of such medical humor more often than physicians in some other medical fields; that male physicians are more prone to engage in this form of joking than women physicians; that nurses as a group do less of it than doctors; and that when they do, it is in a more sequestered, private fashion. However, these are unverified impressions of mine that need further investigation. This humor is an in-group, emotional code through which medical professionals confront, express, release, and handle some of the deepest, most powerful and threatening feelings that their work elicits: anxiety, frustration, anger, fear, grief, despair, and also wrenched tenderness and hope.

Some of the scientific and technical vocabulary of medicine is also an inner language of this sort. Built into it are the same feelings expressed through medical humor. Nurses and physicians speak and write of the "dread graft-versus-host disease reaction" to bone marrow transplantation, for example, or of "rescuing" patients after they have undergone "sublethal doses of total body irradiation," and of "harvesting" organs for human transplantation. Coded into such phrases is their collective chagrin about the macabre nature of some of the activities in which they professionally engage, and about the amount of risk, suffering, and even harm to which they subject patients through their supposedly therapeutic interventions. The fact that such terms not only are used in face-to-face medical and nursing discussions, but also are standard vocabulary in professional publications, printed as if they were neutrally scientific terms, suggests that their relationship to medical stress is not as explicitly recognized by doctors and nurses as is the import of their humor.

There are at least two other characteristics of medical terminology that have some stress-handling functions: the use of initials, on the one hand, and of euphemisms, on the other. The term "end-stage renal disease," usually abbreviated ESRD in the journals, is an example. Calling it "end-stage" rather than "terminal" kidney disease is perhaps more accurate in an era when hemodialysis and/or renal transplantation can keep a patient whose kidneys no longer function indefinitely alive; and referring to it as ESRD saves spoken time and printed space. But, in addition, it protects physicians and nurses from being constantly, verbally reminded that patients in this state are incurably ill, and that, at the present time, all that medicine can do for them is to "rescue" them continually from otherwise death and "maintain" them (as the medical expression goes) by means of so-called "half-way technology." (My insight into the emotionally insulating functions of this terminology was triggered by the way that a group of nurses, physicians, social workers, and technicians working on dialysis and kidney transplant units reacted to my innocent allusion to their patients as persons who were terminally ill with kidney disease. "The patients are *not* terminally ill!" they indignantly insisted. "They have end-stage renal disease!" The response of the physicians was the most vehement of all, and the nurses' was almost as forcible.)

SCIENTIFIC MAGIC

There is one other mode of coming to terms with the stresses of medical work frequently employed by physicians and nurses that I would like to mention. In my publications I have called it "scientific magic,"[5] and have indicated that it characteristically occurs in several highly patterned forms. These are essentially magical ways of behaving that simulate medical scientific attitudes and behaviors, or that are hidden behind them, and that help physicians and nurses to face problems of uncertainty, therapeutic limitation, and meaning by "ritualizing [their] optimism" (as anthropologist Bronislaw Malinowski would have put it). I will mention three such patterns.

First is the tendency of medical practitioners to favor demonstrably vigorous ways to treat patients, and their accentuate-the-positive inclination to be staunchly hopeful and tenaciously confident about the success of their active intervention—even when, and often especially when, a positive outcome is unlikely. Trying hard to "do something" effective about a serious medical problem can have a "self-fulfilling prophecy"-like impact on health professionals, patients, and patients' families alike. Particularly in an energetically melioristic culture like our own, with its "we shall overcome" outlook, it can encourage all concerned to endure, persist, and continue to believe, in ways that can contribute to the stabilization of a patient's condition, to its improvement, and beyond that, to his or her recovery. But this same indomita-

5. Renée C. Fox, "The Sociology of Modern Medical Research," in Charles Leslie, ed., *Asian Medical Systems* (Berkeley: University of California Press, 1976), pp. 102-114.

ble activism can also lead to the nonrational inability to desist, at great physical and psychic, as well as economic, cost to both health professionals and those for whom they care.

Such relentless activism is particularly visible in collective disaster situations in which a number of persons are severely injured or burned. No matter what kind of mobilization of personnel, equipment, and cost it may involve, every effort is usually made to treat as many victims as possible with heroic medical measures. Such extraordinary treatment is not only likely to be initiated, but also to be continued over a prolonged period of time, even for those individuals who, for example, may be burned beyond what would seem to be any reasonable possibility of survival. In part, this is a response to the uncertainty that is inherent to the probability reasoning on which all medical decision-making and action are based: that is, while medical probability statistics foretell the percentage of persons severely burned who may be expected to survive, they do not identify *which* individuals will do so. In the face of this structural ambiguity, the medical team is likely to feel that it "has" to treat each person as if he or she were among the ones destined to survive. The "have to" grows not only out of the cognitive characteristics of the situation, but also out of what physicians and nurses need emotionally to help them function as efficient, composed professionals within it.

The foregoing is related to a second pattern of scientific magic, which I think of as the "game of chance": In the spirit of blasphemous hilarity that I have already described, many physicians and some nurses make wagers on such serious medical matters as the diagnosis of an illness, the impact of therapy on it, or its prognosis; on the outcome of a particularly important or risky experiment on human subjects; and on whether a patient will live or die. The game of chance is a very complicated phenomenon. On one level, it is a collective way of "acting out" the chance elements that are inherent to medical science and practice. It is also a way of "acting on" them, for it involves a group of health professionals in a game-like contest, in which they pit their knowledge, experience, skill, and powers of reasoning and prediction against the unknown, adventitious, hard-to-control factors in the diagnostic, therapeutic, and prognostic aspects of medical work. "Winning" the bet, by "guessing" right, represents a symbolic mastery of these chancy forces, and a schematic victory over them. This wagering is fundamentally ironic in nature. It mimics probability reasoning-based medical scientific thinking, and it is playfully structured around the premise that what physicians and nurses know and do not know, what they can and cannot do, and how their interventions affect patients—all have much in common with a game of chance. At the same time, the betting behavior is self-depreciatory and self-mocking, depicting supposedly professional medical expertise and action as highly speculative, full of guesswork and gambles, and fraught with luck—both good and bad. Finally, the game of chance is both a protest and a petition. It is a ritualized way of declaring that what health professionals know and can do for patients, and whether or not their patients get better or worse, live or die, should have more order and meaning than the throw of the dice or the turn of the roulette wheel.

It is interesting to note that in some hospital contexts—for example, on certain research wards or oncology units—patients who share an especially serious medical predicament, and who have developed a social system around it, may respond to the uncertainty and risk that they face with their own game of chance. The most audaciously macabre version of this game that I have observed was on a ward where patients took bets on whether or not a fellow patient in crisis would survive the night. One of the patients explained to me that "you don't take bets on somebody if you think he has no chance of making it from third to home. So, it doesn't matter if you bet for or against him—you are really rooting for him to make it to home plate."

Through their at once independent and interdependent games of chance, physicians, nurses, and their patients are all rooting for themselves, and for each other.

There is one other form of scientific magic that I call "the celebration syndrome." This refers to the various rites of passage that nurses and physicians create for patients. One of the most common of these is the party to mark the anniversary of a risky surgical procedure that a patient underwent, particularly if the patient was perilously ill at the time and the procedure was highly experimental in nature. In the 1950s, I saw parties like this given for patients who had undergone total bilateral adrenalectomies (the removal of their adrenal glands) for malignant hypertension or terminal carcinoma of the prostate and who had survived for one year. In the 1960s and 1970s, I was a participant observer of many comparable anniversary celebrations for patients who had received organ transplants, particularly heart transplants. Often, these were called "birthday parties," and explicitly related not only to a one-year (or more) survival, but also to what was termed the patient's "rebirth," and "new life."

Some of the deeper feelings involved in such celebrative rites are suggested by a medical team discussion about the pros and cons of putting candles on a patient's one-year survival birthday cake. Shall we put candles on the cake, the team members asked themselves, within the privacy of their conference room. If so, how many candles? Should we light the candle or candles beforehand, and carry the cake through the unit, into the patient's cubicle? Or shall we light the candle(s) *after* we reach the patient's bedside? Behind all this discussion lay the problem of how to make sure that the lights on the cake would not go out before the patient himself had a chance to blow them out. The team was exquisitely sensitive to the negative symbolic meaning the "accidentally" extinguished candles might have for the patient, and for other persons hospitalized on the same unit. As I listened to this discussion, it was also apparent that, in the face of all the uncertainty and risk with which the team was confronted in caring for, and experimenting on, terminally ill patients, and bearing the doubts I often heard them express about the justifiability and fruitfulness of what they were doing, the unplanned and uncontrolled going-out of the birthday cake candles would have been experienced as a bad omen by them, as much as by their patients.

As I have written elsewhere, these and other forms of medical scientific magic make ironic commentary on the apparent lack of order, predictability, and sense in the shared predicament of those who fall ill and those who try to care for them. All express protest against what seems capricious, arbitrary, and existentially absurd in this situation. And all make affirmative petitions that the day will come when the illness and death of human beings are more fathomable and more effectively dealt with by the science and practice of medicine.[6] Their magic, their humor, their use of language, and the ways that these intersect and fit together, suggest that physicians and nurses have created a social world and a subculture of their own structured around common stresses and modes of meeting them.

STRESS AND CONSEQUENCES

What I have briefly presented is far from an exhaustive survey of the special stresses and coping mechanisms of doctoring, nursing, and other forms of medical work. However incomplete this account may be, it does suggest that insufficient attention has been paid to the situation and predicament of health professionals. Insofar as they have been acknowledged, the stresses facing health professionals and the degree to which they react to them have been largely underestimated. Some of the coping mechanisms have been identified and analyzed, but often in ways that do not explicitly connect them with the quality of care that physicians, nurses, and other members of the medical team deliver or fail to deliver. In those instances where such a correlation has been made by commentators on the medical care situation, there is a tendency to *blame* physicians, nurses, and their colleagues for resorting to certain coping mechanisms that supposedly dehumanize care, the patients who receive it, and the practitioners who dispense it. By innuendo, these commentaries imply that there is something arbitrarily willful, as well as

6. Fox, "Medical Evolution," *op. cit.*, p. 778.

undesirable, about the defense-mechanism behaviors in which health professionals engage; that it is neither necessary nor justified for them to act or react in these ways; and that they not only should, but very easily could, "change their ways." The questions of why they collectively use these particular coping mechanisms, and of whether they would be able to do their work and meet the demands of their professional roles with some degree of competence and equanimity without them, are rarely raised. Nor is any serious attempt made to consider whether there are alternative mechanisms that health professionals might use and, if so, what the consequences of these other ways of coming to terms with their professional situations might be for patients and their families, as well as for nurses, physicians, and their teams of co-workers.

I want to reaffirm how important I think it is that more attention be paid to the human condition content of medical work: what health professionals experience in caring for patients, the particular stresses to which they are subject; the means they adopt and do not adopt for handling the stresses; where, when, why, and how they choose, learn, and develop these ways of coming to terms; and the consequences of their stress and coping patterns for the way health professionals relate to and treat their patients, patients' families, and each other.

The thought has been well expressed by Dr. Joel E. Frader, a pediatrician. At the end of his account of a pilot study of the difficulties experienced by physicians working in a pediatric intensive care unit, Dr. Frader made a plea for "reassess[ing] the means" that the medical profession has "developed for coping" with such scientifically, technically, emotionally, and morally stressful situations. Some of these ways of coming to terms with what is distinctive and difficult about medical work, he wrote, lead to "limited focus on data . . . depression . . . possible impairment of function and . . . haphazard consideration of important moral conflicts." If so, he concluded, then "perhaps we can learn to help patients, families, and ourselves."[7]

AN UN-CONCLUSION AND AN INVITATION

I want to end this lecture with a few preliminary thoughts about how the kind of analytic understanding of the condition of health professionals that I have outlined might be used to enhance the human quality of medicine. To begin with, my analysis suggests that simply identifying and selecting "better people" to be nurses and doctors would hardly begin to solve the complex human problems of health, illness, and medicine in our society. Nor does it seem that already-established educational remedies exist to deal with some of

7. Joel E. Frader, "Difficulties in Providing Intensive Care," *Pediatrics* 64, no. 1 (July 1979): 15.

the basic phenomena involved. For example, although after twenty-five years of teaching social science to premedical, medical, and nursing students, and to interns and residents, I still think it is a relevant and important thing to do, I am more convinced than ever that it is not a "magic bullet." Putting more social science (or, as is now being advocated, more medical ethics teaching) in the curriculum will not result in more "human" and humanly competent nurses and physicians, in a simple, cause-effect way. Nor will changing the overall structure in which health care is organized and delivered automatically do so, either.

To deal effectively and constructively with the kinds of phenomena on which I have focused, what must first of all be recognized by medical educators, practitioners, and policymakers, and by all those interested in improving the human quality of medical care is that medicine deals with life and death and suffering, the human body and the human psyche, in physical, emotional, and symbolic ways that are inherently disturbing. No matter how much, or what kind of professional training physicians and nurses may receive, or how experienced they may be, their work confronts them with basic, human condition-associated stresses and dilemmas that cannot be eliminated. For this reason, as I have emphasized, the men and women who fill the roles of physician and nurse cannot go naked into their work. In order to do this sort of work, and do it well, they must develop intellectual and emotional "clothing" that provides them with some degree of detachment and protection. But, ideally, the protective layers they acquire should be porous and permeable. For, if health professionals become too insulated, then their capacity to be concerned—to empathically understand what it is like to be sick and to be a patient—will be seriously restricted.

One of the things to which more attention and thought need to be given is how to help health professionals develop "new clothing" to take the place of some of the overly-detached and self-protective mechanisms that they have classically learned to use. The process of "making the latent manifest" that this entails, however, should not be treated lightly. Something more subtle and delicate is involved than breaking down old defenses and catapulting health professionals and professionals-to-be into supposedly "authentic encounters" with the "true reality" of their work. For, as the surgeon who spoke of the "autopsy smell" in the operating room suggested, a too-conscious and lucid awareness of the fact that a central part of his daily work "really" consists of cutting into the live flesh of fellow human beings would make it emotionally harder and technically more dangerous for him, or anyone else, to do.

But, are there sensitive and skillful means to train health professionals to stay more continually and consciously in touch with the deeper realities of illness and of their own doctorhood and nursehood—ways that would enrich the human quality of the care they deliver without unduly jeopardizing their equanimity? We need more social scientific and educational research and experimentation directed toward this question.

Among the problems that might profitably be explored in this connection are not only whether, and how, this kind of training might be accomplished, but *when,* in the long educational and socialization process that health professionals undergo, it should take place. My own experience in teaching sociology in medical schools has led me to believe that the question of when it is best to deal with what medical educators are disposed to call the "non-biomedical" or "psychosocial" aspects of medicine has been insufficiently considered. I base this primarily on my observation that in most medical schools the required behavioral science course is part of the first-year curriculum—a time when, because of what this phase of their training asks of students, intellectually and attitudinally, they are *least* able to take social science seriously, apply it clinically, or benefit from it personally.

The analysis I have presented also raises questions about the allocation of medical work: how it is divided and distributed, and how it is organized in time. Certain forms of medical work, I have emphasized, are especially hard—physically, mentally, and/or emotionally. They take a heavy toll on the men and women engaged in them. What particular aspects of their work contribute most significantly to the progressive "burn-out" and "impairment" of medical professionals (especially physicians), about which there is now increasing public, as well as professional, awareness and concern? Can anything be done, educationally and administratively, and on a broader, philosophical and policy level, to creatively contravene the damage that the demands of medical work can do to health professionals, and as a consequence, to the persons who are their patients? Are there teamwork and group practice arrangements, time-on-and-time-off modes of scheduling and cycling work, that would help? To what extent can, and should the "on-call-24-hours-a-day" ethos of medicine be modified; and what would be the consequences of doing so, for professionals and patients? Are there certain kinds of medical work that are so exacting, tension-ridden, and/or tragic that no one should be asked, or permitted, to do them for a lifetime?

It would be good if I could give you authoritative answers to these and other questions that this approach to medical work, its distinctive characteristics, and its impact on the human condition of health professionals has opened up. But we have not come that far yet. So, in a spirit of nonconclusion, I want to invite you to consider these questions further, and to work on them in your professional lives—as I intend to continue to do in mine.

"It's the Same, but Different": A Sociological Perspective on the Case of the Utah Artificial Heart

"It was the same, but different," they said. Implicitly and explicitly, this was a theme that was recurrently expressed in our conversations and interviews with members of the team who were involved in the implantation of the Utah artificial heart in Dr. Barney Clark, and in what preceded and followed it.

It was in June 1983 that Judith Swazey* and I spent a week at the University of Utah Medical Center, doing some first-hand field research in connection with the sociological study that we were conducting of the Utah heart implant. Our visit occurred several months after Barney Clark's death, while the team was still in an early phase of its postmortem stock taking. We were struck at that time by their dualistic perspective on what they had undertaken, experienced, and were still in the process of sorting out.

The team's "same-but-different" dualism had multiple origins and mean-

*Judith P. Swazey, historian of science and medicine, was president of the College of the Atlantic, Bar Harbor, Maine, at the time this essay was written. She is currently president of the Acadia Institute in Bar Harbor. Both Dr. Swazey and I are grateful to the Human Qualities of Medicine Program of the James Picker Foundation for the funds that made this field research possible. I also wish to thank Professor Willy De Craemer and Dr. Mary Ann Meyers of the University of Pennsylvania for their critical reading of this paper and helpful comments on it.

This essay originally appeared in *After Barney Clark: Reflections on the Utah Artificial Heart Program*, edited by Margery W. Shaw. Austin: University of Texas Press, 1984, pp. 68-90. Copyright © 1984 by the University of Texas Press. Reprinted with permission.

ings. It reflected their shared ambivalence concerning whether, in the balance, what they had done was right and good. Their almost nostalgic remembrances of their recent Barney Clark past had an "it-was-the-best-of-times-and-the-worst-of-times" feeling about it.

Physicians, nurses, social workers, bioengineers, and members of the University of Utah's Institutional Review Board (IRB) and its Community Relations Department were all still deeply impressed with how "special" Barney Clark, his wife, and family were, humanly and morally, as well as biomedically. But, at the same time, they did not want to imply that they and the center were unaccustomed to caring for such sick patients or to competently mobilizing the complex medical science and high technology that it entailed. And they were concerned about giving the impression that they thought Dr. Clark was entitled to more of their attention, resources, esteem, and affection than so-called ordinary patients. (The intensive care unit nurses were particularly sensitive about these technical competence, distributive justice, and universalism-associated issues. As head nurse Linda Gianelli put it, they preferred to think of Barney Clark as an "extraordinarily ordinary patient.")

Institutional pride and humility were also admixed in the team's twofold outlook. The heart implant, they were convinced, was one of the most important public events, and certainly the most newsworthy one, that had ever occurred at the University of Utah. It had put Salt Lake City, the university, and the medical center on the map, nationally and globally. Yet a number of team members were uneasy about how rapidly and subtly pride can turn to hubris and about the notoriety as well as the fame that being in the public limelight can bring in its wake.

Finally, the "same-but-different" orientation of the team also reflected their collective uncertainty about which aspects of their experiences connected with the artificial heart and Barney Clark were concomitants of trailblazing clinical medical research wherever it occurs and which were particular, if not peculiar, to their own situation. The intricate blend of cosmopolitanism and localism, experience and youthfulness, sophistication and simplicity characteristic of the team, and of the larger Salt Lake City, Utah, environment in which it is embedded, contributed to this felt ambiguity.

In this paper I will identify and briefly discuss some of the socio-medical and cultural ways in which the Utah group's implantation of an artificial heart in Dr. Barney B. Clark resembled other clinical research endeavors and some of the ways in which it significantly differed from them. My angle of vision derives from my continuous, direct relationship as a field-working sociologist to the "experiment perilous" world of medical research and therapeutic innovation, particularly dialysis, organ transplantation, and implantation, since the early 1950s when I made a participant-observation-based study of Ward F-Second, the male metabolic research ward of Harvard Medical School's Peter Bent Brigham Hospital. The reason I chose this topic is that my June visit to Utah persuaded me that clarifying its "same-but-different" dilemmas is a critical part of the unresolved issues that the team faces as it looks back at Barney Clark while contemplating a second heart implant.

LIKENESSES

To begin, How was the Utah artificial heart implant like other clinical research endeavors involving human subjects? As is the case with the first patient-subjects of all radical, experimental procedures, Barney Clark, the recipient of the Utah heart, was a person rapidly moving to his inevitable death from a progressive, chronic disease condition for which there was no further established, effective medical or surgical treatment. The selection of a patient in this state for such a clinical trial was dictated by the uncodified but binding ethical assumption to which medical professionals adhere: namely, that a therapeutic innovation in the earliest stages of moving from the laboratory (or animal barn, as in this case) to the clinic, still fraught with all the uncertainty and risk that this animal-to-human phase of experimentation involves, should only be tried on individuals who are incurably ill, beyond conventional medical help, and close to death.

Barney Clark became what the members of the University of Utah Medical Center referred to as a very "special" patient. In their words, he was a "remarkable man" of great "courage," with a desire "to contribute to medical progress," and "to serve mankind." "He chose the unpredictable experiment over imminent death," they said, although he "knew he might have considerable anguish." Throughout the experiment (which lasted "for 112 days, . . . 2,688 hours, . . . [and] for 12,912,499 [heart] beats"), he displayed what team members described as "stamina, endurance, and persistence, . . . a sense of humor and ability to love (most of all, his wife and children)." Dr. and Mrs. Clark were regarded as "co-investigators with the research team in every sense of the word," and as part of the team members' professional and personal families. "Barney Clark is our hero . . . in this chapter of medical history," spokespersons for the team declared in their final tributes to him—"a pioneer to match these Western lands."[1]

There are striking similarities between the qualities that the Utah team eulogized in Barney Clark and how they related to him, and the way that the metabolic research group of the Peter Bent Brigham Hospital that I studied some thirty years ago felt about and acted toward their own patient-subjects on Ward F-Second. Even the language that they used to praise these patients and describe their relations with them is comparable to, and in many respects identical with, the vocabulary of the Utah team.[2]

The metabolic research group regarded its patients as "special." They were not only viewed as patients and research subjects but also as "colleagues" and "collaborators" whose "understanding" of the experiments in which they participated and unfailing cooperation in these studies made a professional as well as a personal contribution to the research. For the metabolic group, these patients were also "friends," who "at times seemed as close as one's immediate family." The physician-investigators were "impressed" and "inspired" by the "courage, . . . energy," and the dedicated sense of meaning and purposiveness of their patient-subjects. The belief and hope in the "perilous experiments" that patients displayed and their willingness to "suffer stoically" for them in order to "help others in the future," if not themselves, "strengthened [the medical team's] determination," members said, to go on and succeed with the human research they had undertaken. The metabolic group expressed admiration for their "exceptional" patients and a sense of "indebtedness" and "gratitude" to them in various ways. "We celebrate our patients," they declared. They saw to it that their patients received "red-carpet treatment" in the hospital. They acknowledged the role that patients had played as "co-investigators" and "co-adventurers" by citing them in their professional publications. And they portrayed patients as "heroes" and "stars" in the news stories that they released to the press about the trail-blazing research for which the patients had served as subjects.

The observations that I recorded on Ward F-Second, in a Boston, Harvard milieu of the 1950s could have been written about Barney Clark and the medical team that cared for him and experimented on him in Salt Lake City,

1. These quoted phrases used to describe Barney Clark are taken from the interviews that Judith Swazey and I conducted with all the key members of the Utah artificial heart team (other than Dr. Willem J. Kolff, who preferred not to be interviewed) and from the following three documents: "Words Spoken by Dr. Willem J. Kolff at the Funeral Service for Dr. Barney Clark," 29 March 1983; Willem J. Kolff, "Forty Years of Artificial Organs and Beyond" (University of Utah Commencement Address, 11 June 1983); Chase N. Peterson, "Terminal Events," news conference about Barney Clark's death, 24 March 1983.

2. Renée C. Fox, *Experiment Perilous: Physicians and Patients Facing the Unknown* (New York: Free Press, 1959); see especially pp. 85-109.

Utah, 1982. They are also applicable to the many other clinical research settings I have observed over the years. In fact, the "courage-to-fail" ethos of which these physician-patient relationships and values are a part was so characteristic of the organ transplantation and dialysis centers Judith Swazey and I collaboratively studied that it gave us the title for the book we wrote about them. *"The Courage to Fail,"* we explained in our preface, "epitomizes the bold, uncertain, and often dangerous adventure in which medical professionals and their patients are engaged":

> All have a high vested interest in the success of their endeavor. In their shared value system, a primary measure of success is the sheer survival of patients undergoing transplantation or dialysis. Beyond survival, it is hoped that these procedures may give patients an improved state of health that will enhance the quality of their lives. Success also means progress in medical knowledge and technique that may come from the collaborative research. For some of these physicians, and for some of their patients as well, professional and public recognition for their pioneering roles is an integral part of success. But the probability of failure in transplantation and dialysis is high. These therapeutic innovations are in a stage of development characterized by fundamental scientific and medical uncertainties, and they are applied only to patients who are terminally ill with disease not amenable to more conventional forms of treatment. In this context, the death of the patient is the archetype and pinnacle of failure for all concerned. Confronting this situation with courage is an ultimate value shared by physicians and patients. As they themselves recognize, the supreme form of courage that participation in transplantation and dialysis asks of them is "the courage to fail."[3]

In such drastic, path-making situations, there is usually a particular, senior physician–leader on the medical team who, in a charismatic, often tenacious, "don't-quit," indomitably optimistic, "we-shall-overcome" way, embodies this ideology and who exhorts and challenges his colleagues to live up to it. The Utah team has such a figure in Dr. Willem J. Kolff, pioneer over the past forty years in the field of artificial organs: beginning with his invention of the artificial kidney machine in Holland during World War II under Nazi occupation (a machine he built with his own hands, using artificial sausage skin for the cellophane tubing); continuing on to the development of the type of artificial heart that was used in Barney Clark; and extending beyond that to the work being done at present, at the Utah Institute for Biomedical Engineering, on an artificial arm and hand, artificial ear, and artificial blood vessels. "I tried four different machines and the last one became the first artificial kidney practical for clinical use," Dr. Kolff told the graduating class

3. Renée C. Fox and Judith P. Swazey, *The Courage to Fail: A Social View of Transplants and Dialysis,* rev. ed. (Chicago: University of Chicago Press, 1978), pp. xvi-xvii.

of 1983 at the University of Utah in his commencement address to them.

> Of the first sixteen patients, fifteen died. I then remembered the words of William, Prince of Orange, who said, "Even without hope you shall undertake, and even without success, you shall persevere." It was the seventeenth patient whose life was saved by the artificial kidney machine . . . .
>
> A number of doctors were opposed to the artificial kidney and wrote articles against it. I decided not to respond at all and to ignore it.
>
> I still have the same policy now that people tell us that the artificial heart has no future . . . .
>
> What have we learned from Dr. Barney Clark? In the first place, that the artificial heart inside the chest does not hurt. It does not cause any pain or discomfort. Second, the slight noise of the drive system did not disturb him. Third, the circulation could be adequately maintained. Finally, that this artificial heart indeed did fit inside the chest. Dr. Barney Clark has had more than his fair share of complications, most of them not at all related to the artificial heart. In the periods that Dr. Clark felt well, when he could walk and go to the sun room, we know that his spirit was good, that he never lost his zeal for life, his considerable sense of humor, his desire to serve his fellowman, and his love for his wife and children. Therefore, all the qualities of the mind which make life worth living were preserved . . . . Of course, we are disappointed that Dr. Barney Clark did not go home. It is perhaps unfair to expect that the first patient with a permanent artificial heart would be a success, but you can be sure that "even without success, we shall persevere."[4]

Another major figure on the Utah team with a "courage-to-fail" perspective is Dr. William C. DeVries, the principal investigator of the clinical artificial heart program and the surgeon who implanted the artificial heart in Barney Clark. Dr. DeVries' sense of his relative youth (he was thirty-eight years old when he did the heart implant), his attitude of filial piety toward Dr. Kolff (for whom he began to work in the artificial organs laboratory when he was still a medical student), and his reluctance to assume a leadership role that is too moralistic and zealous in tone,[5] have made him more low-key and less public in his expression of these "you shall undertake, persevere, and succeed" values than Kolff. But inside the team (in the words of Donald B. Olsen, the doctor of veterinary medicine who is chief surgeon of the University of Utah Artificial Heart Research Laboratory), DeVries has been "the man of conviction" who risked himself and galvanized the group to implant the first artificial heart in a patient: "He believed sufficiently in our animal research data and survival times, and consistent abilities with the total artifi-

4. Kolff, "Forty Years of Artificial Organs and Beyond."

5. The sociological reasons for Dr. DeVries' wariness about assuming this kind of moral leadership role will be discussed later in this paper.

cial heart in sheep and calves, to gamble his professional future and integrity by implanting the artificial heart in man."[6]

Although DeVries welcomes the pause-for-reflection moratorium that the team is currently undergoing, he feels strongly that the endeavor must continue: "The project is bigger than we are . . . . I have no doubt about the device . . . . It works, and so I have to do it [a second implant]. Like the old Mormon song says, 'I must put my shoulder to the wheel and push along.'"[7] DeVries is actively engaged in trying to reunify the team around this conviction and "put new life" into the medical center's commitment to launching the next implant.

The kind of clinical research situation that the case of the artificial heart represents—with its front lines of life and death and medicine components and its competitive, achievement-oriented ardor both to win against great odds and to be recognized for being the first to attain such success—is a potential seedbed for the sorts of disputes over priority of invention, discovery, and development that so frequently occur among scientists.[8] It is not surprising, then, that the Utah medical center is confronted with a priority dispute over the "paternity" and the eponymy of the artificial heart implanted in Barney Clark.

The dispute centers around the claim made by Dr. Clifford A. Kwan-Gett that he has not received proper credit for his contribution to the model of the artificial heart used in Barney Clark—the Jarvik-7 that bears Dr. Robert K. Jarvik's name, rather than his own. Complicating the determination of who should be recognized and rewarded for making the most important scientific

6. Donald B. Olsen, as quoted in "Total Artificial Heart Development at U. of U." (University of Utah News Service release, 22 December 1982), p.8.

7. William C. DeVries, interview with author, 14 October 1983. Another phenomenon that the Utah team shared with other clinical research groups is the moratorium on artificial heart implants that has ensued since the death of Barney Clark. As Judith Swazey and I have written elsewhere, such "moratoriums have occurred repeatedly in the history of therapeutic innovations. Typically, a moratorium takes place when the uncertainties and risks of a new treatment become starkly apparent and the patient mortality seems unbearable or unjustifiable. Pressure for a moratorium can come from physician-investigators' own reactions to the situation, from their colleagues, from the institution in which they work, or from patients and their families....A clinical moratorium...may last for weeks, months, or years" (*Courage to Fail,* p. 108). See "The Heart Transplant Moratorium" (chapter 5) in *Courage to Fail,* pp. 108-34, and also Judith P. Swazey and Renée C. Fox, "The Clinical Moratorium: A Case Study of Mitral Valve Surgery" in *Experimentation with Human Subjects,* ed. Paul A. Freund (New York: George Braziller, 1970), pp. 315-57. We hope to write a detailed account of the Utah team's moratorium in a future paper.

8. See Robert K. Merton's classic essay "Priorities in Scientific Discovery," first published in *American Sociological Review,* 22 (December 1959): 635-69, and reprinted in Robert K. Merton, *The Sociology of Science,* ed. Norman W. Storer (Chicago: University of Chicago Press, 1973), pp. 286-324.

and technological contributions to this heart is the fact that like other big, modern medical research projects, the heart's development spans many years and has entailed the participation of a large number of investigators from a wide array of disciplines in a team process with a complex, frequently changing division of labor. Within this framework, Kwan-Gett was intensively involved as a member of Kolff's group from 1967 to 1971, during which time he directed the animal studies and engineering research. He developed and laid the groundwork for a pneumatically powered artificial heart system and invented and designed the Kwan-Gett hearts upon which the Jarvik heart, with its superior fit, larger stroke volume, and multiple diaphragm design, was later based. (Jarvik, who initially worked with the Kolff team as a design engineer in 1971, returned to medical school in 1972, and after graduation in 1976 joined the artificial heart research group full-time.)

In his June 1983 commencement speech, with a touch of irony Dr. Kolff obliquely referred to the priority problem in the following way:

> This is the Jarvik type artificial heart such as was used in Dr. Barney Clark . . . . Dr. Tet Akutsu and I kept the first dog in the Western world alive with an artificial heart twenty-six years ago. That was in December 1957 . . . . A great number [247] of different investigators have worked with me on various types of artificial hearts. I cannot possibly give credit to all my dedicated co-workers in this address. I am simply speaking of "we." When an investigator worked with one type of artificial heart, for ease of identification we gave it his name. Therefore, we have had Akutsu hearts, Nosé hearts, Wertzheimer hearts, Donovan hearts, Kwan-Gett hearts and Jarvik hearts. The only thing we have not had is a Kolff heart.[9]

At this writing, the dispute has not been resolved but is being deliberated by a specially appointed university committee. However, it is interesting that a new, smaller artificial heart that was implanted for the first time 4 October 1983 in a calf was not named after a researcher, as many of its predecessors were. It was impersonally called "the Utah 100" heart, because it displaces 100 cc of blood. It would appear that partly as a consequence of the priority dispute it has experienced, the team is now eschewing eponyms.

The Jarvik-7 model of the artificial heart, a number of the physicians and bioengineers who contributed to its development, some of the calves on which it was first tried (Alfred Lord Tennyson and Ted E. Baer, for exam-

9. Kolff, "Forty Years of Artificial Organs and Beyond."

ple),[10] the patient in whom it was implanted, his wife and children, key members of the complex medical team who surgically removed Barney Clark's own heart and replaced it with a mechanical one and who cared for him postoperatively, the University of Utah Medical Center and its various officers and administrators, the mountain-ringed valley of Salt Lake City—all became vividly familiar to the public through the more than 112 consecutive days of media attention that was focused upon them. Although in certain respects this media coverage was exceptional, the fact that one of the first human trials of a therapeutic innovation like the artificial heart proved so newsworthy is neither unexpected nor unprecedented. Health and illness, medical science, technology, and care are front-page feature article, major network news in our society. Increasingly over the last two decades they have become important foci—substantively and symbolically—of basic questions of value and belief with which we are currently grappling in our society. Even in the 1950s, when this was less the case than it is today, the so-called new wonder drugs and new life-saving procedures that were being tried on Ward F-Second and the stories of some of the patients who were experimental subjects were extensively and evocatively reported in newspapers and magazines. Barney Clark, then, was not unique in this regard. Rather, he was an especially large and beloved heroic figure in the American pantheon of tragic

10. The naming of the calves and sheep that have been recipients of artificial hearts is structured by an interesting set of norms and folkloric practices that have developed in the Utah artificial heart laboratory and barn.

The principal surgeon and investigator for a given implant is the person who has the right and privilege of naming the animal-recipient. The name is usually not given to the animal until at least twenty-four hours after the implant has occurred. Dr. Donald B. Olsen, who directs the animal work, attributes this custom to the fact that in the early days of the artificial heart program, there was great uncertainty concerning whether the animal into which a heart was implanted would survive even that long. Investigators say that they try to choose a name that "fits the animal's personality" or the surrounding circumstances under which the implant is done. For example, the name Fred was given to "an extremely ugly animal, with a wonderful personality"; and a female calf who received a heart implant on Columbus day was named Niña after one of Columbus's ships. More often than not, the names chosen are humorous, such as Ali Baa Baa for a sheep. The names in which the investigators seem to take the greatest pleasure are those that make some sort of self-mockingly romantic or ironic commentary on the meaning of their experimental work, such as Alfred Lord Tennyson, Magic, or in the case of twin calves, Charles and Diana. In the last instance, the fact that "Diana gave her heart to Charles" in an experimental heart transplant added a dimension of gallows humor to the significance of their interconnected names.

The observations that I have made in other laboratories over the years lead me to believe that these and other social patterns and cultural traditions that have grown up in the Utah artificial heart group are not idiosyncratic. There is rich sociology of science content in such laboratory behavior that has been largely overlooked by social scientists.

and triumphant research patient-celebrities who have been made famous by the media.

The fact that Barney Clark lost his human heart and that an artificial heart was substituted for it added extra dimensions of meaning and fascination to his case and increased the amount of prominence of coverage that the media accorded to it. In this respect, the kind of attention that it elicited and the way that is was treated by the press resembled the reporting of human heart transplants, particularly in their earlier phases. Along with the rational and factual scientific accounts of the artificial heart implant, certain magico-religious sentiments about the heart, akin to those that came to the surface in connection with cardiac transplants, also appeared. Judith Swazey and I found that "the development of cardiac transplantation . . . revealed that the heart is still widely viewed as the seat of the soul or spirit, the source and repository of love, courage, and the highest, most human emotions."[11] Such feelings and beliefs were apparent in the statements that the media carried about how glad Mrs. Clark was that her husband "still loved [her], even though he now had an artificial heart" and about how the Utah team felt that Barney Clark had "proved that courage and good humor and love of wife and children are sustained by an artificial heart."

There is something of the pathos of the Tin Man in *The Wizard of Oz* in this testimony, as well as magical thinking. For the American school children, who to this day continue to write to the University of Utah Medical Center in great numbers requesting photographs of Barney Clark, the convergence of high technology, one-giant-leap-for-mankind daring, and grandfatherly love that he personified seems to have made him an avuncular astronaut.

These, then, were some of the sociomedical ways in which the implantation of the Utah artificial heart was like other pioneering clinical research ventures. What were some of the differences?

DIFFERENCES

To begin with, the heart team's "special patient," Barney Clark, seems to have been even sicker and closer to death than the usually terminally ill patients who become the first subjects for a high-risk, experimental procedure, device, or drug. He was, in fact, sicker than the members of the Evaluation Committee discerned when they approved his selection as the recipient of the artificial heart. For, in addition to chronic, inoperable, end-stage, progressive, congestive heart failure (in its Class IV phase), it turned out that Dr. Clark also had severe chronic obstructive pulmonary disease that was partly

11. Fox and Swazey, *Courage to Fail,* p. 29.

independent of his heart condition. The fact that the selection criteria established by the Utah medical center stated that such an additional, "incapacitating medical illness" would disqualify a candidate for total artificial heart replacement and that the Evaluation Committee was explicitly charged with "the responsibility . . . to ensure the absence of other illnesses which would threaten the success of the artificial heart and render its implantation a costly but useless exercise" contributes to the inner controversy that the medical center and heart team are still working through, concerning whether or not Dr. Clark should have been chosen for the operation. Could Barney Clark's lung disease have been detected in advance? and Should it have eliminated him as a candidate? are not questions that a sociologist (albeit of medicine) has the competence to resolve or even to comment upon. But it may be of some relevance to note that, sociologically speaking, the individual selected to receive the artificial heart exemplified the "courage-to-fail" values of the Utah heart team. Directly and indirectly, this contributed to his eligibility in their eyes and strengthened his candidacy.

It was not only the biomedical condition of their patient-subject that distinguished the artificial heart team from other therapeutic innovators, but also certain aspects of the team's composition, organization, and functioning. On one level, the Utah group consisted of the whole array of professional persons who make up an advanced modern medical team based in a university hospital. But the team's own definition of its membership was more encompassing than is generally the case. As John Dwan described it: "The Utah artificial heart team extended from the patient and his family down through surgeons, Drs. William C. DeVries and Lyle Joyce, to University Vice President [for the Health Sciences] Chase N. Peterson, to the nurses, the therapists, the laboratory personnel, security, the patient selection committee, the social workers, the operating room staff, to practically every employee of the Utah Medical Center."[12] Dwan and his public relations staff were also considered to be part of the heart team. In effect, virtually the whole medical center was defined as the team, in a way that brought together modern conceptions of bureaucracy and traditional notions of extended kinship, that combined a strong sense of democracy and of hierarchy, and that placed Barney Clark and his family at the summit of the team. These attributes of the heart team's makeup are also basic principles and characteristics of Mormon organization.

In other regards, the team resembled the lonely and heroic situation in which pioneering innovators like Dr. Willem Kolff have historically worked.

12. John Dwan, "The Public Relations of an Artificial Heart Implant," American Association of Medical Colleges News & Comment, typescript.

But the implantation of the artificial heart in Barney Clark was carried out by a surgical group that was unusually small and young when viewed within the time frame of the 1980s. The operation was conducted by thirty-eight-year-old Dr. William DeVries, Utah's chief thoracic and cardiovascular surgeon, and his associate and assistant, thirty-four-year-old Dr. Lyle Joyce (who had come directly to Utah only two years earlier, in 1980, after completing his residency in cardiac surgery and a Ph.D. at Minnesota). Only one house officer, Dr. Charles Berry, chief resident in surgery, assisted in the operating room. Doctor of veterinary medicine Donald B. Olsen, head surgeon of the University of Utah Artificial Heart Research Laboratory, was also present throughout the implant operation in the role of consultant. Dr. Robert K. Jarvik scrubbed in at the point when the artificial heart was inserted in Barney Clark and scrubbed out immediately thereafter. No other surgeons or surgeons-in-training were involved in the heart implant or in the postoperative care of Dr. Clark.[13] In fact, at the time that the implant took place, the center's Division of Cardio-Thoracic Surgery consisted only of Drs. DeVries and Joyce. The University of Utah had a two-year cardiothoracic surgery residency program that it ran jointly with the LDS Hospital in Salt Lake City and which included a rotation at the local Veterans Administration Hospital. However, out of the twenty-four-month training period that this entailed, the surgical residents spent only four months at the University of Utah Medical Center. They were not present at the center during the period of Dr. Clark's hospitalization. Furthermore, the chairmanship of the Department of Surgery was vacant.

The structure and dynamics of the Utah team differed markedly from other groups of therapeutic innovators in still other ways. Rather than centralizing the charismatic influence and authority it had generated through the scientific and symbolic import of its medical trail blazing—as pioneering clinical research groups are wont to do—and consolidating that charisma around the person and role of its physician-in-chief, the artificial heart team divided its charisma and distributed it among four of its members. The allocation and imagery of the team's charisma were also shaped by the media coverage that was accorded to the implantation of the artificial heart and its sequelae. Each of the four charismatic leader figures had his specialized place inside the team, and outside it in the sun of the media-conveyed public attention that the heart implant evoked:

13. In addition, a fourth-year medical student, Patricia McNabb, was present, along with anesthetists and surgical nurses in their vital operating room roles.

- Willem Kolff, venerable and indomitable founding father, master inventor, and historic builder of artificial organs;
- William DeVries, young, modern, all-American, frontier surgeon of courageous conviction, with the physical and personality attributes of a Jimmy Stewart, Gary Cooper, Henry Fonda, and Abraham Lincoln rolled into one;
- Robert Jarvik, principal designer of "Barney Clark's heart"; boyishly glamorous culture hero of bioengineering, in whom the values of the 1960s and of the 1980s seemed to be joined; artist and sculptor, as well as mechanic and physician, who took a long time to commit himself to medicine and to be admitted to medical school, and who, at age thirty-six, achieved Jarvik-7 fame and also business success as president and chief executive officer of Kolff Medical (a company that designs, develops, and produces artificial organs and related devices);
- Chase Peterson, chief medical spokesperson for the Utah artificial heart team, the medical center, and the university; intelligent and articulate, imaginative and candid public relations "star," whose at-once physicianly, teacherly, and pastoral persona conveyed a sense of medical and moral purposiveness, thoughtful responsibility, and team unity to the public.[14]

The development of these division of charisma patterns was given impetus by a phenomenon inside the heart team that was not publicly displayed. This was Dr. DeVries' strong disinclination to claim and control the charisma by organizing it around his status and role as surgeon-in-chief. Although he willingly assumed medical leadership of the team, he felt reluctant about taking on what he called its "moral" leadership. For him, such a moral role broached the domain of religion. As the head of a medical team located in Salt Lake City, Utah, where the Mormon population and Mormon church (The Church of Jesus Christ of Latter-day Saints) are centered, and as a Mormon himself, DeVries was concerned about acting too much like a church elder. In his view, engaging in such morally and spiritually tinged behavior on the basis of his office would be arrogant, particularly for a physician as young as he was. It might also contribute to Mormon–non-Mormon divisiveness on his team. And it could push him into a closer and deeper, personal and institutional relationship to Mormonism than he was ready for at the time of the artificial heart implant.

There are two additional respects in which the social system of the heart team and the way that it conducted itself distinguished it from comparable medical groups: the kind of ethical relationship that the team developed with the Institutional Review Board for Research with Human Subjects (IRB) of

14. In June 1983, after the implantation of the artificial heart in Barney Clark and his subsequent death, Chase Peterson became president of the University of Utah.

the medical center and the degree of familism that it exhibited in its relations with Barney Clark (and his wife, Una Loy) were both unusual. Along with a number of other factors (as in the case of the team's organizational and charisma patterns), the Mormon milieu in which the heart implant occurred latently affected both these two sets of differences.

The most strikingly divergent features of the Utah IRB crystallized around the role of Dr. Ross Woolley, the board's vice chairman, his conception of how the artificial heart implant ought to be ethically monitored, and the means that he used to do so. Dr. Woolley, an engineer with a Ph.D. in evaluation research and a faculty member of the Department of Family and Community Medicine of the University of Utah Medical School, became head of the special subcommittee that was formed to deal with the ethics of human experimentation issues in the case of the artificial heart. He brought to this role the strong conviction that the IRB not only had the responsibility to protect human research subjects and patients but also to protect the rights and principles of the institutions in which human experimentation and medical care take place. He formulated the term "protection of institutional integrity" to express what he regarded as the vital, institutional function of the IRB. Under his influence, the IRB attached greater conceptual and operational importance to this aspect of their obligations and activities than such boards generally do. Woolley and the IRB applied the notion of institutional integrity most vigorously to situations that involved attempts by the media to gain access to certain types of information about the center, especially those that pertained to the proceedings of the board itself and also to matters of so-called paycheck journalism. The chief paycheck journalism issues that the center felt it faced were questions about "the patient's rights to sell parts of his story, versus the institution's obligation to provide the essential elements to the public, versus the physician's rights to protect unpublished scientific data and patient confidentiality."[15]

Dr. Woolley implemented this view of the IRB and of its raison d'être by assuming a monitoring role that has few, if any, counterparts on other IRBs in the United States. By his own testimony, Woolley spent up to four hours a day in the intensive care unit where Barney Clark was hospitalized throughout the entire period that Dr. Clark was a patient there. He made at least one daily visit to see Barney Clark until his death. He became one of Mrs. Clark's confidants and advisors. He read Dr. Clark's chart every day and studied his laboratory values. He made rounds with the heart team in the morning, often came back to the unit in the afternoon, and sometimes returned in the evening as well. He conducted extensive, ongoing, information-gathering discussions

15. Dwan, "The Public Relations of an Artificial Heart Implant."

with a variety of team members. As he put it, he felt that it was his obligation to be very well-informed. The physician *cum* ethicist surveillance role that Woolley adopted took on some of the attributes of a medical and moral watchman. ("He is watching over us to make sure that we are living up to rules that exist in his head," commented one team member with a mixture of respect, irony, and indignation.) There was also an implicit priestly dimension to this role, which surfaced when Ross Woolley gave Barney Clark a Mormon blessing at the time of his death.

Woolley became what Chase Peterson has referred to as "our home-grown ethicist," partly because of the initiative of Dr. DeVries, who first invited him to "monitor the patient" and to act as a moral consultant. Only a few members of the team were aware of this invitation. Some felt uneasy about the scope and nature of what appeared to them to be Woolley's self-appointed activities. But the legitimacy of such a role and its advisability were not challenged by the heart team or the IRB until after Dr. Clark's death. Slowly and hesitantly, partly in response to comments from outside observers, the Utah group began to critically examine this "home-grown" role. Chase Peterson now concedes that it "was not well thought out." William DeVries admits that Woolley's role and behavior "over-stepped bounds." And the IRB has decided that Dr. Woolley's *in situ* monitoring activities, inside the artificial heart team and in intimate contact with the patient-subject, are involvements that conflict with some of his IRB discernment and decision-making functions. Consequently, he has been asked to give up his IRB voting rights on questions that pertain to the artificial heart; and he has done so without rancor. As the team itself appears to recognize, there is something indigenous about the role that Ross Woolley came to play, the process by which it developed, and the fact that although it made some persons uncomfortable, it did not seem either unique or disturbingly aberrant to them. There is a sense in which the at once democratic and authoritatian belief that "every worthy man is a priest," and the moral activism of the Mormon-infused Utah setting in which the implantation of the artificial heart in Barney Clark took place normalized the Woolley role. The Mormon context not only helped to shape this role, it also conditioned the responses of members of the heart team to it so that in the balance they regarded it as more familiar than dubiously strange.

The other singularizing sociological characteristic of the Utah team—what I have called its "familism"—also seems to have been influenced by the fact that the heart implant occurred in a Mormon milieu. I have already indicated that in other "experiment perilous" clinical research units I have observed, medical teams often become involved deeply enough with their patient-subjects to regard them like one of the family, as well as friends, colleagues, and coinvestigators. This was the case in the Utah group's way of thinking about and relating to Dr. and Mrs. Clark and their children. But the saliency of the heart team's sense of family, the ramifying extent to which it encompassed the Clarks, and some of its modes of expression all distinguished the Utah familism from comparable patterns in similar medical situations and groups.

Una Loy Clark was as central a figure to the heart team as her "special patient" husband. She was admiringly seen as the incarnation of an extraordinarily "courageous," "stalwart," "steadfast," "devoted," and "loving" woman, wife, and mother, who displayed great "endurance" and "vision" throughout all the days of "the experiment"; who shared her husband's "strong desire to serve and fulfill his mission," his "great hope," and his "considerable anguish"; and who sustained the heart team as well as Dr. Clark through her unvacillating "support to all." Una Loy Clark was the team's pioneering woman of virtue—their wifely, motherly, and grandmotherly "heroine."[16]

Even more striking was the way that some of the physician members of the heart team involved their own wives and children in firsthand contact and relations with Dr. and Mrs. Clark. At Christmastime, for example, they all feted the Clarks with a family party, complete with gift giving and Yuletide caroling. On New Year's Eve, at least one physician, his wife, and their several children paid a visit to the intensive care unit to see Dr. and Mrs. Clark and wish them a happy new year. Another physician's children visited the Clarks frequently enough to begin to think of them as an additional set of grandparents. There were also a number of times when a doctor's children made evening rounds with their father and when one little boy slept overnight in a hospital room close to the intensive care unit so that he could spend some time with his physician-father who was on around-the-clock call for Barney Clark. By and large, the physicians saw nothing remarkable or problematic in this behavior or in the kinds of family connections they established with the Clarks. Rather, they considered such relations to be supportive and therapeutic for Barney and Una Loy Clark and also for themselves. In spite of the nurses', the social worker's, and the psychiatrist's concern about the disruptive impact of these extra persons and visits on the unit where Barney Clark was hospitalized and about the emotional demands that the team's family relations with the Clarks made upon them, these patterns persisted. The Mormon emphasis on the family as the basic unit of society, on the woman as

16. The quoted statements about Una Loy Clark are drawn from our interviews with members of the Utah artificial heart team and from the various University of Utah documents previously cited.

the vital center of the family, on the desirability and importance of children, and on extended kinship and kinlike group solidarity seems to have shaped and reinforced these medical team attitudes and behaviors. They would be unlikely to occur in this form, or to be permitted to continue if they did, in comparable hospital settings.

In the end, key members of the Utah team flew to the state of Washington to attend Dr. Clark's funeral, and the senior figure among them, Dr. Willem Kolff, delivered a eulogy to Barney and Una Loy Clark on his own and his colleagues' behalf. This was a consummate, ceremonial expression of the artificial heart group's familism. "Speaking for all of the members of our team," Dr. Kolff concluded, "administrators, doctors, nurses, engineers, technicians, physical therapists, dieticians—for all of us who were involved—we thank you, Una Loy, and your wonderful family for your trust and support and wish you Godspeed."[17]

THE "SAME-BUT-DIFFERENT" "COURAGE-TO-FAIL" ETHOS

Underlying the Utah artificial heart team's experimental venture, with its typical and peculiar features, was the "same-but-different," "courage-to-fail" philosophy that motivated and integrated it. The team's "courage-to-fail" outlook was articulated in an especially coherent, collectively self-aware, and thoughtful way. It was pervaded by what appeared to be a faith-filled, but more soberly responsible optimism than usual. This is the tone that Dr. Chase Peterson struck, for example, in his 18 December 1982 press statement: "It seemed to us," he said, "in the quiet of our consciences, that we were very deliberate, not over-enthusiastic, rushing into something that had a technological challenge to it . . . . We are overwhelmed with responsibility for Dr. Clark . . . . It is a milestone for him, a milestone for the human spirit." It was principally through Dr. Peterson that the team's ethos was put into words and communicated to the American public, along with detailed bulletins about Barney Clark's medical course. In his role as public spokesman for the team, particularly in the context of the daily televised briefings that he gave to the media people assembled in the hospital's cafeteria-based news center, Peterson was the key conceptualizer, imagist and integrator of the team's shared perspective. Behind his representative role lay the year-long planning process in which he had involved the team in his capacity as university vice-president of health sciences, and what John Dwan has described as "the countless meetings, the repeated delineating of roles

17. Words spoken by Dr. Willem J. Kolff at the funeral services for Dr. Barney Clark.

and responsibilities, the comparing of written scenarios, the round-table discussions, rehearsals, [and] brainstorming about contingencies" that this entailed.[18]

Below the surface of the team's version of the "courage-to-fail" *geist,* contributing to the unified way in which it was expressed and enlarging its meaning, are the values of Mormonism and the Mormon world view. To say this is not to imply that all or even most of the participants in the implantation of the artificial heart were Mormon. The Clark family, Chase Peterson, William DeVries, Ross Woolley, and Donald Olsen are all Mormons, for example, but Willem Kolff, Robert Jarvik, and Lyle Joyce are not. Nor was the heart team's nursing staff uniquely Mormon. Furthermore, the persons involved in the heart implant who are nominally Mormon vary greatly in the loyalty and fervor of their relationship to the Mormon religion and church and in their relative standing within it. They range from devout, actively involved, high-status lay priests, to alientated, so-called Jack Mormons and include various shades of "fence-sitting-middling,"[19] "lukewarm to cold" varieties of being Mormon that "do not fit into any neat categories."[20] It should not be supposed, either, that the tenets of the Mormon religion shaped the team's perspective and presentation in a totally conscious, deliberate, or doctrinaire way. In fact, as we shall see, the team is uniformly sensitive about any implication that "Mormon cultural or theologic principles," or that the Mormon church and "its life mold"[21] have shaped their undertaking. Mormon and non-Mormon team members alike consider overt references or claims to such influences to be "misleading," and potentially "damaging," regardless of who makes them.[22]

The fact remains, however, that Mormonism is a gathering, a community, a distinctive culture and way of life, as well as a religion in the more conventional sense of the term. It pervades everything in the valley world of Salt Lake City, including the University of Utah, its medical center, and its heart team. The active commitment of the Utah group to developing a permanent artificial heart, its trail-blazing determination to implant the heart in a human patient, the personality attributes and qualities of moral character that the team sought in its first subject and that it found and extolled in Barney Clark, and its style of public reporting and accountability are all highly

18. Dwan, "The Public Relations of an Artificial Heart Implant."

19. This is the way one of the members of the Utah team described his relationship to Mormonism.

20. Thomas F. O'Dea, *The Mormons* (Chicago: University of Chicago Press, 1957), pp. 184-85.

21. The quoted phrases in this sentence are excerpted from interviews with two different Mormon members of the artificial heart team.

22. These quotes come from an interview with a non-Mormon member of the Utah team.

compatible with basic principles of Mormonism. The artificial heart implant dramatically exemplified, in a morality play–like way, fundamental principles of Mormonism: its pioneering, innovating history and perspective; its sense of manifest destiny; the at-once secular and spiritual importance it attaches to health and education; its conception of the human body as a tabernacle; the practical and this-wordly, but transcendental significance it accords to personal and collective improvement, accomplishment, mastery, and progress, through vigorous human effort animated by rationality, knowledge, and intelligence. These values and beliefs were repeatedly expressed in the public briefings the team gave. Occasionally, particularly in Chase Peterson's statements, unobtrusive reference was made to the explicitly religious framework into which these values and beliefs fit: the Mormon theology of progressive self-deification and divinization in an eternal growth process that spans this life and the life that comes after it. ("We express our respect and sympathy to Mrs. Clark and her children, and especially to Dr. Clark who was—and I suspect is—a remarkable man, a pioneer to match these Western lands," said Dr. Peterson in the press conference he gave about Barney Clark's death.[23])

When confronted with this analysis of the relationship and fit between Mormon values and beliefs and those on which the implantation of the artificial heart in Barney Clark rested, members of the Utah team alleged that these principles were as American as they were Mormon. "Mormon culture is uniquely American," Chase Peterson affirmed. "While it may be more vigorously expressed in 1983 in the Mormon land than in Marin county, it is American!"[24] This is indeed true; and herein lies what sociologist of religion Thomas O'Dea has called "one of the great paradoxes of the Mormon experience":

> Despite the marked and genuine peculiarity of Mormonism . . . its typical American quality is no less real . . . . Mormonism [is] in many respects the most American of religions . . . . The Mormon group came closer to evolving an ethnic identity on this continent than did any other comparable group. Moreover, it was a genuine locally and independently conceived, ethnicity, born and nurtured on this side of the water and not imported from abroad. Yet it also has been "an America in miniature." The chief processes of American history have been repeated within the smaller context of the peculiar Mormon experience . . . . When we add to these historical processes the fact that in its values Mormonism offers an analogous spectacle of distinction and similarity, the

23. Peterson, "Terminal Events."

24. This statement was part of Chase Peterson's public response to the version of this paper presented at the conference of the artificial heart implant team in Alta, Utah, 13-15 October 1983.

> strange combination of peculiarity and typicality stands out as the most striking Mormon characteristic.[25]

In this analysis of the Utah team's "same-but-different" profile, the latent influence of Mormon culture and religion has emerged as a significant factor. In largely implicit and unintended ways, Mormonism played a role in shaping the heart team's values, vocabulary, and imagery; its conception of itself; its leadership and organization; and its relationships—to colleagues, to its special patient Barney Clark and his family, to the IRB, to the press, and to the American public. Mormonism in this sense added certain dimensions of meaning and mission to the implantation of the artificial heart in Barney Clark. It also helped to create some of the distinctive phenomena and problems that the heart team developed, such as its familism and its moral watchman role.

One of the earmarks of the Utah team is the exceptional capacity for self-examination and public scrutiny that it has shown. This group candor and openness notwithstanding, the team tends to react with great wariness and strong negative emotion to the suggestion that they were influenced by Mormonism (as I discovered when I shared this part of my analysis with them). The ways in which the team expresses this concern provide valuable further insights into its complex relationship to Mormonism.[26]

The team is convinced that making the Mormon factor manifest would "fragment" and "tear apart" their professional group and the working solidarity that it has achieved despite its potential Mormon–non-Mormon split and the ambivalence of some of its Mormon members toward their own religious tradition and church: "The team has kept [Mormonism] a nonissue . . . . We have worked hard to keep it separate . . . . We have not discussed it. It can only be divisive to get into it."

The team also seems to feel the need both to deny and to resist the controlling power of the Mormon community and church upon them and to take a stand against attempts on the part of Mormon institutions to interpret and use the artificial heart implant too imperialistically or evangelically:

> Can Mormon culture be presumed to be able to influence non-Mormons or the non-religious or atheists? Is Utah culture some sort of Chinese empire which absorbs or converts all those who come to conquer?

25. O'Dea, *The Mormons,* pp. 117-18.

26. The following quotations from members of the artificial heart team come from both public and private discussions that I had with them concerning their reactions to the analysis of the influence of Mormonism on the artificial heart implant. That analysis was presented at the 13-15 October 1983 conference in Alta, Utah, where they were all gathered.

> It's a misuse of people to propagate these values. I don't think it's fair to claim that basic humanness—caring, cooperation, love, family—are exclusive to or even special to Mormons.

> In their way the [Mormon] church recognizes that the purposes of the [artificial heart] experiment were the same as their life mold . . . . The whole valley rallied around it and took it to heart. They saw it as divinely mandated because it fit their principles . . . and also because it put Salt Lake City on the map . . . . People in the church look at Dr. Kolff in a very Mormon way, too. [In their view,] he left Leiden and Cleveland where he was unable to do his work, and he came out here to this beautiful wilderness, where he was left alone . . . unmolested . . . to develop and strengthen a delicate flower . . . his product of modern technology. The church sees Dr. Kolff as a kind of Brigham Young.

Members of the heart team disapprove of what they regard as such religiously self-aggrandizing conceptions. In addition, they worry about how this kind of religious reworking of the meaning of the artificial heart project and its transmission to milieus outside Salt Lake City and the Mormon world could adversely affect their scientific standing and their reputation for objectivity and fairmindedness: "It implies that [our] program is guided by religious influences." The fact that their first patient-subject, Barney Clark, was a Mormon makes them even more sensitively defensive about this issue. "Does it . . . assume . . . then [that we] favor certain patients partly on the basis of religion?" a team member asks.

The heart team is anxiously interested in being seen as scientific, secular, and both medically and entrepreneurially successful in an American way that goes beyond Salt Lake City, Utah, Mormonism, and the cultural and religious tradition of a "peculiar people." As one physician frankly stated, "Wherever I go in my travels, when I say that I come from Salt Lake, people say, 'Mormons.' . . . Salt Lake City is a very growing place. It is to its advantage to become more American and international as well. To the extent that people think the Mormon church controls things here, it's bad."

In the end, it could be said that the Utah artificial heart team's tacit struggle with Mormonism is a microexpression of a more general Mormon and American situation:

> The Latter-Day Saints have successfully created a Mormon community with its own values and social structure, although it is no longer a separate entity but is rather very much part, both geographically and sentimentally, of the larger secular society of the United States. Yet Mormonism retains much of its old peculiarity, and Mormondom remains in many respects a society in its own right and, as such, has been subject to a number of stresses and strains within its own structure . . . . The destruction of the semi-isolation of the last half of the nineteenth century, the growth of the gentile population in the intermountain West, the progress of modern thought, the dispersal of the Saints eastward—in

> short, the reintegration of Mormondom into the parent culture and the accommodation and compromises that it involved—raised once more . . . fundamental questions of "Why?" and "Whither?"[27]

The Utah heart team has entered a moratorium: a time of reflection that is moral and social, as well as medical and technological. However self-searching its current mood may be, it is clear that the team decisively intends to implant another artificial heart in another patient. When it is undertaken, the second implant, like the first, will be done within the framework of Mormon-American faith in "the reality of eternal progression" and belief that "improvement [is] inevitable if man keeps working toward it."[28] In this view, one does not hesitate for long on the edge of a frontier. Rather, in the words of Brigham Young, by courageous and "faithful efforts," one "earn[s] the right to take another step onward."[29] The Utah team's implantation of an artificial heart in Barney Clark and its subsequent pause to reflect on itself constitute such "faithful efforts." The next "step onward" will be their Artificial Heart Implant-2.

27. O'Dea, *The Mormons,* pp. 222, 258.
28. Mary Ann Meyers, "Gates Ajar: Death in Mormon Thought and Practice," in *Death in America,* ed. David E. Stannard (Philadelphia: University of Pennsylvania Press, 1975), p. 113.
29. Brigham Young, as quoted in Meyers, "Gates Ajar," p. 114.

Is Religion Important in Belgium?

"Religion is no longer important in Belgium!" Wherever I travelled in Belgium over the course of 1976-1977, the year of my sabbatical leave from an American university, and my eighteenth consecutive year of fieldwork in Belgian society, friends, colleagues, and informants announced this.

I was particularly puzzled by this statement because I had always considered Belgium to be a society deeply imprinted by religion: by its diffuse Catholicism, and its complex reactions to it. Belgians from the whole range of philosophical, political, linguistic, regional, and social-class milieux in which I had worked knew that this was my considered judgment. Yet, on this visit, they seemed intent on showing me that religion was less important to them, and in their society, than I had supposed. The picture that many Belgians painted was of a society where religion had not merely waned, but spontaneously, and with great rapidity, had virtually disappeared. However much this image intrigued me, neither sociological theory, nor my own first-hand observations on previous trips to Belgium made it seem credible.

But "how important *is* religion in Belgian society today?" I found myself asking, and "what do Belgians mean when they say, 'religion is no longer important in Belgium'?" This essay grows out of a continuing dialogue with Belgians around these questions. It will begin with a descriptive analysis of

From *Archives Européennes de Sociologie* XXIII (1982), pp. 3-38. Reprinted by permission of *Archives Européennes de Sociologie (European Journal of Sociology)*.

what I have observed in Belgian society that I consider to be religious or related to religion, and what has led me to assume that religion is important in Belgium. I will then go on to describe and analyze how Belgians define religion and religious, and what has led them to conclude and assert that "religion is no longer important in Belgium." In the final section of this article, I will try to bring these two perspectives together in an interpretive synthesis.

THE SOCIOLOGIST'S VIEW

Belgium is a Catholic country, even though since its beginning as a nation in 1830, the separation of Church and State has prevailed both in principle and fact. In the first national census of 1846 (designed and initiated by Lambert Adolphe Jacques Quételet), 99.8 percent of the population was recorded as Catholic. And, to this day, the majority of Belgians—approximately 90 percent of the population—are baptized Catholics. The Reformation has played a minor role in Belgian society. What is estimated to be the 50,000 Protestants in Belgium today make up a very small fraction of the total national population of some 9,800,000 persons. There are only 35,000 Jews in Belgium, most of whom (12,000) live and work within the boundaries of the semi-ghetto of Antwerp or in the city of Brussels (18,000) where a less orthodox, solidary, and self-sufficient community of Jews resides. In recent years, the number of Moslems in Belgium has increased to around 120,000 persons; these are migrant workers and their families, primarily from North Africa and Turkey.[1]

Even Belgian Free Thought and Free Masonry (the might-have-been Protestantism of Belgium), the institutionalized opponent of the Catholic Church, and its supposed religio-philosophical antithesis, have been structured and shaped by Catholicism. Whereas Free Thought-Free Mason beliefs in reason and science as the "bringers of light" under whose impact orga-

1. Statistics cited in Jaak Billiet and Karel Dobbelaere, *Godsdienst In Vlaanderen: Van Kerks Katholicisme Naar Sociaal-Kulturele Kristenheid?* (Leuven, Davidsfonds, 1976), pp. 11-28.

Belgium's three leading Protestant churches—the Protestant Church of Belgium, the Reformed Church of Belgium, and the Flemish Reformed Church—were joined together on January 1, 1979, under the name of the United Protestant Church of Belgium.

For a rich ethnographic study of a particular, Chasidic Jewish community in Antwerp, the *Hassides Belz*, see Jacques Gutwirth, *Vie juive traditionnelle* (Paris, Les éditions de Minuit, 1970).

nized religion and "other dark things"[2] will be dispelled represent a deliberate challenge to the basic tenets and world view of Catholicism, on another level they have much in common with the highly positivist, Belgian Catholic philosophical, theological, and intellectual tradition, and with its penchant for scientism. And while the Masonic Lodge was intentionally organized to subvert the influence of the Catholic church, its historical *raison d'être* is symbiotically associated with the dominance of Catholicism in Belgium and its socialist network of health and welfare, economic and political institutions have a mirror-image identity with the Christian (Catholic) set.[3]

But it is not the institutional Catholicism of the country that impresses a non-Belgian sociological observer, as much as the pervasive and evocative "presence" of Catholic images and symbols: churches and cathedrals; convents, abbeys and *béguinages;* church silver and gold-embroidered vestments; painted triptychs, reliquaries, and altar pieces; carved wooden choir stalls; belfries and carillons; printed and sculpted Madonnas, Virgins, saints, and angels; bouquets of flowers and cloistered gardens; conclaves and processions; parchment documents and manuscripts; and the massive oak beams of 800-year-old Sint-Janshospital in Brugge, where Augustinian brothers and sisters nursed the medieval sick. These are more than passively preserved symbols of a church-linked past.

To this day, the bells ring out continually in Belgium. They are an "everlasting language," that mark the hour, proclaim Sundays and holy days, accompany the annual cycle of traditional festivals and processions, joyously announce marriages, solemnly toll for deaths. "Not only religious bells, but civil bells also, those carillons that Flanders invented, both the tragic bells with bloody mouths and the triumphant with golden tongues . . . ."[4] Nor is the language of flowers obsolete. Flowers are indelibly woven into Belgian tapestries, and painted into the portraits, still-lifes, and landscapes of fifteenth- and sixteenth-century Primitive Flemish art: profane bouquets made sacred by Hans Memling, Jan Provoost, Roger Van der Weyden, and the brothers Van Eyck; the Immaculate Conception of the Virgin Mary, her purity, love, and simplicity, expressed through the lily, the red carnation, the

2. These phrases were used by the sociologist Robert N. Bellah to describe the Enlightenment view of religion in modern society. See Bellah, "Between Religion and Social Science," in *Beyond Belief: Essays on Religion in a Post-Traditional World* (New York, Harper and Row, 1970), p. 237.

3. Renée C. Fox, "Why Belgium?" *Archives europénnes de sociologie/European Journal of Sociology,* XIX (1978), p. 209.

4. Michel de Ghelderode, "The Ostend Interviews (Entretiens d'Ostende)," in Michel de Ghelderode, *Seven Plays,* Volume I. Translated from French, and with an introduction by George Hauger (New York, Hill and Wang, 1960), p. 6.

rose, and the humble flowers of the woods and the fields. These are paintings still venerated in Belgium and visited by crowds wherever they hang. The floral displays in the annual flower shows of Ghent, in the windows of the impressively numerous florists of the land, and in the vases in churches and family living rooms perpetuate the painterly tradition of the exquisitely arranged detail and brilliant colors of the "great bouquets." Golden oak remains the favorite wood of Belgians: for *armoires,* ceiling beams, church pews and coffins. When societal issues reach a national crisis point, Belgians continue to summon what they call "conclaves," to negotiate and resolve the problems in an extra-parliamentary way. And parchment has not entirely lost its testimonial and scholastic meaning.

In part spontaneously, in part with conscious self-protectiveness, Belgians present themselves as practical and rational people, stolidly attuned to the everyday world of commonsense reality, and relatively impervious to such ethereal, aesthetic and sentimental things as the music of bells and the message of a rose, or to transcendent moods and meanings. But, in fact, Belgians are highly sensitive and responsive to religious images and symbols—and to imagery and symbolism more generally. Here, for example, is the way that Mr. J., a scientist, intellectual, and financier from Brussels, and a Free Mason, responded to the first "jazz Mass" and one of the few Catholic masses he ever attended.[5] The occasion was the 550th anniversary of the Université catholique de Louvain.[6]

> The setting was perfect: a modern chapel, with simple horizontal and vertical lines, and plain chairs. The cardinal, bare-headed, was dressed in gold-colored vestments embroidered with a motif of wheat. There were lovely, autumnal arrangements of gold, orange, and brown fall flowers on each side of the altar. The other priests were dressed in simple, pure, highly-starched white garments, embroidered with tiny gold crosses. The clothing was as beautifully designed as gowns made by the finest Paris *modiste.* The cardinal did not spoil the aesthetic effect by wearing his red hat. He placed it on the lectern where, throughout the Mass, it gleamed like a gigantic ruby, in that otherwise totally white-and-gold setting. I was stirred by the beat-beat-beat of the music that rose to crescendos

5. The following passage is abstracted from my field notes on an interview that I conducted with Mr. J. in the fall of 1976.

6. The Catholic University of Louvain was founded in 1425. In 1968, as a consequence of the so-called "linguistic" or "community problem" of Belgium, the University "split" into two, autonomous, universities: the French-speaking Université catholique de Louvain (Louvain-la-Neuve), and the Dutch-speaking Katholieke Universiteit te Leuven. The Université catholique de Louvain has been physically moved from the community of Leuven, to Ottignies in Walloon Brabant, and to St. Lambrecht-Woluwe, where its medical faculty has been established. This opening-day exercise was held in Ottignies, one year after the Katholieke Universiteit te Leuven celebrated the 500th anniversary of the Catholic University's founding.

> of joy and contrition. And I thought it remarkable that when the Mass was ended, the entire congregation burst into applause. I must confess that I was bewitched by it . . . .

Or, to take another, less explicitly religious and Catholic example: in the National Library, behind a glass plane, the salon of Michel de Ghelderode, the renowned Belgian playwright, is permanently preserved with all its *objets étranges*.[7]

> . . . masks; marionettes from the traditional puppet theatres of Brussels and Liège; seashells from the beaches of Ostend in Flanders; swords and scabbards; ancient Madonnas; crucifixes, church hangings, a gothic stone frieze reputedly a fragment from the sculpted face of Brussels' *Hôtel de Ville;* discarded dress-shop dummies in various states of theatrical dress and undress; two carousel horses from a carnival or *kermesse* . . . and whole walls of paintings. Paintings—the graphic language of silent Flanders.

Over what Belgians call the 'living museum' that they have made of de Ghelderode's salon, a spotlight moves from one part of the room to another, as the recorded voice of the deceased playwright speaks about the deeper meaning of his *objets* and of his art:

> A being endowed with any poetic sense is sensitive to the supernatural. It is around us; it is in us . . . . You can perceive it, unexpectedly come across its messages in the humblest things, the most everyday things. I have an angel on my shoulder, and a devil in my pocket! . . . [8]

> And [the] fear of the night gives value to our days. But what name can we rightly give to this fear? Let us say anxiety (*angoisse*). This anxiety shows through all my works. Without it, what would be their meaning? They would consist of literary games, little tales . . . neatly parceled up . . . . If I take up my pen, . . . it is more to fix this fear than to deliver myself from it—this fear so old that I believe it was born with the earth, which is so old.[9]

It is "around [them] and inside [them]." But Belgians are not only sensitive *to* symbols and images, and to the rituals that embody and vivify them; they are also sensitive *about* them. "I must confess that I was bewitched by it," is the way Mr. J. put it, reluctantly confiding, with some embarrassment, that he had responded so powerfully to the Mass.

Belgian sensitivity and responsiveness to symbols and images are not confined to those that are explicitly Catholic or religious; and the symbolic

7. The phrase *objets étranges*, is Ghelderode's. Renée C. Fox, "Journal intime belge/Intiem Belgisch Dagboek," *Columbia University Forum*, V (1962), pp. 14-15.

8. Michel de Ghelderode, "The Ostend Interviews," *op. cit.* p. 6.

9. *Ibid.*, pp. 14-15.

imagery to which Belgians are most likely to react strongly is neither random nor adventitious. In fact, the particular kinds of everyday things that light up for them in an emblematic way seem to be systematically related to the cosmic framework within which Belgians experience and order their individual and group existence. "A tiny land, often shrouded in mist, under a huge, continually changing, cloud-and-light-filled sky, swept by westerly winds from the sea, whose inner life as well as its art is pervaded by the everyday images and strange symbols of Breughel and Bosch, Ensor and Magritte."[10] This is the way that Belgium looks through the lenses of its cosmic view.

Belgians are highly aware of the physical landscape within which their daily round takes place, and of the forces of nature that shape its contours and its atmosphere: the sky and the sea; the plains and the hills; the fog and clouds and rain; the wind; the diffuse radiance of the land, and its dazzling bursts of light; its misty greys, and the illumined reds of its roofs, blues of its skies, and greens of its fields; the trees and the birds; the grazing cows and horses; the spaces and sounds; and the language of the country's silences.

Their relationship to nature is complex. It involves both melancholy-in-beauty and joy-in-beauty. It is realistic, romantic, and mystical. It not only focuses on familiar landmarks and vistas, but also on imagined, and hoped-for ones (like the mountains that Breughel painted onto the *pays Brabant,* a region of Belgium that is flat.) It yearns toward the spacious, the solitary, the meditative, and the silent—in a society that is very small, densely populated, enclosing, gregarious, bustlingly active, and that throbs with the sound of hammers, industrial machinery, fast-moving feet, roaring motorcycles, cars and trucks, and loudly-playing radios, phonographs, and television sets. It is rural and pastoral and maritime—in a country that is highly urbanized as well as industrialized and that does not have a seafaring tradition. Miniaturized by the smallness of their society, on the one hand, and by the alchemy of the sky and the light, on the other, Belgians merge into their at once real and idealized landscape, find and lose themselves in it, and are made broodingly anxious by the grip that it has on them. They express all this in painted images, laconic phrases, and a vocabulary of silence.

But the everyday things in the Belgian cosmic view are not all created by nature and anchored in villages. Some of them are fashioned by human hands, are associated with towns and cities and are usually presented by Belgians (with a mixture of pride and self-mockery) as emanations of their burgher spirit. The countless red bricks that Belgians have made for centuries, and all the houses that they have built for themselves with the bricks are central to these aspects of their world view. The bricks and the houses are

10. Fox, Why Belgium?, *op. cit.*, pp. 207-208.

physical and symbolic bulwarks of Belgian mastery, security, privacy, well-being, status, affluence and of progress in life. Wherever Belgians have migrated—whether to Canada, the United States or Central Africa—they have made bricks, and built houses. Some of the early Catholic missions founded by Belgian religious in Congo/Zaire are veritable cities of brick with great brick cathedrals. Whatever one's occupation or social class, one can hardly be a respectable Belgian without a house of one's own, preferably a house that one has planned oneself.

The material significance of the Belgian house is so apparent that it is easy to overlook its more hidden, intangible meaning. Belgians help to make this meaning inobvious through their conspicuous consumption behavior in connection with its building and furnishing, and through their disinclination to speak of its spiritual significance, except under unusually intimate (joyous or tragic) circumstances:

> Unfortunately, the news I have to tell you about Lieve is not so good [Jan wrote in his January letter to me]. Two weeks ago, x-rays showed new complications of her disease. Before, most of the symptoms had disappeared; now some are increasing again. Next week, the doctors will make a decision about intensifying or changing the chemotherapy. For her, and for all of us, this is a new fact, hard to get through after the relative success during the first year of therapy. Fortunately, there are no acute physical complaints of pain. Between therapy sessions, Lieve feels relatively well, and tries to live the life of a normal mother and housewife. One thing that helps us to escape a little bit from that overwhelming threatening feeling and allows us to make and realize some plans for the future is the construction of our new home. It is now in such a stage that we hope to move in during the month of April. So, when you come back to Belgium, we will be able to receive you in our new home.

I returned to Belgium on May 18. Lieve died on May 24, in the new home, of cancer of the bone. She was not quite twenty-five years old. It was from Lieve and Jan that I learned that a Belgian house can be a prayer-in-bricks—but only because they were willing to tell me about the relationship between their house, "that overwhelming threatening feeling," and their hopes and plans for a future.

Numerous other commonplace objects take on a symbolic sense within the framework of Belgians' conceptions of the deeper and wider meaning of human existence. Parlor furniture, family portraits, mirrors, hats, shoes, shaving brushes, combs, casseroles, bottles, test tubes, fans, seashells, *mannequins* [dress dummies], carousel horses, the musical instruments of a *fanfare,* railroad trains, tracks and stations, traffic lights, the gabled rooftops and chimneys of a city street: all of these objects are both more than they seem to be, and not what they seem to be. In Belgian literature, and especially

Belgian painting, both traditional and modern, this collective sense of the mystery of things—of the messages hidden within and behind them—is paramount. Belgians enjoy collecting, owning and being surrounded by many ostensibly ordinary things. Their relationship to the objects that they gather and cumulate is active and transformative. They carefully arrange them, prominently display them, vigorously dust them, and manifestly enjoy them. Belgians are also fascinated by them: some of the surrealistic qualities of everyday objects in Belgian art, for example, derive from a mesmerized kind of concentration on things as things. Under this sort of intense scrutiny, the objects change. They are magnified and seen in peculiar perspective. They become strange, threatening and, sometimes, terrifying. Here, Belgians' love of the mysterious, the subterranean and the fantastic works over the objects like the moving spotlight in the de Ghelderodean "living museum." On another level, this at once imaginative, theatrical, and ironic manipulation of things contains an existential commentary. Behind the everyday semblance of things, beneath their conventional, orderly, and benign appearance, lie curious and potentially dangerous human and extra-human forces. These are unpredictable, disruptive, and essentially unfathomable forces. They cannot be controlled or dispelled by Belgians' customary tendency to dust and scrub all their wordly possessions. In fact, in an allegorical Aladdin's lamp and Pandora's box way, all the rubbing, examining, and coveting of objects may summon up, rather than exorcise, their black-magic powers.

This conception of everyday-things-become-*objets étranges* is connected with another set of Belgian traditions, and the images and symbols that derive from them: Belgian masks and masquerades, carnivals and *kermesses.* The importance of masks in Belgian folklore, festivals, and art is related to a highly developed cultural awareness of the differences between outer appearances and inner reality, and of the omnipresence of façades in human existence. Masks are the faces that people contrive and wear. They cover inner countenances and the chambers of the soul where inhibited tenderness, forbidden passions, and unexpressed capacities for good and evil reside. But Belgian masks are as counterphobic as they are deceiving. They are not beautiful, happy, reassuring faces, or even conventional ones. Instead, they are grotesque and terrifying. They externalize what Belgians feel are some of the most ugly and ominous aspects of the human condition. In this restricted and highly stylized way, the masks represent an unmasking. Like the scarecrows that Belgians construct and implant in their fields, they are make-believe representations of what is frightening in man; and they are symbolically intended to chase away the destructive, black-winged forces in and around him.

Masks and a sense of the grotesque are also a part of Belgian carnivals and *kermesses*. But the carnivals and *kermesses* are less individualistic and more collective than masks. They bring together great gatherings of eating, drinking, singing, dancing, music-making, and parading people for periodic rites of revelry and release. In the Belgian view, however, their symbolic meaning is not purely festive. In painting and literature, the crowds that participate in them are often composed of strange, brutal Breughelian and Boschian figures, carnally uncontrolled and uncontrollable. The elemental behavior of these everyman and everywoman folk has burst through the constraints of self and society to become inhuman and less-than-human.

Closely related to the cosmic meaning of masks and carnivals is the significance of marionettes and of statues in Belgian tradition. For centuries Belgians have been sculptors as well as painters. They have filled their land with statues: of stone and wood and metal; of the Virgin Mary, of Christ, and of certain saints, angels and archangels; of dukes and duchesses, princes and princesses, kings and queens; of warriors and knights, soldiers and generals; of medieval guildsmen, artisans, and tradesmen; and of mythic, legendary, and folkloric figures—like Venus, Till Eulenspiegel, and little Julien, the urinating *Manneken-Pis* of Brussels. Belgian churches, homes, public buildings, squares, parks and cemeteries are rich in statues, shaped into human form out of stone and marble, wood and wax. The Virgin Mary is one of the personages most frequently represented in statuary: carved madonnas on altars and in shrines; doll-like madonnas, dressed in velvet, brocade, and lace, wearing gold crowns, under glass bell-jars, in family parlors and dining-rooms; Bruges madonnas, in niches, watching over the front doors of the medieval houses and streets, beneath the chiming belfries. But most dazzling of all are the buildings of statues, whose stone walls are a Gothic gallery of sacred and profane, patrician and plebian figures.[11]

Belgians admire and enjoy, covet and venerate statues. At the same time, they consider statues presumptuous. In old Brussels dialect, for example, they are called *postures.* The word has a double connotation. On the one hand, it alludes to the human vanity involved in seeking or allowing oneself to be commemorated in this way, and to the absurdity of the poses one must strike in order to be sculpted. On the other hand, it refers to the posturing of the sculptor who dares to suppose that he can create, or even recreate a human form.

Statues, then, have some of the *poseur* attributes of masks. But they are metaphysically more arrogant and dangerous. For the act of fashioning them entails *hubris.* It borders on the assumption that man was not only created by

11. Three outstanding examples of historical Belgian buildings richly decorated with stone sculptures are the town halls of Brussels, Leuven, and Oudenaarde.

God, but that man can create in a God-like way. Though they are silent, static, and composed of inert materials, statues are attempts of human beings to make men and women in their own image.

In the Belgian tradition and cosmic perspective, marionettes are animate statues. Not only do they move and talk, but in contrast to the miniature, schematized puppets of some societies and cultures, Belgian marionettes are realistic and life-sized. From a certain point of view their counterparts are the floating giants that are carried in Belgian processions and carnivals: huge, less earthbound, more grotesque, voiceless, marionette-statues.[12] What fundamentally distinguishes marionettes from statues is their relationship to the puppetmaster. He conceives them; he attaches them to their strings; and he works the strings so that the marionettes speak and listen, shout and whisper, laugh and cry, walk and run, and dance according to the puppetmaster/playwright's script. The animism of the marionettes, the scenario that they are made to act out, the human comedy significance of the play in which they are cast, and their continuing dependence on the script-structured manipulations of the puppetmaster, raise the questions of *hubris* to a higher degree for Belgians than the sculptor-statue relationship. These attributes also summon up another set of cosmic questions—questions that this kind of theatre was designed to evoke. Who is the puppetmaster? Who are the puppets? What is the meaning of the play in which they are acting? And how will it end? More than any other Belgian art form, the marionette theatre leads its audience toward the metaphysical mysteries surrounding the existence of a God; his identity, nature, appearance and intentions; his relationship to man; and his influence over human lives and deaths.

The historic Toone marionette theatre of Brussels clasically embodies the puppeteering tradition of Belgium. The ambiance of this theatre expresses still other dimensions of the meaning of marionettes and their performance. The language of the marionettes is predominantly local dialect—*bruxellois*. Not only is their speech popular and folkloric, but also earthy, impertinent and vulgar. It "calls a spade a spade," and it is full of colorful, exuberant invectives. Even in plays about sacred subjects like the Nativity, Mary and Joseph speak to each other in the cadences as well as the vocabulary of simple but knowing, everyday women and men. The tone is realistic and commonplace. It is also ironic. It is sensually mystical. It is wrenchingly romantic. It is

12. I am indebted to Michel de Ghelderode for this insight. See especially his essay entitled: *"Les gigantesques,"* in Michel de Ghelderode, *Mes statues* (Brussels, Louis Musin, 1978). Each of the essays in this work by Ghelderode is devoted to a different statue in Brussels of which he is particularly fond, or that had special significance for him. The Musin edition of this book is a facsimile of the original, limited edition that was published in June 1943 (274 copies) by Imprimerie Laconti; for Les éditions du Carrefour.

combative. The cosmic stance, deeply rooted in the ordinary, but highly attuned to the extraordinary, is essentially tragi-comic.

Looming behind these general conceptions of existence and humanity, symbolized and expressed through marionettes and statues, carnivals and masks, man-made and natural objects are Belgian images of death. Belgians are both interested in death, and preoccupied with it. On the most manifest level, they approach death with the practicality, good sense, and pride in these qualities that are part of Belgian culture more generally. Belgians make responsible, composed, unmorbid arrangements for their own funerals and burials, as well as those of relatives: for the death announcements and mementos, the floral arrangements, the religious rites (or absence of them), the cemetery plot and the tombstone. The wise and homely pragmatism of certain traditional features of Belgian funerals and cemeteries is striking. In Flanders, for example, the burial is followed by a hearty meal, offered by the bereaved family to all those returning from the cemetery. At this meal (that customarily takes place in the parish hall of the local church), everyone, including the mourners, eats with gusto. An impressive number of *tartines* (white bread-and-butter sandwiches) and cups of strong, steaming coffee are consumed. And just outside many Belgian cemeteries, in Walloonie and Brussels, as well as in Flanders, there is not only a florist shop but also a *café*, or *herberg*. The *café* does a thriving business serving beer, coffee, *tartines* and pastries to the entering and exiting grave-site visitors.[13]

These comfortable, efficient, domestic and entrepreneurial images of death are only part of the total Belgian view. Other aspects of their outlook on death are more anguished and pervaded by a sense of the inscrutability of death. There is a certain rapprochement, even overlap, between the way that Belgians depict the dissembled and the evil in the human condition, and some of the ways in which they see death. Death is often associated with a skeleton dressed in human clothing, a masked personage, a grotesque apparition of the *kermesse*, or with a strange, Breughelian or Boschian figure. Yet, at other times, death seems to be more faceless and impersonal: like a dark, empty field or street, barely visible in the mist, or under the tiny, pale sliver of a Delvaux or Magritte moon. Death may also take on a more human, comely

13. In a way, Belgian *tartines* are the culinary equivalents of Belgian bricks. They are symbolically associated with personal survival, and with the hope of maintaining a healthy, happy, normal family life. There are as many Belgian jokes about *tartines* as there are about bricks. A whole series of such *tartine* jokes, for example, turn around the German occupation of Belgium in World War II, and the wily capacity for surviving and flourishing that Belgians who were imprisoned by Germans supposedly showed. Belgians are depicted as emerging from the jails and camps of the enemy well fed and well clothed, carrying emergency supplies of *tartines*—and numerous other possessions—in their hands.

and feminine form. It may appear in the guise of a delicate and chaste girl, madonna-like in her beauty and purity. Or death may present itself more seductively, as a voluptuous, scantily-clad, Rubens-like woman.[14] Underlying the polyvalence of these images and their shifting, speculative nature, is a fascinated and frightened sense of how enigmatic and elusive the real visage and shape of death are.

In contrast, Belgian images of the suffering and grief that accompany death are more unified, and they are integrally Catholic: Christ on the Cross and the *Mater dolorosa,* holding her crucified son in her arms. The imagery of life after death is more explicitly Belgian and mystically Christian. Hubert and Jean Van Eyck's altarpiece, "The Mystic Lamb" [*L'Agneau mystique/ Het Lam Gods*], in the cathedral in Ghent, is perhaps the supreme expression of how it is traditionally and symbolically conceived. Heaven is portrayed in a quintessentially Belgian way. It is a place that is peopled by golden-haired musician-angels, who form a celestial orchestra and choir. But these angels are opulently dressed, in gorgeous, worldly clothing, painted in meticulous detail. Their faces are not only very human but very Belgian. And the expressions on the angels' faces are neither conventional nor purely seraphic. Heaven, like earth, it would seem, has its share of disagreeable, malcontent, malicious and angry creatures. Neither Christ nor the Virgin Mary appear in the Van Eyck polyptych. Rather, the Crucifixion, and the hope of the Resurrection are embodied in the sacrificial Lamb of God. All the divine and the not-so-divine images of the painting(s) glow with brilliant color and with a wonderful, miraculous kind of radiance. It is in and through the color and, above all, the light that illumines everything, that a transcendent belief in the possibility of a next life is expressed. In its empirical uncertainty, its mystery and its enormity, it surpasses what concrete images can convey.

The robust, zestful, mischievous, and resourceful fashion in which Belgians regard and deal with the universe mitigates their existential unease and anxiety. But it is not sufficient to offset the deep and diffuse *Angst* to which Belgians are prone. The sources of the *Angst* are complex. In that small, particularistic, cloistering, and competitive land, "a certain shyness and discomfort exist between individuals from different categories and groups, along with the anxiety-ridden distrust (*méfiance*) that Belgians themselves

14. In both traditional and contemporaneous Belgian painting, women have been alternatively, but consistently, presented as pure, sacred, and romantic figures, on the one hand, and as voluptuous, sensual, nude, mannikin-like figures, on the other. This painterly view of women—at once "split" and dualistic, as are so many other aspects of Belgian culture—is highly suggestive of an imperfectly fused and reconciled woman-as-Eve, and woman-as-the-Virgin-Mary double perspective. It would be interesting to further explore the imagery associated with women in Belgian painting—its content, historical and cultural origins, and its meaning.

often cite.[15] The *méfiance* is not only associated with specific traits of the Belgian social system. It also has cosmic sources: those facets of their world view that Belgians express through the symbolism of "strange things." Peering out from behind the protectively shuttered and curtained windows of the solid houses that they have built for, and around themselves, Belgians apprehensively survey their familiar but mysterious landscape. The anxiety-provoking signs and signals that they see and hear in the outside world are in part their own creations. They have projected them onto the horizon, where they have taken on "such an aura of factuality" for Belgians, that they have become "really real."[16]

The *Angst* is both circular and reflexive. Belgians turn it back on themselves in a number of ways. They are not only made anxious by their own projections but also by the feelings and moods that their symbolic imagery expresses and reinforces. The force of their feelings is a focus of great existential concern for Belgians. They invest a considerable amount of psychic energy in the culturally-shaped mechanisms that they use to hide and to manage these feelings. The practical and rational, burgher and *bon vivant* dimensions of their society and of their self-presentation provide Belgians with a form of inner protection against the powerful onrush of their emotions. For, in the Belgian view, unbridled affectivity undermines one's capacity to meet and master the challenges and difficulties of everyday life with the fortitude and the *courage/moed* that are basic cultural values.[17] Too strong and uncontrolled feelings also have the potentiality to do harm to others and to one's relationship to others— because of the consuming demands that they make, the powerful bonds that they imply, and because (in a primary process way) there is always the danger that such feelings will be unleashed and become acts.

On a more societal scale, the same kind of *Angst* is publicly and ritually expressed by the irony-tinged doubts that Belgians often voice about "the reality, existence, and survival of their own society." "The sources of this anxiety about the dangers of dissension and the survival of the society and of the propensity for temporizing and for seeking 'quiet,' harmonious ways of resolving conflict are not easy to document . . . . But . . . fundamental to the general Belgian disinclination to allow the divisions, conflicts, and passions present in the country to get too far out of hand [is the] fear that they

15. Fox, "Why Belgium?," *op. cit.*, pp. 211-212.

16. Clifford Geertz, "Religion as a Cultural System," *in* Clifford Geertz, *The Interpretation of Cultures* (New York, Basic Books, 1973), p. 120.

17. The Belgian conception of *courage* and other basic Belgian values will be discussed in the next section of this article.

will ultimately lead to the dissolution of the society.''[18] That fear also contributes to "the caution and suspicion with which Belgians regard cultural and psychological probing.''[19] And it lies at the heart of the fact that although Belgians allow the affective and absurd, surreal and mystical aspects of their cosmic view to "explode" into their art and their carnivals, these are "collectively denied in daily life and systematically excluded from intellectual and scientific work, as if it were both improper and perilous to acknowledge [them] in such commonplace, orderly, and rational contexts.''[20]

One of the most profound origins of Belgian *Angst* is the Catholicism of the country and the feeling of its inescapability that Belgians experience. In this modern, increasingly secularized era, certain formal religious practices like regular attendance at Mass, and participation in the sacraments of communion and confession have diminished. In addition, many Belgians seem to be struggling to free themselves from the deep, subtle, and tenacious kind of grip that Catholicism has on their minds and souls:

> Dr. Z. seems to be haunted by Catholicism; by what he considers to be its "dogmatism," and by the fact that because it has this nature, he cannot be either a "believer," or someone who practices the religion into which he was born and baptized. For him, the doctrine of papal infallibility illimitably extended the Church's dogmatism; and he speaks of this doctrine as if it had been promulgated this summer, rather than in July 1870.[21]

Much has changed in the post-Vatican Council II Church, its doctrine, liturgy, clergy and laity. And part of this change is that not only intellectuals and professionals like Dr. Z. but men and women from wide-ranging Belgian backgrounds and milieux are trying to distance themselves from the Catholicism of their childhood, of their family, and of their forebearers. Yet an older, more orthodox, authoritarian, and admonishing Catholicism lives on in them, in the institutional Church, and in Belgian society. One comes upon it repeatedly, in different settings, in both startling and ambiguous ways:

> After dinner, L. and I visited The Red Mouse, one of the local cafés: a Flemish farmhouse, white-washed on the outside, with well-tended gravel paths and a garden opening onto the fields. Inside, the rooms are woodpanelled, and warmed by fireplaces. The Red Mouse is filled with oak furniture, with madonnas under bell-jars, and with old, Flemish, religious posters. The big, schematic eyes on one of these posters looked disapprovingly down on us. "God is Watching You!" the motto printed under them read. The room in which we sat

18. Fox, "Why Belgium?," *op. cit.*, p. 224.
19. *Ibid.*, p. 225.
20. *Ibid.*, p. 226.
21. Field notes, Summer 1972.

drinking our coffee and our beer had two stained-glass windows, both of them depicting the heads and faces of cats, their eyes gleaming in the sunlight, that filtered through the clouds, on this warm, intermittently rainy, Sunday afternoon.[22]

I took the train from Brussels to Mechelen, for my audience with the cardinal. His palace, located near the cathedral, is a classic, French structure: a white building, with plain glass windows, and a large, inner garden . . . .

I was early, and so I was ushered into a parlor to wait. Its walls and ceilings were painted white. A brass chandelier hung from the ceiling—the sort that one sees in Flemish and Dutch paintings. The furniture was simple, and made of blond wood. A couch and two armchairs, covered in green velvet, were grouped around a coffee table on one side of the room, where a small oriental carpet in matching shades of green and gold-brown was placed on the bare, wooden floor. A small table contained an old-fashioned, black, extension phone. On the other side of the room, near the white marble fireplace, a table, and several hard chairs were grouped. Over the fireplace, a large, white-washed crucifix hung. There were several traditional, Italian-style religious paintings in gilt frames on the walls, and a portrait of the cardinal's face and head by a Belgian artist, painted in dynamic, swirling reds and oranges and golds . . . . The room was restful and immaculate—full of light, and not a spot of dust anywhere. Through the white, net curtains, I could see the old gardener working on the flower beds. The tulips were gone, but there were geraniums and lilacs, and one could see that the roses would be blooming soon . . . .

At 11:30 a.m., the cardinal's priest-secretary took me upstairs in an elevator for my appointment. En route to the cardinal's office, he showed me some of the formal rooms of the house. He opened the door of a huge, long, reception hall, hung with life-sized portraits of previous cardinals. In the center of this enormous room was a throne, shrouded in a faded crimson canopy and curtain. The secretary expressed disapproval of the inappropriateness of the room for these modern times, and indeed, it had a shabby, pale, unused look.

I only had to wait a few seconds in the anteroom of the cardinal's office before the door opened, and he came to greet me. He was dressed in black clergyman, and wore a simple, gold bishop's ring, unjeweled . . . . He was warm, direct, and unclerical in the way that he welcomed me with a handshake . . . . His office is so functional that it is nondescript. It is workaday, with a minimum of metal furniture. I was not conscious of a crucifix on the wall, or of any other religious objects in it . . . . In the course of our conversation, the only gesture of the man behind the desk that reminded me that he was a cardinal, rather than an ordinary, non-princely priest, a college professor, or a business executive, was an occasional fondling of the big, gold, bishop's ring.

The interview lasted for a relaxed, enjoyable hour. Upon my departure, the cardinal got up from his chair, and gave me copies of the prayer that he had composed for the 50th anniversary of his ordination last year, and of his pasto-

22. Field notes, February 1972.

> ral letter for Pentecost . . . . He then shook my hand, and said, "God bless you," and "Goodbye." His secretary accompanied me down the hall to the elevator. On the ground floor, he waited until my taxi came, and waved me off as I rode away.
>
> Despite its summit significance, the cardinal's palace is very Belgian, in a familiar way. The people inside it are the same in many basic, human ways, as those whom I have met outside it. And yet, in a way that is hard to identify or express, the orthodox and controlling presence of the Church pervades this house. The white walls, clear windows, and workaday desk do not dispel that feeling. In this atmospheric and symbolic sense, the crimson throne in the great hall is still in use. Perhaps this, too, is very Belgian. And perhaps it is one of the reasons why Belgians still seem to feel such a compelling need to liberate themselves from the outer and inner influences of the Church.[23]

"It is an invisible lid [*couvercle invisible*] over everything," is the way that one Belgian described the diffuse sense of the controlling influence of the Church. For many Belgians, among the most disturbing features of their Catholicism-pervaded *Angst* is how difficult it is for them to articulate it, to explain it to themselves, and to share it with others. They are also painfully aware of its paradoxical nature. They know that some of their *Angst* springs from the fact that they are reacting against the religious tradition that suffuses their world view, and that has significantly contributed to their ability, as well as their need to find meaning in their individual and collective existence.

These Belgian conceptions of self and others, of man and society, and of the cosmos of which they are part are not only expressed in particular symbols and images, but also through certain values.

It has become apparent that Belgians attach a great deal of importance to material comfort and to ingenuity, both for their own sake, and as means for coping with the difficulties and enigmas of the human condition. In the universe that Belgians envision, what they call *courage* is essential. By this, they mean the capacity to persist and prevail in the face of the many problems, barriers, impasses, and threats that occur in life. Belgian *courage* involves more than the stoical strength to withstand life-difficulties. It also entails the active, manipulative ability to find one's way around challenging, thwarting, and painful predicaments. Thus, *les petits chemins* (the byroads and the "series of adroit . . . tricksterlike means for budging the system or getting around it")[24] that Belgians have developed, and their use of *agent-intermédiaries* to help "them accomplish practical tasks and achieve desired

23. Field notes, May 1978.
24. Fox, "Why Belgium?," *op. cit.*, pp. 215-216.

goals''[25] are not merely expedient. In the Belgian view, they are also morally necessary responses.

Another set of Belgian values is implied here: a reserved and skeptical attitude toward all forms of central authority and power, both civil and religious, and stubborn defiance in the face of oppression and injustice. These values were plainly stated by Monsignor Honoré van Wayenbergh, the last *Rector magnificus* of the Catholic University of Louvain, in his letter of April 29, 1943, to General von Falkenhausen, German Military Governor of Belgium and northern France. (It was written after he and the rectors of the other Belgian universities had been ordered to turn over the names and addresses of all first-year university students to the Germans who had decided to conscript these students for compulsory labor.)[26]

> I cannot be obliged in conscience to betray students who have done nothing wrong and who have adopted a purely passive attitude approved in principle by an occupying power. I have refused to collaborate in the execution of a measure which is unjust, tyrannical and illegal: with far less reason can I yield to intimidation . . . . It has always been my conviction that an honest, dignified and firm defense of rights and justice is . . . triumphant in the end and I do not think that a government is ennobled by having recourse to tyrannical measures like those now being used against our country. If Belgium is at war, it is not because she wanted war. There you have the source of all the sufferings inflicted on us for the past three years: the present situation is the direct outcome of the invasion. A valiant nation, which has had to bow to numerically superior forces and to violence, is not a conquered nation: still less is it a subject one.

The situation in which this response was made was one that Belgium has repeatedly experienced throughout its history: military and political domination by an ''occupying power.''[27] But even when there is no enemy on their soil in this literal sense, Belgians are inclined to deal with the problems and adversities that they encounter as if they were the counterparts of ''sufferings inflicted on [them]'' by ''tyrannical'' forces. It is characteristically Belgian to refuse to capitulate and, if necessary, to employ clandestine, underground means to prevail. It is partly because of its latent moral and metaphysical

25. For further discussion of these and associated mechanisms in the Belgian social system, see Fox, ''Why Belgium?,'' *op. cit.*, pp. 217-218.

26. From a letter sent by Mgr. H. van Wayenbergh, *Rector Magnificus* of the University of Louvain to General von Falkenhausen, April 29, 1943. Reprinted in Appendix II of the English language edition of E. Lousse, *The University of Louvain during the Second World War.* Translated from French by Th. Crowley, O.F.M., Ph. D. (Bruges, Desclee De Brouwer, 1946), pp. 70-74.

27. At different points in its history, Belgium has been occupied by Austria, France, Germany, Holland, and Spain.

significance that using side-roads and intermediaries is not only permitted in Belgian society, but generally admired.

These aspects of the Belgian value system are heroic, in a specially defined and circumscribed way. Not only does the Belgian conception of the heroic accredit certain kinds of deviant and devious behavior; it also opposes what are considered to be *excessively* heroic inclinations. For, the "too-heroic" runs counter to another important complex of Belgian values: *le bon sens.* Translated into English, *le bon sens* means good sense or commonsense. Although they usually refer to *le bon sens belge* with a flash of irony, by and large, Belgians are proud of this value-orientation, which they consider to be one of their most distinctive cultural traits. *Bon sens,* in the Belgian definition of the term, encompasses the pragmatism, materialism, courage, realism, expediency, resourcefulness, chicanery, skepticism, and subterranean defiance already discussed. But its key attributes can best be summed up in two other phrases that Belgians frequently use: "Don't exaggerate" and "Do it quietly." The importance of avoiding extremes, striking a balance, maintaining equanimity, reconciling opposites, negotiating conflicts, creating harmony and, if need be, of making compromises in order to do so are all implied in these phrases. In a society that has repeatedly had to adjust to the conditions of being occupied—one that is also highly particularistic, with a great deal of potential strain between its various ethnic-linguistic, regional, religio-philosophical, and political groups, and that keeps a vigilantly competitive watch over the way resources are distributed to these groups—what Belgians mean by good sense has had adaptive value. In addition, on another level, it is related to the various forms of *Angst* to which Belgians are prone. In this dimension, good sense is an approved, culturally recommended way of dealing with the dangerous emotional and existential states of disequilibrium that can lead to cosmic chaos.

"Solidarity" (*solidariteit/solidarité*) is another basic Belgian value: one that like "good sense" has a special relationship to Belgians' preoccupation with societal and human condition problems of order, integration, harmony, and peace. In a closing address to the 31st National Congress of the Alliance of Christian Mutualities,[28] Léo Tindemans, then Belgian Prime Minister,

28. In addition to the National Alliance of Christian Mutualities, there is also a National Union of Socialist Mutualities in Belgium. Approximately 4,250,000 Belgians, or somewhat more than half of the Belgian population, belong to the Christian Mutualities, and the rest of the Belgian population to its Socialist counterpart. The two networks of mutualities combined represent a powerful entity in Belgian society because they provide and administer health insurance to all Belgians, and manage great funds and a double system of polyclinics to do so.

invoked this value and described its import in the following way:[29]

> I belong to that generation of Flemish for whom the world opened in successive shocks: the confusion of the period before the war [World War II], the terrible ordeal of the war, the contact with another "regime," the reconstruction in the period after the war, economic growth, the progress apparently without limit and now, the crisis, a crisis in many domains. Throughout these years, I have been impressed with the idea of mutual aid, which is Christian in origin, and which values bringing help where it is needed. What is involved . . . are the first steps toward a humane . . . social vision. Today, the Christian Mutualities are an essential element in a Christian vision of society . . . This vision is not a nineteenth-century conception, but on the contrary, it is the most human message that we can launch into the future . . . . Can we not work together to inject a little more heart into our society, more of the human, in the true sense of the word, more of authentic solidarity? . . . In order to further more understanding and more love of man, and to break the taboos and combat the egoism of various groups, that characterize our community. It would also enable us to develop new social conduct [so that] individuals would be truly important, [and] families would be rehabilitated . . . . In sum, a society in which mutual aid would be a determining factor.[30]

"Authentic solidarity" runs counter to self-interest, particularism, inequity, injustice, subjugation, enmity, violence, destruction, confusion, ordeal and crisis. It is the ideal social state that exists when commitment to the common good, concern for social welfare, "mutual aid," cooperation, "understanding," and "love of [one's fellow] man" prevail. In this kind of humane, harmonious, and universalistic society, a "family of man" conception of human relations is exemplified and taught. The worth, freedom, dignity and rights of every individual and group are recognized. Well-being, prosperity, and progress are accessible to all. And peace reigns. As Tindemans states, this Belgian "vision" of solidarity has Christian-humanist roots. It is also Socialist in content and origin (corresponding, for example, to some of the concepts of thinkers like Henri de Man.) And in Belgian society, it is the central set of principles on which both the Catholic and the Socialist networks of institutions for the protection and promotion of social welfare are founded.

In its overall orientation, the Belgian value system is highly active. It could be said that being energetic in the way that one approaches the responsibilities, opportunities, fulfillments, and difficulties of this life is a Belgian value in and of itself. Even Belgian mysticism is vigorous: actively (often sensually)

29. This Congress, which I attended, was held in Antwerp in December 1976. Tindemans' speech was delivered on December 5, 1976.

30. This is my own translation from the French-language text of this speech (delivered in Dutch and French), printed in *La Libre Belgique* (a Catholic newspaper), December 6, 1976, p. 2.

involved in experiences and events of this world, and in their transformation. But it is in Belgians' dynamic relationship to work that their activism and the conceptions underlying it are classically expressed.

Belgians approach work in the spirit of *Als ich can* (If I can): the oft-repeated motto of the painter Van Eyck, that so many of them learned in their primary- and secondary-school classrooms. Belgians work hard, zestfully, efficiently and with craftsmanlike cleanliness and excellence. Work is not only a necessity and a duty for them. It is also a challenge, a pleasure, and it is the most direct and certain means to prosperity and well-being. Work, and the material and immaterial benefits that it brings, confer order, purpose and meaning on the daily round; and in a universe that is often sunless, shrouded in fog, and buffeted by winds from the sea, it is a source of comfort and reassurance. Work is the primary means through which red-brick houses—filled with family possessions, decorated with photographs, paintings and bouquets of flowers, and fragrant with the delicious odors of abundant meals—are built and securely implanted on the landscape of life. Work, then, is a metaphysical as well as a moral and material act: a vital affirmation, pervaded with Belgian *courage* and "good sense." In this regard, the Belgian outlook on work is a more optimistic, less fatalistic version of the Protestant work-ethic.[31]

Along with its activism, the rationalism of the Belgian value system is one of its most salient, general characteristics. For Belgians, a major criterion of the relative worth of acts, ideas, or even feelings, is how rational they are. By rational, Belgians mean in part what is instrumentally related to achieving practical, empirical ends. Rational also has a less applied, goal-directed meaning: modes of behavior and thought that are "scientific," that is, that closely conform to a rigid definition of scientific logic. Belgians assume that this strict positivism has some means-to-ends value. But independently of its utility, they prize rationality because they consider it to be "serious," sober, objective, balanced, and controlled. For Belgians, affectivity is its antithesis. Rationality is regarded as intellectually and morally superior to affectivity,

31. As I have written elsewhere, "Belgium . . . is a Catholic, virtually Protestantless country, which nevertheless has a Protestant ethic-like work ethos" ["Why Belgium?," *op. cit.* p. 227].

Not only the Belgian outlook on work, but also some of the other features of the Belgian value system discussed in the text above resemble aspects of what sociologist Max Weber identified as the Protestant ethic (for example, Belgian conceptions of *courage, bon sens,* material success, rationalism, and activism, and the social, moral and metaphysical importance accorded to them).

The "Belgian case" suggests that Weber may have overlooked, or at least minimized, the degree to which an equivalent of the value and belief system that he associated with Calvinistic Protestantism may also be inherent in certain forms of northern European Catholicism (Dutch and German Catholicism, for instance, as well as Belgian Catholicism).

and as a desirable check on the disorderliness and dangers of the emotional and subjective. As mentioned earlier, Belgian Catholic thought (philosophy, theology, and metaphysics) and Belgian Free Thought are both grounded in what Belgians sometimes term these "spontaneously positivist" assumptions. A strong streak of scientism runs through these two apposite intellectual and religio-philosophical traditions. Belgian Catholics, non-Catholics, and anti-Catholics are equally inclined to view the relationship between religion and science as problematic, as much because they consider *all* religions to be inherently affective and nonrational, as because of what they consider to be the dogmatic aspects of Catholicism and the Catholic Church. One of the historic side-effects that this has had on the intellectual atmosphere of the Catholic University of Louvain/Leuven, especially on its faculties of philosophy and theology, is that a great deal of "apologetics concern" has gone into trying to demonstrate systematically that one can be *croyant/gelovig* (a Catholic believer) and scientific too. As one Louvain philosopher commented, with self-mocking Belgian wit: "Of course, it is considered better to show the existence than the non-existence of God. But that can, and should be done rationally!"[32]

It is not only the importance of rationality for Belgians that accounts for the significance that they attach to science. In addition, as the Belgian philosopher of science, Jean Ladrière, has put it, certain "fundamental presuppositions that are not scientific in and of themselves, but that constitute the principles that determine the scientificness of science" are involved.[33] One of the sets of principles underlying science to which Belgians attribute great value is the free and courageous search to overcome human ignorance, prejudice and suffering that it ideally represents. This was one of the primary reasons for which Corneille Heymans, a Belgian Nobel laureate in medicine or physiology, felt that "Belgium should honor Andreas Vesalius . . . . The historian Singer has so justly said of him, 'One of the most illustrious *savants* in medicine whom the world has ever known is the Belgian Andreas Vesalius.'"[34] In an essay of tribute to Vesalius, Heymans described the way in which his "immortal work, *De Humani Corporis Fabrica* established . . . the fundamentals of human anatomy and opened the way to the discovery of the

32. In addition to its rationalism, the philosophical and theological orientation of Louvain/Leuven can be characterized as non-speculative, reinterpretive, Thomistic, exegetical, and interested in balancing off different philosophical and theological approaches.

33. Jean Ladrierè, "La Raison scientifique et la foi," in Claude Bruaire (ed.), *La Confession de la foi chretiénne* (Paris, Fayard (collection Communio), 1977, p. 99. (My translation from the French text).

34. Corneille Heymans, "L'Anatomiste belge Andreas Vesalius," *Le Carabin,* December 1960, 9-16.

precise physiology of numerous organs." He also emphasized the fact that Vesalius was the "first to straightforwardly break with the medical obscurantism of the Middle Ages and to combat the doctrines of Galen," and that the "revolutionary spirit" and the commitment to "free research" that this entailed, involved Vesalius in the "fierce struggle" that so many scientist-innovators have known.[35] Through his portrait of Vesalius, Heymans expressed patriotic pride in the "Belgian-ness of Vesalius' " [Brussels/*Brabancon*] origins and of his "spirit." At the same time, the portrait implicitly presented Belgium as one of the societal communities where Vesalius had to "combat" the forces of incomprehension and dogmatism.[36]

In an historic speech that he made in 1921 (on the occasion of the 120th anniversary of the establishment of Cockerill, the great metallurgy company of Belgium) King Albert of the Belgians expressed similar sentiments about the moral as well as the industrial and commercial implications of science and about the "veritable crisis of scientific institutions and laboratories" that existed in the country at that time. The symbolic significance of the speech derived in part from the fact that it was associated with the beginning of Belgium's recovery from World War I. But its collective-conscience import does not seem to have been confined to that post-war period; for it is a speech that continues to be invoked and quoted to this day.

> In spite of its narrow frontiers and its resources reduced to coal, the courage, the spirit of initiative of Belgians, and a regime of liberties more extensive than in any other country . . . have worked wonders up to now . . . . [But] modern science opens new and almost infinite perspectives on technique . . . . Our public does not sufficiently understand that pure science is the indispensable condition for applied science, and that nations that neglect science and scientists are destined for decadence. Substantial and sustained efforts, and multiple efforts are necessary, if we want—and we must want it—to maintain our rank and our reputation. In our time, what does not move forward moves backward.[37]

There is still another nonscientific aspect of science that has deep positive meaning for Belgians: the dimension that confers upon science what Ladrière

35. *Ibid.*

36. It is possible that in this aspect of his portrait of Vesalius and his career, Corneille Heymans is implicitly referring to some of the difficult "combats" he himself had to fight in his own scientific career—especially the accusation of being a collaborator with the Germans to which he became subject during the occupation of Belgium at the inception of World War II, just after he had been awarded the Nobel Prize in Medicine or Physiology (an accusation of which he was eventually acquitted).

37. Quoted in Jacques Willequet, "Le Roi Albert et la science," *F.N.R.S. 1928-1978* (Bruxelles, Fonds national de la Recherche scientifique, 1978), p. 18.

has called its "profound existential significance."[38] This dimension was the focus of the address that Albert Claude, a recent Belgian Nobel laureate, gave when he received the prize in medicine or physiology.[39]

> We have entered the cell, the mansion of our birth . . . . It is life itself, and our true and distant ancestor . . . . In the course of the past 30 or 40 years, we have learned to appreciate the complexity and perfection of the cellular mechanisms, miniaturized to the utmost at the molecular level, which reveal within the cell an unparalleled knowledge of the laws of physics and chemistry . . . .
>
> In addition, we know also that the cell has a memory of its past, certainly in the case of the egg cell, and foresight of the future, together with precise and detailed patterns for differentiation and growth, a knowledge of what is materialized in the process of reproduction and the development of all beings from bacteria to plants, beasts, or man. It is this cell which plans and composes all organisms, and which transmits to them its defects and potentialities. Man, like other organisms, is so perfectly coordinated that he may easily forget, whether awake or asleep, that he is a colony of cells in action, and that it is the cells which achieve, through him, what he has the illusion of accomplishing himself. It is the cells which create and maintain in us, during the span of our lives, our will to survive, to search and experiment, and to struggle . . . .
>
> I am afraid that in this description of the cell, based on experimental facts, I may be accused of reintroducing a vitalistic and teleological concept that the rationalism and the scientific materialism of the 19th and early 20th centuries banished from our literature and our scientific thinking.
>
> Of course, we know the laws of trial and error, of large numbers and probabilities. We know that these laws are part of the mathematical and mechanical fabric of the universe, and that they are also at play in biological processes. But, in the name of the experimental method and out of our poor knowledge, are we really entitled to claim that everything happens by chance, to the exclusion of all other possibilities? . . . .
>
> Life, this anti-entropy, ceaselessly reloaded with energy, is a climbing force toward order among chaos, toward light among the darkness of the indefinite, toward the mystic dream of love, between the fire which devours itself and the silence of the cold . . . .

In his account of what man has learned through entering the cell, Albert Claude has evoked many of the images, symbols, values, beliefs and questions with which Belgians are continually preoccupied and that throughout the first section of this paper I have presented as part of their pervasively religious cosmic view. At the end of his speech, Claude expressed the most transcendent aspects of Belgians' "vision of our universe, and the image we make of ourselves":[40] their mystic quest for meaning, growth, lucidity and

38. Jean Ladrière, "La Raison scientifique et la foi," p. 107.

39. Albert Claude, "The Coming of Age of the Cell," *Science,* CLXXXIX (August 8, 1975), 433-435.

40. *Ibid.,* p. 435.

love. It is their "intense longing" for this "other dimension of reality"[41]—a cultural as well as a personal yearning—that Belgians are least likely to call religious, and are most likely to deny.

THE BELGIAN VIEW

When Belgians assert that religion is no longer important in their country, they are usually thinking primarily of certain traditional, Catholic forms of religious practice and behavior that have progressively and significantly changed over the course of the past ten to fifteen years.

Attendance at Sunday Mass has markedly decreased. For example, a survey made of the percentage of the Belgian population between five and sixty-nine years of age who attended Mass on an "ordinary" Sunday (the third Sunday in October) shows the following, progressively downward trend.[42]

	%
1964	44.7
1965	43.9
1966	43.4
1967	42.9
1968	41.8
1969	39.6
1970	37.6
1971	35.6
1972	34.2
1973	32.6

Even among those who regularly attend Mass, very few persons now go to confession and those who do are likely to be over fifty years of age. Baptisms and religious marriages have also declined. Whereas in 1967 the ratio of baptisms to births was 93.6 percent, by 1973 it had dropped to 89.2 percent, and in that same time period, the proportion of church to civil marriages decreased from 86.1 percent to 81.8 percent.[43] Since 1960, the number of young people between the ages of 18 and 30 who live together without being married or before being married, has significantly increased. The use of birth control—especially the pill—has become so extensive that Belgium now has one of the lowest birth rates in Europe (12.58 in 1974, as compared with 15.19

41. Excerpted from a personal interview with a Belgian expert on religion.

42. Jan Kerkhofs, *Morgen Is Er Al: Blauwdruk Voor Een Alternatieve Kerk in Vlaanderen* (Tielt, Lannoo, 1976), p. 17 (Table I).

43. *Ibid.*, p. 18 (Tables 2 and 3).

in 1967).[44] A church-acknowledged "crisis of religious vocations" has developed to the point where the numbers of deaths, and of decisions being taken to leave religious life that are now occurring in communities of priests, brothers and sisters dramatically outweigh the numbers of men and women who are entering the priesthood, brotherhood and sisterhood. Thus, in 1977, as many as 595 deaths occurred among Belgian priests, brothers and sisters; a total of 104 priests, brothers and sisters decided to re-enter lay life; and there were only twenty-seven men and women in the entire country who were in the early, novice stage of their religious training and commitment to become priests, brothers, or nuns.[45]

Not all Belgians are able to cite such statistics; but most are keenly aware of these changing patterns in the family, neighborhood, and work settings of which they are part. There is also widespread recognition of the fact that these patterns are especially prominent in milieux of the young and of the so-called "new middle class" and "new intellectuals," where the Church is having notable difficulty reaching its members through customary means.[46] Belgians are highly impressed by these trends—both because they are traditionally inclined to define religion and to gauge religiosity in terms of such practice-and-behavior indicators; and because these new developments run counter to the active and extensive participation in the life of the institutional Church, and the high level of conformity to its prescriptions and proscriptions that have long been characteristic of the Belgian population.

Although a diminishing proportion of Belgians are baptized, marry religiously, desist from using contraceptives, attend Mass regularly, go to confession, and enter and stay in religious life, their Catholicism or non-Catholicism, Belgians concede, is still a primary criterion of the so-called *famille spirituelle* (spiritual family) or *verzuiling* (pillar, column) to which they belong in the society. Writing about this phenomenon, its persistence and resiliency, Belgian sociologists have described it in the following way:[47]

> Belgium is a society characterized by pillarization. If pillarization were to be defined as the organization of all kinds of social functions and activities on a *religious* basis (as is the case for Dutch society, in the analysis of which the

44. Jan Kerkhofs, *Morgen Is Er Al,* p. 22 (Table 6).

45. *Informissi Bruxelles,* August 1978, I.

46. See K. Dobbelaere and J. Billiet, "Community Formation and the Church," in M. Caudron (ed.), *Faith and Society* (Gembloux, J. Duculot, Bibliotheca Ephemeridum Theologicarum Lovaniensium XLVII, 1978), p. 228; also "Roman Catholic Church and Europe: Some Aspects," *Pro Mundi Vita Bulletin,* LXXIII (July-August 1978), p. 13.

47. K. Dobbelaere, J. Billiet and R. Creyf, "Secularization and Pillarization: A Social Problem Approach," in Joachim Matthes, Bryan R. Wilson, *et al.* (eds.) *The Annual Review of the Social Sciences of Religion,* Vol. II (The Hague, Mouton, 1978), p. 101.

> concept of pillarization was originally deployed), there is only one pillar in Belgium: that of the Catholics. It embraces the majority of schools, hospitals, youth movements, newspapers, libraries, etc. It also has a sick fund, a trade union and a political party—the *Christelijke Volkspartij*—CVP (Christian People's Party.) Although since 1945 this party has been officially non-denominational, it continues to play a central role in organized Catholicism. The two other traditional political parties, however, have developed similar structures, so we can readily identify both a "socialist" and a "liberal" pillar as well. In other words, in Belgium, polarization characterizes the institutionalization of opposing religious and ideological systems, in which the political parties play a central role.

Belgians recognize the fact that the Catholic "spiritual family" with its "pillar association" continues to be a central axis of organization, orientation, and identification in their society. Yet many are strongly inclined to believe that it has "lost" or "abandoned" its "religious and philosophical content."[48] In their view, it has become a socio-cultural community[49] whose links with the Catholic Church, religious practice, and doctrine are so loose and tenuous that there is a question of how real and Christian they are. The processes of desacralization and of secularization have gone so far, they contend, that all that remains that could be called Catholic, or even Christian, in institutions such as the Catholic school, university, hospital, political party, or voluntary association, is the emphasis placed on certain "human values" such as solidarity, compassion, and *Gemeinschaftlichkeit*.[50] Christianity is described as "reduced" to a particular set of values and "ideology."[51]

Belgians' propensity to interpret these developments as signs that what is authentically and deeply Catholic, Christian, and religious is "weakening," "crumbling," or "disappearing" (to invoke some of the phrases they use) stems partly from their tendency to regard secularization more as a process that erodes religion and runs counter to it, than as one that can transform and expand the ways in which religion is expressed. In turn, this is not only related to the inclination of many Belgians to equate religion and religiosity with certain traditional, Catholic forms of religious practice, but also to the historical association that Belgians make between the significant influence and vigorous impact of religion in their society, and a highly militant, actively organized stance on the part of the Church with regard to what are considered

48. Dobbelaere, Billiet and Creyf, "Secularization and Pillarization," p. 107.

49. J. Billiet and K. Dobbelaere, *Godsdienst in Vlaanderen, op. cit., passim.*

50. Dobbelaere, Billiet and Creyf, "Secularization and Pillarization," *op. cit.*, p. 97 and *passim.*

51. *Ibid.*

to be primary institutions and issues. None is more symbolic in this respect than "The School," and what Belgians call the "War" that was waged around it. Whether particular Belgians approved of the school war or not, and whichever side they were on in the confrontations that were a part of it, so long as the Belgian Catholic Church had a quasi-monopoly of the national educational system, or was engaged in conflict and combat with Liberal, Social, and Free Mason groups over the maintenance of such a monopoly, all sectors of the population were convinced that the Church and religion were important and powerful forces in the society. The so-called School Pact of 1958 ended and resolved what were, in fact, two successive "school wars" in Belgium's history (in the late 1870s, and again, in the late 1950s), through the recognition and implementation of the principle that parents have the right to exercise free choice in deciding which kind of school—Catholic or State—they want their children to attend. Most Belgians would define the degree of pacification and consensus, and the kind of freedom and equality that the School Pact entailed, as a religious and moral, as well as a political, legal and ideological achievement. But there is also a sense in which the Pact represents for Belgians one of the national events that diminished the importance of religion in their country. In their logic, resolving the school question not only ended the Church's educational monopoly; it also reduced the intensity and saliency of religious and philosophical conflict in the society; and in so doing, it lessened the significance of religion in Belgian national life.

There are at least three other national developments that Belgians associate with the decline of religion in their society: (1) The fact that the Free Thought/Free Mason "family/pillar" seems to have undergone an evolution paralleling that of the Catholic Church, which has made it less doctrinaire, subversive, and pugilistic in its orientation to the Church than in the past, and less preoccupied with the influence of Free Thought-versus-Catholicism as a societal issue. (2) The end of the Belgian colonial era in Central Africa: although the granting of independence to the Belgian Congo, Burundi, and Rwanda in the 1960s did not entail a massive withdrawal or exodus of Belgian Catholic missionary personnel from these countries, for many Belgians, 1960 signified the "beginning of the end," not only of the missions, but of missionizing in Africa—by the (Free Mason) Lodge, as well as by the Church. In this sense, the loss of their colony and the retreat of religion and religio-ideological issues, are linked in the minds of Belgians. (3) The fact that, since the late 1960s, Flanders and the Flemish part of the Belgian population have been exhibiting the same patterns of decline in religious practice, declericalization and secularization that occurred in Walloonie in an earlier period. This is a trend that has not only spread rapidly but has been accompanied by vociferous questioning of the Church, its organizations, clergy, doctrine, and authority, particularly by young adults, intellectuals, and the upwardly mobile members of what has been called the new "populist bourgeoisie" in Flanders. Because all subgroups of the Belgian population have always considered Flanders to be the center and the stronghold of Catholic practice and faith in the country, these changes are interpreted as one of the most absolute kinds of evidence that religion has finally ceased to be important in Belgium. Here again, Belgians have characteristically attached great significance to certain traditional forms of Catholic practice, action, and behavior.

There is one other major indicator that Belgians are inclined to use when they allege that religion is no longer important in Belgium. These are the characteristic statements about religion that fellow-Belgians repeatedly make—spontaneously or, more often, when questioned on this subject. By and large, when a Belgian person contends, for example, that "religion has nothing to do any more with X or Y or Z," it is likely to be taken at face value by other Belgians who consider it to be objectively and authoritatively true. Rarely does anyone wonder or ask *why* the person who is making such an assertion has this opinion, or what may have led him (her) to verbalize this conviction in this way, in this context, and at this time. Nor is much consideration given to how the attitudes and behavior of Belgian interlocutors or listeners might be influencing such testimony.

A prototypical example of this tendency to rely so heavily and literally on verbal declarations about religion can be found in a recently published study of Gheel, the world-renowned community in Belgium where, for centuries, mentally ill persons have lived and worked with "normal," largely rural families who have cared for them.[52] As the subtitle of the French language edition of this monograph suggests *(Gheel et sa thérapie séculaire)*, one of the author's main theses is that although the foster family and therapeutic community tradition of Gheel has roots in medieval Catholicism, and in the pilgrimages that were made to this area from the year 1250 on to invoke the healing intervention of Saint Dymphna, the fact that there are Gheel families today who continue to care for mentally ill persons in their homes "no longer has anything heroic about it or anything in common with Christian charity."[53] "We conclude [Eugeen Roosens, the anthropologist-author goes on to say] that economic profit, in the largest sense of the term, is an important aspect

52. Eugeen Roosens, *Des fous dans la ville? Geel et sa thérapie séculaire*. Translated from Dutch by Maddy Buysse and Jacques Dumont, in collaboration with the author (Paris, Presses universitaires de France/Perspectives Critiques, 1979). The Dutch language version, *Gheel, Een Unicum in de Psychiatrie,* was published in 1977 (Antwerp/Amsterdam, Uitgeverij de Nederlandsche Boekhandel).

53. Roosens, *Des fous dans la ville?,* p. 40.

of the motivation [of such families] and perhaps even the only decisive reason."[54]

Roosens carefully avoids basing his contention that the family care system in Gheel has nothing to do with religion or religious motivation, exclusively on verbal statements made by Gheel residents in formal interviews. He attributes greater validity and importance to the spontaneous talking that men, women, and children of this community do as they engage in their daily round of activities. Nevertheless, the core of his argument rests on a very literal, categorical interpretation of what people say. The inhabitants of Gheel repeatedly declare that the fact that they take mentally ill persons into their homes and families is not a matter of Christian charity, compassion or high-mindedness, but rather is motivated by the desire "to put a franc aside." Roosens concludes that this is so because the people say that it is. In his view, to use the local Gheel expression, "a franc is a franc," and it cannot be, or mean anything else.

The other major kind of data that Roosens uses to support his argument is what might be called churchly behavior: what the parish priests do and do not do, as well as what they say and do not say; what happens at Mass; what takes place in various Catholic associations, and the like. In contrast to this, the "special atmosphere"[55] of Gheel that Roosens identifies, its "moral code," its collective beliefs in the dignity and worth of "every patient as a human being," its "respect for the human condition of the 'boarder' or the 'sick person.'" and the "system" through which it transmits and enforces them, are considered by him to be "affective" and "humanitarian" but to have no manifest or latent relationship to religion.

There is a "he doth protest too much," and a self-confirming quality to Roosens' analysis that are neither inherently nor generally Belgian in nature. But in other respects, partly because he has a special (and it would appear, strongly-felt) interest in demonstrating through what he calls a "reasoned approach"[56] that "the system of Gheel today . . . no longer has anything to do with the church,"[57] or with religion, his presentation is an exaggerated version of the way that many Belgians think about the presence/absence and the importance/nonimportance of religion in various contexts of their society. Above all, in magnified form, Roosens' approach exemplifies what I have described elsewhere as some of the deepest, most pervasive Belgian culture patterns:[58]

54. *Ibid.*, p. 50.
55. *Ibid.*, p. 54.
56. *Ibid.*, pp. 29-37.
57. *Ibid.*, p. 22.
58. Fox, "Why Belgium?," *op. cit.*, pp. 224-225.

> [There is] a strong tradition of positivism in Belgian intellectual life (that at times borders on scientism) . . . . What it has *not* encouraged is the systematic analysis of feelings, beliefs, values and symbols, of nonrational aspects of social life or of latent structures and processes more generally . . . .
>
> But the reluctance to probe too deeply into questions that directly concern feelings, beliefs and values, the symbolic and that which lies below the surface of social and psychic life, is not purely an outgrowth of positivism and scientism . . . . These reservations and apprehensions are rooted in the kinds of historical experiences and associations that have contributed to the society's pactmaking. The same Belgian apprehension about the society's lacerating conflicts and enmities has also discouraged research and analysis that deal too directly or deeply with its culturodynamic and psychodynamic aspects. There appears to be a high level of latent concern that such inquiries and analyses may exacerbate the destructive and self-destructive conflicts that are prevalent in the social system, or reopen conflicts that have reached some point of settlement and stasis.

Seen in this perspective, the kind of collective denial about their religious motivation in which the people of Gheel engage may be as much a sign that it is present, as that it is absent. What is more, this paradoxical Belgian pattern is reinforced by still another general cultural tendency: that of stating particularly important collective sentiments, values, beliefs, and commitments, negatively rather than positively. An archetypical example of this is the way that Belgians often talk about their country: "It is not really a society"; "it has no culture of its own"; "it has never existed"; "it does not exist"; "it no longer exists." The sources and the implications of these negative affirmations are too complex and far-reaching to discuss here. But it would be culturally erroneous to suppose that they mean precisely what they say and no more than that. For one of Belgium's most distinctive characteristics is that more often than not, both in action and in words, its societal identity and solidarity are expressed negatively. So much is this the case, that it could almost be said that, on the day that Belgians cease insisting that the country does *not* exist, and begin to affirm that it *does,* it will have lost its traditional basis of identity.

AN INTERPRETIVE SYNTHESIS

The juxtaposition of "the sociologist's view" and "the Belgian view" of religion and its significance in Belgium has brought us to a kind of impasse that is historically and culturally familiar to Belgians. Perhaps the best way to resolve it, then, would be to apply core elements of Belgian pactmaking to the question: "Is religion important in Belgium?", and negotiate an answer to it that combines certain elements from each and from both of the two views.

To begin with, as Belgians emphasize, it is clear that over the course of the past twenty years in their country (as in most Western European societies) various traditional forms of Catholic worship, practice, participation, adherence to doctrine, compliance, and commitment have been steadily decreasing. We have already identified numerous of them (attendance at Mass, participation in certain sacraments, membership in various Catholic associations, entry into religious life, etc.). Because this decline is most conspicuous in younger age groups, it is not only likely to continue, but to grow. Furthermore, something like a crisis of authority can be said to exist between Belgian Catholics and the institutional Church over certain issues: notably sexuality, birth control, abortion and other means of terminating pregnancy, cohabitation outside of marriage, and the status and role of women, both in lay life and in the ministry. In Belgium, and particularly in Flanders, anti-clerical sentiments and language are more frequently and widely heard than in the past. On these grounds, in these particular respects, it can justifiably be said, as Belgians do, that the importance of religion in their society has sharply and significantly diminished.

But even within the framework of such Church-circumscribed parameters of religion, the trends are not unilineal. For example, although in Belgium relatively few people go to confession regularly, if at all, there is a marked increase in the number of people who take communion, and who do so without confession. Despite the drop in the church attendance of young adults and in their affiliation with established Catholic organizations, this is precisely the group that, since the 1960s, has become conspicuously involved in new political, community, charismatic, pentecostal, and encounter groups inside the Catholic Church that they also helped to found,[59] and in comparable groups outside the Church, that define themselves as Christian and religious.[60] It is true that only a minority of parents, when asked, give religious reasons for sending their children to a Catholic school; nevertheless, 58 percent of all students in Belgium are enrolled in the Catholic educational system, and as many as 67 percent of the student population in the Flemish region of the country attend Catholic schools. This represents a (modest) rise in the number and proportion of students now receiving their education in Catholic, rather than State institutions. As already indicated, close to 90 percent of the Belgian population is baptized and more than 84 percent are buried religiously. There are still relatively few divorces in Belgium and the

59. For names and descriptions of some of these new groups, see Dobbelaere and Billiet, "Community-Formation and the Church," *op. cit.*, and Billiet and Dobbelaere, *Godsdienst In Vlaanderen, op. cit.*, pp. 23, 38-43, 68, and 93-98.

60. "Roman Catholic Church and Europe," *op. cit.*, p. 13.

national divorce rate is quite low, compared to the rate in other Western European countries, including those that, like Belgium, are predominantly Catholic. What is more, both in Walloon and Flemish Belgium, religious pilgrimages, especially to shrines associated with the Virgin Mary, have greatly increased in recent years.[61]

These data suggest that the diminution of certain traditional forms of religious practice and adherence should not be attributed solely to a progressive loss of religion, loss of interest in religion, and/or alienation from the Church on the part of Belgians. What also seems to be involved is a growing tendency to rely more on individual conscience, and to exercise a greater degree of individual choice in religious practice and participation, to distinguish between religiosity and religious practice, to develop more intimate and affective ways of expressing religious belief and commitment, and to be more critical and ecumenical, and less zealous and militantly evangelical in religious outlook. In certain respects, this "new" Catholicism is less formal, total, and closed, and more selective, personalized, and privatized. It also draws a sharper line between religious and nonreligious domains and issues in individual and social life. One of the consequences of these changes is that some aspects and forms of religious faith, practice, and commitment are less apparent to Belgians than they were in the past. Most Belgians, for example, would be surprised to discover that enrollment in Catholic schools and participation in pilgrimages have risen, and that the majority of Belgians not only are baptized, marry religiously, and are buried with the rites of the Church, but also see to it that their children make their First Communion and are confirmed. Furthermore, if told this is the case (providing that they believed the data cited to be true in the first place), many Belgians would explain away this behavior, characteristically alleging that it had little or nothing to do with religion. The choice of a Catholic school, they would say, is motivated by the desire to give one's children a good education in a setting that maintains high scholastic standards, a tradition of humanism, and more than a modicum of discipline. Baptism, First Communion, confirmation, marriage and burial, they would continue, are "merely" rites of passage: their meaning is largely familial and communal, rather than religious, and social conformity plays a large role in their maintenance. As for the pilgrimages, they would probably

61. The four shrines in Belgium most frequently visited are Beauraing and Banneux in Walloonie, and Scherpenheuvel and Oostakker in Flanders. The most popular pilgrimage that Belgians make outside the country is to Lourdes. Not only in Belgium, but in other European countries as well, such pilgrimages have increased.

For this information on pilgrimages, and for the data in the text above concerning Catholic school enrollment, baptism, burial, and divorce, I am indebted to Jan Kerkhofs, S.J., Secretary General of Pro Mundi Vita (personal communication).

contend these are due to residual pockets of rural piety in the country, and to the increased physical mobility and leisure that Belgians have enjoyed since World War II, due to the advent of the automobile, progressive industrialization, and greater national prosperity. (Belgians would be less likely to point out that owning a car, and having the time and money to take a vacation, do not automatically result in a trip to Lourdes!).

Belgian sociologists who have taken note of these developments have been inclined to interpret them as part of a far-reaching process of secularization. They predict that so long as the spiritual family/pillar structure "is used as a political key in allocating finances for health care, youth care, education, etc., the pillars will continue to maintain themselves in Belgium, even if—ideologically speaking—they have undergone a great change."[62] In their view, a Catholic "socio-cultural community" has survived and will continue to survive, for these reasons. Ultimately, however, they imply, it will be devoid of any relationship to religious belief in Catholic Christianity, or religiously based identification with its message, and its visible church.

It would be presumptuous of me to reject this analysis, or the predictions based on it. However, it seems to me that the changes in Belgian Catholic attitudes and behaviors to which it refers are so mixed in nature—at one and the same time suggesting more, less, and different ways of being Catholic and religious—that a simple conclusion is not warranted. One thing is nevertheless apparent, and here I am in complete agreement with my Belgian colleagues: Belgian Catholicism has changed significantly, and continues to do so. But, unlike them, I would not call these changes primarily "ideological," or make the kind of distinction between "ideological" and "religious" that they do.

This last reflection is related to what is perhaps the most fundamental difference between the perspective of Belgians (sociologists and non-sociologists alike) on religion, and my own. Whereas the Belgian view tends to confine itself to formal, manifest, rational structures and behaviors, explicitly connected with the organization, doctrine, and rites of the Catholic Church, the conception of religion on which I have drawn throughout my discussion is much broader and inclusive. As such it blurs the dichotomy that Belgians tend to make between what is religion and what is not, and it breaks through the boxed-in boundaries that Belgians try to maintain between areas

62. Dobbelaere, Billiet and Creyf, "Secularization and Pillarization," *op. cit.* p. 19.

of the sacred and of the profane.[63] My descriptive analysis of religion in Belgium not only dealt with the dimensions of religion on which Belgians themselves tend to focus, but also with informal, nonrational, unconscious, and latent religious phenomena, outside as well as inside the social system, and the sacred space of the Catholic Church. It included symbols and objects, rituals and performances, feelings and motives, concepts and facts, beliefs and values, and the atmosphere created by "powerful, pervasive, and long-lasting moods."[64] All these elements, I implied, converge systematically, aesthetically, and questingly on what I consider to be the core of religion: the search for transcendent order and meaning in existence, especially in the face of seeming chaos, absurdity, and ephemerality, and of suffering. In turn, I see these as constituent parts of a still larger, religion-infused framework: the way in which a society as an entity—in this case, Belgian society—looks at and relates to the universe: its distinctive world view and cosmic outlook.[65]

Seen from this vantage point, religion in Belgium not only seems important, but also exceptionally pervasive. The economic and political, domestic and everyday life in the country, as well as its art, literature, and science are imprinted with it. Irrespective of the religious sentiments of individual Belgians or of the particularistic social categories to which they belong, the overarching cultural tradition that they share is religiously resonant. That common culture is as Catholic as it is Belgian: not only the "living museums"

63. This kind of dichotomizing and box-making is a fundamental part of all aspects and levels of social organization in Belgium.

I am indebted to Mr. Georges Van den Abeelen, General Advisor to the Fédération des Entreprises de Belgique/Verbond van Belgische Ondernemingen, for pointing out to me that these structural characteristics are so basically and encompassingly Belgian that they have shaped the country's topography in ways that distinguish it from all surrounding territories. Mr. Van den Abeelen provided me with a reproduction of a satellite photograph of a portion of the earth extending from southern Sweden to Nigeria, taken in 1978 by the U.S. Air Force's Defense Meteorological Satellite Program, in which "diamond-shaped Belgium is immediately recognizable by the precise lines of its geometric form." This satellite photo was first published at the end of July 1978 in Thomas A. Croft, "Nighttime Images of the Earth from Space," *Scientific American*, CCXXXIX (1978), 86-96.

64. Clifford Geertz, "Religion as a Cultural System," *op. cit.*, p. 94.

65. My sociological perspective on religion has been significantly influenced by the theoretical and empirical work of Emile Durkheim, Max Weber, Sigmund Freud, and Talcott Parsons; by the monographs of E.E. Evans-Pritchard, A.R. Radcliffe-Brown, and Bronislaw Malinowski; and by the writings of Robert N. Bellah, Willy De Craemer and Clifford Geertz. In addition, my thirty years of experience as a cross-culturally-oriented fieldworker in a number of American, Continental European, and Central African contexts, have shaped my outlook on patterned similarities and differences in the way that religion manifests itself in various social and cultural settings, and contributed to my understanding of the macro-implications of religion—its societal and world-view import.

of church objects and folkloric *fêtes,* but also the meaning of bricks, houses and the family, the relationship to things, to nature, to light, and some of the most basic values of the society, such as courage, solidarity, harmony, compassion and respect for the human condition. "It is an invisible lid over everything": even the existential frustration, anxiety, and protest that suffuses this statement has the ambience of Belgian-ness and Catholic-ness come together.

But if when they speak of religion, Belgians consciously and insistently define it in a more delimited, formal, cognitive, external, orthodox, and doctrinal way, if they deny that there is anything religious about "secular" social values, or the imagery of Belgian art, or even anything religiously Catholic about the country's Catholic universities, or about baptism, first communion, and participation in other church sacraments—then is there any way of reconciling my sociological view and their view of religion, its presence and influence in Belgian society and culture? I believe that there is.

My conception of religion (which has been influenced by certain social science traditions) may be so all-encompassing that it does not easily enable one to identify those aspects of the distinctive and enduring culture of a society that are not historically and integrally associated with its religious orientation and tradition. Here, the Belgian view invites me to make finer and subtler distinctions between religion and non-religion than I have done.

On the other hand, if I allowed myself to be so impressed by the authority of the self-conscious, public statements that Belgians make about religion that I failed to hear what they say about it on less conscious and more private occasions (and also what they do *not* say), or overlooked the fact that, in Belgian culture, denial can be affirmation, inversely expressed, or if I paid insufficient attention to non-verbal behavior and phenomena—then, I would be an incompetent social scientist. What is more, the general rules of sociological inquiry that I followed have special applicability to research on religion in a society like Belgium where, for the historical and cultural reasons I have indicated, there is an indwelling, institutionalized reluctance to talk about beliefs, values, and feelings that might stir up dormant, religious sentiments, conflicts, and questions.

In the end, where does this leave us? In the spirit of Belgian compromise, I offer the following conclusion to the question, "Is religion important in Belgium?": whereas religion may be less diffusely important in Belgium than my analysis has suggested, it is far more important than Belgians say that it is.

Medical Morality is Not Bioethics: Medical Ethics in China and the United States

Renée C. Fox and Judith P. Swazey

Confiants dans les "lumières de la raison naturelle" . . . ils n'ont pas vu qu'ils étaient en présence d'une conception du monde et de modes de pensée fondamentalement différents des leurs et que ces modes de pensée étaient en rapport avec la morale, les attitudes religieuses, l'ordre social et politique des Chinois.[1]

Drawing in part on a medical sociological journey that we made to the People's Republic of China in 1981, this paper examines what the Chinese call "medical morality": the form currently taken by medical ethical interest

1. Description of the problems that the first Jesuit and Franciscan missionaries to China, in the late fifteenth and early sixteenth centuries, had in understanding and analyzing the Chinese way of thought—and their own thought in relation to it (see Gernet, 1982, p. 274).

An earlier version of this essay was presented by Renée C. Fox as the Fae Golden Kass Lecture at Harvard Medical School and Radcliffe College, February 22, 1983. The authors are indebted to Judith Berling and David Smith, Indiana University; James Gustafson, University of Chicago; and Willy De Craemer, Setha Low, and Nathan Sivin, University of Pennsylvania, for their critical reading of the manuscript.

and activity in their society. But our reason for having explored and written about medical morality is not confined to things Chinese. Another primary goal has been to obtain some cultural perspective on what we in the United States term "bioethics." Bioethics is the neologism coined in this country in the 1960s to refer to the rise of professional and public interest in moral, social, and religious issues connected with the "new biology" and medicine and to the emergence of an interdisciplinary field of inquiry and action concerned with these issues. Medical morality not only exemplifies the at-once ancient and contemporaneous "Chinese-ness" of Chinese medical ethics. Seen in a comparative framework, it also helps to illuminate what is characteristically Western about "our" bioethics and highlights some of the ways that it is specifically American.

Our title—"Medical Morality is Not Bioethics"—is a rather mischievous one. It was provoked by an article, "Bioethics in the People's Republic of China," that we read before we went to China in 1981 and reread upon our return (Engelhardt, 1980). It is a traveller's report written by a professor of the philosophy of medicine on behalf of a group of prominent bioethicists (mainly associated with the Kennedy Institute of Ethics, Georgetown University) who made a two-week-long trip to China in 1979. In his report, H. Tristram Engelhardt attributes solely to Maoism-Leninism-Marxism what he loosely terms the "moral viewpoint" of the Chinese scientists, professionals, and intellectuals with whom he and his companions discussed questions of medical ethics. No allusion is made to possible Confucian, Taoist, or Buddhist origins of what the Chinese define as ethical matters or of how they think about them. Instead, Engelhardt expresses puzzlement over what he experienced as the "resistance" of his Chinese interlocutors to "intellectually justifying" their moral outlook within the framework that he considers properly and logically philosophical.

In this regard, Engelhardt's reaction resembles that of the first Christian missionaries who lived and worked in China in the late sixteenth and early seventeenth centuries, and who assumed that the Chinese "do not have logic." Even the most culturally learned and responsive of the Jesuit missionaries, Father Matteo Ricci, did not fully recognize that his Scholastic notion of Reason was not universal or that the Chinese also reasoned systematically within their own internally consistent modes of thought (Gernet, 1982, 327, passim).

Engelhardt's failure to discern the pattern and logic of today's Chinese thought is related to the inadvertent ethnocentricity of the implicit premises on which his article rests. Bioethics, particularly its philosophical aspects, is viewed as largely *a*cultural and *trans*cultural in nature. The author does not seem to appreciate the extent to which the way that he and his fellow voyagers reason about ethics is imprinted with Western and American cultural influences. Furthermore, he, his colleagues, and the editors of the *Hastings Center Report* who allowed him to retain the title of his article took it for granted that bioethics is a sufficiently neutral and universalistic term for it to be applied to medical morality in China or, for that matter, to medical ethical concern in whatever society or form it may now occur.

This kind of cultural myopia disturbs us. Such myopia is not confined to those occasions when American bioethicists venture forth to other lands. Rather, it is a more widespread characteristic of the field of bioethics, one that generally manifests itself in the form of systematic inattention to the social and cultural sources and implications of its own thought.

We consider this cultural nearsightedness, with its implied distortion of vision, to be serious because, from a sociological viewpoint, bioethics is not just bioethics. What we mean by this is that, using biology and medicine as a metaphorical language and a symbolic medium, bioethics deals in public spheres and in more private domains with nothing less than beliefs, values, and norms that are basic to our society, its cultural tradition, and its collective conscience. If this is indeed the case, we have reason to be concerned when bioethicists ignore or misperceive the social and cultural matrices of their ideas.

INTRODUCTION TO CHINESE MEDICAL MORALITY

In the summer of 1981, we spent six weeks doing medical sociology fieldwork in the People's Republic of China, primarily in the city of Tianjin. Our trip was arranged by the program of scientific exchanges created by the American Association for the Advancement of Science in Washington, D.C., and the China Association of Science and Technology (CAST) in Beijing. The focal point of our work was a mini-ethnographic study of a profoundly Chinese urban hospital that is energetically committed to modern scientific and technological medicine. (With characteristically ironic but affectionate wit, the nurses and physicians of Tianjin First Central Hospital, where we did our research, continually referred to us as "the 'Team of Two,' rather than the 'Gang of Four.' ")

The hospital that our Chinese colleagues chose as the base for our research and teaching proved to be the center of medical modernization that we had asked to study—and more. It contained the only free-standing Critical Care Unit in China (Fox and Swazey, 1982), conducted hemodialysis for acute renal failure, included a bioengineering-oriented absorbent artificial kidney group, and had made some forays into the transplantation of human organs.

It was also highly active in matters pertaining to our work in medical ethics—an interest which we had not thought of pursuing in a Chinese setting.

In retrospect, it seems far from accidental that the hospital we were sent to turned out to be as notable for its leadership in what the Chinese term medical morality as in the "fourth modernization" of (medical) science and technology. We soon learned that the First Central Hospital's intensive involvement in medical ethics was partly due to the influence of its vice-director, Madame She Yun-zhu, a remarkable seventy-five-year-old woman who is one of the pioneers of modern nursing in China. "Grandmother-Nurse," as she is respectfully and fondly called, personifies the indissoluble bond that she believes exists between the observance of certain ethical principles, virtues, and rules, and the achievement of greater technical excellence, humanity, and commitment to service, in nursing and in medicine.

But even without the dynamic presence of Madame She, we probably would have been introduced to medical morality as representatives of what our Chinese colleagues conceived to be medical sociology and expected from it—albeit in a somewhat more tentatively conceptualized and less vigorously uplifting way. For, in a number of medical and nursing schools that we visited or about which we were told, first steps were being taken to develop courses that were alternately called "Medical Sociology," "Medical Psychology," and/or "Medicine, Morals, and Society." As the last course title suggests, in China, medical sociology and medical ethics are not only interrelated—they are virtually synonymous. Social relationships and a conception of what one of our hosts termed "the individual as a social community" are at the heart of what the Chinese have always defined as ethics. And ethics is the center of the Chinese world view—its very core and essence in Chinese society today as it has been for thousands of years. What is more, participant observation—which the Chinese recognized as a guiding principle as well as a major technique of our research—is also inherent to their own inductive, humanistic approach to ethics. For them, thinking in an entirely abstract or speculative way about moral or social questions runs the risk of what Chinese scholars historically have called "playing with emptiness." What seems to them more "practical" and "right," as well as comfortably familiar, is to work from everyday, empirically observable human reality, focusing particularly on the relationship between specific, identifiable persons, and on their "lived-in," reciprocal existence.

It was both surprising and satisfying to learn in a first-hand way that, despite the thousands of geographical miles and historical years that separate Chinese society and our own, and their very different cosmic outlooks, these aspects of Chinese thought are compatible with the conceptual and methodological framework in which we observe, analyze, interpret, and evaluate as sociologists. It was also unsettling to feel that (although cross-cultural resemblances can be very deceiving) in these particular respects, we might have more in common with Chinese than with many American colleagues in medical ethics. For, as we will subsequently show, it is the individual, seen as an autonomous, self-determining entity rather than in relationship to significant others, that is the starting point and the foundation stone of American bioethics. Herein lie some of the deepest intellectual and philosophical difficulties that we have experienced as two of the relatively few social scientists who have been professionally associated with bioethics since its inception.

THE COMPONENTS OF MEDICAL MORALITY

Medical morality is "the kind of morality that doctors and nurses should have." It is concerned with three sets of interconnected goals and with the obligation of "medical workers," individually and collectively, to do everything possible, "sparing no effort," to attain these goals. Repairing the moral and intellectual as well as the economic and political damage of the Cultural Revolution (1966-1976) is one of the primary objectives of medical morality. Supreme importance is given to restoring the basic "order" that was "smashed" by the Cultural Revolution (and its personification in the Gang of Four): the "task of straightening things out in every field of [medical] work" that must be accomplished, especially the reteaching of "what is right and wrong." A second basic aim of medical morality is to "scale the heights" of modern medicine and thereby achieve the "golden-dream" benefits that come from applying advanced science and technology to problems of health, illness, and the care of patients. This is the medical facet of the national policy of "Four Modernizations" (agriculture, industry, defense, science and technology) that currently prevails in China. In turn, "order" and "modernization" are part of the third general goal of medical morality: the dynamic and creative continuation of the "Great Liberation," the revolution that established the People's Republic of China in 1949.

As this implies, medical morality fits into a larger societal frame. "Work ethics" and "civic virtues" and their relationship to the integrity and development of the whole society are constantly stressed, ideologically and politically, in every sphere of Chinese life. Nationwide campaigns like the civic virtues month and the *Wujiang Simei* ("Five Efforts" and "Four Beauties") movement have been organized around these themes. Workers of all kinds are continually reminded that they are expected to pay attention to morality. Medical workers are among those who have special ethical responsibilities because their job is to care for patients, "relieve them from pain," help them to recover from their illnesses, and "save them from death." Leading nurses and doctors, in particular, are exhorted to demonstrate "the highest level of ethics" in their own behavior—to be "the first to observe the principles and disciplines" entailed—and thereby to set an example that is "a silent order" to those who work with them.

Medical morality is rooted in a conception of the individual in relation to statuses and roles, enmeshed in the network of human relationships that this involves. In this conception, the individual steadfastly strives to meet his responsibilities and carry out his duties ever more totally and perfectly, guided by certain principles, inspired by particular maxims and exemplars, and in conformity with concrete rules. At the vital center of this morality is the continuous effort that each person is expected to make to perfect this at-once individual and social self through relationships to significant others and the fulfillment of obligations to these persons. The relationships encompassed by medical morality include those of physicians, nurses, other medical workers, and hospital administrators with each other and with patients and their families. It also concerns the relations between the unit or *danwei* (Henderson, 1982) to which medical workers belong and the local bureaucrats and Communist party officials associated with their professional activities. The bedrock and point of departure of medical morality lie in the quality of these human relationships: in how correct, respectful, harmonious, complementary, and reciprocal they are. Here, for example, is the way that Madame She Yun-zhu expresses some of these "relationship" aspects of medical morality in the set of "Requirements for Training Quality Nursing" that she drafted: "Do a good job in building close relationships among physicians, nurses, and patients. Be good at uniting your colleagues to work together. Unite not only those who share your point of view, but particularly those who have different opinions from you . . . . Appoint people on their merits. Treat colleagues equally." In this series of ordered and interconnected relationships that medicine entails (as Madame She goes on to articulate), it is the relations to the patient that have the highest moral status and importance: "Serve the patient wholeheartedly . . . . Put the interests of the patient first all the time . . . . Try to build deep proletarian affection with the patient. Think what the patient thinks, be as eager as the patient is, and be as worried as the patient feels . . . . We should treat our patients as our sisters and brothers . . . . Treat the patient even better than your relatives."

The development and enactment of good moral character, attitudes, and thoughts, and of exemplary professional conduct, are embedded in this skein of relationships and contingent on the way they are handled by medical workers. Scientific knowledge and technical skill are considered to be important ethical as well as intellectual components of excellent medicine. They are morally mandatory. But medical morality and its attainment require more. In the words of Dr. Wang Chin-ta (director of the Critical Care Unit of Tianjin First Central Hospital): "No matter how good doctors and nurses are technically, if they do not have noble thinking, they cannot serve the patient, the people, and the country."

"Noble thinking" is an epigrammatic way of referring to the moral virtues that good medical professionals are ideally expected to demonstrate in their work and work relations. Foremost among these medically relevant virtues are the following:[2]

Humanity, compassion, kindness, helpfulness to others;
Trust in others;
A spirit of self-sacrifice;
A high sense of responsibility;
A good sense of discipline, good order;
Hard, conscientious work that is also systematic, careful, precise, punctual, and prudent;
Devotion, dynamic commitment;
Courage to think, act, innovate, blaze new trails, overcome difficulties;
Alertness, high spirits, optimism, a positive attitude;
Patience;
Modesty;
Self-control, a sense of balance and equilibrium;
Politeness, good manners, proper behavior;
Cleanliness, tidiness, good hygiene, keeping healthy;
Lucidity, clarity, intelligence, wisdom;
Honesty, integrity;
Self-knowledge, self-examination, self-criticism, self-cultivation, self-improvement;
Frankness about difficulties, limitation, shortcomings, and mistakes—admitting them, and working to overcome them.

Seen as a whole, these virtues have a number of patterned characteristics. They are relatively concrete ethical qualities, close to the empirical reality of medical practice and patient care. They are formulated as responsibilities and duties, generally stated as positive "musts" and "can do's," rather than as

2. This list of virtues was compiled from the first-hand data we collected through our participant observation, interviewing, and analysis of relevant documents in China, particularly in Tianjin and at the First Central Hospital. The language used is as close to the original as possible—to the Chinese or the English used by our informants and respondents.

admonitory "must nots" and "do nots." They are punctuated by aphorisms and proverb-like political slogans. A "we shall overcome" moralistic optimism pervades the outlook that they represent. But seen in closer detail, the dynamic nature of these moral virtues is a product of the balancing and blending of the active and passive, traditional and innovative, intellectual and emotional, personal and interpersonal, individual and collective qualities that their fulfillment requires. They are as neo-Confucian as they are Maoist, and more of both than they are Marxist or Leninist.

Particular individuals are singled out because they personify the virtues of medical morality. They are considered to be models whose "example will inspire and encourage others to follow them." At Tianjin First Central Hospital and in the Chinese nursing profession at large, Madame She—"Grandmother-Nurse"— is considered to be such a model. She is esteemed for her pioneering contribution to the establishment and development of modern nursing in China and its rehabilitation after the Cultural Revolution; for her role as "Teacher" (with the ethical as well as intellectual connotations that the term carries in Chinese); and for her unwavering, lifelong commitment to nursing and to improving its quality (even when, at age sixty-two, during the Cultural Revolution, she was sent to the countryside for nine years of "reeducation"). Other valued qualities are her hard, "independent and loyal work"; the "strict demands" she makes on herself and her staff, and her "strict sense of responsibility"; and her "concern for the pain and suffering of patients." Madame She is also recognized for her "obedience to rules and regulations" while "breaking the traditional frame of mind" sufficiently to generate "new ideas"; for her energy and optimism, courage and resiliency; and for her capacity for self-criticism and self-improvement.

One of Madame She's closest younger colleagues, Meng Bao-zhen, the hospital's vice-director of nursing, is another such morally emblematic figure. She is often called "*Doctor* Meng" by the nurses and physicians with whom she works, because during the Cultural Revolution she became a physician and practiced medicine in Inner Mongolia for nine years. Meng was chosen as "Model Worker" of her province in 1974, for which she was awarded a medal and a special diploma by the Committee of Inner Mongolia. In 1979, she was called back to Tianjin and First Central Hospital to help "reconstruct" its nursing. She willingly rebecame a nurse to do so, and it is for this, as much as for her self-sacrificing ardor and "revolutionary humanism" in Inner Mongolia, that she is seen as outstandingly virtuous.

But in keeping with the virtues of modesty, candid self-criticism, and generosity toward others, both Grandmother-Nurse She and Nurse-Doctor Meng insist that they "have not done so much in the First Central Hospital . . . only what our duty required us to do." They cite still another colleague,

Guan Xiao-ying, the director of nursing, as a person whose heroic medical morality surpasses their own (letter from Madame She to the authors; 27 March, 1982):

> It has been only more than three years since we came back from the countryside. We couldn't do much work in such a short period of time. Most work was done by Guan Xiao-ying, the director of the nursing department, and nine middle-aged supervisors who have both ability and political integrity, and thirty-four head nurses. They led over three hundred nurses fulfilling the task of straightening things out in every field of work.
>
> I want to say something about Guan Xiao-ying. She is 53 years old and suffers from coronary disease. She is rich in clinical experience in [a] career of thirty years. She loves her work and usually works 12 hours a day. Really, she takes the hospital as her own home, even pays more attention to her work than to her family. During the period when her husband suffered from cancer, we could still find her working in her post. Compared with her, we still fall far behind.

In the particular settings where nurses, physicians, and their co-workers carry out their medical duties, the principles and virtues of medical morality are translated into specific sets of rules. The ethical importance of these rules is aesthetically expressed through the high quality of their calligraphy, the care with which they are framed, and the prominence with which they are displayed. Here, for example, are the rules of the Critical Care Unit of Tianjin First Central Hospital. Composed by the members of the unit out of their shared experiences, they are written in elegant black script under the title, "Regulations of the Critical Care Unit," which is written in contrasting red ink. Enclosed in an ornate green frame, they hang alone on a wall adjacent to the unit's doorway. The nine sets of regulations are explicit and detailed statements of the unit's work norms, and also of the problematic attitudes and behaviors—the persistent "shortcomings" at work—that have been identified as needing improvement:

1. Patients in this room need critical care. When they are better, they should be transferred to the recovery ward.
2. Care should be given to these patients day and night.
3. The work should be done strictly by the medical workers. They should cooperate. In these ways, they will be able to serve the people wholeheartedly.
4. Medical workers must check the equipment, drugs, and machines on every shift, e.g., ventilator, EKG, tracheal tubes, IV, catheters, abdominal dialyzer, suction, extension cord. Everything must be kept in its place. Do not lend things out.
5. Adhere strictly to regulations. Visiting doctors should make rounds twice a

day, in the morning and in the afternoon. Doctors on duty should carefully observe the patients. They should make careful observations at the bedside in order to discover any developments, and be prepared to give emergency treatment if necessary.

6. The staff on one shift should tell the staff on the next shift about any changes that have taken place with the patients. Explain things clearly for continuing with the next shift.
7. For emergency treatment, use Western and Chinese medicine together. There are four principles to follow in administering Chinese medicine—four things that must be done in time:
   a. Prescription;
   b. Fetching of drugs;
   c. Cooking of prescription;
   d. Administering of prescription.
8. Check regulations, and carry them out strictly, in time. Carry out the doctor's orders, to do well and avoid complications.
9. Perform a case history in time.

The First Central Hospital's various sets of rules, regulations, and requirements are now being organized into a centralized system of total quality control (called TQC) under the direction of the hospital's medical administration office and the Party dialectician who is attached to it. The TQC is an elaborate moral accountancy system, designed principally to apply to nurses and doctors and to raise the overall level of medical care. One of its major features is a "shortcomings control" classification scheme which identifies and categorizes various kinds of "technical" and "responsibility" errors and mistakes that physicians and nurses can make in giving care. It then attaches quantitative weights to them according to how major or minor they are considered to be. "Responsibility shortcomings" are viewed largely as moral errors. They are therefore defined as more grave than are shortcomings judged to be primarily technical in nature and are correspondingly subject to more severe penalties and punishments. Eventually, First Central Hospital hopes to translate the variables of its TQC system into a computer program for calculating individual and group "medical quality scores" in a sophisticated, modern way. The hospital regards the computer not only as an important technological tool in this effort but also as a powerful empirical and symbolic expression of the medical modernization toward which it strives.

Medical morality, with its goals, principles, virtues, rules, and human exemplars, plays an important role in the continuous process of "walking on two legs," a process that dynamically shapes and reshapes the orientation of the whole society (Fox and Swazey, 1982, 700-701):

> A chain of dualities is involved: an intricate balancing of modern Western and traditional Chinese medicine, community public health and individual patient care, central control and institutional autonomy, preventive and curative medicine, primary and tertiary care, acute and chronic illness, rural and urban needs, mental and manual labor, being "Red" and being "expert," proletarianism and elitism, the old and the new, and the balancing of ideas and resources imported from abroad and "made in China." A series of dilemmas . . . are contained in these dualities. Societal precepts constantly shift concerning how the dilemmas ideally should be resolved and what combination of binary elements and states of equilibrium between them this implies. Proper "two-leggedness" in the medical as in all spheres of Chinese society is not only defined and monitored but repeatedly altered by the flow of minor and major national policy directives that emanate from the political leadership in Beijing. In part, these fluctuations in policy are transforming consequences of the interaction between still another set of basic dualities: the canons of Communist party doctrine and the dictates of Chinese pragmatism.

THE "CHINESE-NESS" OF MEDICAL MORALITY

Nothing could more fundamentally epitomize the profound Chineseness of medical morality than the kind of two-legged dualism that underlies it. What it entails is an essentially yin-yang relationship between opposed but complementary opposites. They are the constituent elements and the dynamic force in a moving equilibrium that is continually established and reestablished through their interaction.

The same Chinese principle of dynamic complementarity is also basic to the view of the relationship between self and others, and the individual and society, in which medical morality is grounded. In this view, what it is to be a person and what it is to be in relationship to other persons complete each other and form part of a larger, vital whole.

The central status that medical morality attaches to the primary ethical importance of fulfilling one's duties to specified others in commonplace settings and in everyday acts, and to the continual improvement and perfecting of self in and through these relations and duties, is also anciently and quintessentially Chinese. These are core ideas in the traditional morality: of how striving to perfect one's individual and social being expresses the principle of immanent order in the cosmos and contributes to a society that embodies it.

The "noble" ethical virtues emphasized by medical morality are also closely related to the Confucian virtues that structured the ongoing ethical effort required by traditional Chinese morality (*ren* [humanity], *li* [sense of rites], *yi* [sense of duties], *zhi* [wisdom]). Rules were one of the principal forms in which these ethical obligations were made explicit, as is the case with medical morality. In China's past, they were often developed out of the group experience of a guild or a clan and were posted in temples, clan halls, and schools in a manner comparable to the way that medical morality rules are currently displayed in First Central Hospital.

The stylistic features and ambience of medical morality—with its emphasis on orthodoxy, righteousness, and propriety, its concern about "moral sympathy," its stress on the power of didacticism, its ritualization and bureaucratization, and its preeminently public nature—all have their counterparts and origins in Chinese tradition.

Tianjin First Central Hospital's TQC system has significant antecedents in Chinese history and tradition. It could be said that ancestral versions of TQC existed in the "morality books" (*shanshu*) and the "ledgers of merit and demerit" (*gongguoge*) that were kept by individuals and families in the sixteenth- and early seventeenth-century years of China's Ming dynasty (Berling, forthcoming; Gernet, 1982, 193-197). These were moral account books, based on the self-examination of conscience, the written confession of wrongdoing, and the recording of both good and bad thoughts and acts. Not only were thoughts and deeds morally classified in this positive and negative way, but they were sometimes weighted by a point system. In some ledgers, good points were recorded in red ink, bad ones in black ink. (Since at least the time of the Han dynasty, red had been the color of positive numbers and black of negative ones.) At periodic intervals, the person keeping this moral audit added up the points, thereby arriving at a quantitative score of his current state of ethicality and his cumulated "moral capital." Sinologists identify Taoist and Buddhist influences in these morality books, including concepts of judgments meted out by a "cosmic bureaucracy" that involved one's present life, life span, and rebirth (Sivin).

This is not to imply that medical morality is a pure emanation of Confucianism, Taoism, and Chinese Buddhism, or that Marxism-Leninism-Maoism has played a negligible role in shaping its form and content. Certain precepts of medical morality constitute radical departures from the concepts on which the traditional system of Chinese ethics was built. Most notable are the ways in which the egalitarian and universalistic principles of Marxism have strongly influenced the tenets of medical morality. Doctors and nurses are urged to unite, to work closely together professionally and "transprofessionally," and to treat colleagues equally. This egalitarian view runs counter to the traditional Chinese thesis that morality and public order consist of, and depend on, a series of hierarchically structured relationships and the fulfillment of the duties associated with them. The archetype and the ethical keystone of these superordinate-subordinate relationships was that between father and son; filial piety (*xiao*) was regarded as the model and the source of all other virtues.

Seen from this traditional perspective, perhaps the most revolutionary and un-Chinese aspects of medical morality are those centered on the relationship of nurses and physicians to patients. Medical workers are not only asked to treat their patients as coequals and to identify with them feelingly, "in deep proletarian affection." They are also exhorted to accord such supreme moral importance to their relations with patients that they surpass what have always been the first and ultimate relationships in Chinese society—family relationships, beginning with those between father and son.

The fact that nurses and women, like She, Meng, and Guan, rather than physicians and men, are the leading architects and representatives of medical morality is still another indicator of the impact of Marxist ideas on a society that has been patriarchally as well as hierarchically oriented for thousands of years.

This does not mean that equality between women and men, and the nurses and doctors who work in medicine, is now a de facto achievement in China, or that the ancient and strong cosmic, moral, and social sense of hierarchy has been eliminated from the medical sphere. Chinese nurses complain much the same way that American nurses do about how inequitably they are treated by many physicians—"like servants," they say. An elaborate formal and informal status-rank hierarchy still characterizes work units like First Central Hospital, accompanied and supported by a considerable amount of everyday ritual. Furthermore, hospitals are ranked vis-à-vis each other on a local and a national scale of excellence and prestige. Even medical morality itself is premised on certain hierarchical assumptions, such as the notion that it is "the leadership" of the nursing and medical professions that should set an example for other (nonleaders) to follow. Nevertheless, Marxist ideas of egalitarianism and universalism have made more than a doctrinal difference in medical morality and its implementation.

In the end, it is the essential Chinese-ness of the way that Marxist, along with Taoist, Confucian, and Buddhist, ideas have been blended into medical morality that is the most striking. A distinctively Chinese outlook has been as powerful a determinant of the phenomena and questions that are *not* included under medical morality as of those that are. In contradistinction to American bioethics, as already indicated, Chinese medical morality is not preoccupied with social and ethical problems associated with the advancement of medical science and technology. At the present time, medical modernization—enriched by its incorporation of traditional Chinese medicine—is viewed as morally good, socially desirable, economically necessary, and politically obligatory. Substantive issues that *do* fall under the aegis of medical morality include the population's response to the new, one-child-per-family policy; the wisdom of telling or not telling seriously ill patients (particularly those with cancer) about the gravity of their illness;[3] the role that the family ought and ought not to play in the care of ill relatives who are hospitalized;[4] the causes, prevention, and treatment of suicide attempts;[5] and the problem of obtaining blood donations. All are issues that are encountered by nurses and doctors in the various medical milieux where they currently work. Prominent bioethical concerns, such as human experimentation, the "gift of life" and "quality of life," the termination of treatment, and questions about the allocation of scarce resources associated with therapeutic innovations like organ transplantation and hemodialysis in our own society, are not yet considered to be problems in China. Chinese nurses, physicians, and relevant officials are aware that, as the process of medical modernization goes forward, they may face comparable difficulties. But, in accord with Chinese

3. We had the decided impression that the predominant tendency was *not* to tell patients about serious illness. The expert knowledge that the patients at the Cancer Hospital in Beijing possessed about their conditions, and the pride with which they displayed it to visitors, was a dramatic exception to this general inclination. Nevertheless, there was considerable discussion among doctors and nurses about this "to tell or not to tell" issue. Nurses seemed to us to be more concerned about this problem than doctors, more prone to believe that patients ought to be told, and more disposed to believe that many patients know without being told, particularly when they have cancer.

4. At First Central Hospital, family members were sometimes allowed and even asked to help take care of a relative who was an inpatient, particularly during the night when nursing personnel was more sparse. However, in this hospital and in a number of others that we visited in Tianjin, the days of the week and the hours when patients' families were permitted to visit them were very restricted. From what we could discern, this policy partly stems from the shared sentiment of nurses and doctors that families contributed to the disorder that existed in hospitals during the Cultural Revolution by challenging their medical professional expertise and authority. In addition, many nurses and physicians seemed to feel that the presence and participation of relatives in hospital care introduce "superstitious" and folkloric medical notions into what ideally should be scientific, predominantly modern, medical care in this era of the Four Modernizations.

5. We do not know how great the incidence of suicide attempts and of successful suicides is in China. However, partly because First Central Hospital has a Critical Care Unit, a number of dialysis machines, and absorbent artificial kidney treatment capabilities, it is not uncommon for such cases to be sent to the hospital for emergency care. They are of great concern to the medical staff. One particularly interesting thing that we learned in this connection is that nurses and physicians divided suicides and suicide attempts into two different moral categories: those that were attributed to mental illness and therefore were not considered to be "the fault" of the individual involved; and those that were considered blameworthy, even criminal. These latter included attempts motivated by "lost love," problems with schoolwork and/or in relations to teachers, and difficulties in family relations. Patients who had engaged in blameworthy suicide attempts received severe moral lectures from nurses and doctors, as well as medical care. They and their families were also expected to pay for the medical care given to them.

pragmatism, they are disinclined to engage in abstract speculation about hypothetical problems that may (or may not) develop, and about how they should be handled if they do. It is not until the Chinese face such issues in a first-hand way, and can meet and analyze them as "lived-in experiences," that these matters will become part of their medical morality.

From all the foregoing, it is amply clear that medical morality is not bioethics. It is as Chinese as bioethics is American. We now turn to bioethics, an arena in which we have worked and observed since the mid 1960s.[6] In the final analysis, as we shall see, American bioethics and Chinese medical morality are so culturally dissimilar that they are not sufficiently related to form a yin-yang (opposing, but complementary) pair.

AMERICAN BIOETHICS

In contrast to medical morality, the phenomena with which bioethics is primarily concerned are related to some of the ways in which modern, Western, American medicine has already *succeeded* in what the Chinese call "scaling the high peaks" of science and technology. Bioethics is focused on what we consider serious *problems* associated with these advances, rather than on the achievements they represent or the "golden dream" promises that they hold forth:

> Actual and anticipated developments in genetic engineering and counseling, life support systems, birth technology, population control, the implantation of human, animal, and artificial organs, as well as in the modification and control of human thought are principal [areas] of concern. Within this framework, special attention is concentrated on the implications of amniocentesis, abortion, *in vitro* fertilization, the prospect of cloning, organ transplantation, the use of the artificial kidney machine, the development of an artificial heart, the modalities of the intensive care unit, the practice of psychosurgery, and the introduction of psychotropic drugs. Cross-cutting the consideration . . . given to these general and concrete [spheres] of biomedical development, there is marked preoccupation with the ethicality of human experimentation under various conditions . . . . (Fox, 1979a)

6. The discussion of the cognitive, value, and belief components and characteristics of American bioethics that follows is based on our extensive and intensive work in a variety of bioethical contexts and roles, on a close and continuous knowledge of the bioethical literature, and on a content analysis of the recurrent themes in that literature. As part of this content analysis, we have also been interested in identifying themes that are notable for the infrequency with which they occur in bioethical discussion and publications, or for their consistent absence from bioethics.

Bioethics has also been concerned with the proper definition of life and death and personhood and with the humane treatment of "emerging life and life that is passing away" (Bok, 1982)—especially with the justifiability of forgoing life-sustaining forms of medical therapy. One of the most significant general characteristics of this ensemble of bioethical concerns is the degree to which they cluster around problems of natality and mortality, at the beginning and at the end of the human life cycle.

The chief intellectual and professional participants in American bioethics are philosophers (above all, those who are called "ethicists" in the United States, and "moral philosophers" in Europe), theologians (predominantly Catholic and Protestant), jurists, physicians, and biologists. Lately, the thought and presence of economists have been strongly felt in the field; but relatively few other social scientists are actively involved or notably influential in bioethical discussion, research, writing, and action. The limited participation of anthropologists, sociologists, and political scientists in bioethics is a complex phenomenon, caused as much by the prevailing intellectual orientations and the *weltanschauung* of present-day American social science as by the framework of bioethics (Fox, 1979b).

The disciplinary backgrounds of bioethicists contrast sharply with those of the key participants in medical morality because of historic differences in the American and Chinese cultures as well as current differences in our respective political and economic systems. For example, although one could argue that there are functional parallels between the role of a Chinese dialectician and that of an American theologian, one would hardly expect a theologian trained in the Judeo-Christian tradition to define value and belief issues and make decisions in the same way as someone whose world view is shaped by Confucian, Taoist, and Buddhist thought. Nor does the pivotal place of lawyers and judges in bioethics have its counterpart in medical morality. The status and role of jurists in bioethics are integrally connected with the singular importance that Americans attach to the principle as well as to the fact of being "a society under law, rather than under men."

On the other hand, the control in degree and kind over medical morality exercised by the central government in Beijing is not only an emanation of the Chinese Communist party, its present-day leadership, and its current doctrine. It is thoroughly compatible with the at once profane and sacred power over the order and organization of the entire society accorded to the emperor and his imperial bureaucracy throughout all the dynasties of Chinese history. In the United States, quite to the contrary, the fact that bioethical questions, with their moral and religious connotations, have been appearing more frequently and prominently in national and local political arenas—in our legislatures, courts, and in specially created commissions—constitutes a societal dilemma. Although ours is a "society under law," it is also a nation founded on the separation of church and state as one of its sacredly secular principles. What ought we to do, then, about the fact that bioethics (like Mr. Smith) has gone to Washington? In the light of the religious and even metaphysical, as well as moral, nature of bioethical issues, is it legitimate or wise for our government to deal with them? If so, at what level, through what branch, using what mechanisms? If not, are there other means through which we can try to resolve such matters of our collective conscience, on behalf of the whole society? These are distinctly American questions that are decidedly not Chinese.

The pluralism of American society and its voluntarism have contributed to the development of the numerous centers, institutes, and associations of varying orientations that have been organized around bioethical activities in the United States over the course of the past twenty years, both inside and outside university settings. Most of the persons who are professionally active in the field of bioethics belong to one or several of such groups and participate in their interconnected and to some extent overlapping activities (discussions, research, teaching, consultations, meetings, publications, etc.). In this sense, they form a sort of "invisible college," although not a unified school of thought.[7]

Such a plethora of voluntary associations, organized around common interests, but with somewhat different origins, auspices, memberships, and outlook, is a very American configuration. It embodies a set of culture patterns and social traits, not confined to bioethics, that always have been strikingly characteristic of American society and its conception of democracy. As early as the 1830s, Alexis de Tocqueville, the astute French observer-analyst of our new nation-state, identified our tendency to form and join voluntary associations as one of our most notable societal attributes. Again, for reasons broader, deeper, and older than the particular contemporaneous circumstances that have given rise to bioethics and medical morality, this is

7. Among the best-known and influential bioethics organizations are: The Hastings Center (Institute of Society, Ethics, and the Life Sciences), which publishes the *Hastings Center Report,* one of the most important bioethical journals in the United States; the Center for Bioethics, Kennedy Institute of Ethics, Georgetown University; the Society for Health and Human Values; and the Institute for the Medical Humanities, University of Texas Medical Center, Galveston. Among these associations, the Hastings Center is probably the most interdisciplinary and eclectic in perspective, the Kennedy Institute the most theological and Catholic, and the Society for Health and Human Values the most humanistic, Protestant, and focused on medical education. The Hastings Center and the Kennedy Institute are also strongly influenced by analytic philosophy and analytically trained philosophers; the Society for Health and Human Values is less so.

not a pattern that exists in China or that one would expect to find there.

But above all, it is in the values and beliefs emphasized and deemphasized by bioethics, and in its cognitive framework and style, that its Western and American orientation is both most evident and most fully articulated.

To begin with, as already indicated, individualism is the primary value-complex on which the intellectual and moral edifice of bioethics rests. Individualism, in this connection, starts with a belief in the importance, uniqueness, dignity, and sovereignty of the individual, and in the sanctity of each individual life. From this flows the assumption that every person, singularly and respectfully defined, is entitled to certain individual rights. Autonomy of self, self-determination, and privacy are regarded as fundamental among these rights. They are also considered to be necessary preconditions for another value-precept of individualism: the opportunity for persons to "find," develop, and realize themselves and their self-interests to the fullest—to achieve and enjoy individual well-being. In this view, "individuals are entitled to be and do as they see fit, so long as they do not violate the comparable rights of others" (Gorovitz, 1982). "Paternalism" is defined as interfering with and limiting a person's freedom and liberty of action for the sake of his or her own good or welfare. It is regarded as ethically dubious because, however beneficient its intentions or outcome, it restricts autonomy, involves coercion, implies that someone else knows better what is best for a given individual, and may insidiously impair that individual's ability to decide and act independently.

The notion of contract plays a major role in the way relations between autonomous individuals are conceived in bioethics. Self-conscious, rational, specific agreements by persons involved in interaction with one another, that explicitly delineate the scope, content, and conditions of their joint activities, are presented as ethical models. They are considered to be exemplary expressions of the way that moral relationships, protective of individual rights, can be structured. The archetype of such contractual relations is the kind of informed, voluntary consent agreement between subjects and investigators in medical research which the field of bioethics helped to formulate and that is now required by all federal and most private agencies funding this research. The informed consent contract, though mutual, is asymmetric. It is principally concerned with the rights and welfare of one of the two partners—the human subject, often a patient—because he is the most vulnerable, disadvantaged, and least powerful of the pair. The special contractual obligation to watch over and the safeguard the rights of the person(s) most susceptible to exploitation or harm in this type of exposed and unequal situation is a part of the bioethics conception of individualism and of moral relations between individuals. But little mention is made by bioethicists of what sociologist

Emile Durkheim termed the "non-contractual aspects of contract": that is, the more implicit and informal commitment, fidelity, and trust aspects of social relationships that reciprocally bind persons to live up to their promises and their responsibilities to one another.

Veracity and truth-telling, the "faithfulness" dimension of relationships on which bioethics fixes its attention, is more specific and circumscribed than the Durkheimian concept. In keeping with the overall orientation of bioethics, what is stressed is the right of patients or research subjects to "know the truth" about the discomforts, hazards, uncertainties, and "bad news" that may be associated with medical diagnosis, prognosis, treatment, and experimentation. The physician's obligation to communicate the truth to the patient or subject is derived from and based on the latter's presumed right to know. Discerning what is the truth and what is a lie is seen as relatively unproblematic. And there is a decided tendency to look on the use of denial by the patient as an undesirable defense, because it complicates truth telling and blocks truth receiving. Here, the affirmation that patients have the right to know the truth veers toward insistence that they ideally ought to face the truth consciously and deal with it rationally (in keeping with the particular definitions of "truth" and of "rationality" inherent to bioethics).

Another major value preoccupation of bioethics—and one that it has increasingly emphasized since the mid-1970s—concerns the allocation of scarce, expensive resources for advanced medical care, research, and development. What proportion of our national and local resources should be designated for these purposes, in what ways, and according to what principles and criteria? The resources with which bioethics is chiefly concerned are material ones, mainly economic and technological in nature. The allocation of nonmaterial resources such as personnel, talent, skill, time, energy, caring, and compassion is rarely mentioned. Bioethics situates its allocation questions within a rather abstract, individual rights-oriented notion of the general or common good, assigning greater importance to equity than to equality. The ideally moral distribution of goods is defined as one that all rational, self-interested persons are willing to accept as just and fair, even if goods are allotted unequally. Cost containment is also an essential value-component of this view of rightful distribution. In the bioethical calculus, it is not just a practical or necessary response to an empirical situation of economic scarcity. It has become a more categorical moral imperative.

Finally, what is usually referred to as "the principle of beneficence" or "benevolence" is also a key value of bioethics. This enjoinder to "do good" and to "avoid harm" is structured and limited by the supremacy of individualism. The benefiting of others advocated in bioethical thought is circumscribed and constrained by the obligation to respect individual rights, interests, and autonomy. Furthermore, rather than being seen as an independent virtue, doing good is generally conceived to be part of a "benefit-harm ratio" in which, ideally, benefits should outweigh costs. "Minimization of harm" rather than "maximization of good" is more strongly emphasized in this bioethical equation.

These values are predominant in America bioethics and are considered to be the most fundamental. They are accorded the highest intellectual and moral significance and are set forth with the greatest certainty and the least qualification. Other values and virtues and principles and beliefs that are part of the ethos of bioethics occupy a more secondary and less secure status. They are less frequently invoked and when introduced into ethical discussion and analysis are likely to elicit debate or require special justification.

The concept and language of "rights" prevail over those of "responsibility" and "obligation" in bioethical discourse, and the term "duty" does not appear often in the bioethical vocabulary. As already indicated, the strongest appeals to responsibility are concentrated on requirements for the protection and promotion of individual rights.

The emphasis that bioethics places on individualism and on contractual relations freely entered into by voluntarily consenting adults tends to minimize and obscure the interconnectedness of persons and the social and moral importance of their interrelatedness. Particularly when compared with Chinese medical morality, it is striking how little attention bioethics pays to the web of human relationships of which the individiual is a part and to the mutual obligations and interdependence that these relations involve. Concepts like reciprocity, solidarity, and community, which are rooted in a social perspective on our moral life and our humanity, are not often employed. Characteristically, bioethics deals with the "more-than-individual" in terms of the "general good," the "common good," or the "public interest." In the bioethical use of these concepts, the "collective good" tends to be seen atomistically and arithmetically as the sum total of the rights and interests, desires and demands of an aggregate of self-contained individuals. The fair and just distribution of limited collective resources is the major dimension of commonality that is stressed, often to the exclusion of other aspects, and usually with a propensity to define resources as material (primarily economic), and quantitative. In this view, private and public morality are sharply distinguished from one another in keeping with the underlying essential dichotomy between individual and social. Social and cultural factors are largely seen as external constraints that limit individuals. They are rarely presented as enabling and empowering forces, *inside* as well as outside of individuals, that are constituent, dynamic elements in making them human persons.

The restricted definition of "persons as individuals" and of "persons in relations" that pervades bioethics makes it difficult to introduce and find an appropriate place for values like decency, kindness, empathy, caring, devotion, service, generosity, altriusm, sacrifice, and love. All of these involve recognizing and responding to intimate and nonintimate others in a self-transcending way. Although these principles and qualities are esteemed in bioethics as exemplary and meritorious, they do not fit neatly and logically into its moral framework. There is a real sense in which they fall outside the tight range of variables that are defined as generically "ethical" by this field. For values like these, that center on the bonds between self and others and on community, and that include both "strangers" and "brothers," and future as well as present generations in their orbit, are categorized in bioethics as sociological, theological, or religious rather than as ethical or moral.

These assumptions about what is and is not purely moral are integrally related to the major cognitive characteristics of bioethical thought: to how participants in bioethics actually *do* think, and especially, to what they define as ideal standards of ethical thinking. A high value is placed on logical reasoning—preferably based on a general moral theory and concepts derived from it—that is systematically developed according to codified methodological rules and techniques around select, analytically designated variables and problems. Rigor, precision, clarity, consistency, parsimony, and objectivity are regarded as earmarks of the intellectually and ethically "best" kind of moral thought. Flawed logical and conceptual analysis is considered to be not only a concomitant of moral error but also, to a significant degree, responsible for producing it. This way of thought also tends toward dichotomous distinctions and bipolar choices. Self versus others, body versus mind, individual versus group, public versus private, objective versus subjective, rational versus nonrational, lie versus truth, benefit versus harm, rights versus responsibilities, independence versus dependence, autonomy versus paternalism, liberty versus justice are among the primary ones. Even the field's own self-defining conception of what is and is not a moral problem is formulated in a bipolar, either/or fashion.

Bioethics is an applied field that brings its theory, methods, and knowledge to bear on phenomena and situations deemed ethically problematic. It seeks to identify and illuminate points of moral consideration and provide a way of thinking about them that can contribute to their practical moral resolution through concrete choices and specific acts. Bioethics attempts this by proceeding in a largely deductive manner to impose its mode of reasoning on the phenomenological reality addressed. The amount of detailed investigation of the actual situations in which the ethical problems occur varies. But what philosophers call "thought experiments" are more often conducted in bioethics than is empirical, in situ research. This ordered, cerebral, armchair inquiry is given precedence, partly because the formalistic "data" it generates more closely fit the norms of bioethical logic and rationality than information gathered through first-hand research. Thought experiments are one of an array of cognitive techniques used in bioethics to distance and abstract itself from the human settings in which ethical questions are embedded and experienced, reduce their complexity and ambiguity, limit the number and kinds of morally relevant factors to be dealt with, dispel dilemmas, and siphon off the emotion, suffering, bewilderment, and tragedy that many medical moral predicaments entail for patients, families, and medical professionals.

Within its rigorously stripped-down analytic and methodological framework, bioethics is prone to reify its own logic and to formulate absolutist, self-confirming principles and insights. These tendencies are associated with the disinclination of bioethics to critically examine its own moral epistemology: to searchingly identify and evaluate the presuppositions and assumptions on which it rests. In a scholastic sense, the field of bioethics is knowledgeably aware of the traditions of Western thought on which it draws (e.g., act and rule utilitarianism and various theories of justice). But there is a more latent level on which it nevertheless considers its principles, its style of reasoning, and its perceptions to be objective, unbiased, and reasonable to a degree that not only makes them socially and culturally neutral but also endows them with a kind of universality. Paradoxically, these very suppositions of bioethical thought contribute to its inadvertent propensity to reflect and systematically support conventional, relatively conservative American concepts, values, and beliefs.[8]

These value, belief, and thought patterns of bioethics have developed within an interdisciplinary matrix. But particularly since the mid-1970s, when philosophers began "arriving by the score" in bioethics (and "in applied ethics more broadly" [Callahan, 1982]), moral philosophy has had the greatest molding influence on the field. It is principally American analytic philosophy—with its emphasis on theory, methodology, and technique, and its utilitarian, Kantian, and "contractarian" outlooks—in which most of the philosophers who have entered bioethics were trained. Defined as "ethicists" who are specialized experts in moral problems associated with biomedicine,

8. Several major critiques of the emergence of the new philosophical subdiscipline of applied ethics on the American scene have been published in the *Hastings Center Report* during the past two years, which coincide in numerous respects with our characterization of bioethics, particularly its "seeming indifference to history, social context, and cultural analysis" (see Callahan, 1981; Callahan, 1982; Noble, 1982).

they have established themselves, and their approach to matters of right and wrong, as the "dominant force" (Callahan, 1981) in the field.

This is not to say that all analytic philosophers who actively participate in bioethics think and write in a uniform way, or that every philosopher-bioethicist is grounded in this analytic tradition. Major contributors to bioethics, for example, also include a number of highly esteemed philosopher-scholars whose work incorporates more phenomenological, social, and religious dimensions rooted in the traditions of moral theology and American social ethics. The respect that such individuals are accorded notwithstanding the perspective that they represent has had far less influence on the predominant ethos of bioethics than has analytic philosophy.

The conviction of analytic philosophers that value questions and ethical problems can and should be handled objectively, rationally, and rigorously, with specialized targeted competence, is shared and supported by many jurists, professionally involved with bioethical issues, whose intellectual and moral authority in the field is second only to that of the philosophers. The intricate and controversial, but nonetheless significant, connection that has always existed between law and morality in American society, and the increasing extent to which bioethical issues have been coming before our courts and into our legislatures since the mid-1960s, have contributed to the important status of the law and of lawyers in bioethics. In turn, the rationalism of American law, its emphasis on individual rights, and the ways in which it has been shaped by Western traditions of natural law, positivism, and utilitarianism, overlap with and reinforce key attributes of the philosophical thought in bioethics.

The principles and rules of "being scientific" that physicians and biologists have been educated and socialized to apply to their own professional work, and that they have brought to bioethics, are highly compatible with the positivism of philosophers and jurists. Within the framework of bioethics and its scientific assumptions, this parallelism confers a semblance of "scientific-ness" on the philosophical and legal aspects of its thought and in so doing enhances the validity that it is believed to have.

These same tendencies in the currents of thought that underlie bioethics have played a major role in framing its operational conception of "the moral," in which religious, cultural, and social variables are not only sharply distinguished from ethical ones, but their relevance is minimized. In these respects, despite the significant contributions of theologians to bioethics, its overall orientation is decidedly secular as well as unsociological. When questions of a religious nature do arise in bioethics, there is a marked tendency either to screen them out or to logically reduce them, so they can be fitted into the field's circumscribed definition of ethics and ethical. Through a comparable process of intellectual laundering and reductionism, the social is taken out of its larger cultural, historical, and societal context by bioethics, as well as out of what the field defines as ethical.

The applied pragmatism of bioethics strengthens the common tendency among its participants to cleave to a conceptual framework that focuses on individuals, plays down their interrelationships, rationalizes and simplifies the emotional and social milieus of which they are a part, and limits the range of facts and values considered germane to ethics. Bioethics is oriented to problem solving, decision making, and policy formulation. Bioethicists are continually called upon to serve as expert consultants in numerous biomedical, legal, political, educational, and industrial arenas. In these arenas, physicians, nurses, and other medical professionals, hospital administrators, patients, families, biologists, lawyers, judges, legislators, politicians, business executives, and their associates must make up their minds about what to do or not to do in real-life settings and then act on the basis of their determinations. This advisory role to decision makers has reinforced the cognitive predisposition of bioethics to distill the complexity and uncertainty, the dilemmas and the tragedy out of the situations they analyze. The fact that bioethicists are being asked to help professional practitioners and policymakers arrive at reasonably specific and clear ways of resolving the concrete medical-moral problems they face has given a new, expedient justification for the forms of intellectual and moral reductionism in which it engages.

BIOETHICS IS NOT JUST BIOETHICS

In our sociological view, the paradigm of values and beliefs, and of reflections on them, that has developed and been institutionalized in American bioethics is an impoverished and skewed expression of our society's cultural tradition. In a highly intellectualized but essentially fundamentalistic way, it thins out the fullness of that tradition and bends it away from some of the deepest sources of its meaning and vitality.

In the prevailing ethos of bioethics, the value of individualism is defined in such a way, and emphasized to such a degree, that it is virtually severed from social and religious values concerning relationships between individuals; their responsibilities, commitments, and emotional bonds to one another; the significance of the groups and of the societal community to which they belong; and the deep inward as well as outward influence that these have on the individual and his or her sense of the moral. Social dimensions of ethicality are largely compressed into and meted out through a "do good" and "avoid harm" idea of beneficence. To this narrowly gauged conception of individualism, bioethics attaches an inflated and inflationary value. Claims to individual rights phrased in terms of moral entitlements tend to expand and to beget additional claims to still other individual rights. In these respects, the individualism of bioethics constitutes an evolution away from older, less secularized and communal forms of American individualism.

The outlook of bioethics is also based on a principle of rational calculation set forth as a standard of moral as well as intellectual excellence. Qualities and considerations that do not easily fit into a logico-rational and cost-conserving framework of ethicality are either excluded from bioethics or relegated to a secondary or peripheral status within it. "Qualities of the heart" like compassion and caring that elicit generosity have a lesser place in bioethics than the reason-guided "qualities of the mind" that support frugality. The moral economy of bioethics, like its cognitive system, is governed by a notion of parsimony that borders on penury.

The positivism and the materialism of bioethics integrate it around a narrow range of variables and values. These tight and exclusionary properties of bioethical thought heighten the tension traditional in Western culture and American society between certain pairs of principles. Bioethics splits them further apart and drives them into conflictful dichotomies. Individual and social, self and other, rights and responsibilities, thoughts and feelings, the rational and the nonrational, the material and the nonmaterial, what is ethical and what is religious—all become irreconcilable opposites, among which absolute choices have to be made. We already know the choices bioethics epitomizes. But, "How does one balance a total focus on the needs of the individual with one's responsibility to the whole community? How does one hold together in a kind of creative tension the assurance of faith with the flexibility of tolerance? It is as if one were continually putting up two different poles and letting the sparks fly between. The truth is that we must preserve a readiness to ask new questions and seek new truths in all sphere . . . " (Saunders, Summers, and Teller, 1981).

The reluctance of bioethics to let "the sparks fly between . . . two different poles," to ask such questions, and to "seek new truths in all spheres," is connected with its secularism: "What I am referring to is a process of reductionism that 'thins down' and 'flattens out' the meaning of the individual and person, family and kinship . . . self-giving and sharing, kindness and sympathy, caring and mercy, equality and justice, mutuality and solidarity, communion and community, responsibility and commitment, birth and life, joy and suffering, mortality and death, so that they are progressively stripped of both their primal and transcendent significance, and of their relationship to the common good, the human condition, and the vaster-than-human . . . " (De Craemer).

Bioethics has "sprung loose from that broader [religious] framework" (De Craemer) in which the values of our cultural tradition are historically embedded. In turn, the particular forms that the secularism, the rationality, and the individualism of bioethics take, and the ways in which they interact with each other, contribute to another of the field's constricting features: its provincialism. Bioethics is sealed into itself in such a way that it tends to take its own characteristics and assumptions for granted. It is relatively uncritical of its premises and unaware of its cultural specificity. It is this sort of parochialism, with its mix of naiveté and arrogance, that makes it difficult for bioethicists not only to recognize medical morality and its Chinese-ness when they encounter it but also to perceive the "American-ness" of their particular value-concerns and of how they approach them.

It is unclear whether bioethics truly reflects the state of American medical ethics today and whether it can—or ought to—serve as the common framework for American medical morality.

Beyond this, if, as we suggested at the outset, "bioethics is not just bioethics" and is more than medical—if it is an indicator of the general state of American ideas, values, and beliefs, of our collective self-knowledge, and our understanding of other societies and cultures—then there is every reason to be worried about who we are, what we have become, what we know, and where we are going in a greatly changed and changing society and world.

REFERENCES

Berling, J. Religion and Popular Culture: The Management of Moral Capital in *The Romance of the Three Teachings.* In untitled work edited by A. Nathan, D. Johnson, and E. Rawski. Berkeley and Los Angeles: University California Press, forthcoming.

Bok, S. In discussion at the conference on the Problem of Personhood, organized by Medicine in the Public Interest (MIPI). New York City, April 1-2, 1982.

Callahan, D. Minimalistic Ethics. *Hastings Cent. Rep.* 11:19-25, 1981.

Callahan, D. At the Center: From "Wisdom" to "Smarts." *Hastings Cent. Rep.* 12:4, 1982.

De Craemer, W. See Bok, 1982.

Engelhardt, H.T., Jr. Bioethics in the People's Republic of China. *Hastings Center. Rep.* 10 (April 1980); 7-10.

Fox, R.C. Ethical and Existential Developments in Contemporaneous American Medicine: Their Implications for Culture and Society. In *Essays in Medical Sociology.* New York: Wiley, 1979a.

Fox, R.C. Advanced Medical Technology—Social and Ethical Implications. In *Essays in Medical Sociology.* New York: Wiley, 1979b.

Fox, R.C., and Swazey, J.P. Critical Care at Tianjin's First Central Hospital and the Fourth Modernization. *Science* 217:700-705, 1982.

Gernet, J. *Chine et Christianisme.* Paris: Gallimard, 1982.

Gorovitz, S. *Doctors' Dilemmas: Moral Conflicts and Medical Care.* New York: Macmillan, 1982.
Henderson, G.E. Danwei: The Chinese Work Unit: A Participant Observation Study of a Hospital. Dissertation submitted in partial fulfillment of the requirements of the Ph.D. (Sociology) at the University of Michigan, Ann Arbor, 1982.
Noble, C.N. Ethics and Experts. *Hastings Cent. Rep.* 12:7-9, 15, 1982.
Saunders, C.; Summers, D.H.; and Teller, N. (eds.). *Hospice: The Living Idea.* Colchester and London: Arnold, 1981.
Sivin, N. Ailment and Cure in Traditional China (unpublished manuscript).

Medicine, Science, and Technology

The impact of medical science and technology on our health and illness, our life and death, has become a central preoccupation in American society since the 1960s. Continual discussion about the consequences and implications of the biological and therapeutic "revolution" that modern Western medicine has undergone pervades many spheres of our private, professional, and public activities. Certain biomedical advances are major foci of this ongoing discussion. Principal among them are the entrance of microbiology into the cosmos of the cell and its ultrastructures; the discovery of the double helical structure of deoxyribonucleic acid (DNA), and the deciphering of the genetic code; the development of life-support systems and intensive care units; the evolution of machines (such as computed tomography [CAT] and positron emission tomography [PET] scanners), that can look and hear into the deepest and smallest recesses of the body; the ability to operate on the human heart; the transplantation of live and cadaveric organs from one individual to another; the invention and deployment of the artificial kidney and the artificial heart; the use of powerful psychotropic, anticancer, and immunosuppressive drugs; the emerging possibilities of *in vitro* fertilization; and the prospects of genetic engineering.

A curious mixture of historical awareness and unawareness pervades the ongoing discussion of biomedical revolution. Although it is explicitly concentrated on a series of recent medical scientific and technological developments that have occurred since World War II, the discussion about these advances often proceeds as if they, and the diagnostic, therapeutic, and preventive armamentarium of medicine into which they fit, were centuries rather than four decades old. The chagrin frequently expressed over our medicine's failure to make more progress with the chief life-threatening illnesses that currently afflict us—cardiovascular disease and cancer; the cultural surprise exhibited over the appearance of a new, infectious disease like acquired immunodeficiency syndrome (AIDS); and the propensity to call some 12,900 reported cases of this syndrome an epidemic (Curran et al. 1985)—all suggest a kind of medical historical obliviousness. It ignores the fact that before the discovery of sulfa drugs and antibiotics in the 1930s and 1940s, infectious diseases were commonplace and rampant in our society, and that our medicine could do little for most illnesses of any sort, other than diagnose them, vigilantly follow their course, treat them with hands-on nursing care, and try to anticipate their outcome (Beeson 1980; Thomas 1983, 19-50).

The at-once historical and ahistorical commentary on medical science and technology and on what they have wrought is laced through with ambivalence. On the one hand the commentary is impressed with the knowledge and competence achieved in medicine. It is enthusiastic about the scientific and therapeutic "breakthroughs" periodically announced in professional journals and the media. It is expectant about biomedical progress still to come. On the other hand, it is apprehensive about the bio-uncertainty that these medical advances entail—concerned about the hard-to-predict risk and error, hazard and harm that can ensue from the energetic, manipulative, invasive ways that we bring science and technology to bear on sickness and health. It is harshly critical of the impersonal, relentless technicity of biomedicine. It attributes serious ethical as well as dangerous biological side effects to our medicine, especially to the scientific and technological developments around which so much of the talk about biomedical revolution turns. Alongside these feelings about the beneficial and injurious power of medicine are equally strong sentiments about its inadequacies: the limitations of what it has been able to do for our health and illness, the length and quality of our lives, our well-being, our pain and suffering, and the conditions surrounding our death. Public health measures and changes in lifestyle, it is often asserted, are more responsible for whatever progress we have made in preventing disease, promoting health, and prolonging life than is biomedicine, with its fixation on aggressive, ex post facto, scientific and technological means of treating illness.

What does this social and cultural ambivalence toward biomedicine represent? In part, it is a reflection of how complex and, in many respects, how contradictory the effects of the scientific and technical transformation of medicine have been. To some extent, it is indicative of a crisis of risen expectations that biomedical progress has helped to create: a crisis accompanied and augmented by the sociohistorical tendency, already noted, to "forget" how recent and prolific that progress has been. On deeper levels, the ambivalence is a paradoxical response to a process of change that is more than medical.

The biomedical revolution is part of a much larger social and cultural revolution. It is imbedded in a period of our national history and of the West when unusually massive, profound, and rapid change has challenged our established institutional and organizational structures and shaken our cultural assumptions, calling into question many of our basic concepts, values, and beliefs, and our overarching worldview. Biomedical advance has contributed to this social and cultural ferment. It has also been influenced by this ferment in ways that not only affect the social systems within which biomedical research and therapy are conducted, but also penetrate the scientific content of medicine and color its technical vocabulary. It seems more than coincidental, for example, that at a time when our society is grappling with a variety of issues pertaining to individualism, individuality, personhood, and the relationship of self to others (Fox and Willis, 1983), the medical immunological approach to organ transplantation and the problem of graft reaction is intently focused on how the recipient is able to "recognize" grafted tissue as "not-self," using "individuality markers" to do so.

In this period of disorienting change, medicine (its science and technology, achievements and failures, uncertainties and limitations, promises and dangers, and its bearing on the human condition) has become an important symbolic center in our society. It is a projective screen, a metaphorical language, and a kind of code for the cultural questions we are asking and for our societal worry and perplexity in the face of them.

CHRONIC ILLNESS

There is a wide array of phenomena associated with medical scientific and technological advance through which we are experiencing and pondering such "collective conscience" issues. The medical progress we have made in preventing, detecting, treating, and managing disease, and in sustaining and lengthening life, has altered the sociomedical landscape. Chronic rather than acute illnesses now prevail. Foremost among them are certain medical conditions—cancer, diseases of the heart, disorders of the brain and mind—that have great figurative as well as statistical significance. They affect organs and domains of the body that are anatomically and symbolically integral to our personhood. They are malignant, often insidious bearers of suffering and disability. They can be skillfully overseen, may occasionally abate or be arrested, and are sometimes cured; but by and large, these are illnesses that are incrementally progressive. The battery of drugs, surgical procedures, and mechanical devices that are used for their continuous, long-term care have multiple side effects whose cumulative implications are only beginning to be discerned. Chronic diseases are also harbingers of the physical form in which most of us will die our eventual deaths. They are medical incarnations, then, of what we still do not know, understand, and control in our advanced modern, scientifically sophisticated, technologically ingenious society; of the stubborn persistence of disease; and of our ultimate, mysterious mortality.

The societal impact of chronic illness and of the cultural messages it carries is enhanced because a sizeable proportion of our population (especially in older age groups) is living with these disorders. Never before in history have there been so many people with chronic health problems, wending their way through daily life as best they can, and medical science and treatment enable them to do; or so many individuals in later stages of enduring illnesses receiving prolonged, in-hospital and nursing home care for them. Those who are not personally touched by chronic disease are nonetheless constantly reminded of its presence by its sheer incidence, by its steady, prominent coverage by the media, by the medical predicaments of relatives, friends, and colleagues, and by the underlying awareness that their own freedom from such illness is temporary.

CRITICAL CARE AND SUSTAINING LIFE

Out of the convergence of all that we are medically able and unable to do for chronic illness, a stream of tragic cases has been engendered that represent some of the most basic and awesome problems of life and death, meaning and decision that are now before us. These are cases like that of William F. Bartling, a seventy-year old man, in very poor health for six years, suffering from five chronic, usually fatal diseases (emphysema, arteriosclerosis, a malignant lung tumor, chronic respiratory failure, and an abdominal aneurysm), who was sustained on a life-support system in the intensive care unit of a hospital for six months, and who asked to be disconnected from the respirator. Bartling died on November 6, 1984, just twenty-three hours before his request was heard by a California appellate court that, on December 27, 1984, ruled in favor of what was deemed his constitutional right to refuse treatment. That a person of Bartling's advanced age, afflicted with such a plethora of lethal diseases, survived for the length of time he did is a consequence of the powerful medical technology we have developed and the unremitting expertise with which we wield it. The fact that in a case of this sort, the decision to forego life-sustaining treatment was made by a postmortem court ruling rather than by the patient himself, his family, or the medical professionals caring for him, and that this case is only one of the many related cases that appear regularly in the courts, is indicative of our societal unsureness about what is the right medical and moral thing to do under such circumstances and what is the right way to reach this decision. Through the dramaturgic attention that they have been given by the media, a number of such identified cases have become something akin to societal morality plays, publicly enacting our collective conflicts and anguish over the ethical and existential dilemmas that have been generated by the capacity of our medical scientific technology to maintain life and our strong cultural commitment to be vigorous and tenacious in our efforts to do so.

THE INTENSIVE CARE NURSERY

At the other end of the spectrum of life and age from William Bartling are the infants around whom our medical science and technology have built neonatal intensive care units (NICUs). These infants are at great risk because they were born very prematurely, are of very low birth weight, had their vital functions severely compromised due to perinatal adversity, or are suffering from congenital abnormalities (genetic, environmental, or unknown in origin), such as heart and neural defects associated with or independent of conditions like Down's syndrome or spina bifida. The special, high-technology, intensive nursing, pastel-colored, spaceshiplike (Rostain 1985) hospital units in which this group of infants live out their first days, weeks, and sometimes months, connected to machines (mechanical ventilators, radiant warmers, oxygen monitors, arterial catheters, intravenous feeding apparatus, among them) were recently established—in the 1960s, when neonatology also emerged as a pediatrics speciality. Many of the quarter million infants born prematurely, and with serious birth defects, in the United States each year are now cared for in some 7500 NICU crib-beds, in approximately 600 hospitals. Twenty, or even ten years ago, a sizeable number of these infants would not have survived. With the passage of every new year, these units make further progress in pushing back the limits of survival and of biological viability. It is now possible to keep an infant who is only in its twenty-fourth week of gestation, and who weighs as little as 500 grams (scarcely more than one pound) alive in such an NICU.

We do not yet know the long-term consequences of the efforts and achievements of NICUs: how the infants treated in NICUs will develop, what kinds of health characteristics and illnesses they will have, or what the physical and intellectual, psychological and social qualities of their lives will be. The development of NICUs is so recent that it is only now becoming possible to do follow-up studies of the first cohorts of infants who received this type of intensive care. In a gross, clinical way, however, we do know that many of the infants who survive and leave the hospital do so with permanent physical and/or mental impairments, with continuing susceptibility to neuro-developmental and respiratory problems and to relatively serious, protracted illnesses, and with an ongoing need for specialized care of many kinds. Some of their medical difficulties are side effects of the very lifesaving measures that were taken on their behalf (for example, the blindness and scarred tracheas that may result from the use of mechanical ventilators for premature infants).

The dilemma, To treat or not to treat? and the question, What *are* we doing? hover over NICUs. These problems are as newborn as the units themselves, their infant patients, and the medical technological ability to save such infants from death. Questions about starting, stopping, and foregoing treatment are present in adult ICUs, too, but the NICU situation has added significance and greater pathos because it is associated with the powerful cultural meaning with which our society endows birth, babies, and parenthood. In basic, wrenchingly personified ways, the NICU's tiny patients and their parents represent helpless, innocent, suffering, striving, not-yet-lived human life, and the expectant human family.

This situation is apparent in the intensely emotional, highly polarized reactions to what have come to be known as the Baby Doe cases that have erupted onto the public scene in the past few years. These are cases in which, out of a process of consultation between medical professionals and parents, the decision has been made to withhold some medical or surgical treatment vital to maintaining the life of an infant. The Baby Doe–type cases that have received the most public attention entail two kinds of medical conditions, and treatment options, that epitomize tragic dilemmas. Usually, they have involved infants afflicted either with Down's syndrome or spina bifida, who have both correctable life-threatening defects, such as a blocked intestinal tract, a congenital heart problem, or an open spinal column that can be repaired surgically, and permanent, irreparable handicaps, such as mental retardation, paralysis, or incontinence, that do not jeopardize the infant's survival. Under these circumstances, a decision has been made not to treat a particular infant's remediable life-threatening condition.

Around such Baby Does, highly publicized court cases have occurred; newspapers, magazines, and television have developed extensive coverage; and political and religious as well as medical and ethical controversy has arisen. Over the past three years, no less than the President of the United States, the Department of Health and Human Services (DHHS), the Office of the U.S. Surgeon General, the Justice Department, a number of states and federal courts in different jurisdictions, the House of Representatives and the Senate of the U.S. Congress, numerous organizations of medical professionals (among them, the American Academy of Pediatrics, the American College of Obstetrics and Gynecology, the American College of Physicians, the American Medical Association, the American Hospital Association, and the American Nurses Association), voluntary organizations representing handicapped persons (such as the American Coalition of Citizens with Disabilities, the Association for Retarded Citizens, the Association for the Severely Handicapped, the Disability Rights Education and Defense Fund, and the Spina Bifida Association), individuals and groups of a religion-oriented, right-to-life suasion, and those with civil libertarian commitments have all been involved in the process by which successive versions of federal regulations, called "Baby Doe rules," have been formulated, hotly debated, applied, and altered. Initiated by President Ronald Reagan himself in 1983, these federal regulations extend rulings prohibiting discrimination against handicapped persons, and concerning child abuse prevention and treatment, to disabled infants with life-threatening conditions under care in NICUs. At the present writing (January 1985), all the NICUs of this country fall under the surveillance and jurisdiction arrangements that have been put into place by the rules on health care for handicapped newborns published by DHHS in December 1984, and by a bill passed by the U.S. Congress in October 1984. DHHS rules require a sign to be posted in the NICU declaring that "nourishment and medically beneficial treatment (as determined with respect for reasonable medical judgments) should not be withheld from handicapped infants solely on the basis of their present or anticipated mental or physical impairments." This sign must also list two sets of telephone numbers for reporting suspected violations: those of a hospital review committee and of state child protection agencies. The congressional bill includes the "withholding of medically indicated treatment from disabled infants with life-threatening conditions" under child abuse and neglect, and, in common with the DHHS rules, states that "no heroic measures are required" if treatment would be "virtually futile in terms of the survival of the infant."

Although the foregoing are considered to be final regulations, it is highly unlikely that they are. They have certainly not resolved the maelstorm of questions that surround Baby Does. If anything, they may have added to the societal turbulence over a whole chain of interrelated issues: the irreducibly moral nature of the judgments that enter into decisions about whether treatments are "futile" or of potential medical benefit; the difficulties of making predictions about an infant's prognosis, and the life he or she might lead, particularly in light of the rapid medical technological progress that continues to be made in caring for these infants and the psychosocial, ethical, and existential considerations that such forecasting entails; widely divergent beliefs and interpretations of the meaning of life and death, health and handicap, childhood and parenthood, and the family and its relationships; and the issue of how best to protect the interests of handicapped children, while respecting what the courts have called "the most private and precious responsibility invested in parents for the care and nurture of their children," and parents' associated right to decide on the medical treatment they deem best for their child. What is more, the way that the executive, legislative, and judicial branches of our government have involved themselves with Baby Doe–related questions has raised another set of problems, fundamental to our Constitution and to the nature of our societal community. In a society like ours, with its underlying principles of pluralism and separation of church and state, should our polity be so actively and authoritatively intervening in Baby Doe matters that are as religious and metaphysical as they are medical and moral—taking an official stance and translating that position into rules and statutes that are binding on us all?

In sharp contrast to all the furor over the justifiability of nontreatment decisions in the NICU, very little attention has been paid to the implications of the fact that a disproportionately high number of extremely premature infants of very low birth weight, with severe congenital abnormalities, cared for in NICUs, are babies born to greatly disadvantaged mothers. The women who are at the highest risk for having such infants are poor, nonwhite, single teenagers, underweight and badly nourished, poorly educated, unemployed, who smoke, drink, and are prone to drug abuse, with a history of frequent, closely spaced pregnancies, and who may also be victims of the physical and psychological violence that so often occurs in their milieu. By and large, the public, professional, and private groups that are morally concerned about Baby Does and their life-sustaining treatment are disinclined to regard as *ethical* problems the deprived social conditions out of which many of these infants and their mothers come. And these groups are only weakly motivated, if at all, to recommend and initiate medical, public health, and social action programs that might reduce the likelihood of infants being born in this state and might improve their life chances after birth. Furthermore, the energy that has been devoted to insuring that infants receive life-maintaining care in the NICU far outweighs the interest and activity that have been devoted to developing and funding services that can help families provide the specialized, emotionally and financially expensive care that many of the infants who graduate from NICUs will need for the rest of their lives.

THE ELDERLY

Not only newborn infants at risk have experienced an impressive increase in survival in recent years. A very rapid decline in old-age mortality has also occurred in our society. "The U.S. Census Bureau's 1971 projection anticipated a life expectancy of 72.2 years in the year 2000. But already by 1982, life expectancy was 74.5 years, having increased more than twice as much in 10 years as it was expected to increase in 30" (Preston 1984, 435). The factors contributing to this change in the death rate and longevity of elderly people are complex. Primary among them are the medical, scientific, and technological progress that has occurred during the past twenty years in treating chronic illness and maintaining life, the intensive efforts that have been made to provide and increase access to medical services for the elderly through Medicare and Medicaid, and the development of geriatric medicine and treatment programs.

Between 1960 and 1982, the number of persons in our population aged sixty-five and over grew 54 percent, while the number of children younger than fifteen years of age fell by 7 percent. The decline was due mainly to the drop in birthrate that followed the immediately post–World War II baby boom (Preston 1984, 435). The reduced birthrate is partly a consequence of the deep-structure changes in gender roles, and marriage and family patterns, that have taken place since the 1960s. The birthrate is also integrally connected to biomedicine through its dependency on the development and use of contraceptive drugs and devices, and of methods of abortion. As a consequence of these two converging processes—a significant decrease in the number of children and a rapid increase in the number of elderly—the age structure of the United States has been altered (with an abruptness, to a degree, and in a direction that were not even anticipated by demographers).

Societal responses to these major demographic changes have been admixed. There is much dolorous talk and writing about the number of elderly people in our society who are alone (including shelterless "bag ladies" and "vent men"), with meager financial resources, in frail health, disabled, mentally as well as physically afflicted, with dreaded conditions like Alzheimer's disease, for whom nursing homes are the only recourse. In sharp contrast to this melancholy portrait of the state of the elderly, many references are made to their individual vigor and collective influence. Stories about the robustness, lucidity, and continuing accomplishments of older people abound. There is increasing mention, too, of the political significance of persons over sixty-five years of age, through their active participation in voluntary associations that promote the interests of the elderly, and by virtue of their high rate of voter turnout in local and national elections. This bifurcated image of older Americans reflects different facets of their actual social situation. It also suggests the existence of deeply ambivalent feelings in the American population toward the elderly. Intermingled with palpable concern about what it is like to be an older person in our society, there is a considerable amount of more veiled resentment about the growing salience and importance of the elderly and the sizeable resources being allocated to them. This resentment is present, for example, in some of the commentaries that note the improvement during the past two decades of the social, economic, political, and medical conditions for older people while deploring the deterioration of these conditions for children. It is implied that this situation exists because, both advertently and inadvertently, we have chosen to favor our old at the expense of our young. A questionable notion about allocation of scarce resources underlies such an assumption; namely, if we distributed less of these resources to the elderly, we would necessarily provide more of them to children.

CONTRADICTIONS AROUND THE HUMAN LIFE CYCLE

Birth, infancy, childhood, old age: it is interesting how many of the direct and indirect consequences of the evolution of modern medicine, its science and technology, plunge us into matters of the human life cycle, particularly its beginning and its end. It is around these essences and phases of what it is to be born, live, and die as a human person that our deepest cultural conflict and confusion are being expressed. At one and the same time in our society, we have organized "right to life" movements, and also "right to death" movements concerned with making our medicine- and technology-surrounded deaths more dignified and humane (Fox 1981). We have used legal means both to liberalize access to abortion and to insist that the NICUs of our country do everything possible to sustain the lives of premature infants who are close to the developmental age of previable fetuses, eligible for abortion. Through the relatively new field of perinatal medicine, we are making progress in our capacity to correct certain structural defects and metabolic disorders of fetuses in utero. In addition, we are developing innovative treatments for infertility: various forms of artificial insemination and *in vitro* fertilization. These activities, and the commitments underlying them, are so fraught with contradiction that we are having great societal difficulty in finding a way to reconcile them, or even to make cultural sense of them.

Twelve years after the landmark *Roe v. Wade* decision of the U.S. Supreme Court, which constitutionally supported a woman's right to decide whether to terminate her pregnancy, our society is more embattled than ever over the issue of abortion. Confrontations between so-called prolife and prochoice groups have escalated, as have incidents of violence associated with them. Yet for all this militancy, irresolution about the "rightness" or "wrongness" of abortion, and the consequences of its being legal or banned, seems to have grown. Close to 40 percent of the 757 adults who were polled this January by the Gallup Organization for *Newsweek* magazine answered yes to the question, Do you ever wonder whether your own position on abortion is right or not? Affirmative answers were equally distributed between respondents who support abortion and those who oppose it ("America's Abortion Dilemma" 1984).

NEW TREATMENTS FOR INFERTILITY AND THE CONCEPT OF THE FAMILY

Our struggles over issues surrounding abortion, life-sustaining treatment, remedies for infertility, and the well-being of old persons and children in our society make it clear that we are having problems with our concept of the family as well. Profound disagreements over the value that we attach to the family, and over our beliefs about the rights and responsibilities that should be invested in it, have surfaced. Around the development of artificial insemination by donor (AID), egg donation, and surrogate pregnancy, questions basic to our very definition of a family have arisen. We have only begun to wrestle with our divergent ideas and strong sentiments about how we ought to think and feel about a family unit made up of a wife and a husband, and a child who was conceived and born through "artificial" methods (i.e., fertilization of the egg of the child's genetic mother with semen from a man who is not her husband, or *in vitro* fertilization, followed by implantation of the embryo in the uterus of a woman not genetically related to it). Are these acts inherently adulterous, no matter what the motivation and the quality of consent of the participants may be? Who is this child, biologically, socially, emotionally, and legally? Who are the child's parents? Is the family in which the child is raised "natural" and "right"? If we as a society were more sure about what we consider the core elements of family and of human kinship, other than biological relatedness, we might find these questions less enigmatic.

HOSPITALIZATION AND DEHOSPITALIZATION

All the medical phenomena thus far discussed occur in a system heavily oriented to the hospital as a locus of inpatient and outpatient care as well as a locus of the medical technologies extensively used to diagnose and treat illnesses, and nonillness conditions like pregnancy and infertility. This hospital centeredness coexists with the efforts since the 1960s to "dehospitalize"—efforts made by the women's, consumer health, holistic medicine, and alternative therapy movements, and increasingly by government bodies concerned with health and medical care. To a significant degree, this organized trend away from the hospital has been propelled by a social reaction to what is felt to be the domineering role of doctors, machines, and invasive procedures in hospital medicine, its crushing impersonality, its harmful physical and psychological side effects, its elaborate bureaucracy, and its high costs. An intricate push-pull relationship currently exists between these countervailing hospitalization-dehospitalization patterns. Nowhere is this relationship more starkly and troublingly apparent than in the sphere of the medical care of mental illness. What is usually termed "deinstitutionalization" has been a major movement in psychiatry since the mid-1950s. It has been estimated that over the course of some twenty-five years, from 1955 to 1980, the number of chronically mentally ill patients in large state hospitals has decreased from 559,000 to 138,000 (Gudeman and Shore 1984, 832). The development and use of psychotropic drugs to treat the symptoms of mental disorders, the growing philosophical and ideological conviction about the importance of freeing as many people as possible from the incarcerating control of "total institutions" like mental hospitals, the political advocacy to achieve this goal, and the economic incentives for extra hospital care provided by federal programs have all contributed to the decrease. However enlightened deinstitutionalization may be in some respects, and whatever benefit may be afforded certain categories of mentally ill persons to be released from a hospital-enclosed world, it has also had highly visible, disturbing consequences. During the same period that the patient populations of state hospitals have declined, the admission rates to these same hospitals have grown and accelerated. To a significant degree, this statistic is the result of readmissions of patients who are being hospitalized for shorter periods but who are more often rehospitalized than in the past. Not only has this "revolving door'' phenomenon developed, but many of the unhospitalized persons with serious, chronic, mental disorders are not receiving the extensive, continuing medical and psychiatric care, housing, and vocational and social support services necessary for them to live some semblance of a normal life in the "outside world." Very sick and disabled persons, with flagrant symptoms and behavioral signs of their mental illness, make up a sizeable number of the homeless people who now live on the streets of our cities. The public distress and fear that their presence and predicament evoke have contributed to the romanticization, heard in some quarters, of the assets and accomplishments of mental hospitals and to serious talk about a policy shift in the direction of at least partially restoring these hospitals to the role they formerly played in sheltering, caring for, and treating mentally ill patients.

COST AND COST CONTAINMENT

The issues of hospitalization-dehospitalization, then, like the others we have explored, are surrounded by oscillating social attitudes that conflict and waver. The same kind of ambivalence also characterizes our societal outlook on the sharply rising costs of our science- and technology-driven medical care. Concern about these costs is one of the most prominent and consistent themes that runs through our perennial discussion of health, illness, and medicine. Despite the numerous measures that have been taken, nationally and locally, to reduce and slow down medical care costs, we have not made much progress in doing so. Nor have we arrived at a workable consensus about what the best and most right way to deal with this problem might be. The feelings and views of the American public about controlling medical costs are so split that commentators have ventured to call them "schizophrenic." National public opinion polls indicate, for example, that although most Americans are very troubled by the rising costs of hospitalization and visits to a physician, and although they are discontent with our system of care taken as a whole, they believe that our society is spending too little rather than too much on health and medical care. By and large, they are satisfied with the care that they personally receive (Blendon and Altman 1984).

Still, on a more general value level, cost containment has come to be seen not just as a pragmatically desirable condition but also as a moral virtue in the face of scarce resources, competition for them, and their adequate and equitable distribution. Particularly expensive and scarce advanced medical scientific technologies, such as intensive and critical care, organ transplants, and mechanical organs like the artificial kidney and heart, have become strategic foci of cost-containment/allocation-of-scarce-resources reflection and debate. The state of our economy during the past fifteen years, with its worrisome combination of slowdown and retrenchment, inflation and indebtedness, underlies these considerations; the language in which they are being deliberated is heavily economic in content and tone. How we ought to spend resources for medical care is a question infrequently raised. Saving is emphasized, advocated, and held up as exemplary. Only occasionally are public statements made about the good that can come from spending and the harm that may result from cutting back costs (Blendon and Rogers 1983).

TRANSPLANTATION AND ALLOCATION OF ORGANS

We are using a medical economic framework and vocabulary to talk to each other about essentially moral and religious questions: Who shall live, when not all can live? What is the value and meaning of sustaining life through extraordinary medical treatments in some of the circumstances in which we do so? And what are the nonmaterial costs that these treatments entail for patients, families, and medical professionals?

Nowhere is this framework more apparent than in the field of organ transplantation. Although the surgery, hospitalization, medication, and care that transplantation involves are expensive, the basic scarce resources without which this procedure could never take place are other than financial. They are human organs, live or cadaveric, that become available for implantation in patients with end-stage disease because human donors and/or their families were willing to give parts of themselves to others.

From its inception in the mid-1950s, clinical organ transplantation has been defined and experienced as a gift, at whose center lies overpowering questions of who shall give and who shall receive these supreme gifts of self and life and how, if ever, they can be reciprocated. Fundamental and transcendental issues concerning our individuality and individualism, our interconnectedness and interchangeability with others, our sense of community and society, and our relationship to dimensions of self and other, life and death that are "more than human," have all been called into play by our medical-surgical ability to transplant organs from one human body to another. The biological concomitants of this act (particularly our body's immunological capacity to "recognize" grafted tissues as "not-self," and its propensity to reject them), combined with the psychological, social, and spiritual meanings of transplantation, have endowed it with allegorical cultural significance.

As the range and number of organs that we can transplant have expanded, our public discourse about transplantation has intensified and become more focused on what is felt to be the insufficient supply of organs that our voluntary donation system makes available. Ethical debate is increasingly pitched on a societal level. And like so many other value- and belief-laden medical issues we are discussing these days, this debate is likely to be phrased in economics-influenced, need/supply, scarcity, procurement, allocation/distribution, cost/benefit, market terms. This is the current outer language for the inner questions that are at the core of the transplantation of organs. The "economization" of these questions does not alter their essence (Fox, Swazey, and Cameron 1984, 58):

> What obligations do we have to ourselves as individuals, to the various members of our family, to our close friends, colleagues and acquaintances? And beyond these relationships, what are our obligations to the countless persons in our daily social life, and in our society, whom we do not know? Should we be able to give ourselves to mere acquaintances or strangers in life and death, as we do to our families and intimate friends? Who is my brother, sister, mother, father, child? Who is my friend, and who is my stranger? How are we related to one another? Where does our individuality end, and our interconnection and solidarity begin?

GENETICS AND GENETIC ENGINEERING

The same kinds of thematic questions have emerged around the scientific findings of the "new biology" and their applied, biomedical implications. The field of molecular genetics is an especially striking case in point. In the eyes of both scientists and nonscientists, the fundamental knowledge of genes and their encoding, and the techniques to splice and engineer genes, are "special"—full of exceptional promise and danger, and of high relevance to the "continuous dialogue between the possible and the actual" (Jacob 1982) which the most powerful forms of scientific questing and "tinkering" entail. This outlook on genetics is based on the conviction, as cultural as it is scientific, that the cell and its microcomponents—above all the genes—are the constituent elements of life. Whether in future centuries and other civilizations they will still be seen as such, we cannot predict. But in the here and now of our knowledge and understanding, we believe them to be. Because we do, we accord them a special status, comparable only to atoms and their subcomponents in the physical universe. But partly because of the associations that we make between genes—the deepest levels of living matter, the evolution of life in all forms, and the building blocks of our very humanness—we react to genes and their manipulation with a kind of awe that is different from our sense of atoms. To be sure, we are mindful of the destructive potential in atoms and genes alike if they are handled incompetently, maliciously, or even too innocently by humankind. But it is only the thought of genetic manipulation that evokes something like primal dread and a shuddering sense of metaphysical danger over the mixed beings, hybrid monsters, and Frankensteinian creatures that our hubris-ridden interventions could produce. Because of the relationship that we posit between genes and the "logic of life" (Jacob 1973), advances in genetics have evoked questions concerning our primary conceptions of what and who we are, singly and collectively; how we are distinct from and related to one another, and to other living beings; how mutable and fixed we are; where we come from and where we are going; what we can be said to possess (including our own bodies, its structures, organs, and secretions); and what we can transmit, give, and leave to one another, and to the planet on which we reside.[1]

BIOETHICS

Around the biomedical developments and the value and belief issues that we have reviewed, a field of inquiry and action has developed known as "bioethics." I have written at length, elsewhere (Fox 1974, 1976; Fox and Swazey 1984), about the origins of bioethics, its chief intellectual and professional participants, its research and policy activities, its publications, and its overall ethos. A few aspects of my sociological perspective on the phenomenon of bioethics have bearing on the analysis of the cultural and societal import of the interrelationship between medicine, science, and technology with which this chapter has been concerned.

Bioethics emerged in the late 1960s in the United States, during a period that was marked not only by explosive developments in medical science and technology but also by social and cultural upheaval that extended far beyond biology and medicine. During the past fifteen years, the field of bioethics and the phenomena that it treats have grown in private, professional, and public importance. Much of our individual, personal reflection is now devoted to bioethical questions. Our medical institutions (hospitals, research institutes, health agencies, medical and nursing schools), our classrooms, media, courts, legislatures, and other government agencies are pervaded by collective awareness of bioethical issues and organized attempts to grapple with

1. The foregoing discussion of molecular genetics and genetic engineering is excerpted from the remarks I prepared for my participation in a roundtable discussion titled "The Genetic Revolution," which was part of a colloquium "Recherche Médicale, Santé, Société," held in Paris on October 27-28, 1984, at the Sorbonne, in celebration of the twentieth anniversary of the Institut National de la Santé et de la Recherche Médicale.

them. The full-time professional role of "bioethicist" has emerged. Bioethicists of various disciplinary backgrounds (chiefly philosophers and jurists, and to a lesser extent, physicians and religionists) are constantly asked to give expert opinions and consultant advice in all the contexts where bioethical reflection and debate are ensuing.

The range of matters in which bioethics is involved is not confined to ethics. Bioethics is also concerned with moral questions, including those that lie at the heart of society and culture, and of religion. As time has passed and the field has unfolded, bioethics has dealt increasingly with issues concerning life and death and personhood, at the beginning and the end of the human life cycle.

From the outset, the conceptual framework of bioethics has been marked by tension between the weighty, often overriding emphasis it has placed on individualism—individual rights, autonomy, and self-determination—and the emphasis it has accorded to the social dimensions of our moral life: our caring interdependence with and responsibility for one another that bioethics refers to as "beneficence" and "community." Over the past year, admonitions about a too-singular insistence on autonomy as a moral good have begun to appear in bioethical discussion, along with occasional affirmations about the importance of "building a mature medical ethics that can handle social as well as individual ethical questions" (Veatch 1984, 40). These types of statements have been made in connection with scarce-resources problems, which have become a more dominant bioethical concern. They were also major motifs at the (June 1984) symposium "Autonomy, Paternalism, and Community," with which the Hastings Center, one of the pioneering organizations in bioethics, chose to celebrate its fifteenth anniversary (*Hastings Center Report* 1984). Whether these are signs that the central conflict between individual and social good that has characterized bioethics is beginning to be resolved, in the direction of an ethic that is turning more social, remains to be seen.

CONCLUSION

Around the revolutionary scientific and techological developments that have taken place in modern Western medicine since World War II, and in their application to the delivery of care, deep, far-reaching change has occurred, which has been felt in every sector of American society and by every group in its population. The relationship between this biomedical and social change is complex. Biology and medicine have been as much affected by the change our society has been undergoing as they have been precipitants of it. They have also become important, empirical, and symbolic foci of our efforts to decipher and deal with the implications of the engulfing process of change that we have been experiencing.

It is not only the scope and velocity of this biomedical and social change that have been responsible for its extraordinary impact. Many of its concomitants suggest that it has touched and shaken ideas, values, and beliefs fundamental to our historical and cultural tradition, our worldview, and our conception of our place within it. Taken as a whole, the biomedical issues explored in this chapter have to do with nothing less than societal problems of definition, origin, identity, direction, and meaning—problems that we seem to be having about such elemental matters as our conceptions of life and death, body and mind, self and other, person and human, baby and child, aging and elderly, parent and family, rights and responsibilities, autonomy and reciprocity, solidarity and community. Medicine and its science and technology have given us a common voice and vocabulary to publicly discuss these basic components of personal and social existence. But despite our shared language, a penumbra of uncertainty and confusion, contradiction and conflict, ambivalence and anxiety surrounds our deliberations. We are having great difficulty achieving moral and social consensus about these issues or finding practical solutions to them to which we are mutually willing to consent, whether we privately agree with them or not. Our tendency to dichotomize the individual and the social, and to think in more individual than social terms about ethics and morality, has made this all the harder.

We persist in calling this range of issues "medical ethical," and lately, "medical economic" as well. In fact, the questions that confront us are more, and other, than that. They are also moral, social, religious, metaphysical, and epistemological; they are deeply and encompassingly related to the foundations, the cohesion, and the orientation of our society and culture. Defining these matters as primarily medical, ethical, and economic may make them feel less overwhelming and more amenable to logical analysis and technical solution. But, in the end, the definition masks that what we are grappling with are not just problems of right and wrong, and of dollars and cents pertaining to medicine, but also larger questions about who we are, what we stand for, and where we are going as a total society.

REFERENCES

America's Abortion Dilemma. 1984. *Newsweek,* January 14, pp. 20-29.

Beeson, P.B. 1980. Changes in Medical Therapy During the Past Half Century. *Medicine* 59:79-99.

Blendon, R.J., and D.E. Altman. 1984. Public Attitudes about Health-Care Costs: A Lesson in National Schizophrenia. *New England Journal of Medicine* 311:631-616.

Blendon, R.J., and D.E. Rogers. 1983. Cutting Medical Care Costs: *Primum non nocere. Journal of the American Medical Association* 250:1880-1885.

Curran, J.W., W.M. Morgan, A.M. Hardy, H.W. Jaffe, W.W. Darrow, and W.R. Dowdle. 1985. The Epidemiology of AIDS: Current Status and Future Prospects. *Science* 229:1352-1357.

Fox, R.C. 1974. Ethical and Existential Developments in Contemporaneous American Medicine: Their Implications for Culture and Society. *Milbank Memorial Fund Quarterly: Health and Society* 52:445-483.

______1976. Advanced Medical Technology: Social and Ethical Implications. *Annual Review of Sociology* 2:231-268.

______1981. The Sting of Death in American Society. *Social Service Review* 55:42-59.

Fox, R.C., and J.P. Swazey. 1984. Medical Morality is Not Bioethics: Medical Ethics in China and the United States. *Perspectives in Biology and Medicine* 27:336-360.

Fox, R.C., J.P. Swazey, and E.M. Cameron. 1984. Social and Ethical Problems in the Treatment of End-Stage Renal Disease Patients. In *Controversies* in *Nephrology and Hypertension,* ed. R.G. Narins, pp. 45-70. New York: Churchill Livingstone.

Fox, R.C., and D.P. Willis. 1983. Personhood, Medicine, and American Society. *Milbank Memorial Fund Quarterly: Health and Society* 61:127-147.

Gudeman, J.E., and M.F. Shore. 1984. Beyond Deinstitutionalization: A New Class of Facilities for the Mentally Ill. *New England Journal of Medicine* 311:832-836.

Hastings Center Report. 1984. A selection of the papers presented at the fifteenth anniversary symposium, "Autonomy, Paternalism, and Community," 14:5.

Jacob, F. 1973. The Logic of Life: A History of Heredity. Trans. B.E. Spillman. New York: Pantheon Books.

______1982. The Possible and the Actual. New York: Pantheon Books.

Preston, S.H. 1984. Children and the Elderly: Divergent Paths for America's Dependents. *Demography* 21:435-457.

Rostain, A.L. 1985. Deciding to Forego Life-Sustaining Treatment in the Intensive Care Nursery: A Sociologic Account. Children's Hospital of Philadelphia, University of Pennsylvania, Philadelphia. Typescript.

Thomas, L. 1983. *The Youngest Science: Notes of a Medicine-Watcher.* New York: Viking Press.

Veatch, R.M. 1984. Autonomy's Temporary Triumph. *Hastings Center Report* 14:38-40.

Index